THEORIES OF ADOLESCENCE

The McGraw-Hill Series in Developmental Psychology

Consulting Editor, Ross A. Thompson

THEORIES OF ADOLESCENCE

Sixth Edition

Rolf E. Muuss

Goucher College

With the assistance of

Eli Velder and Harriet Porton

Goucher College

The McGraw-Hill Companies, Inc.

New York   St. Louis   San Francisco   Auckland   Bogotá   Caracas
Lisbon   London   Madrid   Mexico City   Milan   Montreal   New Delhi
San Juan   Singapore   Sydney   Tokyo   Toronto

To my Wife, Gertrude,
and my Children, Gretchen and Michael

McGraw-Hill

A Division of The **McGraw·Hill** Companies

Theories of Adolescence

Copyright © 1996, 1988, 1982, 1975, 1968, 1962 by The McGraw-Hill Companies, Inc. All rights reserved. Printed in the United States of America. Except as permitted under the United States Copyright Act of 1976, no part of this publication may be reproduced or distributed in any form or by any means, or stored in a data base or retrieval system, without the prior written permission of the publisher.

This book is printed on acid-free paper.

3   4   5   6   7   8   9   0   DOC   DOC   9   0   9   8   7

ISBN 0-07-044267-3

This book was set in Garamond Three by Graphic World, Inc.
The editors were Beth Kaufman and Fred H. Burns;
the production supervisor was Louise Karam.
The photo editor was Anne Manning.
R. R. Donnelley & Sons was printer and binder.

Photo credits appear on page v and on this page by reference.

Cover painting by Will Barnet. *Silent Seasons—Autumn,* 1967
Oil on canvas.   43 1/2 × 33 in.   (110.5 × 83.8 cm.)
Collection of the Whitney Museum of American Art
Purchase, with funds from Mr. and Mrs. Daniel H. Silberberg. 73.48
Copyright © 1995: Whitney Museum of American Art
© 1996 Will Barnet/Licensed by VAGA, New York, NY

Library of Congress Cataloging-in-Publication Data

Muuss, Rolf Eduard Helmut, (date).
    Theories of adolescence / Rolf E. Muuss with the assistance of Eli Velder and Harriet Porton. — 6th ed.
      p.   cm.
    Includes bibliographical references and indexes.
    ISBN 0-07-044267-3
    1. Adolescent psychology.   I. Velder, Eli.   II. Porton, Harriet.
III. Title
BF724.M8   1996   95-41242
155.5—dc20

Photo Credits

Rolf E. Muuss received his teaching diploma from the Pädagogische Hochschule Flensburg, Germany, his M. Ed. from Western Maryland College, and his Ph.D. from the University of Illinois. He was a research assistant professor in the Preventive Psychiatry Program at the Iowa Child Welfare Research Station, University of Iowa. From 1959 until his retirement in 1995, he has held the positions of professor, chairman of education, director of special education, and chairman of sociology and anthropology at Goucher College, and the Elizabeth C. Todd Distinguished Professorship (1980–1985). Professor Muuss also taught at The Johns Hopkins University, Pädagogische Hochschule Kiel, University of British Columbia, University of Delaware, University of Illinois, Sheppard and Enoch Pratt Hospital Training Program for Psychiatrists, and Towson State University. Listed in *Who's Who in the World,* he was elected Fellow in the American Psychological Society and two divisions of the American Psychological Association. Certified as a psychologist, he also serves as a Hearing Officer for special education cases in the state of Maryland. He has been a frequent speaker at both the International Congress of Pediatrics and the Congress of Social Pediatrics in Europe.

Professor Muuss has edited four editions of *Adolescent Behavior and Society: A Book of Readings* (1971, 1975, 1980, 1990) and is author of *First-Aid for Classroom Discipline Problems* (1962) and *Grundlagen der Adoleszentenpsychologie* (1982). Previous editions of *Theories of Adolescence* have been translated into Dutch, Hebrew, German, Italian, Japanese, Portuguese, and Spanish. He has published over 100 research studies and articles in medical, psychological, and educational journals in the United States, Germany, England, Switzerland, and Sweden.

C O N T E N T S

ix

FOREWORD

My oldest son, Scott, is age 11 and on the verge of adolescence. At least, I *think* he's on the verge of adolescence. To be sure, he hasn't yet shown the sudden spurt in physical size and the self-conscious clumsiness (the feet that are too large, the elbows that seem to be going in every direction) that I see in some of his friends. On the other hand, his concern about his appearance has become manifested in extensive time in the bathroom—ensuring that his hair is combed "right" and that his clothing has satisfied some ineluctable criterion of appropriateness. I also see signs of impending adolescence in some of Scott's encounters with his family and friends. For some time now, Scott has generalized to his parents an expression of disparaging pity that was formerly reserved only for his younger brother—complete with eyes rolling skyward, an anguished sigh, and a demeanor of needed deliverance from the ignorance of those he is forced to share a home with. When driving Scott and his friends to or from a soccer match, I can faintly overhear whispered references to a teacher, classmate, or another unknowing victim of their discussion that is punctuated by loud, explosive laughter (and what I *can't* overhear causes greater concern!). Scott and I have also had several conversations about the inability of others to truly understand what is going on within him. But there have also been many positive changes in his recent behavior. Conversations with Scott have become a delightful discovery of the insight, yielded by his powers of logic and imagination, into himself, his future, and current events. Quite suddenly, his growing skills and independence have taken him into relationships (with coaches, teachers, peers, and other associates) that are making his world and mine decreasingly alike. And in their best moments, Scott and his friends are models of thoughtful, responsible, and wholly pleasant company.

Are these diverse changes in Scott the markers of adolescence? How can we know whether they are? As a developmental psychologist who is also a parent, I have long been interested in how adolescence is simultaneously one of the best understood and most misunderstood phases of the life course. Asking anybody about the meaning of adolescence will yield a rich network of associations, with the terms "identity crisis," "rebellion," "self-consciousness," "sexual exploration," "generation gap," and "peer pressure" emerging prominently in everyday portrayals of teenagers. This is the adolescence I remember: a period of storm and stress, anxiety, hope, and occasional despair, anger and rebellion, searching and experimenting. But developmental researchers have usually found that the portrayal of adolescence emerging from their research studies is much more benign. More adolescents endorse the same moral, religious, and political values that their parents do, which makes their occasional bickering about musical tastes or hairstyling less portentous. For many teens, the search for identity is a progressive exploration of potential roles rather than the anxious soul-searching that I remember, and perhaps expect to see in Scott. Although some adolescent peer groups provide avenues to delinquency, most help to uphold rather than undermine consensual social values. And adolescence is a period of remarkable achievements in thinking, reasoning, and self-awareness that is often missed in its characterization in the popular culture.

So what are the distinctive landmarks of adolescence? If we look at the lessons of the popular culture, we arrive at a much different set of indicators than when we are tutored by research findings, and integrating the two can be difficult. On such occasions, Kurt Lewin's familiar lesson that "there is nothing as practical as a good theory" seems appropriate. By distilling a welter of human experience into generalizable principles and applications, a good developmental theory cautions against overgeneralizing from the vagaries of personal experience or the lessons of the popular culture, synthesizes apparently discordant aspects of age-related change, and identifies the distinctive features of the developmental pathways characteristic of each stage of life, while also showing the range of individual variability in these pathways. Like a clear and helpful road map, a theory can provide perspective on roads past traveled, what lies ahead, and (perhaps most importantly) the sights we see along the way to the future.

The sixth edition of Rolf E. Muuss's *Theories of Adolescence* is the long-awaited revision of a classic in the field that has attained its status because of its thoughtful, and thought-provoking, examination of the theoretical perspectives that govern contemporary thinking about adolescence. Contrary to many authoritative sources, this author has enlivened each edition by keeping close to the intellectual pulse of contemporary scholarship. In this edition, for example, every chapter has received significant updating, and entirely new chapters have been written to include Loevinger's views on ego development, Lerner's developmental contextualism, Fowler's theory of faith development, and current anthropological perspectives on adolescence. Moreover, readers will find that the chapters on Selman's theory of interpersonal understanding, Bronfenbrenner's ecological view of human development, Bandura's social cognitive theory, and the dual chapters based on Erkison's identity theory have received significant revision. The result is a fresh, current portrayal of theoretical views of adolescence.

More than this, however, Rolf Muuss has provided us with an overview of adolescence in the context of broader developmental pathways. As he notes, few of these theories are exclusively concerned with adolescence, so each chapter provides an overview of how adolescence fits into the broader stream of developmental challenges, changes, and opportunities that characterize the life course. By avoiding a decontextualized view of the teenage years, he enables us to see what adolescence shares in common with earlier and later phases of life, as well as what makes it distinctive. Another noteworthy feature of this book is its organization in terms of intellectual "families" or lineage. Understanding developmental theories requires appreciating how theorists have influenced each other: Kohlberg's moral judgment theory is more comprehensible, for instance, when we appreciate his intellectual debt to Piaget and, in turn, how Kohlberg has been a catalyst to the thinking of diverse theorists like Carol Gilligan (whose gender theory has its origins in her encounters with Kohlberg's work), James Fowler (who developed a close friendship with Kohlberg in his early years), and even Robert Selman. Similar lineage patterns can be traced, in this volume, between different psychoanalytic and neo-analytic theorists, as well as among contextual theorists of various persuasions. Thus a thoughtful reading of this book reveals the intellectual development over the current century of contemporary theories of adolescent development.

Finally, this new edition of *Theories of Adolescence* includes greater attention to the importance of gender as a catalyst, mediator, and context of adolescent change. It provides a reminder that in looking for signs of impending adolescence in Scott, the manner in which his life experience is different from that of Stephanie (the same-age daughter of a faculty colleague) is an important consideration in understanding the adolescent transition of each child. In the creation of this new edition, Rolf Muuss has provided us with a state-of-the-art picture of this multifaceted, variegated, fascinating, and provocative (but often misunderstood) turning-point toward adulthood.

The *McGraw-Hill Series in Developmental Psychology,* of which this volume is a part, has been designed to enrich and expand our common knowledge of human development by providing a forum for theorists, researchers, and practitioners to present their insights to a broad audience. As a rapidly expanding scientific field, developmental psychology has important applications to parents, educators, students, clinicians, policymakers, and others who are concerned with promoting human welfare throughout the life course. Although the fruits of scholarly research into human development can be found on the pages of research journals, and students can become acquainted with this exciting field in introductory textbooks, this series of specialized, topical books is intended to provide insightful, in-depth examinations of selected issues in the field from which undergraduates, graduate students, and academic colleagues can each benefit. As forums for highlighting important new ideas, research insights, theoretical syntheses, and applications of knowledge to practical problems, I hope that these volumes will find many uses: as books that supplement standard general textbooks in undergraduate or graduate courses, as one of several specialized texts for advanced coursework, as tutorials for scholars interested in learning about current knowledge on a topic of interest, and as sourcebooks for practitioners who wish to traverse the gap between knowledge and application. The authors who contribute to this series are committed to providing a state-of-the-art, accurate, and readable interpretation of current knowledge that will be interesting and accessible to a broad audience with many different goals and interests. We hope, too, that these volumes will inspire the efforts to improve the lives of children, adolescents, and adults through research and practice that are much needed in our world.

Theories of Adolescence reflects these goals by offering a sense of the adolescent experience through the lens of gifted theorists, and a gifted interpreter of their views.

Ross A. Thompson
Consulting Editor

P R E F A C E

The general purpose of *Theories of Adolescence* is to provide an overview of selected developmental theories. Its more specific purpose, however, is to highlight the place of adolescence in developmental theories. Very few theories are exclusively concerned with the period of adolescence—even though most see adolescence as the pivotal period in the developmental progression. Theories can help to bring observations, events, and facts which seem random and disconnected into some meaningful relationship and order. Theories examined here are presented within a historical context—therefore, the text begins with the ideas of early Greek philosophers concerning human nature and concludes with modern feminists and multicultural theories of adolescent development.

The sequential organization of chapters has been guided by two principles. First, an attempt was made to present the theories in their chronological historical order. Second, theories that fall into "families" which build upon, modify, or elaborate an original school of thought have been grouped together in family patterns. An appropriate illustration is Freud's theory, whose followers are often referred to by their "family-name": psychoanalysts. Among the developmental theories discussed here, Erikson had his theoretical roots in Freudian thinking. Erikson, in turn, stimulated James Marcia, whose theorizing became the catalyst for the current research approaches to identity formation. Even though identity formation theory has little in common with Freud's original theory, it is possible to trace the roots of identity research back to Freud. The text therefore groups the chapters on Freud, Erikson, and identity theory together. A similar family pattern can be traced from Piaget to Kohlberg and from Kohlberg to Gilligan. Theories also cross-fertilize each other in that ideas are often taken from different schools of thought and integrated into new concepts or even a new and different theory. For example, James Fowler's theory of faith development combines ideas from the theories of Piaget, Erikson, and Selman as well as from specific systems of theology. To the extent possible, *Theories of Adolescence* groups these family patterns together. The hope is that this grouping of theory families will enhance understanding and allow readers to see interrelationships between them.

Because theories are difficult to prove or disprove, theories that have already been declared dead or obsolete may be reconsidered, rediscovered, and reevaluated. Their influence on other theorists is therefore hard to predict. Charles Darwin, Harry Stack Sullivan, Lev Vygotsky, and Kurt Lewin are currently experiencing renewed attention. Darwin has found renewed recognition in the theories of sociobiology and evolutionary psychology. Lev Vygotsky, a Russian psychologist who died in 1934 and was virtually unknown for almost 50 years, is being rediscovered. Parts of his developmental theory are often compared to some of Piaget's ideas. Vygotsky's emphasis on the social-cultural context of development has also left its mark on Bronfenbrenner's writing, especially the research paradigm of his ecological model. This recurring and often reemerging interest in the wisdom of historical theories warrants coverage of classic as well as contemporary theories in this text.

WHY ARE THEORIES USEFUL?

Thomas Jefferson addressed that issue most appropriately when he wrote: ". . . theory is the most practical of men's instruments." The value of theory in developmental psychology is reflected in Kurt Lewin's oft-cited dictum "There is nothing as practical as a good theory." Theory tends to make a unified whole out of many, often piecemeal, bits of accumulated information and research findings. In her memoir of John Bowlby, a noted maturational theorist, his collaborator Mary Ainsworth emphasized Bowlby's belief that theory emerges from and depends on data. "A good theory not only makes sense of a welter of data that has already been observed, but a good theory also plays an essential role in guiding observations [and research] in new and profitable directions" (Ainsworth, 1991: 1). Theories inspire research, guide the formation of hypotheses, influence the selection of assessment procedures, and generate psychological, clinical, and educational insights. Thus, a major purpose of this book may be summarized in a modified version of a statement made by Henri Poincaré: "Our understanding of human development is built out of theories and research findings, just as a house is built out of mortar and stones. But a collection of facts [research findings] without theory is no more a basis for sound understanding than a heap of stones is a house."

WHY DOES DEVELOPMENT REQUIRE SCIENTIFIC EXPLANATION?

Science is the human endeavor that attempts to bring order into diverse, often scattered and meaningless, observations by organizing them into principles, generalizations, and for the purpose of our discussion, theories. Theories encourage the formulation of "if . . . then" statements, (i.e., "if this happens . . . then that results"), which provide explanations, generate hypotheses, and eventually, help in establishing causal relationships. Discovering and identifying these patterns can provide an understanding of the nature of human development and can then be utilized to generate research hypotheses, to provide insight into child-rearing practices, to make practical suggestions for managing children and adolescents, and to construct more efficent learning activities. Intervention—such as therapy, specific skills training or educational programs—guided by theories is more successful than a haphazard approach based on trial and error. Scholars generate hypotheses for empirical research that are based on theoretical considerations. They test their hypotheses and refine existing developmental understandings as a result of what they have learned. Theory and research cross-fertilize each other. "Experiment without theory is blind, theory without experiment is lame" (Eysenck). Throughout this book some of the more important theoretical studies that have an impact on or support basic developmental theories concerning adolescence will be used to support, illustrate, and at times, challenge significant theoretical constructs.

As a science developmental psychology makes certain core assumptions about development: (1) Development follows lawful sequential patterns. Many theories assume that there are age-related behaviors that follow an unvarying developmental sequence. (2) These sequential patterns can be identified and assessed. (3) Developmental outcomes are based on antecedent conditions. For example, a child's development is shaped in part by what happened during that child's earlier life. (4) Factors that contribute to development are often interrelated and interact with each other and we are becoming cognizant that children and adolescents contribute to their own development. Each person's development is affected by many, varied components that depend upon each other and can only be understood in their totality.

HOW HAVE THEORIES CHANGED IN RECENT YEARS?

Early theories of development, especially the historical theories, were created by men from a male point of view, and involved predominantly male subjects. Partly because of the male-centric (androcentric) assumption that what is true for males is equally applicable to females, females were usually neglected or totally ignored. Gender differences, when they occurred, were dismissed or explained by male constructs. Even worse, females were often assigned a role of lesser significance or viewed as deficient in some way. According to the developmental theorist Carol Gilligan (1979: 432), this bias of "adopting the male life as the norm" and considering the female deficient has been pervasive in psychological theories until relatively recently.

This bias against females was prevalent not only in the construction of developmental theories but has also been a pervasive pattern throughout most psychological research. According to Harry Triandis (1994), the majority of the empirical data prior to 1970 reported in the social psychological literature was based on male subjects. Women were relatively invisible in the research literature. It has only been since the period following World War I that female scholars have been more widely recognized for making major contributions to the formulation of developmental theories. Recently, however, girls and adolescent females have become the primary focus of an increasing number of investigations (Archer, 1985; Brooks-Gunn & Petersen, 1983; Brown & Gilligan, 1992; Gilligan et al., 1990).

According to the philosopher Hegel, the nature of the scientific process is that every thesis stimulates an antithesis and eventually these contradictory points of view are resolved into a new synthesis. Developmental theories have followed this process. Earlier theories (such as Arnold Gesell's) emphasized the biological maturational process. In contrast, behavioristic theories, (such as B. F. Skinner's), emphasized external environmental events. The synthesis finds reflection in those interactionist theories that give the balanced credence to organism and environment. Currently, the androcentric view of development (thesis) is being challenged by many and diverse feminist writers (antithesis). One can only hope that a more balanced, more integrated, theory will eventually emerge—one that encompasses both genders accurately, fairly, and equitably. Freudian psychoanalytic theory is often viewed as both offensive to women and, on some issues, as incorrect. Yet it has also been credited with opening the door to the study of feminine issues, including female sexuality. Surprisingly, many of the early contributors to psychoanalysis and to Freud's developmental theory were women: Anna Freud, Helen Deutsch, Melanie Klein, Karen Horney, and more recently, Nancy Chodorow. There hardly exists another psychological school of thought that has produced as many internationally prominent women theoreticians in the first half of this century as psychoanalysis.

Divergent thinking has always been a part of the development of theory. Freud and Skinner are often cited as representing two extreme schools of thought in psychology. Freud focused on internal, conscious, and even unconscious processes; Skinner, on overt, measurable behavior. As a result of their divergent orientation, these theories have little in common and show little agreement. Skinner referred somewhat derogatorily to Freud's model of the inner workings of the mind as the "black box." This same kind of diversity clearly exists among contemporary feminist theories. A feminist is someone who describes herself or himself as one who recognizes women's systematic treatment by society as inequitable. However, beyond this point there is very little that unifies feminist theory. As Sandra Scarr (1994) so succinctly and perceptively points out, there is a broad, overwhelming, and impressive continuum of divergent feminist theories, which fall from "maximizing to minimizing gender differences." In this revised sixth edition of *Theories of Adolescence,* the author has attempted to include those female writers and theorists who focus in their theories on the adolescence of women and who have made theoretical contributions to an understanding of adolescence: Margaret Mead, Carol Gilligan, Jane Loevinger, and Alice Schlegel.

Although it is easy to criticize earlier developmental theories as being male-centered or, by today's terminology, even sexist, one can only judge earlier theories by the knowledge and the sociocultural context that was prevalent when they emerged. This paradigm neither diminishes nor excuses the work done in the past, it simply attempts to explain it.

THEORIES THAT ARE NEW TO THIS EDITION

The revised sixth edition of *Theories of Adolescence* is substantially different from the fifth edition. It not only reflects new developments in the field, it also recognizes those theories which have become more important and seem to have moved into the mainstream of developmental theory. One of the problems encountered in the process of selecting theories for inclusion is the fact that, with the possible exceptions of Margaret Mead, Alice Schlegel, and Harry Barry's anthropological inquiries, few theories are primarily or exclusively concerned with adolescence. Therefore, many of the theories that have been included contribute to an overall understanding of adolescence. Contextualism has become a major theoretical development that is reflected in two new chapters, Urie Bronfenbrenner's ecological model of development, and Richard Lerner's contextualism. Neither theory is exclusively a "theory of adolescence." Both, however, provide a perspective on thinking about adolescent development that cannot be ignored. In addition, two stage theories appear for the first time in the sixth edition: James Fowler's theory of faith development and Jane Loevinger's theory of ego development. In the author's judgment, neither is given adequate recognition in adolescent literature; both are surprisingly neglected in textbooks dealing with adolescent development. These two theories have a common conceptual core and are compatible with each other but emphasize different aspects, e.g. "faith" versus "ego" development. Finally, an entire chapter is devoted to the significant, although controversial, contribution made by anthropology. Particularly significant, in the author's view, is Schlegel's and Barry's broad-based cross-cultural inquiry which focuses exclusively on adolescence.

Ever since the publication of the first edition of *Theories of Adolescence* in 1962, the author's commitment has been to focus on theories and the contribution of specific individuals of schools of thought to the understanding of adolescence. The author's intent remains unchanged and leaves the discussion of tangential domains, such as family problems, peer pressure problems, etc., to more general domain-oriented volumes. This text attempts to enhance the reader's understanding of adolescence as a pivotal stage in human growth and development, and presents the different approaches developmental theorists have used to analyze, explain, and describe adolescence.

Rolf E. Muuss

ACKNOWLEDGMENTS

The first edition of *Theories of Adolescence* was published almost 35 years ago by Random House. The continuous revisions of the book reflect both the importance of theories in explaining developmental phenomena and the ever-changing nature of the field. Since there are not many recent examples of macrotheories of adolescence (such as those of Freud and Erikson), one may assume that the era of global developmental theories has passed. However, a closer look reveals the emergence of numerous microtheories that embrace a more focused and/or narrowly defined aspect of development, such as Fowler's "faith theory." Under the impetus of Kurt Lewin, theories increasingly have expanded to emphasize the ecological field (Bronfenbrenner) and contextualism and diversity (Lerner), and to begin to encompass cross-cultural data for theory formation (Schlegel and Barry). The current edition of *Theories of Adolescence* reflects these new trends.

All of the living theorists discussed in this book have been most generous by providing pictures of themselves and permission to reproduce these pictures. Many have also supplied me with relevant reprints, critical comments, and gratifying encouragement so that I could capture the essence of their life work.

Due to major surgery, I was almost compelled to abandon this project, but McGraw-Hill was kind enough to grant a year's extension as well as additional support. In addition, the project got "back on track" through the competent and enthusiastic collaboration of Eli Velder who revised and wrote the new section for the Kohlberg chapter, and Harriet Porton who did the same for Gilligan. They also read drafts of several other chapters. Much appreciation also goes to Alma Nugent who was initially very involved in the editing and revising of chapters but had to terminate her involvement in the project. I feel very much obliged to these individuals.

I have always felt indebted to the students in my undergraduate course "Adolescent Development" and especially the graduate students in "Theories of Development" who have used previous editions of my book. They have questioned its content, challenged my conclusions, asked for evidence or illustrations, and—in the process—stimulated my thinking. I am especially grateful to Laura Oldham, a graduate student who drew some of the figures for the new edition.

A book of this nature is never the accomplishment of just one person; its creation is nurtured, challenged and stimulated by many individuals. As the author I am especially grateful for the many valuable suggestions, editorial feedback, and critical comments of colleagues, students, and friends who reviewed one or several of the new and substantially revised chapters of the sixth edition: Elizabeth Beckley, Frona Brown, Joan Burton, Christian Carstensen, John Chamberlain, Barbara Gould, Joseph Morton, Richard Pringle, John Rose, Susan Stocker, Jeanie Street, and Robert Williams.

Goucher College granted me a sabbatical leave without which the work could not have been completed in a timely fashion. In addition, I received continuous support from the college computer center; thanks to Robert Dooley, the college library (especially Marjorie Simon), and my always helpful secretary, Madeline Kotowski. My son Michael not only taught me how to use the computer but solved all computer problems with speed and efficiency.

I wish to express my sincere gratitude to the McGraw-Hill support staff, Jane Vaicunas and Fred Burns, but especially to my editor, Beth Kaufman, whose unwavering support, encouragement, and confidence-inspiring enthusiasm for the project helped me to stay on track. She diffused problems easily and made the whole task pleasant.

Through the kindness and generosity of Hank Ketcham I was granted the privilege to use three of his "Dennis the Menace" comics free of charge in honor of his mother Virginia King who was a graduate of Goucher College, class of 1919.

I have benefited greatly from the suggestions, ideas, and guidance of the reviewers and consultants who very constructively criticized early proposals and draft chapters: Sally Archer, Trenton State College; Robert D. Enright, University of Wisconsin–Madison; Karen Howe, Trenton State College; Patricia Jarvis, Illinois State University; Daniel K. Lapsley, Brandon University; David Moshman, University of Nebraska–Lincoln; Beth Paul, Trenton State College; Lawrence B. Schiamberg, Michigan State University; Lawrence G. Shelton, University of Vermont; Peter L. Sheras, University of Virginia; Dennis Thompson, Georgia State University; and Alan S. Waterman, Trenton State College.

Most of all thanks to my supportive and loving family: my wife Gertrude, for support, proofreading, and patience, my daughter Gretchen, and my son Michael.

I also want to express my deepest respect and appreciation to my doctoral advisor Glenn M. Blair, who more than 40 years ago inspired, guided, encouraged, and facilitated my dissertation: *Theories of Adolescence: An Analysis of Selected American and European Positions,* which became the foundation for the first edition and is reflected in all subsequent revisions. Sadly, Glenn M. Blair passed away while the writing for this edition was still in progress.

Rolf E. Muuss

THEORIES OF ADOLESCENCE

1

THE PHILOSOPHICAL AND HISTORICAL ROOTS OF THEORIES OF ADOLESCENCE

Long before psychology became a science, there existed philosophical, theological, and educational theories that contributed to an understanding of human nature and development. As a result of his famous two-volume work *Adolescence* (1916), G. Stanley Hall is considered the father of a scientific "psychology of adolescence." Prior to Hall, it was frequently the philosopher-educator who was especially concerned with the nature of human development and with its implications for teaching and learning. This was the case with Plato, Aristotle, Comenius, Rousseau, Herbart, Froebel, and Pestalozzi.

One difficulty in identifying prescientific theories of adolescent development is that prior to Hall, adolescence was not considered a separate stage of human development. The word "adolescence" first appeared in the fifteenth century, indicating that historically adolescence was subordinated to theoretical considerations about the nature of human development. Contemporary theories of adolescence have their historical roots in more general philosophical ideas about the nature of man and the process of development. Some important ideas about human development come from philosophers who are concerned with the question: What is the nature of man? For example, what Locke and Darwin had to say about the nature of man is so profound that it is reflected in the writings of Rousseau, Hall, and Freud, respectively, and thus provides a philosophical foundation for a theory of development.

EARLY GREEK CONCERN WITH HUMAN NATURE

A historical approach to a theory of adolescence must begin with the early Greek ideas about human development. Their influence remained prevalent throughout the Middle Ages and is still noticeable today. The philosophical idea of dualism, for instance, is essentially Greek. Plato (427–347 B.C.) made a clear distinction between two aspects of human nature: soul and body. He expounded that body and soul are different strata and that although there is some interaction between them, the soul is an entity in itself, capable of leaving the body without losing its identity. The soul can perceive more clearly and reach higher realities when freed from the body; *soma sema* ("the body is the grave of the soul"), he declared. Actually, Plato expressed disdain for the body, favoring the soul which reaches out toward the intangible realm of ideas. The body and sensuality are the fetters that hinder the soul in reaching those higher realities. Body is matter and has all the defects of matter. The idea of dualism between mind and body reappeared later in Christian theology and became of primary importance in the philosophical thinking of the seventeenth century, especially with Descartes, Leibnitz, and Spinoza.

Of greater interest from a developmental point of view is the idea of the layer structure of the soul, which Plato developed in his dialogue, *Phaedo*. According to Plato, the soul has three distinguishable parts, layers, or levels. Thus, probably for the first time in the history of psychology, a threefold division of soul, or mind, is advanced. The lowest layer of the soul is described as man's desires and appetites. Today we might describe this level in terms of drives, instincts, and needs, and its resemblance to Freud's concept of "id" can hardly be denied. According to Plato, this part of the soul is located in the lower part of the body and is primarily concerned with the satisfaction of the physical needs. ". . . [I]t fills us full of love, and lusts, and fears, and fancies of all kinds, and endless foolery, and . . . takes away the power of thinking at all" (Plato, 1921: 450). The second layer of the soul, the spirit, includes courage, conviction, temperance, endurance, and hardihood; aggressiveness and fierceness also originate here. Man has both the first and the second layer in common with the animal world. These two layers belong to the body and die with it. The third layer is divine, supernatural, and immortal; it constitutes the essence of the universe. This is the real soul, which Plato described as reason and which has only its temporary seat in the body. Plato's theory concerning the layer structure of the soul is reflected in several central European personality theories, which are developed on the assumption of a layerlike stratification of personality. They perceive development as a process by which the lower layers mature earlier and are superseded by higher layers as the child grows older. Plato had already postulated such a developmental theory. Reason is latent during the first stage when perception is most important. Among contemporary theorists, Piaget maintains that percepts develop into concepts which facilitate thinking. The second stage of development is characterized by conviction and understanding and brings the second layer of the soul, spirit, into the foreground of psychological development. The third stage, which we might identify with adolescence, but which, according to Plato, is not reached by all people, relates to the development of the third part of the soul, reason and intelligence.

Interspersed in most of Plato's diaologues—but particularly in *Laws* and *The Republic*—are descriptive accounts of children and youth as well as advice concerning the control of their behavior. While this material does not constitute a theory of development as we understand it today, it does give insight into Plato's conception of the nature of development.

During the first three years of life the infant should be free from fear and pain and sorrow. This point of view would be endorsed by many psychologists today. Interestingly enough, in the dialogue, *Laws,* Cleinias suggests that in addition to freeing the infant from pain we ought to provide pleasure. This is in agreement with Plato's basic goal, which is the possession of happiness. However, the Athenian Stranger objects that this would spoil the child, since during the early years "more than at any other time the character is engrained by habit" (Plato, 1953: 359). Plato postulated that some ideas are innate, present in the mind before experiences. Character is formed at an early age because the experiences and impressions leave a lasting influence. However, Plato did admit that "the characters of young men are subject to many changes in the course of their lives." The argument about the consistency of personality versus its modifiability has continued, and proponents of both of Plato's statements, stability of traits versus the power of situational influences, can still be heard today.

From ages 3 to 6 the child needs sports and social contact with age-mates in order to get rid of his self-will. Plato would punish but not disgrace the child. Social development is taken into consideration at this age, and children ought to come together in a kind of kindergarten arrangement under the supervision of a nurse. However, children should find for themselves the "natural modes of amusement" appropriate to their age.

Plato suggested a division of the sexes at age 6. "Let boys live with boys and girls . . . with girls." The boy now has to learn horsemanship, the uses of bow and arrow, the spear, and the sling. Boys will not be allowed to drink wine until they are 18 because of their easy excitability, "fire must not be poured upon fire." A related adolescent desire is argument for amusement's sake. In their enthusiasm they will leave no stone unturned, and in their delight over the first taste of wisdom they will annoy everyone with their arguments. Plato believed that the character is formed through habit at a very early age.

Plato developed his educational philosophy in *The Republic.* He perceived education as the development of the soul under the influence of the environment, "and this has two divisions, gymnastic for the body, and music for the soul." Reasoning in the young child is undeveloped, but since the young child is impressionable, Plato suggested establishing "a censorship of the writers of fiction," since "anything that he receives into his mind is likely to become indelible and unalterable: and therefore . . . the talks which the young first hear should be models of virtuous thoughts" (Plato, 1921: 642). Rational and critical thought develop mainly during adolescence. The training that began with music and gymnastics during childhood was continued through adolescence with mathematical and scientific studies. The latter brought out critical thought and dissatisfaction with direct sense knowledge; during this training students would develop methods of finding the truth and of distinguishing truth from opinion. In *Laws* Plato spoke of education as "that training which is given by suitable habits to the first instincts of virtue in children;—when pleasure, and friendship, and pain, and hatred are rightly implanted in souls not yet capable of understanding the nature of them, and who find them, after they have attained reason, to be in harmony with her" (Plato, 1953: 218). The meaning of education in this view is to provide experiences for children prior to the development of reason that are nevertheless in agreement with reason when it does develop during adolescence. Plato already recognized the importance of individual differences. He recognized that children are born with different abilities and should be guided into those kinds of activities that are in line with their aptitudes.

Plato postulated that the attainment of knowledge might be explained by his doctrine of innate ideas. Though undeveloped, vague, and nebulous, innate ideas are nevertheless present at birth. Learning is a process of remembering these ideas, which once—probably before the soul entered the body—were clear. Sensations help in reawakening these partially lost ideas. The mind-body dualism is of relevance here, since the body contributes sensation while the mind contains the ideas. Through this distinction, Plato's theory of innate ideas opens the discussion about the influence of heredity and environment.

Aristotle (384–322 B.C.), although a pupil of Plato's, challenged many of his master's ideas. Aristotle denied the separation of body and soul and returned to the older Greek idea of the unity of the physical and mental worlds. Body and soul, according to him, are related in structure and function. The relationship between body and soul is the same as that between matter and form; body is matter and soul is form. Soul-life, for which Aristotle used the word "entelechy," is the principle by which the body lives. Aristotle accepted Plato's idea concerning the levels of the soul-life; however, he viewed soul structure from a biological, almost evolutionary, point of view, in that he drew analogies between biological life forms and human nature. The lowest soul-life form is that of the plant, the life functions of which are supply of nourishment and reproduction. The next higher form of soul-life is also found in animals, its additional functions being sensation, perception, and locomotion. The third soul-life function is distinctly human and sets men apart from the animal world. It includes the ability to think and reason. Consequently, there are three layers of soul-life—the food-supplying, or plant, soul; the perceiving, or animal, soul; and the thinking, or human, soul. Aristotle further divided the thinking, or human, soul into two different parts: the practical soul by which we "deliberate about those things which depend upon us and our purpose to do or not to do" (Aristotle, 1925: 1196), and the theoretical soul, which deals with higher and abstract knowledge such as distinguishing between what is true and what is false. Aristotle saw the ability to think and the use of logic and rational powers as the purpose of development and the essence of mankind.

Aristotle advanced a theory of development concerning the layer structure of the soul that appears to have some resemblance to Darwin's more scientific biological theory of evolution, even though it does not include the idea of evolution of one species from another. Furthermore, Aristotle made an impassable division between the different levels of soul-life. Plato, in describing the stages of development, held that the first (plant) soul level developed before the second (animal) soul level and this, in turn, was a prerequisite for the rational (human) soul level. Aristotle followed this idea of the level structure of the soul and applied it to the development of the child.

> As the body is prior in order of generation to the soul, so the irrational is prior to the rational. The proof is that anger and wishing and desire are implanted in children from their very birth, but reason and understanding are developed as they grow older. Wherefore, the care of the body ought to precede that of the soul, and the training of the appetitive part should follow; none the less our care of it must be for the sake of the reason, and our care of the body for the sake of the soul [Aristotle, 1941c: 1300–1301].

Aristotle divided the developmental period into three distinguishable stages of 7 years each. The first 7 years he named infancy; the period from 7 to the beginning of puberty, boyhood; and from puberty to 21, young manhood. This division of the period of development into three stages was generally accepted during the Middle Ages and recurs in some contemporary theories of development.

Infants and animals are alike in that both are under the control of their appetites and emotions. "Children and brutes pursue pleasures" (Aristotle, 1941a: 1053). Aristotle emphasized that moral character is the result of choice, "for by choosing what is good or bad we are men of a certain character. . . ." Even though young children are able to act voluntarily, they do not have choice, "for both children and the lower animals share in voluntary action, but not in choice, and acts done on the spur of the moment we describe as voluntary, but not as chosen" (Aristotle, 1941a: 967–968). This seems to imply that children first go through an animal-like stage of development; what distinguishes them from animals is that children have the potential for higher development than animals, "though psychologically speaking a child hardly differs for the time being from an animal" (Aristotle, 1941b: 635). It is the characteristic of adolescence to develop the ability to choose. Only if youths voluntarily and deliberately choose will they develop the right kind of habits and thus, in the long run, build the right kind of character. By making choices adolescents actively participate in their own character formation. Voluntary and deliberate choice thus becomes an important aspect in Aristotle's theory of development, since it is necessary for the attainment of maturity. Among contemporary writers, M. Mead and E. Friedenberg claim that prolonged education and dependency have reduced choices to the extent that they interfere with the attainment of maturity.

Although Aristotle did not offer us a systematically stated theory of development, however, in *Rhetorica* he provided us with a detailed description of the "youthful type of character," part of which resembles descriptive statements that could have been written by G. Stanley Hall. "Young men have strong passions, and tend to gratify them indiscriminately. Of the bodily desires, it is the sexual by which they are most swayed and in which they show absence of self-control" (Aristotle, 1941d: 1403). Sexuality in adolescence is a contemporary concern and has become an educational and a public-policy issue. Aristotle, in his description of adolescents, commented on their instability: "They are changeable and fickle in their desires, which are violent while they last, but quickly over: their impulses are keen but not deep-rooted" (Aristotle, 1941d: 1403). Among modern writers, Lewin deals with the instability of the psychological field of the adolescent, who stands in a psychological no man's land. This makes many sociopsychological situations unclear, indefinite, and ambiguous, and the resulting behavior is "changeable and fickle." "For owing to their love and honour they cannot bear being slighted, and are indignant if they imagine themselves being unfairly treated" (Aristotle, 1941d: 1403–1404). Adolescent complaints about being "unfairly treated" in home, school, and society in general are so common today that they need no further elaboration. The list of quotes from *Rhetorica* in which Aristotle described the characteristics of adolescence could be continued, and other analogies to contemporary theories would not be too difficult to find. Aristotle discussed, among other issues, adolescents' desire for success, their optimism, trust, concern with the future rather than the past, their courage, conformity, idealism, friendship, aggressiveness, and gullibility, all of which remain contemporary issues in adolescent psychology and some have been researched extensively.

The education of the adolescent in the fourth century B.C. was based on the study of mathematics and included astronomy, geometry, and the theory of music; these subjects taught abstraction but did not require the life experiences and the wisdom considered necessary in order to become a philosopher or a physicist.

Under the early impact of Christian theology, Aristotelian thought seemed to get lost; however, it was later combined with Christian ideas by Saint Thomas Aquinas. The Aristotelian-Thomistic philosophy became dominant in the twelfth and thirteenth centuries, and its influence was felt during the Middle Ages—particularly in the form of Scholasticism. Aristotle is also considered influential in laying the foundation for a more scientific approach to science and psychology.

MEDIEVAL CHRISTIAN VIEW OF HUMAN DEVELOPMENT

The theological view of human nature and development cannot as readily be identified in terms of one man, a specific historical period, or even a particular denomination. We find the idea of original sin expressed by Tertullian in the second century when he spoke of the depravity of human nature. It was emphasized by John Calvin in the sixteenth century and is prevalent in Catholic Scholasticism, Protestant Calvinism, and American Puritanism.

The theological view of human nature as found in the medieval, early Reformation period encompassed several relevant ideas:

1. Mankind's unique position in the universe, being created in the image of God.
2. Mankind's evil due to Adam's original sin.
3. Mankind's dual nature: a spiritual, immortal soul and a material, mortal body. Salvation and life after death places the immortal soul on a higher level of importance.
4. Knowledge as revealed to mankind from without. It comes from God and is revealed to us through the Bible.
5. The homunculus idea of instantaneous creation. The last point is not so much biblical as medieval.

Most of these ideas can be found in biblical sources, but they were also influenced by Greek philosophy, especially Plato's mind-body dualism. We will see later that theories that followed in the seventeenth, eighteenth, and nineteenth centuries, especially those advanced by Locke, Rousseau, and Darwin, can partly be understood as antitheses to these earlier theological ideas.

The idea that God created mankind in his own image and thus gave it a unique position in the universe is expressed in Genesis 1:27-28: "And God created man to his own image: to the image of God he created him: male and female he created them." Furthermore, he gives them the power to rule over all living creatures. Prior to Darwin man was seen as being divinely created and basically different from the animal world.

The second important idea concerning the nature of humanity is the theological doctrine of human depravity. The human being is seen as having innate tendencies toward ungodliness and sinfulness, as fundamentally bad, with the badness becoming stronger during the developmental years if it is not counteracted by stern discipline. The idea of original sin as based on Genesis 3:6-7 relates the sinfulness of each individual to Adam's first sin. And "as sin came into the world through one man and death through sin, and so death spread to all men because all men sinned. . . . Yet death reigned from Adam to Moses, even over those whose sins were not like the transgression of Adam . . ." (Romans 5:12-14).

This pessimistic view of human nature, prevalent in Catholic theology before the Reformation, received a new impetus with Calvin's theology and thus set the intellectual climate for Puritanism. The educational objective in this theory was to bring forth the innate ideas that are God-given—knowledge of his laws and commands. Such a stern disciplinary approach to education was prevalent under the influence of Catholic Scholasticism and Calvinism in Europe and Puritanism in New England. There was little room for individual differences, since the quality of the mind was the same for all individuals, and the child who failed to learn was seen as willfully resisting the efforts of the teacher. The role of the teacher was defined by the teacher's authority and a belief that learning could be facilitated by physical punishment. The role of the child was defined by obedience. Calvin in particular expressed a strong faith in the value of education.

The theological view that mankind is the result of instantaneous creation results in preformationist thinking (Ausubel, 1958). During the Dark Ages, it was believed that the child came into the world as a miniature adult. The difference between a child and an adult was considered to be only a quantitative one, not a qualitative one. If one were to accept this point of view, then it follows that there should be no difference in the physiological functions of the child and the adult. Therefore, girls wore long dresses and corsets of adult style, only smaller in size, as is obvious from many medieval paintings. The qualitative difference in body build, body function, and mental abilities was disregarded. Growth was understood to be only a quantitative increase of all physical and mental aspects of human nature, not a qualitative one. This is a regression of thought when contrasted with the logical theories of Plato and Aristotle. The theory of preformationism held that children had the same interests as adults and therefore should be treated correspondingly, which meant that adult requirements were put upon them and were enforced by stern discipline. According to this view, the child did not "develop" but was preformed. Figure 1.1 illustrates the homunculus concept; it represents a view of the preformed "little man" in the sperm as conceived by seventeenth-century scientists.

> It was seriously believed that a miniature but fully-formed little man (i.e., an homunculus) was embodied in the sperm, and when implanted in the uterus simply grew in bulk, without any differentiation of tissues or organs, until full-term fetal size was attained at the end of nine months [Ausubel, 1958: 23-24].

This idea of homunculism was soon to be challenged by the beginning of modern science and advancements in the field of medicine. It was learned that young children have qualitative and quantitative characteristics of their own and are not miniature adults. One might speculate that the reason for the limited concern of pre-Hallian writers with the basic physiological changes that take place during pubescence—many of these changes are obvious to the keen observer, and their detection does not require medical knowledge or technology—is due to the theoretical position that the child is a miniature adult. In the philosophical realm it was Rousseau who stated that "nature would have children be children before being man. If we wish to prevent this order, we shall produce precocious fruits which will have neither maturity nor flavor, and will speedily deteriorate; we shall have young doctors and old children" (Rousseau, 1911: 54). Thus a new conception of human nature contributed to a more scientific concept of growth and development.

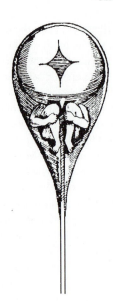

FIGURE 1.1 Drawing of a small man (an homunculus) in a human spermatozoon (adapted from Hartsoeker, 1694).

JOHN AMOS COMENIUS' DEVELOPMENT-CENTERED THEORY OF EDUCATION

The Renaissance may be seen as a revolt against authoritarianism in church, school, and society. The Aristotelian logic, the presupposition of universal ideas, and Scholasticism in general were challenged by Erasmus and Vives. Vives felt that one had "to begin with the individual facts of experience and out of them to come to ideas by the natural logic of the mind" (Boyd, 1965: 179). Learning was no longer seen as a deductive process, but as an inductive process beginning with experiences, and he suggested that an understanding of the learning process came from psychology. Learning, it was believed, was determined by the mind of the learner, and, therefore, education became concerned with individuality in pupils.

Comenius (1592–1670) accepted these ideas of the Renaissance, combined them with Aristotle's classification of development, and advanced a theory of education that was based on psychological assumptions. In his *Great Didactic,* first published in 1657, Comenius suggested a school organization based on a theory of development. Rather than dividing the developmental period into three stages of 7 years, as Aristotle did, Comenius proposed four developmental stages of 6 years each and a different school for each of these four stages.

The suggested school organization was based on assumptions concerning the nature of human development and a specific theory of learning, that of faculty psychology. Interestingly enough, present-day school organization in parts of the United States closely resembles this pattern. Comenius argued that the temporal sequence of the curriculum content should be borrowed from nature; in other words, it should be suitable to the psychological development of the child. "Let our maxim be to follow the lead of nature in all things, to observe how the faculties develope one after the other, and to base our method on this principle of succession" (Comenius, 1923: 257).

In the first 6 years of life children learn at home in the mother-school at their mother's knees. They should exercise the external senses and learn to discriminate among the various objects around them. The nature of the development of the faculty of sense perception is such that it precedes all other faculties, and, consequently, sensory experiences and sensory knowledge should be provided first. The significance of early sensorimotor experiences as the basis for learning and development is emphasized in Piaget's theory.

The child from 6 to 12 attends the vernacular-school and receives a general well-rounded elementary education, which is provided for all children, rich or poor, boy or girl. Included in the curriculum are the correct use of the vernacular language, social habits, and religious training. The program at this level would emphasize training of the "internal senses, the imagination and memory in combination with their cognate organs." Comenius accepted the faculty psychology point of view in respect to memory. "The memory should be exercised in early youth, since practise developes it, and we should therefore take care to practise it as much as possible. Now, in youth, the labour is not felt, and thus the memory developes without any trouble and becomes very retentive" (Comenius, 1923: 152).

For the next 6 years, from ages 12 to 18, which include the adolescent period as we understand it today, education was to be provided in the Latin school. The psychological purpose of the school at this age was to train the faculty of reasoning. The student learned to "understand and pass judgment on the information collected by the senses." Included were judgments about relationships of the things perceived, imagined, and remembered. Understanding here implies utilization of the principle of causality. The curriculum of the school was divided into 6 years, which results in the following six classes: Grammar, Natural Philosophy, Mathematics, Ethics, Dialectics, and Rhetoric.

The following 6 years, from ages 18 to 24, consist of university education and travel, and during this period the faculty of the will is trained. Considering our present conception of will, this appears to be a strange notion and becomes more meaningful only if we consider that the concept of will, as used by Comenius, includes the idea of choice, self-determination and self-direction of one's life. Corresponding ideas can be found in the theories of Erikson and Piaget.

Comenius strongly advocated that the instructional procedure fit the level of comprehension of the child in contrast to the Scholastic education, which he opposed. For Comenius, development is not uniform, continuous, and gradual—as the homunculus theory of development implies—but each stage of development has its own characteristics, "teachable moments" as Havighurst and many developmental stage theorists would say. Development was seen as a process in which the intellectual functions gain progressively more control over the other aspects of the soul.

To attempt to cultivate the will before the intellect (or the intellect before the imagination, or the imagination before the faculty of sense perception) is mere waste of time. But this is what those do who teach boys logic, poetry, rhetoric, and ethics before they are thoroughly acquainted with the objects that surround them. It would be equally sensible to teach boys of two years old to dance, though they can scarcely walk [Comenius, 1923: 257].

The right time for the education of each of the faculties must be chosen correctly, and the sequence must be "borrowed from nature." In Comenius' continuous focus on what children can do, know, and are interested in at each stage of development, one can find the historical roots of a child-centered theory of education.

JOHN LOCKE'S EMPIRICISM

The idea of homunculism with its emphasis on preformationism and Plato's theory of innate ideas—a basic Scholastic principle—was most seriously challenged and opposed by John Locke (1632–1704). Locke was influenced by Thomas Hobbes' (1588–1679) idea that the human being, both body and mind, is part of the natural order; he further expanded Hobbes' theoretical position, known today as empiricism, that all of our knowledge is derived from sensation. Hobbes stated in *Leviathan* that "there is no conception in man's mind, which has not at first, totally, or by parts, been begotten upon the organs of sense" (Hobbes, 1651: 7). Locke further developed the theory that there are no innate ideas. Ideas that can be found in consciousness are either obtained through our senses directly or are derived from those ideas that have been obtained through sensations previously. The child's mind at the time of birth is, according to an analogy used by Locke, a *tabula rasa,* a blank tablet, as the following quote implies:

> Let us then suppose the mind to be, as we say, white paper, void of all characters, without any ideas;—How comes it to be furnished? . . . To this, I answer, in one word, from EXPERIENCE. In that all our knowledge is founded, and from that it ultimately derives itself. Our observation, employed either about external, sensible objects, or about the internal operations of our minds, perceived, and reflected on, by ourselves, is that which supplies our understandings with all the materials of thinking. These two are the fountains of knowledge, from whence all the ideas we have, or can naturally have, do spring [Locke, 1753: 76].

This assumption has had far-reaching influence on social theory and has with amplification become the cornerstone of democracy. Since the mind of each person at birth is a *tabula rasa,* all ideas and knowledge come from experience. Since present differences and inequalities found in people are due to environment and experiences, all are completely equal at birth. Thus the principle of democracy is in part derived from a philosophical-psychological theory concerning the child's mind at birth. Locke discussed his views concerning democracy in *Treatise of Civil Government* (1768). He blamed environmental conditions, such as poor education and poor social environment, for the human misery in the world and gave hope to those who lived under unfavorable conditions. Thus emerged a theory that is an expression of faith in the perfectibility of the human race.

Locke found rather enthusiastic followers in Helvetius and Condillac in France. They carried his empiricism to its extreme, since for them even the powers of faculties of the mind were the result of sensation. Furthermore, since poor living conditions existed for the French lower and middle classes prior to the Revolution, many people in France were especially susceptible to such ideas. Thus, the words *liberté, egalité, fraternité* became the powerful symbols of a new concept of human nature. A new hope emerged, that by changing the environment, human nature could be changed.

Locke's proposition that there are no innate ideas and that the mind is a *tabula rasa* contrasts sharply with several theories of development already discussed. The more outstanding examples are as follows:

1. The doctrine of human depravity and original sin appeared to be in contradiction to Locke's new concept of the human mind. If our mind is formed by experience only, then it follows that whether a child becomes "good" or "bad" is due to environmental experiences. Locke's psychology stresses nurture rather than nature.

2. The medieval class system of Europe was based on what are considered today **hereditary assumptions.** The nobility was noble by birth, regardless of personal merits and qualities. This notion was challenged by the empiricst assumption that "all men are born equal." If everyone is alike and begins life at the same point, then everyone should have the same rights and opportunities to obtain better social positions. King and subject, rich and poor, all begin life at the same point. Therefore, support for social mobility is found in this theory. Locke's early form of environmentalism, even though it is not directly related to behaviorism, social learning theory, and cultural relativism, may be viewed as a historical forerunner to these schools of thought.

3. The doctrine of innate ideas was interpreted during the medieval period to imply that the child is a miniature adult and grows only quantitatively. Locke's *tabula rasa* concept implied that the child at birth is qualitatively and quantitatively different from the adult. If ideas are not innate, then the newborn child is radically different from the adult in respect to intellectual properties. Locke pointed out that the child's personality is different from that of the adult and thus laid the foundation for a new theory of child development; he also urged the scientific study of human nature. Development occurred in a gradual process from mental passivity in the early years of childhood to increased mental activity in adolescence. The rational faculty emerges toward the end of this developmental process and therefore was seen as characteristic of the period of adolescence.

Locke, even though he advanced many important ideas about human nature, foreshadowed rather than developed a specific theory of human development.

JEAN-JACQUES ROUSSEAU'S ROMANTIC NATURALISM

Rousseau (1712–1778) was partly influenced by Locke's ideas, but he developed his own theoretical positions concerning human nature. For Locke reason was the most important aspect of human nature. Rousseau considered human nature as primarily feeling. While Locke was concerned with constitutional government, Rousseau made a strong plea for individualism and individual freedom and directed his critical attack against society and social institutions. Although he, too, was concerned with the social well-being of all, he distinguished between the "will of all" (majority will, determined by vote) and the "general will" (that which is really best for every member of society). Rousseau was not truly democratic, for he was afraid that rule by majority vote could be as bad as any monarchy. Ideally, the majority will and the general will would coincide. This, however, would only be possible if men were educated and wise.

Rousseau brought about a revolutionary change in thought concerning the nature of human development, with its corresponding educational implications, the main ideas of which he expressed in *Émile* (1780). The traditional approach toward childhood education had been to see the child from the adult point of view. Rousseau claimed that such an approach is not only false, it may even be harmful. He started with the needs and interests of the child and saw development as a natural preplanned process, as the following ideas reveal. If one were to free the child from the restrictions, unnatural limitations, and rigid discipline of the adult world, nature would assure a harmonious and healthy development. The child was innately good, but the restrictions of adult society and poor education tended to corrupt the child. To prevent this, he advocated a natural development in a sound and healthy environment, which for him was one that posed few restrictions on the child, especially in the first 12 years. Rousseau was one of the strongest proponents of individualism in education, basing his proposition on a deep faith in the natural goodness of man.

Rousseau advocated a revision of the treatment children received at home and in school as well as changes in the methods of instruction; if development were left to the laws of nature, the outcome would be most desirable. Each of Rousseau's four stages of development had specific psychological characteristics. Consideration of these characteristics resulted in definite educational objectives, the attainment of which helped children grow toward maturity. The educational methods, the content to be taught, and the objectives at each age level were to be determined by the characteristics of the child at that developmental level. Learning was most effective if the child had freedom and could learn and grow according to his own impulses, needs, and abilities.

Rousseau most strongly opposed the homunculus idea and asserted that it was the plan of nature that children play, live, and behave like children before they become adults. "Childhood has its own way of seeing, thinking, and feeling, and nothing is more foolish than to try to substitute ours for them" (Rousseau, 1911: 54). Rousseau advised teachers and parents, "You ought to be wholly absorbed in the child—observing him, watching him without respite, and without seeming to do so, having a presentiment of his feelings in advance" (Rousseau, 1911: 169). Even though Rousseau himself had only limited and not always successful educational experiences—his five children lived in a foundling asylum—his theory had a tremendous impact on educational practice in the latter part of the eighteenth and most of the nineteenth centuries. Rousseau's ideas are obvious in the works of Pestalozzi, Froebel, and Spencer in Europe, and are reflected in the approach of Horace Mann and John Dewey in the United States.

Rousseau, like Aristotle, saw the development of the chid occurring in certain stages; however, he identified four stages rather than three and believed that teaching and training should be in harmony with the developmental nature of each of these stages. According to Rousseau, these various stages are qualitative transformations in the developmental process, and each can be distinguished by its special characteristics and functions. He spoke of a metamorphosis that takes place when the child changes from one stage to another. Thus, Rousseau introduced a saltatory theory of human development according to which the nature of development is seen as change that is more sudden at certain age levels than at others. He, like G. Stanley Hall, spoke of puberty as a new birth. New functions may emerge rather suddenly and become dominant in the psychological organization. This saltatory aspect of Rousseau's theory can be better understood in the light of his own temperamental saltatory experiences.

The first stage, that of infancy, includes the first 4 to 5 years of life. The child is dominated by the feeling of pleasure and pain. This period is called the animal stage, because the child is like an animal in regard to its physical needs and undifferentiated feelings. This idea had been expressed earlier in the writings of Aristotle and later by Freud. Education, such as training motor coordination, sense perception, and feelings, is primarily physical. He advocated that the method of nature be followed in everything and proposed the following rule: "Observe nature, and follow the route which she traces for you. She is ever exciting children to activity; she hardens the constitution by trials of every sort; she teaches them at an early hour what suffering and pain are."

The second stage, which Rousseau characterized as the savage stage, includes the years from 5 to 12. Dominant during this stage is the faculty of sense. Sensory experiences are provided by play, sport, and games, and the curriculum is centered on the training of the senses. During this stage, self-consciousness and memory develop, and human life in the proper sense begins here. The child still lacks reasoning ability and is not yet sufficiently aware of moral considerations. Education during this stage should be free from external, social, and moral control. Formal training in reading and writing are seen as harmful and therefore postponed until the beginning of the third developmental stage. In the first 12 years, education

> . . . ought to be purely negative. It consists not at all in teaching virtues or truth, but in shielding the heart from vice, and the mind from error. If you could do nothing and allow nothing to be done, if you could bring your pupil sound and robust to the age of twelve years without his being able to distinguish his right hand from his left, from your very first lesson the eyes of his understanding would be open to reason [Rousseau, 1911: 59].

Rousseau's method of "negative education," which assumes that there is an innate developmental plan that cannot be improved upon by environmental factors, finds its corresponding modern expression in maturational theories. The defenders of the maturational concept of development frequently advocate, as did Rousseau, a permissive and unrestricted atmosphere for childrearing, and let the child be guided by his/her own inclinations, based on an assumption of "the wisdom of the body."

The third stage, the years from 12 to 15, is characterized by an awakening of the rational functions, including reason and self-consciousness. Youth at this age possess an enormous amount of physical energy and strength. The excess of energy leads to curiosity, which the school curriculum should utilize by encouraging exploratory behavior and the desire to discover what is true about the world. The only book that should be read is *Robinson Crusoe*. Rousseau saw in Crusoe the great model and ideal for the preadolescent, since his style of life was characterized by exploration of the world and a primitive curiosity, which corresponds to the needs and interests of this developmental stage. The curriculum should be geared to the study of nature, astronomy, science, art, and crafts. Rousseau, in agreement with contemporary educational theory, emphasizes the learning process rather than the product. "He is not to learn science, he is to find out for himself." This is the age of reason; curiosity and personal utility are the main motives for behavior; social conscience and emotionality are still undeveloped. It is interesting to observe that, in opposition to other developmental theories, the rational aspect of personality develops prior to the emotional. Rousseau placed great value on emotional development. His theory was a reaction to the historically earlier philosophy of rationalism, with which he differed.

The fourth period, adolescence proper, from the age of 15 to 20, finally culminates in the maturation of the emotional functions and brings about a change from selfishness to social consideration and self-esteem. The adolescent is no longer dominated by self-interest but develops a strong interest in other people and a need for genuine affection. This stage is characterized by the emergence of the sex drive (late by comparison to knowledge about youth today) which Rousseau considered a second birth. "We have two births, so to speak—one for existing and the other for living; one for the species and the other for the sex" (Rousseau, 1911: 193). Now conscience is acquired, and morals and virtues become possible. This is the period of preparation for marriage, which ideally coincides with the attainment of maturity.

Maturity could be considered as a fifth stage in the process, but it is less clearly defined. The faculty that becomes dominant during this period is will. Comenius also placed the development of the will at the time of late adolescence. The will is the faculty of the soul by which we make decisions and choose between alternatives.

These stages of development, according to Rousseau, correspond to certain stages in the development of the human race. Thus, it was assumed by this recapitulation theory that the human race had gone through the stages of animal-like living, the stage of savagery, the stage of reason, and, finally, through a stage of social and emotional maturity. He used the historical development of the race in order to explain the development of the individual child. This hypothesis was further developed by educators such as Froebel and Ziller, as well as by G. Stanley Hall and the Child Study Movement of America.

Critics feel that Rousseau overemphasized the individual nature and the emotional aspect of development and underemphasized the importance of education, society, and culture in the growth process and especially in the formation of the personality. He saw the influence of society and culture as negative forces in personality development; he wanted to remove their detrimental influences to make possible the free, unrestricted, natural unfolding of what is good in the child.

CHARLES DARWIN'S THEORY OF BIOLOGICAL EVOLUTION

A new trend of thought concerning the nature of development emerged with the publication of Darwin's *Origin of Species* (1859). Darwin's (1809–1882) idea of evolution—growth and development from the simpler to the more complex forms of organic life—has been one of the most revolutionary and influential ideas in man's thinking about himself and the nature of his development. Every living organisms from the simplest structure to the most complex, man himself, is brought together under the order of natural explanation. The psychological implications resulting from this biological concept of development were accepted, elaborated, and applied to adolescence by G. Stanley Hall, and also by Freud, thus leading to a science of adolescent development.

Since Darwin's theory is well known and does not propose a psychological or educational theory of development, only its basic principles will be stated. Darwin collected substantial, though not complete, evidence for a theory that claimed that the evolution of biological life is continuous, from a single-cell organism through numerous higher developmental stages to the complexity of human mind and body. This evolutionary theory assumed variability and adjustability in all organisms as well as the overproduction in the number of offspring of each species. Darwin showed that the overproduction of offspring threatened a species' capacity to survive. The result is a "struggle for existence." In this struggle of the selection of some and elimination of others, a "natural selection process" takes place by which the increase in population is checked. The stronger, healthier, faster, more immune, more intelligent, and physically better-adjusted organisms survive and reproduce, while the weak, sick, and less adaptable species perish. In time this leads to the "survival of the fittest." The qualitites that account for the survival of the fittest are inherited by the offspring. Since the conditions for survival frequently differ in various kinds of environments, changes in the organisms occur. Thus in the selection process, variations, new kinds, new races, and eventually new organisms come into existence. This process began with the simple one-cell organism, and from the lower forms of organic life more and more complex forms have developed. The last link in this biological evolution is the human being. Since climatic, geological, and general life conditions change, the evolutionary process is a perpetual one.

This theory of evolution stands in complete contrast to the theological doctrine of the divine creation of humankind. Through Darwin's theory mankind was placed in the order of nature. Most theological and many philosophical positions previous to Darwin's—for example, that of Aristotle—had postulated an essential dichotomy between man and nature. This absolute distinction between human nature and the nature of the organic world was seriously challenged by Darwin. Humans lost their special position and were now seen as part of the organic world, albeit a more advanced and more intelligent species.

G. STANLEY HALL'S BIOGENETIC PSYCHOLOGY OF ADOLESCENCE

G. Stanley Hall (1844–1924) was the first psychologist to advance a psychology of adolescence in its own right and to use scientific methods in his study of adolescence. It can be said that he bridged the philosophical, speculative approach of the past and the scientific, empirical approach of the present.

Hall expanded Darwin's concept of biological "evolution" into a psychological theory of recapitulation. This theory postulated that the experiential history of *homo sapiens* had become part of the genetic structure of each individual. The law of recapitulation asserted that each individual, during his or her development, passes through stages that correspond to those that occurred during the history of mankind. That is, as the child's development progresses he or she relives the development of the human race from early animal-like primitivism, through a period of savagery, to the more recent civilized ways of life that characterize maturity.

Hall assumed that development is brought about by physiological changes. He further assumed that these physiological factors are genetically determined, that internal maturational forces predominantly control and direct development, growth, and behavior. There was little room in this theory for the influence of environmental forces. It follows that development and its behavioral concomitants occur in an inevitable and unchangeable pattern that is universal, regardless of the social and cultural environment. Cultural anthropologists and sociologists have challenged this point and asserted that Hall's position was extreme and untenable. They further refuted the claim that the behavioral predispositions of physiological drives, as expressed in the recapitulation theory, are highly specific. Hall held that socially unacceptable types of behavior—those characteristic of earlier historical phases— must be tolerated by parents and educators, since they are necessary stages in social development. He, like Rousseau before him, and Gesell subsequently, advocated childrearing practices of leniency and permissiveness. However, he reassured parents and educators that unacceptable behavior would disappear in the following developmental stage without any corrective educational or disciplinary efforts.

A corollary of Hall's theory of recapitulation is his concept of stages of human development; the characteristics of a certain age in the development of the individual correspond to some primitive historical stage in the development of the human race. Hall did not divide human development into three stages, as advocated by Aristotle and many present-day "stage" psychologists. He followed a four-division pattern similar to that proposed by Comenius and Rousseau. Hall's developmental stages are infancy, childhood, youth, and adolescence.

The period of infancy includes the first 4 years of life. While children are still crawling, they are recapitulating the animal stage of the human race when the species was still using four legs. During this period, sensory development is dominant; the child acquires those sensorimotor skills that are necessary for self-preservation.

The period of chidlhood—the years from 4 to 8—recapitulates the cultural epoch when hunting and fishing were the main activities of man. This is the time when the child plays hide-and-seek, cowboys and Indians, uses toy weapons, slings, and bow and arrows. The building of caves, shacks, tree houses, and hiding places parallels the cave-dwelling culture of early history.

Youth—from 8 to 12—includes the period that today is referred to as "preadolescence." During this stage the child recapitulates the "humdrum life of savagery" of several thousand years ago. This is the period when the child has a favorable predisposition to practice and discipline, when routine training and drill are most appropriate.

> Never again will there be such susceptibility to drill and discipline, such plasticity to habituation, or such ready adjustment to new conditions. It is the age of external and mechanical training. Reading, writing, drawing, manual training, musical technic, foreign tongues and their pronunciation, the manipulation of numbers and of geometrical elements, and many kinds of skill have now their golden hour, and if it passes unimproved, all these can never be acquired later without a heavy handicap of disadvantage and loss [Hall, 1916: xii].

Adolescence is the period from puberty until full adult status has been attained. According to Hall, it ends comparatively late, between the twenty-second and twenty-fifth years. Hall described adolescence as a period of *Sturm und Drang,* "storm and stress." In German literature, the period of *Sturm und Drang* includes, among others, the works of Schiller and the early writings of Goethe. It is a literary movement full of idealism, commitment to a goal, revolution against the old, expression of personal feelings, passion, and suffering. Hall saw an analogy between the objectives of this group of writers at the turn of the eighteenth century and the characteristics of adolescence. In terms of recapitulation theory, adolescence corresponds to a time when the human race was in a turbulent, transitional stage. Hall described adolescence as a new birth, "for the higher and more completely human traits are now born" (Hall, 1916: xiii).

The characteristics of adolescent *Sturm und Drang* are pictured in detail by Hall in the chapter, "Feelings and Psychic Evolution" (Hall, 1916). He perceived the emotional life of the adolescent as an oscillation between contradictory tendencies. Energy, exaltation, and supernatural activity are followed by indifference, lethargy, and loathing. Exuberant gaiety, laughter, and euphoria make place for dysphoria, depressive gloom, and melancholy. Egoism, vanity, and conceit are just as characteristic of this period of life as are abasement, humiliation, and bashfulness. One can observe both the remnants of an uninhibited childish selfishness and an increasing idealistic altruism. Goodness and virtue are never so pure, but never again does temptation so forcefully preoccupy thought. Adolescents want solitude and seclusion, while finding themselves entangled in crushes and friendships. Never again does the peer group have such a strong influence. At one time the adolescent may exhibit exquisite sensitivity and tenderness; at another time, callousness and cruelty. Apathy and inertia vacillate with an enthusiastic curiosity, an urge to discover and explore. There is a yearning for idols and authority that does not exclude a revolutionary radicalism directed against any kind of authority. Hall (1916) implies these antithetical impulses of Promethean enthusiasm and deep sentimental *Weltschmerz* (sorrow and sadness about the state of the world) in his use of the concept of *Sturm und Drang,* which for him is so characteristic of the adolescent.

In late adolescence the individual recapitulates the stage of the beginning of modern civilization. This stage corresponds to the end of the developmental process: the adolescent reaches maturity. Hall's genetic psychology did not see the human being as the final product of the developmental process; it allowed for indefinite development.

2

THE PSYCHOANALYTIC THEORY OF ADOLESCENT DEVELOPMENT

INTRODUCTION TO PSYCHOANALYTIC THEORY

Sigmund Freud (1856–1939) developed a comprehensive theory of psychopathology, of personality, and of human development and founded the psychoanalytic movement. His theory was revolutionary, since it fundamentally changed the conceptual foundation of psychology and psychiatry of his time; it has remained influential to this day. Psychoanalysis was based on concepts and on insights into the workings of the human mind that had received little systematic attention in pre-Freudian psychology. The new ideas of physics and biology emphasized energy and dynamics and were prevalent toward the end of the nineteenth century. Darwin's notion of evolution influenced Freud's thinking and became part of his psychodynamic theory. He believed that all psychological events are tied to energy, drive, and instincts based on biological characteristics.

Freud's theoretical assumption concerning the nature of man has dramatically changed man's conception of himself. Freud is often identified as one of the most important thinkers of the twentieth century, comparable in influence to Copernicus and Darwin. Copernicus changed our geocentric view of the world. Darwin's theory removed the human race from its special position in relationship to God and placed it within the continuum of natural evolution as part of the animal world; humans were seen as no more than just another animal with specific survival mechanisms. Freud, in turn, made explicit that humans were not the rational, logical, and intelligent beings they were believed to be but instead were irrational and influenced by hidden, unconscious motives of which they themselves were often not aware. Freud implied that the crucial psychological reality is desire rather than reason.

The significance of Freud's work is not limited to psychology, psychiatry, and psychoanalysis proper; his ideas have also become influential in literature, art, advertisement, philosophy, sociology, medicine, and education. His contributions to our understanding of the mind have penetrated many areas of modern Western culture and thought to such an extent that his ideas have become part of people's "implicit psychology" to a much larger extent than is commonly acknowledged. Freud's contribution to our understanding of the nature of the mind contains several identifiable ideas:

1. All behavior is motivated, often by unconscious dynamics.
2. Freud's theory of dreams emphasized the meaningfulness of dreams as manifestations of the unconscious mind.
3. Similarly, Freud ascribes meaning to errors, forgettings, slips of the tongue, and other unintended behavior, believing that they are expressions of unconscious forces.
4. A major motivating force in human behavior is sexuality, including the idea of infantile sexuality. Freud emphasized the conflictual relationship between sexuality and civilization.
5. Early childrearing experiences, especially in weaning, toilet training, and the role of the family in the handling of sexuality and aggression, are seen as significant factors in development.
6. Freud gave new hope to the treatment of psychopathology and changed social attitudes toward the neurotic and psychotic.

After completion of his medical training, Freud began his medical career in Vienna as a research scientist in neurology, hoping to become a professor rather than a practicing physician. However, because he saw limited opportunities for advancement in the university setting and since he needed to support his family, he was forced to practice medicine. As a medical specialist in neurology, he began to see patients with neuropsychological problems. The treatment of nervous disorders was a branch of medicine that was, at that time, primitive, and few treatment modalities existed that could successfully be used in dealing with patients with mental aberrations.

Freud's scientific inclination led him to the discovery and development of new treatment methods. He systematically collected observational and case study data, supplementing them with his own famous self-analysis, to which he devoted the last half hour of each day from 1897 until his death in 1939. Freud's theory evolved only slowly and was a multifaceted theory of various models and explanatory systems of psychopathology, the nature of dreams, human motivation, and the inner workings of the mind. Like the theories of Copernicus, Darwin, and other revolutionary thinkers before him, Freud's formulations were met with bitter resistance and objections from other scientists.

A rather careful review of the empirical research literature attempting to test Freud's theoretical assumptions concludes:

> Large masses of experimental information are available for testing psychoanalytic propositions. We have been amused by the fact that while there is the stereotyped conviction widely current that Freud's thinking is not amenable to scientific appraisal, the quantity of research data pertinent to it that has accumulated in the literature

Sigmund Freud (1856-1939)

grossly exceeds that available for most other personality or developmental theories. We have actually not been able to find a single systematic theory that has been as frequently evaluated scientifically as have Freud's concepts [Fisher and Greenberg, 1977: 396].

While not all of Freud's concepts receive unequivocal empirical support, many do, and many others receive at least partial support. Apparently, Freud's concepts of the oral and the anal personality, several aspects of the Oedipus complex theory, and his theory of the origin of paranoid delusions seem to find substantial support from empirical investigations. Other aspects of Freud's theory, such as the nature of dreaming, the effectiveness of psychoanalytic therapy, the psychology of women, and sex differences are not borne out by empirical studies. In general, there is much more support for Freud's overall theoretical propositions concerning human nature and personality development than for his practical suggestions about conducting psychotherapy (Fisher and Greenberg, 1977).

Space does not allow a discussion of the entire system of psychoanalytic theory. Therefore, in the context of theories of development and especially theories of adolescence, only those models especially relevant to an understanding of personality development will be discussed.

1. The topographical model of the mind consists of three layers: the conscious, the preconscious, and the unconscious. This conceptualization of the tripartite organization of the mind grew out of Freud's book, *The Interpretation of Dreams* (1990/1953).
2. Another tripartite model of the mind, which Freud later developed in *The Ego and the Id* (1923/1961), was based on the structural hypothesis. It comprises the id, the ego, and the superego. These two systems are not only compatible but have been integrated into a more dynamic view of the inner workings of the mind and thus contribute to an understanding of personality development as well as to the dynamics of psychopathology.
3. The psychosexual stages of human development are the oral, anal, phallic, latency, and genital stages. These are of particular significance for our concern with theories of adolescence, since they constitute the cornerstone of Freud's developmental theory.
4. The mechanisms of defense: repression, displacement, identification, rationalization, reaction formation, introjection, projection, undoing, and denial. These are mechanisms by which the ego defends against the unacceptable and painful or anxiety-arousing wishes of the id. Anna Freud considered asceticism and intellectualization especially characteristic of pubescence. O. Rank also viewed asceticism as typical for adolescents but contrasts it with its opposite, promiscuity.

Freud's theory of psychosexual development has stimulated considerable research interest and further theoretical development in personality development in general and adolescent development in particular, research was carried out by such psychoanalysts as Hartmann, Horney, Sullivan, Winnicott, Fromm, Reich, Rank, A. Freud, Erikson, and Blos. Freud himself, partly because of this preoccupation with the role of infantile sexuality in normal and abnormal development and partly because of his emphasis on the importance of the first 5 years of life in human development, climaxing in the Oedipus complex, placed relatively little emphasis on pubescence and adolescence. Many neo-Freudians seem to agree with this neglect of the period of adolescence in Freud's original theory. Among the neo-Freudians, E. Erikson and P. Blos in particular have rectified this theoretical neglect by placing particular emphasis on the period of adolescence.

CONSCIOUS—PRECONSCIOUS—UNCONSCIOUS

The first tripartite model of the mind emerged from Freud's efforts to explain the psychology of the dream processes. The mind, according to Freud (1900/1953, 1915/1957), consisted of three layers: the conscious, the preconscious, and the unconscious. This early comprehensive theory of personality and development is referred to as the "topographical model."

The *conscious* is that layer of the mental apparatus of which the individual is aware. It provides contact with both the external world—through perceptions, motor activity, and feelings—and with the internal personal world of dreams, images, and thoughts. Consciousness itself contains only a very small and limited part of the mental life. The metaphor often used is the iceberg, of which only a very small part floats over the surface while most of it is under water. (See Figure 2.1.) Freud emphasized that only a very limited part of our mental activity takes place in the conscious at any one time. However, the conscious also has the function of censorship, admitting or excluding thoughts and ideas from awareness.

The much greater part of our mental activity remains more or less inaccessible in the lower regions of the mental structures. One of the major tasks of psychoanalytic treatment is, according to Freud, the uncovering of this hidden material to make unconscious content, motives, and dynamics conscious. It is assumed that only the patient's conscious understanding of these hidden dynamics makes a realistic and thoughtful adjustment possible, and this is the task of psychoanalytic therapy.

The *preconscious,* in a certain sense, is part of the unconscious, since the individual is not aware of its content. Yet much of it, particularly in the upper regions of the preconscious, is easily accessible to the conscious, since the content can voluntarily be retrieved by directing one's attention to it. This can be achieved by asking relevant questions or by providing appropriate stimuli. The preconscious constitutes much of the mental warehouse of information and experiences, accessible through memory and, therefore, basically accessible to the conscious on request. Most of the ideas that are not at present in our awareness but that can, through the process of memory, retrieval, and thinking, be brought back into our conscious mind are in our preconscious.

The preconscious, however, is not a passive storehouse of information but is actively involved in many mental activities. According to Kubie (1958), sudden insights into complex problems or creative thoughts and discoveries do emerge from preconscious processes. Often the solution to a problem does not emerge while one is deliberately working on it but seems to pop into one's mind from the preconscious, without any conscious effort, when one is relaxed or about to go to sleep, and sometimes solutions emerge even when one is not consciously aware of the problem.

The *unconscious* contains experiences and information that cannot readily be brought into awareness by volition, but require special efforts, treatment, hypnosis, or interpretation to be brought back into the conscious. However, for Freud, the unconscious was the

LEVEL OF AWARENESS   LEVEL OF RECALL

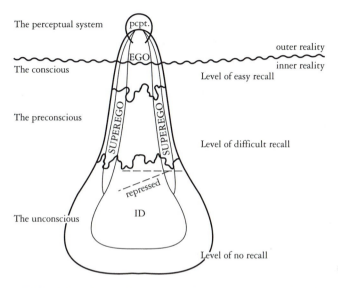

FIGURE 2.1 Freud's model of the mind. A schematic presentation of Freud's theory of the mind in which the structural model and the topographical model are combined (adapted from S. Freud [1933/1964] and Kaplan and Baron [1952]).

dominant force in the mental apparatus, especially in psychopathology. The pathway between the unconscious and the conscious is normally blocked, but the pathway between the preconscious and the conscious is at least partially open. The content of the unconscious (traumatic experiences, unacceptable impulses, and such) are kept in the unconscious by repression; however, they are not dormant but remain dynamic and active. Although the constant process of repression itself is not conscious, it consumes psychological energy. However, repression is unable to restrain the unconscious impulses permanently, hence these impulses and experiences manifest themselves in distorted, nonrecognizable form in dream content, errors, accidents, and neurotic symptoms. Thus, an accident may be understood as an unconscious desire to punish oneself for forbidden thoughts or deeds. The craving for sweets is viewed as an unconscious, symbolic, repressed desire for human love. Dreaming is a process by which the repressed unconscious wish (the latent dream content) finds a distorted conscious manifestation in the dream experiences (the manifest dream content).

    Scientific evidence supports Freud's basic assumption that motives, wishes, feelings, and fantasies exist in an individual without conscious awareness of these hidden dynamic forces; furthermore, these hidden forces are known to influence behavior (Fisher and Greenberg, 1977).

ID—EGO—SUPEREGO

Later Freud developed in *The Ego and the Id* (1923/1961) another tripartite model of the mind that is closely related to the topographical model of conscious, preconscious, and unconscious. Each component of this id–ego–superego model emerges during different stages of psychosexual development (the developmental model will be discussed later). In the structural model Freud conceptualizes the structure of the mind as consisting of three major systems: the id (biological), the ego (psychological), and the superego (social). In the healthy adult person, these three systems—id, ego, and superego—form an integrated personality pattern, which aids the individual in conducting daily interactions with the environment and allows satisfaction of basic needs and desires within socially prescribed limits. In the neurotic person, these systems are in conflict, necessitating the use of defense mechanisms or maladaptive manifestations, and thus reducing the efficiency of that person's everyday functioning.

> A number of psychoanalysts assert that some of the reemergence of infantile or childish behaviors that may occur in early adolescence is due to regression. Faced on the one hand by the problem of coping with a sudden upsurge in sexual and aggressive drives and the anxiety that they create, and on the other hand by greatly increased social demands, the adolescent may temporarily abandon anxiety-producing and not always successful efforts at more mature responding, and retreat to more "primitive" responses that were successful and rewarding in an earlier, simpler period [Conger, 1977: 84].

The id is present at birth and governed by the pleasure principle. The id provides the mind with its psychological energy, impulses, and motivation to act. It represents the biological component of the mental apparatus, including untamed passion. It contains irrational instinctual appetites and impulses, and its purpose is to gratify basic instinctual and bodily needs and reduce the tensions produced by these biological needs. The contents and the processes of the id are primarily but not exclusively unconscious. Tension reduction, which comes about when basic biological needs are gratified, is pleasurable. Hence, the object that reduces bodily tensions becomes attached (or cathected) to the id. Freudians speak extensively of libidinal object finding, and the object can be a thing, the self or part of the self, or another person: oral object choice, anal object choice, parent object choice, Oedipal object choice, same sex and opposite sex object choice. In the young infant the drive of the id is not yet restrained by moral or practical considerations but is directly oriented toward drive gratification. The operations of the id are, therefore, referred to as "primary processes."

Even later in life, an id-dominated personality asserts little or no control over instinctual wishes and sexual desires. Such a person's behavior is mainly influenced by the immediate gratification of the pleasure-seeking motive and would show little concern either for the demands of reality or for social or ethical values. The acting-out juvenile delinquent as well as the promiscuous sexual behavior of the adolescent seem to be illustrations of id-dominated behavior.

■ Development of the Ego

The ego develops in part out of the id during the end of the first through the second year of life and is defined by its reality-testing functions. The most important function of the ego is the adaptation of the individual to reality (S. Freud, 1933/1964).

Toilet training advances ego development since it contributes to the delineation of body boundaries or, in a more general sense, to a distinction between the self and the outside world. The ego represents the psychological component of the personality, but the id still remains the dominant element in the partnership between id, ego, and superego. This emergence of the ego out of the id takes place when the demands of the id are not met and transactions between the organism and the outside world become necessary to discharge tensions. When needs are not satisfied, two consequences can occur:

1. The infant remains in a state of tension.
2. The id, having to cope with unresolved tension, is transformed into a new structure, the "I" or the ego, which takes into account the external reality that does not allow the uninhibited gratification of impulses, and in the process the maturing child learns to cope with the tensions stemming from the needs of the id that are in conflict with the demands of reality.

The ego serves several functions in the mental apparatus. First and foremost, the function of the ego is to compromise between the inner world of subjective experiences, the id, and the demands of the external (objective) world. It obeys the reality principle. The ego has a reality-testing function; that is, it delays, inhibits, restrains, and controls the demands of the id—not permanently, however, but only in order to maximize its gratification at the appropriate time and place, when short-range as well as long-range consequences are being considered, and when the gratification of a desire is actually in the individual's best interest. The ego also considers whether the object is appropriate for the gratification of the needs of the id. The ego takes on several other functions. It prevents the drive discharge when such behavior would not be in the individual's best interest; that is, it helps the individual develop impulse control and frustration tolerance. It also controls the ideas that enter consciousness. Furthermore, through various defense mechanisms at the disposal of the ego, ideas that are dangerous or arouse anxiety may be prevented from entering the conscious or may be distorted. The ego thus guides the behavior of an individual toward goals that are realistic and are assumed to have no negative consequences. In that sense all cognition is a function of the ego. Finally, the ego encompasses logical thinking.

The ego represents the external world to the id. It consists of reason, common sense, and reality-testing functions, but serves the purpose of the id from which it borrows its energies. The metaphor used by Freud was that of the horse (id), constituting instinctual drive and energy, and the rider (ego) who controls where and how fast the horse can go.

> The ego's relation to the id might be compared with that of a rider to his horse. The horse supplies the locomotive energy, while the rider has the privilege of deciding on the goal and of guiding the powerful animal's movement. But only too often there arises between the ego and the id the not precisely ideal situation of the rider being obliged to guide the horse along the path by which it itself wants to go [S. Freud, 1933/1964: 77].

On the other hand, there often are no real differences between the goals of the id and the ego, only differences in the way these goals can be attained. The ego tries to avoid the negative consequences that could result from an uninhibited gratification of the id impulses.

■ Development of the Superego

Later in human development, during the latency period, the superego develops, primarily as a function of the resolution of the Oedipus complex. Freud (1923/1949) views the superego as the "heir of the Oedipus complex."

Research findings suggest that the development of the superego is less a direct outgrowth of oedipal tensions and conflicts with the father than Freud suggested. Instead, the mother's and other people's standards play a larger role and are more positively assimilated and gradually integrated in the self-structures than Freud had theorized. The oedipal struggle itself is resolved most effectively, not out of fear of the father (castration anxiety) but out of the nurturant, friendly attitude on the father's part (Fisher and Greenberg, 1977).

The superego represents the social-moral component in the personality. It represents the ideal rather than the real and strives for perfection. The individual's internalized moral code develops out of a process of identification with one's parents and their standards as to what is good or bad, virtuous or wicked. Later, the superego becomes the internal representation not only of parental mores but, in a more generalized sense, of societal rules and cultural restrictions on the expression of instinctual drives. The development of the superego approaches its completion at the beginning of puberty, which means that self-control begins to replace the control through reward and punishment by parents, and anxiety and guilt become the self-administered punishment of the superego. The superego has two components. The *conscience,* which reacts to moral transgressions by producing guilt feelings when internalized moral values are violated, and the *ego-ideal,* which produces pride and satisfaction when behavior corresponds to internalized standards. At this point of development, when the tentative balance between id, ego, and superego is just beginning to emerge, the awakening sexual tensions of puberty demand id gratification and thus produce serious conflicts in the personality structure.

The sueprego serves three functions:

1. To inhibit, especially the aggressive and sexual impules of the id that are not approved by society
2. To persuade the ego to substitute moralistic goals for realistic goals
3. To strive for perfection (Hall, 1954)

Considering the relationship between the topographical model of the conscious, preconscious, and unconscious to the structural model of the id, ego, and superego provides a more dynamic understanding of the mental apparatus. The id corresponds most closely to the unconscious in the topographical model. The ego is not sharply distinguished from the id, but its lower portions flow into the id and the unconscious. Repressed ideas merge into the id but are sharply segregated from the ego by the resistance of repression. The ego cuts across all three layers of the topographical model; it is obviously present in the perceptual system of conscious. "It may be that much of the ego is itself unconscious, only part of it, probably, is covered by the term preconscious" (S. Freud, 1923/1961).

The superego is also located in all three layers of the topographical model, and while it interacts with the ego, it also decides what part of the id may be allowed into the region of the ego.

It must be emphasized that the model in Figure 2.1 is obviously only a human construct, developed to explain the inner workings of the mind. It is not material or physiological, and the dividing lines are not as neat and clear-cut as the illustration suggests. What are depicted are functions of awareness, not locations in the brain.

SIGMUND FREUD'S STAGES OF PSYCHOSEXUAL DEVELOPMENT

Psychosexual development, according to Freud, begins in early infancy and passes through a series of predetermined, highly differentiated stages, named according to the body zones or erogenous zones that provide libido satisfaction during a particular developmental period (Figure 2.2). Freud assumed that these stages are universal, in that each individual, regardless of society and culture, must move through this invariable sequence of psychosexual experiences to reach maturity, almost as if it was part of human nature. Development progresses because the child derives pleasure from different parts of the body at different times and therefore, each developmental stage is identified by the psychosexual mode of the body area that dominates in its urge toward pleasure and satisfaction: oral, anal, phallic, and genital. During the latency period the libidinal drive is repressed. Even the personality structure of some adults can be classified by their preferred mode of libido gratification: the oral (eating, smoking, talking), the anal (saving, hoarding or giving away), the phallic (aggressive-intrusive), and the genital types.

This sequential order of normal development can be disrupted by *fixation or regression.* Fixation can occur at any point in development, with the individual remaining at least partially at an immature level of libido gratification and not moving on to more mature levels. Illustrations of oral fixation are alcoholism, excessive smoking, or compulsive eating. Regression takes place when the individual encounters serious frustration in psychosexual development and therefore returns to less mature and safer stages in order to attain libido satisfaction. The typical example is the child's return to thumb-sucking when a younger sibling is born.

The adolescent unsuccessful in dating or sexually rejected may regress to less mature behaviors, play with younger children or age-inappropriate toys. Fixation and regression occur when progress toward more mature levels of sexual development encounters serious frustration from the environment. Fixation can also result from overgratification at a particular stage; thus, spoiling the child may impede progress toward heterosexual maturity.

■ The Oral Stage

During the first year of life the oral region is the primary source of pleasure. The child gets pleasurable autoerotic stimulation not only from sucking, drinking, and eating but also through oral activity not motivated by hunger, such as thumb-sucking and sucking a pacifier or various other objects placed in the mouth. At this age the mouth is the dominant

A. Libidinal Localization (erotogenic zones)	B. Aim, or Mode of Pleasure-Finding	C. Libidinal Object-Finding		
INFANCY PERIOD				
Pregenital Period	*Infantile Sexuality*	*Auto-eroticism*	*Narcissism*	*Allo-eroticism*
1. Oral Stage				
a. early oral	Sucking, swallowing (incorporating)	at first objectless		Oral object-choice
b. late oral	Biting, devouring (destroying, annihilating)		Primary Narcissism	Oral-sadistic object-choice
2. Anal Stage				
a. early anal	Expelling (rejecting) (destroying) · looking exhibiting handling inflicting pain			Anal and anal-sadistic object-choice
b. late anal	Retaining (controlling) (possessing) · submitting to pain			
Early Genital Period (phallic stage)	Touching, rubbing, exhibiting and looking at genitalia, investigating, comparing, questioning, fantasizing (tender affection)			Parent object-choice Oedipus-phantasies
LATENCY PERIOD				
No new zone	Repression Reaction-formation Sublimation Affectional trends	Further decline of auto-eroticism	Diminished Narcissism	Develop-ment of social feelings
ADOLESCENT OR PUBERTAL PERIOD				
Late Genital Period Revival of zone sensitivity of infancy period	Reactivation of modes or aims of infancy period	Revival of auto-eroticism	Fresh wave of Narcissism	Revival of Oedipus object-choice
Later, functioning of vaginal zone	Emergence of adult mode of pleasure-finding			Homosexual object-choice
				Heterosexual object-choice

FIGURE 2.2 Freud's view of normal development. The theoretically normal development of children according to Freud's hypotheses of psychosexual development (From *The Structure and Meaning of Psychoanalysis* by William Healy, Augusta Bronner, and Anna Mae Bowers. Copyright 1930 and renewed 1958 by Alfred A. Knopf, Inc. Reprinted by permission of the publisher.).

erogenous zone. Displeasure is expressed by spitting out. Libidinal energies are directed toward an oral object choice. The love object at this early stage of development is the self. Self-love often precedes object love, since the young infant has no perception of objects in the outside world as separate from the self. Self-love is narcissistic, a concept Freud adopted from Greek mythology. During this stage the ego remains undeveloped, and the energies of the id seek satisfaction with little concern for reality or even awareness of possible dangers.

Oral characteristics manifest themselves later in life through overeating or by finding primary satisfaction through drinking, smoking, kissing, or talking. Even the aggressive component of this stage can express itself in making "biting" remarks or in oral sarcasm.

■ The Anal Stage

During the second year of life, partly as a result of the social demand for toilet training, the primary erogenous zone shifts from the oral to the anal region; libido is now invested in an anal object choice. During this stage the infant must learn to regulate bodily impulses and to postpone immediate gratification in order to meet the demands of the external reality; hence, the ego develops. From anal activity the infant may derive not only pleasure but also a feeling of power over the mother from both "holding back" (prolonging evacuation in order to obtain stronger sensations) and "letting go" (experiencing relief and pleasure from evacuation). The oral and the anal stages are basically autoerotic phases.

Depending on the severity and the method of toilet training, anal attributes may emerge as personality characteristics. Fixation at the anal stage or regression to this stage may produce anal-erotic conflicts, which manifest themselves in one of the two modalities of the anal stage: retention or expulsion. The retentive component is most obvious in the stingy person who holds on to all kinds of objects, especially money. This person is most likely stubborn, overcontrolled, fussy, and excessively concerned with neatness, cleanliness, and orderliness. The expulsive type, in contrast, lets go, both emotionally and physically (emotional outbursts, temper tantrums, and rage). This person is a spendthrift, and is rebellious, unclean, messy, and disorderly.

Factor analytic studies have demonstrated that clusters of traits corresponding to the basic qualities of the oral or anal personality, such as parsimony, neatness, and obstinacy, do occur together in children and adults as would be predicted on the basis of Freud's theory (Fisher and Greenberg, 1977). There is a paucity of data, rather than negative evidence, to clearly show that the oral and anal personality traits originate in these crucial early developmental stages. Scattered bits of evidence including anthropological data (Triandis, 1994) suggest that such a relationship between early childhood experiences and adult personality patterns does indeed exist.

■ The Phallic or Infantile Genital Stage

Although the oral and the anal stages are basically pregenital stages, children in the phallic stage, from about age 3 to 6, become interested in their own sex organs and feelings; fantasies and preoccupations with sexuality begin to predominate. Touching and manipulating one's sex organs is experienced as pleasurable, and playful masturbation can be expected at this stage, even though it does not necessarily lead to orgasm. The oral, anal, and phallic stages are narcissistic stages, since all libido satisfaction is derived from stimulation of one's own erogeneous zones. However, during the phallic stage the object of the libido begins to change. The self as the love object is replaced by a parent object choice, and the parent object is the opposite-sex parent, leading to the *oedipal situation.* In Greek mythology, Oedipus kills his father and marries his mother. Since the reproductive organs of the sexes are different and since the roles each parent plays in the life of the child are different, the events that occur during the phallic or infantile genital stage are also different for the two sexes. However, Freud is much more explicit in explaining the events in the boy, and his account of the male's oedipal situation is generally better known and receives stronger empirical support than the Electra complex which represents the girl's experience.

During the phallic stage the male child begins to take pride in his penis; he values and idealizes it. With increased sexual desire, his love for his mother becomes erotic, and he begins to view his father as a rival. Wanting exclusive possession of his mother leads to the oedipal conflict. His feelings toward his father are ambivalent. On the one hand he identifies with his father and loves him; on the other hand he sees his father as an obstacle to his incestuous wishes and has aggressive feelings toward him. Since he knows his father is more powerful than he is, he fears that the father may cut off the offending sex organ, something that apparently must have happened to girls, who lack the protruding penis. This insight leads to a fear that Freud identified as *castration anxiety.*

As an outgrowth of castration anxiety the incestuous wishes for the mother are repressed. Three additional factors contribute to the resolution of the Oedipus complex: (1) the realization that social taboos forbid him to possess the mother sexually, (2) disappointment from the mother, and (3) maturation. Eventually the child resolves the conflict by identifying with his father, hoping to become like his father, so that he too can eventually possess a wife. Through the resolution of the Oedipus complex the child begins to incorporate parental and later social moral values into his personality structure, thus contributing to the development of the superego during the latency period, which follows.

Fisher and Greenberg (1977: 400) report, based on their extensive review of the research literature concerned with the oedipal concept, that there exists fairly convincing evidence "that men do have differentiated attitudes about their parents that mirror a history of sexually tinged rivalry with father for mother as a love object. The male does, as Freud proposed, experience castration anxiety, and this anxiety is intensified by exposure to erotic stimuli."

The processes in the female referred to as the Electra complex are reversed, less complicated, less dramatic, begin later, and last longer than in the boy; and Freud is less specific in identifying the underlying dynamics. He has also received less empirical support for these conceptualizations. The girl, like the preoedipal boy, loves her mother. With the increasing awareness of her sex organs she discovers that she lacks something the boy has, feels castrated, and blames her mother for her missing organ. As her relationship with her mother weakens, she turns her love to her father and develops an attitude of both jealousy and sexual attraction, referred to as *penis envy.* Again, confrontation with the impossibility of attaining the desired penis and aided by maturational processes helps the girl under normal circumstances resolve the Electra complex. However, the resolution of the Electra complex proceeds more slowly and continues throughout the latency period into adolescence.

Empirical evidence suggests that the female is more likely to resolve her oedipal conflict out of fear of loss of love than the male and is less motivated by castration anxiety. In general, fewer empirical investigations have tested the oedipal theory as it applies to females; some of Freud's assumptions about sexual development have been criticized and challenged, especially as they apply to female sexual development.

The phallic stage is somtimes referred to as "little puberty." Apparently, Freud felt that in terms of evolutionary theory, the human race had evolved from a species that reached its reproductive maturity at the human age equivalent of about 5 or 6. Thus, the "little puberty" is a hypothesized remnant of sexual development in evolutionary terms. Even the body zone identified by the names given to these two stages—"phallic" for "little puberty" and "genital" for "actual puberty"—refer basically to the same body zone. The masculine term "phallic" in the earlier stage reflects the strong male orientation of much of Freud's theory. However, the implications of this evolutionary aspect of Freud's theory allow for interesting comparison. "The phallic stage is then the vestige of that prehuman adolescence. The period between these two adolescences has some stability, while the periods before and after latency are full of rapid change, conflict, and psychological problems stemming from urgent libidinal demands" (Baldwin, 1967: 368).

■ Sexual Latency

With the successful resolution of the Oedipus complex, the child enters the relatively calm period of latency; the libido drive is less urgent, and more importantly, no new object choice emerges. It is during latency, as a by-product of the resolution of the Oedipus complex, that the identification with the parents become strong, and hence the superego develops. The period itself covers the elementary school years, although there are individual age variations. During this period the aggressive impulses, the sexual instincts, and the libidinal forces go under cover. The traumatic experience of having been deprived of fulfilling the sexual desires during the oedipal situation restrains the child for several years from seeking an overt affectionate relationship.

Several writers disagree with Freud's assumption of a period of sexual inactivity and sexual latency during this stage. White states:

> His assumption about the quiescence of sexual energies seems to be simply wrong. Anthropological evidence and better observation in our society have combined to cast grave doubt on the hypothesis of a biologcially determined sexual latency. For once we can almost say that Freud underestimated the importance of sex [1960: 127].

The latency period, during which the child identifies with parents, is viewed by psychoanalysts as a period when important social and moral values are acquired. Schooling greatly facilitates learning general cultural values and acquiring fundamental social skills. New roles are tried in games and in play, and the development of motor ability is encouraged. Psychoanalysts are quick to point out that this is the period in the human life cycle when all known societies provide some formal training in essential skills, even though not necessarily the academic schooling of most Western societies.

Toward the end of the latency period, orientation of interests, games, and play activities enter a homosexual phase in which friendship ties to one's own sex grow strong and often involve an exclusion of the opposite sex. During the transition from latency to puberty and with the increase in sexual tension, sexual awareness, and sexual interests, even these same-sex friendship patterns may become erotic in nature. Hence, homosexual activity in the form of genital exhibitionism, genital exploration, and masturbation are not uncommon during this prepubertal or early pubertal phase.

■ Puberty, or the Genital Stage

Adolescence proper, brought about by the biological maturation of the reproductive system, is characterized by a rapid increase in sexual tensions demanding gratification. The sexual needs and fantasies become more explicitly concerned with tension release, and later, with the sexual union of male and female. However, these inclinations are restrained by the social demands for adaptation to the moral values of society and the norms of the community. The magnitude of this situation becomes obvious if one considers that pubescence requires—for the first time since birth—that a basic biological drive, which acquires full strength only as a result of the pubescent growth changes, must be integrated into the personality structure of the young, still-developing adolescent. This fact is complicated further by the traditional social-moral-religious standards, which demand that the heterosexual gratification of this drive be postponed until marriage, often as long as 10 to 15 years after the drive acquires its full biological strength. In terms of psychoanalytic conceptualizations, this means that the "id impulses" seeking gratification with new urgency clash with the recently developed and still formative "superego," producing guilt feelings because the superego finds the demands of the id unacceptable. The ego, unable to satisfy both, feels crushed between the two powerful contenders. Thus, the new balance between id, ego, and superego, recently established during the latency period, is suddenly thrown out of balance, producing conflict, turmoil, and a psychological disequilibrium. These conflicts can be internal, a struggle between temptation and conscience, or they can be external, between parents and self. The ego attempts to cope with these conflicts, on the one hand, by denying the demands of the id through such mechanisms as repression or denial or, on the other hand, by quieting the superego through intellectualization, rationalization, asceticism, and regression.

Sexual attraction, once more as in the phallic stage, turns to the opposite-sex parent, and Freud does speak of a revival of the oedipal situation during puberty, accompanied by the reawakening of castration anxiety (S. Freud, 1925). However, during latency the development of the superego has proceeded to the point at which an internalized "incest barrier" will no longer allow these taboo feelings into full consciousness, and hence the ego uses defense mechanisms, especially displacement, to divert the incestuous demands of the libido toward somewhat more acceptable love objects. Freud (1925) commented that during early adolescence, a boy's first serious love object is most likely a mature woman—not unlike his mother—a common theme in French literature and movies. In much the same way the pubescent girl often falls in love with older men (as seen in her crushes on and infatuations for teachers, movie stars, and entertainment heroes) before she shows much interest in boys of her own age group. Thus, the first opposite-sex love object of the adolescent is often, symbolically speaking, a mother or father figure, allowing the oedipal wish an acceptable nonincestuous substitute. And even later in adolescence, when the sexual object choice begins to turn to an opposite-sex partner of the same age, the choice is often unconsciously motivated by patterns and traits prevalent in one's own parents. This idea is expressed well in the song, "I want a girl just like the girl that married dear old dad." Thus, unconscious motives determine the adolescent's attraction to a particular individual when falling in love, allowing the fulfillment of the oedipal wish.

Related to this second oedipal situation is the adolescent task of freeing the self from emotional dependency on one's parents. The boy's libidinal attachment to his mother must be released, and he must also free himself from the dominance of his father. This process of detachment from the incestuous love object brings the "problem of the generation" into the foreground and gives it its psychoanalytic explanation. This process of emotional detachment results, at least for a time, in rejection, resentment, and hostility toward parents and other authority figures. The conflict between the generations has been a frequent theme in the literature on adolescence and is a fairly common, everyday experience in many families. A fundamental task of the adolescent, as seen by psychoanalytic theory, is the "attainment of genital primacy and the definitive completion of the process of nonincestuous object finding" (Spiegel, 1951: 380). In other words, only through the emotional detachment from parents does the more permanent libidinal attachment to an opposite-sex partner become possible.

MECHANISMS OF DEFENSE

One of Freud's major contributions to an understanding of the dynamics of the mind—widely recognized, even by professionals who tend to disagree with other assumptions of psychoanalysis—is the identification of defense mechanisms. They help the ego cope with anxiety, frustration, and unacceptable impulses and help relieve tension and inner conflicts. Since anxiety is likely to increase during periods of rapid developmental changes and since adolescence is such a period—old ways of responding no longer seem to work and new patterns of adjusting have not yet been tried—the need for defense mechanisms is heightened during adolescence (Conger, 1977). Individuals develop such mechanisms, especially if they cannot deal with anxiety in a rational fashion, to defend themselves against the demands of the id or against conflicts with society. Some mechanisms of defense, such as denial, reaction formation, and projection, are considered more primitive, since their use suggests being out of touch with reality; others, such as sublimation, undoing, rationalization, displacement, identification, and intellectualization, represent higher (closer to normal) levels of functioning. Everybody seems to utilize some defense mechanisms at one time or another to cope with conflictual situations and to protect the personality from the stresses, anxieties, and frustrations of everyday living. It is only when a particular defense is used exclusively to deal with the tension between inner psychological reality and the demands of the external world that use of defense mechanisms becomes symptomatic of adjustment problems, neurotic tendencies, and even psychopathology.

Of course, no individual makes use of all the possible mechanisms of defense; each person merely selects certain of them, but these become fixated in his ego, establishing themselves as regular modes of reaction of that particular character, which are repeated throughout life whenever a situation occurs similar to that which originally evoked them [S. Freud, 1937/1950: 340].

The most common defense mechanism, widely used even by normal people, is *rationalization,* a process in which one advances more or less plausible reasons to justify an act or an opinion, concealing to others and even to one's self the true reason or motive. Sometimes this mechanism is referred to as the "sour-grapes reaction," based on the famous fable in which the fox who cannot reach the luscious grapes claims that he doesn't want them after all because they are sour.

The adolescent unable to attain a date with a highly desirable girl will tend to rationalize that he is better off without her because she talks too much or is too spoiled or is too popular or is likely to lose her pretty figure at an early age. The high school girl ignored by the student council president may rationalize that the latter does not recognize her because he wears glasses and is probably nearsighted, when in fact the school leader does not even know she exists (Lambert et al., 1978).

Rationalization can help us to cope with disappointment in two ways: (1) it provides an acceptable justification for what we did, or what we believe, or what we really wanted but could not attain, and (2) it helps soften the anxiety and the disappointment connected with unattainable goals. We often rationalize failure by blaming circumstances rather than ourselves; we thus avoid the feeling of anxiety and guilt that would result if we acknowledged our own failures and inadequacies. Rationalization aids the ego by providing an excuse for something unattainable, unpleasant, or unacceptable. Methods of rationalization are used, especially if we are criticized or called upon to explain unacceptable or undesirable behavior. Adolescents use it vis-à-vis parents, and students vis-à-vis their teachers. However, frequent use of rationalization makes it impossible to learn from error and avoid mistakes, since such an approach impairs our coming to full awareness of our errors, mistakes, or other shortcomings. One avoids ownership of deficiencies. By rationalizing, one is denying a personal responsibility for one's shortcomings. Students who fail the exam but blame the test or the teacher rather than themselves free themselves from anxiety but also absolve themselves from studying harder next time, having convinced themselves that it was not their fault.

Repression to some extent is the purpose of all mechanisms of defense, and repressive components do accompany most of them. Repression deals with impulses from within, while denial relates to events that happen in the outside world. Repression should also be distinguished from suppression. Suppression is a conscious effort not to let ideas or impulses surface to awareness. Repression, in contrast, is an unconscious process of refusing to let into awareness the traumatic event, the stressful incident, or the unacceptable impulse. It was one of Freud's earliest constructs. Repression is less reality-oriented than rationalization since the impulse is cut off from awareness but remains dynamically operative in the unconscious. Most people are unaware of their earlier sexual feelings toward the opposite-sex parent. Socially taboo and highly traumatic early sexual experiences such as incest or rape may be repressed but dynamically operative in the adolescent's attitude toward sexuality. "Thus, for example, a girl who is sexually attracted to her father will simply remove this intolerable incestuous thought from her consciousness. It may come up again in her dreams, but upon awakening these too will be repressed" (Calhoun, 1977: 35). Repression is the metaphorical rug under which we sweep the garbage of our life to hide it, and although the garbage is no longer visible, it is still there.

Displacement is a very important psychoanalytic defense mechanism used to explain how the affect or libidinal energy toward one object is transferred to a substitute object, which, while logically inappropriate, is quite appropriate for unconscious thinking. The original emotions remain the same, but the object to which the emotions are directed changes. An adolescent girl who experiences an intense fear of snakes may be displacing her underlying fear of a male's sexual organ. Displacement seems to be common when the original impulse or object is accompanied by a high degree of guilt or anxiety or when libidinal energy is blocked. For example, the libidial drive toward masturbation during adolescence may be transferred to a compulsive need to wash one's hands. The connection between the two behaviors appears inappropriate. However, the hand is the body part that executes the masturbatory behavior, and since masturbation at Freud's time was viewed as a "dirty habit," hand washing is an unconscious undoing of masturbation. It cleans what is dirty, it relieves anxiety, and some of the libidinal energy seeking release in masturbation may actually find discharge in the substitute behavior. Even the motions of the hands around the soap may contain some similarity to masturbatory behavior. In a more general sense, the unavailable or unattainable gratification of sexual needs may find displaced expression in oral activities, such as smoking, kissing, applying lipstick, drinking, whistling, singing, talking, chewing gum, and spitting. The adolescent's first serious infatuation with a somewhat older, motherly teacher may be viewed as a displacement of the unacceptable love impulse toward his mother. However, since even the teacher is unavailable and socially unacceptable as a love object, a further displacement directs the love need to a more readily available girl of a similar age; however, she, too, may possess some characteristics of his mother. Thus, in the search for a mother substitute, one displacement may be put on top of an earlier displacement.

Identification is a process by which characteristics and qualities of an external object, frequently another person, are absorbed into one's own personality. Freud prefers the term "identification" over the term "imitation" since identification implies the involvement of deeper, more significant layers of the personality as well as a more permanent change. Imitation, which is part of identification, is superficial copying of behavior. The person with whom a child identifies changes as the child moves through the developmental stages. The successful resolution of the oedipal conflict requires an identification with the same-sex parent, a process that greatly enhances superego formation. However, with the beginning of adolescence, parental identification dramatically declines and identification with movie heroes, entertainment personalities, and famous athletes as well as coaches and teachers is common, a process that aids in achieving independence and establishing a personal identity. A primitive form of identification finds expression in eating something in order to become more like the object eaten. Thus, the hunter may eat the lion's heart in an attempt to become as brave as the lion. In the Christian sacrament the body and blood of Christ are eaten in order to become more Christlike.

In *isolation* or *intellectualization* the actual impulses reach the conscious, but they are isolated from the strong affect that usually accompanies such impulses. Feelings and intellect are separated so that a threatening situation loses its emotional impact. The feelings are repressed and the problem is viewed in abstract inellectual terms. The psychoanalyst refers to the process as "decathexis," since the object has lost its cathexis. Cathexis is the concentration of mental energy on a specific idea or object. In other words, affect has become separated from content, as in a person who is insulted but does not feel anger. Isolation of affect means that mental activities that usually occur together are separated, a phenomenon not at all uncommon in adolescent sexual development when, for example, sexual-sensual needs are gratified with one person (for example, a prostitute), while the erotic affectional feelings are reserved for the beloved virginal sweetheart. In a religious, scientific sense, isolation would find expression in a dual incompatible belief system by the same person who as a religious person believes in the biblical story of creation and as a biological scientist believes in the Darwinian theory of evolution. Patients in therapy may develop an elaborate and abstract self-analysis of their problem but have no real feelings about it; instead, they try to convince the therapist of how much insight they already have even though the problem behavior remains unchanged.

Among the many defense mechanisms that the ego can use, Anna Freud (1948) considers two especially characteristic of the adolescent coping with the onslaught of sexual tensions: *intellectualization* and *asceticism.* Both may be used before pubescence, but they become especially important during this period of sexual disequilibrium. Asceticism is characterized by rigor, self-denial, and mortification of the flesh. It is typically seen as a phase in puberty, where it indicates a fear of sexuality and a simultaneous defense against sexuality. Asceticism in an adolescent results from a generalized mistrust of all instinctual wishes. This mistrust may go far beyond sexuality and may include eating, sleeping, and dressing habits. The increase in intellectual interest and the change from concrete to abstract interest (thinking) are accounted for in terms of these defense mechanisms against the anxiety produced by the libido.

Otto Rank (1945) contrasts promiscuity with aceticism as the two adolescent defense mechanisms that aid in maintaining independence. Having just freed themselves from the emotional dependence on parents, adolescents avoid any kind of strong emotional attachment, including an intimate personal love relationship, since it implies a new kind of mutual dependency. Being promiscuous satisfies sexual urges without the loss of the newly acquired independence, since such sexual gratification takes place without genuine love, personal commitment, and ego involvement. Separating the physical side of sexuality from its emotional component, as the practice of promiscuity implies, is of course a form of intellectualization as defined by Anna Freud. By being ascetic, adolescents retain their independence because they willfully reject any kind of personal, intimate involvement. Periods of asceticism may alternate with periods of instinctual gratification. In both instances the adolescent avoids the real love relationship in which self-restraint, self-subordination, and dependency are necessary to maintain permanent intimacy.

In *reaction formation*—"reversal into the opposite"—the unacceptable impulse is repressed from consciousness but readmitted as its very opposite. Thus, the hostility an unmarried teenage mother may feel toward her newborn baby is unacceptable and is replaced by too much kindness, resulting in overprotection. Over-compensation often accompanies reaction formation, so that, as in this illustration, too much kindness is provided. The expression "killed with kindness" aptly illustrates the tendencies that underlie this kind of defensive kindness. The function of kindness is not really to help other people but to release the anxiety and guilt associated with the true feeling of hostility.

Similarly, hate may be transformed into love. The question arises, how can the new defensive emotion of kindness or love be distinguished from true kindness or love? Several characteristics suggest that an emotion may be the product of reaction formation: extreme forms of the defense emotion; some inconsistency, since the negative emotions may break through when one is off-guard; extravagant showiness; and compulsivity. The extreme and intolerant crusades against various vices are often a reaction formation against unconscious impulses toward that very same vice. The individual inclined toward criminal behavior may, through a reaction formation, become a highly effective police detective. Unacceptable homosexual tendencies may manifest themselves as extreme disgust and crusading against homosexuals. The puritanical censor of pornographic films and books may gain secret satisfaction from viewing the suspect material.

Introjection (internalization) has certain similarities to identification, such as the internalizing of outside events or characteristics of other people into the protagonist's personality structure for defensive purposes. However, introjection is more limited in scope. The whole personality is not restructured, only a specific part, as when an individual internalizes society's values as a guide to behavior. An extreme form of introjection is the "identification with the aggressor," seen even in concentration camps among older, surviving inmates who assumed the behavior and the values of the hated Gestapo. Apparently, an attitude of "if you can't defeat your enemies, join them" prevailed.

Projection is the opposite of introjection in that one attributes or projects to somebody else impulses unacceptable within oneself. In other words, we ascribe to others those feelings that we ourselves have but find unacceptable. Projection is, in certain respects, similar to rationalization. The adolescent boy, for example, claims that none of his peers like him, when actually he likes neither himself nor others. This mechanism of defense serves a dual purpose: (1) we free ourselves of the unacceptable and frustrating feeling (relieve anxiety) and (2) we get rid of some of our tension and frustration by complaining about the nastiness of the individual to whom we have assigned our own unacceptable impulse, and we can pretend that we are the innocent party. A highly irritated adolescent girl, for example, angrily accuses her parents of being inconsiderate and ill-tempered. If asked what the parents did, she might respond, "They irritate me." Or to take another example, if we dislike someone, projection allows us to interpret everything that individual does as an expression of that person's dislike for us.

Although almost all mechanisms of defense distort reality in one way or another, *denial* is the most primitive defense because it not only distorts the cognition of reality but denies the existence of some emotionally significant part of reality. We refuse to acknowledge that the source of our distress actually exists. In contrast to repression, denial focuses on external reality; however, it does seem to serve a function quite similar to repression. This defense is not comon in very young children, since they have not learned to distinguish between fantasy and reality. It begins to appear in the anal stage and is very common in neurotics and psychotics. In its extreme form, denial means that an existing sector of reality is blotted out. An example is the rejected bride in one of Dickens's novels who kept the wedding table set and her wedding gown on for years after the groom left her waiting at the altar. Another is the boy who plans and talks of graduate school and of becoming a laywer even though he barely receives passing grades in his academic high school subjects. Still another is the girl who has no boyfriends but sits anxiously near the telephone every Friday evening in the hope that "someone may want to invite me out tonight."

Because the process of denial is unconscious, the person is not lying. The most common form of denial is blocking a past event out of memory; we say "I don't remember," and we actually do not, but everybody else remembers quite well. Less serious use of denial seems to occur when we attempt to avoid unpleasant events in our real environment; we look away from an unpleasant or disgusting sight. Another form of denial is postponing an unpleasant task, such as writing a term paper (or studying for an exam) without much concern for the consequences, until the work is due.

There is some debate as to whether *sublimation* ought to be considered a defense mechanism, since it is basically a constructive and adjustive process. On the other hand, sublimation is really a specific kind of displacement. In sublimation the libidinal instincts, rather than being displaced in neurotic behavior, are rechanneled into constructive and socially acceptable behavior. The libidinal impulse, even though it is transformed, is actually discharged. In the sense that the unacceptable impulse is discharged, sublimation differs from all other defense mechanisms where the energy is repressed or distorted. The common illustration is the creative artist who sublimates his anal impulse to smear feces all over by painting a beautiful picture on canvas. More to the point, Freud maintained that the gorgeous male and female nudes created by Renaissance painters were really the result of sublimated erotic impulses. Lincoln chopped wood to sublimate his anger. For Freud, the development of civilization was the result of sublimation of instinctual energies. Sublimation takes place if a socially acceptable and closely associated substitute object can be found for a libido force, so that partial satisfaction can take place. This process of seeking and finding a substitute activity is still an unconscious one (except when the football coach demands sexual abstinence from his players two weeks before the big game). Psychoanalytic treatment is intended to direct the patient toward sublimation. The final goal of psychoanalytic treatment is to have the patient accept his or her desires and wishes, sublimate them in a socially acceptable way, and find a normal way for sexual satisfaction.

Undoing takes the form of atonement, penance, repentance, apology, restitution, and being punished or punishing oneself. When an unacceptable impulse has broken through and manifested itself in actual behavior, through the process of undoing we attempt to counteract the undesirable acts or desires or thoughts and to reduce our anxieties.

Children are taught at an early age that when they engage in socially disapproved behavior they are punished, or they have to make up for it, since it is only through punishment or atonement that the misdeed can be negated and the individual can start over with a clean slate. If this cleansing process does not take place, the anxiety, guilt, and self-debasement will threaten the ego. Hence, the individual tends to "undo" what has been done, just as one erases a misspelled word to start over.

Freud provided an illustration of undoing. "His patient, while walking down a country road, kicks a stone onto the middle of the road. He then reflects that when his beloved's carriage comes down the road it will hit this stone, overturn, and kill her. To undo this potenital murder, he now kicks the stone off the road. On reflecting further, he decides this is all very silly, and so he kicks the stone back to the center of the road. He repeats this sequence endlessly" (Corsini, 1977: 31).

The outcome of the use of defense mechanisms is a reduction in drive and anxiety. Defense mechanisms satisfy immediate needs and do reduce frustration, but often their benefit is short-lived. The damaging effects are evident in their long-range consequences and their negative impact on other people. Frequent use of defense mechanisms impedes learning, personal growth, and satisfactory interpersonal relationships, since most defense mechanisms tend to increase the social distance between the individual and others. Quite commonly the attitudes and behaviors expressed through such mechanisms are evaluated by observers as defensive, immature, unrealistic, and neurotic.

EDCUATIONAL IMPLICATIONS

Freud assumed that "frustration of normal sexual satisfaction may lead to the development of neurosis" (S. Freud, 1900/1953). Even at the risk of over generalizing, the psychoanalytic argument may be stated as follows: therefore, if parents do not want their child to be neurotic, they must not discipline their child in a frustrating manner. This statement implies that educators should avoid frustrating adolescents unnecessarily and question the prudish Victorian attitude toward sexuality prevalent at Freud's time. But since "sexuality" for Freud is defined rather broadly—that is, to include everything that relates to and grows out of a person's love life—one might go one step further and assume that parents and educators should keep frustrations to a minimum, especially those frustrations that block the satisfaction of basic human needs. What is needed instead is an atmosphere of leniency, love, affection, approval, and attention in which the child can grow up feeling secure, wanted, and loved.

A similar idea was expressed in Rousseau's natural romanticism and especially in his emphasis on "negative education." More recently, psychoanalytic ideas have been influential in the creation of a variety of educational experiments, the best known of which was A. S. Neill's school, Summerhill. Summerhill attempted to remove all restrictions and frustrations from the educational process, including many of the common restrictions on children's sexual curiosity and exploratory sexual behavior. The school was designed to fit the child rather than to make the child fit the school, and the intent was to make Summerhill the happiest school in the world.

But even for the regular classroom teacher in a more conventional setting, some of Freud's ideas can be applied for the benefit of the pupil and the educational process. By applying psychoanalytic thought to classroom management, discipline becomes less authoritarian and therefore less frustrating. Even when the kind of freedom provided in Summerhill may be inappropriate, there can be a genuine concern with the underlying causes and dynamics of disturbing, disruptive, antisocial, acting-out behavior. Even for a teacher with only rudimentary understanding of psychoanalytic principles, misbehavior can no longer be viewed as arbitrary, as simple meanness or a personal affront, but rather it must be seen as a symptom of underlying conflicts and causes (Muuss, 1962). What an individual does or says is not meaningless but has a cause. Just as errors in conceptual development reflect lack of understanding, use of a false method, or incorrect reasoning, so lack of self-control, rudeness, moodiness, and disobedience may serve a psychological purpose. A basic assumption of psychoanalytic theory is that all behavior is meaningful. Dreams, neurotic behavior, even a slip of the tongue, and forgetting and losing things are motivated; if there is no conscious motive, they are assumed to be unconscious.

Education has been slow in providing a place for the "affective domain" in its structure and curriculum. However, much of the recent efforts to legitimize emotions in the educational process have their roots in the writings of Freud and are made explicit by some of his followers—Anna Freud (1948), Lawrence Kubie (1960), and Richard Jones (1960).

> The child's fifth freedom is the right to know what he feels; but this does not carry with it any right to act out his feelings blindly. This will require a new mores for our schools, one which will enable young people from early years to understand and feel and put into words all the hidden things which go on inside of them...[Jones, 1960: vii-viii].

Psychoanalytic theory assumes that talking about and playacting dreams, fears, and aggressive or hostile feelings not only brings them out into the open but cleanses them and reduces their magnitude. In addition, openly sharing emotional problems in a classroom of peers leads to the realization that others have similar, if not the same, fears and feelings. "The freedom of one individual to express what another individual inhibits often results in freeing the latter" (Jones, 1960: 16). In their concern about normality in regard to physical development, sexual needs, social sensitivities, and their intimate problems adolescents can benefit from the realization that their thoughts are not really too different from those of their peers.

The inhibition of sexual energies that most Western societies demand of their youths is the basis of Freud's concept of sublimation. Damming up libidinal energies "must swell the force of the perverse impulses, so that they become more powerful than they would have been had no hindrance to normal sexual satisfaction been present" (S. Freud, 1953: 319). It follows that early infantile sexual activities should not be repressed or pushed into the unconscious, lest normal sexual development be perverted. If libidinal energies are forced to regress to earlier stages of sexual development and denied any normal satisfaction, substitute satisfactions in the form of fetishism, sadism, masochism, narcissism, or other neurotic symptoms may manifest themselves. Yet, psychoanalytic theory does not advocate uninhibited gratification of sexual impulses. Freud suggested redirecting sexual energy by means of sublimation. Most Western cultures oppose unrestricted sexual gratification in their young and assume that uninhibited sexuality would create new and different problems. Furthermore, since society's values are already represented in the adolescents' personality structure by means of the superego—which develops during the latency period—the sociosexual conflict is a psychological, internal one, a conflict of the conscience. Freud does not make a specific statement about adolescent sexual gratification. But since during this time the sexual drive and internal and external forces controlling the expression of sexuality are strong, sublimation can be a means of guiding these energies into productive activities, thus contributing constructively to the learning process.

In practicing sublimation an individual finds substitute forms of satisfaction and tension release for unsatisfied libidinal energies. It is assumed that nonsexual aims and socially useful activities absorb some of the sexual energy. Hence, many educationally desirable activities may be stimulated by denying sexual gratification. For a long time football players and athletes have been advised prior to major sports events to abstain from sexual activity.

Through sublimation "sources of sexuality are discharged and utilized in other spheres, so that a considerable increase of psychic capacity results" (S. Freud, 1925: 95). The connection between sexual energy and productivity in the fields that appeal more to emotion, such as music, art, poetry, and literature, is another of the assumptions of psychoanalytic theory. Freud developed a theory of culture and civilization in which all human creations—from the learning of language to the composition of symphonies and scientific inventions—are due to sublimation. "Sexual impulses have contributed invaluably to the highest cultural, artistic, and social achievements of the human mind" (S. Freud, 1953: 27). Since sexual urges appear to be strongest in the late adolescent period—if Kinsey's "outlets" are taken as an indication of the strength of sexual drive—and since internal and external restrictions are also strongest during this period, at least for middle-class American youth, sublimation appears to be one important educational objective during this period. If society can use sublimation to provide a harmonious balance between realistic denial of gratification and fulfillment of basic needs without repression and utilization of sexual energies and thus avoid the two extremes of maladjustment—neurosis and delinquent behavior—the productivity and creativity of the individual could be vastly increased. Sublimation remains a theoretical model, and Freud stated quite frankly that very little is actually known about the physiological and neurological process of sublimation.

Freud (1933/64) believed that applying psychoanalysis to education was most important. But he admitted quite openly that he had no "special understanding of it." He did credit his daughter, Anna, with making this aspect of psychoanalysis her life work and thus expanding his theories. Anna Freud's interest in child psychoanalysis and education is expressed in many of her publications, but was most explicitly developed in her lecture, "The Relation Between Psychoanalysis and Pedagogy" (A. Freud, 1931).

3

ERIK ERIKSON'S THEORY OF IDENTITY DEVELOPMENT

Erik H. Erikson's (1902–1994) theory reflects in part his psychoanalytic training, but it embraces society's influence and the social aspects of development to a much larger extent than did Freud's. With little more than a German high school education, Erikson attended art schools and traveled in Italy, apparently in search of his own identity. Erikson's later writing popularized the concept of "identity," and he applied it especially to the period of adolescence. After Erikson returned to Germany, where he studied art and prepared to teach art, he was offered a teaching position in a private school in Vienna that served the children of patients of Sigmund and Anna Freud. Peter Blos, a friend of Erikson from the time they attended the Gymnasium together, also worked as a teacher in the same school and it was Blos's idea to offer Erikson the position. During his tenure as a teacher, Erikson was invited to undergo psychoanalysis with Anna Freud, and during this process his interest expanded from art and teaching to also include the study of psychoanalysis. While in Vienna, he also studied Montessori education, which later influenced his psychoanalytic studies, such as the organization of objects in space. Erikson graduated from the Vienna Psychoanalytic Institute in 1933 as a lay analyst since he held no medical or academic degrees. Later that year, he immigrated to the United States and became associated with the Harvard Psychological Clinic.

Erikson has published extensively, his best known and most widely read book being *Childhood and Society*, published in 1950 and revised in 1963. Of particular significance to an understanding of adolescence is his *Identity: Youth and Crisis* (1968). Erikson's more recent book, *The Life Cycle Completed* (1982), encompasses an integration of much of his earlier work, but with the explicit purpose of exploring development by beginning with old age and to make sense of the "completed life cycle." He also explained that the new organization reflects his view that, because all stages grow out of previous stages, tracing the antecedents backward would highlight these relationships. The idea of identity formation has remained the focus of much of his work and appears in other book titles, such as *Identity and the Life Cycle* (1959). In addition, he has examined the identity issue of historical figures, such as Martin Luther (1962), Mahatma Gandhi (1969), and Thomas Jefferson. In these psycho-historical studies he is concerned with the identity crisis of each of these men as well as with the respective national identity issues at the time of their most notable contributions. Revealing his basic philosophy, he maintains that one cannot separate "the identity crisis in individual life and contemporary crisis in historical development because the two help to define each other and are truly relative to each other" (Erikson, 1968: 23). The word *crisis,* as Erikson uses it, is not just an emotional turmoil or emergency; it also has (as it does in Chinese), the meaning of "opportunity," an idea that is essential to an understanding of the word *crisis* as Erikson sees it. Erikson has also written about his own identity crisis as well as the philosophical and psychoanalytic foundation of the concept in "Autobiographic Notes on the Identity Crisis" (1970).

In his famous chapter, "Eight Stages of Man," Erikson (1950) modifies and expands the Freudian stages of psychosexual development by placing much greater emphasis on the social context of development. Erikson also is the first person who proposes a life-span theory of development that encompasses the entire life cycle. His modifications were inspired by anthropological findings and a concern with the social origins of these stages, which contribute to a shift from the sexual nature of man to a theory of psychosocial development. The core concept in this theory is the acquisition of an ego-identity, and the exploration of identity issues becomes the outstanding characteristic of adolescence. Although the specific quality of a person's identity differs from culture to culture, the accomplishment of this developmental task has common elements in all cultures. The establishment of a true sense of a personal identity is the psychological connection between childhood and adulthood. In order to acquire a strong and healthy ego-identity, the child must receive consistent and meaningful recognition for his or her achievements and accomplishments.

Humans develop according to the *epigenetic principle of development,* borrowed from embryology, which states "that anything that grows has a ground plan, and that out of this ground plan the parts arise, each part having its time of special ascendancy, until all parts have risen to form a functional whole" (Erikson, 1968: 92). Epigenesis, for Erikson (1982: 28) involves much more than a sequence of stages: "It also determines certain laws in the fundamental relations of the growing parts to each other. . . ." Every element must arise at the appropriate time; the failure to do so will jeopardize the development of "a succession of potentials for significant interaction" with significant others and the "mores that govern them." Unless normal development takes place, the individual cannot grow into a psychologically healthy person. Obviously, the significant others and the individual interact, so the ongoing process is mutual and reciprocal. In other words, the epigenic plan which arises from within the human organism is supported (or interfered with) by social demands. It basically identifies the developmental interaction between maturational advances and the social expectations made upon the child. For example, at about age 2–3 the social demand placed upon children to control elimination (an issue in the autonomy stage) dovetails with the child's maturational ability to exercise the necessary sphincter control. Furthermore, every stage is related developmentally to every other stage, "whether in the form of an earlier condition or of a later consequence" (Erikson, 1982: 61).

In the epigenic model (Figure 3.1), the basic ground plan of increasing psychosocial differentiation is depicted. The diagonal axis, beginning with "Trust vs. Mistrust," shows

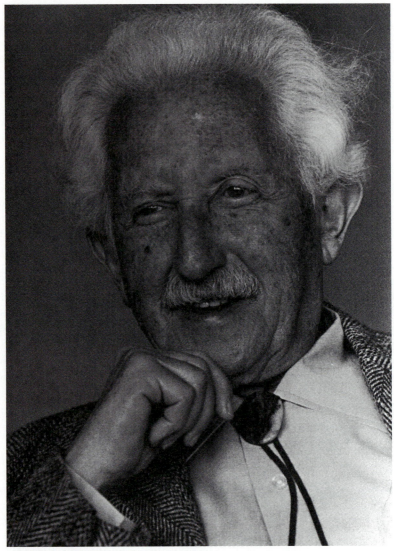

Erik Erikson (1902-1994)

the developmental sequence of the well-known eight stages of man. Movement upward along the diagonal axis represents normal development and shows the successive differentiation of the original undifferentiated structure, and thus represents increasingly more mature levels of functioning. This diagram demonstrates that:

1. Each item of the vital personality is systematically related to all others; they all depend on the proper development in the proper sequence of each item.

	1	2	3	4	5	6	7	8
VIII								INTEGRITY vs. DESPAIR
VII							GENERATIVITY vs. STAGNATION	
VI						INTIMACY vs. ISOLATION		
V	Temporal Perspective vs. Time Confusion	Self-Certainty vs. Self-Consciousness	Role Experimentation vs. Role Fixation	Apprenticeship vs. Work Paralysis	IDENTITY vs. IDENTITY CONFUSION	Sexual Polarization vs. Bisexual Confusion	Leader- and Followership vs. Authority Confusion	Ideological Commitment vs. Confusion of Values
IV				INDUSTRY vs. INFERIORITY	Task Identification vs. Sense of Futility			
III			INITIATIVE vs. GUILT		Anticipation of Roles vs. Role Inhibition			
II		AUTONOMY vs. SHAME, DOUBT			Will to Be Oneself vs. Self-Doubt			
I	TRUST vs. MISTRUST				Mutual Recognition vs. Autistic Isolation			

FIGURE 3.1 Erikson's epigenetic diagram (from *Identity: Youth and Crisis*, by Erik H. Erikson, with the permission of W. W. Norton & Company, Inc. Copyright © 1968 by W.W. Norton & Company, Inc.).

45

2. "Each item exists in some form before 'its' decisive and critical time normally arrives" (Erikson, 1968: 93, 95). Thus, the horizontal and the vertical axes entries in Figure 3.1 identify how earlier development contributes to identity in adolescence.

Each of the eight developmental stages is characterized by a conflict, and each conflict contains the possibility of bipolar outcomes. Erikson suggests that the individual must actually experience both sides of the conflict and must learn to subsume them into higher synthesis. This bipolar nature of the social crisis gives each stage its name, rather than the body zone that gives pleasure as in Freudian theory. If the conflict is worked out in a constructive, satisfactory manner, the syntonic or positive quality becomes the more dominant part of the ego and enhances further healthy development through the subsequent stages. For Erikson, the growth of a positive self-concept is directly linked to the psychosocial stage resolution that constitutes the core of his theory. However, if the conflict persists past its time, or is resolved unsatisfactorily, the dystonic or negative quality is incorporated into the personality structure. In that case, the dystonic or negative attribute will interfere with further development and may manifest itself in impaired self-concept, adjustment problems, and possibly, psychopathology.

Erikson (1982) substitutes the terms *syntonic* and *dystonic* for initially used terms *positive* and *negative,* but they will be used interchangeably. The reader should bear in mind that Erikson emphasizes the necessity and healthiness of an individual actually having both syntonic and dystonic reactions depending on the situation. For example, a person walking the streets in the dark of any major U.S. city will more likely avoid becoming the victim of an assault if he or she has a healthy sense of mistrust and behaves accordingly. Thus, as Erikson states (1982: 80), "both syntonic and dystonic and both sympathic and antipathic potentials are necessary for human adaptation. . . ."

Each crisis or conflict is never completely solved but appears to be most pronounced at the age at which it emerges. However, as in psychoanalytic theory, these stages occur in a sequential order, as implied in Erikson's use of the principle of epigenetic development. Ego "identity is never 'established' as an 'achievement,'" as something static or unchangeable, but is a "forever to-be-revised sense of reality of the Self within social reality" (Erikson, 1968: 24, 211). Although the identity crisis is most pronounced during adolescence, and gives that age its stage name, identity issues remain a lifelong concern. A redefinition of one's ego-identity emerges quite commonly when major role changes occur, such as when college freshmen leave home and have to make their own decisions, often for the first time. Other issues that tend to renew identity concerns are: one's first job, marriage, parenthood, the death of one's parents, divorce, unemployment, serious illness, widowhood, and retirement. The ability to cope with these later identity issues that result from major changes in one's role in life may well depend on the degree of success with which one has mastered the adolescent identity crisis.

The vertical sequence in Figure 3.1, beginning with "Mutual Recognition vs. Autistic Isolation" and ascending until it coincides with "Identity vs. Identity Confusion" in the diagonal sequence, demonstrates how each of the four preceding stages contributes significantly to the development of ego-identity or identity diffusion during adolescence. Thus, "Mutual Recognition," "Will to Be Oneself," "Anticipation of Roles," and "Task

Identification" are secondary outcomes of the earlier stages of psychosocial development that are essential contributing factors to the achievement of a syntonic identity in adolescence. On the other hand, failure in the earlier stages resulting in "Autistic Isolation," "Self-Doubt," "Role Inhibition," and a "Sense of Futility" may contribute to a personal estrangement or identity confusion in adolescence.

The horizontal sequence in Figure 3.1 beginning with "Temporal Perspective vs. Time Confusion" depicts the derivatives or earlier relative achievements that now become part and parcel of the struggle for identity. Erikson notes, "It is necessary to emphasize . . . [that] . . . the early achievements must be . . . renamed in terms of the later stages. Basic Trust, for example, is a good and a most fundamental thing to have, but its psychosocial quality becomes more differentiated as the ego comes into the possession of a more extensive apparatus, even as society challenges and guides such extension" (Erikson, 1959: 141).

The symptoms of confusion that make up the dystonic alternative on the horizontal sequence represent the earlier failures to progress normally and to resolve conflicts; they become, therefore, part of the identity confusion issue. The experience of time confusion (or simple obliviousness to time) during adolescence, for example, can arise out of the undifferentiated mistrust that may have occurred much earlier. Time confusion may develop in an attitude of not trusting time or of interpreting unnecessary delay, lateness, or forgetting time for a scheduled meeting as deceit.

THE RELATIONSHIP OF ERIKSON'S "STAGES OF MAN" TO ADOLESCENT IDENTITY

■ Trust versus Mistrust

During infancy—Erikson's first stage in the human life cycle—the major developmental crisis (that is, opportunity) is between becoming a trusting or a mistrusting person. The development of trust includes becoming trustful of others and developing a sense of one's own trustworthiness. The necessary healthy experience for the development of trust is maternal love and care. Initially, the infant "lives through, and loves with his mouth" (Erikson, 1968: 97). Being fed regularly does contribute to trust. However, the infant is receptive to maternal love in many ways besides orally. Children learn to trust because mother does come and take care of them regularly. They ideally experience living in a predictable, secure world in which their basic needs are consistently satisfied. This emerging sense of trust facilitates all subsequent development. Later, as motor skills develop and children are given freedom to explore their environment, they also learn to trust themselves and their own bodies, especially as they begin to control body movements such as grasping, holding, reaching, and later, crawling, standing, and walking.

The mistrust of time and *time confusion* that Erikson sees as "more or less typical for all adolescents at one stage or another" (Erikson, 1968: 182) grows out of unhealthy experiences at this early stage and tends to be related to the regularity of the cycle in which the infant's basic needs are satisfied. Repeated delay or irregularity in essential body satisfactions results in mistrust of time. In addition, Erikson maintains that adolescents may challenge the sense of time that was established during the earlier stages.

The conviction that emerges from this receptive state is, "I am what I am given," and it is an incorporative stage. The healthy syntonic outcome is the ability to trust others and to trust oneself, and thus, to have hope. Fowler's theory of faith development (see Chapter 13) draws on these earlier forms of trust and hope as the early, essential components of faith. Late in the life cycle, the capacity to experience faith, "the last possible form of hope" (Erikson, 1982: 62), is based on positive experience in this early stage. This clearly demonstrates Erikson's perception that all stages are related and that early experiences have definite consequences later in life. The trusting infant has developed the first requisite for later developing confidence, optimism, and finally, a feeling of security. The trusting infant comes to recognize the self in the mother's reaction to it, her smile, her face, her eyes, her acknowledgement of the child, and her ministrations. *Mutual recognition* and *mutual trustworthiness* are the earliest and most undifferentiated experiences of what will later become a sense of identity. No one can get an identity all by oneself. Even in adolescents, identity is never an individual achievement, but an outgrowth of mutual recognition; and just as for the infant, identity grows by being acknowledged and appreciated by others. This notion of "psychosocial reciprocity" as implied in the words *mutual recognition* and *mutual trustworthiness* pervades Erikson's thinking and highlights the importance of social relationships in development.

The dystonic outcome is mistrust of others and/or mistrust of oneself. Lack of trust in infancy may find expression in statements of self-debasement and may contribute to identity confusion in adolescence. Absence of experiences leading to the development of trust in early childhood may impair the "capacity to feel identical" with others during adolescence (Erikson 1968: 105). *Autistic isolation* in infancy is the earliest contribution to identity diffusion in adolescence (Figure 3.1).

■ Autonomy versus Shame and Doubt

The issue at the second stage in the human life cycle is between becoming an *autonomous, creative individual* or a dependent, inhibited, and *shameful individual* filled with *self-doubt.* The stage falls approximately between the ages of 18 months and $3\frac{1}{2}$ years. During this stage, children, although still dependent on others in many ways, begin to experience an autonomy of free choice. They now develop motor ability and the intellectual capacity to experience themselves as entities in their own right. They realize that they are different from father and mother. This newly gained sense of autonomy is often used in an exaggerated fashion, which can lead to social conflicts. The battle for autonomy may show in stubborn refusal, temper tantrums, and the "yes-no" syndrome. An important task is to begin the mastery of self-control; particularly important in this process is the control of body waste products. Toilet training means "holding on and letting go" when the child wishes, representing highly autonomous activities over which nobody else has control. The child can—and at times does—retain body waste even though the caretaker may want him or her to let go. On the other hand, the child can release them even though the parents wish him or her to hold back. However, with proper training, the child can develop a feeling of mastery for a job well done and a sense of autonomy of choice in regard to toilet training, but also in a much more general sense of making his or her own decisions.

The conviction that emerges during this stage is "I am what I will be," reflecting the child's new sense of autonomy. The syntonic attributes that are commonly gained during this stage are pride, control, self-assurance, autonomy, *self-certainty,* and *the will to be oneself.* The development of a rudimentary form of *the will to be oneself* during the autonomy stage later becomes an essential prerequisite for the development of a mature ego-identity during adolescence: "There are clinical reasons to believe that the adolescent turning away from the whole childhood milieu in many ways repeats this first emancipation" (Erikson, 1968: 114). The autonomous attributes gained during this period contribute to the formation of an identity during adolescence, leading to the conviction: "I am an independent person who can choose freely and who can guide my own development and my own future." Obviously, such a conviction enhances further development.

The dystonic outcome at this stage is *shame, self-doubt,* dependency, *self-consciousness,* and a meek compliance resulting from too many restrictions, unfair punishment, and the parents' inability to cope with the budding—and at times frustrating—*autonomy* of their young child. The identity crisis of adolescence revives and grows out of these earlier unresolved autonomy issues. Since autonomy is one of the essential ingredients for the development of identity, the battle for autonomy becomes more and more an important issue in the adolescent's struggle for independence from the family; it functions also as a recapitulation of earlier attempts at self-determination. This involves two problems. Adolescents may become so self-conscious and lacking in autonomy that they are afraid of being seen in an exposed and vulnerable situation. They may question their self-worth and the reliability of the whole experience of their childhood, and therefore, be unable to form an appropriate identity. On the other hand, entering adolescence with too much of their immature autonomy still unresolved may contribute to brash and shameless defiance of parents, teachers, and other authorities.

■ Initiative versus Guilt

The psychosocial conflict in the third stage of life is the development of a sense of *initiative versus a sense of guilt.* A conflict arises now between an aggressive intrusion into the world by way of activity, curiosity, and exploration or an immobilization by fear and guilt. The child from about $3\frac{1}{2}$ to 6 years of age normally shows a great deal of exuberance, a feeling of power, curiosity, a high level of activity and surplus energy. In play activities, the child moves around much more freely and more aggressively and develops an increasingly larger radius of operations. In the process of developing initiative, goal setting emerges and activities become increasingly guided by a purpose. This is also the stage during which language develops rapidly. Early in this stage, the child asks an endless number of "what" questions. These questions are basically learning tools since new words, concepts, and a basic understanding is acquired in this fashion. In addition, one can observe aggressive manipulation of objects, especially toys. The child takes things apart to see what is inside, not necessarily because of destructive tendencies, but out of curiosity. However, if this curiosity is interpreted as destructiveness, if the child is punished and made to feel guilty, initiative may wane. Children will also explore and manipulate their own bodies as well as those of friends, and this exploratory behavior does involve curiosity about sex organs. Social criticism and punishment may foster the development of guilt feelings in regard to sexual exploration. The aggressive behavior, including exploration of the bodies of other people, is accompanied by a rudimentary form of cooperation with others in play activities and games. During this stage of development, gender differences originate because of the role that anatomy plays in oedipal and Electra conflicts. Like Freud before him, Erikson focused more on male development and does not sufficiently differentiate between the genders; this paragraph and the one that follows reveal this bias.

The conviction that emerges from this intrusive mode is, "I am what I can imagine I will be." The intrusive (male-biased) mode is characterized by a variety of thoughts, fantasies, and behaviors: "(1) the intrusion into space by vigorous locomotion; (2) the intrusion into the unknown by consuming curiosity; (3) the intrusion into other people's ears and minds by the aggressive voice; (4) the intrusion upon or into other bodies by physical attacks, and (5) and often most frighteningly, the thought of the phallus intruding into the female body" (Erikson, 1968: 116).

If the crisis of this stage is mastered successfully, a sense of purpose and initiative emerges that will, later in adolescence, become the basis for curiosity, ambition, and *experimentation with different roles,* just as the child's play activities often reflect an *anticipation of different roles.* The sexual self-image and the differentiation between what Erikson refers to as masculine-making and feminine-catching initiative become important prerequisites for the sexual identity crisis or exploration during adolescence. The ability to take the initiative contributes to the development of an identity in adolescence since it fosters the anticipation of what one might become and one's future role in life by "freeing the child's initiative and sense of purpose for adult tasks which promise a fulfillment of one's range of capacities" (Erikson, 1968: 122). The issue of the "intrusive" and "inclusive" mode is implied in the protruding male structures and the enclosed female structures graphically represented in preadolescents' play constructions which Erikson researched. (See Figures 4.2 and 4.3 in Chapter 4.)

A dystonic outcome is likely if parents restrain, resist, and punish the newly developing initiative too much, for example, by making the child feel guilty for taking toys apart or exploring his own or someone else's body. If the child's exploration and initiative encounter severe reprimand and punishment, the result may be a more permanent immobilization by guilt, inhibition by fear, *role inhibition, role fixation,* and over-dependence on adults. Since these attributes interfere with identity formation during adolescence, a negative outcome at this stage would contribute to the emergence of identity diffusion in adolescence (Figure 3.1).

■ Industry versus Inferiority

The task at the fourth stage is the development of a *sense of industry versus the emergence of feelings of inferiority.* Erikson partly adopted Freud's idea of the Oedipus complex followed by a period of sexual latency. Unable to marry his mother, the boy must learn to become a potential provider so that he eventually will become a husband who has his own sexual partner. Therefore, this period between school entry and puberty becomes a period of learning and mastering the more basic skills needed in society. Children now acquire much fundamental knowledge and even more important, they learn to take pride in their work and acquire an attitude to do well in their work. This period is therefore described as *the apprenticeship of life.* In all known cultural groups, children receive instruction during this time, although not necessarily the kind of formal schooling provided in Western societies. The child must learn to win approval, recognition, and a feeling of success by producing things and doing the job well. An important component of becoming industrious is the "positive identification with those who know things and know how to do things" (Erikson, 1968: 125). The free play of the earlier period now becomes subordinated to rules and regulations and more structured activities. The child must learn to follow and respect rules and to become committed to the ideas of cooperation in team effort and fair play. Through team activities, games, and cooperative play, the child learns to anticipate the behavior, roles, and feelings of others. The developmental significance of role-taking receives further emphasis in the theories of Selman (Chapter 11) and Bronfenbrenner (Chapter 15).

The conviction that emerges during this apprenticeship is: "I am what I will learn" or even more production-oriented: "I am what I can learn to make work." If the *sense of industry* is established successfully, the child will need and want accomplishments and strive for completion of tasks and for recognition of work well done. The child will develop a sense of duty, a feeling for workmanship and work participation, and an attitude of wanting to do well that is based on industriousness and a desire for success. The contribution that this stage makes to identity formation is "the capacity to *learn* how to be, with skill, what one is in the process of becoming" (Erikson, 1968: 180), that is, an *identification of the task* ahead and a willingness to learn and master it (Figure 3.1), a feeling of competence.

If the child fails in the task to acquire a feeling of success and a desire for recognition for work well done, there will be a lack of industriousness and a feeling of usefulness. Such children may not develop the feeling of enjoyment and of pride for good work. On the contrary, they may be plagued by feelings of inadequacy and inferiority and may become convinced that they will never amount to much. As a result, there is *work paralysis* and a *sense of futility* that will most likely contribute to ego diffusion in the next stage.

■ Identity versus Identity Confusion

Adolescence has been characterized by Erikson (1950) as the period in the human life cycle during which the individual must establish a *sense of personal identity* and avoid the dangers of *role diffusion* and *identity confusion*. Identity achievement implies that the individual assesses strengths and weaknesses and determines how he or she wants to deal with them. The adolescent must find an answer to the identity questions: "Where did I come from?" "Who am I?" "What do I want to become?" Identity, or a sense of sameness and continuity, must be searched for. Identity is not readily given to the individual by society, nor does it appear as a maturational phenomenon when the time comes, as do secondary sex characteristics. Identity must be acquired through sustained individual effort. Unwillingness to work actively on one's identity formation carries with it the danger of role diffusion, which may result in alienation and a sense of isolation and confusion.

The search for an identity involves the establishment of a meaningful self-concept in which past, present, and future are brought together to form a unified whole. Consequently, the task is more difficult in a historical period in which the anchorage of family and community tradition has been lost and the future is unpredictable. In a period of rapid social change, the older generation is no longer able to provide adequate role models for the younger generation. Mead (1970) describes in detail the changing relationship of adolescents to parents as societies move from post- to co- and prefigurative cultures (see Chapter 6). Keniston (1965) has even suggested that in a rapidly changing society, the search for an identity is replacing the socialization process, since the latter implies that there actually exist stable, uniform, socially defined roles and values into which the adolescent can be guided.

The older generation no longer provides effective role models to the younger generation in the process of searching for a personal identity. If the elders do provide them, adolescents may either reject them as personally inappropriate, or follow them—in what will later be discussed as a "foreclosed fashion"—that is, seeking to fulfill their parents' aspirations for them, without appreciating the search for an identity as a personal opportunity. Thus, the importance of the peer group in helping the individual to answer the identity question, "Who am I?" cannot be emphasized enough. The answer to this question depends on social feedback from others who provide the adolescent with their perception and their evaluation of him or her. Identity is based on psychosocial reciprocity. Therefore, adolescents "are sometimes morbidly, often curiously, preoccupied with what they appear to be in the eyes of others as compared with what they feel they are and with the question of how to connect to earlier cultivated roles and skills with the ideal prototype of the day" (Erikson, 1959: 89). Adolescents' preoccupation with the thinking of others is the basis of Elkind's (1967) theory of egocentrism.

Since an identity can be found only in interaction with significant others, a process Erikson refers to as psychosocial reciprocity, the adolescent often goes through a period of a great need for peer group recognition and almost compulsive peer group involvement. Conforming to the expectations of peers helps adolescents find out how certain roles fit them, but peer group conformity can also create a new kind of dependency, so that the individual accepts the values of others too easily without really addressing the identity issue of how well they do fit him or her. The peer group, the clique, and the gang, even the lover, aid the individual in the search for a personal identity since they provide both a role model and very personal social feedback. The seemingly endless telephone conversations during adolescence and later, the bull session in college, can serve genuine psychological purposes by providing this kind of personal information. As long as the adolescent depends on role models and feedback, the in-group feeling that the peer group provides will remain quite strong. Also, behaviors of conformity to the expectations of the peer group reflect the learned skill of not making oneself an easy target of "catty remarks" or to avoid being "mocked out." The ensuing clannishness and intolerance of "differences"—including petty aspects of language, gesture, hair style, and dress—are explained by Erikson as the "necessary defenses" against the dangers of self-diffusion that remain prevalent as long as the identity has not yet been achieved. Particularly during the time when the body image changes so rapidly, when genital maturation stimulates sexual fantasies, and when intimacy with the opposite sex appears as a possibility with simultaneously positive and negative valences, the adolescent relies on peers for advice, comfort, companionship, and uses peers as a personal sounding board. Eventually, adolescents must free themselves from this new dependency on peers—which has just replaced their dependency on parents—in order to find themselves, that is, to attain a mature identity. Such an identity, once found, gives the young adult "a sense of 'knowing where one is going' and an inner assuredness of anticipated recognition from those who count" (Erikson, 1959: 118).

Pubescence, according to Erikson, is characterized by the rapidity of body growth, genital maturity, and sexual awareness. Because these changes are qualitatively quite different from those experienced during childhood, an element of discontinuity from previous development may emerge during early adolescence. Youth is not only confronted with an internal "physiological revolution" that interferes with the easy establishment of a new body image, but also confronted with a "psychological crisis" that revolves around issues of identity and self-definition. Erikson maintains today that the study of identity has become more important than was the study of sexuality in Freud's time. For the searching adolescent, identity—the establishment and reestablishment of sameness with previous experiences and a conscious attempt to make the future a part of one's personal life plan—seems to be subordinated to sexuality. Adolescents must establish ego-identity and learn to accept body changes as well as new libidinal feelings. Identity exploration depends at least in part on these psychophysiological factors. If ego-identity is not satisfactorily established during adolescence, there is the danger that role diffusion will inhibit further healthy ego development: "Where this is based on a strong doubt as to one's sexual identity, delinquent and outright psychotic incidents are not uncommon" (Erikson, 1950: 228). Erikson believes that those youth who are attracted to delinquent behavior have a poorly formed sense of personal identity and low self-esteem; they doubt their occupational skills and are unable to resolve core psychological tasks or to carry deficits from the previous psychosocial stages. Many of the social and behavioral problems adolescents encounter (substance abuse, acting out behavior, suicide or suicide attempts, eating disorders, teenage pregnancy, dropping out of school, etc.) can be viewed as reflecting earlier difficulties with mistrust, shame and doubt, guilt, and/or inferiority feelings. The successful way of coping with the challenges of adolescence (academic mastery, dating, individuation, renegotiating relationships with parents, wholesome health habits, etc.) all seem to build on earlier experiences of trust, autonomy, initiative, and industriousness.

Falling in love, a common occurrence at this age, is seen by Erikson not so much as a means of satisfying sexual needs, as it might be at a later age, but as an attempt to project and test one's own diffused and still undifferentiated ego through the eyes of a beloved. The various love affairs through which an adolescent passes may thus contribute to the development of an identity. The personal feedback that is mutually shared in a love relationship aids the individual in defining and revising his or her own self-definition and encourages him or her to clarify and to reflect on a personal definition of the ego. Thus, the numerous crushes and infatuations, not at all uncommon at the high school and even the college level, serve a genuine developmental purpose: "That is why many a youth would rather converse, and settle matters of mutual identification, than embrace" (Erikson, 1950: 228).

Of great concern for many adolescents is the issue of developing a vocational identity, and during the initial attempts some unrealistic choices based on role diffusion are not uncommon. The problem, identified through empirical investigations, is that early and even middle adolescents hold highly glamorized, idealized, and often unrealistic conceptions of the vocational roles they dream about. Furthermore, goal aspirations are often much higher than warranted by the individual's perseverance, skill level, and ability. Frequently, the adolescent is attracted to vocational goals that are attainable by only a very few: models, actors, actresses, rock musicians, athletic champions, car racers, astronauts, and other socially glamorized "heroes." In the process, the adolescents overidentify with and idolize their models and heroes to the extent that they forsake their own identity to imitate the heroes. At this point, youth rarely identify with their parents; on the contrary, they often rebel against parental control, value systems, and intrusions into their private life. This is a necessary part of growing up, since youths must separate their own identity from that of their family and develop autonomy in order to attaint maturity. Erikson (1982) notes that the particular strength of early adolescents is *fidelity,* which connects back to infantile trust and reaches forward to mature faith. Erikson sees fidelity as a virtue that can become a dimension of adolescent ego strength, the search for something and somebody to be true to. Fidelity can only emerge through the interplay of social experiences in the individual's development. Fidelity is the capacity to sustain freely given loyalties even when confronted with inevitable contradictions between one's own and other people's value system. Fidelity defines what we are faithful to, what we identify with, and what, in turn, we are identified by. Fidelity raises and answers important questions: "What is so important in my life that I am willing to commit to it?" What matters so much, that I pledge my faithfulness to it?" "What project is so crucial that I identify with it, and pledge my fidelity to live it, to seek it with integrity?" "What (and whom) shall I be faithful to?" (Lapsley, personal communication). According to Erikson (1965), fidelity must find its ascendancy during the period of identity formation and is a "strength inherent in the age of youth"; it is part of the human equipment that evolved through man's social and evolutionary history. Fidelity is essential for autonomous behavior.

The adolescent's search for a personal identity also includes the formation of a personal ideology or a philosophy of life that will give the individual a frame of reference for evaluating events. Such a perspective aids in making choices and guiding behavior, and in this sense a personal identity based on a philosophy of life may greatly influence the value orientation of the individual. In a society such as ours, where many different ideologies compete for followers and new ideologies emerge constantly, the formation of a personal ideology that has both consistency and conviction is made increasingly difficult. While it is easy to adopt a ready-made existing ideology, such a philosophy is often less flexible and less effective than a personally developed one. The adopted ideology rarely becomes fully integrated into the personality and can, therefore, lead to foreclosure in identity development.

A syntonic or positive outcome of the identity crisis depends on the young person's willingness to accept his or her own past and establish continuity with previous experiences. To complete the search for an identity, the adolescent must find an answer to the question "Who am I?" and must also establish some orientation toward the future and come to terms with the questions, "Where am I going?" and "Who am I to become?" The adolescent must develop a commitment to a system of values—religious beliefs, vocational goals, a philosophy of life—and accept his or her sexuality. Only through the development of these essential components of an ego-identity can intimacy of sexual and affectionate love, deep friendship, and personal self-abandon without fear of losing ego-identity emerge and thus make possible the developmental advance to the next stage in the human life cycle: *intimacy versus isolation.* The intimacy stage has been explored in considerable detail by Orlofsky (1975) and Orlofsky, Marcia, and Lesser (1973).

The adolescent who fails in the search for an identity will experience self-doubt, role diffusion, and role confusion; such an individual may indulge in a self-destructive one-sided preoccupation or activity. He or she will continue to be morbidly preoccupied with the opinion of others or may turn to the other extreme of no longer caring what others think and withdraw or turn to drugs or alcohol in order to relieve the anxiety that role diffusion creates. Ego diffusion and personal confusion, when they become permanent, can be observed in the chronic delinquent and in pathological personality disorganization. In its most severe form, the clinical picture of identity diffusion may lead to suicide or suicide attempts: "Many a late adolescent, if faced with continuing diffusion, would rather be nobody or somebody bad, or indeed, dead . . . than be not-quite-somebody" (Erikson, 1959: 132). The increase of suicide attempts among adolescents in the last decades is well documented and appears to parallel the widely reported increase in identity diffusion.

■ Intimacy versus Isolation

Once a personal identity has been achieved, the need for personal intimacy moves into the foreground of the psychosocial development of the young adult. The conflict at this higher level of development is between finding *intimacy or isolation* in interpersonal relationships. At this stage, peer group conformity has lost much of its earlier importance. The peer group may aid the young person in finding an identity and may even be helpful in making contacts with the opposite sex. However, intimacy is a personal matter and involves the establishment of emotional closeness to other people as a basis for enduring relationships. Physical closeness and sexual and affectional intimacy are only part of the issue. A basic theoretical insight emerges from the sequential order of Erikson's stages: the prerequisite for genuine and lasting intimacy is the achievement of an ego-identity, since intimacy implies the fusion of the identities of two people. At least in the typical male pattern, an ego-identity must be established before the possibility of marriage can be realistically considered. Erikson (1959: 95) holds that "only after a reasonable sense of identity has been established that real *intimacy* with the other sex (or for that matter, with any other person . . .) is possible." Subsequent research has shown that at least some females work on identity and intimacy issues simultaneously. (Theory and research related to this issue will be discussed in Chapter 4.) Generally speaking, one must first find an answer to the question, "Who am I?" before one can find a partner to become complementary to this "I." As long as the "I" remains undefined or is still forming, the selection of a permanent partner appears futile: "The giving of oneself to another, which is the mark of true intimacy, cannot occur until one has a self to give" (Constantinople, 1969: 359). If marriage is begun before one or both partners have established an identity, the chances for a happy, lasting marriage are low.

The conviction that emerges during the intimacy stage is: "We are what we love." The use of the plural pronoun "we" rather than the singular "I" is a significant reflection of the mutuality of the relationship. The syntonic outcome of this stage is intimacy, including sexual intimacy, genuine friendship, stable love, and lasting marriage. The dystonic outcome is isolation and loneliness, and, if intimacy is not based on a permanent identity, divorce and separation may result. Young adults who still have uncertainties in their identity will shy away from interpersonal relationships or may seek promiscuity without intimacy, sex without love, or relationships without emotional stability. As a counterpoint to intimacy, detachment and distancing in interpersonal relationships may emerge, that is, "the readiness to repudiate, isolate, and, if necessary, destroy those forces and people whose essence seems dangerous to one's own" (Erikson, 1968: 136).

■ Generativity versus Stagnation

The developmental polarity of adulthood is the achievement of *generativity;* the dystonic possibility is *stagnation.* This stage encompasses the productive years of the human life cycle, and generativity is the driving force in human behavior. Generativity is a productive creativity in terms of vocational and professional contributions to society. Marriage, giving birth to children and guiding their growth are such creative, productive activities. The successful resolution of the conflict implies that the mature person wants to be useful and productive, wants to be needed. In this stage, a new virtue, that of "care," emerges from the dialectical relationship of generativity versus stagnation. Erikson (1982: 67) sees this as "a widening commitment to take care of the persons, the products, and the ideas one has learned to care for." The generative caring may find healthy expression with "a more universal care concerned with a qualitative improvement in the lives of all children" (p. 68), for example, of those in developing countries. In addition, it finds expression through one's contributions to family, work, and community. The conviction that emerges is: "I am what I create," or "I am what I can produce." The giving of oneself to another person, an ideal, or one's work leads to an expansion of ego interests. If failure should occur at this stage, there would be no further development. Stagnation would be the outcome. Stagnation implies a routine repetition in vocational activities and stereotypical repetition in social relationships. The individual becomes egotistical, self-absorbed, and self-indulgent and, in turn, expects to be indulged. Stagnation means that "individuals, then, often begin to indulge themselves as if they were their own . . . one and only child" (Erikson, 1968: 138).

■ Integrity versus Despair

The last stage of the human life cycle encompasses old age and retirement from the productive years of life. The developmental task of this stage is between the achievement of *ego integrity* and its antithesis, *disgust and despair.* The conflict here is between combining, integrating, and appreciating all previous life experiences or becoming bitter, resentful, and negative. The successful resolution of the seven preceding stages culminates in integrity. The conviction that emerges is: "I am what survives of me." The syntonic outcome at this last stage of life is an acceptance of one's self and one's life without bitterness and regret and coming to terms with the approaching finality of life. Ideally, there is independence, autonomy, and maturity rather than a regression to childlike dependency. Erikson (1982: 62) defines wisdom as the "informed and detached concern with life itself in the face of death itself." Ego integrity is based on self-discipline and results in the wisdom that can give old age its positive or syntonic quality.

The negative or dystonic outcome, on the other hand, is confusion, helplessness, and a feeling that one's life was wasted, of being finished. What results is a basic discontentment with one's life, one's self, and others. There is fear of death and a regression to childhood dependency that characterizes the disintegration of old age, resulting in disgust and despair.

The question inevitably arises, does an individual have to acquire all of the syntonic or positive qualities of the preceding stages in order to move successfully to the next higher stage and eventually achieve the integrity that is the final and crowning experience of the human life cycle? If this were so, most people would be doomed to "despair." Not only can Erikson-type therapy help in reconstructing missed opportunities and aid the individual to acquire syntonic outcomes later, but psychosocial experiences may serve the same corrective function. Most people experience both syntonic and dystonic challenges and work on both, quite commonly past the time where they constitute the pivotal developmental issues that gives each of the eight stages its name. As was pointed out in the early part of this chapter, most important to consider is that both syntonic and dystonic opportunities are essential for development. Autonomy, the will to be oneself and to control oneself coincide with the physical readiness for bowel and bladder control and hence, most social groups emphasize toilet training during the second stage. Entering school and being required to produce work, the issue of industry cannot be avoided. Approaching sexual maturity, the issue of intimacy becomes paramount. Entering adulthood; the social expectation of becoming self-supporting brings to the foreground the issue of productivity and generativity. Thus, there appears to be a good fit between epigenetic potential and social demands that make Erikson's stages plausible. However, new social demands may create a crisis and a developmental opportunity, and Kroger (1993) hypothesizes—and provides case-study-type evidence—that personal crisis (which has to be resolved) facilitates the transition from one stage to the next higher stage. The adolescent identity crisis emerges when the individual is confronted with fundamental role changes, most globally the change from childhood to adulthood; also from dependence on parents to emotional independence, there are the social expectations to define one's future, one's gender role, and one's sexuality. According to Erikson (1965: 23), during adolescence the life history of the individual youth and the cognitive awareness of personal past and future plans interact and intersect with social history. Therefore, "individuals are confirmed in their identities, societies regenerated in their life style."

Another issue is, when and and why do individuals move from one stage to the next higher one? (And why does the identity crisis emerge during adolescence?) Erikson devotes considerable space to a description of the stages, but is much less specific in identifying the nature of these structural transitions. The epigenic ground plan suggests that maturational, biological forces propel the organism toward the development of more mature physical, cognitive, social, and emotional potential. Social expectation, child-rearing practices, and education generally speaking match these latent potentials.

Erikson has continued to expand and modify his theory, responding to criticism and clarifying issues where he seems to have been misunderstood. In addition, his theories have generated both considerable theoretical expansion and remarkable support from empirical research. However, Erikson himself never fully endorsed the research efforts, operationalizing and measurement attempts that claim to have been stimulated by his theory. He felt that the existing research methodologies were unable to really capture the full complexity of his constructs. These attempts to submit Erikson's theory to empirical tests began with James Marcia's (1966) efforts to refine the identity issue by postulating four distinct identity statuses. Also, Orlofsky's (1975) work, which broadened, subdivided, and refined the late adolescent/early adult intimacy issues (intimate, pre-intimate, stereotyped relationship, pseudo-intimate, isolate), has offered a new perspective of different levels of intimacy. Some of these expansions of Erikson's theory on contemporary thinking will become the focus in the following chapter.

4

THEORETICAL EXPANSION AND EMPIRICAL SUPPORT FOR ERIKSON'S THEORY

JAMES MARCIA'S EXPANSION OF ERIKSON'S STAGE "IDENTITY VERSUS ROLE DIFFUSION"

Erikson's theory remains in many important ways the starting point for most of contemporary identity research since it provides the foundation for understanding the processes underlying adolescent identity formation, and thus sets the standards against which scholars compare their findings. Much research has emerged that has validated Erikson's psychosocial stages by testing his theoretical assumptions empirically; in addition, this process has generated new ideas and refined old ones. However, it is important to bear in mind that Erikson never endorsed the empirical research intended to explain and validate his theory. By moving into more and more specific and refined substages of Erikson's "Eight Stages of Man," these efforts have tended to trivialize Erikson's theory and tended to fragment "identity formation" into increasingly more specific domains. Current identity formation researchers are becoming increasingly aware of what might have been Erikson's critique: "We have been stretching this construct in a myriad of directions in terms of its definitions, contexts, behavioral expressions, relationship with other components of living" (Archer, 1994: 10).

The early efforts to operationalize Erikson's theory and to develop a structured *Identity Status Interview* to determine identity formation comes from James Marcia. His dissertation "Determination and Construct Validity of Ego Identity Status" and the numerous subsequent research studies by him and his followers (Marcia; 1966; 1967; 1968; 1976a; 1976b; Marcia & Friedman, 1970; Marcia, et al., 1993; Schenkel & Marcia, 1972; Toder & Marcia, 1973) constitute such an expansion and elaboration of Erikson's theory and focuses especially on his theoretical construct of the adolescence stage of *identity versus identity confusion.*

Marcia identifies various patterns and common issues operating in youths who are exploring the adolescent identity issues. In addition, Marcia's conceptualizations have stimulated others to pursue identity-status research. In part, these scholars have relied on Marcia's interview assessment technique (which, as the most commonly used assessment technique, will become the primary focus in this chapter) and, in part, they have developed alternative ways to measure identity as well as new theoretical constructs for identity-status research.

Marcia's pioneering methodological and empirical contributions to the theory of identity formation are widely recognized. Marcia's conceptualization of identity statuses are assumed to have a "high degree of construct validity and predictive utility" (Archer & Waterman, 1990: 107).

Marcia (et al., 1993) calls for an awareness that theory builders such as Erikson and Blos did not intend developmental issues to be conceptualized as either-or propositions. For example, Marcia has dropped the "versus" from Erikson's original stage labels of his "Eight Stages of Man" in favor of the connecting word "and": Trust and Mistrust, etc. Erikson (1982: 55) actually meant "versus" to express the idea of "complementarity." Marcia argues that Erikson saw the psychosocial stages as a connected series of progressions in "forms of relatedness" as well as separation, as an option for males as well as for females. He calls for dialectical language that lets one see the "both . . . and" rather than the "either . . . or" nature of each of the outcomes of the psychosocial stage.

According to Marcia, the criteria for attainment of a mature identity are based on two essential variables that Erikson had already identified: crisis/exploration and commitment.* Crisis/exploration refers to the time during adolescence when the individual actively examines developmental opportunities, identity issues, and questions parentally defined goals and values, and begins to search for personally appropriate alternatives in respect to occupation, goals, values, and beliefs. Commitment pertains to the extent that the individual is personally involved in, and expresses allegiance to, self-chosen aspirations, goals, values, beliefs, and occupation (Berzonsky, 1989; Bilsker & Marcia, 1991; Marcia, 1967). In applying these criteria of the absence or the presence of crisis/exploration as well as that of commitment to Erikson's adolescent stage *identity versus role diffusion,* four identity statuses emerge (Figure 4.1). They provide the conceptual structure for Marcia's taxonomy of adolescence and represent four distinct modes for conceptualizing the identity issue of adolescence (Marcia, 1980).

1. The *identity-diffused or identity-confused subject* has not yet experienced an identity crisis or exploration nor made any personal commitment to a vocation or a set of beliefs. Identity issues have not yet been a significant issue, or if they ever did become an issue, they were never resolved.

2. The *foreclosure subject* has not yet experienced an identity crisis/exploration but has made definite commitments to goals, values, and beliefs. These commitments emerge from both an identification with parents or significant others and from socialization efforts, pressures, and indoctrination of parents and others. The motivation leading to a foreclosed commitment usually is a reciprocal one. However,

---

*In order to avoid the negative connotations of the term *crisis,* the synonym *opportunity* should be considered; the recent literature also substitutes the term *exploration.*

Commitment

	No	Yes
No	Diffusion	Foreclosure
Yes	Moratorium	Identity Achievement

Crisis/Exploration

FIGURE 4.1 Marcia's four identity statuses.

the commitments that emerge—in contrast to the commitments of identity achievement—are not the result of any truly personal searching and exploring. In other words, foreclosed commitments are accepted without working (and suffering) through the fundamental existential questions and choices.

3. The *moratorium subject* is in an acute state of crisis/exploration and is actively searching for values to eventually call his or her own. In other words, the moratorium subject is actively struggling to define personal identity by experimenting with alternative roles and beliefs but has not yet made a commitment, or has developed only very temporary tentative kinds of commitments.

4. The *identity-achieved subject* has gone through the process of exploration/crisis but has resolved the identity issues on his or her own terms. As a result of the resolution of these explorations, the individual has made a well-defined personal commitment to an occupation, a religious belief, a personal value system, and has resolved his or her attitude and values toward sexuality.

The specific content areas or decision-making issues that the adolescent is exploring or has made a commitment to are referred to as *domains*. The traditional domains—already identified by Erikson as areas in which adolescents have to make choices—provided the focus for much of the earlier identity research: occupation, ideological views in regard to religious beliefs, and political values. In addition, sex roles and sexuality are significant identity issues for adolescents because reproductively mature sex drive emerges during puberty and makes sexuality an identity issue.

Erikson studied psychosocial development in terms of changes in structure as reflected in the resolution (or lack of resolution) of the developmental tasks posed in each of the stages. The formation of an identity from a structural perspective involves development of overall ego strength; all functions increase as identity develops. In other words, the four identity statuses define the internal structure of the adolescent's ego; however, neither Marcia nor anyone else ever intended them to be used as a rigid typology. Rather than a static entity, each identity status is always an ongoing process. By definition, the *process* by which an individual established a sense of identity is developmental progression through these four stages. The ease or difficulty with which an individual moves (or does not move) through the identity statuses may well be a function, at least in part, of the effectiveness with which the child resolved (or did not resolve) Erikson's four preceding psychosocial stages. To the extent that mistrust, shame and doubt, guilt or inferiority issues linger on into the time of adolescence, a smooth and easy resolution of identity issues is impaired, and some of the adolescent's psychosocial problems (school problems, substance abuse, delinquency, suicide and suicide ideation, sexual promiscuity, etc.) can be understood as the result of developmental deficits from these earlier stages.

Identity statuses may be perceived as a developmental sequence, but no one status is necessarily and inevitably a stepping stone for another, as is the case in Erikson's "Eight Stages of Man." Only the moratorium appears to be an essential and inevitable prerequisite for the achievement of an identity, because an authentic personal identity cannot emerge without the kind of searching and exploring that is the defining characteristic of this stage. Regressive changes from higher to lower statuses in follow-up studies, e.g., from foreclosure or moratorium to identity diffusion, and also from identity achievement to either identity diffusion or moratorium, have been reported in the literature (Adams & Fitch, 1982; Waterman, 1982; Waterman, Geary, & Waterman, 1974) and as one's roles in life change, identity issues may change or reemerge. Apparently, no one has a permanent identity. Marcia introduced the term *status regression* to characterize the return from higher to lower statuses, which is contrary to theoretical expectations. However, since research has shown that the process of developing an identity actually involves movement back and forth between the stages, this recursive pattern appears to be part of forming and later reestablishing an identity for at least some individuals.

Any one of these identity statuses could become terminal, but the foreclosure subject is in greater danger of closing his or her development than the moratorium subject. However, a basic assumption is that, initially, as children enter into adolescence, they have not yet considered identity issues, hence they are diffuse. Their life goals are still vague, unclear, and undefined. Erikson's postulation of this developmental process from identity diffusion to identity achievement during adolescence is well documented. Identity achievement is, of course, not a terminal status, but always functions as a component of the overall progression of Erikson's eight stages. Within that frame of reference, bringing to successful completion the struggle for an authentic identity greatly enhances one's ability to establish a genuine intimate relationship in Erikson's next stage, *intimacy versus isolation,* as Orlofsky (1975) has demonstrated. However, the progression toward the intimacy stage takes place according to the epigenic plan, even though an individual may not have successfully achieved an identity.

Individuals in the process of moving to higher statuses may exhibit some of the characteristics of two or perhaps even three statuses at the same time. For example, a young person may already have developed a goal and a clear commitment to a vocation based on personal choices, while at the same time he or she may still actively search for a personal value system and remain committed to a puritanical attitude toward sex that reflects indoctrination by parents. Marcia found that, as students moved through the four years of college, the proportion of identity-diffused subjects declined significantly while the proportion of identity-achieved subjects increased steadily. This movement toward more mature identity statuses was not a function of college selectivity but of increased psychosocial maturity. This developmental progression from identity diffusion to identity achievement as a function of age and maturity during adolescence is a widely reported research finding. Constantinople (1969: 367) reports "consistent increases in successful resolution of identity, both from the freshman year to senior year across subjects and from one year to the next within subjects." Meilman's (1979) investigations of the age changes in identity status confirmed Erikson's and Marcia's theoretical assumptions. Meilman found that 12-year-olds were identity-diffused (68 percent) or foreclosed (32 percent), but by age 24, the majority (56 percent) had achieved an identity. Even then however, the other statuses were still represented: moratorium, 12 percent; foreclosure, 8 percent, and identity-diffused, surprisingly, 24 percent. Consistent with Meilman's earlier finding, research has repeatedly reported that high school students tend to be predominantly in the foreclosure of the identity statuses (Archer, 1989b). Marcia maintains that the late adolescent years (18 to 21) are the crucial time for identity formation.

Marcia created a semistructured *Identity Status Interview* that he developed as a research tool to assess identity thinking and decision making in the various domains. As such, the interview methodology has contributed in large measure to the understanding of identity formation and has generated much empirical knowledge (Marcia, 1966; 1967; 1968; 1976a; 1976b). The interview is administered individually and designed to sample the subject's commitment to a personal value system and religious and political beliefs, the extent to which the subject has experienced a personal crisis or identity exploration and how he or she has made decisions in regard to any of these. More recent revisions of the interview include more detailed questions to be used as a follow-up for responses that need further exploration. These follow-up questions are designed to unearth and clarify identity issues. Marcia's interview initially covered three core domains: (1) vocational choices, (2) religious beliefs, and (3) political philosophy. When he worked with females, Marcia added two domains: (4) family and career conflict (Marcia & Friedman, 1970), and (5) beliefs about sexual expression (Schenkel & Marcia 1972). Supplemental domains that appear with increasing frequency in the literature and—depending on the purpose of the research—are administered in conjunction with the core domains are: (6) gender role attitudes (Matteson, 1974), (7) avocational interest (Meilman, 1979), (8) relationships with friends and dates (Grotevant & Cooper, 1985), (9) role of spouse (Archer, 1981), (10) role of parent (Archer, 1981), (11) priorities assigned to family and career goals (Marcia & Friedman, 1970), and (12) ethnic identity (Rotheram-Borus, 1989).

IDENTITY DIFFUSION

The identity-diffused individual has no apparent personal commitment to occupation, religion, or politics and has not yet developed a consistent set of personal standards for sexual behavior and, by implication, for any of the goals, values, and choices of the other domains. The diffused subject has not explored identity issues actively nor gone through a genuine struggle in terms of reevaluating, searching, considering, and deciding personal alternatives. Consequently, identity diffusion can encompass a variety of different behavior patterns, from an aimless drifting, to a manipulative selfishness, to a morbid self-preoccupation. Archer and Waterman (1990: 96) actually subdivide the identity-diffused status into "precrisis, apathetic, alienated, pathological, marginally involved and commitment-avoiding types." This appears to be one reason why some of the research findings concerned with identity-diffused subjects are not always consistent.

For the child entering adolescence who has not yet been confronted with identity decisions, diffusion appears to emerge due to a precrisis lack of commitment, which, therefore, may be a common experience, perhaps developmentally necessary. Apparently, it is a kind of psychological instability typically experienced by early adolescents, as the data by Meilman (1979) and Archer (1989a, 1989b) convincingly demonstrate. There is also the narcissistic type of identity diffusion. These youths are primarily involved in their own lives, their motto is "to live and let live," and in their selfish approach "use" others for their own advantage and try to get for themselves whatever they can get away with. Apparently suffering from an unresolved ego crisis of Erikson's first stage, *trust versus mistrust,* unable to trust people, they use them. In addition, some identity-diffused subjects avoid anxiety, exploration, and confrontation by means of alcohol or drugs or by otherwise avoiding and/or denying that these issues need to be worked through. Others are alienated from their social, educational, and political world without actively challenging or questioning these institutions. Still other diffused subjects are in a state of psychological fluidity. Uncommitted to a personal system of values, they are open to all kinds of influences. When opportunities arise, they may take advantage of them, often without design or purpose, certainly without any personal commitment. Such individuals may take a "smorgasbord" approach to ideological systems and be most influenced by and overly receptive toward whichever politician or minister they last heard. Diffused college students can become quite vehement in their demand that the professor tell them which of the various theories is best, which is right, or which they should believe. Erikson (1968) maintained that identity diffusion is not the diagnosis of a psychological problem but the description of normal developmental process. Only if it persists over an extended period of time into late adolescence and adulthood could diffusion be considered a pathological condition; the most common diagnostic categories would be: delinquency, schizophrenia, and suicidality.

The classical example of identity diffusion in literature is Shakespeare's Prince Hamlet. He appears confused about his sex role: "Man delights me not, no, nor woman either." He is also estranged from love and procreation: "I say we shall have no more marriage." Finally, Hamlet feels alienated from the ways of his country: ". . . though I am native here, and to the manner born . . ." (Erikson, 1965: 6). In Arthur Miller's *Death of a Salesman,* Biff admits his identity diffusion quite succinctly: "I just can't take hold, Mom, I can't take hold of some kind of life."

FORECLOSURE

Foreclosure status is the most frequently observed identity status during adolescence, and while it declines with increasing age, it remains prevalent even in adulthood. Foreclosure subjects are committed to goals and values, an occupation, and a personal ideology. Consequently, in everyday life they superficially may appear very much like identity-achieved subjects, with whom they actually share some characteristics. However, foreclosure subjects differ from identity-achieved subjects in that they have not gone through the reflective process of intensive searching and personal exploration. They have never seriously considered other values and other alternatives for themselves. The goals they aim for and the values and beliefs they endorse are those adapted from parents or other "models," such as relatives, media personalities, ministers, or peers. Usually, the choices leading to foreclosure are made relatively early in life. "E.g. ever since I was seven I knew I wanted to be a

By permission of Doug Marlette and Creators Syndicate.

marine biologist" (Waterman, personal communication). When a young man is asked what he wants to become, he may answer: "I want to be a dentist" and when asked why, he may respond: "Because my father is a dentist." And even further probing would not change the essence of that response. No personal reason is given, no personal searching seems to have taken place. Foreclosure subjects were "socialized" by or "identified" with their parents, to the extent that parental values rather then personally explored convictions defined their commitment. College serves mainly to reconfirm the childhood value system and to provide an opportunity to attain the individual foreclosed goals rather than as a conscious process to explore vocational options.

The danger is that foreclosure subjects become so solidified in their position and in their attitudes that their identity status becomes terminal, and hence, they do not move easily toward reaching the status of identity achievement. Marcia refers to this phenomenon as "structured foreclosure" as distinguished from the more normal and temporary "developmental foreclosure." There appears to be a certain rigidity in foreclosures' personality structure. If the subjects are not sufficiently challenged to question their preprogrammed assumptions and values, foreclosure may become a permanent part of their personality structure. Waterman (1993) has pointed out that parents, teachers, or friends may effectively influence an individual's life work decisions that actually will bring out the highest potential in that person. Thus, parents may often be quite accurate in assessing their child's needs. (However, authoritarian and/or foreclosed parents may also misjudge their children's needs and exert pressures that reveal their own preferences.) Furthermore, Waterman notes that someone who has found satisfying life work without personal exploration should probably not deliberately disrupt it unless that foreclosure status interferes with the life work and no longer brings fulfillment. If that should happen, then the individual should be encouraged to explore more potentially rewarding possibilities.

Responses from Marcia's interview protocol may illustrate the commitment of foreclosure subjects to parental values. One interviewee commented on his political affiliation with a Republican ideology quite similar to that of his parents: "You still pull that way, Republican, if your parents are that way. You feel like it is where you should be." Another foreclosed adolescent who holds the same religious beliefs as his parents states: "Maybe it's just a habit with me, I don't know. I've thought a lot and you meet all kinds of people here, but I really haven't changed any of my beliefs . . . I plan to bring up my children in the church, just the way dad did with me" (Marcia, 1968: 329).

The foreclosure status is most widely viewed as being shaped through the reciprocal influences of identification processes with, as well as the socialization efforts of, parents. However, the dynamics do not inevitably involve the parents; they could be applied to other potent influential forces, such as a church or the individual's peers. For a certain developmental period, peer group conformity is common, and young adolescents may yield to their family values but lose their budding identity to the peer group. In this situation, foreclosure occurs because the individual's identity submerges too readily and without exploring other alternatives into the roles prescribed for them by others. As a result, adolescents define themselves primarily by their group membership; they act, dress, select food and entertainment, and use language and slang expressions in conformity to peer group standards, expectations, and pressures. Explicit or implicit peer group suggestions may lead to intolerance and even cruelty toward those who behave differently, especially in the junior high school years. When, outside the peer group context, the individual is confronted by parents or teachers with such behavior, he or she may feel ashamed and not understand his or her own cruelty.

The youth group movement of totalitarian systems, such as the Hitler Youth or the Pioneers/Komsomol in Communist Russia, provides such group identity with uniforms, flags, songs, rituals, beliefs, and even heroes as models. A similar vicarious identity is provided by belonging to a gang, a "hood" subculture, a sports team, and other less structured youth groups. Many junior high school students conform rather unquestioningly to the dress and behavior standards of their peer group in order to be accepted, to benefit from the feeling of solidarity with others, and to boost their immature identity through identification with the peer group. In the process, they often overidentify with the peer group, with its heroes and idols, to the extent that they may lose for some time their own personal value system and even the capacity to make independent decisions. According to Keniston, if the "conformity to peer group norms merely replaces conformity to parental norms . . . adolescent development is foreclosed before real self-regulation and independence are achieved" (Keniston, 1971: 377).

The youth group of the totalitarian system may serve as an illustration of political foreclosure, since the youth movement provides the adolescent with a ready-made system of beliefs and even a personal identity that the democratic society does not provide. It is no coincidence that totalitarian systems have large and very active youth groups often with idealistic commitment, while such politically committed youth groups rarely exist in democratic societies. Democratic identity is much harder to attain because it is based on freedom of choice. Rather than supplying a ready-made identity, democratic societies insist on self-made identity. Adolescent imagery, which frequently tends to reduce complex realities to black and white, has an affinity to the totalitarian system, which encourages this kind of absolute dichotomy. The democratic system allows for many different shades of ideological beliefs—and tolerates them all—and therefore provides more ambiguity. Is even tolerates totalitarian belief systems, such as the Moonies, Hare Krishna, Koresh's Davidians, Bagwadinians, etc., which cater to the needs of some adolescents for a ready-made value structure. The democratic value structure requires that individuals develop their own ego-identity in order to withstand ambiguity as well as the persuasive arguments of totalitarian ideologies; the problem is that it provides little help to the individual in establishing an identity.

MORATORIUM

The word *moratorium* is defined as a period of delay granted to somebody who is not yet ready to meet an obligation or make a commitment (Erikson, 1968: 157). The moratorium of adolescence is defined as a developmental period during which commitments either have not yet been made or are rather exploratory and temporary. However, applied to identity formation, the concept suggests that there are still many unresolved questions and much ongoing personal exploration. The individual is in an active struggle to find answers, to search, to explore, to try on different roles, and to play the field. In the process of actively pursuing identity concerns, the individual is willing to explore new ideas, new behaviors, and to change. This openness to unconventional, even regressive, alternative experiences (e.g., tolerance for unfamiliar ideas and unconventional behavior, fantasy, imagination, artistic creativity, subjectivism, distrust of logic and certainty, etc.) are used in the service of the ego. If such temporary adaptive regression leads to rational evaluation and purposeful selection, these experiences contribute to the achievement of a constructive synthesis of identity elements. Moratorium subjects, especially moratorium women, have a greater tendency to use "adaptive regressive experiences" in the identity exploration process (Bilsker & Marcia, 1991). Adaptive regression used in the service of ego development involves a temporary withdrawal from reality in order to master a higher-level synthesis.

Erikson and also Margaret Mead (1961) postulate that the adolescent period is a psychological moratorium, or an "as-if period" when individuals can experiment with different roles "as if" they were committed to these roles. However, since it is only an "as-if period," they are not really held fully responsible for errors that they might make in trying out new roles. Moratorium subjects can still change their values and modify their commitments, and they frequently do, in the process gaining new experiences and exploring a variety of new roles. Therefore, the "as-if period" is the delay society grants to youth to try on different roles—like trying on clothes—to see which fits best. It is in this spirit that the moratorium may try out radical political philosophies, nontraditional religious beliefs such as Oriental mysticism or Hare Krishna-belief, or even different vocational activities such as social work or the Peace Corps. The moratorium may try different interpersonal relationships, cohabitation, homosexuality, bisexuality, and heterosexuality. It is in this sense that the moratorium status is considered the adolescent issue *par excellence.*

If, while exploring moratorium issues on an uncommitted basis, adolescents have sufficient opportunities to search, experiment, play the field and try on different roles, experience and absorb the consequences, the chances are very good that they will eventually find themselves. They will develop an identity, and emerge with commitments to politics, religion, a vocational goal, and a more clearly defined gender role and sexual preference. These more permanent commitments, which lead to identity achievement, are frequently much less radical than some of the tentative and exploratory commitments during the moratorium. According to Marcia, moratorium is truly an essential and necessary prerequisite for identity achievement. However, while the adolescent is in the process of trying out different, new, and unconventional attitudes, values, beliefs, and behaviors, the world does not look very stable or predictable and does not appear to be a very desirable place; rather, the youth views the world and the social institutions as badly in need of improvement. Experiencing moratorium issues often creates subjective discomfort. Moratorium subjects are inclined to express their disenchantment by challenging what they see and hear. Their desire is to change government, politics, the church and education, in short, the system. While they are frequently very good diagnosticians and effective critics who can point to limitations, inconsistencies, and imperfections of the "system," moratorium subjects are not equally effective in producing viable, realistic alternatives because to do so requires life-experiences, identity, willingness to compromise, and a more permanent commitment.

Mead, Friedenberg, and Elkind have expressed concern that society's emphasis on rapid success, visible progress toward some goal, and achievement—as symbolized by scout badges, good grades, promotion, honors, recognition, awards, and diplomas—exerts too much pressure on youth. Such pressure deprives them of the opportunity to experience a true moratorium, an "as-if period" without the necessity of accountability.

IDENTITY ACHIEVEMENT

After an individual has experienced a psychological moratorium and has explored identity issues and crises and, as a result, has begun to develop more permanent personal commitments, he or she has achieved an identity. The achievement of a personal identity inevitably contributes to an increment in ego strength. Successful achievement of an identity means that adolescent development comes, at least for the time being, to completion. The progression to young adulthood, Erikson's *intimacy vs. isolation* stage, will emerge regardless of the successful or unsuccessful resolution of the identity issues, because stage progression is determined both epigenetically and socially. However, the ability to establish genuine intimacy is very much enhanced if an identity was achieved during adolescence (Orlofsky, 1975).

An identity has developed after the individual has seriously and carefully evaluated various alternatives and has considered different options, but has found a personal value structure and made his or her decisions on his or her own terms. In actuality, it is not at all uncommon for such an individual to choose a position that is fairly close to the parents' values; however, unlike the foreclosure subjects, achievers have considered various options, tried more liberal and often even more radical positions, but finally accepted or rejected them on their own terms. This identity formation process contrasts with that of the foreclosure subject, who remains, often by choice, very close to parental values and expectations and willingly accepts the parental ideology without seriously challenging parental beliefs. The achievement of an identity gives the individual an awareness and acceptance of personal continuity with the past and a more stable orientation toward the future. Identity means that the adolescent has found a new synthesis that "will link the past, the present, and the future" (Keniston, 1965: 212). The function of this sense of identity is to create a new outlook toward the self, to provide inner self-sameness and continuity, and to stabilize values and purposes. Once an identity has been achieved, there is an increase in self-acceptance, a stable self-definition, a willingness to make commitments to a vocation, a religion, a political ideology, and also toward intimacy and a personal commitment in an intimate relationship. Orlofsky, Marcia, and Lesser (1973) were able to show that the identity-achieved subjects have by far the greatest capacity for engaging in interpersonal intimacy. Those subjects still at lower levels of identity have a much greater probability of being stereotyped, pseudo-intimate, or even isolated in their intimate relationships. To achieve a mature ego-identity, the individual must overcome both "his irrational rebelliousness as well as his irrational urge to conform" (Keniston 1971: 364).

Stephen, Fraser, and Marcia (1992) maintain, however, that the individual who has achieved an identity will not necessarily—or even likely—remain in that status without changing. Identity achievers can reenter a period of exploration or crisis if the chosen identity element does not work out for some reason or if more appealing alternatives come up that could precipitate a crisis over whether or not to change. This could set off a moratorium-achievement-moratorium-achievement (MAMA) cycle. Even if this does happen, the identity achiever will probably process the new crisis/exploration issues somewhat more constructively than someone just beginning moratorium crisis/exploration, because that person would already have established effective methods of weathering the upheaval. The earlier success at resolving moratorium issues would most likely help the identity achiever to successfully resolve the situation again. If the MAMA cycle becomes too frequent, however, the individual may come to the conclusion that decisions are only temporary. This could lead to rather tenuously formed commitments.

In addition, adult identity achievers sometimes appear to move back even to the identity-diffused status. This happens because the established commitment lost its importance and its vigor over time. A committed love relationship gone sour can create interpersonal and intrapersonal diffusion. Regression to earlier stages may occur if the person experiences "burn out," for example, on the job or for economic or psychological reasons and therefore can no longer remain with the original commitment. The identity diffusion status for a persons at mid-life is not a true regression to early adolescence, but may actually be an enactment of Erikson's stage 7 (*generativity versus stagnation*) crisis/exploration. The adult who burns out is not at all like the drifting identity of the early adolescent-diffused subject.

Individuals who have attained an identity feel in harmony with themselves, accept their capacities, and even more important, their limitations. Such an individual realizes "where he fits (or knowingly prefers not to fit)" into social situations in terms of his own personal preferences.

SUMMARY OF IDENTITY STATUSES RESEARCH

A summary of the ego-psychoanalytically oriented identity research, such as the review publications by Adams (1992), Bourne (1978), Marcia (1980), and Waterman (1982) shows the extent to which Erikson's theory has stimulated contemporary research and the extent to which the concept of "identity status" has become a major research construct, leading to a broad range of investigations of personality development in adolescents (including college students and young adults). Much of the early research has been conducted with males, a problem that is rectified especially through Archer's (1989a, 1989b, 1993) more recent research. However, in general, males and females show similar patterns in the process of identity formation; some of the minor differences will be discussed later.

As a generalization, it appears valid to conclude that those who have achieved an identity (and to some extent, but less so, this is true for moratorium subjects), tend to possess desirable psychological and mental health attributes and to have developed effective ways of adapting. Archer (1989b: 348) identifies some of these positive correlates: "autonomy, re-flection, self-esteem, postconventional moral reasoning, mature intimacy, cultural sophisti-cation and internal locus of control." To this list one could add that these individuals are less conforming and demonstrate integrative complexity in social-cognitive reasoning.

The less advanced identity statuses, especially identity diffusion (and, to a lesser ex-tent, foreclosures), are characterized by lower levels of psychological functioning, and may have greater difficulties in coping with everyday problems, but also with mental health is-sues. Archer (1989: 348) defines some of these problem areas: "authoritarianism, precon-ventional and conventional moral reasoning, an external locus of control, less self-directed-ness, stereotyped interpersonal relationships, a preference for cognitive simplicity . . . and impulsivity." They also tend to be more conforming and less able to integrate information from multiple perspectives (Berzonsky, 1989; Waterman, 1982).

These generalizations imply a hierarchical ordering of identity statuses from the more sophisticated (identity-achieved, moratorium) to the less advanced stages (identity-dif-fused, foreclosure). The above generalization finds solid support for the two extreme groups: identity-achieved and identity-diffused. But it may need some modification for the two in-termediary statuses where the patterns are not as unequivocal. Since foreclosures actually have an identity, albeit not from their own explorations, they sometimes, at least superfi-cially, appear similar to identity-achieved. They experience less anxiety, are less likely to use drugs, but are more authoritarian and are described as "best behaved" but less able to deal with complexity and ambiguity. Moratorium subjects, in contrast, experience a great deal of anxiety, but they are not very authoritarian.

Finally, gender differences may be more relevant to the comparison of the intermedi-ary stages than to the two extreme statuses, where gender differences are minimal. In some research reports, foreclosure appears to be associated with more positive mental health in-dices for females, while for males the moratorium status had more positive correlates. Waterman (1982) maintains that male moratoriums look more like identity-achieved sub-jects and both groups are quite different from foreclosure and identity-diffused. Females re-veal a more complex pattern, but at least in some respect foreclosed females are more like identity-achieved, however, in other respects moratorium females resemble more the identity-achieved.

RECENT EXPANSIONS AND MODIFICATIONS OF IDENTITY THEORY

Grotevant (1993) has contributed to the theory of identity by suggesting that scholars can research identity as an integrated orchestration of domains, including "assigned" ones (e.g., social-class, gender, ethnicity) and "chosen" ones (e.g., vocation, political ideology), by making use of the narrative approach. Scholars, notably Marcia, but also Archer and Wa-terman, have examined the same processes but using slightly different terminology. Marcia et al. (1993) explain *conferred identity,* those elements of identity about which the subjects become aware over time, they are assigned not chosen (i.e., "I am the child of these par-ents," "I am the possessor of these skills and needs," etc.). In contrast, *self-constructed identity* elements are "chosen," they require decisions, i.e., about occupation, beliefs, values (i.e. "I want to become a teacher," "I view life as a continuous challenge"). Individuals with a self-constructed identity not only have a sense of inner coherence, they also know how they came to be the way they are. Those with conferred identities "experience the future as the fulfillment of expectations; those [with] . . . constructed identities experience their future as the creation of self-relevant forms" (Marcia et al. 1993: 8). This means that the individual actually tells his or her own life story to the researcher. Typically, researchers have focused on the structure, content, and function of the life story. Grotevant proposes more attention to the process of telling the story itself because identity is developmental, contextual, and life-span in scope, as Erikson (1959) noted. For example, the study of the life story allows scholars to see how the individual makes connections between/among elements of life that he or she plans for (e.g., college) and those that just seem to occur (e.g., serious illnesses of parent).

Kroger (1993) also emphasizes the importance of the life story. She notes that most longitudinal studies report findings from interviews spaced 2 to 12 years apart. She expresses concern that no one has conducted an ongoing detailed study of the process of structural change, that is, the transition from one level or stage to another in the individual's life story. By conducting a case study of "Ellen," a woman in mid-life, to research structural change, Kroger focused especially on the transitions between developmental stages. An intelligent and articulate subject, Ellen's exploration of her life story allowed her to study elements of identity formation, especially ones that seem universal, like conflict. A universal element would characterize development for everyone regardless of variables such as age, sex, race, culture, etc. Kroger suggested that the presence of conflict as the individual moves from one stage to the next may be one such universal element of development. She calls for more analysis of structural transformations that comprise a person's life story to see how and why people progress from one stage to the next or regress to earlier stages.

Waterman (1993) suggests that researchers must go beyond Erikson's theory to better understand the process of personal identity formation. Waterman's work represents an example of the "new wave of forthcoming scholarship" (Adams, 1992: 8). He proposes that Erikson posited identity as "something to do" rather than as "something to be." Waterman also attempts to go beyond Marcia's work on exploration and commitment to what he calls "personal expressiveness." This is the individual's own unique way of presenting an authentic sense of self in daily life. He wants to explain why some individuals seem satisfied to find "something to do" while others seem compelled to find "someone to be." He relies on eudaimonist philosophy, which demands that the individual consistently bring out the best that is in him or her, as this leads to happiness because it is good and ethical. If an individual manifests in daily life the very best that is within him, this philosophy holds that self-esteem and serenity will result. Waterman examines the individual's psychological make-up to see how one best realizes one's great potentialities. Why, for example, do some students consistently give their best effort to homework, while others complete assignments in a rather perfunctory manner, without caring about their own learning. Why do some try to bring compassion, tolerance, and understanding to their dealings with their peers, while others openly ridicule and taunt those whom they perceive as different in some way, ranging from someone not wearing the "right" clothes or having the "approved" hairstyle to someone having a disability or deformity.

Archer (1982, 1989a, 1989b, 1993) has emerged as an important scholar of identity status, who has contributed to identity theory by investigating the process of identity formation for both boys and girls. She concludes that similarities, not differences, abound in terms of boys' and girls' identity formation. With minor exceptions, males and females seem to follow similar patterns in the process of developing an identity. In addition, her work has focused systematically on males and females during the early and middle adolescence period. She notes that 12-year-olds lack the sophistication of 18-year-olds when they respond to the *Status Interview Schedule* questions about vocation, marriage, and parenting. However, even within a group of 12-year-olds, great diversity in identity status exists. And like others before her, Archer (1993) observed that many individuals in a group of adolescents will be in different identity statuses at the same time, depending on which domains are being assessed.

Identity formation, of course, is a complicated developmental process that is normative during the period of adolescence. Scholars generally divide the adolescent stage into early (11/12–15), middle (16–18), and late (18–22) periods. Archer (1993) has studied exploration and commitment in early and middle adolescence, a developmental period during which identity formation is in process, because young teenagers in this age range typically experience events that would precipitate identity development, e.g., the physical changes of puberty, infatuation, individuation, peer group pressures, etc. These are, therefore, the developmental periods for exploring, searching, and "playing the field," rather than for commitment. Archer chose to study males and females about to change schools (sixth-, eighth-, and twelfth-graders). Most of the adolescents were diffused and foreclosed, which suggests that younger teenagers must have time for exploration and can make only tentative commitments to occupations, religious beliefs, political philosophies, and personal definitions of sexual attitudes. The study showed a large number of foreclosures in the sex-role area, perhaps as a result of relatively limited opportunities to experience and develop consistent, personal, sexual values.

Archer suggests the use of five criteria for exploration/crisis and six for commitments (with some overlap) to assess the identity status of the younger adolescents. For exploration/crisis, these criteria include: (1) knowledgeability, (2) activity directed toward information-gathering about various alternative choices, (3) the weighing of advantages and disadvantages, (4) the emotional tone, and (5) whether or not the adolescent wishes to make an early decision about commitment. To illustrate these criteria, Archer uses the example of a sixth-grader, a high school senior, and a college senior considering marriage and a family and a career. Obviously, the responses of teenagers will become more realistic, more sophisticated and complex as the sixth-graders develop into late adolescents.

The younger adolescent will probably not respond at all like his or her older counterpart in terms of emotional tone and the desire to make an early decision about commitment. The younger adolescent's emotional tone conveys naive curiosity and uncritical excitement because the young person does not face the immediate need to implement any decisions. Older adolescents may likely express some uneasiness and concern about the pressure they experience, perhaps from parents and teachers, that they should make decisions that conform to the ideas of these others about appropriate choices.

But younger adolescents generally do not experience these pressures until later. Thus, younger adolescents usually will remain unwilling to make decisions about specific alternatives in various domains. Because they will not be acting on their choices for some time, they typically express an open-endedness as they consider their choices, an entirely suitable approach since, as many adults advise, their preferences will most likely change. So, for a 12-year-old and a 17-year-old, the process of choosing a college will probably involve very different criteria. But perhaps, depending on the specific denomination and the parents' values, a 12-year-old and a 17-year-old could possibly make similar decisions about religion.

The other dimension for assessing identity status in younger adolescents is commitment, which refers to "a stable investment in one's goals, values, and beliefs evidenced in supportive activity" (Archer, 1993: 181). The criteria Archer suggests for the assessment of commitment are: (1) knowledgeability, (2) activity directed toward implementing the chosen identity element, (3) emotional tone, (4) identification with significant others, (5) projection into one's personal future, and (6) resistance to being swayed. Note that the criteria of the weighing of advantages and disadvantages is absent from the list for evaluating commitment because the committed young person has already made his or her choice. Hence, the weighing of pros and cons has ceased. Note also that the activity for commitment is directed toward implementing the identity element, not toward finding out about that element as would be the case for the still-exploring adolescent. Finding important role models, projecting into the future to see how the commitment will work, and resisting attempts from others to change the commitment are criteria that Archer establishes to assess commitment only, not exploration.

1. *Knowledgeability* requires that the young adolescent have some personally relevant information about the domain being investigated. The information may be inaccurate; it will surely be limited and simplistic. Archer gives the example of a vocational choice, a science career. Using information gathered, perhaps from parents, teachers, family members, peers, the media, personal experiences, etc., a young person in sixth grade may have a very disoriented view of the rigors of a scientific education and career. But a college senior who has taken science courses will have acquired some actual appreciation about the difficulty of a career in science.

2. For the younger adolescent, *activity aimed at actualizing the chosen identity elements* may consist of conversing with knowledgeable people in the area, reading, making visits to appropriate sites, finding friends who share the interest, pursuing a hobby related to the interest, or joining or even forming a "future nurses" club, for example.

3. The *emotional tone* of the younger adolescent who is still exploring will differ from both that of the older adolescent who has made a commitment and the adolescent who has not yet began to explore making a commitment. In general, the younger adolescent will sound curious and enthusiastic; the committed adolescent will sound calm and stable, less so if the choices have resulted from conflict with parents, teachers, etc.

4. Parents, teachers, media personalities, peers, siblings, clergy, etc., may all serve as *role models* for adolescents. The foreclosure subject, who by definition has not yet undergone identity exploration/crisis, typically finds role models especially influential in the process of establishing commitment; however, a foreclosure commitment is a shortcut without any direct personal exploration of alternatives. Identity achievers may also find inspiration from role models, but they will usually com-

bine their own observations of characteristics of a number of respected models into a personal blend that reflects their own personality. For example, a foreclosed mid-adolescent would likely mention his or her mother, a liberal democrat, as the source of his or her own party preference. An identity achiever might point to a parent, several teachers, and even a political figure who may have influenced his or her choice about politics. Most likely, he or she would look up to each of these role models for different reasons, i.e, the esteem afforded to them in the community, their dedication, their perspective on important problems, etc.

5. Mid-adolescents can tentatively *project their plans into the future* in general outlines as far as their mid- to late-twenties. Early adolescents, on the other hand, can only very vaguely imagine their lives after high school or college graduation. But their general ambitions can, even in a very tentative condition, support their futures as they envision them.

6. But when young adolescents have the leisure to explore before they must begin to commit, they show relatively *little resistance to being swayed* in other directions than the originally selected identity element. Discussions of various vocational options that an adolescent might choose may not precipitate much of a commitment. During such a discussion of vocational alternatives, the adolescent may offer only: "Yes, I might be better off, choosing some other option, but I most likely will not because. . . ." In contrast, the foreclosure typically will resist being influenced by alternative arguments, even more so than the identity achiever, perhaps because identity achievers have already examined options on their own terms; hence, their commitment is less likely to be threatened.

GENDER DIFFERENCES IN THE ACHIEVEMENT OF AN IDENTITY

Before 1980 most research did not adequately address the issue of sex differences in adolescent identity formation (Waterman, 1985). Early research tended to consider only males or only females, but not both sexes together. Earlier studies also emphasized different domains for females (e.g., sexuality) than for males. Typically, different research instruments were used for each sex. Recent research on gender differences has shown a greater emphasis on methodology to ensure that both sexes receive attention and to ensure reliable empirical instruments for studying identity formation across gender.

Generally, more recent scholarship (Archer, 1989a; Archer & Waterman, 1988; Waterman, 1982) shows that:

1. In most traditional domains (e.g., vocational choice, religious beliefs, political ideology), males and females follow a similar pattern of identity status distribution.
2. The timing of identity formation for both sexes appears to be about the same.
3. The personality correlates of each of the identity statuses (e.g., authoritarianism, anxiety, concept formation, etc.) tend to be the same for both sexes.

The similarities between males and females are more pronounced than any reported difference in terms of the process, the timing, and the correlates of identity formation. Some relatively minor gender differences emerged in some domains, especially sexuality, as well as some of the domains that have been added more recently. Apparently, females confront a more complex task in forming their identity than do males: Not only are females concerned with their own sense of self, but they are more concerned than males with the impact of their self on significant people in their lives. Within a different theoretical framework this idea is elaborated in the work of Carol Gilligan. Much more than males, females are likely to have experienced an exploration/crisis period in terms of defining their sexual identity. They also tend to experience greater complexity in terms of making decisions pertaining to family and career choices than do males (Archer, 1985, Waterman & Nevid, 1977).

Erikson suggested that identity precedes intimacy for males, but that identity follows intimacy for females or that both emerge simultaneously. He maintained that identity remains incomplete for a female until she bonds with a man: ". . . something in the young woman's identity must keep itself open for the peculiarities of the man to be joined and of the children to be brought up" (Erikson, 1968: 283). Research advances various conclusions about the relationship between identity and intimacy in males and females. Not all of the relevant findings are entirely consistent. The earlier research, in line with Erikson's theory, had emphasized that identity precedes intimacy for males, but that the sequence is reversed or occurs simultaneously for females. Others have observed that only more assertive females follow a pattern similar to that of males (Dyk & Adams, 1989; Matteson, 1977, 1974, 1993).

Dyk and Adams (1990) maintain that gender alone does not explain the link between identity and intimacy. Females with a predominantly masculine orientation show a pattern of identity/intimacy like that of both masculine-oriented and feminine-oriented males. Females with a feminine orientation showed more merging of identity and intimacy, which suggests a simultaneous rather than sequential developmental pattern. Dyk and Adams (1990), and Matteson (1993) do note that the progression in relation to identity and intimacy may be reversed for females, that is, they may develop intimacy before identity. The reason may be that females actually develop a caring intimate orientation in interpersonal relationships earlier in life than males do.

Carol Gilligan's (1982) notion that there are two fundamentally different voices, a characteristic masculine (justice) and a feminine (caring) voice seems to have implications here. Both genders can speak with both voices, but males are much more likely to speak only with the masculine voice, while females speak with both voices. A distinction that may be reflected in the timing of identity and intimacy issues. Gilligan proposes that, while for males, identity emerges before intimacy, for at least some females, identity and intimacy are apparently fused.

However, for females who scored above the median on masculinity in Dyk and Adams's (1990) investigation, identity preceded intimacy. But the feminine-oriented women in this study showed fusion between identity and intimacy. This finding seems to support Gilligan's argument that men and women exhibit contrasting patterns of identity/intimacy development. It also suggests that identity/intimacy patterns may vary for females. Dyk and Adams (1990) question why feminine-oriented and masculine-oriented females differ in their development of identity/intimacy. Specifically, they want to know how masculine-oriented females are like males. Perhaps a biological, hormonal component may eventually explain this. Dyk and Adams (1990) maintain that some studies (Baucom et al., 1985) suggest the presence of higher levels of testosterone in those women who score male-oriented.

Thus, Gilligan and other researchers (Josselson, 1990: Unger and Crawford, 1992) may be correct in contending that more than one pathway may lead to identity development for females. However, Archer (1989a: 117) found in three studies that both males and females "use the identity status (process) comparably, except for foreclosure, which characterized males significantly more than females." Archer focused on the process of identity formation domains and timing. She found virtually no differences in the domains of vocational orientation, religious beliefs, and sex-role orientation. However, she reported that males tend to be more foreclosed and females more diffused with respect to political ideology. Females are more likely to be in moratorium or identity-achieved status than males when the research focuses on family roles. Archer observed no gender difference in the timing of identity status in two of her three studies. The last study revealed that the process of identity development may become more complicated for some high school female seniors as they grapple with both intrapersonal and interpersonal goals. Still, Archer (1989a: 136) noted that "adolescent females did not put aside identity tasks because of their interpersonal concerns," nor did the "males forge ahead . . . to self-definition." Actually, Archer found that females were more likely to use multidimensional, complex decision-making processes in the domains of family roles and sexuality. Archer proposed that these contrasts might result from sociocultural expectations: If men had to care for children while they pursued their careers as frequently as women do, these differences might disappear or become significantly less delineated.

Waterman and Nevid (1977) found that women seem to examine the content of their sexual identity more carefully than men and invest more exploration and develop firmer commitments. Besides sex roles, participants considered occupation and politics. Matteson had found that the integration of masculine and feminine personality traits must occur in order for males and females to achieve optimum identity development. Matteson (1977) reported that sexual ideology did not seem more necessary (though it may be more difficult) for women's identity formation than for men's, but was important for both genders. Working through this task is essential for the identity of both genders. Matteson (1972) did report that a higher percentage of females as compared to males are in crisis across all domains. He found also higher levels of commitment among females in all domains except politics, in which only a slightly higher commitment prevailed among males.

Waterman and Nevid (1977) found no such pattern in their study of college students that included the domain of premarital sex. Like Erikson, Waterman and Nevid found that females were more likely to have undergone a sex identity crisis, whereas males were much more likely to be foreclosed in regard to the domain of premarital sex. However, males and females were both more likely to be committed about their sexual values than any other area.

In summary: Except for the resolution of a personal value system regarding sexuality, male and female identity development patterns seem virtually identical. Obviously, the continued double standard requires females to make careful sexual decisions since they bear the social and often economic consequences of contraception and abortion (or single unwed parenthood). Waterman and Nevid propose that Erikson's elaboration of women's "inner space" concept may provide the explanation.

WOMEN AND THE INNER SPACE

Erikson (1968) dealt with gender issues in a chapter entitled, "Women and the Inner Space," in order to address differences in identity formation between males and females. He maintained that the sexes form different identities because they experience differences in the ground plan of their reproductive physiology, differences which pervade their lives and the very essence of their existence in space. The core concept in defining woman's sexuality and, more generally, her identity, is her "Inner Space." As she forms her sexual identity during puberty and the following decade, she must develop her sexual values and standards and decide whether, when, under what circumstances, and whom to permit entry into her "Inner Space."

At least in part, Erikson illustrates his theory with reference to his repeated observations of 150 boys and 150 girls over a 2-year period as they constructed an imaginary movie scene from simple toys (Figures 4.2 and 4.3). The study was conducted in the 1940s at Berkeley and grew out of Erikson's curiosity to explore whether and to what extent his theories were relevant to nonclinical subjects. The primary purpose was to study life cycle changes and neurotic tensions in these prepubertal subjects. The children were instructed to construct a playful scene with toys, such as human figures, animals, furniture, vehicles, and blocks and tell the plot. Even though gender differences were not the primary purpose of the study, Erikson was struck by the fact that boys and girls tended to structure their space quite differently. "Girls emphasized inner, boys outer space." Girls structured their scenes as interior rooms or enclosed areas, often with decorative gates and with people inside the enclosed space (Figure 4.3). Boys emphasized protrusions, cannons, cones or cylinders, or high structures (that collapse); people, animals, and vehicles were on the outside (Figure 4.2). Erikson compares the construction of such playfully created images through the arrangements of toys or blocks to parallel the morphology of the male and female reproductive systems.

"The existence of a productive inner-bodily space safely set in the center of the female form and carriage" (1968: 267), for Erikson, has greater theoretical meaning than Freud's concern with the missing organ. The uniqueness of a woman's individuality, "her somatic existence, and her social potentials . . . demand that the feminine identity be studied and defined in its own right" (Erikson, 1968: 290). At least partial empirical support (Lerner & Brackney, 1978: 232) suggests "greater salience of the inner body for females than for males."

In his chapter, "Once More the Inner Space" (1975), Erikson thoughtfully attempts to reply to the critical writing that his "Inner Space" concept has generated. While acknowledging that a new womanhood is evolving and that new and more universal identities for women are emerging, he recognized his obligation to expand the ideas of "Inner Space" and "Outer Space" to include both sexes. However, Erikson basically reaffirms his commitment to the "Inner Space" construct.

In addition, Erikson continued to argue that interpersonal concerns create the core of female identity, with vocational and ideological issues remaining much less important. He also emphasized that a woman's identity remains in process. Accordingly, issues of identity, intimacy, and generativity could be dealt with simultaneously rather than sequentially; Pat-

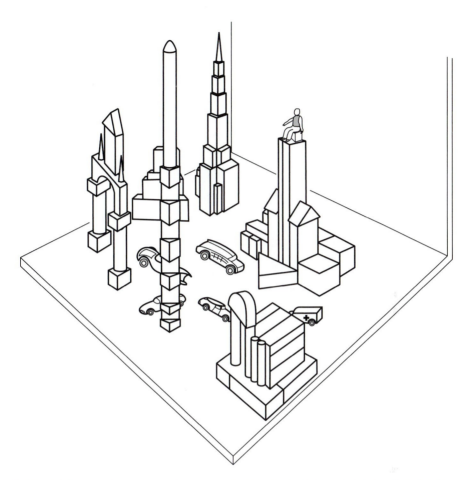

FIGURE 4.2 Typical boy's construction of space. (Reprinted from *Childhood and Society* by Erik H. Erikson, with the permission of W. W. Norton & Company, Inc. Copyright 1950, ©1963 by W. W. Norton & Company, Inc., renewed ©1978, 1991 by Erik H. Erikson.)

terson's (1992) research confirms this idea. Current scholars frequently demand the predominance of research protocols and models that include both sexes so that an inclusive model can represent the feminine side of development (Archer, 1993; Gilligan, Lyons, & Hanmer, 1990; Kroger, 1993).

Since Erikson's original study was conducted half a century ago, "Women and the Inner Space" has become a controversial construct and has not only been the target of criticism but has also inspired further research, validating the use of play constructions to assess gender differences and in general supporting Erikson's findings. He felt that his ideas were misunderstood by feminist scholars (Blackman, personal communication). Especially in his later work he emphasized the theme of empowering women and considered it essential that women be their own person and not be subordinated to anyone. At the same time he felt that investigating gender differences is crucial to understanding the symbolic mean-

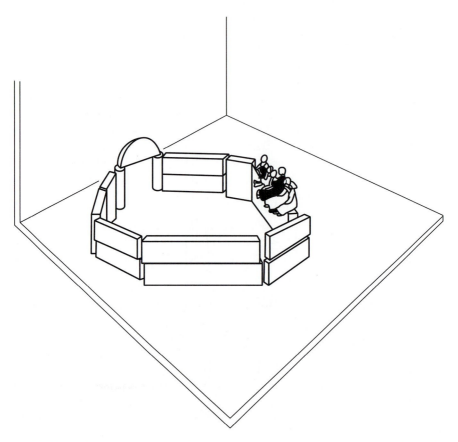

FIGURE 4.3 Typical girl's construction of space. (Reprinted from *Childhood and Society* by Erik H. Erikson, with the permission of W. W. Norton & Company, Inc. Copyright 1950, ©1963 by W. W. Norton & Company, Inc., renewed ©1978, 1991 by Erik H. Erikson.)

ing revealed in preadolescents play constructions. Play constructions are rich in metaphoric content and Erikson interpreted them as latent manifestations of subjective psychosocial feelings and interpersonal themes that are deeper than those found in conscious awareness.

Nancy Blackman in an unpublished paper "Inner Space Revisited and Outer Space Reconsidered in the Preadolescent" reviews much of the follow-up research generated by Erikson's earlier investigation at Berkeley of preadolescents play constructions. She asks: What fiction and what truth do these gender differences reveal and more specifically, to what extent are they influenced by chronological age and by the social changes of the intervening decades?

Blackman systematically replicated Erikson's research design and found support for his earlier observation that pronounced gender differences exist in the construction of play materials. Boys are more likely to build exterior designs, towers, protrusions, and high buildings. The creation of girls, in contrast, are more likely to be a block high, surrounding an inner space without a roof, but with an entrance. Often contained in the interior space are people, animals, and furniture.

Blackman's fourth-grade boys built exterior "masculine structures" and revealed patterns of violence and aggression quite similar to those reported by Erikson earlier. The creations of fourth-grade girls showed enclosed walls, no doors, and no roofs. In general, these were less "feminine structures" than those built by sixth-grade girls, because some of the fourth-grade girls created buildings that revealed elaborate exterior "masculine structures." Sixth-grade boys tended to construct exterior scenes as they had in the earlier study, but there were exceptions and if they built interior spaces they often were uninhabited, lacking both people and animals. The constructions created by sixth-grade girls had become even more feminine than those in the Berkeley study: low walls, encapsulated interior space with people, animals, and furniture. Almost totally absent in their constructions were male models or father figures. However 12-year-old girls were preoccupied with the theme of intruders violating the "inner space" or attacking the sedentary female doll.

These findings are interpreted as revealing both a great deal of consistency with the earlier observations reported by Erikson as well as those of other researchers, but they are also viewed as representing subtle influences of social changes on the processes of pubescence. The shortened period of childhood, the prepubertal girls' freedom to participate in masculine activities, and the dilemmas created for youth through the erotification of the content of the mass media and the ambiguous meaning of sexuality and gender roles may account for the changes noted. Modern feminists acknowledge that "boys and girls arrive at puberty with a different interpersonal orientation and a different range of social experiences" (Gilligan, 1982: 11). A different interpretation of the observed play habits may reveal a girl's need for relationship and the need for "room" for relationships. ". . . women . . . define themselves in a context of human relationships" (p. 17). Since gender differences have remained an issue for scholars, the need for further, thorough, continuous, and vigorous investigations into the process of identity formation and gender is obvious.

ETHNIC DIFFERENCES IN IDENTITY DEVELOPMENT

According to Erikson (1975), identity formation during adolescence is not just a task that an individual can accomplish in isolation, but a process that is compounded by the individual's place in society and in history, as well as by what Bronfenbrenner refers to as the "ecological niche": sex, social class, community, ethnicity, and culture. Awareness of the role of ethnicity in the process of identity formation and the assessment of the new domain, "ethnic identity" (Rotheram-Borus, 1989), has only recently attracted the attention of scholars in the field. Phinney (1990) noted that much of the earlier research focused on white ethnic subgroups, such as Greek-Americans, Italian-Americans, French-Canadians, and the most extensively studied white subgroup, Jews. A review of the current literature leads her to conclude that overall ethnicity-focused research is still quite fragmented. Scholars tend to work with particular ethnic groups in isolation from each other and, therefore, generate findings that are of only limited generality. Follow-up studies are rare and so are comparative studies across ethnic groups.

Phinney and Alipuria (1990) conducted an investigation to study the identity processes of search/exploration (moratorium) and commitment in relationship to ethnicity among college students. Specifically, they hypothesized a positive relationship between commitment to one's ethnic identity and self-esteem. Earlier studies had reported that low levels of ethnic identity among black youth were related to anxiety and feelings of insecurity. Phinney and Alipuria's subjects included males and females from Asian-American, African-American, and Mexican-American ethnic backgrounds as well as a comparison white group. The search/exploration of ethnic identity issues emerged as a central concern among the minority group members as compared to the white students. Thus, the data support the hypothesis that an "ethnic identity search" was more pronounced in the three minority groups as contrasted to the white majority. This generalization was also reported by Rotheram-Borus' (1989) research. According to her, exploring one's ethnic identity appears to be an important issue for minority adolescents, while it is not a salient feature for those who are in the majority and who consequently may show little awareness or have given little thought to their ethnic roots.

In the Phinney and Alipuria study, for African-Americans and Mexican-Americans, an active search for an ethnic identity was related to self-esteem. Finally, those who had not only explored but also successfully established an ethnic identity commitment scored significantly higher on self-esteem, a finding that was more pronounced within the three minority groups. Apparently, self-esteem is related to both ethnic identity search (blacks and Mexicans) and ethnic identity commitment (all minority groups). For whites, ethnic identity was rated less important than the other four identity domains that were assessed (occupation, sex role, religion, and politics). For all groups, occupation and sex role were the important domains, but for the minority groups, religion and politics were less important than ethnic identity. The researchers suggested that additional research with multicultural populations and with different educational and age levels is needed to confirm these results.

However, the integration of an ethnic identity into one's personality appears to proceed in accordance with Erikson's theory of ego-identity development. Identity formation in minority youth apparently progresses from a lack of interest in ethnic identity issues—also referred to as an unexamined identity diffusion/foreclosure—through a stage of active ethnic identity search/exploration (moratorium), and culminates in a commitment to self-selected ethnic values (identity-achieved). The achievement of such an ethnic identity is defined as "a secure commitment to one's group, based on knowledge and understanding obtained through an active exploration of one's cultural background" (Phinney & Chavira, 1992: 272). In a small-scale follow-up investigation, Phinney and Chavira showed that ethnic identity—assessed at ages 16 and 19—tends to progress along these identity statuses. Most of the lower stage individuals moved to higher stages in the 3-year period, while those at the higher stages remained there.

In general, research has examined such components of ethnic identity as positive and negative attitudes toward one's own ethnic group, the relative position of the ethnic identity domain in relationship to the more traditional identity domains among members of minority groups, personal involvement in ethnic practices, the relation of the individual's ethnic identity to the majority culture, ethnic identity and gender, etc. Phinney (1990: 511) calls for more research in order to better understand "the psychological impact of . . . diversity" on the process of identity formation.

EDUCATIONAL IMPLICATIONS

One basic question regarding education during adolescence that emerges from Erikson's theory is: To what extent and how do educational institutions enhance youths' efforts in self-finding, or does traditional education actually interfere with identity development? Numerous critics of the educational system—Dennison, Elkind, Friedenberg, Goodman, Holt, Silverman, and others—have maintained that, rather than foster a moratorium-like exploration of individual growth experiences, schools require adolescents to suppress their creativity, individuality, and identity exploration to the routines of a skill- and knowledge-oriented curriculum. Thus, schools seem to be encouraging foreclosure to the extent that they demand conformity to the status quo and submission to authority rather than aiding the adolescent in the search for and exploration of a personal identity. Indirect support for this idea comes from the Waterman and Waterman's (1970) findings, which suggest that foreclosure subjects felt more comfortable in school and held more positive attitudes toward their educational experiences, while the uncommitted, searching, and experimenting moratorium subjects evaluated their educational experience rather negatively. Apparently, the structure of the school—the curriculum, schedules, attendance requirements, grades, hall passes, and so on—encourage foreclosure rather than efforts directed toward self-finding and self-definition, all of which leads to questioning and challenging of existing patterns, values, and authorities. One might speculate whether the widespread indifference of adolescents toward school and their frequent discontent with the educational establishment and with their teachers in part result from the lack of concern of many educators with what Erikson and his followers consider a fundamental educational/developmental issue, namely, the exploration necessary for the resolution of the identity crisis. Educators have recognized that the problem of adolescents dropping out of school is not simply a matter of lack of ability or even a lack of school achievement; it is due to a dislike of school, a desire for independence, a need to find a job, a search without a goal, an expression of inner discontent and restlessness. Even in college, students' dissatisfaction with their school, their questioning of the value of their education, the increasing pattern of "dropping in and dropping out," as well as the common pattern of transferring from one college to another do suggest moratorium-like explorations. These behaviors make sense in view of Erikson's "identity crisis/exploration" concept; all of this is also compatible with the related assumption that "moratorium and Wanderlust" and exploration are essential psychological prerequisites for the development of a mature identity.

The increasing demand for relevance in the curriculum and in the total educational experience might also be better understood in view of the moratorium issues: developing a sexual identity, exploring religious values and alternatives, selecting career goals, and developing a commitment to a political ideology. The adolescent often has difficulties in seeing the relationship among these burning existential issues and conjugating French verbs, studying ancient Rome, proving the Pythagorean theorem, and examining the finer points of Shakespeare's *Macbeth*. Teachers, in turn, are often remiss in failing to make such personally significant relationships obvious, even in those content areas where they are readily apparent. At a minimum, the subject matter of any course provides ample opportunity to explore vocational opportunities in that field. Explicit suggestions have been made to reorganize the school curriculum so as to facilitate rather than impair adolescents' identity achievement (Dreyer, 1994).

The junior high and even the senior high school student's choices of personally relevant courses are limited, and the adolescent has relatively little to say about the curriculum. The curriculum should become more closely related to the adolescent's search for self-understanding by including more identity-development-relevant topics. This could include interpersonal social skills, health education, drug education, and sex education, areas in which considerable misinformation exists even among sophisticated youth. Furthermore, such topics as human development, family relationships, sociology, consumer economics, social organization, career opportunities, ecology, diversity, gender roles and sex stereotypes, and a study of values could aid the adolescent in developing a philosophy of life. All of these topics could be taught in ways that make them academically respectable as well as personally meaningful. In their English courses, high school students could study the period of adolescence as reflected in the rather extensive literature dealing with the problems and issues of growing up. In addition, present teaching styles frequently include lectures, rehearsing, reviewing, drill, quizzes, tests, and assignments—which means that, even when these activities are meaningful, they are teacher-directed, so that the learning activities remain under the control of the school authorities. Consequently, the high school student often ends up in a docile and submissive role. School provides limited exploratory opportunities for moratorium subjects, and foreclosures receive little or no encouragement to move out of their stagnant position; they may actually receive rewards for foreclosure behavior. Identity formation thrives when there are opportunities for exploration of divergent ideas, controversial issues, and alternative ways of thinking and behaving. An identity-enhancing curriculum would encourage individuals to assume personal ownership of their work, in the way students do who prepare exhibits for science fairs.

In contrast to Freud's emphasis on the danger of frustration and the possible contribution of frustration to neurosis, Erikson distinguishes between meaningful and necessary frustration as contrasted with neurotic frustration. Meaningful frustration actually serves constructive educational purposes. Thus, even though the adolescent initially might not see possible solutions to the teacher's questions, problems, or assignments—and consequently may feel stressed and frustrated—he or she can find the solution, with work, perseverance, and help. The process does contribute to growth. The teacher who has become an effective frustrator does not contribute to neurosis, but instead helps the student to develop frustration-tolerance. This idea finds clear expression in the words of Bruce Barton: "Frustration and denials which seem to youth cruel and unfair often provide important equipment for life." In a similar vein, the banished Duke in Shakespeare's *As You Like It* praises the use of frustration: "Sweet are the uses of adversity" (II, i, 12).

Therefore, parents and teachers might introduce more personally meaningful frustrations and insist that the adolescent resolve problems with genuine effort and grow in the process. As part of the process of growing up, children must learn to accept some of the necessary and inevitable limitations and restrictions that initially appear very frustrating. Erikson objects to a frustration-free educational environment—like Summerhill—in which children's natural tendencies and interests determine the learning activities and the curriculum. An educational policy characterized by the child's freedom to learn—as implied in the often quoted "Teacher, *must* we do today what we *want* to do?" (Erikson, 1968:

127)—can be as detrimental to the establishment of a healthy identity as the overemphasis on duty, obedience, self-restraint, and arbitrary rules. Learning occurs most effectively and the development of identity is most enhanced in an educational climate that avoids the pitfalls of both of these extremes. Youth do benefit from being "mildly but firmly coerced into the adventure of finding out that one can learn to accomplish things which one would never have thought of by oneself, things which owe their attractiveness to the very fact that they are not the product of play and fantasy but the product of reality, practicality, and logic" (Erikson, 1968: 127).

In the past, societies (Chapter 17)—through puberty rites, initiation ceremonies, the apprenticeship-journeyman system, bar/bat mitzvahs, and coming-out parties—have offered some fairly clearly defined social roles that once gave the individual a kind of ready-made identity (foreclosure) by providing socially defined roles and a structure which allowed self-definition. As these ready-made social role definitions have virtually disappeared—and as confirmation and bar/bat mitzvahs have become primarily private, religious matters—the individual's search for his or her own unique identity and the exploration of where he or she fits into society have become the expected route toward adulthood. Hence, the burden now falls upon the individual to define his or her own social roles, goals and values, and identity: "Some of the adolescent difficulties in Western societies may be better understood if one considers the adolescent as the marginal man who stands in a psychological no-man's land without clear understanding of what is expected of him, struggling to attain adult status" (Muuss, 1980: 503). This quote also suggests that the emergence of identity issues occurs during the second decade of life, because childhood roles are no longer appropriate and thus, identity formation becomes the inevitable struggle to work on the definition of new adult roles. The adolescents' struggle to attain an identity and achieve adult status can be a stressful experience. Society, educational institutions, and teachers may well ponder how they can make this a more meaningful and less stressful, but nevertheless growth enhancing experience.

5

HARRY STACK SULLIVAN'S INTERPERSONAL THEORY OF ADOLESCENT DEVELOPMENT

Harry Stack Sullivan (1892–1949) proposed a social psychiatry theory of human development that highlights the importance of interpersonal relationships and communication. Unlike the traditional intrapsychic theories, which emphasize internal dynamics, his model accentuates the social component, the interaction between personality development and culture. He maintains—and therein lies one of his major contributions to personality theory—that the intrapsychic component of personality cannot be observed directly except through interpersonal interactions (which may take place in reality or in fantasy). His concern about interpersonal conflicts and tension extends far beyond individual and psychotherapeutic matters to include international conflict and prejudice. He presented his most important paper on the topic of international understanding, entitled "Tension Interpersonal and International" (Sullivan, 1964), shortly before his death in Paris.

"Comfortable, successful interpersonal relationships are what life is all about," according to Sullivan. A complete understanding of Sullivan's ideas requires a conceptual framework of "field theory" (see Chapter 7). His view that psychiatry covers "much the same field as . . . social psychology, because scientific psychiatry has to be defined as . . . interpersonal relations" (Sullivan, 1953: 368) is unique, and advanced a truly American, interpersonal psychiatry, quite different from the psychodynamic approaches that had grown out of psychoanalysis. Social scientists C. H. Cooley and G. H. Mead exerted strong influences on Sullivan. Especially noteworthy is Mead's idea that the self develops through the reflective appraisal of significant others; this became a major component of Sullivan's theory. His emphasis on the significance of interpersonal influences and his assertions that "every human being has as many personalities as he has interpersonal relations" (1964: 221) seems to anticipate the insights of social psychology.

Sullivan underwent analysis with C. Thompson and participated actively in the American Psychoanalytic Association; however, his theory was most strongly influenced by sociological and anthropological thinking. He renounced many of the psychoanalytic constructs as insignificant explanations of human behavior and gave them a subordinate role in his theoretical model. In addition, he introduced his own unique terminology (e.g., defense mechanism became security measures) because he felt that many of the psychoanalytic concepts carried a heavy, loaded burden of meaning. In contrast, the influences and terminologies of sociology, anthropology, and field theory permeate Sullivan's writing. He created a model that combines clinical, social-psychological, field-theoretical, and cognitive components.

Instead of explaining the primary forces in human development in terms of biological conditions, sexuality, internal conflicts, or aggression, Sullivan, more than any other theorist of that time, builds his developmental theory out of the social context of human experiences. While he does not deny that constitutional factors play a role (as, for example, in schizophrenia), he plays down their significance because not much could change them. The social component of human development begins with a fundamental state of interpersonal relatedness in infancy and continues unabated throughout adulthood. Interpersonal relationships are the essential ingredients for normal human development; moreover, their destructive, anxiety-arousing manifestations provide explanations for immaturity, deviance, and psychopathology. The individual learns to behave in particular ways and learns to modify his behavior not because of biological imperatives but as a result of socialization. The major tenet of Sullivan's interpersonal theory, that a person does not and cannot exist without other people, becomes a recurring theme.

Sullivan's model of psychiatry is identified as "social psychiatry," and some commentators said that he really was a social psychologist whose specialty happened to be psychiatry. This notion fits in well with our present concerns with adolescence: peer-group conformity, friendship patterns, peer pressure, and intimacy. Some current researchers of peer-group influences (Bronfenbrenner, 1986b; Kandel, 1986; Youniss, 1980) agree with Sullivan's theory that effective and meaningful peer relationships, especially during adolescence, are essential prerequisites for healthy and psychosocial development. Even the reverse receives much research support: that is, poor peer relationships contribute to poor adjustment and depression. Furthermore, they are associated with delinquent behavior, poor school achievement, dropping out of school, running away from home, drug use, early sexual behavior, mental illness, and behavior disorder.

INTERPERSONAL RELATIONSHIPS

The quality and the nature of interpersonal relationships constitute the foundation of Sullivan's theory. *Interpersonal Theory of Psychiatry* (1953), his most important developmental book, published posthumously, is the major source for this chapter. According to Sullivan, interactions with other people are enormously important both in normal and pathological development. Sullivan's psychiatric research dealt with schizophrenic patients; and he ran a spectacularly successful special ward for schizophrenic patients at the Sheppard and Enoch Pratt Hospital in Baltimore. During this period, in the early 1920s, his new theory emerged, that mental illness is due to social factors. However, absence of mental illness is also due to social factors and his theories of normal development, especially adolescent development, will receive emphasis here.

Harry Stack Sullivan (1892-1949

Our relationships with other people influence how we develop and what we are. Sullivan defines personality as "the relatively enduring pattern of recurrent interpersonal situations which characterize a human life" (Sullivan, 1953: 111); this definition captures the significance of the "interpersonal," which is the core of his theory. He perceives the satisfaction of interpersonal needs as even more important than that of sexual needs. Successful and positive interpersonal relationships are essential for a happy and satisfying life.

Sullivan virtually equates the personality of an individual as the outcome of interpersonal relationships of that individual, almost to the extent of questioning whether a "unique individual self" independent of interactions with others actually exists. He is concerned that the significance of "entrenched feelings of independence and autonomy" have interfered with our understanding of interpersonal relationships, and he speaks of the "delusion of a unique individuality," an idea which he emphasized in "The Illusion of Personal Individuality" (1950).

The effects of interpersonal relationships can, of course, be both constructive and destructive. According to Sullivan (1953), the benefits of interpersonal contacts depend upon positive feedback. The knowledge that others value us and consider us attractive and worthwhile provides a feeling of security. However, when interpersonal relationships, especially in infancy and childhood, create a great deal of anxiety, the security measures (defenses) one develops may impair relationships with other people. Hence, almost by definition, social relationships are reciprocal in nature, and "one can find in others only that which is in the self" (Sullivan, 1947: 22). An adolescent who already has a low opinion of himself or herself and feels inadequate tends to reject friendly overtures by others and remains hostile and distrustful. However, experiences, that are negative, threatening, and anxiety-arousing create feelings of insecurity. Positive, supportive, tension-reducing experiences with significant other people produce feelings of security.

People can be understood only within the context of identifiable social interaction patterns. Depending on who they are interacting with, individuals differ in the way they see themselves and in the way they behave. Thus, adolescents may—and often do—behave dramatically differently in their interaction patterns with parents, teachers, relatives, peers, valued friends, or members of the opposite sex. In other words, interpersonal relationships provide the most significant key to understanding human behavior.

THE SELF-SYSTEM

Closely related to Sullivan's general emphasis on interpersonal relationships is his specific use of the "self-system." Sullivan's notion of the self-system strongly reflects the influence of the social scientists concerned with the development of the self, especially C. H. Cooley and G. H. Mead. Since the self has a social origin, its theoretical primacy reflects the importance Sullivan accords to the interpersonal as well as social and cultural experiences. Our sense of self is shaped by the manner in which "significant others"—people who are most influential in our lives—see us and treat us. The self is first and foremost a social self, formed by others; in turn, the self becomes the instigator of social relationships. The self-system organizes life experiences within the personality. The self-system constitutes a very important part of personality, particularly significant in fending off anxiety; however, it is only part of personality, not identical to it.

The self-system develops out of cultural, social, and interpersonal experiences; in the process it absorbs cultural values and becomes a "selective filter" through which experiences are incorporated in or excluded from awareness. "The origin of the self-system can be said to rest on the irrational character of culture or, more specifically, society" (Sullivan, 1953: 168). A self consists of the "reflected appraisal" by others. "If these [appraisals] were chiefly derogatory, as in the case of an unwanted child who was never loved . . . then the self dynamism will itself be chiefly derogatory. It will facilitate hostile, disparaging appraisals of other people and it will entertain disparaging and hostile appraisals of itself" (Sullivan, 1947: 22). The "reflected appraisal," the way significant people appraise the individual over an extended period of time, eventually becomes the way he or she appraises himself or herself. There can be no standard for the evaluation of self, other than the feedback received from others. In Shaw's play, *Pygmalion,* Eliza Doolittle astutely describes this relationship when she says: "you see, really and truly . . . the difference between a lady and a flower girl is not how she behaves, but how she's treated. I shall always be a flower girl to Professor Higgins, because he treats me like flower girl . . . But I know I can be a lady to you, because you always treat me as a lady." Sullivanian analysis of Eliza's insight would go further. Eliza Doolittle is not only influenced by how others perceive her but also reacts to that perception (as the quote implies), which influences those who perceive her, which, in turn influences her . . ., and so on. The relationship enters into an endless loop of continuing social interactions.

According to Sullivan, "all that is the self-system arises in interpersonal relations" (1953: 200). The earliest experiences involve interactions with the "mothering one," experiences that can be tender and harmonious or forbidding and anxiety-arousing. As development progresses, both the kind of individuals with whom one interacts and the nature of the interactions increase in complexity. Furthermore, the self-system organizes these experiences and integrates them into a screening filter through which the individual perceives and evaluates events, especially whatever seems most relevant to one's self-appraisal. A human being without a self-system through which experiences are filtered is beyond imagination.

One of the important functions of the self-system is to provide satisfaction and to reduce the anxiety so often connected with the many experiences of disapproval or anticipated disapproval that accompany the socialization process. The self-system evolves in order to minimize anxiety in dealing with others (Sullivan, 1964). A coherent system that tends to perpetuate itself, the self-system is essential to the adjustment of the person in that it maintains self-respect, contributes to security, and is extremely important in warding off anxiety. After an equilibrium has been established in the self-system, it resists changes, because modifications can prove disturbing and threatening to the individual's sense of well-being. Unpleasant, anxiety-arousing experiences are dissociated from the self-system by a mechanism called "selective inattention." This mechanism renders us unable to observe the importance of those events that challenge established features of the self-system. Thus, while selective inattention reduces anxiety, it increases our "failure to profit from experiences." Because it resists change, the self-system can reduce anxiety; however, it can also interfere with an individual's ability to learn new but uncomfortable ideas, to try new approaches, and to live more effectively with others. Selective inattention also explains the great faith we have in our own prejudices and how we maintain them: "The self-system is the principal stumbling block to favorable changes in personality . . . [but] also the principal influence that stands in the way of unfavorable changes in personality" (Sullivan, 1953: 169). Even though the self-system resists changes, Sullivan emphasizes repeatedly that it can and does undergo significant modifications, especially early in each of the transitions from one stage to another. Psychotherapy can offer another important route to enhance positive self-system changes.

The self-system seeks the kind of information that contributes to self-protection and the maintenance of the equilibrium. Thus, it becomes of paramount importance in understanding the dynamics of interpersonal relationships. Not only is the self-system initially formed by the way important others treat us, but the reverse also holds true: our self-system guides our attention and influences how we perceive others. People with chronically low self-esteem inevitably anticipate that others also have unfavorable opinions about them. The self-system becomes the filter through which we continuously evaluate our social environment as well as ourselves.

Healthy development is the process of transforming the undifferentiated and often anxiety-ridden self-system of the infant into the stable and secure self of the mature adult, in which various dynamisms are successfully integrated. The essential experience that enhances this transition is based on mutually satisfying interpersonal relationships.

DYNAMISM IN SULLIVAN'S THEORY

Dynamism is a small component of the self-system. Sullivan defines dynamism as "relatively enduring patterns of energy transformation which recurrently characterize the interpersonal relations . . . which make up the distinctively human sort of being" (1953: 103). Both "enduring" and "recurrent," dynamism seems to approximate what in other systems has been referred to as "habit," "trait," "permanent attitude," or "consistent pattern of behavior." Dynamisms introduce an element of permanence, predictability, and stability into the self-system. Since dynamism is defined as a "pattern of energy," it does create tensions that disturb the individual. Furthermore, dynamisms do change over time, so that at various stages new patterns of interpersonal interactions develop. These changing patterns of interpersonal needs are the forces that move the child from one stage to the next. Actually, the deinvestment of energy from established interpersonal relationships allows the reinvestment of energy in new social endeavors. Particularly just before and during the early adolescent period do we see a deinvestment of energy from certain relationships (parents and family) and a reinvestment in new social relationships (chums and friends). The quality and nature of interpersonal relationships emerge and change as a result of being closely interwoven with dynamics.

All human beings basically have the same dynamism by which they try to maintain self-esteem and security; Sullivan emphasizes this similarity that all human beings—even psychotic patients—share, especially in contrast to other species. "Everyone is much more simply human than otherwise . . . the differences between any two instances of human personality—from the lowest-grade imbecile to the highest-grade genius—are much less striking than the differences between the least-gifted human being and a member of the nearest other biological genus" (Sullivan, 1953: 33). He has even spoken of the delusion of uniqueness and the illusion of individuality (1950). However, the extent to which humans reveal this dynamism and the way they do so demonstrate individual variations. Individual differences in the manifestations of dynamisms depend on earlier life experiences, on the developmental stage of the individual, and on the social, interpersonal context.

Sullivan refers to a great many different dynamisms that become important during development. However, the following distinctions need to be made: (1) the zones of interactions that are defined by specific areas of the body (oral dynamism, anal dynamism, etc.) and (2) the direction of interaction, which can be disjunctive, isolating, or conjunctive.

A *disjunctive dynamism* produces repetitive destructive energy patterns—for example, the dynamism of malevolence, in which the individual habitually behaves hostilely or aggressively toward other people.

An *isolating dynamism* moves the individual away from other people because it becomes detached from interpersonal relations—for example, the lust dynamism, which seeks sexual gratification primarily through masturbation or without regard to the partner's feelings.

The *conjunctive dynamism* involves behavior patterns that benefit the self-system, contribute to the expansion of the self, and build constructive interpersonal relationships. Examples of conjunctive dynamism include a nurturing dynamism, expressed by a recurring desire to care for others; an affinity dynamism, characterized by seeking close friendships with other people; and an intimacy dynamism, which develops during preadolescence and implies a close intimate relationship with just one other person.

TENSION: NEEDS, ANXIETY, ENERGY TRANSFORMATION

Sullivan views personality as an energy system whose goal is to reduce tension. Tensions arise from such basic needs as food, water, oxygen, sleep, and so on, but they also result from anxiety-provoking interpersonal situations. The alternating pattern of increasing and declining tensions creates an impetus toward development. Tensions fall along a continuum. At one extreme is absolute tension, a rarely observed state of panic, as when one suddenly faces the possibility of injury or death. At the other extreme is absolute absence of tension, experienced as utter well-being or euphoria. The illustration that Sullivan provides for absolute absence of tension is the infant in a state of deep sleep. The relationship between tension and euphoria is inverse: the higher the level of euphoria, the lower the level of tension or anxiety, and vice versa.

Tensions provide the organism with the potential for action; some tensions arise out of biological needs (e.g., oxygen, water, food, etc.). Tensions lead to energy transformations that dissipate the tension and create a mental state of satisfaction. The tension, by way of energy transformation, finds its outlet in work or overt action, when one is fully aware of what one is doing. Energy transformation may also take place in less obvious ways, as in scratching one's head, when there is no awareness of that particular behavior. Many patterns of tension and energy transformation are learned; they are culturally based and depend on what is socially approved and expected.

There are several kinds of tensions. Some arise from general, usually physical needs (hunger, thirst, etc.). Others, called zonal needs, emerge from specific body zones (oral, anal, etc.). Still others, which arise from anxiety, originate from social difficulties. Whereas general and zonal needs usually lead to integrative behavior, tension arising from the anxiety of interpersonal difficulties may lead to disjunctive or disintegrative behavior.

Anxiety is a particularly significant tension because it always interferes with the reduction of other needs and the achievement of a feeling of satisfaction. The anticipation of unfavorable evaluation of one's current behavior by significant others whose opinion we value creates anxiety. It always relates to what Sullivan (1953) calls "the whole interpersonal field." Anxiety is created by the way in which other people meet, or—more importantly—fail to meet the needs of the individual. Anticipatory anxiety is an emotion that we create in anticipation of negative events that may never happen or are very unlikely to happen. The distinction between fear and anxiety is important in this context. The origin of fear (such as fear of a biting dog) is known, but the origin of anxiety is unknown. Fear increases performance in the form of fight or flight. Anxiety is often accompanied by loss of energy and memory, and the inability to concentrate interferes with performance. Fear can be postponed, especially while we are struggling with the object of fear. Anxiety is not postponable except through security measures (defenses). Although the negative emotions associated with fear and anxiety are similar, these concepts cannot be used interchangeably.

Human beings seek security more than any other state. Sullivan elevates striving for "freedom from anxiety" to be the major motivating force in humans, an idea most clearly expressed by the existential philosophers, especially Kierkegaard. From the early experiences with the "mothering one," anxieties evolve out of interpersonal relationships, and anxiety remains the most pervasive interpersonal force in the human life cycle. The corollary is also true: an imagined threat to one's security produces anxiety. The more severe the threat, the greater the anxiety. As our anxiety level increases and our ability to benefit from experience, to plan ahead, and to communicate decreases, we resort to private, symbolic emotional fantasy or nonsymbolic responses. Anxiety can create disintegrative behavior; it blocks communication, which in turn, increases the level of anxiety.

The reduction of needs is a transformation of energy that dissipates tension and produces a feeling of satisfaction (Sullivan, 1950: 85). Adolescents frequently experience a clash between various tensions, such as the desire for sexual behavior and the need to be free of anxiety. The sexual activities, to the extent that they are socially disapproved, increase anxiety. However, even if encouraged by the peer group, they may create anxiety in regard to interpersonal intimacy or in anticipation of other events (e.g., loss of reputation, pregnancy, AIDS, etc.). To avoid this anxiety, therefore, means to avoid the sexual activity.

MODES OF EXPERIENCE

According to Sullivan, experience—and basically all cognition—occurs in one or more of three modes. These modes, the prototaxic, the parataxic, and the syntaxic, represent the elaboration of events in inner thought: they emerge in a developmental pattern that becomes increasingly complex. However, at times of difficulty, we all return to more primitive patterns of thought. Psychiatric patients commonly function at the lower levels.

The prototaxic mode is the crudest, most primitive, simplest, and—developmentally speaking—lowest form of awareness; it is also very common. It involves sensory experiences that are discrete, momentary, and unconnected to other events. Dreaming is a good illustration of the prototaxic mode. Prototaxic thinking is presymbolic and incapable of formulation or conceptualization. Communications by "emotional contagion or empathy," as between mother and child, are prototaxic. This mode involves primitive feelings of body states, sensations, and emotions that are not lost but become part of the unconscious. For example, tactile sensations from my buttocks inform me that I am sitting in a chair and also that I have been in that position too long.

The parataxic mode is more differentiated; however, it is primarily private in that the experience makes sense to the individual but not necessarily to others. Events are connected in a temporal sequence, as when a feeling of hunger leads to the anticipation of feeding. The parataxic mode involves private thought, private speech, fantasies, magical thinking, daydreams, and superstitions. Autistic speech is a typical manifestation of the parataxic mode, as is the belief that "the black cat crossing the street will cause me bad luck." Distortions that we hold about other people or groups of people—in terms of stereotypes, prejudices, or personifications—represent parataxic thinking.

The syntaxic mode involves language that clearly conveys thoughts to other people and enhances interpersonal communication. The child now understands physical and spatial causality. Syntaxic symbols and syntaxic language can be illustrated by gestures and speech that have been consensually validated. They are logical and rational, and others, who function in the syntaxic mode, have no difficulties in following the ideas expressed.

PERSONIFICATION

Personification refers to the mental image that a person has of himself or herself (e.g., good-me, bad-me, not-me) or of another individual (e.g., good-mother, bad-mother). Such mental pictures may have some correspondence to reality; however, they may also be distorted by the individual's needs, disturbed experiences, and/or anxieties. These mental pictures develop from a group of interrelated attitudes, emotions, and evaluations that grow out of experiences such as praise, support, tenderness, need satisfaction, but also threats, criticism, punishment, and anxiety. Based on experiences with the "real" mother, the infant may differentiate her into two personifications.

The good-mother emerges as a differentiation of the good and satisfactory nipple (being nursed and cared for). She provides tenderness, love, security, and satisfaction. More generally, any satisfaction of basic needs without undue anxiety tends to create a "good" image of the caregiver. On the other hand, *the bad-mother* is the symbolic representation of the mother whose presence arouses anxiety. She punishes, scolds, criticizes, disapproves, makes forbidding gestures, and actually provides an "anxious" nipple.

The differentiation of the "me" results in three kinds of personification: the good-me, the bad-me, and the not-me, all of which grow out of the child's increasing awareness of his body. *The good-me* is based on interpersonal experiences conducted in a way that invites tenderness, love, appreciation, and encouragement from others. Later, actions that receive social approval produce the good-me awareness. Good-me personifications are conscious and find expression in "I am . . ." statements completed by positive attributes. *The bad-me* forms by habitually being the recipient of negative comments, punishment, criticism, and anxiety. As others consistently disapprove certain of the child's behaviors—such as touching certain parts of the body, refusing to eat certain foods, or doing things that annoy caretakers—bad-me feelings are produced; eventually, just the impulses toward such behaviors may create bad-me feelings. *Not-me* has a different quality and consists of dissociated behavior that lies outside of conscious awareness. Experiences of being totally disapproved, feelings of being unwanted, or overwhelming anxiety contribute to the development of a "not-me" personification. Unacceptable behaviors that we do not recognize as "ours" are not-me, as are parts of ourselves so alien or so hideous that they must be denied. When an individual does or says things of which he has no awareness or knowledge, "not-me" dissociation is at work. It is a common experience during dreams, especially nightmares, rage, severe temper tantrums, or drunkenness. Similarly, thought processes during severe schizophrenic episodes are examples of "not-me" dissociations.

Personification provides the individual with helpful guidelines for coping with other people who show attributes that are similar to, for example, the bad-mother. Any demanding and authoritarian male may be perceived as a symbolizing part of the "frightening father," and any nurturing and warm female is recognized as a representation of the "good-mother." These personifications guide the child's behavior toward such people. Personification, therefore, can help the infant and later the child in coping with anxiety and guiding behavior when confronted with social complexity. However, later in life these earlier personifications may be retained, even when they have become too simplistic and are no longer appropriate. The result is that distorted attitudes stemming from experiences in the past are transferred to people in the present; such attitudes are parataxic.

Personifications shared by a larger group of people are referred to as *stereotypes*. They are the generalized attitudes that find expression in the use of such derogatory classifications as "dumb blond," "irresponsible student," "obnoxious teenager," "absent-minded professor," and so on.

SULLIVAN'S HEURISTIC STAGES OF DEVELOPMENT

Like many of the major theorists of development, Sullivan assumes that human development progresses through a sequence of stages from infancy to adulthood. However, in line with his fundamental social science orientation, he readily admits that his stages are primarily applicable to Western societies; he makes no claim to universality. In addition, his division of the stages differs from that of other theories. For example, the "latency period" is subdivided into two important stages that receive special attention. The terms commonly used to describe children of different ages provide the names of most of Sullivan's stages; they seem devoid of any heavy theoretical message. Each of these developmental stages has a unique quality of interpersonal relationships. The movement from one stage to another involves a qualitative shift in the orientation toward "significant others." Each stage—revealing once again the interpersonal nature of the theory—is characterized by a specific person or social group that has a predominant influence on the child's self-evaluation: infancy (the mothering one), childhood (family + parents), juvenile era (school + peer group), preadolescence (chum), early adolescence (friends, beginning opposite-sex orientation), and late adolescence (lover).

According to Sullivan, the forces that propel the child from one stage to the next are not primarily sexual (Freud), or maturational (Gesell), or cognitive (Piaget), nor do they constitute social crises (Erikson). Instead, they are based on the child's growing ability to cope with basic feelings of anxiety that are the inevitable result of changing interpersonal relationships. Maturation, the child's social experiences, the development of new interpersonal needs and new social relationships—all these play an important part in the process. Sullivan highlights "the interpersonal dimension of human existence," and the crucial experiences for the more permanent formation of interpersonal orientations are very much a function of preadolescent and adolescent events.

As in Erikson's psychosocial theory, so in Sullivan's interpersonal theory of development: the mastery of tasks, especially the learning of interpersonal skills, influences the success of development in the following stage. Important developmental deficits from earlier stages can produce problems in future adjustment. But successful or supportive encounters (e.g., with a chum, a peer group, an understanding teacher, or a psychotherapist) can correct such deficits, facilitate readjustment, and redirect the individual toward normality and health.

Anxieties begin early in life when parents disapprove of some behaviors in their infants; the reduction of tension by avoiding disapproval is a major motivating force. However, the quality and nature of interpersonal relationships give each stage its unique meaning and specific interpersonal focus. Social forces produce interference or enhance the progression from one stage to the next. This focus on interpersonal and socialization processes reflects Sullivan's belief that interpersonal needs are more important than biological needs. The process of socialization, which depends on absorbing social values from significant other people, contributes greatly to the process of development. The movement from one stage to the next occurs because the skills and characteristics acquired in earlier stages suddenly become "actually inadequate" as new, more complex social relationships develop. For example, during early adolescence, as the social needs of friends change, friendships become vulnerable to breakup. As interest patterns diverge, former partners require different kinds of interpersonal relationships; as a result, new friendships are formed, often in rapid succession. In order to succeed in becoming a normal, civilized human being, an individual's social relationships must become increasingly more complex and differentiated. Sullivan's stages of development reflect this increasing interpersonal complexity and the process of social differentiation that occurs between infancy and adulthood.

■ Infancy

Infancy is the period between birth and the maturation of "articulate speech, however uncommunicative or meaningless" (Sullivan, 1953: 33). The infant's basic drives, its need for food and bodily comfort, and its more global needs for security create tension that can be satisfied only by other people, especially the "mothering one." The manner and extent to which these fundamental needs are satisfied become the determining factor in the development of the individual's self-system. If the mother is tender, supportive, and responsive to the infant's basic needs without arousing anxiety, the infant will feel secure—even "euphoric"—and will develop a good-me personification. Experiences based on the deprivation of bodily needs becomes the initial catalyst for the development of anxiety as a personality characteristic. Furthermore, through gesture, tone of voice, or behaviors, the mother will communicate her own inevitable anxieties, creating bad-me feelings in the infant. Sullivan states this idea as a theorem: "The tension of anxiety, when present in the mothering one, induces anxiety in the infant" (1953: 41). This process is "empathy," which means the infant actually "reads" the mother's feelings. The transfer of anxiety is further complicated because even the infant's crying increases the mother's anxiety. (This is especially true if she cannot account for the infant's discomfort. Her increased anxiety then, in turn, is communicated back to the child.) By way of this empathic linkage, the infant's crying may contribute to its own anxiety. From such early anxiety-arousing experiences with the "mothering one," tension and anxiety later evolve in the course of interpersonal relationships.

■ Childhood

Childhood is the period from the beginning of meaningful speech to the appearance of a need for interaction with playmates or compeers—that is, of companions or cooperative individuals of approximately one's own status. The major developmental accomplishment during this stage is the emergence of symbolic capacity in the cognitive area. The child begins to use words, language, and gesture in such a way that the meaning is understood; however, language is still used in a parataxic way. The learning of language, in particular, facilitates the formation of the self-system and enables the child to identify and express emotional states. At this stage, the child has a very active imagination. In the absence of actual interpersonal relationships or the presence of loneliness, the child may turn to a rich fantasy life, create imaginary playmates, and have imaginary conversations. To the extent that children play with other children, they tend to interact in an egocentric, basically self-centered way. They are primarily concerned with their own welfare, their own pursuits, and their own needs.

Parents now increase their efforts toward socialization and teach their values, thereby directing the child in the acquisition of acceptable cultural patterns and attitudes. The most significant accomplishments of this stage are the learning of cooperation in interpersonal relationships, carrying out instructions, and doing simple chores in order to avoid anxiety. Mastery of these social skills places the child on the threshold of the next higher stage. However, to the extent that the child does not live up to the parents' expectations, he or she may experience disapproval and feel fear and shame, which contribute to the internalization of parental standards. The experience of obedience and approval—being called cute, clever, smart, or charming, for instance—contributes to the good-me personification. Repeated disapproval creates anxiety, until eventually the breaking of a social rule arouses anxiety even if the parents are not present.

The child learns some of these skills and attitudes through punishment, which may be effective as long as the child perceives the chastisement as fair. Nevertheless, in this process, the child may also learn to conceal from authority figures those events that are known to bring on punishment or anxiety. These efforts at concealment take on the form of "verbal excuses" and private fantasy, but they also create a "social distance" and, to the extent that they reflect low self-esteem, may lead to social isolation. Punishment perceived as unfair, as well as disapproval (being called bad, clumsy, stupid, naughty, etc.), leads to rebelliousness and the development of the bad-me personification.

If the punishment is severe, callous, degrading, and arbitrary, the child will feel that he or she lives among adversaries and will not trust people. The punished behavior may eventually be concealed, dissociated from the personality, no longer recognized as part of the self, and submerged into the not-me personification.

■ The Juvenile Era

The juvenile era is a period characterized by the broadening of social and interpersonal relationships. During this stage the need for playmates emerges and develops. Chronologically, the juvenile era encompasses the early elementary school years. It ends when, due to maturation, the child desires to deepen social relationships. The young person then longs for deep, intimate interpersonal relationships, usually with just one person of a status comparable to his or her own.

Sullivan ascribes extraordinary significance to this and the following chumship period: "The importance of the juvenile era can scarcely be exaggerated, since it is the actual time for becoming social" (1953: 227). The youth moves away from the family into the larger social world and enters school. He has opportunities for a variety of new social experiences, but he also becomes vulnerable to socialization efforts and social pressures from peers. In the course of learning true cooperation in play activities as well as sharing and communicating experiences with peers, the youth comes to adopt the syntaxic mode. However, since the compeers are now becoming a particularly significant reference group, the "threat of ostracism" and the fear of being excluded by them become powerfully felt threats to security and self-esteem. The widely recognized individual differences in development, residential area, family background, and other factors, contribute to the formation of "in-groups" and "out-groups." Being a member of the out-group creates considerable anxiety, arousing fears of ostracism, isolation, loneliness, exclusion, and harassment. "Most people have had in the juvenile period an exceedingly bitter experience with their compeers . . . the fear of being accepted by no one of those whom one must have as models for learning how to be human" (Sullivan, 1953: 345).

Because many of the earlier social experiences occur with parents, older or younger siblings, or imaginary playmates, the child has had relatively little opportunity to develop a sensitivity to the actual feelings of his or her personal worth as seen by peers. They, therefore provide basically new interpersonal experiences and, in the process, contribute a different kind of socialization experience. In addition, compeers contribute some corrective experiences for those children who were overprotected as well as those who were petty tyrants, overly docile, or overly obedient at home. Thus, during the juvenile era and under favorable circumstances, peer groups can still help to correct serious distortions carried over from childhood. At times, the peer group's efforts are not benevolent and its socialization pressures—in the form of teasing, bullying, and ostracizing—increase anxiety and pain and may become debilitating themselves. The juvenile peer group calls for the acquisition of habits of competition, cooperation, compromise, and teamwork toward some common goal; such requirements are seldom imposed in the same uncompromising way by parents. Peer disapproval can be more devastating than that of parents. The juvenile faces opportunities to compare the values, attitudes, and behaviors of family members with those of peers and other people. As the circle of social contacts outside the home enlarges, young people are likely to question parental infallibility and to change their perceptions not only of their families but also of themselves.

In a process Sullivan refers to as learning "social subordination," the child at this stage learns to respect and obey the demands of new authority figures, such as teachers, coaches, and Cub Scout leaders. Later, there are further contacts with people who are, think, or behave differently and who thereby expand the youth's horizons. Such interactions may teach tolerance toward social diversity and give rise to a more differentiated self-image.

One of the outcomes of training by parents and other authority figures during the juvenile era is the emergence of stereotypes. That means taking from others the inadequate and often inappropriate mental picture of a group of people—one that is not based on observation, experience, analysis, or some form of personal validation. Stereotypical thought provides shortcuts that simplify social complexities, but it remains at the parataxic level. "Overemotional—just like a female" or "another aggressive, competitive male" both illustrate this parataxic mode. One particular stereotype that is quite prevalent during the juvenile and the preadolescent periods is the blind acceptance of the peer group's idea of the opposite sex. Sullivan explains that "in spite of all experience which was contrary to the stereotype, you almost had to adopt, by the time you were on the verge of preadolescence, what might be described as the juvenile stereotype of the 'girls' or the 'boys'—whichever the other sex was—and govern yourself accordingly—publicly at least" (1953: 238). The juvenile peer group holds distorted ideas of what the opposite sex is like, creating animosity and social distance that can interfere with opposite-sex intimacy later on. Since stereotypes include prejudicial attitudes, they foster intolerance, fear, hatred, aversion, and revulsion toward an alleged class of people, and they encourage the juvenile to disregard personal experience and to ignore individual differences. Unfortunately, once such stereotypes have become a more permanent fixture of the self-system, they are resistant to change. They interfere with the establishment of successful and satisfactory interpersonal relations with members of the stereotyped class. Sullivan expresses concern not only with the individual aspects of stereotypes but also with their social and international implications.

The unique importance of this period finds expression in Sullivan's division into two distinct stages of what is commonly referred to as the latency period: the juvenile and preadolescent eras. Psychoanalytic theory considers latency a period of consolidation and superego development, but it receives less attention than the periods that precede or follow it. By contrast, Sullivan regards this period as one of paramount importance, not only for learning social skills, developing social sensitivity, learning social subordination and social accommodation, and developing academic and intellectual skills, but also for very important personality changes. According to Sullivan, personality is not fixed in the first few years of life; rather, it continues to remain open to modification: "Everything that has gone before becomes reasonably open to influence; this is true even in the organization of the self-system, which . . . is remarkably inclined to maintain its direction" (1953: 227).

■ Preadolescence

In Sullivan's theory, preadolescence is depicted as an exceedingly important period, even though, chronologically speaking, it is of short duration. It begins with a powerful change in social orientation, a newly emerging need for an intimate one-to-one relationship with a playmate of the same sex. Preadolescence ends "with the eruption of genital sexuality" as a result of puberty.

The individual now moves away from the broad need for a larger group of playmates that prevailed during the juvenile era. A new need emerges—for interpersonal intimacy and the intimate sharing of thoughts, feelings, and ideas with just one playmate who is similar to oneself. Sullivan defines intimacy as the "type of situation involving two people which permits validation of all components of personal worth" (1953: 246). Intimacy always involves interpersonal closeness but not genital contact. This best friend—a "chum" who also becomes a confidant—would be of the same sex, the same social status, and approximately the same age. Thus, the preadolescent experiences, often for the first time, genuine love, loyalty, opportunity for self-disclosure, and intimacy, but in an atmosphere still uncomplicated by the lust dynamism. As Sullivan explains, "The quiet miracle of preadolescence, the changes of character of interpersonal relations . . . includes an interest in the satisfactions and security of another person which approaches . . . one's interest in one's own satisfaction and security" (Sullivan, 1950: 103). In this new chum-relationship, the two friends find themselves more and more able to talk about those things and to express those thoughts that they had learned during the juvenile era never to discuss. The chum becomes of great importance to the self in almost every area. There emerges a new quality of deeper interpersonal mutuality that was lacking in the juvenile era. The youth, in confronting the views held by the valued playmate, acquires information about himself or herself that can help to correct autistic ideas, fantastic perceptions, and distorted personifications. Sullivan maintains that because of this corrective influence of the "chum," many individuals avoid serious mental disorders. The fact that someone approves of and finds them attractive and worthwhile may counteract the low opinion they have of themselves or that others have. In addition, this process of revealing virtually everything about oneself (things that had previously been kept secret) can relieve the sometimes morbid, egocentric thought: "I am quite different from everyone else." As the preoccupation with the chum relationship gains in importance, preadolescents tend to distance themselves from the family. They begin to look at the family more objectively, often more critically, and share this new perception with their chum.

Sullivan describes this relationship revealingly:

> All of you who have children are sure that your children love you; when you say that, you are expressing a pleasant illusion. But if you will look very closely at one of your children when he finally finds a chum—somewhere between eight-and-a-half and ten—you will discover something very different in the relationship—namely, that your child begins to develop a real sensitivity to what matters to another person. And this is not in the same sense of "what should I do to get what I want," but instead "what should I do to contribute to the happiness or to support the prestige and feeling of worth-whileness of my chum." So far as I have ever been able to discover, nothing remotely like this appears before. . . . Thus the developmental epoch of preadolescence is marked by the coming of the integrating tendencies which, when they are completely developed, we call love, or, to say it in another way, by the manifestation of the need for interpersonal intimacy [1953: 245–246].

Later on, heterosexual adjustment may be impaired if intimacy with a chum of the same sex and same age has never been experienced during preadolescence, if loneliness is never dispelled before puberty brings the lust dynamism into the foreground during the early adolescent stage. Sullivan maintains that almost all adult males who have difficulties in relating to other men—who are unaware of what members of the same sex are thinking about them—never had the opportunity to benefit from such a chumship during preadolescence. The integration of the lust dynamism with the intimacy dynamism in late adolescence will be impaired if intimacy in relation to a chum has never been experienced. Achieving such a deep, intimate relationship with a member of the same sex, therefore, is the major developmental accomplishment of the preadolescent period. For Sullivan, this is an essential growth-enhancing experience, because once true intimacy with a chum has been learned, heterosexual relationships become possible. Chumship also provides the opportunity to work through the problem of loneliness and to validate one's own personal worth. Erikson (1950, 1968), G. H. Mead (1934), and M. Mead (1961) agree that genuine friendship between same-sex friends in childhood and early adolescence serves an important purpose in the development of a healthy self and facilitates the development of a positive identity. Early same-sex friendships contribute significantly to the emergence of love and intimacy in heterosexual relationships later on. Gilligan (1982, Gilligan et al., 1992) also feels that the intimate friendship between girls in early adolescence is a better preparation for love and heterosexuality than too-early and often-shallow involvement with boys. Gilligan seems to identify interpersonal processes in girls that parallel, in some ways, Sullivan's more male-oriented description.

The preadolescent's great need for intimacy and love must be viewed against its opposite force, which also reaches its peak during this period—loneliness. Since human beings are basically social creatures, they experience throughout life a recurrent need to be with others. This need may take on various qualities and involve numerous people, including imaginary playmates; nevertheless, to seek contact with others remains a powerful force at all ages. The infant craves tenderness and physical contact, the child wants adult participation in play activities, the juvenile has a need for compeers, the preadolescent craves a chum, and the adolescent pines for sexual intimacy and love. The lack of satisfying personal contacts is experienced as loneliness, which the individual feels with great intensity during preadolescence and which, later in life, may become even more terrible than anxiety. Although the lonely child often has a rich fantasy life, this may contribute to social isolation, which increases anxiety about the process of seeking companionship. In the juvenile era, reporting one's fantasies to peers can invite ridicule, ostracism, and avoidance, all of which tend to perpetuate social isolation. This leads to more fantasy and creates a vicious circle that discourages a reality orientation vis-à-vis other people and contributes to the derailment of the socialization process. Sullivan himself, because of his Irish Catholic background, his homosexual tendencies, and his life on an isolated farm in an all-Protestant rural community, in all likelihood experienced an acute sense of loneliness as well as ostracism; he was probably in the "out-group" as an adolescent.

■ Early Adolescence

Puberty and the eruption of genital maturity determine the onset of early adolescence. As a result, the individual experiences a conflict and collision between the intimacy dynamism and the newly emerging lust dynamism. Early adolescence ends when interest shifts from a person of one's own sex, the chum, to one of the opposite sex.

A zone of the body that until now was experienced primarily in terms of excretion suddenly becomes significant for exciting interaction in physical interpersonal intimacy. In addition, the genital drive in its pure form is now experienced as a feeling of lust, resulting in tension. Out of this lust dynamism emerges a growing desire to attain intimacy with a member of the opposite sex, following the pattern established during preadolescence.

In the normal pattern of social development, especially in early adolescence, a need emerges that requires a shift in the object of intimacy. For the preadolescent, that object is an "isophilic choice," someone quite like oneself, the chum. During adolescence, that changes to a "heterophilic choice," someone who, in very significant ways, is quite different from oneself. However, this move toward opposite-sex intimacy initially involves a great deal of insecurity, fumbling, and unrealistic wishful thinking; it is complicated not only by the adolescent anxieties about rejection by the opposite sex but also by the stereotyped views of the opposite sex acquired during the juvenile stage. In actuality, there is much fantasy about the opposite sex, but the individual may still spend a great deal of time with same-sex chums and friends.

Thus, three highly significant and powerful, but, at this stage, still incompatible needs begin to collide during early adolescence; it is usually not until much later that these needs are effectively integrated and become compatible. Their collision provides some real understanding of the various interpersonal difficulties so commonly experienced during this period. These still separated needs are (1) the new need for sexual satisfaction, (2) the preadolescent need for intimacy, and (3) the need for personal security in the form of freedom from anxiety. A collision of these needs may occur on different levels.

Lust, which, as a result of puberty, emerges as a new dynamism in the self-system of early adolescence, collides with the already established security dynamisms in the personality. The most powerful conflict is created through "the collision between one's lust and one's security." Security encompasses self-esteem, a feeling of personal worth, and the absence of anxiety. The threat to one's security comes from general cultural patterns as well as from earlier established personal values such as embarrassment, humiliation, puzzlement, and shame. The genitals until now were not an incorporated and integrated part of an approved and worthy social self. Thus, a revision of the self-system is required, because the feeling of arousal and sexuality has to become an accepted component of the self-image. But there also exist, at least in some individuals, more serious primary phobias in relation to the genitalia; these generally stem from the parents' punitive efforts to prevent the child from handling, exploring, or showing these body parts.

In addition, "the intimacy need may collide with the need for security." Often the family brings pressure to bear against the establishment of intimacy with members of the opposite sex, a pressure that was not applied against earlier preadolescent chum relationships. These pressures may take a variety of forms, from objecting, criticizing, nagging, and threatening to ridiculing; they can be very powerful and devastating threats to one's security. In addition, anxiety involves the fear of disapproval—disapproval from the opposite sex being a strong possibility in the imagination of the early adolescent. Thus security needs are threatened by the often quite awkward initial attempts to find a suitable opposite-sex partner. Many intended invitations are never extended because the young adolescent fears rejection more than he or she desires intimacy.

Finally, there is the "collision between intimacy and lust." Sullivan identifies four types of awkwardness that contribute to conflicts between these two dynamisms in early adolescence: first, the awkwardness in interpersonal situations commonly experienced during early adolescence (when lust is not yet a fully integrated part of the self); second, lack of self-confidence; third, excessive precaution in what Kurt Lewin refers to as an unknown situation (see Chapter 7). All these factors make intimacy highly unlikely if not impossible.

The fourth type is characterized by an exaggerated confidence, leading to particularly crude advances toward the desired object of intimacy. This approach is often so obnoxious that it prompts embarrassment and withdrawal in the person being approached and thereby precludes any further interpersonal progress.

Failure to integrate the lust and the intimacy dynamisms may lead to the splitting of these motives into two separate forces, which are then directed toward two different types of people. For the young man, one of these is the "good girl," who can provide friendship, love, and untarnished intimacy; she may be seen as a potential marriage partner. The other is the "bad girl," the prostitute or the "sexy" female, who satisfies genital needs but not the needs for intimacy. The opposite sex is divided into two groups, one that can help overcome loneliness, reduce anxiety, and provide intimacy and another that can satisfy lust. However, this arrangement occurs at the expense of self-esteem, because a boy cannot have an affair with a "bad girl" and love his "sweetheart" without loss of self-respect. Such an arrangement precludes the easy integration of the genital needs into the personality, "which is in itself an extremely unfortunate way of growing up" (Sullivan, 1953: 269). The conflicts experienced in the fumbling attempts to establish intimacy with the opposite sex are not only "internal" but also the result of interpersonal difficulties, stereotypes, and communication problems. Observation of middle-school boys and girls in cafeterias, hallways, or other gathering places gives testimony to the teasing—the clumsy, awkward, and sometimes exaggerated attempts to capture the attention of the opposite sex.

Sullivan observes both the delay that some individuals experience in the timing of puberty and the very serious personality disturbances that may result if being out of step developmentally becomes a major issue in establishing acceptance and friendship in the peer group. The effects of maturation can become a major threat to one's self-system because of negative evaluation by peers. Furthermore, during early adolescence girls are quite advanced in the development progression through puberty, to the extent that, when the boys finally awaken to an interest in girls, "most of the girls are already fairly wound up in their problems about boys" (Sullivan, 1953: 266).

Early adolescence continues until a way has been found to satisfy lust or the genital drive. Inability to resolve the conflict between security, intimacy, and lust creates crisis and feelings of loneliness. Masturbation appears to be the one easy solution to tension created by the lust dynamism, but leaves the interpersonal needs unsatisfied.

■ Late Adolescence

Late adolescence begins when the individual has established a pattern by which to satisfy his genital needs. It ends when the capacity to reproduce and the need for tenderness and intimacy begin to merge and the task becomes the integration of both into a mature interpersonal relationship. When all the partially developed aspects of personality fall into their proper place and form a more integrated pattern, including a vocational identity, the individual is ready to leave adolescence behind. In adulthood, lust and intimacy have been fused and the individual can now form a stable, lasting relationship based on love; this means that the other person has become "as significant, or nearly as significant, as one's self" (Sullivan, 1953: 34).

Sullivan believes that "late adolescence extends from the patterning of preferred genital activity through [numerous] . . . steps to the establishment of a fully human or mature repertory of interpersonal relations, as permitted by available opportunity, personal and cultural" (1953: 297). During late adolescence, people explore what they prefer in terms of genital activity and how it will fit into their lives. Sullivan assumes that genital activity is essential to the establishment of mature, intimate interpersonal relationships based on mutual respect. The late adolescent needs to experiment with all of the components of the self-system in order to form a functioning unity.

A disjointed or compartmentalized self is like living behind a "mask." According to Sullivan,

> The adolescent may begin the "life behind a mask" that tends to characterize numbers of urban denizens. The mask, however, requires so much energy for its successful maintenance that personality growth is apt to end with its successful construction. As the necessities for masking certain motivations vary from one interpersonal situation to another, it may be easier to avoid further integration of the self, and to develop, from this point onward, specialized accommodations and interest for various groups [1972: 210].

In order to become an adult, the individual must institute effective security measures (defense mechanisms) that help him or her to cope with anxiety and sublimate tension. This task is "all-absorbing, all-frustrating," and requires the development of effective mechanisms for coping with anxiety and achieving a sense of respect for self and others. A major obstacle to further development occurs if the individual attempts to escape the anxiety of adult responsibility by avoiding reality-oriented behavior and engaging in daydreaming and fantasy or, more seriously, through disassociation from personal and social difficulties. Late adolescence can also become the precipitating event of personality disorder, eating disorder, depression, or suicide, especially for those who suffer from loneliness, low self-esteem, anxiety, or who enter the period inadequately prepared by preceding inappropriate interpersonal events.

The demarcation between early and late adolescence is not biologically determined but does involve an achievement: "the achievement of adequate and satisfactory genital activity" (Sullivan, 1953: 297). Religious, legal, political, and personal restrictions can create obstacles to the achievement of this progression; hence, not everybody reaches late adolescence. Interpersonal problems experienced earlier in life, especially the lack of a chumship, can contribute to a poorly developed affectional growth pattern and may produce a stumbling block in interpersonal relationships. In late adolescence, the capacity to reproduce ideally should merge with the capacity for tenderness and intimacy.

To the extent that tasks of late adolescence are mastered successfully, there is "great growth in the experience in the syntaxic mode." Colleges and universities especially foster the expansion of the syntaxic mode of thinking by providing extraordinary opportunities for the widening of cognitive and symbolic horizons. Mastery of these late-adolescent tasks prepares for the successful transition into adulthood.

RELATIONSHIP TO OTHER SYSTEMS

Sullivan was able to effectively integrate rather diverse psychological, psychiatric, anthropological, field-theoretical, and sociological thoughts into a systematic statement about the nature of human development that emphasizes the importance of the adolescent and preadolescent periods. Nevertheless, his theory hardly seems to have received the attention it deserves. In part, this neglect has resulted because his system is quite complex and does not easily fit existing models; it integrates clinical, social, and cognitive psychology in unconventional ways and uses unfamiliar terminology. Finally, the richness of his thought is not matched by the clarity of his writing style. Sullivan was aware of this: "Some of my critics say that I do not write clearly" (Perry, 1982: 212).

Since Sullivan presents a new interpersonal theory of development, it appears appropriate to contrast some of his basic ideas with other systems, especially psychoanalysis. Although Sullivan identified with the psychoanalytic movement, he was hardly a psychoanalytic thinker in the traditional sense. He refused to compare his theory with psychoanalysis. When asked whether his self-system corresponded to the Freudian ego or the superego, Sullivan basically rejected such parallels because his self-system and Freud's contributions are based on fundamentally different assumptions. The ego is an intrapsychic construct while the self-system is social and interpersonal. Obviously, Sullivan's self-system cannot easily be translated into the id, ego, superego model. Nevertheless, he conceded that there may be some commonalities; however, he left it to others to define them.

Sullivan did not deny that biology plays an important role in human, especially adolescent, development (puberty); nevertheless, he emphasized the socialization process and acculturation—the nature and quality of interpersonal relations—much more than almost any other theoretical system, except social learning theory (see Chapter 14). Sexuality is not seen as the major driving force in human behavior; a much more important motivating force is the continuous struggle to overcome the feeling of anxiety. According to Sullivan, anxiety is the central motivating force in human behavior. Since anxiety is the result of interpersonal difficulties, interpersonal needs appear to be more significant than sexual needs. Infantile sexuality is not a major issue in Sullivan's theory, while the ability to establish an intimate personal relationship from infancy on—and especially during preadolescence and adolescence—becomes a major factor in the movement toward maturity, adulthood, and adult sexuality. In general, Sullivan deemphasized past events; he regarded as much more important the "here and now" of the contemporary interpersonal field. Interpersonal relationships, communication, and social factors promote or thwart the individual's advancement from one stage to the next. Rather than emphasizing trauma, conflict, and crisis, Sullivan placed greater emphasis on the positive forces in development. Furthermore, he saw development as continuous. Even the names of his stages imply more continuity than the body zones that give libido satisfaction (Freud) or the psychosocial crises that need to be resolved (Erikson). Sullivan believed that important personality changes may occur, certainly up to and including adolescence, but can, under favorable circumstances, even later in life.

Sullivan's theory of development was written, as were many of the other major developmental theories, primarily from the male's viewpoint. The uniqueness of the female experience of adolescence especially seems to have been neglected. Female development, or at least the experiences of the female that correspond to those described for the male, are seldom mentioned and never made as explicit as those of the male. One gets the impression that there are many similarities in the development of the sexes but also that important differences exist. Neither similarities nor differences are made sufficiently clear. In the development of the characteristics of each of the stages, Sullivan was unequivocally concerned with the male, especially in his description of the two stages that precede adolescence. Sullivan made a revealing statement that, although written in a very specific context, seems to be an appropriate self-critique about the general attention given to female development in his theory: "I am confining my remarks to male . . . because the female picture is more complicated and I have less material on it" (1953: 248). Many of Sullivan's reviewers and critics took him to task for not having sufficiently developed in his writing his thoughts on female development. However, Mullahy (1970) claimed that Sullivan "possessed keen insight into feminine psychology."

The last quote makes particularly good sense in view of Carol Gilligan's (see Chapter 10) research on sex differences in moral judgment. She was able to show that females make moral judgments differently than males. Compared to males, females are guided much more by their concern and empathy for other people, their efforts to communicate, and in general, their emphasis on interpersonal relationships than by their focus on abstract universal principles. Kandel (1986) too has observed that girls are more receptive to interpersonal influences than boys. Looking at Sullivan's theory from Gilligan's and Kandel's perspectives implies that his theory has much greater relevance to a "psychology of women" than do the traditional psychoanalytic theories, with their emphasis on the primacy of genitality and sexuality. Many authors have claimed that for the female—as in Sullivan's theory—the interpersonal quality of an intimate relationship is much more important than the lust dynamism. For Sullivan, anxiety grows out of actual or anticipated interpersonal disapproval, and sexuality reaches maturity only when it involves intimacy and concern for the other person. Regrettably, Sullivan did not make some of the feminine values that are implied in his theory more explicit in his writing. However, a comparison of Gilligan's (see Chapter 10) more recent writing with Sullivan's theory would provide a rich exploration of both gender differences and gender similarities in early adolescence.

6

MARGARET MEAD: CULTURAL ANTHROPOLOGY AND ADOLESCENCE

BIOLOGICAL VERSUS CULTURAL DETERMINISM

A major controversy about human nature arises in the early part of the twentieth century and has substantial implications for developmental theories. It is against the controversial question of "biological destiny" versus "cultural destiny" that cultural anthropology emerges as a major developmental theory. The issue over which the battle was being fought is relevant to the theme of this book: Is adolescence a biologically determined period of storm and stress, or is storm and stress simply a reaction to social and cultural conditions?

Biological determinism had its roots in Darwin's theory of evolution (see Chapter 1), which Sir Francis Galton, through his ideas of "race improvement," had applied to humans. At about the same time, the rediscovery of Mendel's law of heredity and Goddard's very influential work on the Kallikak* family advanced the then powerful eugenics movement. Eugenics had as its goal the improvement of the human race through selective breeding. Numerous states actually passed sterilization laws for the retarded and the deviant, laws which had strong racial overtones. These ideas, quite prevalent in the United States, found their most despicable expression in the Eugenic Sterilization Laws in Nazi Germany. Galton had claimed—and these legal efforts toward eugenics are based on this assumption—that nature is five times as influential as nurture.

---

*Goddard researched the family tree of Kallikak (a fictitious name of Greek origin, meaning *good-bad*). A civil war soldier, Kallikak first conceived a child with a bar maid with a "bad" reputation, producing 480 descendants, most of whom became alcoholics, prostitutes, or mentally retarded, even criminals. Later, he married a respectable and socially prominent "good" woman, and their offspring became the social and political leaders in New Jersey. Goddard's books contributed greatly to the belief in heredity and had a profound influence on the eugenics movement and the passage of sterilization laws.

In psychology, biological determinism found expression in the belief in instincts (William McDougall). Freud, who had claimed that his developmental stages were universal, emphasized biology. G. Stanley Hall's (see Chapter 1) influential theory of adolescence was based on evolutionism. Adolescence—the period in which "storm and stress," "crisis," "turmoil," and "conflict" were the inevitable effects of the process of physical and sexual maturation—was natural, and hence biologically determined. Hall's thinking had a profound influence on Gesell's maturational theory of development. Freud's biologically rooted theory greatly influenced the psychoanalytic thinkers who followed, particularly Blos and, to a lesser extent, Erikson who combines psychoanalytic theory with insights obtained from anthropology and the social sciences.

Franz Boas, professor of anthropology at Columbia University, was influenced by the German philosopher Immanuel Kant and the liberal and enlightened ideals of the German revolution of 1848, in which his uncle participated. Boas most strongly opposed the supremacy of biology. His theory of extreme cultural determinism postulated "the independence of cultural achievement from race" and claimed that "the social stimulus is infinitely more important than the biological mechanism"; he took a point of view opposite to Galton's. Boas's theory constituted a major intellectual and theoretical challenge to the thinking prevalent at about 1917 and eventually led to the separation of cultural anthropology from biology. However, Boas's theory had never been empirically tested. The testing ground for the validity of cultural determinism became adolescence. Specifically, whether adolescence proved a universal period of storm and stress, turmoil and crisis (biologically determined), or whether, as Boas assumed, a "negative instance" could be found to demonstrate that adolescence could be a smooth, happy, carefree time, at least in some societies. The task fell upon Margaret Mead (1901–1978), a doctoral student of Boas's, to undertake a field study in the South Seas to search for such a "negative instance," that is, a counterexample in which adolescents did not categorically experience crises, nor storm and stress. Mead landed in 1925 in Pago Pago, Samoa, with the goal to determine whether adolescent turmoil was a universal product of puberty, and hence biologically determined, or could be modified by the cultural context. She studied the process of growing up in Ta'u, a remote small island in the eastern part of the Manu'a Archipelago. Mead refers to Ta'u as "the most primitive part of Samoa." Upon her findings rested the fundamental claim of cultural determinism, namely that "human behavior could be explained in exclusively cultural terms" (Freeman, 1983: 44,48). Her purpose became to demonstrate Boas's claim that human behavior is understandable primarily in the context of social and cultural patterns. The question that guided her ethnographic research appears to have been: "Are the disturbances which vex our adolescents due to the nature of adolescence itself or to the civilization? Under different conditions does adolescence present a different picture?" (Mead, 1928/1950: 17).

MEAD'S SAMOA AND FREEMAN'S CRITIQUE

At the time of Mead's research, Samoa was assumed to provide the classic example of a society in which many of the behaviors, attitudes, and values of the average adolescent were allegedly casual and stress-free, almost the opposite of the storm and stress assumed to be universal and the prevalent pattern in the United States. Mead's famous report of her

Margaret Mead (1901-1978)

landmark investigation, *Coming of Age in Samoa* (1928), became the most widely read anthropological book ever published (millions of copies were sold in sixteen translations). Part
of the ensuing controversy generated by that book resulted because it was written, particularly three chapters, for popular consumption rather than as a scientific treatise. Samoa became the earliest and most widely quoted example of Franz Boas's theory of "cultural rela-

tivism," in which he maintained that environment, culture, and socialization are the primary determinants of human personality and behavior. Boas's theoretical position must be understood as a reaction against the biologically based developmental, psychological, and psychiatric theories of that period. He emphasized that the diversity in childrearing, family patterns, and the broader sociocultural setting exerted an influence much greater than had been believed, and that a uniform, universal, biologically based human nature simply did not exist. Mead's field study of 50 adolescent females in Ta'u conducted in 1925-1926 was the first major anthropological investigation to report about a society in which the transition from childhood to adulthood appeared fundamentally different (relaxed and casual) from the expected and, presumably, natural pattern of that in the United States. Mead's pioneering ethnographic research seemed to demonstrate that whether or not adolescence becomes a period full of stress, conflict, and sexual difficulties or one of harmonious, pleasurable, sexually uninhibited experimentation does depend on the cultural context. Hence, Mead's findings became a primary argument supporting "cultural relativism."

Mead's observation of adolescent girls in Samoa has been cited frequently as evidence that the turmoil, the crises, the sexual frustration, and the storm and stress associated with growing up in the United States—and considered universal by many of the major developmental psychologists of that time—is far from being an inevitable, universal condition, and actually resulted from particular expectations, cultural setting, social environment, and childrearing practices. Mead's description of life in Samoa (1928/1950), a life characterized by carefree, unpressured, and harmonious interpersonal interactions, a "lack of deep feeling, . . . is the very framework of all their attitudes toward life" (133), without jealousy and stress. "Love and hate, jealousy and revenge, sorrow and bereavement, are all a matter of weeks" (132). The relationship between adolescents and their parents seemed easygoing—like life in Samoa—where "disagreements between parent and child" end with "the child moving across the street" (132). Mead described the transition to adulthood as smooth and unencumbered by conflicts. Ta'un society encouraged free love and uninhibited sexual explorations among youth; hence, sexual expressions and sexual experimentation occurred without fear, shame, guilt, or social sanctions. On the Ta'u island, "sex is a natural, pleasurable thing" (134). Mead explains the differences between Samoa and the United States in terms of the relaxed and laid-back nature of Samoan culture, the lack of competitiveness, low level of violence and the easygoing, carefree nature of Samoans and the "general casualness of the whole society" (132).

In a more general sense, Mead described Samoa as a patient, gentle, and peaceful society where "no one is hurried along . . . or punished harshly" (132). Samoans experienced no religious or sexual conflicts, no jealousy; by extension, Mead concluded that the carefree behavior of the adolescent can and must be explained in terms of cultural learning, childrearing, and socialization. Cultural conditioning, and thereby "nurture," became the principal mechanism by which to explain such human diversity. According to Côté (1992, 1994), Mead inappropriately and inaccurately generalized from the very small, very remote island of Ta'u with its unique characteristics, to Samoan culture in general. Mead herself invites such harsh criticism by ignoring the possibility of differences between individuals, villages, and islands. ". . . because one girl's life was so much like another's, in an uncomplex, uniform culture like Samoa, I feel justified in generalizing although I studied only 50 girls in three small neighbouring villages" (Mead, 1928/1950: 17). Even Ta'u in the 1920s had its own geographic, historical, political, social, and economic conditions that set it apart from the main part of Samoa. It seemed to have been chosen because it was the most primitive island and had less contact with American-Samoan culture. Mead would have been more accurate and less vulnerable to criticism if she had titled her book, *Coming of Age in Ta'u,* and confined her generalizations to adolescent girls in Ta'u.

In a highly critical analysis, *Margaret Mead and Samoa: The Making and Unmaking of a Myth* (1983), Derek Freeman questions the validity not only of her generalizations but also many of her specific findings, and sets out to show that *Coming of Age in Samoa* seriously misrepresented the Samoan culture and the character of the Samoan people. An Australian professor of anthropology who spent 6 years in Samoa (Mead spent only 9 months), Freeman maintains that many of her assertions "are fundamentally in error and some of them preposterously false" (1983: 288). Mead's findings about Samoa had been criticized in the social science literature before. Even during her lifetime "she never provided a full defense of her position" (Côté, 1992: 503). However, Freeman places into question not only the validity of her specific findings, he also develops a picture of Samoa and Samoan youth diametrically opposed to Mead's. The reader needs to be aware that Freeman collected his data in the 1960s and mainly on the island of Upoln, 30 times larger than Ta'u and with a population of 90,000, as compared with 600 in the Ta'u villages studied by Mead in the 1920s. In addition, Freeman's theoretical orientation led him to attack the "nurture" side of Mead and Boas's argument. Freeman demonstrates that, indeed, as much—if not more—violence, competition, guilt, and repressed sexuality permeates Samoan culture just as it does many Western cultures. Samoan parents beat their children and continue to beat them if they do not stop crying. Vividly describing the significance of the official deflowering of the virgin bride at her wedding ceremony, Freeman speaks of a "virginity cult" and maintains that virginity is of great social importance, not something casually and carelessly done away with as Mead's descriptions implied. Based on official documents, Freeman shows that Samoans do have a surprisingly high rate of homicide, rape, and assault, and are prone to jealousy.

The discrepancy between these two accounts speaks to the vulnerability of anthropological research and the geographic significance of 70 miles' distance of often turbulent seas, and to the influence that 40 years of social change may have on anthropological observations. Since Margaret Mead is deceased, showing how she would defend her findings may be difficult. The controversy that has ensued since the publication of Freeman's book has again brought the issue of "nature versus nurture" once more into the foreground of the debate. Those who tend to ascribe greater significance to the environment attempt to defend Mead against Freeman's more recent collection of evidence; the hereditarians, such as Nikolaas Tinbergen, 1973 Nobel Prize winner, praise Freeman's work "as a masterpiece of modern scientific anthropology." The Mead/Freeman controversy has stirred much interest both in the popular press and in the academic world, not because of what actually happened in Ta'u in 1925-1926, but because of the underlying theoretical issue of "biological determinism" vs. "cultural relativism." Côté (1992, 1994), in a very careful analysis, identifies the major factors that may have contributed to the escalation of the Mead/Freeman controversy into a major social science debate. He maintains that the nature of the controversy in its own right has become an issue of sociological interest. On a personal, anecdotal level, Ala'ilima, an American married to a Samoan who has written a book about her adjustment to the Samoan way of life, says:

I have seen days (and nights) like Margaret Mead's and moments of Mayhem like Freeman's. No one who has lived in Samoa long could doubt the existence of both. My only problem is with people who, like the blind men and the elephant, feel for one aspect or another and draw conclusions about what Samoans really "are" [Ala'ilima, 1984: 91].

Some of the factors that influenced Mead's research are well known. A young anthropologist who at the age of 23 went to Ta'u, Mead was philosophically committed to "cultural determinism" advanced by her mentor, Franz Boas. Obviously, he perceived of Samoa as proof that what is thought of as human nature is not common everywhere. And since Mead is the first of the emerging scientists of anthropology to provide substantial evidence for the theory of "cultural relativism," Boas praised her lavishly in his foreword to *Coming of Age in Samoa.*

The anthropologist doubts the correctness [that adolescence is a period of unavoidable difficulty] but up to this time hardly any one has taken the pains to identify himself sufficiently with a primitive population to obtain an insight into these problems. We feel, therefore, grateful to Miss Mead for having undertaken to identify herself so completely with Samoan youth that she gives us a lucid and clear picture of the joys and difficulties encountered by the young individual in a culture so entirely different from our own. The result of her painstaking investigation confirms the suspicion long held by anthropologists, that much of what we ascribe to human nature is no more than a reaction to the restraints put upon us by our civilization (Boas, 1928/1950).

Besides Mead's determination to find evidence for Boas's theory of "cultural relativism," others have raised questions about her methodology and the generality of her findings. Rather than opening her inquiry with an overall assessment of the more general Samoan culture, Mead started immediately with her research in Ta'u, focusing on the sexual adjustment of adolescent girls. She did not live among the natives, but with expatriate Americans. The girls from three villages often came to the naval medical dispensary, where Mead had her headquarters; she talked to her informants in this setting. Samoan teenagers may have let fantasy color their reports of what happened in the bushes just as adolescents in our society often improve the quality of their sexual adventures when they report them to others. Perhaps Samoan teenagers may have teasingly improved the sexual encounters and "provided her with a skewed view of Samoan culture" (Côté, 1992: 506). According to Freeman (1983), teasing or duping someone is a pastime that greatly appeals to Samoans. As a woman, Mead was excluded from the meetings of the chiefs held to discuss important issues. Freeman, in contrast, became the adopted son of Lauvi Vainu'u, a senior talking chief. Later, a chiefly title was bestowed on Freeman which allowed him to participate in the meetings of the chiefs. However, that may also have influenced him to take a more authoritarian and more conservative approach, since he felt that the reputation of the Samoans was at stake. Furthermore, he cites numerous educated and knowledgeable Samoans who, appalled after reading Mead's account of their society, provided evidence that Samoan culture in general and in the 1960s in particular is full of stress and strain. Freeman had access to diverse historical and anthropological data, to documentary evidence as well as to official crime records. In a special effort to avoid the problem arising from his visiting Samoa

14-42 years later than Mead, Freeman traces the major Samoan traits discussed by Mead from 1830 to 1980.

If Mead had stated more explicitly that she was not writing about Samoa in general, but about three small, remote villages on the island of Ta'u, some of the controversy could have been avoided. Thus, in Hegelian terms, one can look at the biological determinism espoused by Darwin, Galton, Mendel, Goddard, McDougall, G. Stanley Hall, and Freud as the thesis. Boas, Mead, and Benedict challenged this thesis and advanced cultural determinism as the antithesis. Freeman argues for a synthesis "in which there will be, in the study of human behavior, recognition of the radical importance of both the genetic and the exogenetic [cultural] and their interaction, both in the past history of the human species and in our problematic future" (Freeman, 1983: 302).

Freeman's critique of Mead's *Coming of Age in Samoa* is extensively documented but his argument for a synthesis between biological determinism and cultural determinism seems to come too late to have a major impact. The synthesis has already taken place; although proponents of culture or biology may emphasize one more than the other, most contemporary theorists view development as an interaction between nature and nurture. Adolescent turmoil, storm and stress, and crises are no longer considered inevitable, not even for adolescents growing up in the United States. And, regardless of whether or not Mead was correct about Samoa, other anthropologists have observed societies in which adolescence is not a turbulent period of storm and stress. And even for the United States, considerable evidence has accumulated that adolescence can be a happy and harmonious period of life, at least for a not insignificant portion of youth. Thus, the physiological changes of puberty and sexual maturation alone are not categorically responsible for adolescent difficulties. Anxieties, insecurities, social pressures, social expectations, and cultural, educational, and family factors all may contribute to adolescent stress.

RUTH BENEDICT'S THEORY OF CULTURAL CONDITIONING

Ruth Benedict (1887–1948), in "Continuities and Discontinuities in Cultural Conditioning" (1938/1980) and in *Patterns of Culture* (1934), advanced a theory of development from the perspective of cultural determinism sometimes also referred to as "cultural relativism," a perspective particularly well suited to illustrate, anthropologically, the transition from childhood to adulthood. This theory of cultural conditioning is based on various field investigations which Mead conducted in the South Seas. By combining the theoretical writing of Benedict with relevant anthropological field studies, we derive a systematic statement concerning the importance which the early "cultural relativists" ascribe to environmental and social factors in the developmental process. "Cultural relativism" is a term more appropriately applied to the earlier writings of Mead, when she rather firmly believed in the sovereignty of culture over biology, in shaping the raw material of human personality. In her later writing, she modified her extreme position to give some credence, though limited, to the importance of biology and recognized universal aspects of development (e.g., an innate pattern of growth, menarche as a biological event of social significance, incest taboo). Mead's earlier findings—even though they have been challenged by Freeman—did contribute the revolutionary idea that adolescence is not a biological but a cultural phenomenon. Benedict, a contemporary of Mead and also a student of F. Boas, wholeheartedly endorsed the emphasis on the importance of environment and socialization, or as her book title suggests, on cultural patterns.

Benedict argued that human beings show far greater plasticity and modifiability than animals. She accepted the Boasian principle that humans, above everything else, were from the time of birth on, conditioned by the cultural setting into which they were born. This ability to adapt accounts for the progress the human species has made as well as for wide intercultural differences. The constitution of man does not determine particular patterns of behavior, chromosomes and genes do not transmit culture. Cultural relativists claim that few, if any, human traits are universal; even if there are universal traits, they may not be biologically determined.

Benedict (1938/1980) offered as a theoretical construct "continuities and discontinuities" as a means of analyzing the socializing influences of a given culture on the development of individual personality. If natural growth is uninfluenced by social-environmental forces, Benedict perceived that growth was a gradual, smooth, and continuous process; however, to the extent that social groups introduce requirements, restrictions, differential treatment, and expectations, she predicted that discontinuities would emerge. Newborn infants depend on other people for support and survival. From this early infantile dependency, they must grow into a state of relative independence; as adults they must function to maintain themselves and must provide for and protect their own offspring. The patterns by which the child reaches independence vary from one culture to another. In some cultures, such as the American, the difference between a child and an adult—and even between adolescents of different ages—is delineated sharply, by legal definition, by different schools, and different grades for different ages. Benedict referred to this as an *age-graded society.* Advancing from one "grade" or one group to another, and especially from one type of school to another, introduces anxiety and insecurity and often requires the formation of new interpersonal relationships. This creates discontinuity in social, emotional, and personal processes. The famous cross-cultural study of crime by Bacon, Child, and Barry (1963) supports Benedict's claim of the disadvantage of discontinuity. These scholars were able to demonstrate that the abruptness (discontinuity) of the transition from dependence to independence in the patterns of training children accompanies the observed frequency of personal crime. Lewin (see Chapter 7) also accounts for many adolescent adjustment problems in terms of the cultural dichotomy between children and adults. Lewin conceptualizes adolescence as having only a "marginal" status between these groups, being different from both.

One example of this discontinuity in our society—at least in the past—involved the emphasis on exclusion of sex for the child as contrasted with the sexual orientation of the adults. Children never, or very rarely, witnessed childbirth, sexual intercourse, or death; with pregnancy camouflaged, evacuation veiled with prudery, breast-feeding hidden, and some girls menstruating for the first time without knowing what was happening, they had few or no opportunities to learn about such realities. Television and movies have changed much of this, but only in a vicarious, impersonal, and out-of-context sort of way. Children still get an incomplete understanding of the life cycle of the sexes, and emerging sexual feelings during puberty still clash with prevailing social values, thus producing discontinuity. The sexual explicitness of the mass media from *Playboy* to prime-time TV stimulates sexual feelings and contributes to the clash with the preaching of parents and the church.

In contrast, children in some primitive societies follow a relatively continuous growth pattern. Youths have an opportunity to observe birth and death near or in their own home. They may have seen a partly developed fetus, occasionally stolen glimpses of adult sexual activity, and certainly observed the sexual copulation of their animals. Considered natural and pleasurable, sex is not repressed by some societies. Thus, certain societies provide a relatively gradual, continuous sequence of experiences without severe interruptions or restrictions, making for continuity in the developmental process. By contrast, in Western societies many experiences approved for or tolerated among adults remain forbidden to or hidden from children. Attitudes, values, and skills that children have learned must be unlearned when they become adults. Such transitions may be stressful.

Benedict discussed three specific aspects of discontinuity versus continuity in cultural conditioning. The major changes relevant to these three occur during adolescence in Western Society. They are:

1. Responsible versus nonresponsible status role
2. Dominance versus submission
3. Contrasted sexual roles (Benedict, 1938/1980: 15)

The issue of work and play demonstrates the difference between continuity and discontinuity in behavior from *responsible to nonresponsible status roles*. In American society, especially in urban areas, work and play are considered separate and distinct. A child rarely makes labor contributions to the subsistence of the family and is protected by law from employment outside the family. But when young men and women graduate from high school or college, they must compete—sometimes for the first time in their life—on an equal basis with other adults and suddenly must assume dramatically different roles from those of student. On the small family-owned farm of the nineteenth century, this transition proved much more continuous. Play and work were not exclusive activities for children. For example, turning the hay, harvesting potatoes, or driving the cows to the fields involved playfulness and fun as well as some work, the work increasing as children grew older. In many contemporary primitive societies, development from a nonresponsible to a responsible status role similarly proceeds gradually. Play and work are not necessarily separated; they often involve the same activities. Among the Cheyenne Indians, a boy received a bow and arrow at birth. As he grew, he received larger and larger bows. His relatives feasted to celebrate his first contribution of a snow bird to the family meal. The boy's contribution had value to the family even if his father brought home a buffalo. Nor did the boy's status change when he finally brought home a buffalo himself. The family regarded his killing of the buffalo as part of a natural, predictable sequence.

In Samoa, the girls, sometimes as young as 6 or 7 years old, accepted responsibility for caring for and disciplining their younger siblings. Thus, each girl was socialized to develop responsibility by her early involvement in family duties. The boys at an early age learned the simple tasks of reef fishing and canoeing while the girls, after they were released from their duties as nursemaids for their younger siblings, worked on plantations and helped carry food to the village. No basic change took place during the adolescent period; the degree of responsibility, and the amount and quality of work increased as the child grew and matured. In our society (especially in urban and suburban communities), the transition from nonresponsible play to responsible work occurs during late adolescence and is often experienced as a rather sudden shift. This can create anxiety and even conflict in the adolescent, since he or she enters a heretofore unknown field. In addition, employment requires a redefinition of essential roles if not the essence of one's identity.

The difference between *dominance and submission* is also extreme in our culture. The child must relinquish his or her childhood dependency and submission and adopt its very opposite—dominance—in adulthood. Often, emotional attachments that are hard to break later enforce submission to parental authority. Our emphasis on respect for parents and elders creates strong elements of discontinuity because the submissive child must eventually become a dominant parent. Nowadays, people even take "assertiveness training courses" to unlearn submissive behavior.

During adolescence, a rather sudden shift takes place from submission to dominance. Frequently, only a short time elapses between the adolescent submitting to parental wishes or demands and leaving home to begin his or her own family. At times, the adolescent who is ready to leave home consciously experiences this change as discontinuity. Since he or she typically has received little or no training for independence, he or she may experience homesickness or actually return home. In contrast, some primitive societies have patterns of continuous conditioning in respect to submission-dominance. Benedict reported a case among the Crow Indians in which a father boasted "about his young son's intractability even when it was the father himself who was flouted; 'He will be a man' his father said. He would have been baffled at the idea that his child should show behavior which would obviously make him appear a poor creature in the eyes of his fellows" (Benedict, 1938/1980: 17). In Samoan society the 7-year-old girl dominates her younger siblings as their nursemaid, but she herself may still be under the dominance of older sisters. As the child becomes older, she dominates and must discipline younger children; in turn, older children restrict and discipline her. If a youth gets into a conflict with his parents, he may move to his uncle's house without stigma or emotional trauma. Parents have only limited influence over their children because discipline is the job of an older sibling. As a result, the intensely emotional conflicts between dominance and submission so common in our society remain relatively unknown in Samoa.

Another important discontinuity in the life cycle in our culture involves the child's need to learn to assume a sexual role leading to parenthood. Benedict did not deny that *the discontinuity in gender role* has an important biological root, based on the distinction between infertility before and fertility after puberty. However, whether the contrasted gender role of child and adult are experienced as continuous or discontinuous is determined not only by physiological maturation but also by social expectations and cultural patterns which alter the influence of physiological factors. Our culture emphasizes the discontinuity of the sexual role. Childhood sexual experiences are legally prohibited, socially disapproved, and labeled "sinful." Although practiced only to a limited extent, virginity and sexual abstinence until marriage are upheld as social ideals. Clinical evidence suggests that the virginal bride frequently cannot make an instantaneous sexual adjustment after her wedding because she has failed to unlearn the "danger" and "evil" of sex that she learned while growing up. Benedict defines continuity in the sexual roles to mean "that the child is taught nothing it must unlearn later" (Benedict, 1938/1980: 19). Mead's account of Samoa has for many years provided an alluring portrayal of a society in which the happy, uninhibited, carefree sexual experimentation and free love of the Samoan girl was cited as an illustration of continuity in sexual development. Mead concludes that Samoan adolescents have the smoothest and happiest sexual adjustment of any society on earth and do not experience maladjustments, moral conflicts, or "adolescent turmoil." However, as discussed earlier, Freeman (1983) maintains that many of Mead's conclusions were "fundamentally in error." He questions whether sexual adjustment in puberty can be totally smooth, harmonious, and anxiety-free. Freeman suggests that the Tahitians are actually sexually less inhibited than the Samoans. Even among Western societies, we find a more open and accepting attitude toward sexuality among Swedes and Danes in contrast to the puritanical and ambivalent attitude in the United States.

Benedict (1938/1980) maintained that significant discontinuity in childrearing necessarily results in emotional strain, whereas cultural conditioning characterized by continuity is more likely to promote smooth, healthy, and harmonious growth. Western societies that are based on discontinuous cultural patterns foster conflict, crises, turmoil, and storm and stress during adolescence. Primitive societies that are continuous in their childrearing patterns, where the child does not have to unlearn anything as he or she matures and becomes an adult, foster happy, healthy, conflict-free development. Societies that emphasize discontinuity are identified as *age-graded societies,* which means that those from whom we expect similar behavior or the learning of similar material are grouped together. Presumably, these groups of children have distinct characteristics and approximately the same skills. In age-graded societies, stages in development become observable because social institutions and the law expect or demand different behaviors at different age levels. Children in a certain age-grade are grouped in formal institutions such as schools, Scouts, and informal play and peer groups. Their activities are organized around behaviors considered appropriate for that age; the more formal training a society requires, the more discontinuity ensues. Individuals often "graduate" from one group or school to another, receive certificates, social recognition, and at a clearly demarcated point in time, become legally entitled to drive, to buy cigarettes, or to vote, all of which introduce elements of discontinuity.

MEAD'S POSTFIGURATIVE, COFIGURATIVE, AND PREFIGURATIVE CULTURES

Mead's conceptualization of postfigurative, cofigurative, and prefigurative cultural patterns is relevant to the consideration of peer group influences versus parent influences on the individual adolescent, and also relevant to some of the fundamental changes in the structure of the modern family, identified by Bronfenbrenner (1986b). Mead's terms require definition: the prefixes "post" (the past), "co" (the present), and "pre" (the future) refer to the type of world youth will inherit when they grow up. "Figure" is a model or representation of that world. Thus, postfigurative culture means that the adolescent will grow into a world that very much is modeled after the past, an idea related to the concepts, "folk society" or "preindustrial society." The cofigurative culture is modeled after the present world, a phenomenon sociologists identify as the "industrial society." Mead's prefigurative society represents the emergence of an unknown future, an idea expressed by sociologists as "postindustrial society." Mead's patterns, concerned with the speed of cultural change and the transmission of cultural information from the older to the younger generation, are crucial to an understanding of adolescence. Adolescents stand on the boundary between childhood and adulthood where the individual moves from the younger to the older generation. In addition, adolescence is the connecting link in cultural patterns between tradition (the past) and innovation (the future).

■ Postfigurative Cultures

The historically earlier, and preliterate cultures are *postfigurative cultures.* These basically static cultures experience relatively little, if any, change. In such cultures children and adolescents grow up in a world very much the same as that of their parents and grandparents. Life will still be the same when adolescents have become grandparents. Postfigurative cultures depend on the presence of three generations, who live in the same village if not the same abode. Frequently, the children follow in their parents' footsteps in vocational choices. Parents and adults possess the basic knowledge, skills, and values required to function effectively in such a stable and unchanging world; therefore, they are knowledgeable and respected for knowing how to live. The requirements for the young person to become a self-governing adult are quite clear because they remain easily identifiable. A different future lies, literally, beyond imagination. The parents are the most experienced guides, able to pass on their information, skills, ideas, and vocational roles to their offspring. Children and adolescents cooperate through their willingness to absorb the skills, knowledge, and values passed along by their elders because their future depends on that transmission. Finally, a stable cultural pattern emerges in which adolescents are adult-oriented. Often, they enter adulthood relatively early. Puberty rites play a particularly significant role in postfigurative societies. Clarifying at what point youth is prepared to take on adult roles, the rite makes this transition socially visible.

> A postfigurative culture is one in which change is so slow and imperceptible that grandparents, holding newborn grandchildren in their arms, cannot conceive of any other future for the children than their own past lives. The past of the adults is the future of each new generation; their lives provide the ground plan. The children's future is shaped in such a way that what has come after childhood for their forbears is what they, too, will experience after they are grown (Mead, 1970: 1-2).

Examples of such cultures are the mountain Arapesh of New Guinea, Australian aborigines, as well as many of the preliterate and basically unchanging cultural groups. And even within our own societies, postfigurative communities exist that emphasize tradition and resist change, such as the Amish in Pennsylvania or the Hutterites in North Dakota.

■ Cofigurative Cultures

Because of migration or religious conversion, as technology advances and intercultural contact and commerce increase, a break in the postfigurative system occurs; cultural patterns begin to undergo modification. *The cofigurative culture* experiences a moderate rate of social change. The assumption that life for the new generation will differ from that of the older generation begins to take hold. The family structure changes from the extended (three-generation) family pattern to a nuclear family pattern and the influence of grandparents diminishes even if they live in the same home. The peers and age-cohorts rather than the elders begin to represent the future for an adolescent. The sense of interconnectedness and mutual respect and support between older and younger generations prevalent in the postfigurative family declines, replaced by isolation. Parents no longer provide the sole or even major models for teaching important skills, knowledge, attitudes, and values useful in the future. The function of passing along cultural knowledge and skills becomes increasingly supplemented and eventually replaced by schools and formal education. The actual introduction of formal education for all inevitably accelerates the rate of social change. In addition, no less important, the same age peers provide informal teaching-learning opportunities. The adolescent shifts in his or her orientation away from parents, who are no longer perceived as models nor as the source of wisdom; increasingly the adolescent looks to his or her peers for guidance and information. Peers become the models, at least in some areas of life, namely, those that are particularly relevant to social adaptation outside the home, especially those areas in which adults often have little knowledge and experience. Illustrations from our cofigurative culture would include: the use of drugs, adolescent fashion, athletics, adolescent entertainment and music, as well as topics about which parents are unwilling to communicate, such as heterosexual relationships, sexual behavior, sexually transmitted diseases, etc. Mead described the relationship between the older and the younger generation in the cofigurative culture in the following terms:

> In . . . cofigurative cultures the elders are still dominant in the sense that they set the style and define the limits within which cofiguration is expressed in the behavior of the young. There are societies in which approbation by the elders is decisive for the acceptance of new behavior; that is, the young look not to their peers, but to their elders for their final approval of change. But at the same time, where there is shared expectation that members of a generation will model their behavior on that of their contemporaries, especially their adolescent age mates, and that their behavior will differ from that of their parents and grandparents, each individual, as he successfully embodies a new style, becomes to some extent a model for others of his generation (Mead, 1970: 32-33).

As a result of these changes, adolescents express less interest in the past, both in terms of family tradition and cultural history, and more interest in the future. Hence, a gap develops between the parents, who often cherish the past and tradition, and adolescents, who value the future. Different thinking along generational lines has divided many families, especially after the turn of the century, most intensely the post-World War II family. Cofiguration is most pronounced in first-generation immigrant families where parents still try to hold onto Old World tradition and try to maintain control. Adolescents in such families experience particular anxiety to adapt to the New World; they perceive their peers as better and more knowledgeable models than parents and resent their parents' control.

■ The Prefigurative Culture

Consider the splitting of the atom, the invention of the computer, the discovery of the pill, space travel, the disintegration of family patterns, the deterioration of the cities, and the slow but steady destruction of the environment—as the pace of technological and social changes accelerates, new cultural patterns emerge with increasing rapidity. Major events are communicated around the world instantaneously to reach every corner of the globe. As a result, a world community develops, a community united "by shared knowledge and danger," creating a situation that has never existed before. For this new world community the future no longer exists as a predictable extension of the past. The role of parents as models declines further because their skills, knowledge, and values have become dated. *The prefigurative culture* is a conception of the future, an era that—at least in some segments of our society—we are about to enter. Family disintegration continues to erode family support and cohesiveness, propagating rootlessness and alienation. The older generation becomes isolated from the younger generation and has less and less to offer in terms of guidance, advice, and values. Mead did emphasize that love, trust, and dependence remain important, at least for the younger child. Even though the future is all-important, a great deal of uncertainty about the unknown future means that the young have to chart their own course without much guidance from the parents. The past no longer has much meaning and provides no answers: ". . . it will be the child—and not the parent and grandparent—that represents what is to come" (1970: 88). A feeling prevails that nothing out of the past is meaningful. Cofigurative parents used to say: "You know, I have been young and you have never been old" (1970: 63). Prefigurative youth may respond: "You never have been young in the world I am young in, and you never can be" (1970: 63).

Adolescents—if they attend effective schools—now actually know more and are more up-to-date on current scientific advances than their parents. Learning begins to take place without guidance, and sometimes even without the understanding, of the parents. Roles begin to reverse, and adults learn much from their young. The best illustration—depicted in the comic *The Family Circus*—is computer technology, where parents, if they understand anything about computers, come to their children for advice.

Even in other areas of life, adults begin to imitate their offspring rather than the other way around, in fashion, entertainment, sexual behavior. Parents no longer can advise children or help them solve problems, they may even respond helplessly to questions, "you better figure that one out for yourself." As the new patterns of cultural change and cultural transmission emerge (changes that differ fundamentally from the postfigurative and cofigurative changes), inevitable clashes between values, groups, ideologies, and beliefs may take on violent forms. A clear illustration involves the clash between those who unyieldingly and with dogmatic fervor oppose abortion and hold onto the idea of the sanctity of life, no matter how and under what circumstances conception took place. And at the other extreme are those who view abortion as no more than a belated, just slightly more expensive form of birth control.

> As I see it, children today face a future that is so deeply unknown that it cannot be handled, as we are currently attempting to do, as a generation change with cofiguration within a stable, elder-controlled and parentally modeled culture in which many postfigurative elements are incorporated (Mead, 1970: 62).

According to Mead, while we are still retaining some of the characteristics of the cofigurative culture, and maybe even remnants of the postfigurative culture, we are moving slowly but inevitably into a prefigurative culture. In education, change affects not only who instructs whom and where information may originate, but the very the mode of learning

THE FAMILY CIRCUS. **By Bil Keane**

"If you help me with history, I'll help you with the computer."

Reprinted with special permission of King Features Syndicate.

shifts from the "what" of learning (knowledge) to the "how" of learning (the method of discovery). The ability to cope with change becomes of paramount importance. Education changes from product orientation to process orientation. To face an uncertain future, flexible problem-solving strategies are the most important tools that the older generation can give to the young.

GENDER ROLE PATTERNS IN DIFFERENT CULTURES

Prior to World War II Mead described in "Sex and Temperament" (1935/1950) the differences in gender role patterns in three primitive societies in New Guinea. Quite in line with her theoretical commitment to cultural relativism, which means that the attitudes and characteristics of adolescents vary greatly from one cultural group to another, Mead challenged the belief that masculine and feminine traits are based on biological factors. Basically, she attacked the "cultural assumption that certain temperamental attitudes are 'naturally' masculine and others 'naturally' feminine" (p. 14). Instead, she tried to demonstrate that particular gender role behaviors are a function of the social and cultural conditions under which children and adolescents grow up. Her findings greatly contribute to our understanding of sex-role development because she did present evidence to show that masculine and feminine traits considered typical are actually less "natural" and more culture-bound. She focused on the relationship between the sexes and gender role development in three different tribes in New Guinea: The Arapesh, the Mundugumor, and the Tchambuli.

■ The Mountain Arapesh

The Mountain Arapesh lived in a steep, inhospitable, and unproductive mountain region of New Guinea. Poor and undernourished, they had to struggle to produce enough food. Food gathering efforts became a major preoccupation because the possibility of starvation was always present. Because of the threat of not having enough to eat, they spent much of their time helping their neighbors; men and women displayed equal commitment to such group efforts. Their major interest is growing things: children, pigs, and coconut trees. They treated their infants as a "soft, vulnerable, precious little object, to be protected, fed, cherished" (Mead, 1949: 65). Among the Arapesh, both male and female displayed some of the characteristics that in Western societies are often associated with the feminine gender role. Mead described the Arapesh male and female as cooperative, unaggressive, peaceful, noninitiatory, warm, docile, contented, and responsive to the needs of others.

Boys and girls absorbed these social values and emerged into adolescence with happy, trustful, confident attitudes toward life. Sex differences during adolescence were few, though boys enjoyed somewhat greater freedom in expressing aggression and girls learned to be more passively accepting of the way things were. The major adjustment crisis for the Arapesh girl did not occur during adolescence, but when she lost her husband or her husband's affection. Such an event made her most vulnerable because she had been supported and protected all her life. As the children reached puberty, they become self-conscious of their sexuality and observed the cultural taboos. For the still growing young Arapesh, sex was forbidden, not because of moral reasons, but because it was believed that it stunted growth; therefore, it is dangerous for the young. Sex is good, but only for adults who have completed their growth.

■ The Mundugumor of the Yuat River

The Mundugumor were cannibals who lived on the banks of the swiftly flowing jungle river, the Yuat, in New Guinea. Their food-gathering expeditions led them down the river, where they prey upon the malnourished bush people who live on poorer land, to capture "fresh meat." The Mundugumor illustrate a social organization where both male and female were trained to display an exaggerated form of masculine characteristics. Both men and women were ruthless, quarreling, aggressive, assertive, competitive, domineering, and unresponsive to the needs of others. Except for rare cooperative interludes for ceremonial occasions and against a common adversary, it was each man's hand against the other man's. The social structure of the Mundugumor was founded on the hostility between all members. Assisted by boys, women provided much of the food, went fishing, harvested sago, and climbed coconut trees, leaving the men free to plot and to fight. Women despised bearing and rearing children and did not cherish their maternal roles. While men did a little hunting and fishing, they carved, painted, and decorated wooden figures much of the time.

The culture into which a Mundugumor child came was hostile, a world where welcome was always uncertain, where maternal rejection was likely. Emphasizing individuality, the treatment from the beginning was harsh and hostile, the training Spartan. The youth learned that success in life depended upon one's capacity to defend oneself, to fight, and to be able to avenge an insult. Society placed a value on virginity; if a girl was known to be no longer a virgin, her value had been damaged. Passion without tenderness characterized love affairs of unmarried youth. Such affairs remained short, secretive, and impersonal because of the ever-present danger of discovery. Foreplay was expressed by violent scratching and biting, which produced a maximum excitement in a minimum of time.

■ The Lake Dwelling Tchambuli

The Tchambuli, a very small tribe, built their houses on the shores of the beautiful lake Tchambuli, which is connected to the Sepik River in New Guinea. Though they had gardens, they depended mainly on fishing and trading of foods. Among the Tchambuli, the women performed most of the labor. Therefore, Tchambuli society may serve as an illustration of the reversal of gender roles typically found in Western societies. The Tchambuli were an agricultural and an artistic tribe. However, the stern, dominant, matter-of-fact, determinedly busy, and impersonal women pursued fishing, weaving, planting, harvesting, cooking, and the rearing of children. Their attitude toward men was one of kindly tolerance, but women held the real positions of power: "Tchambuli women, brisk, unadorned, managing and industrious, fish and go to market; the men, decorative and adorned, carve and paint and practice dance-steps" (Mead, 1949: 54). Slender, narrow-bodied, submissive, emotionally dependent, involved in petty bits of insult and gossip, the men were less responsible than the women but more responsive to the needs of others. They stay at home creating new dances, fixing their hair, pursuing various forms of artistic endeavor, and planning the ceremonies.

Surprisingly, in Tchambuli society, where the sexes behave so differently, boys and girls, until the age of 6 or 7, received identical treatment from the women who trained them. The girls learned womenly skills and responsibilities and fairly soon formed a solid identification with their own gender. Boys between the ages of 7 and 12 had no clearly defined role, but began to join the men. A ceremonially, but painful cutting of patterns on a boy's back emphasized this transition, but often young males returned and took refuge with the women. They found themselves on the edge of society, often excluded from the men's activities, sitting around on logs, sulking and quarreling with each other, and sometimes getting chased away by bigger boys. There was a piecemeal admission to the "secrets," which turned out to be little more than what they already knew. However, this experience of exclusion and neglect became a male pattern that prevailed even later in life, so that men remained sensitive, easily hurt, and quick "to burst into hysterical vituperations." As they grew older, they learned to play the flute and to pursue other artistic endeavors typical of men.

■ Historical Changes in Gender Role Patterns

These illustrations from New Guinea offer vivid illustrations that gender role is not solely determined by biology, and can be modified. On the other hand, societies such as the Arapesh, Mundugumor, and Tchambuli are the exception, not the rule. The more common gender role patterns, even in preliterate societies, are similar to our own: males tend to be more dominant and do the heavy work while females tend to be more nurturant, cook, do the housework, garden, and care for the children. However, gender roles in our own society are in a process of continuous change. What is socially expected, appropriate behavior, demeanor, and apparel for males and females has changed substantially over time and continues changing at an accelerated rate. At the time of the Revolutionary War, a man, especially a gentleman of status, did wear hose, a powdered wig, and even a lace-trimmed shirt. This clothing did not appear odd or feminine. Women in the early part of the century could not smoke in public, did not cross their legs, and unmarried girls did not go out unchaperoned with males. On the plantations in the South, when young, nubile unmarried females stayed overnight, all unmarried males had to move for the night into another building.

These changes, under the influence of the Women's Liberation Movement, have intensified in the last two decades. The trend today is toward greater equality and increasing overlap of gender roles, a phenomenon referred to as "androgyny," which means combining, accepting, and expressing both masculine and feminine traits, regardless of the sex of the person. In terms of vocational choices, this means that adolescent males may become nurses, househusbands, and caregivers for the young. Adolescent females today aspire to become busdrivers, astronauts, and business executives. A girl may join the previously all-male wrestling team in her high school and win the match.

As a result of these social changes, assumption that males should act "masculine" and females should act "feminine" has been questioned. However, many people, and adolescents in particular, continue to be committed to some degree of gender role differentiation. On the other hand, an overly rigid identification with the traditional gender role of one's sex may be associated with negative psychological characteristics. The especially feminine female tends to show more signs of anxiety, low self-esteem, and low self-acceptance. While the overly masculine adolescent may initially be less disadvantaged, later in life he is more likely to show anxiety, neuroticism, and low self-acceptance.

Even among technologically advanced societies, substantial sex differences have been observed. Communist and socialist countries have advocated equality and encouraged women to enter the labor force. They often provide child care and even household assistance. Actually, less gender role differentiation has been observed in Sweden and Denmark as compared to the United States (Block, 1973). However, even in the Soviet Union, where sexual equality is a political goal and women have entered many of the so-called masculine jobs, females often end up in the lower-paying jobs and are not proportionally represented in the leadership roles. For example, in typically male professions, the following proportions are women: 36 percent of the engineers (but only 12 percent of the plant supervisors), 72 percent of the schoolteachers (but only 23 percent of the school directors), and 45 percent of the scientists (but only 204 members of Soviet Academy of Science). In Japan in contrast, the role of women has changed more slowly, and women find themselves in the more traditional roles of housewife and secretary, higher education remaining less accessible to them.

Obviously, the patterns of gender role differentiation or gender role similarity very much reflect the influence of historical and social changes, environmental and cultural factors; biology may play less of a role than has been assumed.

EDUCATIONAL IMPLICATIONS

Mead (1961) and Benedict (1938/1980) were convinced that cultural, social, and environmental factors account for the adolescent's difficulties in American society, such as the "discontinuities of cultural conditioning" and even the "contradictions and unevenness of physical puberty." Since identifiable conditions in the United States produce stress, strain, crisis, anxiety, and instability in the adolescent, Mead suggested modification of these conditions through social planning and education.

In modern Western societies, which Mead considered "prefigurative cultures," the rate of social and technological change has accelerated rapidly. Adolescents confront many—often, too many—alternatives and choices with little—and often inadequate—guidance. Consequently, problem situations involving genuine choices with far-reaching consequences arise more frequently than they do in primitive societies. The possibility of inappropriate choices is always present. Adolescent difficulties in complex societies relate to "the presence of conflicting standards and the belief that every individual should make his or her own choices, coupled with a feeling that choice is an important matter" (Mead 1928/1950: 154). This conflict of choice becomes intensified and further encumbered because physiological puberty now occurs earlier than in the past and because a number of behaviors involving important choices (such as dating, partying, smoking, drinking, drug use, and sexual intimacy) arise with increasing frequency at increasingly earlier ages. At the same time, the expectation for prolonged and advanced education are increasing. The earlier and earlier imitation of "adultlike" behavior among adolescents, in combination with an extended period of education and the prefigurative rapidity of social change, have increased the duration of social adolescence and created a "mass adolescent culture pattern" in which the influence of parents has declined; "today the elders can no longer present with certainty moral imperatives to the young" (Mead, 1970: 82), while the significance of the peer group as guides and models has increased.

Mead felt that junior high school has especially contributed to adolescents' increased anxiety and insecurity about growth, body image, peer acceptance, and appropriate sexual behavior. Since females mature significantly earlier than boys, the slow-maturing male suffers special vulnerability to anxiety. He may be pressured into premature romantic associations with members of the opposite sex at a time when he is not psychologically or physiologically ready. The formation of deep personal friendships and associations with members of his own sex would help him to develop his own masculine identity, an idea that Mead, Blos, and especially Sullivan emphasize. These theorists perceive intimate same sex friendship in early adolescence as prerequisites for heterosexual adjustment later. Consequently, Mead felt that boys and girls begin too soon to depend on each other for "social and intellectual companionship" (1961: 44). Mead postulated that, because of premature and early heterosexual intimacy, the young adolescent learns to distrust his male companions as competitors in the dating process. Because junior high school invites and the peer group expects early interest in the opposite sex, junior high may contribute to the development of negative attitudes and hostility between the sexes. It lays "the basis for hostility to females on the boys' part and, on the girls' part, pressure toward marriage combined with contempt for males" (Mead, 1961: 38).

With Erickson (1959) and other contemporary writers, Mead maintained that the major task facing adolescents is the search for a personal identity. This task becomes immeasurably more difficult in a modern multifarious society than in primitive cultures. The behavior and values of parents in a prefigurative society no longer provide adequate models, since they are outmoded as compared with the models provided by the mass media. And while the entertainment and mass media models often have a great deal of temporary appeal to the young, they often do not provide realistic and desirable models for a permanent, personal identity. Furthermore, adolescents in the process of freeing themselves from dependency on parents are not only unresponsive, but frequently antagonistic to their parents' admonitions. Since adolescents have learned to evaluate their behavior against that of their age-mates, they often discard or ignore the advice of their parents and exchange the values of their parents for those of their friends. Rapidity of social change, exposure to various secular and religious value systems, and modern technology make the prefigurative, postmodern world seem overwhelming to the adolescent, far too complex, too relativistic, unpredictable, and dangerous to provide a secure frame of reference for the future. In the past society provided adolescents with a period (e.g., apprenticeship, travel, trying a job without commitment), which both Erikson and Mead called a "psychological moratorium" an "as-if" period, during which youth could tentatively experiment with various options without being asked to show "success" and without emotional, economic, or social commitment. The adolescent's loss of such an experimentation period to explore various identity issues makes establishing an identity more difficult. As a substitute for a personal identity, youth utilizes peer-group symbols to establish a semi-identity by way of special clothes, special hair styles, most dramatically illustrated in our time by the punk hair style, punk language, and punk attitudes toward the world. The reason that identity formation is difficult today is that education has become functional, compulsory, and success-oriented. Consequently, the goals and values of adolescents are directed toward economic success, security, immediate gratification of desires, conformity, and social acceptance, with little room for "playing the field," "fooling around," experimentation, idealism, utopianism, and personal martyrdom. "Failure to adapt our educational and social system . . . may be held responsible for . . . negative identities, . . . characteristic of this present group of young people" (Mead, 1961: 49).

Mead criticized the American family for its too intimate organization and its crippling effect on the emotional life of the growing youth. She believed that too strong family ties handicap individuals in their ability to live their own lives and make their own choices. She suggested that "it would be desirable to mitigate, at least in some slight measure, the strong role which parents play in their children's lives, and so eliminate one of the most powerful accidental factors in the choices of any individual life" (Mead, 1928/1950: 141). However, even though she objected to the pattern of the American family that produces too much conformity and too much dependency in children, she considered the family an important social institution and demonstrated that it is almost universal. Mead knew of no better way to produce wholesome individuals than through a tolerant family system in which father and mother may disagree with each other, without a resulting quarrel, and in which adolescents can challenge their parents without a resulting loss of love and self-respect or an increase of emotional tensions.

Mead also demanded more emphasis on mental and physical health in the classroom. Making choices has become an important component of growing up in America, especially for adolescents at that period of development when sexual urges begin to intensify, often years before society would condone sexual behavior. The adolescent will be increasingly confronted with conflicting choices, in sexual as well as in many other matters. The lack of a definitive, generally accepted social canon in American society and the conflicting advice offered by parents, teachers, peers, the mass media, and commercials complicate the choice situation considerably for the adolescent. Consequently, many choice situations produce anxiety during adolescence. To help youth in overcoming this dilemma, a special education effort to train adolescents to think critically and to consider options, alternative solutions, and consequences when confronted with a choice situation ought to be made. "Children must be taught how to think, not what to think" (Mead, 1928/1950: 161). The new model of education should teach adolescents "not what to learn, but how to learn and not what they should be committed to, but the value of commitment" (Mead, 1970: 92).

Returning to the theory of continuities and discontinuities in cultural conditioning, the implications are self-evident: our educational practices in the home as well as in school should emphasize continuity in the learning process so that the child acquires the same set of values and behaviors in childhood that will be expected from him or her in adulthood. The child should be taught nothing that he or she will have to unlearn later in order to become a mature adult. The implementation of this idea is obviously difficult in modern, age-graded, and complex society. Our culture expects each of us to change behavior, often to an extent that constitutes a discontinuity, as we move from elementary to high school, from college into the marketplace, and from the suppression of sexuality before the wedding to sexual bliss afterward.

7

KURT LEWIN: FIELD THEORY AND ADOLESCENCE

Kurt Lewin (1890–1947) was a student of the early Gestalt school of psychologists at the University of Berlin. He was also influenced by Freud's psychoanalytic theory, particularly in regard to the importance of motivation in human behavior. However, Lewin's theory of adolescence is conceptually quite different from any of the theories discussed so far. Lewin's field theory—especially as it relates to social psychology and learning theory—is widely known and frequently discussed in the psychological literature, but comparatively few references are made to his theory of adolescent development, which is explicitly stated in "Field Theory and Experiment in Social Psychology" (1939). His field theory explains and describes the dynamics of behavior of an individual adolescent without generalizing about adolescents as a group. His constructs help to describe and explain, and—if the field forces are known—to predict the behavior of a given indiviudal in a specific situation. In a sense, the field theory of adolescence is expressed explicitly and stated more formally than other theories of adolescent development. At the same time, however, Lewin's theory strongly opposes those conceptual schemes that require placing the phenomenal world in rigid and mutually exclusive categories.

Lewin assumed the "lawfulness" of all psychological events, even those that occur only once. He maintained that general psychological concepts and laws derived on the basis of frequency of occurrence created a dilemma, since these laws are abstracted from many individuals and are generally true in terms of probability only. Such laws may or may not apply to any one specific individual. Therefore, no individually useful application results from these generalizations except by way of probability.

DEVELOPMENTAL CONCEPTS OF FIELD THEORY

One of Lewin's core concepts is the law "that behavior (B) is a function of the person (P) and the environment (E), $B = F(P,E)$, and that P and E in this formula are interdependent variables" (1951: 25). Person and environment continuously and mutually influence each other. This idea has found explicit expression in Bronfenbrenner's ecological theory. How children (P) perceive their environment (E) depends on the stage of their development, their past experiences, their personality, and their knowledge. An unstable psychological environment during adolescence brings about instability in the behavior of the individual. Therefore, to understand a child's behavior, one must consider the child and the environment as a constellation of interdependent factors. The sum total of all environmental and personal factors in interaction is called the "life space" (LSp), or the "psychological space." Behavior is a function of the life space and not only of the physical stimuli, $B = F(LSp)$. The life space includes physical-environmental, social, and psychological factors, such as needs, motives, goals, and real as well as imagined obstacles, all of which determine behavior. To demonstrate the dynamics of the life space, Lewin introduces two constructs that are to represent the situation of a particular individual at a particular time in a particular environment:

1. A map or geometrical representation of the life space, in which the person, available goals, and possible barriers between an individual and his goals are depicted (see Figure 7.1).
2. A representation of the forces that act on the individual and bring about locomotion toward or away from a goal.

Within the life space, objects or goals can have a positive (attraction) or negative (repulsion) valence. If goals allow the fulfillment of needs and desires, they have a positive valence; barriers that interfere with the attainment of a goal produce resistance or negative forces. If the attracting forces of two equally desirable goals are in balance, a person experiences conflict. If the forces are not in balance, they produce locomotion and the individual moves, psychologically speaking, toward or away from the goal. When several forces act simultaneously, the locomotion is called a "resultant." A barrier between an individual and the goal may increase the individual's efforts to reach the goal, but it may also result in frustration.

In Figure 7.1, the person (P) is strongly attracted to the goal (G1), such as passing a course or getting a good grade in high school. However, to reach this goal various barriers

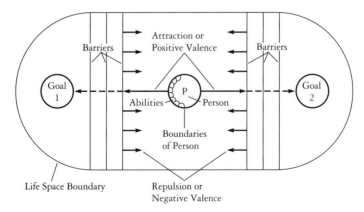

FIGURE 7.1 An individual's life space in a conflict situation.

Kurt Lewin (1890-1947)

exist and may have negative valences, for instance, quizzes, exams, papers, and reports which require effort and time must be completed. If another attractive goal (G2), wanting to earn money, is operative at the same time and also requires overcoming barriers—namely, mowing the lawn, washing the car, and so on—the adolescent may experience conflict if these forces are in balance. Actual behavior would be determined by the strength of the forces, as one individual may be more attracted to earning money, whereas another may be more interested in passing the course or may actually enjoy writing the required paper.

The psychological field, or the life space, includes the individual with his biological and psychological dimensions as well as the environment with its social relations and physical objects. Since person and environment are seen as a constellation of interrelated factors, this theory achieves harmony among the many aspects of development by combining biological, sociological, environmental, and psychological factors in the concept life space. Field theory has successfully integrated the biological and sociological factors, which are frequently considered contradictory (for example, the nature-nurture issue). Lewin made explicit his position on this issue in several of his publications: "the social aspect of the psychological situation is at least as important as the physical" (Lewin, 1946: 793); "the psychological influence of environment on the behavior and development of the child is extremely important" (Lewin, 1931: 94); "psychology in general [is regarded] as a field of biology" (Lewin, 1935: 35). "Psychological ecology" is seen as the biological science that deals with the relationship between the organism and its environment or, as Lewin states the issue, "the relation between psychological and non-psychological factors" (Lewin, 1951: 170). Thus he attempts to combine biological, social, and environmental forces into one integrated system, and he accomplishes this with the construct of the life space, which can be readily illustrated as a map of the objects, goals, and valences that are operative on an individual in a specified situation. Lewin's writing was frequently illustrated by numerous drawings that demonstrate the versatility and the explanatory power of the life space.

In infancy, a child's life space is unstructured and undifferentiated; the child depends on outside help and external structuring of the environment by other people. As the child grows older and as the life space increases in structure and differentiation, the child learns to be more and more self-reliant. An individual's space of free movement is limited by "(1) what is forbidden to a person, (2) what is beyond his abilities" (Lewin, 1936: 217). As the child matures, fewer restrictions are placed on his or her freedom to move; in addition, the ability to deal effectively with the increased life space grows. To acquire maximal differentiation of life space, the child must have the freedom to advance into new regions, to explore and include new experiences. Lack of freedom of movement will place restrictions on the child's attempt to expand his or her life space; psychological rigidity of personality may result. Conversely, if the life space, especially in early childhood, remains unstructured, the personality will lack integration and organization. Thus, Lewin not only emphasizes the child's developmental need for independence but also adds the idea of a developmental need for a kind of dependency that provides the child with structure and guidance toward favorable personality development. The importance of the dependency need and the structure in the home contributing to the socialization of the child is a major concern of social learning theory. Research findings reported by Harris (1958) support this idea. Studies were made of the feelings, attitudes, and ideas of adults who, as children, attended the University of Minnesota Nursery School in the late 1920s. Those who had been reared in structured situations were decisive, confident, self-accepting, and achievement-oriented. Those raised in an unstructured home situation were indecisive, distrustful, pessimistic, and perceived success and failure in terms of good or bad luck. Similarly, Bronfenbrenner observed that adolescents from egalitarian, permissive families received lower ratings than those from structured (patricentric or matricentric) families in terms of responsibility and self-reliance.

The space of free movement—that region in the physical and psychological life space that is accessible to an individual—differs from person to person both in scope and nature, thus providing for a conceptualization of different experiences and thereby explaining individual differences (see Figure 7.2). But even more important are the restrictions that limit free movement. Individual differences in forbidden and permitted regions are important in understanding the achievement of independence which is a crucial factor in healthy personality development. As the adolescent's life space increases, many more regions become potentially accessible (see Figure 7.3). But often it is not at all clear to adolescents whether or not they are supposed to enter these regions. Sometimes they enter such a forbidden activity when they are not supposed to and experience conflict; at other times they do not enter a new region when they are supposed to and experience reprimand. The difficulty arises because these regions are no longer "beyond their ability"; because these regions may not be explicitly allowed or explicitly forbidden, they are part of the space of free movement but remain undefined and unclear. If they are forbidden, adolescents realize that these regions are not forbidden for some of their peers, and hope that their own restrictions will soon be lifted. For example, some of their peers may already be allowed to date, to stay out late in the evening, to drive, or even to drink and smoke. Consequently, the definition and redefinition of the space of free movement in the adolescents' life space may take innumerable hours of discussion and argumentation between them and their parents, and may deal with the issue of what behavior is allowed, appropriate or inappropriate, and what is forbidden. This uncertainty of the undefined space of free movement illustrated in Figure 7.3 is the psychological construct by which field theory explains the unpredictability of some adolescent behavior. The undefined regions in Figure 7.3 are "new psychological situations."

Lewin speaks of developmental stages, but his conceptualization of stages is quite different from the stages of Freud, Erikson, Sullivan, and Piaget. Lewin's stages relate to differences in the scope of the life space and the degree of life space differentiation. In accordance with the ecological definition of the life space, these developmental differences are concerned with the psychological environment as well as with the individual, his body, his goals, and his self-perception. According to Lewin, the differences between developmental stages as a function of increasing age manifest themselves in the following ways:

1. An increase in the scope of the life space in regard to
   a. what is part of the psychological present
   b. the time perspective in the direction of the psychological past and the psychological future
   c. the reality-irreality dimension
2. An increasing differentiation of every level of the life space into a multitude of social relations and area of activities
3. An increasing organization
4. A change in the general fluidity or rigidity of the life space [1946: 797–798]

Figure 7.4 illustrates the change in life space as a function of age, comparing the child's (a) life space with that of an adolescent (b). Several important developmental differences become obvious from this comparison. (1) The main difference is the increased differentiation in the life space of the adolescent as compared to the undifferentiated and unstructured area of the child's life space. Both the child and his or her perception of the environment become differentiated and structured in the process of growing older. This holds true in respect to many different aspects of development, such as language skills, social relations, and emo-

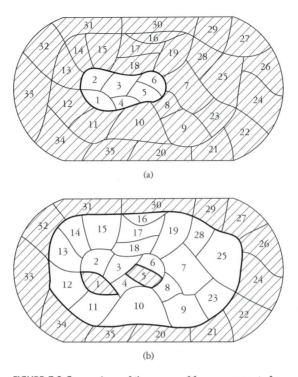

(a)

(b)

FIGURE 7.2 Comparison of the *space of free movement* of child and adult. The actual activity regions are represented. The accessible regions are blank; the inaccessible shaded. (a) The space of free movement of the *child* includes the regions 1-6, representing activities such as getting into the movies at children's rates, belonging to a boy's club, etc. The regions 7-35 are not accessible, representing activities such as driving a car, writing checks for purchases, political activities, performance of adults' occupations, etc. (b) The *adult* space of free movement is considerably wider, although it too is bounded by regions of activities inaccessible to the adult, such as shooting one's enemy or entering activities beyond one's social or intellectual capacity (represented by regions including 29-35). Some of the regions accessible to the child are not accessible to the adult, for instance, getting into the movies at children's rates or doing things socially taboo for an adult which are permitted to the child (represented by regions 1 and 5) (from Kurt Lewin, The Field Theory Approach to Adolescence. *American Journal of Sociology,* 1939, *44,* 868–897. Reproduced by permission from The University of Chicago Press).

tions, as well as the child's cognitive understanding of his or her world. The adolescent knows more people, is familiar with a wider geographic area, and has more and better social, physical, and intellectual skills than the child. Change in the differentiation of the life space occurs slowly at certain times and more rapidly at other times. Slow changes result in relatively harmonious periods of development, whereas rapid changes are more likely to re-

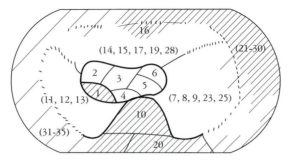

FIGURE 7.3 The *space of free movement* of the *adolescent* as it appears to him. The space of free movement is greatly increased, including many regions which previously have not been accessible to the child, for instance, freedom to smoke, returning home late, driving a car (regions 7-9, 11-13, . . .). Certain regions accessible to the adult are clearly not accessible to the adolescent, such as voting (represented by regions 10 and 16). Certain regions accessible to the child have already become inaccessible, such as getting into the movies at children's rates, or behaving on too childish a level (region 1). The boundaries of these newly acquired portions of the space of free movement are only vaguely determined and in themselves generally are less clearly and sharply differentiated than for an adult. In such cases the life space of the adolescent seems to be full of possibilities and at the same time of uncertainties (from Kurt Lewin, The Field Theory Approach to Adolescence. *American Journal of Sociology,* 1939, *44,* 868–897. Reproduced by permission from The University of Chicago Press).

sult in periods of crisis. Adolescence is characterized by a relatively rapid change in the structure of the life space, and changes occur in several different domains: cognitive, physical, emotional, and interpersonal. The rapidity of the changes in the life space during adolescence may be responsible for the so-called adolescent crisis. (2) The comparison between (a) and (b) in Figure 7.4 makes clear that the time perspective has expanded, since it now includes an awareness of a more distant future and a more distant past. Such change in time perspective is a fundamental aspect of development; it has far-reaching consequences for education, the curriculum, and vocational planning. The adolescent develops the ability to understand the past, adopt a new outlook toward the future, and plan his or her own life more realistically. (3) Since the life span differentiates and the time perspective expands, the reality-irreality level also takes on new dimensions. The reality-irreality dimension is an important concept of Lewin's (1946) theory. "Irreality" refers to fantasies, dreams, wishes, fears, and certain forms of play. Young children are not able to distinguish clearly between reality and phantasy, wishes and facts, hopes and expectations. As they grow older, their understanding of reality enables them to distinguish with increasing accuracy between truth and falsehood, perception and imagination. One characteristic of adolescents is that they have obviously learned to distinguish between reality and irreality.

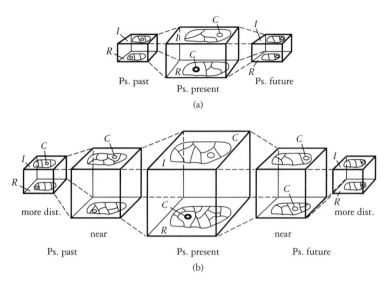

FIGURE 7.4 The life space at two developmental stages. (a) Represents the life space of a younger child. (b) Represents the higher degree of differentiation of the life space of the older child in regard to the present situation, the reality-irreality dimension, and the time perspective. C, child; R, level of reality; I, level of irreality; Ps past, psychological past; Ps present, psychological present; Ps future, psychological future (from Kurt Lewin, Behavior and Development as a Function of the Total Situation. In L. Carmichael (ed.), *Manual of Child Psychology.* © 1946 by John Wiley & Sons, New York. Reproduced with permission).

LEWIN'S THEORY OF ADOLESCENT DEVELOPMENT

Fundamental to Lewin's theory of development is the view that adolescence is a period of transition during which adolescents must change their group membership. While both the child and the adult have a fairly clear concept of how they fit into their group, the adolescent belongs partly to the child group, partly to the adult group, without belonging completely to either group. Parents, teachers, and society reflect this lack of clearly defined group status; and their ambiguous feelings become obvious when they treat the adolescent at one time like a child and at another time like an adult. Difficulties arise because certain childish forms of behavior are no longer acceptable. At the same time some of the adult forms of behavior are not yet permitted either, or if they are permitted, they are new and strange to the adolescent. The adolescent is in a state of "social locomotion," moving through an unstructured social and psychological field. Goals are no longer clear, and the paths to them are ambiguous and full of uncertainties—the adolescent may no longer be certain that they even lead to the desired goals. Such ambiguities and uncertainties are illustrated well by the boy asking or hesitating to ask for his first date. Since the adolescent does not have a clear understanding of his or her social status, expectations, obligations, or how to cope with rejection, his or her behavior reflects this uncertainty.

A life space—as illustrated in Figure 7.1—has different regions that are separated by boundaries with varying degrees of permeability. For example, the adolescent is confronted with several attractive choices that at the same time have relatively impervious boundaries. Driving a car, smoking pot, dropping acid, having sexual relations are all possible goals with potentially positive valence, and thus they become part of the adolescent's life space. However, they are also inaccessible because of parental restriction, legal limitations, or the individual's own internalized moral code. Since the adolescent is moving through a rapidly changing field, he or she does not know the directions to specific goals and is open to constructive guidance, but is also vulnerable to persuasion, seduction, and group pressure. Unfamiliar situations cause crises that can produce withdrawal, sensitivity, and inhibition as well as aggression, inappropriate emotional outbursts, rebellion, and radicalism. Consequently, because of a lack of cognitive structure, the adolescent frequently is not sure whether certain behavior can help in moving toward or away from a particular goal nor what its consequences may be. This concept of "lack of cognitive structure" helps explain some of the uncertainty and unpredictability in adolescent behavior.

The self-image of individuals depends on their bodies. During the normal developmental process body images are so slow that the self-image remains relatively stable. The body image has time to adjust to these developmental changes so that individuals know their own bodies. During adolescence changes in body structure, body experience, and new body sensations and urges are more drastic, so that even the well-known life space of the body image becomes less familiar, unreliable, and unpredictable. Adolescents are preoccupied with the normality of their bodies and how their bodies are perceived by others; they are concerned about and may actually be disturbed by their body image. They spend considerable time studying their image in the mirror and are concerned about the development of primary and secondary sex characteristics in relationship to age-mates. This is understandable; obviously, the body is especially close to and vital to one's feelings of attractiveness, stability, security, and one's gender role. In addition, body appearance is used by peers to evaluate physical strength, physical-sexual maturity, and attractiveness. Negative feelings about one's own body are related to a negative self-concept and may lead to emotional instability that can change one's orientation toward life. Due to these uncertainties, adolescent behavior is characterized by an increased plasticity of personality that can lead to personality changes and even religious conversions.

The change in a child's life space from being limited in scope but relatively structured to the increased but less structured and often unknown regions of the adolescent's life space may generate insecurities; but it includes also more extensive social relationships, a new body image, and expanding geographic surroundings, as well as an increased perception of the future and a better understanding of the past.

Field theory defines adolescence as a period of transition from childhood to adulthood. The possibility of moving from one social group to the other is determined informally by one's physique: looking like an adult makes it easier to get adult privileges. Formally, adult privileges and responsibilities are determined by law and come at legally established ages. This transition is characterized by deeper and far-reaching changes, a faster rate of growth, and differentiation of the life space as compared with the preceding stages of late childhood. The transition is also characterized by the fact that the individual enters a cognitively unstructured region that results in uncertainty of behavior. Transition from childhood to adulthood is a universal phenomenon (see Chapter 18), since children change their social roles and eventually become mature adults in all societies. However, the shift from childhood to adulthood can occur in different patterns. It can take the form of a sudden shift, such as has been observed in primitive societies in which the puberty rites end childhood and signify the beginning of adulthood. Mead reports, for example, that for the Manus girl, puberty "means the beginning of adult life and responsibility" (Mead, 1953: 107). There can also be a gradual shift, especially if the child group and the adult group are not as clearly separated and defined as they are in our society. Thus development would be continuous and the adolescent crisis would be less dramatic. If the transition period is prolonged and if the children as a group are clearly distinguished from adults, as they are in Western societies, ado-

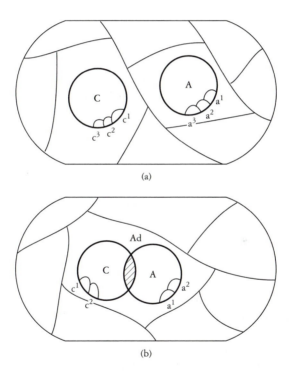

(a)

(b)

FIGURE 7.5 The adolescent as a marginal man. (a) During childhood and adulthood the "adults" (A) and "children" (C) are viewed as relatively separated groups, the individual child (c^1, c^2) and the individual adult (a^1, a^2) being sure of their belonging to their respective groups. (b) The adolescent belonging to a group (Ad) which can be viewed as an overlapping region of the children's (C) and the adults' (A) group belonging to both of them, or as standing between them, not belonging to either one (from Kurt Lewin, The Field Theory Approach to Adolescence. *American Journal of Sociology*, 1939, *44*, 868–897. Reproduced by permission from The University of Chicago Press).

lescents find themselves in a social situation in which their group membership is not clearly defined. The adolescent in such an in-between situation is referred to by Lewin as the "marginal man," and the adolescent's in-between standing is represented in Figure 7.5 by the overlapping area (Ad) of the child region (C) and the adult region (A). The assumption of the marginal-man concept is that the adolescent no longer belongs to the social group of childen and does not want to be considered a child; yet he or she is not yet accepted into the social group of adults, and to the extent that this in-between situation is operative in his or her personal life space, his or her behavior will reflect this marginality. Being a marginal man implies that the adolescent may at times act more like a child, often when he or she wants to avoid adult responsibilities; at other times he or she may act more like an adult and request adult privileges. Parents and teachers, too, may interpret the marginal-man situation in their own way; however, they are more likely to remind the adolescent to be mature, grown-up, and adultlike when the issues involve responsibilities, chores, work, and study. They perceive their charges as "still so young" and "immature" when it comes to adult rights and privileges. Such a situation is most characteristic of youth in Western society, and it is partly responsible for some of Western society's "adolescent difficulties." The marginal man, topographically speaking, stands on the boundaries that separate two groups. "They are people who belong neither here nor there, standing 'between' the groups" (Lewin, 1948: 179). Marginality, even in other social situations, increases social tensions. Minority group members may find themselves in such a situation when they attempt to establish close personal relationships within the majority group—that is, by changing their group belonging. The psychological problems confronting the marginal man are both internal—instability, uncertainty, and self-hate—and external—a constant conflict over group belonging and a lack of role definition, with ostracism by either group possible.

From these basic assumptions about the nature of human development, Lewin (1939) derives a number of statements that describe, explain, and if the field forces are known, predict adolescent behavior:

1. Adolescents may show shyness and sensitivity but at the same time aggressiveness, mainly because of the unclearness of the situation and the disequilibrium in their life span.

2. As a marginal man, the adolescent experiences a continuous conflict among different attitudes, values, ideologies, and life-styles, since he or she is shifting his or her orientation from the childhood group to the adult group, but he or she really does not belong to either. Therefore, he or she experiences lack of social anchorage except in relationship to his or her peer group.

3. These conflicts in values, attitudes, and ideologies result in increased emotional tension.

4. There is a predisposition in the adolescent to take extreme positions and to change behavior drastically; consequently, one can find radical, rebellious attitudes and actions side by side with sensitivity and withdrawal tendencies.

5. "Adolescent behavior" can be observed only if and to the extent that the structure and the dynamics of the life involve the following: (1) expansion and differentiation of the life space; (2) marginal-man standing in relationship to childhood and adult groups; and (3) biologically determined changes in the life space, as a

result of body changes. The particular type of behavior that emerges and the degree of "adolescent behavior" depend greatly on the strength and nature of these conflicting forces. Above all in importance is the amount of difference between—and the factors that separate—adult society and child society in a particular culture.

The question of universality of the adolescent phenomenon is one of statistical frequency. Lewinian field theory (1935) considers this question irrelevant as well as the question of whether heredity or environment is the greater influence on development. Both nature and nurture can be depicted in the life space of an individual, and one can be more important than the other for a particular goal or a particular behavior.

What is . . . important to the investigation of dynamics is not to abstract from the situation, but to hunt out those situations in which determinative factors of the total dynamic structure are most clearly, distinctly, and purely to be discerned. Instead of a reference to the abstract average of as many historically given cases as possible, there is a reference to the full concreteness of the particular situations [Lewin, 1935: 31].

The dynamic aspect of adolescent behavior and the individual situation, not the statistical frequency of one event or another, is the concern of field theory.

According to Lewin, specific characteristics of individuals cannot be classified in categories of overt behavior. Field theory moves away from an Aristotelian system of classification that dominated scientific endeavors of the past. Lewin follows the Galilean field-theoretical notion that emphasized process and that assumes individual variations that defy easy categorization. Field theory sees as its objective the systematic explanation of these differences. Sensitivity to environmental influences varies greatly among people. The speed with which the differentiation and structurization of the life space take place also varies considerably in different people. Therefore, we must expect great individual variations in behavior. Furthermore, since sensitivity as well as rate of change in the life space increases during the adolescent period, we must expect that behavior changes also will differ widely and probably be more noticeable than at other times.

Moreover, field theory assumes not only individual differences, but cultural differences as well. Thus, while the life span varies from individual to individual within a given culture, the differences from culture to culture are even greater. Two aspects that will be relatively stable within a given culture but quite different from culture to culture are: (1) the ideologies, attitudes, and values that are recognized and emphasized and (2) the way in which different activities are seen as related or unrelated; for example, religion and work are more closely related in Mennonite society than in American society as a whole (Lewin, 1942).

Another factor that may account for cultural differences in adolescent behavior is the varying length of the adolescent period from culture to culture and from social class to social class within a culture. Increased demand for education results in prolonged dependency and thereby increases the length of adolescence. Furthermore, the degree to which the child group and the adult group are differentiated in a given culture has far-reaching consequences for adolescent behavior. The more clearly the groups are separated, the more difficult the transition.

EDUCATIONAL IMPLICATIONS

Adolescents and their problems are related to the change in group belonging. They no longer belong to the child group and are no longer considered children. Nor do they yet belong to the adult groups and receive their privileges, even though some adult activities may have a positive valence for them. Thus, adolescents are in a stage of social locomotion; they are transferring from one group to another but do not belong to either one. The term "marginal man" implies that adolescents are "social outcasts," to use a somewhat extreme term. This condition necessarily makes them more dependent on their own age group for support, inspiration, fellowship, and idols than either children or adults are dependent on their age groups. These insights gained through field theory may be used as psychological arguments in favor of the junior high school, since this is the age group in which the accelerated change in body maturity and the shift in group belonging are most obvious. Counterarguments concerning the negative psychological effects of junior high school are advanced by Mead and were presented in the previous chapter.

An important factor in adolescent development is the enlargement, differentiation, and conceptualization of the time perspective. The young child lives mainly in the present; the past and the future include only a few days or weeks and have relatively little impact on long-range vocational and personal planning. As a child grows older, and especially during the adolescent period, he or she develops a time concept that makes the past significant; historical occurrences can now be understood in their chronological sequence. Lewin's concept of the enlargement of the time perspective during adolescence coincides with the teaching of history at the onset of adolescence and has been supported by research studies. But the time concept expands not only into the past but also into the future, which now becomes meaningful for the individual, who begins to form a life plan and set goals. The adolescent has to make choices in training and preparing for a vocation. This bespeaks the necessity for vocational guidance.

Adolescence is a period in which reality and irreality should be clearly distinguished, even though irreality will not necessarily disappear completely from the thought of the adolescent. It is important for the educator to emphasize the understanding of reality and to confront the adolescent with facts when thoughts and ideas appear to be fabrications based on fantasy or irreality.

Adolescents' social awareness of group belonging undergoes great change, as do their bodies and body images. The child "knew" his body or showed little interest in it, but sexual maturity disturbs the adolescent, and the new bodily dimensions, qualities, and functions are sometimes threatening. Thus, a very close and vital part of life space, one's own body, becomes foreign and produces tension. Since body image is a fundamental region in the life space, this change can lead to confusion, conflict, and uncertainty of behavior. Preoccupation with one's body and body image disturbances in their extreme manifestations take pathological forms, such as anorexia nervosa and bulimia (Muuss, 1990), which usually begin during adolescence. Education probably will not be able to overcome all the difficulties related to body change, but it can at least prepare the adolescent boy or girl for these changes by helping them understand human growth and by giving them knowledge of the great normal variations in physical development.

The infant and child have much of their life space structured by their parents and other adults. But as they grow older, the restrictions and limitations should be removed slowly so that young adults are allowed to structure their own world. From an educational point of view, this means that the adolescent should be encouraged to develop independence and responsibility and learn to make choices, set personal goals, and explore methods to attain these goals.

Field theory presents the total situation, with all the aspects that make up the child's life space. If teaching is to be successful and produce the maximum amount of learning, the activities involved should have a positive valence for the student. Field theory holds that success in teaching depends on all of those conditions of learning that have been singled out by one or another educational theory—the social atmosphere, the amount of security, the interest and meaningfulness of the material, its psychological appropriateness for the developmental level of the learner, and the atmosphere in which the material is taught.

Lewin suggested, as do other phenomenological-oriented psychologists, that what is more important psychologically speaking is the subject's perception of an event rather than the objective reality. This implies that a teacher must make a genuine effort to understand the student's perception of the situation—that is, to try to empathize with the adolescent's point of view. An illustration is the not uncommon observation that two students perform about the same on an examination and both receive a B grade. However, their psychological experience of success or failure is not so much dependent on the objective reality of their performance, but on their expectation. The student who expected an A is disappointed and perhaps even angry. The student who feared a C or worse is encouraged and feels elated. Understanding behavior is only possible through a reconstruction and understanding of the perceptual field of the behavior. Facts acquired in this way may be quite different from those obtained by an objective approach. Psychoanalysis, clinical psychology, Gestalt psychology, and field theory have applied this method within its natural limitations. The phenomenological point of view means that, within the obvious limits of this approach, the educator and the counselor would attempt to see and understand the world of the adolescent from the adolescent's perspective.

C H A P T E R

8

JEAN PIAGET'S COGNITIVE THEORY OF ADOLESCENCE

AN INTRODUCTION TO PIAGET AND HIS DEVELOPMENT

Jean Piaget's (1896–1980) contribution to our understanding of human development is reflected in the continuing attention that developmental psychologists have devoted to his theory. Stimulated by Piaget's theory, alternative theoretical approaches for cognitive development which have moved beyond his original contributions have proliferated since the 1970s. In his earlier work, he emphasized cognitive development in infancy and childhood. During his middle research period, systematic attention was devoted to the more advanced levels of cognitive reasoning characteristic of adolescence. His theory of adolescence and much of the follow-up research it has generated is based on the formal operations tasks described in the book, *The Growth of Logical Thinking from Childhood to Adolescence* (Inhelder & Piaget, 1958). Although Piaget and some of his followers have moved beyond that approach, this volume remains the standard work for understanding the formal reasoning of adolescence as seen by Piaget.

Characterized as a "zoologist by training, an epistemologist by vocation, and a logician by method," Piaget is best known for his contributions to developmental psychology. He regarded himself as an interdisciplinary thinker; perhaps the identification "genetic epistemologist" best describes his orientation. Epistemology is the branch of science concerned with the methods, limits, and validity of knowledge. The term *genetic* is used in the sense of genesis or development; indeed, Piaget did not study the genes of his subjects, and the idea of genetic influences on the acquisition of knowledge applies only in a very broad sense. In regard to the nature-nurture controversy, Piaget was neither a maturationalist nor an environmentalist, but is better characterized as an "interactionist" or "constructionist." He emphasized that development is an interaction between individual and environment and the resulting mental structures are constructed by the child as a result of this interaction. Piaget (1953: 16) shares with Vygotsky the notion that "The organism and the environment form an indissoluble entity" and that the "two [are] inseparable from each other." In addition, Piaget added the new and, at that time, innovative idea that children themselves actively participate in the construction of their knowledge. Thus, he has developed a constructionist explanation for the development of knowledge: Knowledge is neither innate nor learned, but is constructed from experiences.

After completing his dissertation, Piaget worked in Paris on the standardization of intelligence tests. Even though he showed little interest in the psychometric procedures essential for test construction, he became fascinated with the underlying reasoning that children revealed while trying to solve test problems. He found their explanations of incorrect responses particularly revealing. According to Piaget, to understand intelligence, one must examine two factors: (1) One must explore how a person acts upon the environment, that is, how a child answers the test question or solves the problem. This has been the approach of the traditional test makers. (2) One must also ask why a child acts the way he or she does or why a person gives a particular response to a problem or a test question. This second approach, investigating the underlying cognitive structure to discover why a person acts or responds as he or she does, is the essential focus that sets Piaget apart from much of the traditional psychology of his time. This emphasis on the cognitive thought structures that underly overt responses has occupied much of Piaget's research, and the qualitative changes in cognitive structure later became the defining criteria for his developmental stages. This distinction between overt performance (function) and internal structure is crucial for understanding his theory. The conventional test that requires specific answers is assessing the child's declarative knowledge. Piaget's questioning of students' answers, in contrast, delves deeper because he challenges his subjects to explain their answers. Thus, subjects lay bare their underlying thinking to reveal their cognitive structures which control their understanding and, by extension, their answers. Piaget assumed that similar thinking process applied to or generalized to a variety of problems at the same level of difficulty, a principle that has been referred to as "inter-task generality," or as the "unity hypothesis of cognitive development."

The developers of Piaget-type assessment tools still maintain that standardized test questions lead to stereotyped responses, none of which will disclose the underlying thinking processes. Piagetians, instead, gather data through a "clinical method" that assesses thought processes rather than declarative knowledge by requiring children to explain the reasons behind their answers. Psychologists (Pinard & Laurendeau 1964; Furth & Wachs 1975; Patterson & Milakofsky 1980; and Copeland 1988) have developed Piaget-type cognitive assessment batteries, which emphasize not the correct answer, but focus on the reasons that children give to explain their answers, whether correct or incorrect. Because this type of assessment often takes the form of an interview, it requires much more time to administer and to evaluate than a standard information-based test. Piaget's preoccupation with qualitative, structural changes in children's thought processes is obvious in much of his work: "Much of Piaget's research was a logical and philosophical exploration of how knowledge structures might develop . . ." (Sternberg & Powell, 1983: 364).

Among contemporary schools of psychology, Piaget takes a relatively unique and independent position. Apparently, he never took a course in developmental or general psychology. Nevertheless, the contributions of a number of scholars influenced his thinking, especially Kant's epistemology and Bergson's metaphysics. Piaget translated Kant's

Jean Piaget (1896-1980)

epistemological question, "How is knowledge possible?" into a developmental query that pervaded his life work: "How is knowledge constructed and transformed in ontogenesis?" (Beilin, 1992: xi). Furthermore, the question of how children change in their comprehension of such phenomena of the world as time, space, speed, causality, and quantity dominated his inquiries. From this, he developed the corollary that knowledge is always a process, never a static fact.

Though Piaget read Freud, he did not share the psychoanalyst's interest in the unconscious, in conflicts, or in the affective aspects of development. He focused on the conflict-free, rational side of development and he emphasized thought processes, the structure of intelligence, and the development of logical thinking. Nevertheless, his concept of "egocentrism," which characterizes the language, thought, and social judgment of developing children, is quite compatible with some psychoanalytic notions, such as subject-object differentiation. Piaget also stimulated the ongoing concern with moral judgment and social cognition.

The development of Piaget's theory can be divided into four broad but distinguishable periods (Montangero, 1985). The first period encompasses the works published between 1923 and 1932 and focuses on a "social explanation" of knowledge. During this time, he studied the influence of the social and physical world on the child's responses. For example, young children, through repeated experiences, eventually learn that crying will bring one of their parents even though originally they cried without knowing that this behavior would result in their parents' coming.

During his second period, including most of the works produced during the 1930s, Piaget began to move toward "a theory of adaptation" (Beilin, 1992). His research focus shifted from the social environment and the responses it elicited to the internal processes of adaptation that determine the child's reactions. He noted that adaptation allows the child to survive and also provides a mechanism for cognitive development. Intelligence is described as adaptation to the environment.

Piaget's third period covers his work from the 1940s until the 1960s. Here, his interest turned to structural analysis to explain knowledge. He emphasized logico-mathematical structures as the foundation of cognitive development. During this period, Piaget concentrated on the differences between the child's and the adolescent's cognitive development. For example, confronted with a glass tank of water and numerous objects of various density, shape, size, color, and weight, the subject is to explain why some objects float and some sink. Elementary school children may be quick in classifying the objects into those that float and those that sink. However, they may have some real difficulties in explaining why some small objects sink while some larger, apparently heavier objects, float. Only adolescents can explain the phenomenon, since they have more advanced and complex logico-mathematical cognitive structures to perform formal operations, which involve the kind of abstract, hypothetico-deductive thinking required in logic and mathematics.

The final period extends from the 1960s until Piaget's death in 1980. During this period he produces his least known contributions, which constitute "a radical departure from the earlier theory" (Beilin, 1989). Piaget gradually came to see the functions he studied in his earlier period and the structure he studied in his middle period as equally important contributions to cognitive development. He has always shown interest in both functions and structures even though one or the other might have received relatively more emphasis at various points in his life. Piaget's final vision revealed a balance between functions and structures (Beilin, 1992).

Because Piaget's unique methodology as well as his theoretical conceptualizations seemed suspect from a positivist's point of view, they were very slow to be absorbed into mainstream psychology. However, he was remarkably successful in his use of naturalistic, ecologically valid observations of children. His research method, which has a subjective element, was based on "clinical interviews" in which each question is guided by the subject's answer to the previous question. The "clinical method" requires a semester of graduate training and is more like a psychiatric interview than the more objective research method of the American experimental psychologist, and hence, has remained a source of criticism.

As his method and theory became better known in the late fifties and sixties, they exerted considerable influence on developmental psychologists all over the world; nevertheless, they have remained controversial. Actually, Piaget revolutionized the English-speaking world's understanding of children's acquisition of knowledge. While his theory has been exposed to a continuous barrage of criticism and seems to have lost some of its earlier popularity, there is no imminent danger that his thinking will easily be superseded. Complex and multifaceted, his ideas cannot easily be evaluated by controlled empirical investigations; however they have tended to polarize cognitive psychologists into the Neo-Piagetians and their critics. Like Darwin and Freud before him, Piaget's influence—partly in terms of stimulating new theories such as Kohlberg's, Elkind's, Selman's, Fowler's, and others', partly in terms of stimulating challenging or opposing propositions—will remain an intellectual, philosophical, and theoretical force to reckon with during much of the twenty-first century.

THE DEVELOPMENTAL CONCEPTS OF PIAGET'S EARLY THEORY

■ Piaget's Stage-Independent Theory of Development

Piaget advanced a system of interrelated concepts borrowed primarily from biology that comprise his stage-independent theory of development. The stage-independent theory focuses on small advances in development. These advances occur continuously, and are seldom noticed; nevertheless, they accumulate and contribute to development. Thus, his view of development encompasses both the notion of continuity as identified in his stage-independent theory as well as the idea of qualitative changes in cognitive structure as expressed through his stage-dependent theory. Piaget focused on adaptation because adaptations occur constantly through each of the developmental stages. Important constructs characterized as adaptation include: schema, structure, operation, assimilation, accommodation, equilibrium, and disequilibrium. These adaptive processes cut across all levels of the stage-independent theory, and apply to early sensorimotor development as they do to the advanced logical thought processes of the mature adult. They explain the minute progressions in the developmental process rather than the major qualitative advances that define each of the stages.

Schemata and Structures

The first two concepts of the stage-independent theory are *schema(ta)* and *structure*. A schema is a generalized or established pattern of meaningful and repeatable behavior patterns, such as the sucking schema, the grasping schema, and later in adolescent thinking, the "all-other-things-being-equal" schema. As children interact with their environment, their simple, early schemata become broadened and modified and/or combined with other schemata. Schemata, therefore, are not static, but are continuously growing. Appropriately, they are referred to as "mobile schemata." According to Martorano (1977: 666) schemata are defined by the following characteristics: "(a) They are general concepts or psychological abilities which can be applied to many content areas, (b) They are derived from the underlying cognitive structure rather than from objects in the environment." When referring to the thought processes of adolescence, a third characteristic needs to be added: "(c) They all show some logical relationship to the combinatorial system and the INRC group" (to be discussed later).

When referring to the thought processes of adolescents, Piaget uses such terms as *cognitive schema, operational schema, anticipatory schema.* In "formal operations schemata," the schemata reflect the underlying structure of logic. Schemata and structure become nearly synonymous, except that schemata refer to the behavioral equivalent, and structure refers to the corresponding internal problem-solving strategies. The structures are the organizational properties of thought that determine the nature of the child's actions, especially the more complex cognitive responses. Throughout his life, Piaget has been preoccupied with the basic cognitive structures of thinking that reveal the child's conceptual development. His major research interests focused on the Kantian categories of knowledge and became book titles: physical causality (1930), numbers (1952), space (with Inhelder, 1967), geometry, movement, and speed, as well as the child's level of moral judgment (1932b), language development (1932a), and the child's conception of the world (1929). "It is possible to discern synchronized structures of operational development manifesting themselves in such diversified fields as logic, space, time, etc." (Inhelder, 1966: 304). Thus, the theory focuses on the expanding changes of intellectual structure from birth to maturity. The integration of simpler, less mature structures into new, more advanced structures provides the continuity for cognitive development (Flavell, 1963b) and are reflected in such diverse topics as: intelligence, memory, perception, mental imagery, play, dreams, and imitation.

Piaget has always been interested in how the acquisition of knowledge is possible and what the guiding principles are for the progression from one level of knowledge to the next higher level. Individuals create the epistemic structures (from the Greek word *episteme,* meaning *knowledge*) as a consequence of their interaction with others and with environmental experiences. From these experiences, the individual constructs increasingly more sophisticated knowledge structures; this construction follows a sequential developmental progression. The individaul uses the base of earlier experiences to actively participate in constructing more complicated ways of knowing. For example, infants at birth have virtually no knowledge structures. They may know only sensory qualities or objects. As individuals develop, they manipulate objects, these behaviors are repeated, become habitual or automatic, and thus become schemata. After many repetitions of such actions, individuals make an abstraction about what will happen if they perform such behavior again. An illustration of such an abstraction is children's realization that a toy will be outside of their crib if they throw it out. Such experiences become more sophisticated and produce increasingly more complex epistemic structures (Kitchener, 1986).

Kitchener (1986: 184) argues that Piaget's genetic epistemology is "firmly committed to a biological epistemology" because all living organisms must adapt to their environments at least somewhat, or they cannot survive. In adapting to the environment, the organism must "accommodate itself to change and modify itself, including its cognitive structure."

Virtually all commentators on Piaget's theory agree that, for him, the essential components responsible for cognitive development are:

1. the maturation of the nervous system, a biological component,
2. experiences gained through interaction with physical reality,

3. the influence of the social environment, and
4. the child's active participation in adapting to environmental experiences and in constructing his or her knowledge out of these experiences (Sutherland, 1992).

The Equilibration Process

The maturation process of development constitutes only a general background for Piaget's disequilibrium equilibrium model; the dynamic interaction between the developing child and his or her physical and social environment receives major emphasis. Social factors may not have received the systematic treatment as many other elements of the theory; nevertheless, even logical development is an adaptation to social as well as other factors: "Social life is a necessary condition for the development of logic. We thus believe that social life transforms the individual's very nature" (Piaget, 1977: 239). Cognitive adaptation and intellectual growth are based on a continuous interaction between experiences (social experiences included), internal maturation, and the child's active participation in his or her responses to these environmental conditions. For Piaget, growth in knowledge is not a function of innate tendencies, nor the simple result of environmental experiences or reinforcements. "The organism and the environment form an indissoluble entity, that is to say . . . there are adaptational variations simultaneously involving a structuring of the organism and an action of the environment, the two being inseparable from each other" (Piaget, 1953: 16).

To intellectually assimilate "reality is to construe that reality, and to construe it in terms" of one's existing cognitive structure (Flavell, 1963a: 48). Piaget and his followers have built a database for a constructionist epistemology, that is, a constructionist theory of the development of knowledge. Knowledge is not just a replication or a memory of reality, such as making a mental copy or an image. For Piaget, to acquire knowledge means to act on, to modify, to transform the new information. It is this process of transformation which requires a constructionist approach that leads to genuine understanding. Thus, it is an interiorized action—an operation—which is the essence of the process of acquiring knowledge. In order to accommodate and to reestablish an equilibrium, children must actively reconstruct assimilated experiences and events. That is, they have to make them part of their cognitive structure. Piaget came to recognize this process from assimilation and disequilibrium through accommodation and a new equilibrium as cognitive adaptation. Disequilibria can be viewed as "the principal 'motor' of developmental changes" (Beilin, 1989: 111). This equilibration process is defined as "leading from certain states of equilibration to others, qualitatively different, and passing through multiple 'nonbalances' [disequilibration] and reequilibrations" (Piaget, 1972: 1).

The discrepancy between assimilation and accommodation should never be too great because only moderately discrepant events, experiences, and ideas can easily be accommodated. For example, in school, an assignment may not be understood, that is, assimilated, if it is too difficult because the student's skills and background knowledge are inadequate so that no accommodation can take place. Good teaching implies that the gap between assimilation and accommodation should neither be too large nor too small. Cognitive growth will occur only if assignments are appropriately challenging for the learner. Or, to state the problem differently, only when the organism is ready for a learning experience can it benefit from that experience.

Piaget borrowed the "assimilation-accommodation" concept from biology, and biology provides an appropriate analogy: The organism assimilates food by chewing, swallowing, and breaking down. In this process, food is restructured to fit the biological needs of the organism. However, in the process, the organism also changes. The organism accommodates food by incorporating (digesting) it into its own structure. As a result, the organism itself is restructured; it has more energy, and it grows. Assimilation and accommodation are complementary processes. They bring about conceptual adaptation and cognitive growth through their continuous interaction. It is through these processes of assimilation and accommodation that the intellectual structure expands. Balance between assimilation and accommodation produces a state of equilibrium.

The concept of equilibrium is essential in Piaget's (1962b: 120) definition of intelligence as a "form of equilibration . . . toward which all functions lead." Piaget (1985) maintained in *The Equilibration of Cognitive Structures* that knowledge does not come from empirical experiences with objects only, nor does it come from any *a priori* program inherent in the individual. Rather, it comes from a sequence, a progression of cognitive structures that, in turn, generate additional new structures. Indeed, Piaget came to see the striving for equilibration or balance as "the moving force behind all cognitive development" (Lerner, 1986: 248). The progression from one disequilibrium to a higher order equilibrium generates development and is referred to by Piaget as "the equilibration process." Equilibration is defined as an internal compensation for an external disturbance. There must be an equilibrium between the influences of the environment on the individual and the way the individual adapts and changes in the constant influx of new information and experiences that the environment engenders. Thus, knowledge is both behavioral and cognitive adaptation. "To know an object or a happening is to make use of it by assimilation into an action schemata" (Piaget, 1971: 6).

Equilibrium is the harmony between sensory information and accumulated knowledge, or harmony between the individual and the environment. As new sensory information—in the form of questions, assignments, and problems—disturbs existing or incomplete knowledge, the equilibrium is thrown into a new disequilibrium. A new assimilation-accommodation process begins. As these questions or problems are taken into the existing structure (assimilation) and the existing structure grows, changes, and expands in the process (accommodation), a new higher-level equilibrium is attained. The accommodation of new experiences produces modifications in the structure and the schema, a process which means that children gain thinking tools and reasoning ability that allow them to make more sophisticated observations, to solve more difficult problems, or to advance to higher-level generalizations. Thus, the theory allows for continuous progressive cognitive development. Oliver Wendell Holmes captured the essence of the assimilation-accommodation process: "Man's mind stretched to a new idea never goes back to its original dimensions." Assimilating and accommodating environmental experiences lead slowly but steadily to cognitive growth. Piaget views children as active participants in their own development. He expresses this concept well in his often quoted statemet: "Every time we teach a child something, we keep him from reinventing it. On the other hand, every time a child discovers it for himself, it remains with him for the rest of his life."

Intelligence comes into play (as opposed to instinct and habit) only when intentionality is involved. Intelligence requires intentional recombinations of behavioral or cognitive methods used to reach a goal, and the advance from a strictly sensory-motor approach to preoperational reasoning at about the age of 2 makes intentional recombinations possible, such as using a stick to get an out-of-reach object. Piaget (1985) regarded mental operations as self-regulatory thinking mechanisms because the individual who can anticipate events can correct mistakes even before he or she makes them in reality. The thinking individual can conceptualize various actions and foresee their potential consequences without actually doing anything. So, those conceptualized behaviors that produce unfavorable consequences in anticipated thought never find expression in performed actions.

Operations

According to Piaget, when schemata and structures have developed to the extent that they can be used by interrelated systems of logic, they are called *operations.* Operations are interiorized actions that one performs in one's mind. Operations allow the subject to mentally perform actions that previously had to be performed physically. As operations mature, they increasingly approximate the rules of logic and reflect the underlying organizational structure of the mind. Piaget defines an operation as a reversible action or a reversible transformation of one structure into another. Consequently, operations are more complex and more differentiated than schemata. Operations can be applied to a much wider spectrum of problems than schemata. For example, memorized formulas that a student applies to a series of identical problems correspond to schemata. However, when students are able to solve dissimilar problems in a different context or to use different symbols, or when they can understand the relationship of each piece of information to the whole problem, they demonstrate operational thinking. In operational thought, the reliance on the memorized formula becomes unnecessary because the meaning of the problem is understood. To the extent that operations have become meaningful parts of the cognitive structure, students show resistance to forgetting them and can apply them to a variety of different problems. Operational thought has two characteristics:

1. Operational thought is reversible. Logical operations can be reversed by canceling an operation. The operational child understands that subtraction can cancel the process of addition just as division can cancel multiplication. The addition $6 + 7 = 13$ can be canceled by its reversal, $13 - 7 = 6$. One can reverse an operation by reciprocity and return to the starting point. The same water that was poured from the low, wide glass into the high narrow glass can be poured back into the low, wide glass. That is, the process can be reversed without a change in the quantity of water.

2. Operational thought is associative. Thought is not limited to only one avenue, but has the flexibility and the freedom to pursue a problem by way of different routes or detours and/or by way of a variety of methods and approaches. For example, the problem 25×25 can be solved in a number of ways: $(25 \times 20) + (25 \times 5)$; or $20(2) + (2 \times 20 \times 5) + 5(2)$; or 25×100 divided by 4; and so on.

The distinction between operational and preoperational thought constitutes the most fundamental dividing line in Piaget's stage-dependent theory. Piaget speaks of the child prior to this age as the *preoperational child,* who relies predominantly on perception and in-

DENNIS THE MENACE

"MAKE UP YOUR MIND. FIRST YOU TELL ME 3 PLUS 3
IS SIX, AND NOW YOU SAY 4 PLUS 2 IS SIX!"

Dennis the Menace® used by permission of Hank Ketchum and
© by North American Syndicate.

tuition. After the age of about 7, the child enters the *operational stage of development* and begins to use systems of operations which are conceptualized as internalized actions that constitute a system of organized and related thoughts. Operational thoughts correspond to the operations of mathematics and logic. In the comic Margaret understands the associative nature of problem solving; Dennis does not, since he still thinks preoperationally.

The distinction between the operational thought of the child and the formal operations of adolescence is that the former can deal with problems that are presented concretely, while the latter can deal with abstract ideas and use more involved logical processes. Scholars seem to have underrated "the essence and sophistication of formal operations" (Gray, 1990: 247). Inhelder and Piaget (1958) identified the four major components of formal operations:

1. conceptions of possibilities
2. hypothetical deductive reasoning
3. interpropositional thinking
4. combinatorial or systemic thinking

Each is important and each describes formal operational adaptation, but the ability to think of possibilities without implementing these possibilities in actual behavior is an ability that emerges during adolescence. As Gray (1990: 248) elucidates, "by their very nature, formal operational adaptations must require a considerable amount of energy, effort and possible knowledge" because they are internal adaptations to possibilities, not just relations or properties of the physical or social environment. Gray argues that individuals will not automatically develop formal operational procedural competency if less complex and less vigorous adaptations will work. Unless biological/psychological survival or social/educational demands within an environment propel individuals to develop formal operational capabilities, they may not progress. Many adolescents and adults, in fact, do not encounter a sufficient number of circumstances that require formal operational competency. Therefore, they will not automatically progress to formal operational thinking, but will remain at less mature levels: "They will necessarily adapt in the most appropriate way: concrete operational, preoperational or sensorimotor" (Gray, 1990: 248).

■ The Concept of "Stages" in Piaget's Theory

The concept of "stages of development" permeates many of the theories discussed in this book. Furthermore, the concept of stages in general, as well as Piaget's use of stage theory, has been criticized and frequently challenged, especially by theorists from other schools of thought, such as Bandura's social cognitive theory and Lerner's contextualism.

For Piaget, developmental stages simply mean that a sequential progression in the cognitive structures, which underly problem-solving operations, takes place. Thus, stages emerge in an orderly, invariant sequential pattern, and no stage can be skipped. Stages cannot be advanced by designing experiences; they are characterized by a "whole structure" rather than by a dominant feature as is characteristic of Freud's and Erikson's stages (Beilin, 1989). The earlier stages provide essential building material that the individual integrates and transforms in the process of moving to the next higher level. Significant is that the problem-solving skills that characterize a given stage are qualitatively distinguishable from those found in stages that precede as well as those that succeed it, e.g., elementary school children can solve the same problem when presented in concrete terms that high school students can solve when presented abstractly. And it is this qualitative change that elevates Piaget's theory from simply a description of age-related changes in reasoning to a stage theory: "Each stage is characterized by an overall structure in terms of which the main behavior patterns can be explained" (Piaget & Inhelder, 1969: 153). For example, adolescents deal with learning tasks and with their world in substantially different, more abstract, ways than elementary school children because their cognitive structure is different. The appeal of Piaget's stages is that they identify a comprehensive system of different features in the developmental progression of reasoning ability. Furthermore, the developmental progression identified by Piaget is characteristic of most individuals found in a broadly defined age range. The idea of a "stage" does not negate the well-known fact of the existence of intraindividual, interindividual, and intercultural differences; however, it does mean that a given stage-defining operation follows the same sequence in all individuals. There is an assumption that a phase-specific equilibrium must be reached before the individual can advance to the next higher stage. In other words, each higher level stage integrates and builds upon the accomplishments and the underlying structure of the preceding stage. This process can be gradual; it does not have to be abrupt, nor must it introduce a major discontinuity, as some critics (Linn, 1982; Sutherland, 1992) claim that any stage theory implies. Piaget's stage theory implies only that the schemata and the operational processes at the next higher stage have become qualitatively different from those of the previous stage. The stage progression is not simply biologically determined but depends on the joint interactive effect of both environmental experience and also endogenous and maturational factors. Furthermore, the speed with which an individual progresses through these stages depends upon intellectual ability, educational experiences, cultural and social context, as well as other factors. However, the sequential progression through the stages itself is not a function of these factors, but is invariant. Children who possess low intelligence, come from preindustrial cultures or from dysfunctional families, or have limited educational experiences may progress at a slower rate and may not reach the final stages. The age levels suggested for these stages are not norms, but allow for considerable variations, and therefore, should be treated as approximations. Nevertheless, the proportion of adolescents who can perform successfully on the Piagetian-like tasks that define formal operations increases as a function of age (Eckstein & Shemesh, 1992). Linn's (1982) critique, that "Stages in reasoning as defined by [Piaget's] theory do not emerge crisply," is certainly correct, but there never was an assumption that stages ought to emerge "crisply." Piaget himself places less emphasis on the stages than his critics imply: "psychologists have relied too much on the notion of stage" (Piaget, 1971: 17), and especially in his later years, he downplayed—although he never gave up—the notion of stages. Finally, it must be emphasized that Piaget's stage-independent theory implies continuity of development, so that he cannot easily be considered as just another stage theorist who emphasizes discontinuity.

PIAGET'S STAGE-DEPENDENT THEORY OF DEVELOPMENT

The landmarks of Piaget's stage-dependent theory, based on major qualitative advances in cognitive structure, are: sensorimotor, preoperational, concrete operational, and formal operational stages. Originally, the theory focused on infancy and childhood but was later expanded to include adolescence. Some of Piaget's followers (Arlin, 1975; Richards & Commons, 1984) have even proposed a more advanced, but relatively rare, adult stage of reasoning. The interrelationship of the various facets of Piaget's theory requires a brief presentation of characteristics of the earlier stages. The adolescent period, characterized by formal operational thought, will be described in more detail and become the primary focus of this chapter. The stage-dependent theory has to be understood in light of the continuing disequilibrium-assimilation-accommodation-equilibrium process which provides the conceptual model for continuity in development. The stage-dependent theory is the core of Piaget's initial systematic theory of development, and is by far the most widely known and most often discussed part of his theory; nevertheless, it has come under critical reconstructionist attack.

■ The Sensorimotor Stage

The *sensorimotor stage of development* (from birth to age 2) is subdivided into six developmental phases. The first phase (birth to 1 month), the *reflex phase,* consists primarily of exercising inborn reflexes such as the sucking reflex, which, as it becomes modified to meet the demands of different situations, becomes the sucking schema. During the second phase (1 to 4 months), which Piaget calls the phase of *primary circular reactions,* reflexes are slowly replaced by voluntary movements. Children may tirelessly practice an emerging schema, such as grasping, since they are motivated by "function pleasure"—a concept quite different from the behavioristic notion of "drive reduction" or "reinforcement." In the third phase (4 to 8 months), that of *secondary circular reactions,* infants begin to pursue objects and events unrelated to themselves—for example, following slow movements of an attractive toy. Or, if an infant learns through trial and error to grasp a cord and make a bell jingle, he or she may repeat such behavior. That such an action can be repeated is evidence of the beginning of intentionality and even an incipient form of goal-directed behavior. The fourth phase (8 to 12 months), that of *coordination of secondary schemata,* is characterized by the emergence of an understanding of means-ends relationships. The child reaches for a box in order to obtain the toy that is inside. When the child begins to search for a toy hidden under a blanket, the concept of "object permanence" is beginning to emerge. During the fifth phase (12 to 18 months), *tertiary circular reactions,* the concept of "object permanence" becomes more stable. The child will search for and find the object even though in the process of hiding it, it may have been moved through a series of displacements. The last of the six phases (18 to 24 months) is that of *internalization of sensorimotor schemata.* The child begins to use foresight and symbolic representation in solving sensorimotor problems. For the first time, the child may investigate whether a hole is big enough before attempting to push an object through it, thus giving evidence that the strictly sensorimotor approach to problem solving is being replaced by thought. The progression from the primarily sensorimotor approach to life to the beginning use of thought is the qualitative difference between this and the preoperational stage.

■ The Preoperational Stage

The second period of development (2 to 7 years), called the *preoperational stage,* is a transition period from the predominantly egocentric and sensorimotor stage of early childhood to rudimentary forms of social behavior and the beginning of conceptual thought. Children learn new concepts on the basis of direct, first-hand perceptual experiences—that is, they are still at the mercy of what they see and hear. Reality is what they perceive; other alternatives are not available to them. When a chocolate bar is broken into pieces, they think there is more chocolate, because the pieces look like more candy than the solid bar. Similarly, Dolly in *The Family Circus* comic bases her question solely on her perception.

During this phase, to about age 4, children's language develops at a phenomenal rate. From the rather rudimentary usage of a number of appropriate words at the age of 2, children develop language skill well enough to communicate their thoughts by the end of the stage; however, their speech remains primarily egocentric. The words they hear and use become associated with objects and relationships and thus contribute to conceptual and language growth.

Preoperational children are too dependent on sensory impressions and they do not yet comprehend the *principle of conservation:* a given quantity remains the same, even though the way that quantity has been arranged has changed. One commonly used illustration is the

THE FAMILY CIRCUS® By Bil Keane

12-9

© 1991 Bil Keane, Inc.
Dist. by Cowles Synd., Inc.

"How come PJ got 4 sandwiches
and I only got 2?"

Reprinted with special permission of King Features Syndicate.

pouring of water from a low but wide glass into a tall but narrow glass in full view of children. Even though they actually observe the water being poured, preoperational children think there is more water in the tall glass because it looks like more (See Figure 8.1). They do not think in terms of a hierarchy of classes and supraclasses. A child may maintain, "We are not in Baltimore; we are in Maryland," without comprehending that one can be included in the other.

The judgments of preoperational children are still intuitive and subjective, but they are beginning to deal with more complex issues. Preoperational children manipulate objects, tools, and toys effectively, express thoughts, and ask questions. Nevertheless, accurate judgment and thought is limited by several factors:

1. Basically, children are still heavily dependent on sensory experiences.
2. They cannot consider two or more dimensions at the same time, rather, they focus on one aspect and consequently neglect to consider the other. A corollary is their directional thinking, also referred to as one-way mapping or one-way functioning, which interferes with mental reversibility.
3. They cannot rearrange or reorganize information in their minds.
4. They are quite limited in their ability to take the point of view of another person.

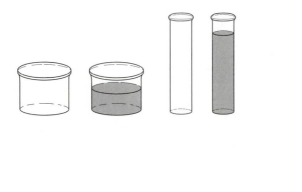

FIGURE 8.1 The beakers and the clay material used in assessing children's understanding of the concept of conservation.

■ The Concrete Operational Stage

At approximately age 7 or 8, a major qualitative shift in children's conceptual development
takes place. They are now beginning to perform *concrete logical operations* in their mind. This
period (from 7 or 8 to approximately puberty) is referred to as the *operational stage in logical
thinking.*

During the operational stage, using concrete content, the child learns to master basic
logical operations. "Concrete" in this context does not mean that the child can deal only
with tangible objects, but that any problem has to be tied to reality. The major limitation
evident in the thinking at this level is the child's inability to think abstractly about a problem. Since concrete operations can be performed mentally, overt trial and error becomes unnecessary. For the first time, the child begins to think in accordance with a model of logical reasoning. The important elements of concrete logical operations are:

1. The logic of classes, which is based on an understanding of whether or not an object
belongs or does not belong in a given class. This enables children to solve problems of classification. They become concerned with the relationship between the parts and the whole.
Understanding and classifying parts that belong together help children to gain a better understanding of the whole, the supraclass. Their ability to hold several pieces of information
in mind and to reverse their thinking enables them to understand hierarchy of classes and
supraclasses.

2. The logic of relations, which makes it possible to order and organize several objects in
relationship to one another, according to specific criteria. In a test situation, the child is
asked to order a series of objects, such as dolls or sticks, according to their size. Such an "operation of serializing" is similar to the classification of a hierarchy, since it involves some

understanding of the structure of the whole: "There is no class without classification; there is no systematic relation without serialization" (Piaget, 1962b: 126). The logic of relations receives elaboration when the child is asked to set two series of objects into correspondence with one another. For example, matching a series of dolls of increasing size with a corresponding set of hats or sticks (see Figure 8.2). Possessing the "logic of relations," the operational child is able to organize objects according to their size, height, or weight as long as objects are presented concretely. Not until adolescence can such operations be performed abstractly.

3. *The principle of conservation,* to which Piaget attached great importance, is probably the most extensively researched cognitive operation (see Figure 8.1). Realizing that changing a clay ball into a sausage or flattening it out into a pancake does not change its mass, weight, or volume, the operational child now begins to develop an understanding of the principle of conservation. The concept of conservation of mass is established first; weight is of intermediate difficulty; volume is the most difficult and may not emerge during the concrete operational stage (Elkind, 1961a; 1961b). Elkind showed that the conservation of volume concept appeared later in American adolescents than suggested by Piaget; however, he did agree with Piaget that formal operations are necessary for the attainment of the conservation of volume concept. Being able to conserve reveals that the child can actually perform mental operations and consequently has attained an operational cognitive structure.

4. *The reversibility of thought processes* implies that the child has acquired "the permanent possibility of returning to the starting point of the operation in question" (Inhelder & Piaget, 1958: 272). With an understanding of the principle of conservation, the child can construct a chain of different color beads, copying the original pattern in reversed order. Awareness of the concept of reversibility is critical to operational thought: "An operation is an action capable of occurring internally and of which . . . the essential characteristic is its

FIGURE 8.2 Piaget's dolls-and-sticks problem. Can the child establish a correspondence between the size of the dolls and the size of the sticks?

reversibility. Cognitive activity becomes operational when it acquires a mobility such that an action (or transformation) can be annulled in thought by an inverse action or can be compensated for by a reciprocal action" (Inhelder, 1966: 302). The ability to return to the starting point of an operation—which is implied in the concept "reversibility"—constitutes an important milestone in the intellectual development of the child. Operational children use addition and can reverse the findings by subtraction. Alice in Wonderland, after eating one side of the mushroom, demonstrates the idea of reversibility when she nibbles on the other side in order to reverse her height. As a result of having reversible operations, the operational child can use various approaches to solve a problem without becoming committed to any one possible solution.

At the same time that the concrete operations emerge, the child's language, which until approximately age 7 had been predominantly egocentric, has become primarily sociocentric. Sociocentric language implies a genuine effort to understand other people and to communicate thoughts objectively: "The child really exchanges his thoughts with others, either by telling his hearer something that will interest him and influence his actions, or by an actual interchange of ideas by argument or even by collaboration in pursuit of a common aim" (Piaget, 1932a: 9-10). Research does not substantiate the dramatic transformation from egocentric to sociocentric speech as neatly as the shift from preoperational to operational thought suggests, but research does support the more general idea that, with the beginning of schooling and with increasing age, the proportion of egocentric speech decreases and that of sociocentric speech increases.

Even adults retain some egocentric thinking at certain times and under certain circumstances: "Children begin development by being cognitively 'egocentric'" (Piaget, 1932a; Flavell, 1992: 107), which means that they do not differentiate among concepts, perceptions, and feelings. Especially through confrontation with peers, children learn about their own and others' points of view (Youniss & Damon, 1992). Piaget (1962a) maintains that the egocentric thinking of children usually decreases as they mature; however, older children and adults retain egocentric thinking, especially when undergoing new experiences or encountering new and challenging situations.

The change from egocentric to sociocentric thought is not only reflected in children's language, but permeates their thought processes as well. Sociocentric children can place themselves in the situation of other persons and take those persons' points of view. When confronted with a model of three differently shaped mountains, children can identify correctly what the mountains would look like from other positions (Figure 8.3). They can rotate objects in their mind and might spontaneously ask, "What does the other side of the moon look like?"

Piaget identifies the properties of concrete operations and applies the term *elementary groupings,* or *group-like structures,* to the different ways in which a child's thought processes can manipulate classes and relations. Since Piaget postulates a direct relationship between logic and a child's cognitive processes, the concepts he introduces are conveyed in terms of logic and mathematics. An important set of four concrete group-like structures, follows:

Combinativity. Two or more classes can be combined into one larger, more comprehensive class. For example, all men and all women equal all adults. Logical relationships, such as A is a larger than B and B is larger than C; therefore, A is larger than C, can be compre-

Position 3

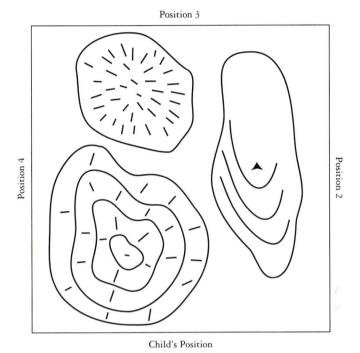

Child's Position

FIGURE 8.3 Schematic presentation of the three differently shaped mountains. The question is: When can a child accurately identify what the mountain range looks like from positions 2, 3, and 4?

hended. The ability to understand classes and to combine subclasses into supraclasses is essential to assemble or disassemble a hierarchy of classifications.

Reversibility. Every operation is reversible. Every operation has an opposite operation that reverses it. Supraclasses can be taken apart so that the effect of combining subclasses is reversed: All adults except all women equals all men. The child's ability to reverse thought processes is an important indicator of cognitive development.

Associativity. Children whose operations have become associative can reach a goal in various ways. They can make detours in thought, but in such a fashion that the results obtained by these different routes remain the same. For example, $(3 + 6) + 4 = 13$, and $6 + (3 + 4) = 13$ (see comic, p. 149).

Identity or nullifiability. An operation that is combined with its opposite becomes nullified. Illustrations of nullifiability in mathematics are: give 3 and take 3 away results in null, or 5 times X divided by 5 equals X. If I drive one mile west and one mile east, I am where I started; my actions are nullified.

Primary groupings make combinativity, reversibility, and associativity in thought possible and thus aid a child in achieving a structural equilibrium that is considerably more mobile and flexible than the thought process of a preoperational child. Thus, the approach to problem solving is no longer intuitive or impulsive but rational and logical. However, reasoning is not yet integrated into a single total system of interrelated propositions.

Late in his career, in collaboration with Inhelder, Piaget enlarged his theory of logical reasoning by emphasizing the algorithmic level of analysis and developing his understanding of cognitive processes more exactly. The most recent presentation of the theory (Piaget, 1987a, 1987b) states that the subject possesses two cognitive systems, the competence system and the procedure system. The competence system works to make sense of environmental experiences. The components of the cognitive understanding of the environment remain stable and more or less permanent. The cognitive structures are complete, as when an adult has developed the capacity to reason deductively, or they remain incomplete, as in concrete operational logic (Overton, 1990). In contrast, the procedure system actively works to solve problems. The components of this system do not last because the work of the procedure system is to reach a goal, or to solve a problem. So, time and context become crucial variables. Acquired procedures (such as sewing a dress) are sufficient or insufficient, not complete or incomplete. Piaget rejected a mechanistic metaphor for the subject; he described growth "as originating in organized activity and proceeding according to processes that result in the differentiation and hierarchic integration of systems and subsystems" (Overton, 1990: 15).

Gray (1990) noted that researchers have significantly minimized the complexity of incorporated concrete operations because scholarship has focused primarily on the very early concrete operations: conservation, reversibility, classification, and seriation. This almost overwhelming concentration on the initial development of concrete operations seems to have led to the incorrect inference that concrete operations, in general, are not nearly as important for effective day-to-day functioning as are formal operations. Many people do not need to perform formal operations in school or at work, to function successfully (Gray 1990; Keating, 1980). Almost everyone needs to perform concrete operations daily, making the ability to use concrete operations extremely important throughout life.

■ The Formal Operations Stage

The final stage of cognitive development of Piaget's theory is the *stage of formal operations,* which typically emerges during adolescence. Piaget's formal operations include, among others, the use of propositional thinking, combinatorial analysis, proportional reasoning, probabilistic reasoning, correlational reasoning, and abstract reasoning. The concept *formal* implies that what matters is form and logic rather than content. With the progression through these stages, mental operations become increasingly more abstract, more complex, more logical, and the boundaries of the mental structures become more permeable and thus, provide thought processes with greater flexibility. The major source of information about adolescent cognitive development is *The Growth of Logical Thinking* (Inhelder & Piaget, 1958). This volume provides the most comprehensive presentation of Piaget's research and his ideas of formal operations and the logical thinking on which they are based.

Piaget subdivides the stage of formal operations further into substages III-A, almost full formal function (11 or 12 to 14 or 15 years), and III-B, full formal function (14 or 15 years and up). This division of the adolescent period at age 14 or 15 implies another restructuring and a disequilibrium, which then leads to a higher level of equilibrium and intellectual structure during late adolescence. The earlier substage (III-A), corresponding to early adolescence, appears to be a preparatory stage in which individuals may make correct discoveries and handle certain formal operations, but since their approach is still cumbersome, they are not yet able to provide systematic and rigorous proof for their assertions. By the time adolescents reach substage III-B, they have become capable of formulating more elegant generalizations and of advancing more inclusive laws. Most of all, they are now able to provide more systematic proof for their assertions since they understand the importance of the method of control. The difference in approach and reasoning of adolescents in substages III-A and III-B may be illustrated by actual responses.

In one of Piaget's tasks, "The Law of Floating Bodies . . . ," which involves volume displacement, the subject is presented with a variety of objects. The problem is to distinguish those that float on water from those that sink, and to provide proof:

> Jim, who is 12 years and 8 months and in substage III-A, approaches the task of grouping those objects which float or sink "according to whether they are lighter or heavier than water."—"What do you mean?"—"You would have to have much more water than metal to make up the same weight."—"And this cover?"—"When you put up the edges, there is air inside; when you put them down, it goes down because the water comes inside and thus makes more weight."—"Why does the wood float?"—"Because it is light."—"And that little key?"—"No, this piece of wood is heavier."—"So?"—"If you measure with a key [= with the weight of a key], you need more wood than lead for the weight of the key."—"What do you mean?"—"If you take metal, you need much more wood to make the same weight than metal" [Inhelder and Piaget 1958: 38].

The subject who has reached substage III-B sees the problem more specifically in terms of units of measurements that are provided and uses the measures spontaneously. Furthermore, the subject appreciates that the weight of the object in relationship to the weight of the water that it displaces determines whether it floats or sinks. There is a reduction in trial-and-error reasoning, and proof is provided with greater elegance and precision, as the following protocol illustrates:

> Lamb, who is 13 years and 3 months old and in substage III-B, is more efficient in identifying those objects that sink: "I sort of felt that they are all heavier than water. I compared for the same weight, not for the same volume of water."—"Can you give proof?"—"Yes, I take these two bottles, I weigh them . . . Oh! [he notices the cubes] I weigh this plastic cube with water inside and compare this volume of water to the wooden cube. You always have to compare a volume to the same volume of water."—"And with this wooden ball?"—"By calculation."—"But otherwise?"—"Oh, yes, you set the water level [in the bucket]; you put the ball in and let out enough water to maintain the original level."—"Then what do you compare?"—"The weight of the water let out and the weight of the ball" [Inhelder & Piaget 1958: 44].

As these illustrations show, the reasoning from substage III-A to III-B becomes increasingly more abstract and shows a more sophisticated mastery of formal operations. Since Piaget postulates a direct correspondence between the structure of logic and the structure of cognitive operations, there is a developmental approximation of the operational thought process of an adolescent to the formal system of modern logic. The significance that Piaget attaches to the change from concrete operations to formal operations is even reflected in a change in the symbols of logic; for example, A + B used for concrete operations, changes to the symbols of logic "p ₒ q" for the same abstract operation. These changes in thought processes are seen as being related to maturational changes in the cortex that accompany puberty. While a child at the concrete operational stage is able to reason on the basis of objects, an adolescent begins to reason on the basis of verbal propositions. The principal difference between the operational and the formal operational stages is that an adolescent gains the ability "to reason in terms of verbally stated hypotheses and no longer in terms of concrete objects and their manipulation" (Piaget, 1980: 72). Formal thought, by definition, involves the ability to reason abstractly, to think of all possibilities, to perform hypothetical deductive thought processes, to reason interpropositionally, to combine thought, to reason contrary-to-fact, to solve proportional reasoning problems, and to understand social and environmental events (Gray, 1990). These newly emerging formal reasoning processes allow the adolescent not only to think in terms of logical necessity in which the force of logic makes the conclusion necessary (e.g., If A is larger than B, and B is larger than C, then A is larger than C); they also allow the adolescent to think in terms of possibilities. That is, adolescents can think of a variety of possibilities that lie in the future as well as possibilities in their social world.

Formal operations require the individual to integrate all of these specific operations, a process which results in a "structured wholeness" of the thought processes (Gray, 1990: 236). This concept of "structural wholeness," developed by Piaget and commented on by his critics, has precipitated disagreement because testing of such a complex network of ideas is difficult, if not impossible. Any given cognitive problem could typically require the individual to use all of the various modes of logical thinking to solve it. And the subject probably will not consciously be aware of the numerous types of reasoning employed as he or she works through, for example, what to do or what not to do if a particular set of circumstances is obtained. The adolescent will now make hypothetical deductions and entertain the idea of relativity: "Formal thought reaches its fruition during adolescence. An adolescent, unlike the child, is an individual who thinks beyond the present and forms theories about everything, delighting especially in consideration of that which is not" (Piaget, 1947b: 148).

Adolescents not only think beyond the present but analytically reflect about their own thinking. Piaget calls this type of reasoning "second-degree thinking"; it involves operations that produce "thinking about thinking," "statements about statements," or more significantly, "operations on operations." Byrnes (1988) maintains that formal operational reasoning only becomes possible through this kind of "second-degree thinking," that is, the utilization of information in the reasoning process, that are themselves the result of formulations which grow out of earlier cognitive processes rather than concrete real-life experiences. Such operations allow a set of all possible combinations to emerge, which then make possible the construction of new knowledge out of previously acquired knowledge by way of propositional thinking. Thus, the interrelationship of actual observation, learning and vicarious learning, and the layering upon layering of knowledge eventually makes hypothetical reasoning possible and allows the construction of theories. The adolescent's theories may at times still seem to be oversimplifications of reality. Nevertheless, most adolescents in substage III-B have social and political theories and at least some also have religious, philosophical, and scientific theories.

Formal operations give the adolescent the ability to understand and even form theories and "to participate in society and the ideologies of adults; this is often accompanied by a desire to change society and even, if necessary, destroy it (in his imagination) in order to elaborate a better one" (Piaget, 1980: 72).

Moshman and Franks (1986), in one research study, distinguish between "inferential validity," that is, conclusions that are logically necessary (necessity) from "empirical validity" that are either true or false. Inferential validity has the same meaning here that it has in logic and requires reasoning from a premise rather than from a fact. Thus, inferential validity can be tested by arguments that are empirically true (or false) and logically valid (or invalid). One of several such arguments, used in testing adolescents, may serve as an illustration. The argument has logical validity even though one of its premises is empirically false:

> If dogs are bigger than elephants
> And elephants are bigger than mice
> Then dogs are bigger than mice.

Moshman and Franks found that fourth-graders cannot effectively use the concept of validity; seventh-graders show quite diverse levels of logical reasoning; most college students demonstrate some understanding of the concept of inferential validity, even though they do not consistently apply it. Piaget identified hypothetico-deductive reasoning—in this illustration, reasoning based on premises that are false—with the emergence of formal operations. Moshman's data support the notion that seventh-graders begin to understand logical validity, and that during the period between fourth grade and college these competencies emerge.

In their thoughts, adolescents can leave the real objective world behind and enter the world of ideas. They now can control events in their minds through logical deductions of possibilities and consequences. Even the directions of thought processes change. Preadolescents begin thinking about reality by attempting to extend thoughts toward possibility. Adolescents who have mastered formal operations begin by thinking of all logical possibilities and then considering them in a systematic fashion; reality becomes secondary to possibility because adolescents reduce reality to a subset of possibility. To emphasize this point further, one could say that, in operational thinking, reality is the foreground and possibility remains in the background. In formal operational thinking, this relationship is reversed—possibility has become the foreground and reality has become simply one of the many possibilities: "The most distinctive property of formal thought is this reversal of direction between *reality and possibility;* instead of deriving a rudimentary type of theory from the empirical data as is done in concrete inferences, formal thought begins with a theoretical synthesis implying that certain relations are necessary and thus proceeds in the opposite direction. . . . This type of thinking proceeds from what is possible to what is empirically real" (Inhelder & Piaget, 1958: 251). This reversal of the direction of thought between reality and possibility constitutes a turning point in the development of the structure of intelligence, since it leads to an equilibrium that is both stable and more flexible.

An illustration may serve to contrast preadolescent reasoning based on concrete operations with adolescent reasoning based on verbal propositions (see Figure 8.2). The 9-year-old can arrange a series of different-size dolls according to their height and can even supply each doll with a stick of a corresponding size from a series of different-size sticks, even if the sticks are presented in reverse order. Not until the formal operations have developed can a similar, abstract problem be solved: "If B is not as bad as C, and C is not as good as A, then who is worst?"

The attainment of formal operations is a gradual, not an abrupt process. Between the ages of 11 or 12 and 14 or 15, considerable modification, systemization, and formalization of thought processes emerge. The complexity of problems that the individual can handle increases substantially during these years and reaches an equilibrium after the individual attains substage III-B.

Piaget distinguishes between the concrete elementary, or primary, groupings discussed earlier and formal, or second-degree, groupings characteristic of the formal stage. He also refers to these more advanced groupings as operations to the second power, or the proposition-about-proposition attribute. Implied in the proposition-about-proposition concept is the idea that adolescents think about their own thoughts in a reflective way. Turning to a description of the formal operational schemata, one ought to remain aware that adolescents, even though they think operationally, do not have a basic understanding of the kind of *formal logic* by which Piaget analyzes and describes adolescent thought processes. The two important theoretical foundations of the formal logic are:

1. *The combinatorial system of operations,* defined as "the matrix of all possible combinations of all possible values of all possible variables inherent in the problem" (Dulit, 1972: 288). A task illustrating combinatorial analysis is the request to determine which combination of five chemicals produces a yellowish-brown liquid, and which returns the liquid to its original colorless state. The difference between the concrete and the formal operational structure is revealed by the trial-and-error approach of the concrete thinker, while the adolescent who has reached the formal operational stage will approach the tasks by systematically trying all possible combinations and thus quickly discovering the right answer.

2. *The INRC group of operations.* Piaget considered the INRC group as representing the capabilities of most adolescents and normal adults in mathematical-logical or deductive reasoning.

Piaget saw deductive reasoning as a significant part of his entire system. The cognitive design that supported deductive reasoning was identified as the "INRC group," or "second order operational structure" (Overton, 1990). Made up of four categories, the INRC group is a formal set of transformations that develops as part of the propositional logic of the adolescent. Each of the four letters represents one of the logical transformations that can be performed on a proposition, changing it into a different operation. The acquisition of the INRC transformations is an important component of the development of logical thought in adolescence and makes propositional logic possible. An understanding of these four transformations is necessary in order to solve problems of proportionality and contribute to higher order reasoning.

1. *"I"—Identity or identity transformation.* The identity transformation is also referred to as the "null transformation" since it results in no fundamental changes; the original proposition retains it identity, hence, its name. One of Piaget's experiments may provide an illustration. In a balance-type weighing scale, different-size weights can be attached to sev-

eral points on the crossbar (Figure 8.4). The problem is to develop an understanding of the concept of equilibrium, which is based on an awareness of proportionality. In an "I" transformation the subject may simultaneously increase the weight and the distance in such a way that the balance itself remains unaffected. An identity transformation would be of such a nature that the basic relationship between the elements—the equilibrium of the scale—retains its identity.

2. "N"—Negation or inversion. A negative transformation means an undoing of the original operation. In an "N" transformation, everything in the initially given proposition is changed into the opposite of the original proposition. "All assertions become negations, and vice versa, and all conjunctions become disjunctions, and vice versa" (Flavell, 1963a: 216). The inverse to "all vertebrates" is "all nonverteates." Inversion or negation cancels out an operation and consequently constitutes one form of reversibility. Reversibility by inversion or negation means that the result of an operation is annulment. For example $+ 6 - 6 = 0$, or $+ n - n = 0$ (Piaget, 1980). In the crossbar experiment (Figure 8.4), an "N" transformation would be to "reduce the distance while increasing the weight or diminish the weight while increasing the distance or diminish both" (Inhelder and Piaget, 1958: 178).

3. "R"—Reciprocal or reciprocity. Reciprocity transformation means undoing the results of the original operation; however, in this transformation it is accomplished by changing some other variable in the system. The reciprocal of a proposition transforms the proposition without changing the conjunction or disjunction that joins the part of the proposition. In an "R" transformation, "A is twice as large as B" becomes "B is twice as large as A." Reciprocity does not cancel a factor in the sense that negation does; rather, it neutralizes one factor, which makes it possible to vary the other. It allows for systematic testing of hypotheses and makes possible the experimental manipulation of variables. In the crossbar experiment (Figure 8.4), "R compensates I by increasing both weight and distance on the other arm of the balance" (Inhelder and Piaget, 1958: 178). Reversibility by reciprocity involves operations of relationships. "For example, if A = B, then B = A, or if A is to the left of B, then B is to the right of A" (Piaget, 1980: 71). A good illustration is Piaget's ring ex-

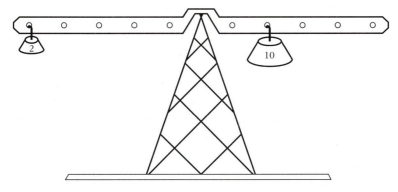

FIGURE 8.4 The balance scale used to assess children's concepts of proportionality. Different weights can be hung at different points on the crossbar.

periment, in which the subject is given a screen, a light source, a board with holes, and a series of different-size rings with pegs. The task is to place two rings on the board, producing only one shadow on the screen. Ring size and distance from the screen bear a reciprocal relationship. One must compensate for the increase in the size of the ring by increasing the distance from the light source.

4. "C"—Correlative. Correlative transformation simply means the negation of a reciprocal. Piaget refers to the correlative as the "inversion of the reciprocal," or the "reciprocation of the inverse"; in other words, the relationship of "C" to "R" is the same as that of "N" to "I." This transformation changes the conjunction or disjunction that joins the parts of the proposition but does not transform the remainder of the proposition. In the crossbar experiment, "C cancels R in the same way that N cancels I" (Inhelder and Piaget, 1958: 178).

These theoretical "building blocks" are comparable in significance to the "logic of classes" and the "logic of relations" in the operational stage.

■ Criteria for Operational Reasoning

Murray (1990), utilizing both Piaget's more recent revisions as well as the traditional criteria for genuine operational thought, proposes the following criteria:

- *Duration.* For the same problem, a truly operational thought will produce the same results even after an extended period of time has elapsed; it will endure. Children who truly understand that a round clay ball flattened must necessarily weigh the same as the ball in its original round shape will report this long after the original assessment was conducted. This is the principle of necessity—there is no possibility for deviation.
- *Resistance to countersuggestion.* Children who truly understand that the flattened ball must weigh the same as the round ball will not change their original response, when confronted with counterevidence, persuasion, and arguments because they have grasped the necessity of the weight remaining constant regardless of its shape.
- *Specific transfer.* If children have to solve the same kind of problem with other materials rather than the flattened and rounded ball, they will understand that the same principle of conservation can be applied equally to the new and different materials.
- *Nonspecific transfer.* Children will face tasks in different domains such as the narrow but high and the wide but flat water glass, and will recognize that all conservation tasks have the same theoretical structure as long as they have acquired an understanding of the principle of conservation.
- *Necessity.* Researchers ask whether or not the flattened mass of clay and the round ball will always weigh the same. This tests children's certainty about their judgments. Children who understand the concept of necessity will realize that the same amount of clay will always weigh the same. Thus, the concept of necessity has become an important element of operational thinking. Adolescents begin to demonstrate an understanding of necessity at age 13, but seldom before (Murray, 1990).

ARE THERE ADULT STAGES OF COGNITIVE DEVELOPMENT?

Generally, it has been assumed that formal operations that develop during adolescence and constitute Piaget's most advanced and final stage in cognitive development are also characteristic of the thought processes of most adults. Moshman (1993) concludes on the basis of empirical evidence that the formal reasoning abilities of adolescents correspond to those of normal adults.

Inevitably, the question was raised whether there exist cognitive structures that extend beyond and are different from formal operations, possibly moving the end of cognitive development into adulthood. Earlier research (Arlin, 1975) reported postformal operational ability, which was based on theoretical as well as empirical evidence. Identified as the "Problem-finding stage," this structure included problem-defining skills assumed to constitute a new level of reasoning more advanced than the stage of formal operations. The problem-finding stage is described as a creative stage that involves the ability to raise new questions and to discover new ideas and methods.

More recent approaches to the issue of an "adult stage" take a different approach. However, since this rather extensive work is not by Piaget and does not deal primarily with adolescents—and applies only to a relatively small segment of a particularly bright, well-educated and/or creative segment of the college and adult population—only a brief introduction will be offered. The interested reader is referred to *Beyond Formal Operations* (1984) edited by Richards and Armon.

In that volume, Richards and Commons (1984) make "A Case for Stages of Reasoning beyond Formal Operations" in which they claim that progression from Piaget's formal operational stage can actually move on to qualitatively distinct higher levels of thinking in adulthood. They report the emergence of three postformal operational stages in a small proportion of the population. These more advanced adult stages are identifed as: (1) systematic level, (2) metasystematic level, and (3) cross-paradigmatic level. Each more advanced level is constructed out of the structure and the function of the preceding level. Moving from the lower to the higher of these levels, one finds they become increasingly rarer and actually very few individuals ever reach the paradigmatic level. If the assumptions of these postformal stages were proven, it would challenge Piaget's assertion that the adolescent stage of formal operation needs to be seen as a "general form of equilibrium [that] can be conceived as final in the sense that it is not modified during the life span of the individual" (Inhelder & Piaget, 1958: 332), and formal thinking would lose its special status as the "final equilibrium." However, in Piaget's defense, it must be pointed out that his concern has always been with the general patterns of cognitive development, not with the exception and these three postformal levels appear to be so rare that they are unique rather than the norm.

Richards and Commons (1984) used four stories as research-assessment tools. The subject has to explain which stories appear to them most similar and most dissimilar and why, and establish an order for the relationship of the elements of the stories. Typical adolescents in *the formal operational stage,* who have not moved into a postformal stage, can deal only with some of the possible similarities and dissimilarities in these stories and establish some relationships, but they cannot evaluate the group of stories as an integrated and interrelated whole; they have difficulties in viewing "the system as a whole" in producing a good Gestalt. At *the systmatic level,* the subject understands each story as an integrated whole and can use possible relationships between elements for purpose of comparison. At *the metasystematic level* a subject cannot only consider all of the elements to determine relationships but can also create a structure that allows him or her to determine how like or unlike each story is to each other story. Finally, at *the cross-paradigmatic level* the entire inter- and intra-relationship of all aspects of all stories are now fully understood and can be explained.

In terms of the increasing complexity and rarity in the adult population of these post-formal levels, Richards and Commons (1984) reported that few undergraduate students display the capacity for systematic or metasystematic thinking. Graduate students exhibit a much greater capacity for reasoning at these advanced levels. Disciplines such as science, mathematics, literature, history, philosophy, anthropology, and music all require such an assessment of whole systems and a comparison of systems within a multisystem arrangement. Thus, individuals who want to make contributions to their fields need at least some level of postformal operation.

FROM NECESSITY TO POSSIBILITY IN OPERATIONAL THOUGHT

During the last two decades of his life, Piaget continued to work on revisions and expansions of his work and emphasized cognitive functions in addition to cognitive structure, an endeavor which suggests that he never viewed his theory as a completed, finished model. Piaget's final books (published in the 1980s) and only recently translated, propounded a revised version of his earlier theory. Continuing the original emphasis on "truth testing," his more recent theory also explores new components: "logic of meaning," a movement away from knowing (i.e., cognitive structure) to procedures for acquiring knowledge and to performance by action, in other words, to cognitive functions. "There is no structure without function, and no function without structure" (Beilin, 1989: 90). Being able to classify objects into specified groups is a procedure, and some children can do it almost intuitively. However, the ability to give a logical reason for each classification reveals the underlying cognitive structure. Also, in his later years, Piaget shifted his attention from "logical necessity" (the way things must be), to an increasing awareness of "the role of possibilities" (the way things might be), as well as procedures and strategies to consider "possibility" as the foundations of logical processes. For Piaget (1987a, 1987b), operations have increasingly become a blending of possibility and necessity. While these ideas of necessity and possibility have always been part of his theory, they do assume an increasingly larger role in his later writing and appear even as the title of his more recent books.

Piaget originally thought that "the understanding of necessity and possibility occurred in the formal stage of cognitive development. But he later came to realize that even children understand certain forms of possibility and necessity . . ." (Inhelder & de Caprona, 1990; Murray, 1990). Even the infant has some understanding of "the 'real' (that which is), the 'necessary' (that which must be) and the 'possible' (that which might be)" (Overton, 1990: 17). The adolescent can understand possibility because sometimes one outcome will occur conditional to something else. "If" sentences may express an awareness of possibility:

"If it rains, we will not go to the ball game even though we usually go on Saturdays." Such and similar "if" statements reveal an understanding of possibility that develops during the preadolescent years (Scholnick, 1990).

Adolescents can imagine possible consequences of behaviors without actually trying them out in real life. For example, they can consider how their grades would fall if they did not study for the exams. They can imagine their parents' disappointment, perhaps even disapproval, in terms of loss of privileges, like the use of the family car. They can imagine all such possibilities, as well as others, without ever having to skip studying for the final exams. The ability to imagine possible outcomes is particularly powerful when one thinks of the consequences of unprotected and/or promiscuous sex, alcohol and drug abuse, and other risk-taking behaviors.

The work Piaget produced during his late years is still being translated. An important book, *The Equilibration of Cognitive Structures,* was not translated into English until 1985, clearly shows that Piaget's thinking had changed extensively. From the early 1970s until his death, Piaget's publications show a fundamental change in some of his theoretical formulations. As a matter of fact, some of these revisions are so pronounced that Beilin (1992) actually speaks of a "new theory." These changes can be summarized:

1. Piaget's move away from the truth testing of logical propositions to intentions, meanings, and inferences reveals the directions of his revisions (Beilin 1992: 1). The analysis of the ability to anticipate the relationship between two different actions, that is, to make logical inferences, to understand a meaning in terms of two actions in relation to one another, became the focus of the revision (Piaget & Garcia, 1991). Children understand that pulling a toy toward themselves is only one of various possibilities—they can push it away, or leave it where it is. Children learn to understand various possible implications of moving the toy, or other actions they perform.

2. A move away from "logical necessity to . . . possibility and its consequences for constructivist theory" (Beilin, 1992: 1) constitutes a major change. Logical necessity is based on formal logic: A is larger than B, B is larger than C, therefore, by the compelling necessity of logic, A is larger than C. This is true everywhere at all times and under all circumstances. Logical necessity differs from empirical truth, which may be true in one place or at one time, but need not always be true. It is certainly true that there are more Senators than Supreme Court Justices. For the United States this is an empirical truth, but not a logical necessity, since the relationship could possibly be different in other places (Moshman & Timmons, 1982). This illustration demonstrates the differentiation between the real (that which is) and the necessary (that which must be). In his later life, Piaget became increasingly aware of the importance of possibility. In this process he emphasized accommodation. What is (reality) does not have to be, so it is not the same as what must be (necessity). What is no longer remains a possibility because reality requires actualization, not potentiality. The individual tries to infer what has to be and what might be and what is the difference between the two (Beilin, 1992). Thus the individual can construct more complex structures, and the new more complex structures allow for more understanding of all the potential alternatives that are not yet actualized. Indeed, understanding possibility is crucial for the development of knowledge and the anticipation of possible events for making decisions.

3. An ongoing concentration on "rationality and its place in current discussions of ideology" (Beilin, 1992: 1). Piaget saw children as rational beings: "Cognitive development emerges with . . . increasingly sophisticated and powerful rational forms" (Beilin, 1992: 16). Piaget increasingly saw the child as rational; he continued throughout his life to show the increasing capacity of children for logical reasoning. Children are rational because they are continuously revising their incomplete knowledge of the world in order to create a better and more rational fit between their knowledge and reality. Such a revision is essential when they are confronted with discrepancies and contradictions between their own limited understanding of reality and new information or unexplainable experiences. Resolving such discrepancies requires rationality and produces cognitive growth.

Because Piaget supported a constructivist explanation of knowledge, he has always rejected one-sided conceptualization of development, such as: nativism or empiricism or information coming across solely through the social environment. The constructionist position is that the child, based on previous experiences and on already existing structures, actively pieces information together, bit by bit. The success and the level of sophistication in this constructionist approach are dependent on the intellectual maturity and the underlying structure of the individual's mind. Social constructivism expands this notion to include the perspectives and the contributions of others, peers, parents, teachers—as an inevitable dimension of this knowledge-building process. Thus, development occurs through cooperative exchanges between subjects and their social world. Actually, Piaget's theory has been social constructivist since the beginning, but this fact has not been recognized until recently (Youniss & Damon, 1992). Scholars argue whether one can today refer to only one Piagetian theory or whether one must distinguish between several Piagetian interpretations and/or distinguish between different constructivist theories. Case (1992)—who might be considered a Neo-Piagetian himself—argues that Neo-Piagetians (rather than Piaget himself) have advanced "hybrid theories" because they have incorporated some of their own ideas and research findings and selectively used parts of Piaget's conceptualizations. Not everyone demonstrates that same level of competence—or even any competence—all of the time (Gray, 1990); individuals will develop only those cognitive abilities that prove to be advantageous for them in their situation. Thus, Neo-Piagetians emphasize domain-specific concepts, including skills, limited memory capacity, and automaticity while Piaget emphasized generality in formal operations across various tasks.

EVALUATION AND CRITIQUE OF PIAGET'S FORMAL THINKING STAGE

Piaget's theory is multifaceted and complex and has its roots in biology, logic, and philosophy. During his lifetime he pursued different purposes and topics and used different approaches, so that different theories or at least different interpretations of development exist. Piaget's data, especially in the earlier periods were based on the "clinical methods" which left room for subjective interpretations. Piaget did not provide the detailed description of his subjects and his methodology that would allow easy replications of his findings. All of these factors, inevitably, invited critical scrutiny of his work. Consequently, scholars have questioned several components of Piaget's system, and much criticism has been directed against specific constructs as well as against the theory as a whole.

A major controversy involves whether or not discreet stages of cognitive development actually exist as Piaget (1947b, 1952, 1953, 1955, 1962a; Inhelder & Piaget, 1958) has always argued, although he placed less emphasis on stages in his more recent work. For example, Sutherland (1992) has criticized the clear division of stages, suggesting that the boundaries separating them are not nearly as clear-cut as Piaget proposed. Piaget's assertion that egocentric language dominates the preoperational stage and becomes sociocentric as the child acquires operational thought has also elicited strong disagreement (Vygotsky, 1986). For further discussion of this issue see the section, "The Concept of 'Stages' in Piaget's Theory."

A related concern of critics is the question whether the "Formal Operational Stage" can actually be considered a stage in the same sense as the preceding stages. Evidence suggests that the proportion of adolescents—and even of adults—who actually attain full ability to master the kind of logical operations that Inhelder and Piaget (1958) so skillfully described is limited. Both Arlin (1975) and Kuhn (1979) cite the widely demonstrated estimate that only approximately 50 percent of the late adolescent and adult population actually attain the full stage of formal thinking (III-B).

In spite of evidence critical of his assumptions, Piaget (1980: 75) maintains that "all normal individuals are capable of reaching the level of formal operation" as long as the environment provides the necessary cognitive stimulation. However, Piaget does admit to a differentiation in cognitive aptitude with increasing age, depending on interest, motivation, and environmental stimulation, so that some adolescents may show their operational skills in logic, mathematics, or physics, while others may show it in literature, linguistics, or artistic endeavor; still others may show it in practical skills performed by a carpenter, a locksmith, or a mechanic, for example. Nevertheless, it is important to keep in mind that Piaget's theory has been studied, tested, and developed in the adolescent age range primarily with content material that came from science and mathematics. Piaget has shown little concern with the question of how formal operations might manifest themselves in artistic and literary endeavors. Yet, disciplines other than science and mathematics clearly require advanced reasoning skills (Richards & Commons, 1984).

As with many of the so-called stage theories, there is a debate whether Piaget's theory is universalist or cultural relativist. Piaget's own interpretation, as well as the suggestion of many who have conducted cross-cultural research, seems to support a universalistic position (Piaget, 1947b, 1952, 1957, 1980). There actually exists considerable cross-cultural evidence—assuming the specific tasks are adapted to different cultural patterns—that the developmental changes in cognitive structure which are identified as Piaget's major stages are indeed universal or near-universal. The four major stages of cognitive development seem to emerge in the same order in all cultural groups that have been studied. However, it is less clear that the advance within each of the major stages follows an invariant sequence in different cultures. Nevertheless, according to Eckstein and Shemesh (1992), the pattern of formal operational problem solving was remarkably similar in the United States and in Israel, and numerous other cross-cultural studies support that observation.

Keating has criticized Piagetian-like testing of formal operational structures as being applicable only to adolescents. Younger children in particular perform much more successfully than predicted when nonlogical elements of the task (e.g., memory demands, attention, familiarity of content, and so on) are changed. Keating (1990: 300) argues "that there are fundamental limits to the Piagetian—or to any structuralist—theory of mature logical thought." Criticizing the empirical tests of formal operational thinking, Keating (1990: 303) questions the result of such testing because it "presumes that the formal operations tasks are rather pure measures of logical competencies." He maintains that the task of formal operations, as used in Piagetian research, does not unequivocally establish an underlying generalizable logical structure that can be applied to different kinds of problems.

The poor performance of some adolescents, college students, and adults (Keating, 1980) might result from lack of familiarity with the content of the task. There also appear to be intraindividual differences in the performance on different formal operations tasks that Piaget and Inhelder developed. Keating suggests that content related to social or interpersonal relationships might allow some individuals to display the formal reasoning skills they possess; however, they may not be able to demonstrate these formal operations on the traditional tasks, involving logic and a scientific way of problem solving. Reporting that "it is not clear that older adolescents do any better on tests of interpersonal reasoning," Keating (1990: 305) concludes that "performance on designated tasks of concrete formal operation cannot be used directly to diagnose the underlying structures." Based on a review of the relevant literature, Kuhn (1979) suggests that the formal operations stage of adolescence, quite in contrast to the preceding childhood stages of Piaget's theory, may never be attained by a significant proportion of the general adolescent population. Piaget (1980) readily admits that the subjects of his study were "from the better schools in Geneva" and that his conclusions were based on a "privileged population." However, he ascribes differences between his own studies and those of others to "differences in speed of development without any modification in the order of succession of the stages."

Piaget's stages have come under attack, principally for his assertion that every one of the features of a stage must be present for that stage to exist, i.e., "the doctrine of the structure of the whole" (Campbell et al., 1986: 51). The "all or nothing" requirement suggests that if all but one characteristic are present, then that stage structure does not exist. Critics have questioned this crucial "all or nothing" assumption, namely, whether and to what extent changes in the subjects' problem-solving approach to Piaget's various cognitive tasks (e.g., the pendulum, the floating bodies, colorless chemicals, the projection of shadows, the flexible rods, and others) develop synchronously. The issue is whether the performances on the operational tasks correlate with one another. If they do correlate substantially, one could assume that such similarities are the result of changes in the underlying cognitive structure, referred to as "inter-task generality" or the "unity hypothesis of cognitive development," which assumes that the various schemata of formal operation appear concurrently. It must be emphasized that, while the "unity hypothesis" has been researched extensively, the findings remain controversial. Some of the reported correlations for inter-task performances vary, but fall in the $r = .30$ to $.40$ range, not a very convincing piece of evidence for the existence of a coherent, underlying, and generalizable formal structure. Bart (1978) had hypothesized, in agreement with Piaget's theory, that the content of a test of formal reasoning should have little or no effect on formal reasoning performance. However, contrary to this hypothesis, he found that the correlations between three formal reasoning tests, quite different in content but structurally equivalent, were only .46, .51, and .65, actually lower than the inter-task generality hypothesis would predict. He concludes that formal reasoning is not necessarily generalizable across content areas. Therefore, Neo-Piagetians have argued that Piaget's general logical structures—referred to as the "structure of the whole"—need to be replaced by structures that are domain-specific. Such a conceptualization of domain-specific cognitive structure would account for the observation that not all structures develop in a synchronized fashion but show considerable unevenness in the age of the domain-specific acquisition. Domain-specific structures would be better suited to explain inter- and intraindividual differences.

On the other side of the controversy, in a review of formal reasoning research, Lawson (1985) finds strong evidence for the "unity hypothesis." Edelstein and Shemesh (1992) compare the ability to solve operational tasks in both the United States and Israel and find equally strong support for the "unity hypothesis" in both countries. Piaget's theory has changed substantially during his lifetime, and while much supportive evidence (e.g., Eckstein & Shemesh 1992; Lawson 1985) has accumulated, his theoretical ideas continue to stimulate research and theory building; nevertheless, many of the specific issues remain controversial. To rephrase a comment recently written about another famous theorist: "Piaget's cognitive developmental theory, even though repeatedly declared dead, taken as a whole has not only survived the criticism but continues to demonstrate vitality and scientific fervor."

Byrnes (1988: 66) expresses the concern of contemporary scholars, the problem of "the stage of formal operations is that the model has lost a good deal of its explanatory value." The general move away from Piagetian theory as well as recent changes in the nature of research programs assessing formal operations may help to explain this assertion. Byrnes (1988: 66) further notes that scholars now seem more interested in "views of conceptual development which explain age differences in terms of domain specificity and the acquisition expertise." Domain specificity refers to the particular area under investigation, for example, the individual's ability to complete algebra problems or solve interpersonal relationship problems. Byrnes observes that this new concern over domain specificity is especially significant because a particular improvement of "formal thought over concrete thought" is "the capacity to reason about any content whatsoever" (Piaget & Inhelder, 1969).

EDUCATIONAL IMPLICATIONS

In his interaction with children in various experimental situations, Piaget observed that children often show resistance to learning from traditional instruction. Apparently, the subject's cognitive structure determines the degree of understanding that the individual can bring to the solution of a problem and the utilization of instructions. Using specific clinical methods, Piaget was very skillful in challenging his subjects to the limits of their understanding. Nevertheless, children seem incapable of being guided, even through careful questioning, beyond the limits of their cognitive structure. And even if suggestions with explicit explanations are provided, children appear to return to their own level of cognitive functioning as indicated by their earlier responses rather than to produce any generalized cognitive growth that would readily transcend the earlier established limits. Lovell (1961) investigated the influence of teaching on the child's ability to solve Piaget-type problems and the long-range benefits of such strategies. Apparently, the knowledge that a child might acquire before developing the corresponding cognitive structures either disappears very rapidly or, if it is retained, is retained as rote memorization without real understanding.

The interaction between a child and the experimenter, as reported by Piaget (1963: 294-295), may serve to illustrate the subject's resistance to change as a result of information that is still beyond his or her cognitive structure. The child is presented with an open box that contains 20 wooden beads; 18 of these beads are brown and 2 are white. The child is asked: "Which are there more of, brown beads or wooden beads?" The preoperational child, who cannot yet classify and cannot consider two dimensions of a problem simultaneously, cannot distinguish brownness as a subclass to woodenness as a supraclass and consequently is most likely to answer: "There are more brown beads, because there are only two white ones."

Following such a typical preoperational response, Piaget might go to great length explaining the situation and the task to the child. Introducing an empty box he might ask: "If we were to put all the wooden beads in the box, how many would be left?" Whereupon the child might reply: "None, because they are all wooden." It thus becomes apparent that the child knows all beads are wooden. So Piaget continues: "Now, if we were to put all the brown beads in this box, how many would be left?" The child's reply would be: "These white ones," or "Two." Apparently the subject now clearly understands the situation that all beads are wooden, that most of the beads are brown, and that two are white. After these instructional efforts, the initial question is asked once more: "Which are there more of, wooden beads or brown beads?" The child may hesitate, indicating that he is more aware of the nature of the problem; nevertheless his response remains the same: "There are more brown beads, since there are only two white ones." Even though the elements necessary for solving the problem have been explained, the child before age 6 to 7 is still unable to consider both the color and the woodenness of the objects and is unable to free his thinking from the perceptual dominance of the many brown beads.

Development is seen as an increase in complexity, mobility, and systematization of schemata and logical structures, which result from equilibrium disequilibration processes, but advances in cognitive structure cannot be substantially accelerated by instruction. Obviously, in the assimilation-accommodation process, education plays a very significant role. However, the assimilation-accommodation process must move in very small logical steps in order to enhance learning. If the gaps in the presentation of educational material are too large or too advanced for the child, the individual cannot accommodate. The teacher has to be skillful in maintaining the proper level of tension between assimilation and accommodation, in starting at the child's level, and in progressing in small steps in order to foster genuine conceptual and cognitive growth. On this particular issue Piaget appears to be very close to a maturational interpretation of development and reveals a somewhat conservative outlook on education. His objection to what he referred to as "the American question"—"How can we accelerate the child's progression through your developmental stages?"—is, that to do things faster or earlier is not necessarily a desirable thing and may be even worse than doing nothing.

Interestingly enough, it is on this issue that some of Piaget's close associates seem to depart from his interpretation. Bruner, who was influenced by Piaget's theory, seems to take almost the opposite point of view when he says: "We begin with the hypothesis that any subject can be taught effectively in some intellectually honest form to any child at any stage of development" (Bruner, 1960: 33). On the other hand, Bruner appears to agree with Inhelder's statement that it may be worthwhile to devote 2 years of a schooling "to a series of exercises in manipulating, classifying, and ordering objects in ways that highlight basic operations of logical addition, multiplication, inclusion, serial ordering, and the like" (Bruner, 1960: 46). Such an approach implies a rather direct structuring of the school curriculum in accordance with Piaget's theory.

Kamii, Clark, and Dominick (1994: 673) propose that a return to Piaget's (1973) vision of the development of autonomy as the goal of education would go a long way to help address the problems in the American educational system today. With the national emphasis on performance on tests, the focus has moved away from the child/adolescent (where Piaget insists it should be) to the teacher as the authoritarian dispenser of knowledge. The six national goals of education initiated by former President Bush and the National Governors' Association have attempted to define "values and priorities." Kamii et al. (1994) rely on Piaget's theory as they call for education to support the child in his or her attempts to realize the ability to become self-governing. Students and teachers must work together to enable the child's acquisition of knowledge, a process of "constructing [it] . . . from within," not taking it from the social demands or the external world. The reward and punishment methods that most teachers use (Kamii et al. 1994: 674-675) persuade children that only the authoritarian teacher knows how to answer correctly. This results in children's lack of confidence in their own abilities.

The teacher can habitually use three methods to enhance student autonomy (Kamii et al. 1994: 676-677). The teacher is no longer the only source of knowledge, and students are encouraged to become active participants in decision making and problem solving.

1. "Encouraging children to make their own decisions and to enforce their own rules."
2. "Fostering intrinsic motivation." According to Piaget, children will work harder when the problems and questions are relevant to them and arouse their curiosity.
3. "Encouraging children to exchange viewpoints." The teacher would not merely identify correct and incorrect responses, since this inhibits thinking, but guide the child in his or her self-construction of knowledge and values.

When children do make mistakes, asking for an explanation of their thought process or asking the class to comment on their findings could stimulate more sophisticated understanding and generate critical thinking as students share perspectives. These Piagetian guidelines would help children to develop autonomy, which is the prerequisite for the solution of many educational and social problems.

Some research does provide evidence that Piagetian-type problems can be taught and that teaching such concepts does accelerate cognitive growth. Richards and Commons (1984) found that graduate rather than undergraduate students exhibit postformal operational capacity, suggesting that education and experience contribute to the development of cognitive reasoning. If this is true at advanced levels, might it not also be true at the earlier stages? Ojemann and Pritchett (1963) have shown that guided learning experiences, such as teaching preadolescents the reasons why objects sink or float, significantly affect children's thought structures. Aebli (1963), a former associate of Piaget, has taken his teacher's theory of development and expanded it toward an education theory. Aebli uses the sandbox in which the subject looks at three mountins of different shapes and is asked what the scenery would look like from different angles (Figure 8.2). He demonstrated that the method of presentation and the number and nature of significant cues were as important as the child's cognitive structures in facilitating solutions to the problems and learning. He varies the complexity of the problem by providing the subject with the following: (1) the contours of the mountains only, (2) contours and different surface structure of the mountains, and (3) contours, surface structure, and color of the mountains.

Aebli and Bruner do not maintain that the child's logical structures can easily and substantially be accelerated through educational procedures. They are, however, somewhat more optimistic than Piaget in attributing a greater importance to the organization of the curriculum material and the methods of teaching, since they feel that complex concepts can be simplified and presented so as to fit the logical structure of the child. The task of the teacher then becomes that of the "translator" who has to present the curriculum content on such a level and in such a way that it corresponds to the cognitive structure of the child; the goal is to correlate the curriculum systematically to the child's ability to assimilate and accommodate the material. Such a translation implies that, for a specific problem, the preoperational child should be presented with the problem in the form of direct sensory experiences, whereas the preadolescent would be able to work with concrete problems, and the adolescent could master abstract ideas, verbal propositions, and combinatorial analyses. More specifically, the formal operations found in the adolescent constitute the prerequisite for teaching geometry, proportionality, propositions, and probabilistic reasoning. A Piagetian approach to teaching would make it mandatory for the educator to assess the operational structure of pupils. Piaget-type assessment and test materials (Burk, 1973; Copeland, 1988; Furth, 1970; Patterson & Milakofsky, 1980; Pinard & Laurendeau, 1964; Uzgiris & Hunt, 1976) and curriculum material constructed with Piaget's developmental and educational theory in mind (Furth & Wachs, 1975; Lavatelli, 1970; Petrone, 1976; Sund, 1976; Weikart et al., 1971) have become available and have been used in educational settings.

Piaget is concerned with fundamental questions of genetic epistemology and the sequence and orderliness of cognitive changes and not with the variables that have always been of concern to the educational and developmental psychologist: individual differences, sex, socioeconomic class, IQ, reading level, and so forth. Piaget's theory has stimulated considerable research into these traditional developmental variables. For example, sex differences on Piagetian-type problems are rather minimal, and where they have been reported, they seem to be limited to very specific tasks. Males do seem to perform better on some of the tasks that have a strong spatial reasoning component. However, overall, on abstract logical competencies which constitute the core of Piaget's formal operations tasks, sex differences are minimal or nonexistent.

Piaget devoted little attention to such variables. He never denied that they might exist; he simply focused on a different set of questions. "The order of succession of these stages has been shown to be extremely regular and comparable to the stages of an embryogenesis. The speed of development may vary from one individual to another and also from one social environment to another . . . but this does not change the order of succession of the stages through which they pass" (Piaget, 1980: 70-71). It is the order of succession in the acquisition of knowledge that was the focus of Piaget's research. However, knowledge of Piaget's theory gives the educator insights into the limitations and abilities of children at various stages in their cognitive development. Piaget made it clear that children think differently at various age levels and think quite differently from adults. Did it occur to anyone that children might think—assuming equality exists—that there is more milk in a thin, tall galss than in a wide, low glass, before Piaget's experiments became widely known?

Not only the content of Piaget's theory and the substance of his findings but also his methods are relevant to the educator. He collects data by what is frequently referred to as the "clinical method," which means that children actively search for the solution to the problem. The examiner stimulates and challenges the children to reflect and elaborate on their answers and to use this discourse as a means to clarify thinking. Piaget believes in the autonomy of children and in their active participation in their own cognitive growth—an idea he shares with John Dewey. "There are two basic and correlated principles from which an educator inspired by psychology can never depart: (1) That the only real truths are those that one builds freely one's self and are not those received from others, and (2) that moral good is essentially autonomous and cannot be prescribed" (Piaget, 1947a: 5).

C H A P T E R

9

LAWRENCE KOHLBERG'S COGNITIVE-DEVELOPMENTAL APPROACH TO ADOLESCENT MORALITY

PIAGET'S CONTRIBUTION TO AN UNDERSTANDING OF CHILDREN'S MORAL JUDGMENT

Piaget, in *The Moral Judgment of the Child* (1932b), postulated that the development of children's moral judgment follows the same basic pattern as that of cognitive development. The moral schemata develop out of existing cognitive structures, and the moral judgment is always based on the necessary level of conceptual-cognitive development. The development of moral reasoning depends on such cognitive skills as the perception of reality, the organization and evaluation of experiences, the ability to take the other person's point of view, and during adolescence, the ability to think abstractly.

Piaget and Kohlberg (1927–1987) were primarily interested in moral judgment, which differs significantly from moral behavior. Moral judgment refers to the intellectual or reasoning ability to evaluate the "goodness" or "rightness" of a course of action in a hypothetical situation. Moral behavior refers to the individual's ability in a real-life situation to help others, to resist the temptation to steal, cheat, lie, or commit other immoral acts. Piaget and Kohlberg have assumed that the structure underlying verbal moral judgment and actual moral behavior, while related, are not identical. Because a person intellectually can identify morally right behavior does not guarantee that he or she will actually behave in accordance with moral principles. Various research studies have demonstrated that the correlation between moral judgment and moral behavior is not very high (Hartshorne & May, 1928–1930); however, others have actually reported positive relationships (Rubin & Schneider, 1973), and juvenile delinquents rather persistently score lower on cognitive moral reasoning tasks than their nondelinquent peers (Hains & Miller, 1980; Kohlberg, 1969).

Piaget has observed that a remarkable change in the quality of children's moral reasoning takes place when they progress from preoperational to operational thinking and, at the time of puberty, from concrete operational to formal operational thinking. Piaget identifies the morality of the preoperational stage, before the age of about 7, as "morality of constraint" or "moral realism," and describes a child at this stage as advocating blind obedience to authority. The child perceives justice as resting in the person of authority; this idea is referred to as "ethics of authority." The moral concepts of children develop partially out of the parental teaching of what is right and what is wrong. Preoperational children do not have the intellectual structure to consider other alternatives, nor do they have the emotional capacity to empathize with others. Children at this stage are not yet able to decenter—that

Lawrence Kohlberg (1927-1987)

is, they do not yet have the capacity to move from one point of view to another or to take into account the view of another person.

With the shift from preoperational to operational reasoning, the ability to decenter increases. Children become more altruistic and more aware of the needs of others in orientation and behavior (Rubin & Schneider, 1973). While preoperational children approach moral dilemmas from an "objective" viewpoint—that is, they are primarily concerned with the objective amount of damage resulting from an act rather than with the intent or the motivation of that behavior, the moral judgment of the operational child, "morality of cooperation," reflects the change to a social orientation, an "ethics of mutual respect." Moral judgments shift from an objective to a subjective orientation: the primary concern is no longer simply the objective amount of damage caused by the immoral act, but the intent or motivation now becomes more important. Children begin to take into consideration the viewpoint of others and to appreciate the reciprocity of relationships. In one of Piaget's stories, children must decide who is naughtier: John, who opens a door and accidentally breaks fifteen cups that were behind the door; or Henry, who tries to snatch some cookies, climbs on a chair, and in the process, breaks one cup. Preoperational children judge John to be naughtier because they are primarily concerned with the objective amount of damage. Operational children feel that Henry is naughtier because the subjective intention receives more weight than the objective damage.

The moral judgment of preoperational children has two basic characteristics, moral realism and immanent justice. Moral realism implies that moral rules have an existence of their own and cannot be changed (Piaget, 1932b). Immanent justice involves the child's belief that immoral behavior inevitably brings pain or punishment as a natural consequence of the transgression. For example, if a child steals and later, on the way home, falls and hurts himself, he may see the fall as punishment for the stealing. The transition from moral "realism" to moral "relativism" takes place when the child no longer blindly follows orders but considers the intent of any act rather than the letter of the law. The child realizes that the laws, or the rules that govern behavior, can be changed by consensus.

For Piaget, the highest stage of moral development, characteristic of adolescence, is "moral autonomy." Dependent on the attainment of formal or abstract reasoning ability, moral autonomy commonly begins at puberty. In a game situation, the adolescent reveals interest not only in the rules by which the game is played but also in possible new rules to make the game more interesting or more challenging. There emerges an anticipation of all possible alternatives to which these rules apply. Since abstract thought is possible, the adolescent begins to develop a sense of ethical and moral responsibility based on abstract principles of what is right or wrong.

■ Philosophic Considerations

What is the nature of morality? Is there an absolute definition of "dos" and "don'ts" which would apply to all people at all times wherever they may be? Or, is morality determined by the individual, by the situation, or by the social climate? Is morality absolute, or is it relative and therefore changing according to specific conditions and cultures? If the latter, then what is considered morally right or good in one society may or may not be defined as good in another. Similarly, what may be morally correct for one individual in one situation may not be right for someone else or for another situation. This position of moral or cultural relativism is one which disturbed Kohlberg and initiated a lifelong search for a better definition of morality. He felt that the majority of American social scientists were influenced by behaviorism and by Freudian psychoanalytic approaches. By dealing with methods of transmitting morality rather than emphasizing issues of moral philosophy, these approaches, he maintained, lend support to a position of moral relativism. Kohlberg strongly rejects this position. How can one who accepts relativism argue against cannibalism or Nazism? If a given society accepts these actions as being valid, then by the standards of relativism these practices would be considered morally correct. Relativism for Kohlberg was, therefore, inadequate to provide a basis for moral thinking. What was needed were some universal principles that would provide some guidance in defining morality.

Would a more absolutist approach specifying lists of agreed behaviors such as honesty, patriotism, service, responsibility, etc., offer an answer to relativism? This "bag of virtues," as Kohlberg called such lists, was also rejected by him for two reasons. First, since it would be difficult to reach a consensus on what characteristics should be included in this "bag," we would doubtlessly find ourselves agreeing to disagree; and as a result, we would back into a position of relativism. Secondly, the character education movement in the earlier part of this century was based on just such an approach and the studies by Hartshorne and May (1928-1930) clearly indicated that the virtues taught did not affect moral behavior in daily life (Kohlberg, 1981). Hence, both an absolute and a relative definition of morality were unacceptable to Kohlberg. "Ultimately," he wrote, "we must ask ourselves, 'Are our values universal? Is there a hierarchy of values that everyone does or should accept?'" (Kohlberg, 1981: xxviii).

Kohlberg and Elfenbein (1981: 274) did find an answer to these questions in Kant's categorical imperative: "Act only according to that maxim by which you can at the same time will that it should become a universal law." How does one do this? Since we are rational human beings, we can by the use of reason and by following a general rule or a "practical imperative" (to use Kant's words) arrive at universal notions of morality. This practical imperative: "Treat each person as an end, not as a means" (Kohlberg & Power, 1981: 337) then becomes the principle by which we can make moral judgments.

Building on this Kantian foundation, Kohlberg incorporates elements of Plato and Dewey in his pursuit of finding guiding principles in the development of moral judgment. From Plato he adopts the notion of justice as the ultimate goal of morality, and from Dewey he adopts the concept of education contributing to moral development. By exposing students to dilemmas or conflicts, the educator stimulates modifications in the subject's thinking patterns. Thus

> morality is neither the internalization of established cultural values nor the unfolding of spontaneous impulses and emotions; it is justice, the reciprocity between the individual and others in the social environment (Kohlberg & Mayer, 1981: 54-55).

With Kant's categorical and practical imperatives combined with a rational search for principles by means of questioning and reflection, we would be able to arrive at a consensus as to what constitutes justice. "The question of what is morally right or good action . . ., is defined by valid universalizable moral principles . . . of justice like that of respect for people and their liberty and dignity or like that of utility or the greatest welfare for the greatest number" (Kohlberg, 1984: 393).

KOHLBERG'S THEORY OF MORAL DEVELOPMENT

Having established a philosophic base and inspired by Piaget's cognitive developmental approach to moral development, Kohlberg and his collaborators expanded the structural cognitive approach through longitudinal, cross-cultural, social class, and educational research (Kohlberg, 1963, 1969; Kohlberg & Blatt, 1972; Turiel, 1969). From these findings emerged a more inclusive and systematic theory of moral judgment than Piaget's. Initially, Kohlberg based the theory on the moral reasoning responses of 72 male subjects age 10, 13, and 16; the adolescent years rather than the childhood years became the critical period for the development of advanced levels of moral reasoning. His initial bias favoring males as research subjects was reflected in the construction of his theory since it was inspired by their responses. Adolescent males seemed to score higher (and reach level 4 earlier, "morality based on abstract principle") than adolescent females (who reach level 3, "social orientation"). This gender difference has become a lasting issue of contention and provided the initial impetus for Carol Gilligan's critique of Kohlberg and the creation of her own theory, which assumes morality speaks in two different voices. Kohlberg based his classification of individuals into moral reasoning stages on the resolution of moral dilemmas presented to the subject. The following story illustrates one of these moral dilemmas: A woman is dying of cancer. The local druggist has discovered a new drug that could save her life. The pharmacist, who has not invested much in this cure, sells it for $2,000, an amount which is 10 times greater than his cost. Heinz, the sick woman's husband, tries to borrow money from a friend, but he can raise only $1,000. He approaches the druggist, asking him to sell the remedy for half the price or to let him repay him at a later time. The pharmacist refuses. In desperation the husband breaks into the store and steals the medicine. Should he have done so? Why? The subject must explore the rightness or wrongness of the husband's decision, the rights of the druggist, the duties of the husband, the appropriate punishment for the husband, and the obligations an individual has toward relatives and nonrelatives.

Kohlberg based classification of responses not on the particular solution the subject proposed, but on the moral reasoning that leads to the proposed answer—in other words, on the moral structure underlying the response, or in his words, "on the form, not the content." This means that all classifications depend on the subject's verbal reasoning and may not be related directly to actual moral behavior. Other stories (there are a total of twelve) place the conflict between satisfying a personal need and keeping a promise, respect for an individual versus concern for the group welfare, obedience versus keeping a promise, etc. Most of his dilemmas, as critics have pointed out, do not involve typical, everyday adolescent issues and conflicts.

STAGES IN MORAL DEVELOPMENT

Kohlberg began his research on the stages in moral development in the fifties and presented his theories as a doctoral dissertation in 1958. Kohlberg's (1963) findings were published a few years later and immediately stirred considerable interest among philosophers, psychologists, and scholars interested in the field of moral development. As a result of criticisms, empirical data, and philosophical and educational reactions appearing in the 1970s, Kohlberg incorporated a number of these scholarly evaluations and ideas into a revised description of his stage theory. Different versions of these stages and different scoring protocols have therefore appeared during Kohlberg's life.

Kohlberg's theory distinguishes three basic levels of moral development: the preconventional or premoral level; the conventional or moral level; and the postconventional or autonomous level. Moral development begins in young children as an undifferentiated, selfish and egocentric idea, but, with increasing maturity, it becomes more sophisticated and sociocentric as the individual moves through a series of sequential stages of moral thinking. In some individuals moral judgment may reach an awareness of both universal values and ethical principles of justice. Kohlberg subdivided each of these three general levels into two stages to create a highly differentiated and elaborate theory of moral development of six stages. Each stage of moral reasoning represents a distinct moral philosophy that has implications for education, social and political organization, and can serve as a typology of moral orientation even among adults at different moral judgment stages.

■ Level 1: The Preconventional or Premoral Level of Moral Reasoning

Most prevalent during childhood, this level is concerned with external, concrete consequences of an act to the self. It commonly includes the ages of 4 to 10 but may characterize the moral reasoning of some adolescents and even adults. Children at this level respond to the definitions of "good" and "bad" provided by their social reference group. Although the children are often well behaved, their moral structure is still undeveloped and undifferentiated; indeed, the reasons underlying the moral judgments of those at the preconventional level are different from the reasons of those who have advanced to higher levels. Moral decisions are primarily egocentric, hedonistic, and based on self-interest, fear of punishment, anticipation of reward, or material considerations. Individuals at this level interpret behavior as good or bad in terms of what Piaget has termed "objective judgments."

Level 1, Stage 1: The Heteronomous Morality

At the lowest level of moral reasoning, the main motivation for obeying a rule is to avoid punishment and achieve gratification. "Good" and "bad" are defined by obeying and disobeying authorities and rules. Initially, Kohlberg actually referred to this stage as the "obedience and punishment orientation." The child's conscience is based on a primitive, egocentric fear of punishment. Children at Stage 1 manifest submission to superior power and try to avoid trouble. Still unclear about human values and human life, they value people in terms of the benefits which they can provide and in terms of their physical attributes or social status. You should, for example, listen to your father because he is bigger. Or, you should steal to save a life of an important person. The actual physical damage of an act rather than the underlying intent becomes primary in the child's evaluation of goodness or badness. This confusion of the physical with the social-moral world corresponds to what Piaget calls "moral realism." If Heinz in the previously described dilemma operated at this level, he might fear that God will punish him if he lets his wife die.

Level 1, Stage 2: Individualistic, Instrumental Morality

Children can now distinguish between the physical damage and the psychosocial intent; however, they still confuse individual needs with what they think is right or wrong. At Stage 2, revealing a hedonistic orientation, morally right behavior depends on what satisfies one's own personal desires. There is, therefore, a moral relativism during this stage; and, as a result, an individual has difficulty in deciding among conflicting claims and in establishing priorities. A major motivating force becomes the manipulation of others in order to obtain the desired reward; for example, being good before Christmas in order to maximize the number of gifts one will get. The notion of reciprocity is beginning to emerge; consequently, under certain circumstances, when it will be to one's benefit, the needs of others receive consideration. Reciprocity, then, depends on an exchange of powers and favors rather than on considerations of loyalty and justice. The prevailing philosophy seems to be, "You scratch my back and I'll scratch yours." Fairness, reciprocity, and sharing do exist, but exclusively in pragmatic and utilitarian terms. Tom Sawyer's episode of the whitewashing of the fence provides a classic illustration of this stage of moral development. The criterion for making moral decisions depends on selfish desire, as in the case of the child who believed the man should steal the drug for his ill wife because, if she did die, nobody would take care of his needs. Stage 2 subjects cannot decenter their thinking sufficiently to consider the position of another person objectively.

■ Level 2: The Conventional or Moral Level

At this level, children become concerned about meeting external social expectations. Children base moral orientation on an acceptance of the existing social order and on a clear recognition of the rights of others. Kohlberg describes the child at this level as conforming to social conventions, desiring strongly to maintain, support, and justify the existing social order. Most adolescents and even the majority of adults function on the conventional level. However, as an individual progresses into adolescence, the association of a specific chronological age with a specific level of moral reasoning becomes increasingly more difficult. Many adults continue to function primarily at the conventional level, while relatively few mature adolescents reason at the postconventional level.

Level 2, Stage 3: Interpersonally Normative Morality

This is the stage of the conventional level in which the egocentric orientation is replaced by one that is sociocentric, a fundamental reorientation. Kohlberg refers to Stage 3 as the "good boy-good-girl," approval-seeking orientation in moral development. The golden rule—Do unto others as you would have others do unto you—is often the criterion in making moral judgments. Personal needs and morality can be distinguished, but the confusion is now between social approval and right and wrong. Living up to the expectation of others becomes more important than "goodness." Good behavior now becomes that which pleases or helps others, and children will try to behave, not because it is the right thing to do, but in order to win the approval of others. Because the ties that individuals have to their social group now define morality, adolescents may break the laws of the larger society in order to win the approval of their peers. Actions are "right" if they win approval and "wrong" if they elicit disapproval from significant others.

The need to win the approval of the immediate social group and to live up to the perceived expectations of the significant others becomes the yardstick for moral decisions in smoking, alcohol and drug use, sex, and abortion. Subjects conform to what they believe to be the opinions of those they identify with on "natural behavior." Seventh-grade adolescents in Stage 3 tend to conform more than age-mates who actually were at either a higher or a lower level of moral reasoning. Like individuals in Piaget's subjective stage, those in Stage 3 judge behavior by the underlying intentionality, a perspective frequently expressed by the adolescent's explanation that "he means well." Often, like Charlie Brown in *Peanuts,* adolescents overuse this argument. Stage 3 also includes the Mary Poppins type of morality. As adults, females remain at Stage 3 longer than do males, a finding that has been reported for other societies as well (Reid, 1984) and has become the major challenging issue in Gilligan's theory of moral reasoning in females.

Level 2, Stage 4: Social System Morality

Characteristic of morality at Stage 4 is a strong belief in law, order, duty, and legitimate authority. The individual views the existing social order as a primary value. Moral rules and a focus on duty become distinguishable from feelings of approval. However, rather than involving abstract principles of justice, at Stage 4 the rules are concrete, "Thou shalt not . . . ." One obeys and respects the law to avoid the penalty that legitimate authority can impose; one also realizes that others have legitimate rights. Breaking the law produces guilt. Therefore, both personal guilt and fear of legitimate censors motivate moral behavior. The moral orientation involves believing in existing authority, obeying the law, doing one's duty, showing respect for authority, and maintaining the social order at any price. This emphasis on duty motivates Colonel Saiti in *The Bridge over the River Kwai;* the colonel rigidly maintained his lifelong orientation toward duty, authority, and the social order—even when it was no longer appropriate and had become counterproductive. According to Kohlberg (1970: 184), "Life is conceived as sacred in terms of its place in categorical moral and religious order of rights and duties." In Heinz's moral dilemma, a Stage 4 reasoning might be: Since marriage is an institution essential to society and based on law, the Stage 4 subject may consider it his lawful duty to steal the drug.

■ Level 3: The Postconventional or Autonomous Level

The autonomous individual identifies the primary concern as self-chosen moral principles. At this advanced level the approach to moral problems—no longer based on selfish needs, nor on conformity to others or the social structure—depends upon autonomous, universal principles of justice that retain validity even beyond existing laws, social conventions, or one's personal social reference group. At this highest level of moral reasoning, moral judgment and behavior reveal more internal congruence than at earlier levels.

Level 3. Stage 5: Human Rights and Social Welfare Morality

Moral reasoning at this postconventional level depends on fundamental principles such as individual rights, equality, a human dignity, contractual agreement, and mutual obligation. Consequently, Kohlberg refers to this stage, which is based on formal, abstract, operational thinking ability, as the principled stage of moral thinking. Moral behavior reflects a concern for the welfare of the larger community and a desire for community respect. Because the individual believes the law should preserve human rights and serve the larger community, unfair or unjust laws must be changed. Laws and rules for behavior are no more and no less than an agreed-upon social contract; they are not right in and of themselves. In contrast to the individual in Stage 4, the postconventional thinker views the law as modifiable and works for changing the law, as long as these changes reflect consensus and follow rational deliberations and considerations of social utility. Stage 5 reasoning is represented by the moral philosophy underlying the American Constitution. However, although democratic government is philosophically based on the moral judgment identified as Stage 5, Kohlberg estimates that only 20 to 25 percent of adult Americans actually reach this level of moral development. In literature, Shakespeare's Prince Hamlet reveals a postconventional level of morality when he challenges the legitimacy of King Claudius' claim to the throne. The Stage 5 husband may decide that Heinz should steal the drug in order to save his wife, perhaps reasoning that he and his wife have promised to love each other regardless of the circumstances; furthermore, society sanctions their moral commitment to each other.

Level 3, Stage 6: Morality of Universalizable, Reversible, and Prescriptive General Ethical Principles

Morality at this most principled stage of moral reasoning assumes a conscience that is based on self-chosen ethical principles that place the highest value on human life, equality, and dignity. Rules are binding only to the extent that they represent these ethical principles. Rules that violate ethical principles must be broken and the penalty willingly accepted. Stage 6's concept of justice goes beyond any particular existing social order. Consistency, logical comprehensiveness, and universality characterize the ethical principles of Stage 6 subjects. No one can attain the individual principled level without having operated first at the social contractual level and without having clearly understood the basic contractual nature of the existing social order.

The individual governed by universal ethical principles may practice civil disobedience, not out of disrespect for the law, but out of respect for a morality higher than the existing law. Unjust laws will be broken because Stage 6 morality is grounded not in legality, but in ethical principles of justice and in respect for the rights of the individual. In practicing civil disobedience, the individual willingly accepts the penalty in order to demonstrate to the society at large that principles of justice, human rights, and dignity of the human being are more important than the law. Stage 6 individuals feel that no law, no contract, no moral obligation, and no fear of punishment can interfere with their desire to save those they love. The husband in the dilemma will steal the drug, first, to save the life of his wife; and second, to demonstrate to society that the right to live is so fundamental that it must and should take precedence over the right to make a profit; and third, to exemplify his willingness to accept the penalty. Visionaries and moral leaders such as Joan of Arc, Abraham Lincoln, Henry David Thoreau, Nelson Mandela, and those who sacrificed their lives opposing Hitler, such as Hans and Sophie Scholl and Claus Schenk von Stauffenberg, seemed to have accepted universal ethical principles that challenged the existing morality of their societies and time.

The thinking of an individual oriented toward universal moral principles receives clear expression in an excerpt from Martin Luther King's (1964: 86) "Letter from Birmingham Jail."

> I do not advocate evading or defying the law, as would the rabid segregationist. That would lead to anarchy. One who breaks an unjust law must do so openly, lovingly, and with a willingness to accept the penalty. An individual who breaks a law that conscience tells him is unjust, and who willingly accepts the penalty of imprisonment in order to arouse the conscience of the community over its injustice, is in reality expressing the highest respect for the law.

SUBSEQUENT DEVELOPMENTS IN KOHLBERG'S THEORY

These stages represent the type of reasoning used by people when presented with moral dilemmas. Kohlberg assumes that all individuals move through these stages at different speeds. Some plateau at a specific stage and progress no further. Generally speaking, the movement through these stages is sequential and no stage is skipped. This invariant sequence is hierarchical in nature whereby the higher stages incorporate the approaches of the lower ones but allow the person to make moral judgments on a more mature, rational, principled level. Since these stages represent the form or structure of moral reasoning rather than the content or issues of a moral dilemma, they are universal and not affected by cultural, religious, or societal contexts (Kohlberg, 1981). Some of these assumptions about stage developments were subsequently challenged and these challenges will be discussed later.

In the earlier formulations of his stage theory, Kohlberg stressed that the criteria for each stage were not based on the content or the specific details of the dilemma presented to the subject. Instead, the scoring of the responses was determined by the form, the structure, the reasoning of the individual. In the 1984 formulation of the stages of moral development, however, Kohlberg found that some of the moral reasoning fell somewhere between the form and the content. Consequently, he developed two substages which theoretically could appear in some of the existing stages. Substage A represents the heteronomous individuals who depend on authority and rule in their approach to morality and whose moral reasoning is similar to that described in the early stages of moral development. Substage B describes the methods used by the autonomous individuals. Although some of these characteristics have been included in the description of the stages quoted above, a brief summary of the autonomous type may be useful. The criteria for autonomous reasoning are:

1. *Choice.* Moral choice should be based on the more "just" course of action as determined by logical, rational, and principled reasoning.

2. *Hierarchy*. Following Kant, one should treat others not just as means but at the same time as ends. "As such, the right of life, the value of acting on one's conscience, and the importance of promise keeping . . . are all placed above any other considerations" (Kohlberg 1984: 677).

3. *Intrinsicalness*. While resolving a moral dilemma, one should bear in mind the intrinsic moral worth and respect for people.

4. *Prescriptivity*. Moral decision would include responsibility and obligation and as such would become a basis for prescribing moral action.

5. *Universality*. Moral judgments would be equally applicable universally to all people in similar situations or circumstances.

6. *Freedom*. An individual should be free to make moral judgments without appealing to existing norms of authority.

7. *Mutual respect*. All persons are to be treated with respect.

8. *Reversibility*. Moral decisions should be based on consideration of all points of view. In the dilemma quoted above, the individual should "play musical chairs" by putting himself in the role both of Heinz and of the pharmacist before making his or her moral judgment.

9. *Constructivism*. Although rules may be beneficial, the autonomous individual should go beyond these rules to construct a rational principled moral position.

An example of a Stage 4, Substage B approach might be helpful. In considering the morality of the pharmacist interested in maximizing his profits and the husband who steals the drug to help his wife who is dying from cancer, a Stage 4 adolescent would typically support his decision on the basis of social system morality. A Substage B response would go further and include such things as respect for both the needs of the husband as well as the pharmacist, the possible support for the husband since the right to life is essential, and the recognition that individuals may at times take actions that go beyond the existing norms of society. The development of these substages thus extends the original theory of moral development to include some of Gilligan's findings of care and responsibility and provides an opportunity to include moral action as well as moral judgments in scoring individuals' responses. "Subjects using B substage reasoning would be more likely to engage in the moral action they believed to be just, than would users of A substage reasoning" (Kohlberg, Levine, & Hewer, 1984: 252-3).

In addition to creating Substages A and B in response to scholarly criticism and empirical data, Kohlberg found it necessary to institute further changes in the stages described above. As a result of a number of longitudinal studies and the revised scoring system (Colby & Kohlberg, 1984), Kohlberg concluded that in order to attain the post conventional level of principled reasoning, one had to have adult life experiences. The data support this conclusion in that none of the studies reports Stage 5 thinking before the age of 20. Moral development, therefore, does not stop at adolescence but seems to continue into adulthood (Kohlberg, Snarey & Reimer, 1984).

While Stage 5 has now been postponed until later years, Stage 6 has disappeared completely because the longitudinal studies using the new scoring system found no one operating on this level. Kohlberg explained that in the earlier versions of the stage theory, he did find some philosophically trained individuals who, as a result of their sophisticated studies dealing with moral issues, were responding to the dilemmas on a Stage 6 level. Moreover, his readings of Plato's descriptions of Socrates and the writings of Martin Luther King led him to conclude at that time that Stage 6 constituted a realistic level of moral development. In spite of the disappearance of this stage, Kohlberg still includes it in his typology of moral development so that it may serve as a "theoretical construct" or a "theoretical end-point of justice reasoning" (Kohlberg, Levine, & Hewer, 1984: 271). Stage 6 characteristics, however, have not totally disappeared since a good bit that was included in this stage is now being subsumed under as Substage B.

■ Carol Gilligan's Criticism of Kohlberg's Stage Theories

Carol Gilligan's research and theorizing provide a major impetus for the rethinking of both developmental theory and the role of gender differences in our theoretical conceptualizations. For a number of years, she was associated with Kohlberg; she participated in his earlier research on moral judgment. However, Gilligan eventually did redefine Freud's and Kohlberg's notion that what is ethically normal in females "is different from what it is in men," postulating a new theoretical conceptualization of women's moral development. She does not deny that gender differences exist: quite the contrary, she develops her theoretical model in an effort to explain these gender differences and goes so far as to say that we really need two different theories to describe both sexes accurately. However, she differs significantly from Freud and Kohlberg, because she does not conceptualize these gender differences as "lower" or "higher," "better" or "worse," but as complementary. In Gilligan's system, the fact that feelings for the other person influence women's judgment is not at all a moral deficit but a moral quality, a unique and valuable moral asset. Thus, she redefines the issue: the female level of moral judgment is not "lower" than that of men but does require a different theoretical explanation.

Gilligan has demonstrated that males and females approach moral and other interpersonal issues from fundamentally different perspectives. They construct their relationships to self, others, and society in different ways. Men tend to organize social relationships in a hierarchical order and subscribe to a morality of rights in their judgments. Based on repeated responses to the Kohlbergian dilemmas, men respond to "an injunction to respect the rights of others and thus to protect from interference the right of life and self-fulfillment" (Gilligan, 1977: 511). In contrast, oriented toward interpersonal connectedness, females base their morality on care, sensitivity, and responsibility to people rather than on abstract principles of justice. For females, the moral imperative that recurs in the interview protocols involves "an injunction to care, a responsibility to discern and alleviate the 'real and recognizable trouble' of this world" (1977: 511).

Gilligan designed a series of studies to define more precisely the nature of these gender differences, the divergent male and female developmental patterns, the female perception of morality, and the way in which females make moral choices. She uses her findings to construct a theory quite different from those of her male predecessors—a feminist theory.

In all human experience and human judgment, Gilligan maintains, two different voices utilized by the majority of males and females emerge. One of these voices, the one most commonly identified with the masculine world, speaks of preserving rights, exercising justice, obeying rules, and upholding principles; logical and individualistic. This male voice advocates equality, reciprocity, autonomy, and individuation; in short, this represents the justice orientation. The other voice, more common in women than in men, speaks of caring for others, sensitivity to others, concern for others, connectedness to others. It emphasizes responsibility to human beings rather than to abstract principles and advocates avoiding hurt and violence, maintaining relationships and attachments even if self-sacrifice becomes necessary. In short, this female voice represents the "interpersonal network" or care orientation. Gilligan (1977, 1982) is describing two different voices which represent different ways of viewing the world, people, self, and morality. According to her theory of moral development, the first voice, the masculine voice, which represents the justice orientation, has become the standard for evaluating both males and females; Gilligan argues against this as prejudice to women. Since the interpersonal network or care orientation tends to be more salient in women, researchers in the past have portrayed women as deficient or even deviant in moral judgment because they have evaluated everyone against the masculine justice orientation.

At first Kohlberg felt that Gilligan's criticism belonged in the field of ego development rather than in his theory of moral development. However, as a result of further studies and reactions, Kohlberg accepted Gilligan's position and his revised stage theories include a Substage A and B (Kohlberg, Levine, & Hewer, 1984). The latter substage includes, among other things, Gilligan's criteria of caring, connectedness, and responsibility to people. Furthermore, the description of the new hypothetical Stage 6 contains a number of her suggestions.

As one would expect, the proposition of two different moral voices advocated by Gilligan produced a series of empirical studies. We shall restrict our summary of these studies to two questions: (1) Are there really two major orientations to moral judgment: the one of justice and rules as originally proposed by Kohlberg; and the one emphasizing care and responsibility to human beings as suggested by Gilligan? and (2) Are these two orientations gender-related?

Are there two orientations? The findings in most of the studies support the existence of both the justice and the care orientation. Considering the second question—whether these two approaches are gender-related—one discovers conflicting and inconclusive evidence. There are a number of studies (Haan, Langer, & Kohlberg, 1976; Lyons, 1983; and Parikh, 1980) which show a definite tendency for men to select a justice and rule approach and for women to choose the care and responsibility orientation. On the other hand, there are a significant number of studies that indicate that the choice of these two orientations is not related to gender (Snarey et al., 1985; Kohlberg, Snarey, & Reimer, 1984; Donenberg & Hoffman, 1988; Walker 1982, 1989, 1991). Men and women in these studies utilized both the justice and the caring approaches in making their moral decisions.

At one point Kohlberg suggested that those findings that did show gender differences did not control for education and job status. Snarey et al. (1985) tested this hypothesis and found that when these two factors are controlled, the gender differences did disappear (Kohlberg, 1984). These differences, however, do seem to appear under specific circumstance. After reviewing 27 studies, Walker (1984) found that while generally there does not seem to be any differences among men and women in their approach to moral judgments, some differences emerge when he analyzed the sub-groups. Among the adult subjects, women tended to resort to the care and responsibility orientation more often than men. Similarly, while no differences appeared in response to the somewhat theoretical dilemmas, women again more often used Gilligan's approach when confronted with real-life situations (Gilligan & Murphy, 1979; Murphy & Gilligan, 1980).

Several researchers surveyed the empirical literature with the hope that a broader perspective might yield some more reliable answers to the question of gender differences. Donenberg and Hoffman (1988) analyzed twelve studies and found that six revealed gender differences and six did not. Rothbart, Hanley, and Albert (1986) did a similar review of the literature and also concluded that the evidence is conflicting. They found that both men and women use care as well as justice responses; "however, the balance of women's arguments tends to be more care oriented than men's" (p. 651). Finally, Broughton (1983: 619) concluded, "overall the findings indicate that the existence of a sex difference in moral development, at least of the Kohlbergian variety, is still open to question, especially for the age group prior to adulthood."

■ Evaluation and Criticism of Kohlberg's Stage Theory

As mentioned earlier, Kohlberg (1970) claimed that his stages of moral judgment represent an invariant developmental sequence because they are universal and the thinking of any one moral stage remains fairly consistent in a variety of situations. Development inevitably progresses from the lower to the higher stages in an invariant sequence; the child moves sequentially and inexorably step by step through these stages. Theoretically, according to Kohlberg, these stages are constant, and normal development requires each in sequence.

Kohlberg maintains that these stages are universal. He believes that the moral structure reflected in the decisions in his dilemmas do not involve mastery of cultural values. He argues that the sequential patterning of these stages occurs under varying cultural conditions and that the principles of justice reflected in postconventional reasoning are free from culturally defined content.

These basic assumptions undergirding Kohlberg's stage theory have been subjected to considerable analysis and study. Scholars in such widely divergent fields as ethics, philosophy, sociology, and social and developmental psychology have engaged in lengthy debates about the validity of this moral theory. We will restrict our summary of this debate primarily to the empirical studies with an occasional detour into some philosophic issues.

■ Cross-Cultural, Socioeconomic, and Political Differences in Moral Reasoning

In support of his claim of universality in moral reasoning, Kohlberg (1964; Nisan & Kohlberg, 1982) and others have conducted research with adolescents not only in the United States but also in the Bahamas, Great Britain, Canada, Honduras, India, Israel, Kenya, Mexico, New Zealand, Nigeria, Taiwan, and Turkey. Although the sample includes few truly primitive societies, the findings support his claim of the universality of the developmental stages.

Later studies, however, raise questions about the universality of Kohlberg's stage theory. If his stages were truly universal, why do cultural differences appear in many cross-cultural studies? Tietjen and Walker (1985: 982) examined whether Kohlberg's reasoning applies to a "collectivistically oriented small scale, traditional society" and found that such an ideology is not part of his scoring. Even his own cross-cultural and longitudinal study (Kohlberg, Snarey & Reimer, 1984) in Israel revealed that the kibbutz ideology affected the moral reasoning of the subjects but there was no provision to score those responses in the Kohlberg manual. Snarey et al. (1985) reviewed forty-two cultures outside the United States and concluded that higher stage thinking appears far less frequently in non-Western cultures. Kohlberg explained these seemingly cultural differences as differences in content, not in form. He suggested that, while the specific content of responses is culture-bound, the moral reasoning (form) is basically the same across all cultures (Blum, 1990).

The concept of invariant stage sequence is an extremely important one in Kohlberg's theory of moral development and there is considerable evidence to support this notion (Kohlberg & Nisan, 1984; Kohlberg, Snarey, & Reimer, 1984; Rest, 1983; Snarey et al., 1985; Walker, 1982; 1989). However, Gilligan and Murphy (1979; Murphy & Gilligan, 1980) found regression to the less mature moral stage among some of their subjects. Kohlberg explains this regression as an indication of the faults in his scoring method which were corrected in 1984 (Colby & Kohlberg, 1984). Since then, however, the invariance of stage has been questioned once more by Levine, Jakubowski, and Côté (1992). Krebs et al. (1991) found that 87 percent used four or more substages in response to the dilemmas presented. Other studies likewise report the use of different moral stages in different situations (Levine 1976; 1979; Levine, Jakubowski, & Côté, 1992). Thus, the moral reasoning appears to be more domain-specific and less a matter of moral structure. The issue of domain specificity versus underlying structure is reminiscent of the same controversy in Piaget's theory (see pages 168–171). Rest (1983), after reviewing twelve studies, concludes that the evidence for an invariant stage is "inconclusive."

As noted previously, principled reasoning is essential in Kohlberg's theory of moral development. In our discussion of universality, we noted how cultural differences influence the use of this type of reasoning. In addition, such factors as job status and responsibility, level of education, and social climate affect the extent to which principled reasoning is utilized. Kohlberg, in *The Psychology of Moral Development* (1984: xxxv) admits that "[m]y earlier writing was, in part, an overstatement of the case for rational individual moral development."

One final concept needs to be examined. Justice, as we have seen, is a fundamental principle in Kohlberg's approach to resolving moral dilemmas. Once again, more recent studies raise some questions about this approach. We have already noted that Kohlberg's development of substages incorporated, in addition to the criteria of justice, such factors as care, responsibility, etc. Shweder and Haidt (1993) indicate that cultural psychologists have found sophisticated postconventional thinking that does not utilize the principle of justice. The Japanese, for example, emphasize group harmony and are willing at times to make a judgment in favor of the group that compromises justice (Markus & Kitayama, 1991). Indians too sacrifice justice because of the moral obligation to meet one's proper social role (Miller & Bersoff, 1992; Shweder & Much, 1991). Studies dealing with American subjects also raise the question whether justice is the principal criterion for moral judgment. Perlmutter and Shapiro (1987) argue that such factors as political climate, mass media, religious institutions, schools, and the psychological context of the "adolescent's individuation experience of attachment and separation within the family" (p. 201) all affect individuals as they make their moral judgments. Finally, Levine, Jakubowski, and Côté (1992) propose a "value consistency thesis, which states that certain characteristics of persons (such as ego qualities or ways of making moral judgments) persist through time and varying concrete circumstances as a result of the role played by internalized values" (p.293). It is these internalized values, they contend, rather than justice that are the determinants of moral choice.

In light of these questions concerning some of the basic assumptions of Kohlberg's work, must one reject his stage theories of moral development? Even his most vociferous critics do not endorse such a position. Shweder and Haidt (1993: 360), for example, in their review of Kurtines and Gewirtz's *Handbook of Moral Behavior and Development* (1991) point out that "[t]he 40 chapters contained in the *Handbook* make it clear that the voice of Kohlberg still dominates the current scene. The reference lists contain 143 references to his work, more than twice the number for any other author." Kagan (1993: 358), in another review of the *Handbook*, discusses methods of measuring moral development. "The most popular measurement procedure during the last 20 years," he writes, "was the product of Kohlberg's bold ideas, which lie in the shadow of almost every chapter in this trilogy on moral development."

In the process of making projections into the "post-Kohlbergian era," Lapsley provides a critical evaluation of Kohlberg's work. While attempting to combat moral relativism, he argues, Kohlberg made two "wrong turns." The first was to describe the ideal moral agent in Kantian terms. Such an individual "is an abstraction . . . and not a *psychological* being at all" (Lapsley, 1992: 175). The second wrong turn was his rejection of character education based on teaching specific values and virtues. It is interesting to note that while initially arguing against the "bag of virtues" approach, Kohlberg in one of his revisions of his stage theory does "admit . . . that this emphasis on the virtue of justice in my work does not fully reflect all that is recognized as being part of the moral domain. We may note that, in addition to justice, the moral domain also includes reference to a virtue emphasized by Christian ethical teachings" (Kohlberg, Levine & Hewer, 1984: 227). In a similar ironic twist, Lapsley points out that while Kohlberg's principal motivation in his study of moral development was to counter the position of the moral relativist, he nevertheless did conclude that some form of relativism in the context of social and cultural differences did exist. What, then, will the post-Kohlbergian era look like? He suggests that an all-encompassing theory like that of Kohlberg is not likely to emerge. Instead, he argues, scholars will probably work on smaller, more specific aspects of morality and moral development (Lapsley, 1992).

In spite of these wrong turns, Kohlberg's work appears to continue as one of the most important advances in our understanding of moral development and is likely to remain a major contribution to the field of moral development in the future.

EDUCATIONAL IMPLICATIONS

Though Kohlberg's theory of moral development has stimulated much thinking and much discussion about moral education in the classroom, it has not resolved many of the controversial issues that surround the teaching of morality. Parents fear that educational systems may impose arbitrary values upon their unsuspecting children, or worse, that the values taught in school are ones they might oppose for religious, political, or philosophical reasons. Consequently, the teaching of moral issues often becomes disguised in such "value-neutral" approaches as mental health, life adjustment, personality development, and more recently, "value clarification." Other parents, partly because of their own confusion as to what is right and partly because of their inability to teach those moral values that they accept, increasingly demand that values and moral behavior be taught in school. However, little consensus exists as to what those values are and how they should be imparted. Teachers and schools have been reluctant to teach moral values, partly because the teaching of middle-class values may confuse or offend the child who is exposed to lower-class values at home and partly because of the wide endorsement of a relativistic moral philosophy, not only among adolescents ("do your own thing"), but also among theologians in the form of "situational ethics." A teacher might say: "I will expose my children to my moral philosophy, but I will not impose it upon them. Who am I to say that I am right, and they are wrong?" Obviously, no easy solution to this dilemma seems likely.

The relativist philosophy of "doing your own thing" questions the school's right and obligation to teach morality. Historically speaking, American schools have progressed from the formal teaching of Christian moral values in the strict Puritanical tradition of the seventeenth century. A more subtle and indirect approach to morality appeared in the form of moral fables; in the McGuffey readers in the middle and the latter part of the nineteenth century, misbehavior inevitably resulted in painful consequences. During the early part of the twentieth century, emphasis fell on teaching virtues such as honesty, service, duty, and self-control. More recently, schools and teachers have declined the role of teaching virtues and values, especially when "values" seemed to mean only "white middle-class values." Some have construed that the Supreme Court's interpretation of the First Amendment concerning school prayer intends to eliminate not only religious education, but any form of moral and ethical education from public schools (Ball, 1967). By contrast, Kohlberg (1967) believes that the school can no more be committed to value neutrality than can the law, the Constitution, or the government. Two people obviously have the right to hold different values, but that does not mean that both are equally valid. Indeed, to believe that because a person maintains a sincere commitment to a set of values, these values are necessarily valid, sound, mature, or beneficial, involves an egregious fallacy. Public schools have a commitment to the development of the idea of justice, and Kohlberg attempts to make this commitment explicit. Furthermore, schools frequently have a "hidden moral curriculum" that becomes obvious in the kinds of behaviors that teachers reward and punish. Students learn to be obedient, to wash their hands, to avoid disturbing neighborhoods, to avoid fighting. The underlying moral assumptions regarding what behavior to reward and what to punish may actually remain unconscious on the teacher's part, involving no recognition of the reinforcement of explicit moral values.

The early version of moral education consisted of teaching a "bag of virtues." These included honesty, service, self-control, friendliness, and truthfulness. Aristotle had proposed a similar cluster of virtues including temperance, liberality, pride, good temper, and justice. More recently, the Boy Scouts advocate honesty, reverence, cleanliness, and bravery.

Traditionally, children were encouraged to practice virtuous behavior. They learned about the benefits and rewards of good behavior and about the harm or the punishment that would come if they were not virtuous. To illustrate the point, teachers used didactic stories in which good little children received rewards and bad ones received punishment. According to Piaget and Kohlberg, this experience amounts to training for an immature (Stage 2) level of moral development, since in more mature reasoning the abstract moral principle is more important than the material reward. The bag-of-virtue approach to moral education cannot be effective because virtue is not a psychological trait; virtues, such as honesty, are labels for abstract qualities not consistently reflected in behavior. The famous Hartshorne and May study (1928-1930) demonstrated that participation in the character-education program as provided in schools, churches, and Scouts did not contribute to improved moral behavior as measured by simulated situations involving honesty, self-control, and service. For example, almost all children cheated no matter what their moral education had been. Far from being a consistent trait, cheating depended upon the situation and the likelihood of being caught. Though some children cheated in one situation, this did not predict their behavior in other situations. Follow-up studies have supported these observations that moral knowledge and moral behavior often show low correlations. Children who did cheat were just as likely to say that cheating was wrong as those who did not cheat. When asked, "How can one teach morality?" Kohlberg answered as Socrates might have answered: "You must think I am very fortunate to know how virtue is acquired. The fact is that far from knowing whether it can be taught, I have no idea of what virtue really is" (Kohlberg, 1970: 144).

Kohlberg believed that educational procedures can facilitate moral reasoning; some of these have been tried experimentally. The goal of this approach is to aid children to take the next step to greater moral maturity, to assist them in developing the natural tendency toward which they are already predisposed. Kohlberg's suggestions to the teaching of moral values represent radical departures from those used in teaching a "bag of virtues" (which included preaching, rewarding, punishing, cajoling, and demanding). Far from being a "bag of virtues," morality for Kohlberg becomes an understanding of justice; consequently, schools must become concerned with moral development, moral reasoning, and an understanding of justice.

Prior to Piaget and Kohlberg, the belief that moral development functioned as a part of the socialization process dominated. Kohlberg assumed that progress from one stage to the next—like development in Piaget's theory—results from adaptation to a cognitive disequilibrium. The advance from one moral stage to the next is not simply a matter of socialization, of more or better understanding, but a reorganization and restructuring of earlier moral challenges. Working through moral conflicts which often emerge in interactions with peers can facilitate moral development, especially if the moral ideas and ideals of one's peers are slightly ahead of one's own conceptual development. In addition, Kohlberg (1969) sees moral development as a function of role-taking ability, an idea congruent with Selman's theory. Through role-taking, people learn to restructure their own moral schemata and incorporate those of others. Consequently, role-taking opportunities and interaction with peers will facilitate moral development. Keasey (1971) investigated these hypotheses and found that the stages of moral development of early adolescents showed a positive relation to the degree to which individuals rated highly in social participation and social interaction. Adolescents with significant peer group involvement, role-taking opportunities, and social interaction advanced more rapidly through the moral stages than the children who were withdrawn and lacked social participation opportunities. Selman (1971a), too, found that "the ability to understand reciprocal social perspectives"—that is, role-taking skills—

related positively to higher levels of moral thought and constituted one precondition for progression in moral development (see Chapter 11).

Teaching moral values involves several steps: first, creating in students a feeling of dissatisfaction about their present concept of good and bad, right or wrong. This cognitive disequilibrium results from exposing adolescents to situations involving moral conflicts for which they have no readily available solutions or which contradict their own point of view. The second step is to engage them in a discussion with their peers, a discussion in which different interpretations, disagreements, and conflicts are freely expressed, thereby inviting role-taking. Ideally, the moral arguments advanced should be one stage beyond the subject's own moral development, since arguments two or three stages ahead of a person are not easily assimilated and sometimes not even fully understood. Children and adolescents can understand the moral argument of all stages preceding their own and actually prefer the moral reasoning which they can comprehend (Rest, 1973); however, they rarely comprehend an argument that is more than one stage ahead of their own (Turiel, 1969). This position has recently been challenged by Walker (1982), where he showed that programs using two stages above the subject's moral development were equally effective. By creating a cognitive dissonance and having the subject listen to the arguments of others, the individual will see aspects of moral dilemma that were inaccessible to him before. As adolescents think about the problem, they are likely to incorporate into their thinking suggestions proposed by others. Cognitive conflict brings about the advance to the next level since resolution of conflict leads to a reorganization of structure—an idea not unlike Piaget's progression from equilibrium through disequilibrium to a higher level of equilibrium (Turiel, 1969) in cognitive development.

Research (Kohlberg & Blatt, 1972) utilizing this technique has demonstrated that 50 percent of the experimental subjects moved up one stage and an additional 10 percent moved up two stages. In a control group not exposed to such teaching of moral thinking, only 10 percent moved up one stage in the same period of time. Follow-up data suggest that the gain in moral structure was not temporary, but permanent. An experiment involving juvenile delinquents (Hickey, 1972)—who originally were at the preconventional level, espoused an "If I'm not getting nothing, I'm not giving nothing" philosophy—showed that most had moved to a Stage 4 law-and-order morality after exposure to this method of creating cognitive dissonance.

Kohlberg is concerned that schools themselves often do not espouse a very highly developed institutional moral philosophy in their actual day-to-day operation. All too often, school management seems to blend a fear of punishment (Stage 1) with an ever-present concern for law and order (Stage 4).

In an effort to raise the moral level of these kinds of schools, Kohlberg suggested the creation of "just communities" where decisions would be arrived at by group consensus in a democratic moral atmosphere. Students thus would have to listen to divergent opinions, encounter disequilibrium, reach a shared decision, and thereby learn to assume responsibility for their judgments. In the process they would be helped in moving forward to a higher stage in moral development. Kohlberg experimented with this approach with prisoners and found that such a communal approach was effective in raising the levels of moral reasoning (Jennings & Kohlberg, 1983). However, by applying analysis of covariance on the latter study, Lapsley et al. (1989: 124) found that "there was *no* significant differences between the just community and the behavior modification programs." Other studies (Higgins 1991; Power et al., 1989; Kohlberg, 1985; Kauffman, 1990) have found that the moral atmosphere approach was quite effective and therefore represents a promising development in moral education.

During the last decade, another approach, based on the distinctions between morality and social convention (Nucci 1982, 1989; Nucci & Weber 1991; Turiel, 1983; Turiel, Killen, & Helwig, 1987), has appeared. Morality is defined in Kohlbergian terms and deals with questions of justice, rights, and welfare which are universalizable. Social conventions, on the other hand, pertain to behaviors expected by a given society. Thus, questions of proper dress, manners, "forms of address, sex roles . . . are the arbitrary and agreed-upon uniformities in social behavior determined by the social system in which they are formed" (Nucci & Weber, 1991). These social conventions are not universal, but vary from society to society. Unlike the moral domain, social conventions can and do change, or in the words of Kohlberg, moral decisions are based on form (principled reasoning) while social conventions emphasize content. Based on this distinction between the moral domain and social convention, a new approach to values education was developed during the past 15 years. The goal of this domain approach is to help the student to recognize differences between moral issues and social conventions. Teachers present the students with issues in both the moral and social domains. In small discussion groups, the students are helped to identify the domain of that specific issue and learn to apply different criteria. When discussing moral issues the students are encouraged "to focus on underlying justice or human welfare considerations of the episode." When considering issues of social convention, the students are directed to concentrate "on the role of social expectations and social organizational function of social norms" (Nucci & Weber, 1991: 255).

Nucci and Weber investigated the effectiveness of this domain approach to education. They report that social convention and morality are indeed two "distinct conceptual systems" and that students who participated in this domain-appropriate program that emphasized the difference between questions of morality and those of social convention showed significant progress. These investigators conclude, "If we have learned Kohlberg's lesson, and the teachers we work with successfully integrate domain-appropriate values education in their teaching practices, we will have demonstrated that attention to domain is accessible to teachers, and can be made a part of a practical approach to values education" (Nucci & Weber, 1991: 264).

10

A FEMINIST PERSPECTIVE: CAROL GILLIGAN'S THEORY OF SEX DIFFERENCES IN ADOLESCENT DEVELOPMENT

There is increasing awareness and increasing evidence that most major developmental theories, written as they are from the male perspective, reflect a gender bias. The reasons are numerous and are due partly to the following: the creators of these theories have been predominantly male; the theoretical models have been based on research data collected from males; female data have not easily fit into the established male model (see Chapter 3); and historical writings, social values, and cultural prejudice and stereotypes seem to have influenced psychological and developmental thinking in the past (see Preface).

Initially, like many of the developmental theorists who preceded him, Kohlberg conducted his research on moral development with male subjects and developed his scoring method from male responses. Based only on males' resolutions of moral dilemmas, Kohlberg's theory necessarily reflects a bias against females. Eventually, Kohlberg did administer the moral dilemmas to females as well, and he does observe gender differences in the development of moral judgment. However, he identifies these differences primarily in quantitative, not qualitative, terms. Kohlberg and Kramer (1969) and others have rather consistently observed—and cross-cultural data support their observations—that the average adolescent female is more likely to attain a moral judgment rating corresponding to Stage 3 (the good boy-nice girl orientation); frequently, this becomes the terminal stage for females. In Stage 3, the stage in moral development referred to as "interpersonal normative morality," the subject perceives morality in terms of interpersonal relationships; goodness implies helping or caring for and pleasing others. Adolescent boys of the same age typically score approximately one stage higher, with an average at Stage 4 (the law-and-order orientation). In Stage 4, subjects base their moral judgments on whether the behavior maintains or violates the existing social order. In addition, according to Kohlberg and others, more male than female adolescents move beyond Stage 4 to the higher postconventional level of

Carol Gilligan (1936–   )

development in their moral judgment. This gender difference in the past used to be explained as a deficiency in the female's ability to apply advanced principles of moral judgment. To put the argument in different terms, Kohlberg's system appears to penalize women for their greater sensitivity to others and their caring attitude, and to reward males for their preference for abstract principles of justice.

GENDER DIFFERENCES IN PERCEPTIONS OF VIOLENCE

Susan Pollak and Carol Gilligan conducted an interesting related research study, "Images of Violence in Thematic Apperception Test Stories" (1982). Stories written by college students in response to four TAT (Thematic Apperception Test) pictures were analyzed for violence. Violence was defined as inflicting actual harm, such as homicide, suicide, accidental death, rape or forcible violation, physical assault, etc., on others.

Two of the four TAT pictures used as stimuli represent "affiliation themes" and depict people in close interpersonal relationships: (1) a man and a woman sitting next to each other overlooking a river; (2) a man and a woman in a trapeze act, the woman in midair, grasping the man's wrist. The remaining two pictures, representing "achievement themes," show (3) a man alone at his desk in a high-rise office, with a picture of his wife and children on his desk; and (4) a group of women working in white coats in a lab, with an older woman in the background supervising the group.

The stories were scored by two different methods. First, the researchers looked for the presence or absence of violent imagery in each of the situations depicted. Second, an independent score was based on whether, in the violent stories, the subject associated danger with the affiliation or with the achievement situations. Horner (1972), in her research, had observed that women often wrote violent endings to situations exhibiting competitive academic success. Pollak and Gilligan found that men often created violent stories for pictures suggesting affiliation and possible intimacy. From these initial observations about gender differences, they developed the initial hypothesis that men are more likely to experience "fear of intimacy," to see danger in interpersonal closeness, and to project violence into situations that depict affiliation and intimacy. In contrast, if women experience "fear of success," they are more likely to see danger in being alone and to project violence into competitive achievement situations.

The findings supported the existence of gender differences both in the quantity of aggression and also in the distribution of violent imagery in response to affiliation or achievement themes. As expected, and as has been reported elsewhere, the occurrence of violence in the stories of college men was much more common (51 percent portrayed violence in at least one story) than in women's stories (22 percent). However, more interesting than these expected quantitative differences are the gender differences in violence elicited by affiliation-versus-achievement themes. Gilligan and Pollak based their scoring criteria on the situations depicted in the pictures. The male students' responses to the two pictures showing interpersonal affiliation and possible intimacy revealed more violence (26 percent) than the females' stories (only 6 percent). For the pictures suggesting achievement themes, these findings were reversed. In response to the achievement pictures, 16 percent of the women created violent stories as compared with only 6.8 percent of the men. In addition, some men but no women perceived violence in both the affiliation and the achievement situations. Pollak and Gilligan assert that these data support an interpretation of qualitative differences between males' and females' perceptions of violence.

A somewhat different scoring approach was obtained when the researchers analyzed the content of the stories in terms of where males and females perceive danger. In general, these independently derived data follow the same trend as those found in violence studies, but they demonstrate even more dramatic gender differences. In the affiliation situations, 26 percent of the men but none of the women (0 percent) perceived danger. In contrast, in the achievement situations 12 percent of the women but only 1.1 percent of the men perceived danger. In the stories of both the male and the female students, the victims of the violence tended to be females, a trend that was even more pronounced for the female students, who seldom created stories in which the victim was a male.

Pollak and Gilligan concluded from these data "that men and women perceive danger in different situations and construe danger in different ways" (1982: 164). In a more general sense, and quite consistent with the overall theme of Gilligan's research and her emerging theory, men seem more likely to see danger in interpersonal connectedness and may fear being entrapped, rejected, humiliated, or betrayed; men perceive competitive achievement as less dangerous than do women. Women, in contrast, see danger in the separation from others which comes with competitive success; they fear being left alone, isolated, or separated. Gilligan speaks of the tremendous sensitivity to abandonment in women, who tend to view interpersonal affiliation and intimacy as safe and nonthreatening. For many women, interpersonal care and intimacy are very important personal goals and their interpersonal network is something that they want to protect.

Thus, this study of college students' violent imagery and their perception of danger complements the moral judgment studies summarized above and gives additional credence to the theory that men and women structure their environments differently, show different orientations to affiliation and achievement situations, and speak with "different voices."

TEENAGERS' MORAL REASONING WITH SEXUAL DILEMMAS

Most of the past research concerned with moral judgment utilizes Kohlberg's standard moral dilemmas such as Heinz's Problem. Only an expensive drug available in the pharmacy can save his dying wife, but Heinz cannot afford the price. Critics of Kohlberg's methodology have suggested that the content of dilemmas and the nature of his moral problems make the likelihood of such occurrences improbable in the daily experiences of the average adolescent. In other words, Heinz's dilemma and others like it seem quite unrelated to the decisions and choices that people actually have to make. Therefore, one may question whether or not the exercise constitutes detached intellectual reasoning with a moral content or whether it really assesses a personal, existential moral judgment. This issue is crucial because the assessment of moral development depends on the subject's actual rather than hypothetical choices.

The question underlying this distinction involves whether or not adolescents can apply their impersonal moral reasoning skills equally effectively in a context that may correspond to real life situations. Gilligan, Kohlberg, and several others conducted a study to investigate this issue. The researchers developed three new, more personally applicable sexual dilemmas describing situations with which teenagers are more likely to identify, situations which they might actually experience.

Such a sexual dilemma, with abbreviated questions assessing moral reasoning, might illustrate the personal relevancy of the underlying conflict:

A high school girl's parents are away for the weekend and she's alone in the house. Unexpectedly, on Friday evening, her boyfriend comes over. They spend the evening together in the house and after a while, they start necking and petting.

1. Is this right or wrong? Are there any circumstances that would make it right (wrong)?
2. What if they had sexual intercourse? Is that right or wrong? Why?

3. (If applicable:) Why do you think petting is OK but sexual intercourse is wrong?
4. Are there any circumstances that would make sexual intercourse right (wrong)?
5. Suppose the girl is less willing than the boy to have sexual intercourse. The girl thinks sex before marriage is OK for boys but not for girls. What reasons does she have for thinking that way? What is your thinking about this?
6. The girl's parents return and find out that the couple had sexual intercourse. What should the parents do?
7. Do you think these issues about sex have anything to do with morality and immorality?
8. Where do you think your ideas about what's right and wrong come from?
9. There is a lot of talk these days about the new morality and the sexual revolution. What do you think about this? (Gilligan et al., 1971: 151–152).

Three such sexual dilemmas along with Kohlberg's standard moral dilemmas were administered to 25 male and 25 female high school juniors from a higher and a lower academic group of a suburban high school. As critics had suggested might be the case, the level of Moral Maturity Scores (MMS) on Kohlberg's standard dilemmas was significantly higher than on the sexual relationship dilemmas with which adolescents are more likely to identify personally. On the standard MMS, subjects scored about halfway between Stage 3 and Stage 4; however, on the sexual dilemmas they clearly scored on Stage 3. Fifty percent of the subjects reasoned on the same stage when working out both sets of problems; however, of those who demonstrated any changes, 80 percent exhibited a lower level of reasoning when asked to respond to the sexual dilemma. This was equally true for both sexes, but comparing the impersonal MMS with the personally relevant sexual dilemmas, the boys obtained greater differences than the girls. For example, 13 boys fell two stages, 6 declined three stages, but none of the girls dropped more than one stage. The evaluations for girls on the sexual dilemmas remained closer to their general MMS than those for boys. Girls in general tended to be somewhat more conservative in their reasoning of the sexual dilemmas, a characteristic which in this hypothetical situation appeared to be in their own best interest.

The decline in moral reasoning from Stage 3.5 to Stage 3 is both statistically and theoretically significant. Stage 3 implies a great deal of influence of significant others, peer group pressure, conformity to those who matter in life, and desire to be accepted by doing what others expect. Obviously, in a situation involving sexual temptations, these kinds of pressures can influence practical decisions. Gilligan et al. conclude that "the affective involvement of the adolescent with sex depresses his ability to reason at a level comparable to that shown on more abstract issues" (1971: 149).

ABORTION AS A MORAL DILEMMA

In a related study, Gilligan and Belenky (1980) examined the moral reasoning of young women involved in making a personal, existential abortion decision, a very difficult moral choice. The abortion decision, obviously a central issue in women's moral choices, emphasizes the conflict between self-interest and concern for others.

Abortion and pregnancy counseling services referred to the investigators 29 women whose pregnancy had been confirmed and who were seriously considering abortion. Their ages ranged from 15 to 33, and they represented diversity in ethnic and social class background. The researchers administered several of Kohlberg's standard hypothetical moral dilemmas to them and interviewed them in some depth about their reasoning in regard to whether or not to terminate the pregnancy. The issue was not whether they decided to abort or to have the baby, but the moral reasoning that led to their eventual choices. Using criteria based on Kohlberg's theory, the investigators scored the subjects' responses according to the underlying level of moral reasoning.

The first interview took place during the first trimester of the pregnancy, followed by a similar interview with 24 subjects of the initial group one year later. These data allowed the analysis of several related issues:

1. The relationship between the level of impersonal moral reasoning on Kohlberg's dilemma (Moral Maturity Score = MMS) and the level of moral reasoning underlying their personal abortion decision.
2. The changes in moral reasoning that took place between the first interview and the second interview a year later and how the patterns of relationship identified under 1 (above) related to changes in moral reasoning.

Three different patterns emerged from the data:

1. For one group of women, the MMS and the abortion reasoning scores were about the same. These women applied their moral reasoning equally effectively to impersonal issues and to their own personal abortion dilemma.
2. For a second group of women, reasoning about personal decisions operated on a more mature level than more generalized moral reasoning.
3. A third group of women scored higher on the impersonal, traditional moral dilemmas and lower in respect to their own personal abortion decision. Apparently, they were unable to apply their moral reasoning ability when they themselves were directly and personally involved in the issue of having to make an existential choice. This third pattern corresponds to that of many of the adolescents responding to the sexual dilemmas whose scores dropped lower when confronting more personal problems.

Group 2, those for whom the reasoning about their own personal abortion issues had been higher than the more traditional MMS, experienced the greatest amount of growth in moral reasoning during the intervening year. Apparently, working through a personal moral issue facilitated maturation; in addition, even the more general life circumstances of those in this group had improved during the intervening year.

For the remaining two groups, (Group 1, traditional and abortion reasoning on the same level, and Group 3, traditional reasoning higher than the abortion reasoning), there really was no significant downward or upward trend in moral reasoning during the intervening year. Their level of moral reasoning had remained unchanged. Even though they did not experience a change in overall moral reasoning ability, the third group, whose MMS had been significantly higher and the level of abortion reasoning lower, did give evidence that they were unhappy both about life in general and the abortion decision in particular.

They also had experienced a decline in emotional and mental health a year after the initial interview.

GILLIGAN'S PARADIGM: A THEORETICAL CONSOLIDATION

Based on an analysis of the moral reasoning of women confronted with the abortion issue as well as gender differences in perceptions of violence and sexual dilemmas (some of which used Kohlberg's traditional moral dilemma situations), Gilligan suggests that we replace Kohlberg's male-oriented preconventional, conventional, and postconventional levels of moral reasoning with different constructs for males and females. The redefined female levels are based on interpersonal relationships in women's moral reasoning, not on Kohlberg's principles of justice based on the moral judgment of males. Gilligan developed her own model for levels of moral reasoning. Although Gilligan's interest in the differences between male and female levels of moral reasoning continued into her later research, her more recent studies reflect her concern for the crises she observed as young girls became adolescents.

GILLIGAN'S REVELATION: THE MISSING VOICE

Gilligan taught at Harvard with Erikson and Kohlberg during the Vietnam war. She worked on a traditional longitudinal study to see if Harvard students facing the draft fit Kohlberg's theory of identity and morality. When the war was over and the Supreme Court legalized abortion, she began a different study of women who were facing very personal decisions relating to their pregnancies. Gilligan discussed her "revelation" in an interview. She was at home with her children that year and was looking through the women's interviews when a friend and colleague visited. "And I said, 'Dora, these women—they are constructing self and they're constructing what's a moral problem differently—and that's why they weren't fitting into the whole discussion of self in Freud and Erikson . . . and that's why women were falling through the sieve of Kohlberg's categories'" (Kitzinger, 1994: 409). Gilligan's friend suggested that she write about her observations. Gilligan said, "I did. I mean for nothing; for no-one. I just sat and wrote an article called 'In a Different Voice: Women's Conceptions of Self and Morality' (Gilligan, 1977). And it was then that I realized something that was just *stunning* to me, because I had never noticed that Erikson's work on identity was done with an all-male sample (returning war veterans); that Freud's work had a male voice . . . that Piaget had all boys in his *Moral Judgment of the Child* and Kohlberg's 20-year longitudinal research, heavily funded, was done with an all-male sample" (Kitzinger, 1994: 409).

THE EMMA WILLARD SCHOOL STUDY

As a result of the insights regarding gender differences gained by Gilligan and others, the Harvard Project on the Psychology of Women and the Development of Girls was created. The project is specifically designed to include girls' and women's voices in the study of human psychological development by listening to and attempting to record what girls and women really think. Although Gilligan conducted two of her well-known studies at private schools, the Emma Willard School and the Laurel School, the conclusions she reached have been validated by her more recent research with urban adolescent girls considered to be at risk.

The first program undertaken by the Harvard Project began at the Emma Willard School in Troy, New York. Robert C. Parker, the school's former principal, approached Gilligan and asked for help. "The school had a question . . . 'How can we make intelligent decisions about girls' education without knowing about their psychological development?'" (Prose, 1990:13). Gilligan's research clearly validated Parker's concern. It became obvious that there had been a longstanding inequity between the great amount of research done on adolescent males and the sparse amount done on adolescent females. Since her work at the Emma Willard School, Gilligan's research has been primarily focused on female adolescent development. Her goal is to fill the gaps created by the gender bias of prior research.

Gilligan and her colleagues conducted a five-year longitudinal study which included extensive interviews and a standard sentence completion test. The research team investigated girls' understanding of the world around them, their relationships with others, and their ability to distinguish between authentic and fraudulent feelings. The researchers conducted one-on-one interviews with the girls and asked these girls the same questions over a five-year period. The girls were given Loevinger's Washington University Sentence Completion Test (WUSCT). (See Chapter 12 for a discussion of methodology and theory.) They were asked to finish the standard 36 incomplete sentences such as: "A woman should always———"; and "Rules are———."

Gilligan's findings caused her to revise her description of women's developmental sequence in moral judgment. "The developmental sequence I had traced—three levels: survival, goodness, and truth, and two transitions: repairing relationship by correcting an exclusion of others, or of self—did not jibe with my observations of younger girls. In short, the sequence that I had traced by following adolescent girls and adult women through time and through crisis did not seem to be rooted in childhood. Instead, it seemed a response to a crisis, and the crisis seemed to be adolescence" (Gilligan, Lyons, & Hanmer, 1990: 9).

■ What Happens to Girls as They Go Through Adolescence?

According to the data collected at Emma Willard, adolescence creates a crisis for girls because it forces a showdown between what they know to be true about relationships and responsiveness to others, and the demands made on them to "grow up" and assert their independence by disconnecting and separating from others. For girls, the experience of this crisis in connection is often devastating. Gilligan relates this to an increased incidence of depression among adolescent girls, and an increase of female suicide attempts and suicidal ideation during adolescence. As many studies and clinical observations have revealed, girls are more self-disparaging than boys when evaluating their physical appearance, and female eating disorders begin during adolescence.

Gilligan and her colleagues identified three developmental stages. Stage One, characterized by a confident world view, occurs in childhood. Young girls, ages 7 to 10, tend to be forthright in their observations, claim their authority without hesitation, and describe their world without inhibitions.

By the time girls approach eleven, they enter Stage Two. Gilligan refers to girls at this age as "Whistle Blowers." At 11 girls become astute observers and outspoken critics of "where and when women speak and when they are silent. As resisters, they may be especially prone to notice and question the compliance of women to male authority . . . " (Gilligan et al., 1990: 25). As Stage Two girls observe the interplay between males and females, they are especially tuned in to compliance and capitulation on the part of adult women. They do not like it and feel compelled to "blow the whistle" on acquiescence and applaud assertiveness. One teacher shared a story with Gilligan that clearly illustrates this behavior. A female teacher was working with a male colleague who had made a new rule that he announced to the students without her knowledge or consent. The students resisted the rule, but the female teacher felt compelled to uphold the other teacher's authority. One day when it was clear that the rule was senseless, the female teacher excused the students from obeying the rule. " 'Good for you,' the girls said, 'we're proud of you.'" (Gilligan et al., 1990: 25). The students had accurately observed everything and were proud of the female teacher for finally standing up for what she believed was right.

Stage Three, revealed by personal confusion, occurs during adolescence. Gilligan found that adolescent girls learn to understand the human social world, but they distance themselves from their knowledge by "regularly prefacing their observations by saying, 'I don't know'" (Gilligan et al., 1990: 14).

Gilligan says, "Eleven year olds are not for sale," (Prose, 1990: 12) but 15- and 16-year-old girls bury their knowledge and parts of themselves in an intricate, repressed underworld. It is during adolescence that "girls are in danger of losing their voices and thus their connection with others" (Gilligan et al., 1990: 25).

According to Stern, a researcher involved in the Emma Willard School study, adolescence for girls is a time of great paradox. By virtue of being adolescent, they are expected to separate from their families and become autonomous; however, by virtue of being female, their need for connection has not abated. Stern's studies reveal girls' complicated systems of maintaining connections and relationships while developing a sense of autonomy. One student in the study described her own system of independent relationships with great clarity, "I'm going to become more independent, and I'm going to be able to continue to see it as more of a relationship . . . As I realize that my mother's not just there for me and as I become more independent, that's going to cause me to stop seeing it as just taking my mother for granted . . . " (Gilligan et al., 1990: 83).

When asked to describe themselves, many participants included information about other people, especially in terms of the girls' relationships with others. However, using the presence/absence response count, Stern noted that 19 of the 23 participants described themselves as independent at some point over the years of the study. Although theorists such as Peter Blos believe that being independent and being connected are in opposition to each other, the young women in this study discussed the need to assimilate both. "Relationships without independence become just as problematic as independence without relationships" (Gilligan et al., 1990: 85).

Making Connections: The Relational Worlds of Adolescent Girls at Emma Willard School, edited by Gilligan, Lyons, and Hanmer, is a compilation of essays written by members of the Harvard Project research team. The research at the Emma Willard School was started in 1981 and completed in 1984. During this project, the team employed standard research design procedures. Using random assignment, two groups were established. The experimental group was given a series of open-ended questions and encouraged to talk freely. The control group was asked to respond to hypothetical dilemmas and standard probe questions. "The . . . study as a whole was designed to permit both cross-sectional and longitudinal analyses" (Gilligan et al., 1990: 161). Longitudinal analysis of the data was possible because the same girls were studied over the 3-year course of the research. Cross-sectional analysis was possible because different-aged subgroups were also studied. The stages described were consistent both in longitudinal and cross-sectional analyses.

THE LAUREL SCHOOL STUDY

The original goal of the research at the Laurel School in Cleveland, Ohio, was to study younger girls, to continue research on adolescent girls, and to verify the connections between interview data and other standard measures used in developmental psychology (Brown & Gilligan, 1992). When the team went to the Laurel School and described their research plan, the students' reaction forced the scholars to redesign their research model and their relationship with their subjects.

Soon after the arrival of the 13-member research team, "the word was out: there are two interviews—the personal one and the one with 'the little stories'" (Brown & Gilligan, 1992: 9). The students began preparing for their interviews, telling each other what to say, and virtually "rehearsing their lines." The girls' underground system sent shock waves through the school and through the research team. The hypocrisy of learning about girls by standing apart from them and then commenting about girls' needs for relationships was obvious. "We needed, it seemed, to create a practice of psychology that was something more like a practice of relationship" (Brown & Gilligan, 1992: 15). As a result of the girls' resistance, the comments made by the girls to the team, and the researchers' own observations, the research staff made significant changes in their research design. "Clearly we needed a different way of working and a method which did not interfere with our ability to listen to ourselves and to others but which enabled us to bring our knowledge as women and as psychologists into relationship with our work" (Brown & Gilligan, 1992: 15). The team believed that their new approach to studying development helped their efforts to clarify and embellish the three stages which they had already identified at the Emma Willard School.

Gilligan let go of the traditional research design and by implication let go of the standard practices of authority, distance, and order. In their place, they created a "Listener's Guide—a voice-sensitive way of working that allowed us to follow girls' thoughts and feelings and to hear girls' struggle at adolescence" (Brown & Gilligan, 1992: 16).

As a result of the revised research design, the girls became more open, more outspoken, warmer, more playful, and more genuine in their relationships with the researchers. In effect, the students were no longer "research subjects" and became instead research partners.

■ Centering on Voice

Gilligan's new technique required the listeners to ask questions in order to learn about the storyteller, her sense of the relationships being described, and her social and cultural background. Each person's story was then recorded and listened to at least four times. The first time, the research team listened in order to understand the plot. The second time, they listened for the "I" in the story, the emotions, and the speaker's sense of self. The third and fourth time, they listened for the relationships described in the story.

Using this technique during a 5-year study, Gilligan and her colleagues could describe the changes they heard in their interviews. When the girls were young, Stage One, they were outspoken. As preadolescents, Stage Two, they expressed frustration with the adult women who appear to them as being submissive and compliant to male authority. When they reached adolescence, Stage Three, their voices expressed ambivalence, confusion, and denial.

Stage One girls speak with clarity. They are willing to voice painful and difficult feelings. They maintain their friendships by being direct. One 8-year-old girl described what she would do if she were playing at a friend's house and felt left out. ". . . I would say, 'This is really making me feel bad, for leaving me out. Can you please play with me too? . . . I will go home if you don't, cause this isn't any fun for me, just sitting here'" (Brown & Gilligan, 1992: 54).

On the border of adolescence, Stage Two 11- and 12-year-old girls are astute observers. They are aware of what they know. However, simultaneously they are becoming sensitized to the discrepancy between that knowledge and what they hear adults, especially women, say and do. They resist the notion that a woman has to accept being compliant to male authority. With impressive accuracy, these young women point out their frustrations while watching the adult women in their lives capitulate, cover, and reconfigure reality. One woman teacher at the Laurel School described a painful conversation between her and her 11-year-old daughter. The youngster said she was angry with her mother because whenever the girl's parents fought, the mother gave in. The mother said she felt humiliated by the accuracy of her daughter's observation.

The pivotal time in girls' adolescence appears to be 12 and 13. Gilligan speculates that in part it is girls' fear of being exposed to attention and anger that triggers the onset of this dilemma. "Aware of the realities of physical violence and also of psychological violation, girls have reason to fear arousing other people's anger" (Brown & Gilligan, 1992: 173).

On one hand, girls at this age speak about strong feelings and describe their relational conflicts accurately and with precise insights. On the other hand, they use the phrase, "I don't know." Sometimes they really don't know, but much more often it is a signal that precedes perceptive observations. According to Gilligan, girls must choose between the knowledge they have gained and the voices of authority, especially women's voices, who express conflicting versions of that knowledge.

The researchers concluded that adolescent girls struggle with their desire to have authentic relationships in which they can express themselves freely and their fear that a free expression of feelings and thoughts will jeopardize and endanger their relationships with their peers as well as with the adults in their lives. Caught in this trap, they are afraid to bring their real voice into adult womanhood. This conflict creates the "unauthentic" voice of adolescence. "The erosion of girls' capacity to stay in relationship with themselves and with others becomes clear . . . [As] girls struggle with relational conflicts and exclusive choices—choices that destroy relationship whichever way they turn. The either-or framing . . . marks an inner psychological split or division" (Brown & Gilligan, 1992: 176-177).

In interviews with the same girls at 15, an entirely different voice is heard. At 15, girls describe fraudulent, idealized relationships. Buried under what they know and feel and think is a constant barrage of "I don't know." Some girls model themselves on the image of the "perfect, nice girl" who does not want to hurt anyone or appear defiant. Many adolescent girls lose their sense of who they are, how they feel, and what they know. One young woman in the study said: "'The voice that stands up for what I believe in has been buried deep inside of me'" (Brown & Gilligan, 1992: 40).

During adolescence, girls are encouraged to cover strong feelings under calm and quiet behavior. Words that had clarity—"friend," "love," "caring,"—get lost in a system where everyone is supposed to be a friend. In the process, many girls separate what they know and feel so they only experience what nice girls are supposed to know and feel. This separation between their existential self and their socially acceptable self creates turmoil, confusion, and inner conflict.

According to Gilligan, the result of this stage is a type of double vision. Many adolescent girls cannot really see what they see or feel what they feel, or they will not fit their idealized model of the perfect girl. The images portrayed for girls from the popular culture, TV, and listening in to what adults are saying encourage many girls to label their childhood feelings as "selfish" or "self-centered." Instead, they are drawn to the image of the lovable, selfless, self-silenced perfect girl. Many adolescent girls speak in their unauthentic voice in order to fit their image of the nice, perfect girl. In this voice they are not selfish, unkind, or real. "Poised at the edge, and suspecting that people prefer the 'perfect' girl to the real one, these girls experiment with her image and the protection and security and happiness she promises" (Brown & Gilligan, 1992: 100).

Gilligan's findings at the Laurel School verified her findings at the Emma Willard School. However, at Laurel she uncovered the impact of the image of the "perfect girl" in the development of physical and emotional pathologies in some female adolescents. She knew from her work at the Emma Willard School that adolescent girls lost their voice, but the insights gained at the Laurel School helped her to explain why and how.

As a result of her work at the Laurel School, Gilligan moved from behind the traditional research screen of the third person, objective observer, and wrote *Meeting at the Crossroads* with her collaborator in the first person. This movement away from what Gilligan refers to as the "hidden, oracular voice" to the relational first-person voice created a fundamental systemic change. The team chose to let go of their planned experimental-control group design and replace it with what they describe as being an unpredictable and vulnerable ongoing relationship model which is both disruptive and more genuine, unsettling and more sensitive (Brown & Gilligan, 1992). In this work, the voices of the research team join with the voices of the girls, and a community of learners share their life's experiences.

Gilligan's experiences at the Laurel School led her to further her study of girls and women sharing their experiences. Using their "voice-centered relational method" in a research study of urban adolescent females considered to be at risk, Gilligan and her research team confirmed many of her findings at the Emma Willard School and the Laurel School. Urban girls describe the same problems in trying to maintain relationships and trying to stay connected to their own knowledge as those described by girls attending private schools.

Gilligan found that it is through connections with women that girls are often able to sustain ". . . their knowledge of their own thoughts, feelings, and relationships. A number of the girls speak about the importance of adult women in their lives who are able to listen, confirm the validity and value of their experience, and help them think about their futures. Alternatively, the girls who appeared to be in the most psychological distress reported few or no ties to adult women" (Gilligan et al., 1992: 270).

Although this study was conducted with women educators and urban adolescents, Gilligan does not make the point that it is just women educators who can add the connecting ties that young women need. Any woman who will listen, validate, and encourage can make the difference between risk and resilience in a young woman's life.

EDUCATIONAL IMPLICATIONS

In an address given at Fordham University in 1994, Gilligan discussed the idealized implications of her work; however, she does not provide the practical strategies necessary to reach her goals. Using Toni Morrison's novel, *The Bluest Eyes*, as one of her analogies, Gilligan says that when we look at the way we live with each other, and the way we live with those who are different, the need for radical cultural changes becomes apparent. " 'How' is the naturalist's question, and also the novelist's question. It is deeply scientific and creative. To understand how something happens may point to how it could *not* happen" (Gilligan, 1994: 30). In order to end the process which leads to adolescent girls' experiencing increased depression, eating disorders, and suicide attempts, girls will need to belong to social, educational, and familial systems that do not require them to choose between voice and relationships. In Gilligan's vision of her "how it will *not* happen model," girls will not have to face political, psychological, or physical attacks, or at least will not have to face them alone. Men will no longer have to disconnect from women, and women will no longer have to dissociate from themselves. The relationships between men and women will resonate, and education will become more vital.

CRITIQUE OF GILLIGAN'S THEORY AND INFERENCES ABOUT OTHER THEORIES

Intriguing as Gilligan's theory is, the empirical basis is weak, especially the empirical support from researchers whose primary concerns are gender differences in moral judgment. The invariant and developmental sequential nature of her stage theories have been called into question, even by Gilligan. Critics have even questioned Gilligan's basic assumption that female children and adolescents score consistently lower on the traditional moral dilemmas Kohlberg originally developed. Existing research data are much less clear-cut in supporting Gilligan's notion that males' moral judgments tend to be governed by a principled justice orientation and that of females show more empathy, altruistic concern for the other person and a greater interpersonal orientation. The data reveal that both voices express care and justice themes. However, females do tend to voice more care and relational themes, and males voice more justice/injustice themes.

Gilligan presents data relevant to her basic argument in four areas: moral judgment, sex differences in violence, sexual dilemmas, and the abortion decision. However, by inference, much of what Gilligan has to say about the limited applicability of Kohlberg's theory of the development in females of moral judgment suggests that similar shortcomings may exist in many other theories of adolescent development presented in this book. Gilligan suggests that past models of human development have often failed to give the female experience its unique place and its proper value in our theoretical conceptualizations. By extension, Gilligan suggests that we might need to theorize differently for males and females.

Sullivan's theory (see Chapter 5) is relevant to this discussion. His stages—specifically what happens just before and during adolescence—do seem to present primarily in a male perspective. However, his remarkable insight and continuous emphasis on the significance of others, or interpersonal relationships and communication and care seems to have anticipated many of the same elements which Gilligan now identifies as the female experience.

In summary, Gilligan believes that during childhood, both boys and girls feel free to express their thoughts and feelings. However, at around age 11, girls become aware of the differences in the way adult men and women express anger, compliance, and power. By the time girls reach adolescence, many experience a crisis which Gilligan refers to as a loss of "voice." Using a barrage of "I don't know," many adolescent girls disown what they know and disconnect from their essential selves.

The main criticisms of Gilligan's later work revolve around several issues: (1) her movement away from standard research practices; (2) the criteria she uses for defining her concepts, for example, authentic and unauthentic voice; (3) the absence of male subjects in any of her recent studies; and (4) her selection of private school subjects in her earlier studies. Critics also have attacked her for developing a closed system which can only confirm, never invalidate, her theory.

Although Gilligan no longer uses an experimental-control group design which requires the researcher to stand apart from the study, she describes her work as empirical and data-driven. Gilligan's work with the Harvard Project on Women's Psychology and Girls' Development was an outgrowth of her awareness of the existence of gender bias of earlier studies. The primary goal of her project is to express the female voice which had been missing in earlier research. Clearly, her work at the Emma Willard School and the Laurel School was based on a selective population; however, two recent studies she conducted on urban adolescents have helped to broaden her subject base and support the generalizability of her earlier private school findings. She encourages fellow researchers to stop trying to invalidate each other's work, and instead ask each other more searching questions that will generate better research.

C H A P T E R

11

ROBERT SELMAN'S THEORY OF INTERPERSONAL UNDERSTANDING

SOCIAL COGNITION

The complex and multifaceted concept of social cognition has been embraced by many psychologists. Generating constructs such as empathy, altruism, egocentrism, self-recognition, role-taking, social competency, social rules and conventions, etc., social cognition theory cannot be considered one single theory nor one precisely definable conceptual domain. Instead, the concept of social cognition is best understood as a rather diverse group of mini-theories, constructs, and submodels, each pursuing its own agenda, emphasizing a different or at least an independent orientation, and relying on a different methodology. Therefore, interpersonal cognition or social intelligence cannot be perceived as one uniform, consistent, theoretical construct such as the original theories developed by Erikson or Piaget. Social cognition theory constitutes the integration of several trends, combining and cross-fertilizing some of the insights gained from cognitive and moral development theory as well as the accumulated empirical knowledge about social development in general. Selecting Robert Selman's (1942–) work on interpersonal understanding as the primary emphasis allows the presentation of a focused and meaningful discourse within this context of *Theories of Adolescence*. Selman's theory of interpersonal perspective taking was chosen for inclusion here since both his original theory and the more recent clinical expansion considers preadolescence and adolescence in more detail than most other social cognition theories.

Selman's theory of social cognition must be understood as a direct outgrowth of Kohlberg's theory of moral judgment and, of course, Piaget's theory of cognitive development. Furthermore, it is also influenced by Heinz Werner's theory of orthogenesis, according to which development is viewed as a progression toward greater differentiation and hierarchical integration (Selman & Schultz, 1990). The social dilemmas used to assess

Robert Selman (1942-   )

interpersonal understanding are reminiscent of Kohlberg's moral dilemmas. Social cognition focuses on the ways in which children gain knowledge about their social world and identifies their social reasoning processes. Underlying all social cognition issues is the assumption that with increasing age, children and adolescents apply more advanced cognitive skills and social strategies to understanding interpersonal situations and social problem-solving tasks (Selman et al., 1986; Youniss, 1975). Social cognition addresses issues such as anticipating or predicting how another person may feel or respond in a social situation. However, social cognition asks additional questions: How does the child learn to understand what other children and adolescents think about others' behavior? How does an individual conceptualize and express his or her understanding of the thinking of others? What kind of intervention programs can facilitate the development of interpersonal problem-solving strategies?

The theoretical concept of "social role-taking" as a significant construct in social psychology goes back to George Herbert Mead (1934), who emphasized that social interactions and role-taking are essential elements that contribute to the socialization process. Moreover, children's development progresses by increased consideration being given to the thoughts, feelings, and actions viewed from the other person's perspective. Selman refines this idea by identifying distinct developmental stages in perspective taking.

Two concepts from Piaget's developmental theory are directly related to social cognition: egocentrism and decentering. Both are applicable to impersonal tasks such as Piaget's famous mountain range where the child has to determine what the silhouette of the mountains looks like from different positions. However, egocentrism and decentering apply equally to interpersonal issues, such as putting oneself into another person's position. A common expression of taking the other person's perspective can be found in the saying, "You need to walk in my moccasins for a day before you can understand where I am coming from." In Piaget's view, the emergence of social role-taking ability must be viewed as a by-product of cognitive decentering. Selman, however, defines role-taking or perspective-taking as the core concept of social cognition.

An important question must be raised: "Are social objects and physical objects known in the same or in different ways?" (Youniss, 1975: 173). Much information about social behavior, like much information about the physical world, will be acquired through observation, trial and error, exploration, direct first-hand experiences, and discovery. However, the correlation between IQ and Interpersonal Negotiation Strategies (INS) are only moderate ($r = +.38$), suggesting that interpersonal reasoning is substantially different from intellectual reasoning that is applied to social dilemmas (Selman et al., 1986). However, there appears to be some parallel in the structural changes that accompany the development of impersonal and interpersonal cognition. Byrne (1974), for example, demonstrated a close relationship between logical stages, moral stages, and role-taking stages. A certain level in logical thinking appears to be necessary before the equivalent stage in moral judgment is reached, and a certain level in role-taking is a prerequisite for the corresponding level of moral judgment. "Logical stages may be in evidence without the equivalent role-taking or moral stage, but the role-taking or moral stage rarely occurs without the corresponding stage of logical thinking" (Byrne, 1974: 564B).

However, as Piaget (1932b) pointed out, there is one important distinction between physical knowledge and social understanding: scientific knowledge is objective and factual and can be proven or disproven by scientific methods. Social knowledge, in contrast, is relative to the situation, social rules can be arbitrary, and appropriate social behavior is determined to a very large extent by the specific social context, as well as by social, cultural, and even subcultural definitions and expectations. Learning social protocol is dependent on approval and disapproval of significant people. Because social rules are less uniform, less specific, and more situation-dependent than the laws governing physical phenomena, they are less easily predictable and more complicated to understand. For adolescents it can be quite an eye-opener to realize that their friend's mother has quite different social rules and expectations than their own mother.

There is considerable debate in the literature about whether and to what extent physical knowledge and social cognition are associated, and about whether scientific problem-solving skills and social problem-solving skills are correlated or relatively independent (Keating, 1978; Keating and Clark, 1980). At this point we are not justified in assuming that problem-solving skills in the domains of the physical sciences can easily be transferred and applied to social problem-solving skills. Many scholars claim that social problem-solving skills function independently of and are really different from intellectual problem-solving skills and need to be taught in their own right. Shure and Spivack (1980) provide evidence that the cognitive abilities involved in interpersonal problem solving are not the same as those measured by conventional intelligence tests. Furthermore, the improvement in social adjustment that resulted from interpersonal skills training programs was not dependent on the child's level of intellectual functioning. Selman (1976b) reports that when a poorly adjusted clinical group of preadolescents was compared to a matched group of normally functioning peers, no differences in level of cognitive functioning were found, but the poorly adjusted group scored substantially lower than the normal group in interpersonal and moral reasoning skills.

The emotionally immature individual with social problems or a deficient ego is known to have greater difficulty in differentiating between physical and social reality. Such individuals are at times surprisingly capable of figuring out problems posed on an impersonal, factual level, but they are unable to solve corresponding problems of social living. For example, they fail to comprehend how their own aggressive behavior might have a negative impact on another person or group. Present knowledge about the relationship between physical knowledge and social knowledge can best be summarized by a quote from Selman: "The development of social conceptions, reasoning, thought—social cognition—is distinct from, though not unrelated to, the development of nonsocial cognition" (1980: 14). Therefore, the investigation of social cognition development, independent of reasoning ability, constitutes an exciting and fruitful contribution to developmental psychology.

Although many writers on social cognition refer to the works of Piaget, Kohlberg, Bruner, and Heider, new and more specific social cognition theories of development have emerged, particularly in the writings of Chandler (1973), Flavell (1974; 1977), Shantz (1975), Selman (1976a; 1976b; 1977; 1980), and Selman and Schultz (1990), to mention just a few.

Flavell's (1977) model of social cognition is a "general information processing model," rather than a developmental theory. He identifies four components that are necessary for drawing inferences about the perspectives of other persons: the existence component, the need component, the inference component, and the application component. The *existence component* simply implies that a subject recognizes the existence of psychological experiences or events in the other person and realizes that the other person's perspective of such experiences or events may differ from one's own. "There scarcely can be any thinking about social-cognitive phenomena if the very existence of such phenomena is not yet represented by the thinker" (Flavell, 1977: 120). The *need component* expands and includes the idea that the goal-directed behavior of another person is now understood as being motivated by a need. Other people are now being seen as having existence, feelings, and needs. The *inference component* leads to the construction of a representation of another person's subjective experiences. In other words, there is an attempt to figure out what the specific nature of the other person's needs or feelings may be. This kind of social thinking requires observing clues, integrating the clues, and reasoning probabilistically about the clues. The *application component* requires the subject to apply the information obtained from the inference. Behavior adjustments are needed, for example, in game strategies when new information results in new or different inferences.

A decision about an interpersonal problem must go through all four steps. For example, assume that an adolescent boy riding in a train is sitting next to a teenage girl reading a book. He first becomes aware of her and finds her attractive. His interest increases until he is aware of little else. To assess her need component, he may begin to observe whether and how much she is absorbed in her reading, what she is reading, what she is wearing, whether she is wearing an engagement ring or other evidence of being attached, whether or not she looks at him, the openness and closedness of her body posture, and so on. He infers that she might be interested in talking to him. The young man may never dare to make the necessary application and talk to her, in which case he will never know the correctness or incorrectness of his inferences. However, if he does complete the fourth step and makes the application by saying, "Hi, I see you are interested in science fiction—so am I," he may find out whether his inferences about her were correct. She may look at him, smile, and begin a conversation. On the other hand, if she abruptly turns the page or stares away from him without responding, he may be forced to reassess his initial inference.

Shantz (1975) develops her theory around five related questions that identify some of the fundamental issues of social cognition:

1. *What is the other person seeing?* This calls for the ability to make inferences about a person's visual perception of objects in space.
2. *What is the other person feeling?* The focus here is on understanding the emotional state of the other person; this involves empathy.
3. *What is the other person thinking?* At issue is the ability to make inferences about the thought processes of other people and to distinguish them from one's own.
4. *What is the other person intending?* This particular social cognition skill requires inferences about the motivation of the person.
5. *What is the other person like?* This social cognition skill involves person perception and can deal with overt physical characteristics, such as size, strength, physical maturity, and covert personality traits, such as friendly, warm, outgoing aspects of the other person.

The insights that can be ascertained from these social cognitive developmental issues provide an exciting model for understanding social behavior and social development (Selman, 1980). Taking the social perspective of someone else, a major component of this theory, appears to be at the very core of social cognition.

DEFINITION OF SOCIAL
OR INTERPERSONAL COGNITION

Social cognition can be defined as "how people think about other people and about themselves," or how people come to know their social world. Social cognition is concerned with the processes by which children and adolescents change in their conceptualization of others: their thoughts, their intentions, their emotions, their social behavior, and their general points of view. Social cognition involves role-taking, perspective taking, empathy, moral reasoning, interpersonal problem solving, and self-knowledge. Shantz has provided a formal definition of social cognition: "the child's intuitive or logical representation of others, that is, how he characterizes others and makes inferences about their covert inner psychological experiences" (Shantz, 1975: 1). Implied in the concept of social cognition is an ability to make inferences about other people's capabilities, attributes, expectations, feelings, and potential reactions. These inferential processes of social cognition are referred to as "role-taking," or social perspective taking, which Selman defines as the question of what social or psychological information may look like from the position of the other person. More broadly defined, this involves an "understanding of how human points of view are *related* and *coordinated* with one another" (Selman, 1980: 22).

SELMAN'S STAGE THEORY OF SOCIAL COGNITION

Selman (1971b; 1976a; 1976b; 1977; 1980; Selman & Byrne 1974; and Selman & Schultz 1990) advanced a stage theory of social cognition based on the concept of an ontogenetic, invariant sequence of predictable stages in social perspective taking. Selman coalesces ideas which came from George H. Mead's theory of self, from Harry Stack Sullivan's theory of interpersonal relationships, from Piaget's theory of cognitive development, and from Kohlberg's theory of moral judgment. "Conceptually, role-taking can be described as a form of social cognition intermediate between logical and moral thought" (Selman, 1976a: 307). The developmental changes in logical structure seem to manifest themselves first in the thinking related to physical events, later in the thinking concerned with social events, and still later in the thinking concerned with the moral domain.

Selman's model focuses on the individual's ability to draw interpersonal inferences about somebody else's perceptual or conceptual social awareness and to apply interpersonal negotiation strategies to social dilemmas. It is based on an investigation of the developmental changes that take place in social perception or role-taking skills. Social role-taking skills are defined as the ability to differentiate between the perspective of self and others, accurate perception of the thinking of others, and interpersonal negotiation strategies (INS). The assumption, well supported by empirical evidence, is that social role-taking skills increase with age at least into adolescence (Selman et al., 1986).

Social role-taking is viewed by Selman (1971b) as a prototypical social cognitive skill. The basic theoretical issue rests on the belief "that the unique aspect of social cognition and judgment that differentiates human from sub-human functioning is 'role-taking,' the ability to understand the self and the other as subjects, to react to others as like the self, and to react to the self's behavior from the other's point of view" (Selman and Byrne, 1974: 803).

The role-taking stages identified by Selman and Byrne are logically related and follow in a fixed developmental sequence, thus meeting the criteria for a structural developmental model. Similar to Piaget's theory, a structural model focuses not so much on the achievement of specified learned social skills as on the underlying structural level of social, moral, and cognitive understanding. The structure reveals itself most frequently through the justification of a decision, rather than in the individual's answer as to how he or she would handle the situation. The structure, which remains relatively consistent across different issues and circumstances, emerges in the same sequence and at approximately the same age for all normal children. Selman makes an important distinction between the structure and the content of thought. What is being reasoned about is the content; in contrast, how the social reasoning is carried out refers to the structure. It is the structure of social reasoning that constitutes the basis for Selman's "Structural-Developmental Model of Social Cognition" (1977). Selman hypothesizes that "each level of social perspective taking provides the structural basis for a stage in the development of conceptions of interpersonal role relations" (1976b: 160). Originally, Selman identified only four developmental levels of social perspective-taking skills between the ages of 4 and 12. In his follow-up work (Selman, 1976a; 1980; Selman et al., 1977), a fifth stage was identified, corresponding to adolescence and reaching into adulthood.

Selman's model of interpersonal understanding is a direct outgrowth of Kohlberg's theory of moral development. The crucial and stage-defining variables are the qualitative changes in the child's ability to see the world from the perspective of other people. The names, approximate ages, and the identifying characteristics of these stages are:

Stage 0. The egocentric undifferentiated stage (ages 3–6)
Stage 1. The differentiated and subjective perspective-taking stage (ages 5–9)
Stage 2. Self-reflective thinking or reciprocal perspective-taking stage (ages 7–12)
Stage 3. The third-person or mutual perspective-taking stage (ages 10–15)
Stage 4. The in-depth and societal perspective-taking stage (ages 12 to adulthood)

These stages constitute the developmental structure in Selman's theory, and the assumption is that advances from a lower to the next higher stage are characterized by qualitatively different levels of perceiving the relationship between self and the other person. Research clearly demonstrates that there is an age-related progression from undifferentiated egocentric to social perspective taking and mutual collaboration from childhood to adolescence (Selman et al., 1986).

The progression through these stages is assessed, analyzed, and described in terms of four distinct social domains. They are:

1. The individual concepts domain
2. The friendship concepts domain
3. The peer-group concepts domain
4. The parent-child concepts domain

These content domains provide the conceptual frame of reference within which the structural changes are investigated. The responses revealing the child's social awareness are elicited in an individual interview through stories containing social dilemmas. The purpose of the interview is to assess the child's stage of social cognition. However, the analysis of the child's responses to these stories is complex, and hence, the scoring is labor-intensive. The following is an illustration of a dilemma from the individual concepts domain (self-awareness):

Eight-year-old Tom is trying to decide what to buy his friend Mike for his birthday party. By chance, he meets Mike on the street and learns that Mike is extremely upset because his dog, Pepper, has been lost for two weeks. In fact, Mike is so upset that he tells Tom, "I miss Pepper so much I never want to look at another dog again." Tom goes off, only to pass a store with a sale on puppies; only two are left and these will soon be gone (Selman, 1980: 94).

The dilemma that Tom faces is whether or not to buy the puppy and he wonders how Mike would feel about receiving such a gift. After posing such dilemmas, the interviewer follows up first with standard questions, then with less structured questions to clarify the

Individual	Friendship	Peer Group	Parent-Child Relations
1. *Subjectivity:* covert properties of persons (thoughts, feelings, motives); conflicts between thoughts or feelings within the person	1. *Formation:* why (motives) and how (mechanisms) friendships are made; the ideal friend	1. *Formation:* why (motives) and how (mechanisms) groups are formed; the ideal member	1. *Formation:* motives for having children and why children need parents
2. *Self-awareness:* awareness of the self's ability to observe its own thoughts and actions	2. *Closeness:* types of friendship, ideal friendship, intimacy	2. *Cohesion–loyalty:* group unity	2. *Love and emotional ties:* between parents and children
3. *Personality:* stable or predictive character traits (a shy person, etc.)	3. *Trust:* doing things for friends; reciprocity	3. *Conformity:* range and rationale	3. *Obedience:* why children do as their parents tell them
4. *Personality change:* how and why people change (growing up, etc.)	4. *Jealousy:* feelings about intrusions into new or established friendships	4. *Rules–norms:* types of rules, and reasons for them	4. *Punishment:* the function of punishment from the parent's and the child's perspective
	5. *Conflict resolution:* how friends resolve problems	5. *Decision-making:* setting goals, resolving problems, working together	5. *Conflict resolution:* optimal ways for parents and children to resolve their differences
	6. *Termination:* how friendships break up	6. *Leadership:* qualities, and function to the group	
		7. *Termination:* why groups break up or members are excluded	

FIGURE 11.1 Issues of interpersonal understanding related to concepts of the individual, close friendships, peer-group organizations, and parent-child relations (Selman, 1980) (© 1980, Academic Press. Reproduced with permission).

child's level of social reasoning. Sample questions are: "'Mike said he never wants to see another puppy again. Why did he say that?'" Depending on the child's response, the interviewer might pursue the issue through 'stage-related' follow-up questions, such as: 'Can someone say something and not mean it?' 'Is it possible that Mike does not know how he feels?' 'Can you ever fool yourself into thinking you feel one way when you really feel another?' (Selman, 1980: 94).

This dilemma assesses the issue of *self-awareness* in the individual concepts domain. In each of the four social domains there are between four and seven issues (a total of twenty-two) that make up the practical concepts for assessing social cognition. Thus, for example, the six practical issues in the friendship domain are:

1. *The formation of friendships.* How and why are friendships formed and what might make an ideal friend?
2. *The closeness of friendships.* What are the different types of friendship? What constitutes the ideal kind of friendship? What is intimacy in friendship?
3. *The role of trust in friendship.* Under what circumstances does one do something for a friend and what is the role of reciprocity in friendship?
4. *Jealousy in friendship.* How does the person feel about the intrusion of others into an established friendship relationship?
5. *Conflict resolution.* How do friends resolve their conflicts when there is disagreement?
6. *Termination of friendships.* How and why are friendships terminated?

A similar group of issues are identified in the assessment of the other three social domains: individual, peer-group, and parent-child relations. In the following discussion of Selman's developmental stages of interpersonal understanding, at least one issue from each domain will serve as the focal point in order to provide illustrations. The issue of *self-awareness* will be the focus in the individual's concepts domain. *Conflict resolution and trust* will be used to illustrate the friendship concepts domain. *Leadership and group loyalty* are the issues in the peer-group concepts domain and *punishment* in the parent-child concepts domain.

■ Stage 0. Egocentric Undifferentiated Stage of Social Perspective Taking (Ages 3-6)

At the *egocentric undifferentiated stage* of social perspective taking, children cannot make a clear distinction between their own interpretation of social situations and another person's point of view. Nor can they understand that their own perception may not be the true or correct perspective. In social perspective-taking tasks, subject and object are not yet differentiated, but they are viewed egocentrically from the subject's perspective. However, young children do seem to realize that the preferences and subjective experiences of others may be different from their own. Lacking still are the inferential skills necessary to figure out what those subjective states of others might be. At Stage 0, children do not clearly distinguish between the physical and the psychological attributes of another individual. This confusion between subjective psychological and objective physical characteristics leads to difficulties in differentiating feeling from behavior, and it also interferes with the ability to distinguish intentional and unintentional behavior. While children understand that each person can have different feelings, they do not yet have the ability to determine how the thoughts and feelings of others might differ from their own.

Characteristic of egocentric thinking is the cognitive inability to differentiate between various points of view. The differentiation between oneself and another can only be accomplished in respect to physical qualities: the psychological characteristics remain undifferentiated. Since the subjective psychological perception remains undifferentiated, children are not aware that another person may interpret a social event quite differently (see Figure 11.2). Lacking is the awareness that another person possesses different perspectives. Young children cannot, so to speak, get "under the skin of another person," nor can they see the cause-effect relationship between thinking and behaving in other people. A girl may give her mother jelly beans for her birthday, not just because she herself likes jelly beans, or because she thinks her mother might like jelly beans, but because she views jelly beans as "things that are liked," without differentiating between her own point of view and that of others. To be able to choose an appropriate gift for another person requires the ability to take the other's perspective and to assess the needs of the person for whom the gift is intended.

Self-Awareness in the Individual Concepts Domain. Stage 0 children are unable to differentiate an inner psychological experience from the more concrete nature of external experiences. They do possess an awareness of self; however, that self has quasi-physical attributes—for example, one part of the body tells another part what to do. When asked, "'When you think, where do you think?'" the child may answer, 'In my mouth,' or when asked, 'How do you think?' the answer may be, 'My words tell me' (Selman, 1980: 95).

Conflict Resolution in the Friendship Concepts Domain. The child at Stage 0 uses two methods to resolve conflict. The first may be characterized as noninteractional; the child may say, "Go play with another toy," or just "Go away." The going away is not thought of as a cooling off period but as an "out of sight, out of mind" approach to conflict resolution. The second approach is physical attack—"Go and hit him." No reflective considerations are given to such psychological variables as motives, feelings, or attitudes. Conflict is viewed not as a disagreement between two parties, but as a situation where one party does not get to do what he or she wants because of the behavior of the other.

Leadership in the Peer-Group Concepts Domain. The young child views the leader as the one who has the physical power to tell group members what to do, and they must do it.

Punishment in the Parent-Child Concepts Domain. Although the Stage 0 child seems to be aware of the fact that punishment follows misbehavior, he or she is unaware of the parents' motives for punishment. The egocentric undifferentiated child confuses punishment as a cause and punishment as an effect. Instead of thinking, I was punished because I did something wrong, the Stage 0 child thinks, I did something wrong because I was punished.

FIGURE 11.2 Self and other—egocentric view. The other person is seen egocentrically, or undifferentiated from the self's own point of view.

The egocentric undifferentiated social perspective-taking stage seems to parallel closely the preoperational thinking structure in Piaget's theory of cognitive development and, in turn, seems to correspond to the premoral stage in Kohlberg's theory of moral judgment (see Figure 11.7 later in this chapter).

■ Stage 1. The Differential or Subjective Perspective-Taking Stage or the Social Informational Role-Taking Stage (Ages 5-9)

Children at this stage realize that another person can have cognitive or social perspectives different from their own. One's subjective experiences are differentiated from the experiences of others; however, judgment of the other person is still based on physical observations. The awareness dawns that others can interpret the same social situation differently. Children understand that other people may feel or think differently because they are in a different social situation or have access to different information. However, children are still unable to determine accurately what the other person's perspective looks like. In other words, they cannot maintain their own perspective and simultaneously assume the perspective of another. The interpersonal perspective of the other is conceived and conceptualized in one-way, unilateral terms (see Figure 11.3). Even through children realize that different perspectives of an event do exist, they still assume that there is only one correct point of view, either their own or that of the "authority." In the cartoon (p. 221) Dennis superimposes his thinking on the fish, suggesting that they are aware of his existence as he is of theirs.

There are three distinctive features in this level of social perspective taking. First, children become aware that they themselves and their own inner thoughts can be the object of another person's thinking, but they cannot accurately judge their own behavior as seen from the perspective of another person. There is no reciprocity between perspectives of self and others; perspective taking is a one-way affair. Only physical experiences can be understood as a two-way reciprocity. For example, the child who is hit, hits back. Individuals react to the actions of other people with the same action.

Second, the Stage 1 child, in contrast to the Stage 0 child, distinguishes between the physical and the psychological dimensions of another person and between intentional and unintentional behavior; thus, the Stage 1 child begins to consider personal reasons as causes of actions. The child now realizes that others have their own unique psychological life, understands the concept of these reasons, and recognizes that personal reasons are the cause of choices.

Third, Stage 1 children are capable of inferring the other person's intentions, feelings, and thoughts with some degree of accuracy. They also realize that other people have their own reasons for their thoughts and actions; however, the reasons themselves are not apparent to the outside observer, and since these children base their judgment of the feelings of others on physical observations, they are not always correct.

Self-Awareness in the Individual Concepts Domain. Since Stage 1 children are not yet able to distinguish between overt physical behavior and psychological experiences, they do not yet understand that people may hide their true inner feelings. They know how to lie and know that others lie; however, they are not yet cognizant "that one can *purposefully* misrepresent one's inner experiences" (Selman, 1980: 96). Even though these children are aware that intention and behavior are different things, they assume that the internal feelings eventually must manifest themselves in overt behavior. This

DENNIS THE MENACE

"WE KNOW THERE ARE FISH IN THERE, BUT THEY KNOW THAT WE'RE HERE, TOO."

"Dennis the Menace" ® used by permission of Hank Ketcham and
© by North American Syndicate

is well illustrated by the child's responses to questions about the previously cited missing dog:

HOW DOES MIKE FEEL INSIDE? Sad.
HOW DO YOU KNOW? Because of the way he looks.
COULD HE LOOK SAD AND BE HAPPY INSIDE? He could but you would be able to tell if you watched him long enough, he'd show you he was happy [Selman 1980: 97].

Finally, the distinction between awareness and unawareness is still quite vague and different from the more advanced levels that follow. "Fooling oneself" in the dilemma is seen more as changing one's feelings rather than being unaware of them.

FIGURE 11.3 Self and other—interpersonal view. The other is seen as different from the self, but the other person's perception of the self is still undifferentiated.

Conflict Resolution and Trust in the Friendship Concepts Domain. The child begins to realize that the subjective or psychological effects in a conflict situation may be as important as the physical, which is the focus of attention of the Stage 0 child. However, awareness of the psychological effect is still a one-way proposition; that is, it can be applied to one of the two individuals involved in the situation. Thinking now expresses itself in two different approaches to the conflict situation: (1) to undo the actions that caused the conflict ("Give him back what you took from him"); (2) to perform a positive substitute action ("Give him something nice"). The problem at this level is that the child assumes that a conflict is started by one person and that the conflict should be resolved by the conflict-instigating person; thus, conflict is still basically a one-way proposition.

Trust in a friendship relationship continues to be a one-way proposition. The trust in a friendship is based, rather egotistically, on getting the other person to do what the child wants "his friend" to do. Selman quotes a child, "You trust a friend if he does what I tell him" (Selman et al., 1977: 268).

Leadership in the Peer-Group Concepts Domain. The child at Stage 1 of social perspective taking sees the leader as someone who (1) has the best skills and knowledge and (2) helps the other members of the group to acquire these skills ("He teaches them tricks"). Group leadership is still based on unilateral authority. Cooperation and coordination of activities are not yet evident.

Cohesive loyalty in the Peer-Group Concepts Domain. Loyalty to the group becomes important at this stage, but the child defines loyalty as the "unilateral obedience to the dictates of a leader or other group members." One of Selman's 8-year-olds defines loyalty as "always doing what you are told, 'cause they kick you if you don't'" (Selman et al., 1977: 269).

Punishment in the Parent-Child Concepts Domain. In contrast to the earlier stage, the child now considers the parents' motives for punishment; however, this too is seen as a one-way proposition, since the child does not yet consider the punished child's reactions toward punishment. The child views punishment as serving three functions: (1) parents might punish to teach their children a lesson; (2) parents might use punishment as a method to protect their children from danger; and (3) parents might punish as a way of restoring the equilibrium—that is, "setting things straight" or "paying someone back."

The beginning of decentering in perspective taking characteristic of the transition from Stage 1 to Stage 2 seems to find its counterpart in Piaget's transition from preoperational to operational thinking and corresponds to Kohlberg's "Heteronomous Morality." For Selman, the transition to actually taking the perspective of another person (Stage 2) constitutes a major advance in social cognition, and on a more practical level, is a prerequisite for making and maintaining friendship.

■ Stage 2. Self-Reflective Thinking or Reciprocal Perspective Taking (Ages 7-12)

During late childhood and preadolescence, the individual who realizes that others possess their own cognitive or social perspective because they think or feel differently also becomes aware that the other person thinks about the subject's thinking and in turn can take his or her role. Thus, the crucial developmental advance from Stage 1 to Stage 2 consists in the ability to leave oneself mentally and to take the perspective of another individual. The thought processes themselves can best be illustrated by the quote of a Stage 2 subject: "I know that she knows that I know she knows."

Individuals can now make inferences about the perspectives of other people; they can reflect about their own behavior and their own motivation as seen from the perspective of someone else. There is a self-reflecting anticipation of the other person's behavior toward the subject's own thought and purposes. However, such reflections about their own behavior and that of others are still limited since they occur sequentially, rather than simultaneously. Furthermore, the subject is aware that the other person can do the same thing (see Figure 11.4).

This new ability to reciprocate social perspectives introduces an awareness of relativity, since each person might have quite different goals, values, ideals, feelings, and thoughts. No single individual's social perspective is necessarily correct or valid in an absolute sense. Another person's point of view may be as correct as one's own.

In contrast to the mutual role-taking ability that develops in Stage 3, perspective taking at Stage 2 is still based only on a two-way reciprocity. The preadolescent thinks only within the frame of reference—"I think; you think"—and cannot yet take a more general third-person perspective or understand a more general social relationship system.

Other people are now seen as operating on multimotivational levels rather than being motivated by one factor. The preadolescent becomes cognizant of the fact that one can experience two opposing emotions at the same time; for example, he or she might simultaneously be repulsed by and attracted to the same person or the same object. Furthermore, the preadolescent can differentiate thoughts from feelings, and thus can understand that one might do some things that one did not intend to do. Preadolescents establish a hierarchy of motives and perceive the possibility that altruistic and instrumental motives may conflict with one another, both in their own mind and in the minds of others. They can take into account the hierarchy of motives in a situation where a person wants to do one thing but actually does another. A person's behavior may be the expression of different layers; outward clowning, for example, may be a cover-up for true hidden feelings of insecurity or unhappiness.

Self-Awareness in the Individual Concepts Domain. The Stage 2 preadolescent clearly distinguishes between outer-physical and inner-psychological reality and becomes aware that the two do not need to be congruent. Individuals may cover their true inner feelings to save face or to avoid social embarrassment. Since preadolescents can take the perspective of another person, they can now monitor their own thoughts and actions from the perspective of another person. There emerges a new sense of priorities in that inner self-awareness matters more than outer appearances.

Conflict Resolution and Trust in the Friendship Concepts Domain. The preadolescent in Stage 2 becomes aware that quite commonly both parties contribute to a conflict. Therefore, it be-

FIGURE 11.4 Self and other—reciprocal view. The self can take the perspective of another person and becomes aware that the other person can also take the perspective of the self.

comes obvious that both parties must cooperate in seeking an effective solution. This is often done by appealing to the individual's sensitivity and good judgment. Lacking still is the notion of conflict resolution by mutual consensus. As in Stage 0, he or she may suggest a resolution of the conflict by getting away from one another; however, the idea in this suggestion is the establishment of a psychological space or a cooling-off period.

Trust at Stage 2 is based much more on reciprocity between two friends than it was in Stage 1. However, self-interest still dominates the quality of trustworthiness in a friendship relationship, finding its clearest expression in the simple thought or statement, "If you do something for me, I will do something for you."

Leadership and Loyalty in the Peer-Group Concepts Domain. The preadolescent sees the issue of leadership as a reciprocal relationship. Leadership is based on bilateral equality and a reciprocity of interest. The role of the leader is that of mediator, organizer, and coordinator of group efforts. The leader encourages the efforts of group members through friendliness, recognition, support, and reward.

Peer group loyalty, like trust, is based on an even exchange of favors or mutual expression of affection, such as, "I like you, if you like me," or "If he is loyal, the guys will be nice to one another."

Punishment in the Parent-Child Concepts Domain. Punishment by parents may now be seen as an expression of the parents' concern for the child's well-being. He or she can conceptualize that parents punish to communicate with their children; thus, one purpose of punishment may be to make the child think about certain behavior. "Punishment functions as a message sent from one self-reflecting and judging being to another" (Selman, 1980: 125). In addition, punishment is also seen as a deterrent in that it is likely to instill fear, which will become an internal agent of control when a similar situation arises.

The self-reflective perspective taking of Stage 2 finds its developmental parallel in Piaget's stage of operational thinking and sets the stage for the movement to Kohlberg's Stage Two, "Individualistic, Instrumental Morality." (See Figure 11.7 later in the chapter.)

■ Stage 3. The Third-Person or Mutual Perspective-Taking Stage (Ages 10-15)

The perspective-taking skills of early adolescence lead to a capacity for a more complex type of social cognition. The adolescent moves beyond simply taking the other person's perspective in a back-and-forth kind of approach and begins to see all parties from a more generalized third-person perspective. The third-person perspective "allows the adolescent to abstractly step outside an interpersonal interaction and simultaneously and mutually coordinate and consider the perspectives (and their interactions) of self and other(s)" (Selman, 1980: 39). In other words, the emerging concept of mutual role-taking implies that adolescents can consider the mutual relationship involved, even as one of the participants (see Figure 11.5). As third-person observers they see themselves as both actor and object. Adolescents know that both they and their thoughts can also be the object of the other person's thought, and vice versa.

Furthermore, there emerges the ability to distinguish between one's own point of view and a more generalized perspective that might be taken by an "average" member of the group. Adolescents can assume the role of such a disinterested average spectator and view

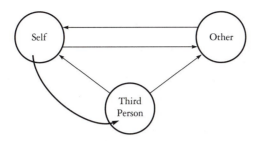

FIGURE 11.5 Self and other—objective view. The self can view the self–other interaction from the perspective of a neutral third person.

the social interaction between themselves and somebody else from that spectator's position; they can see each party's perspective simultaneously and mutually. Furthermore, they can reflect on their own self interacting with the self, an idea that Selman characterizes as "the observing ego."

Self-Awareness in the Individual Concepts Domain. The degree of self-awareness increases and the mind is seen as the observer of the self-aware self. Thus, the mind becomes the active psychological manipulator controlling the inner life. In other words, the mind is now viewed not as a storehouse of information but as an active participant in deciding which ideas go where and which are kept out. Indeed, it becomes possible to fool the mind through an act of will. Thoughts and feelings may emerge even when opposed by will and mind. There is now a much more basic comprehension of the relationship between the self-as-subject and the self-as-object (Selman, 1980).

Conflict Resolution and Trust in the Friendship Concepts Domain. Friendship is no longer viewed as a process of reciprocal back scratching but as a series of interactions over an extended period of time. Relationships validate mutuality and involve emotional support and sharing of common feelings. Conflicts are seen as a natural, almost inevitable, part of a friendship relationship since each individual is unique and has different needs and values. Conflicts are not just a problem of one individual. To resolve conflict in a friendship relationship, both sides must feel satisfied and be able to place themselves in the other person's shoes. Disagreements are seen as possibly emerging from different personality characteristics, and a permanent conflict resolution might require some personality changes. In addition, conflict resolution may actually contribute to strengthening a friendship—especially if there is a mutually satisfying way to work out the disagreement and find a harmonious compromise. Effectively working through a mutual disagreement seems to strengthen the commitment to the relationship. The adolescent can distinguish between the superficial nature of mere acquaintances and the value of the long-term affectionate relationship. The more permanent bond that constitutes the friendship between individuals becomes a factor contributing to conflict resolution. Mutual perspective taking, characteristic of early adolescence, implies an "active interpersonal communication and sharing" and relies on "verbal or mental rather than physical-action resolutions" (Selman, 1980: 112).

Friendship and trust during Stage 3 are no longer defined as a fair exchange of favors. Friendship is built on a more basic and lasting mutual support system. More personal concerns and intimacies are shared; the relationship has more lasting consistency, and one friend will stand up for the other "through thick and thin" even if there is no immediate benefit. "One thirteen-year-old said that trust in a friendship is, 'When they get it off their chest if they talk to you; things that are going on in your life and in the other person's life'" (Selman et al., 1977: 269).

Leadership and Loyalty in the Peer-Group Concepts Domain. The group is viewed as a social system, and the role of the leader is to coordinate the efforts of the group, to hold the group together, to express the feelings of the group, and to encourage group solidarity. The leader encourages a sense of community and acts as a catalyst in that process.

Loyalty to the group now requires a willingness to contribute to the welfare of the peer community, a kind of all-for-one loyalty. The underlying philosophy can be expressed by paraphrasing John F. Kennedy's famous statement: "Ask not what the peer group can do for you, but what you can do for the peer group."

Punishment in the Parent-Child Concepts Domain. Adolescents in this stage clearly distinguish between punishment as a general childrearing procedure and punishment that might be applied to themselves. They often feel that punishment is less applicable to them than to younger children. At this stage punishment is mutually perceived as serving a need for parents and a purpose for the child. Both parent and child have needs, characteristics, interests, and personalities that must be considered and, ideally, carefully weighed in a punishment decision. Adolescents now recognize that there may be methods other than punishment to achieve control or obedience and to ensure safety.

The mutual role-taking advances of adolescence seem to indicate the transition to formal operations in the impersonal thinking domain and also make possible the development of an "Interpersonal Normative" and a "Social Systems Morality" in Kohlberg's moral judgment theory (see Figure 11.7 later in the chapter).

■ Stage 4. In-Depth and Societal Perspective Taking (Adolescence To Adulthood)

During adolescence the individual may move to a still higher and more abstract level of interpersonal perspective taking, a stage which involves the "coordination of all possible third person perspectives—a societal perspective." The adolescent can conceptualize that the subjective perspectives of persons toward other persons not only operate on a level of common expectations and awareness but exist "simultaneously at multidimensional or deeper levels of communication" (Selman, 1980: 40). Thus, role-taking is raised from the level of didactic relationships between people to the level of an overarching general social system. "At this level the subject can compare and qualitatively contrast different sets and levels of perspectives" (Selman, 1976b: 160). Adolescents reaching this level become aware of the relativity of perspectives held by themselves as well as by the social group. Social facts are now understood as being interpreted by each individual according to that individual's own system of analysis (see Figure 11.6).

Stage 4 subjects understand that each person can consider the shared point of view of the "Generalized Other" or the social system, an ability which, in turn, makes possible accurate communication with and understanding of other people. Furthermore, the notion of law and morality as a social system depends on the idea of consensual group perspective, implied in Stage 4 role-taking ability. "At this level, the adolescent or young adult can ab-

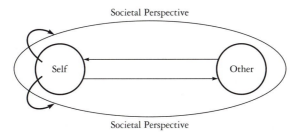

Societal Perspective

Societal Perspective

FIGURE 11.6 Self and other—societal perspective. The self can take a generalized societal perspective of the self–other interaction.

stract multiple mutual (generalized other) perspectives to a societal, conventional, legal, or moral perspective in which all individuals can share" (Selman, 1980: 40).

There are two distinguishing features of the Stage 4 subjects' advanced conception of other people. First, they become aware that motives, actions, thoughts, and feelings are shaped by psychological factors. This notion of psychological determinants may now include the idea of unconscious processes, although adolescents may not express this awareness in psychological terminology. Second, they begin to appreciate the idea that a personality is a system of traits, beliefs, values, and attitudes with its own developmental history.

Self-Awareness in the Individual Concepts Domain. Since adolescents are now discovering the idea of the unconscious mind, they become cognizant that there may be influences on thoughts, feelings, and motivations that they are not aware of and that, therefore, are not available for self-analysis. This means that beneath the inner reality of feelings and fantasies there may exist an even deeper reality that the individual is not aware of but that influences actions and behavior.

Conflict Resolution and Trust in the Friendship Concepts Domain. The Stage 3 conception of friendship was characterized by an awareness that friendships are based on close-knit mutuality. The adolescent in Stage 4 seems to reject that idea of mutuality partially, at least as long as it interferes with the autonomous growth and development of the individual. A striving for independence may result in a rejection of overdependence and overbonding characteristic of Stage 3. However, just as mutuality based on overdependence is not ideal, total independence is not the goal either. There is a striving for a balance between independence and dependence with a focus on the mutual relationships in the sense of "keeping the lines of communication open." The adolescent actually becomes aware that conflicts within one person may cause conflict between that person and his or her friend.

Adolescent and adult trust in friendship relationships becomes an ongoing process. "Trust means openness to change and growth, as well as stability in a relationship" (Selman et al., 1977: 269). The idea is well expressed by a college student who said, "Trust means that you've got to grow to let your friend grow. The more you hold on, the less you have. You have to have confidence in yourself as a good friend, then you'll have trust in your relationship" (Selman et al., 1977: 269).

Leadership and Loyalty in the Peer-Group Concepts Domain. The leadership position is seen as being created by the group, and the leader's role is to enhance the collective good of the group. The leader is thus viewed as the embodiment of the group, and the function of that person as an individual is clearly separated from the leadership function. Leadership serves a fundamental social purpose that is abstracted from the members of the group. Furthermore, in Stage 4 there is a clearer understanding and differentiation of several different kinds of leadership.

Loyalty to the group takes on the quality of a contractual agreement. Loyalty presupposes that an individual member of the group is willing to relinquish personal goals for the benefit of the collective goals. "Loyalty is the unity of the group; that means each member is willing to make a sacrifice for the good of the group—a sacrifice of himself" (Selman et al., 1977: 269).

Punishment in the Parent-Child Concepts Domain. The one new idea that seems to emerge in the adolescent's conception of punishment is that punishment now may be seen as an unconscious effort to maintain psychological control over others. The social perspective-taking ability identified as Stage 4 will not be reached by all adults; it constitutes the final and mature stage in social cognitive development.

Byrne (1974) investigated the relationship of these stages to Piaget's stages of logical development and Kohlberg's stages of moral judgment (see Figure 11.7). He found that a relationship exists between Piaget's logical thinking stages and Selman's role-taking stages. However, the adolescent may reach a certain level of logical thinking without having reached the equivalent role-taking stage or moral judgment stage. On the other hand, rarely can an individual reach a given role-taking or moral judgment stage without having first attained the corresponding level of logical thinking. Furthermore, an individual may reach a certain social role-taking stage without evidence of an equivalent attainment in moral judgment, but it is unlikely that a specific moral judgment stage can be reached without the necessary role-taking stage. It thus appears that role-taking is an intermediate step in the development of social cognition that falls between the development of logical operations and the development of moral judgment during the years from age 10 to adulthood.

During adolescence, girls are more aware of interpersonal relationships and score higher on the interpersonal negotiation strategies, even when age and IQ are controlled (Selman et al., 1986). Perhaps this is due to the earlier physical maturation of girls and their more intimate friendship patterns based on dyadic relationships. Gender differences in interpersonal skills are more pronounced in the lower IQ ranges and may be the result of the social relationship concern emphasized in the socialization of girls (Gilligan, 1982).

Adolescents use higher levels of social reasoning in dilemmas involving peers than in those involving adults. The former most likely involve conflicts based on equality, whereas the latter often represent unequal social relationships based on authority or power. Similarly, they do better on personal dilemmas than on work-related dilemmas, perhaps because many have not had significant work-related experiences (Selman et al., 1986).

FACILITATING FRIENDSHIP DEVELOPMENT THROUGH PAIR THERAPY

Since the earlier research and publication of the normal stages of interpersonal perspective taking summarized above, Selman's investigations and theory development efforts have moved toward the application of these social-cognitive stages to clinical problems in

	Piaget's Stages of Cognitive Development	Selman's Stages of Social Perspective Taking	Kohlberg's Stages of Moral Judgment
Stage 0	Sensorimotor and preoperational stages	The egocentric undifferentiated stage of social perspective taking	The premoral stage
Stage 1	Beginning of concrete operations	The differential or subjective perspective-taking stage or the social-informational role-taking stage	The heteronomous morality
Stage 2	Well-developed concrete operations	Self-reflective thinking or mental perspective-taking stage	The individualistic, instrumental morality
Stage 3	Beginning formal operations (Piaget's stage III-A)	The third-person or mutual perspective-taking stage	The interpersonal normative morality
Stage 4	Well-developed formal operations (Piaget's stage III-B)	The in-depth and societal perspective-taking stage	The social systems morality
Stage 5			The human rights and social welfare morality
Stage 6			The morality of universalizable general ethical principles

FIGURE 11.7 Parallels between systems. The parallels between Piaget's stages of cognitive development, Selman's stages of social perspective taking, and Kohlberg's stages of moral judgment. According to Byrne (1974) at each stage, cognitive development appears to be a prerequisite for the corresponding stage of social perspective taking, which in turn precedes the emergence of the corresponding stage of moral judgment (adapted from Selman [1976a] and Papalia and Olds [1979]).

adolescence, especially the processes underlying friendship formation. Thus, while his approach still remains committed to the underlying social perspective-taking theory, it has become more practical, more clinical, and more focused on the interactive aspect of interpersonal negotiations. The clinical intervention approach utilized to facilitate the development of interpersonal skills necessary for forming friendships is quite unique in that it is especially suitable to late childhood and early adolescence, when making and having friends become particularly important. Although Selman and Schultz (1990) have coined the term "pair therapy" for this process, the approach goes beyond the immediate goal of facilitating friendship in that it enhances the development of interpersonal negotiation strategies (INS) for social relationships. As such, Selman and Schultz's approach becomes the mediator for social competencies and social adjustment.

Based on the theoretical understanding of the development of friendship, Selman became increasingly more committed to the clinical, counseling, and educational question of how to facilitate growth in friendship-making skills. The answer is particularly significant for those adolescents who have a great need for a friend but who have problems in their interpersonal relationship strategies and who find it difficult to form lasting friendships.

In the clinical pair-therapy model, how the individual (the self) thinks about others (the cognitive domain) remains important, but the emphasis shifts and more explicitly focuses on how the individual actually interacts with others (the social and emotional domain). Even among perfectly normal individuals, there sometimes exists a gap between their knowledge about forming or maintaining interpersonal relationships and their actual behavior. In specific situations and for their own personal reasons (defensiveness, habits, past experiences, revenge, etc.), people act contrary to their actual knowledge in ways that actually impair friendship formation and endanger intimacy. Everyday observation suggests that at times some social situations "bring out the worst in us" in an almost predictable fashion. Peter in B.C. (p. 231) lacks the skills for friendship formation and could benefit from pair therapy. If the gap between thought and action remains pervasive and appears in diverse social situations, such individuals have no friends and may be considered deviant if not outright pathological. For these individuals, the underlying social structure can be modified and enhanced through the guidance of a therapist (Nakkula & Selman, 1991; Selman & Schultz, 1990). Thus, in the strict sense of the word, "pair therapy" is somewhat of a misnomer, since the therapist is a vital third person and actually serves as a catalyst in the therapeutic process.

In general, the goal of pair therapy is to enhance growth in social perspective taking so that eventually the individuals involved can regulate their mutual interaction without the support of an adult therapist. They learn to balance their needs for autonomy and intimacy. Individuals who have poor peer relationships are provided with a safe context in which they can try strategies for getting along better and negotiating their needs on a give-and-take basis. Pair therapy guides them into positive interpersonal experiences and, eventually, into mutual collaboration so that healthier patterns of social interactions develop. Thus, participants learn how to make friends and how to maintain friendship relationships. "The goal of therapy is to aid the pair in working through the obstacles to their becoming or remaining friends. 'Working through' includes reflections upon what 'I' (the self) bring to this conflict with 'you' (the other), and what each must do to resolve it" (Nakkula & Selman, 1991: 180).

The therapist's contributions in this process are guided by the social maturity and the social strategies initially displayed by the pair. Guiding the pair to resolve their disagree-

By permission of Johnny Hart and Creators Syndicate, Inc.

ment in a less contentious manner, the therapist might, for example, suggest alternatives for dealing with the other person or help the pair to redefine their goals so that they become common goals. In suggesting interpersonal negotiation strategies, the therapist would suggest a strategy that is just one level higher than the one currently employed. The suggested strategy may not be particularly attractive and would certainly not be the one the therapist would employ. Although not necessarily socially desirable, even the change from overt physical aggression (Level 0), to a demanding "bossy" one (Level 1), is developmental progress. Indeed, there is much evidence that supports the notion that intervention programs are more effective if they encourage the child to move just one step (or level) above the one on which they currently function (Yeates & Selman, 1989).

The more immediate purpose of pair therapy is to facilitate building-up relationships between the pair so that the two play and interact in a more constructive, mutually satisfying fashion. Thus, the therapist is laying the foundation for friendship formation. If interactions become more satisfying and more reciprocal—often only after months of therapy—the therapist may leave the room and watch through a one-way mirror to see if the pair can continue to function effectively on their own. The therapist returns only if the interaction patterns become destructive again, in order to make further corrective suggestions. Pair therapy is much more than a change in behavior, as is the goal in social skills training; its aim is to alter the pair's "interpersonal ethics," to reach deeper more basic structural levels, and to contribute to restructuring personalities in a way that allows the integration of self-protective needs (autonomy) with the need to care for the other (intimacy) (Nakkula & Selman, 1991). The ultimate goal is to achieve relatively permanent and mature relationships with other people, that is, interaction patterns that are based on collaboration and equality.

Working as the director of the Manville School of Boston's Judge Baker Children's Center, Selman had ample opportunities to observe the friendship-making skills (or their lack) in adolescents who were enrolled in the Center because they required a special educational intervention program to treat their emotional, social, and interpersonal difficulties. Children with "special needs," such as those admitted to the Manville School, often have difficulties establishing lasting friendships because they still lack the ability to recognize the inappropriateness and/or ineffectiveness of their own social strategies. In addition, they do not understand the social perspective of those with whom they interact, both on an emotional and a cognitive level. In their daily interactions they may function on an age-inappropriate level of social perspective taking and try to utilize strategies in influencing others that may be characteristic of much younger children.

Research has supported the idea that emotionally disturbed, delinquent, and socially maladjusted adolescents often exhibit patterns of deficit in social skills and social-cognitive development (Selman & Schultz, 1990: 294; Chandler, 1973; Chalmers & Townsend, 1990; Dodge, 1980; Gaffney, 1984; Gaffney & McFall, 1981; Selman, 1980; Shantz, 1983). That is, these troubled adolescents seem to suffer from low-level self-understanding and hence they react to others like much younger children. In addition, troubled adolescents often function inconsistently and are highly vulnerable to regression to socially inappropriate actions.

Against this background of dealing with personal, social, and developmental inadequacies of adolescents who, even though in need of a friend, often lacked the necessary skills to make friends, Selman shifted from his earlier concern with cognitive stages of "interpersonal thought" to the more complex but clinically rich concept of "interpersonal action." This shift is accompanied by a corresponding methodological change: from verbal responses to hypothetical social dilemmas to an examination of interpersonal strategies actually utilized in a real-life context, taking personal background and changes over time as the therapy progresses into account. Thus, the practical issue becomes: How do children actually negotiate conflict? What strategies do they use in influencing others? How do their actions repulse others? How do they impair friendship-inviting overtures? And, how can friendship-enhancing skills be encouraged?

Initially, Selman and Schultz (1990) focused on small groups of 6–8 students; however, even in a group that size, social interaction patterns occurred so fast that it became impossible to analyze all that was happening. Frustrated by the interpersonal complexity of small groups of disturbed adolescent boys, they decided to reduce further the size of the group and work with pairs of youngsters under the supervision and guidance of a therapist. Their goal was twofold: First, they hoped to better understand the nature of interpersonal behavior and the effect of such behavior on the other person. Their analysis focused on the contextual and the historical nature of the interaction, "each piece of information is predicated on that which came before and has implications for all that follows; nothing is understood in temporal isolation" (Nakkula & Selman, 1991: 181). Thus, a major purpose was to enhance the theory of interpersonal development. Second, they intended to study the clinical-therapeutic approaches that could facilitate change in social strategies and perspective-taking skills. Thus, "friendship pair therapy" emerged as a clinical application of Selman's initial theory of stages in social perspective taking.

Yeates and Selman (1989: 71, 87-88) identify four necessary steps to deal with a specific social problem. (1) Encoding the social cues in order to define the nature of the social problem as seen by the child. (2) Generating different problem-solving strategies that might be utilized to solve the social problem. (3) Choosing the strategy that appears most appropriate (at least from the perspective of the child) and implementing it. (4) Evaluating the result so that, if the outcome does not solve the problem, a new problem-solving strategy can be applied until a satisfactory outcome is achieved.

Pair therapy has been in operation for over 10 years and has been integrated with Selman's "Theory of Social Cognition." While the empirical support is still limited, the anecdotal, clinical, and observational results are most encouraging and provide an exciting model through which social-cognitive theory merges with pair therapy. Such a merger has far-reaching implications for helping socially inadequate adolescents, as well as for counseling, and by implication, for education. The general approach of providing intervention aid to teach interpersonal negotiation strategies and enhance the child's ability to learn to use social perspective coordination is not limited to pair therapy. Indeed, it can be utilized with any child who faces intrapersonal and/or interpersonal difficulties in a social setting, including children in regular classrooms (Yeates & Selman, 1989).

Pair therapy is the clinical application of knowledge about the dynamics of interpersonal cooperation to the formation of friendship in the narrowly defined dyadic unit of the pair. These individuals are placed in a therapeutic setting, literally a pair-therapy room, because they have not progressed appropriately through the normatively defined levels of interpersonal skills. Thus, they may still be incapable of taking the perspective of another person or unable to make the important distinction between intentional and unintentional behavior. Such a distinction cannot easily be taught in an explanatory, cognitive style, but requires personal experiences and guidance that eventually lead to deeper emotional, structural changes. Results lead to a higher order equilibrium and hence become generalizable. The influence of Piaget's and Kohlberg's theories in these ideas is undeniable.

Selman and Schultz (1990) richly illustrate their theoretical analysis with case study information from the actual behavior and verbalization of adolescents in pair therapy sessions. Their descriptions capture the nature of the interaction followed by a theoretical analysis of the strategies used by the individuals. A detailed discussion of pair therapy goes beyond the scope and purpose of this book, and since space permits only a brief citation of a few selected illustrations, the interested reader is referred to the innovative presentation of pair therapy in *Making a Friend in Youth: Developmental Theory and Pair Therapy* (Selman & Schultz, 1990).

■ Strategies for Interpersonal Negotiations

Through their verbal exchange and their social behavior in pair interaction (including voice quality, gestures, and facial expression), adolescents and older children in pair therapy reveal their interpersonal negotiation strategies in dealing with the other person.

Selman classifies these strategies for interpersonal negotiation by two dimensions: *Orientation* and *level*. The orientation can be *other-transforming*, which asserts the importance of the self over the other, such as the command, "Give me that doll," meaning the other-transforming efforts are directed toward changing the other person's action. A *self-transforming orientation* implies a submissive stance toward the other person's request. It manifests itself in the change of the self's behavior, such as a passive acquiescence or withdrawal from interpersonal conflict. In the self-transforming situation the needs of the self are considered secondary to the demands of the other. Actually, self-transforming and other-transforming negotiation strategies need to be viewed as the two end points of a continuum.

Alex may illustrate a submissive self-transforming strategy.

The therapist asked him: "Do you still get teased?"
Alex: Yea, I don't like standing up for myself. It doesn't do any good.

Jamie [Alex's more assertive pair partner]: You don't stand up for yourself Alex. You let everyone push you around.
Alex: Why should I stand up for myself? What good will it do? (Nakkula & Selman, 1991: 193).

Alex's verbalizations reveal an other-transforming interpersonal style, although many pair-therapy sessions later, he had learned to become more assertive. In pair therapy, matching someone who is primarily other-oriented (such as Jamie) with someone who tends to be self-oriented (such as Alex) seems to work effectively according to Selman and Schultz (1990).

Adolescents with interpersonal difficulties seem to function primarily in one orientation, avoiding the other, while normal adolescents show greater flexibility in their use of both self- and other-transforming actions. There is no assumption that either self- or other-transformations are better, but troubled adolescents often show a strong almost rigid commitment for one and the goal of pair therapy is to increase flexibility between assertiveness (other transformation) and submissiveness (self-transformation). However, the distinction between self- and other-orientation appears to be more pronounced at the lower levels. Later, at the higher levels of interpersonal understanding *collaborative orientation* or a we-transforming style, emerges at about the same time that the pair begins to think and act in terms of "us".

Selman's other dimension known as *the levels* basically follows the pattern of his cognitive stages of interpersonal perspective taking. In pair therapy, they are not assessed on the basis of cognitive explanations of dilemmas but on the basis of actual, practical, social-emotional behavior strategies, that is, on how they reveal themselves in interpersonal actions. Obviously, the verbalizations and behaviors of the self inevitably are influenced by the behavior of the pair-partner. Each partner has a strong influence on the level of thought and the organizational strategies of the other member of the pair. The actions of self and other are interactive, so that the strategies used by one have an impact on the strategies used by the other. In pair therapy, the level of thought changes frequently, both up and down levels. The orientation of the interaction may change also from self-orientation to other-orientation (see Figure 11.8). The intent is not to classify the person, but to identify the strategies, the verbalizations, and the interaction sequences which the individual utilizes. If Andy demands, "Give me that toy!", the other child may respond by a Level 1 counter-challenge: "You just try and make me. Ha! Ha!" However, another child may respond to Andy's command in a relationship-enhancing fashion: "We need to share these toys. I will give you the toy in 5 minutes, but until then you need to find yourself another toy." Such a response might diffuse Andy's immediate demand. In addition, interactions occur in a context of the physical room with its toys and objects, relate to preceding actions, and depend on the forcefulness or the timidity of words and actions. The following levels of interactions need to be understood in relationship to Selman's stages in social cognition (see pp. 218–228).

■ Level 0: Demanding Egocentric Goals by Unreflective, Impulsive, Physical Abuse

What is characteristic of the interpersonal behavior at the "Egocentric Undifferentiated Stage" is an unreflective, impulsive strategy to reach one's goal and control the situation. Things must be done according to the desires and needs of the self. Social conflicts are re-

Other-Transforming Orientation	Self-Transforming Orientation
Level 0	
A. Forcefully blots out other's expressed wish B. Unprovoked impulsive grabbing C. Absolute repulsion of other	A. Takes impulsive flight B. Uses automatic affective withdrawal C. Responds with robotlike obedience
Level 1	
A. Uses one-way threats to achieve self's goals B. Makes threats of force C. Criticizes other's skills as a rationale for self's activity	A. Makes weak initiatives with ready withdrawal B. Acts victimized C. Appeals to source of perceived power from a position of helplessness
Level 2	
A. Uses "friendly" persuasion B. Seeks allies for support of self's ideas C. Goal-seeking through impressing others with self's talents, knowledge, etc.	A. Asserts self's feelings and thoughts as valuable but secondary B. Follows but offers input into other's lead C. Uses self's feelings of inadequacies as a tool for interpersonal negotiation
Level 3	
A. Anticipates and integrates possible feelings of others about self's negotiation B. Balances focus on relations with focus on self's concrete goal	

FIGURE 11.8 Some prototypical interpersonal strategies coded at developmental levels 0-3 in each orientation. (From R. L. Selman and L. H. Schultz, *Making a Friend in Youth.* The University of Chicago Press, Chicago 60637, The University of Chicago Press, Ltd., London; © 1985 by the American Psychological Association. Adapted with permission.)

solved by impulsive fight or flight strategies (Nakkula & Selman, 1991). The perceptions of the self and the other are not differentiated and the child is not yet capable of distinguishing between the self's point of view and that of the other person. There is no concern about the impact the self's actions may have on the other person and there is no attempt to communicate the self's perception to others, nor is there any internal dialogue within the self.

Self-orientation at this level may manifest itself in impulsively and unreflectively leaving the scene or the room. The other-orientation mode may be displayed through regressive out-of-control impulsivity, such as screaming, drowning out any opposition by shouting, "Shut up, shut up, shut up . . . ," thus denying others the opportunity to express their opposition. Other examples include: pulling an object out of the hands of another child, ignoring the other child's objections and even the teacher's reprimand: "Please give it back!" physically shoving the other person away from the resources or intruding into and dominating interactions among others that are in progress. A request to finish one activity in order to begin another is totally ignored. Such attempts to control the events as well as other people in an unreflective fashion are the dominant theme at Level 0.

A more delightful and age-appropriate illustration is provided by Selman. The young child is sitting in the mother's shopping cart and approaching the supermarket checkout counter. Requesting a piece of the invitingly displayed candy, the child observes his mother shaking her head "no" whereupon the child takes the mother's head, moving it up and down, which the child knows, means "yes." The child assumes that this other-transformation, that is changing the direction of the head gesture, will produce the desired candy. Apparently, the child is still unable to differentiate between the mother's head movements and the underlying intention. This level of behavior appears to be based on the assumption that by changing the physical gesture from "no" to "yes," the mother's intention has also been changed.

Another rather benign form of Level 0 interaction (or the lack thereof) is mutual silliness without planning, coordination, or communication. Selman identifies a Level 0 friendship relationship as "Momentary Playmanship." A Level 0 attempt at making friendship may simply consist of offering a toy, a candy, or money.

■ Level 1: Negotiation for Control by One-Way "Will Driven" Power

The need to dominate others and to get one's way is still present, but the Level 1 child is dictatorial rather than tyrannical (Level 0). The domination of others is based more on ordering and verbal threats than on physical impulsive actions. There is a beginning awareness that the perception of the other may be different from the self, but the perceptions of the other and the self cannot be considered simultaneously; they are unilateral (Nakkula & Selman, 1991), and the necessity of a "give-and-take" in interpersonal relationships is not yet part of the cognitive structure. "Good friendship" is defined as the other person doing what the self wants. Jimmy asserts: "John is not my friend anymore!" When asked why, his answer reveals a Level 1 structure: "Because he doesn't do what I want him to."

The self-transforming strategies at Level 1 often involve a nonassertive stance (as in the case of Alex, p. 233) or a submissive compliance to the demands of others. The child who is being bossed gives in quickly and without resistance.

A common and simple other-transforming strategy at the subjective perspective-taking stage is telling the other person, in a one-way fashion, what to do. However, there is now an attempt, not present at Level 0, to use "relationship-oriented resources of power, assertiveness and control to get" one's way (Selman & Schultz, 1980: 80). Examples of this would be a withdrawal of friendship: "If you want me to be your friend, you must give me back that toy . . .," or simple bribes such as, "You can have some of my cookies, if you . . . ." The other person is fully acknowledged and efforts are directed toward changing the other person's behavior (hence, other-transformation); however, the other person's feelings and intentions in the matter are still disregarded. Battles are fought over which activity to pursue, who plays with what toy, who goes first, and who cheated. The issue becomes a matter of "mine versus yours" or who controls whom. Often the motives determining such demands seem to be more to obtain control and to get one's way, rather than to receive the goods, services, or resources that—at least on the surface—appear to be in dispute. Both individuals have separate wills and often separate goals (or the same goal, wanting the same object at the same time to play with) and through forcefully ordering the other, through threat, bribe, or psychological manipulation, the self tries to force the other to do what the self wants. A common observation supporting this self-wanting-control idea is one in which the other child who has the toy-in-demand relinquishes it and picks up another toy. At this point the self also loses interest and now demands the new toy that the other child has just selected. In a more benign fashion, Level 1 play activity is one in which each of the pair pursues his or her own goal, neither of the pair accommodating to the other. The personal feelings are not differentiated from the situation, so that the child who does not get his or her way sees the final outcome as a matter of "unfairness." Only after the other person's feelings, interests, intentions, and points of view are being considered, and there are some two-way negotiations with an appeal to turn-taking or fairness, has Level 2 been reached.

■ Level 2: Negotiation for Influence by Conscious Reciprocal Persuasion

The needs of the other person are now clearly acknowledged and reciprocal exchanges and reflections take both the self and the other into consideration. Selman describes Level 2 friendship, a process in which both parties participate, as the "Two-Way Fair-Weather Cooperation." There is an attempt to persuade and convince, rather than to order the other person to do what the self wants. Selman distinguishes between attempts to control or coerce the other person's will (Level 1) and efforts at modifying, making deals, or manipulating the other person's interest and intentions, so that the other person agrees with the self (Level 2). Level 2 negotiation appears to be a genuine attempt in seeking the other person's support for one's own ideas; however, Level 2 does not exclude the possible use of manipulative attempts. At times, and as long as the other person appears receptive, these other-transformations may be constructive, and they are not at all uncommon in normal children, adolescents, and even much of adult social interactions. Illustrations of Level 2 negotiations include: (1) appealing to fairness, such as "Let's flip a coin to see who goes first!" or "you can have the toy first, me second"; (2) past experiences, "we always have had fun playing it this way"; (3) common interest, "we both really like the game"; or (4) the expertise of the other, "you are really good at this." However, the goal of the self still remains of primary importance and the process of getting to the goal is secondary. Self-interest is still more important than mutual interest. If friendly persuasion doesn't work, the self may turn to somewhat more deceptive methods, such as using the guilt trip strategy: "Come on Kate, lots of time I've done stuff because you wanted to. I think it's your turn to do what I want" (Selman & Schultz, 1990: 86). Conformity pressure, "everybody plays this game now," can also be used to persuade the other to do what the self wants. Stage 2 individuals understand jealousy in others and can identify with the feelings of a child who has been excluded from a social event.

■ Level 3: Negotiation for Collaborative, Mutually Satisfactory Ends

Individuals at this mutual perspective-taking level attempt to establish a collaborative orientation. Disagreements are resolved through mutual negotiations on a "give-and-take" basis. Self and other can be understood from the perspective of a third person. Self and other reflectively communicate their thoughts and feelings, and there is now some willingness to compromise by sharing power, material possessions, and even attention. The outstanding characteristics of Level 3 are the mutuality of the negotiation, collaboration, and sharing. Selman refers to Level 3 friendship as "Intimate Mutually Shared Relationship." The individual seems to be able to step outside the one-to-one relationship and consider from the outside (the perspective of a neutral observer) how each individual feels about the other's suggestions. Relationships are based on sharing and a sense of "we" or "our." The goal is to openly negotiate; the other person's feelings (yes, even his or her objections) are respected. There appears to be an underlying feeling that the closeness of the pair is of primary importance rather than who gets his or her way. However, this exclusive intimacy can result in possessiveness, jealousy, and dependency. Harry Stack Sullivan (1953) has coined the term "chumship," which is very appropriate for this dimension of friendship development, when the attachment to a "chum" becomes very powerful and when the desire to maintain the relationship and to be sensitive to the other person's needs are more important than whether or not one gets his or her way in a particular activity. Level 3 is rare in pair therapy, because when Level 3 interpersonal negotiation strategies can be used with any consistency, maturity has been reached and pair therapy is no longer needed. The mutual, collaborative, and reciprocal level of social understanding that is characteristic of Level 3 is not generally expressed by adolescents until they are in seventh or eighth grade.

It is no coincidence that, with the attainment of Level 3 social understanding, mutual perspective taking, and collaborative efforts, the earlier childhood preoccupation with who gets to play with what toy or who goes first begins to take on somewhat of a secondary role to the preoccupation with having a friend and maintaining that friendship. Thus, the goals themselves are changing from self-interest to having friends and belonging to a group of peers. Increasingly, there emerges at this level a beginning concern with more stable boy-girl relationships, a situation which really could not endure for any length of time on Level 0, 1, or 2, except if one partner tolerates the domination and exploitation of the other. The frequency of marital discord and divorce can be understood if one or usually both of the couple function at these lower levels. Negotiating, validating, and communicating one's feelings become a particularly significant aspect of dating, going steady, engagement, and marriage, and involve mutually agreed-upon levels of physical intimacy as well as an understanding on the exclusion or inclusion of friends, parents, relatives, and others in the relationship.

■ Level 4: Negotiation for Intimacy in Relationship Through Interpreting and In-Depth Understanding of the Other Person

The in-depth social perspective-taking stage which is based on the most advanced strategies of interpersonal negotiation may be the ultimate goal of pair therapy; however, Level 4 hardly ever appears in the therapeutic process and hence, has not been studied in sufficient detail. Level 4 interactions are less common in the daily interactions of typical early and middle adolescents. Obviously individuals who function at this level are not in need of pair therapy.

Level 4 is, of course, the most mature of the five levels and requires "the need to cope with the powerful emotions and doubts that can be generated when people attempt to share their deepest and most uncertain experiences with one another" (Selman & Schultz, 1990: 94). Intimacy in this context is certainly not limited to sexual intimacy but refers also (maybe even more) to relationships in which people have made deep existential commitments to each other. This kind of relationship requires flexibility and means that the self can be both dependent on the other, as well as supportive of the other; indeed the orientation between the self and the other combine into a mutual orientation and become integrated. The common conflicts in most relationships between autonomy (I need more space) and intimacy (I need more love, more support, and more emotional sharing) are acknowledged. Hence, Selman refers to this level as "Autonomous Independence." Each partner provides emotional and psychological support, but simultaneously respects the need for both autonomy and dependence. As one person summarizes the essence of this level: "You have to be able to support and trust and give, but you have to be able to let go, too" (Selman & Selman, 1979: 72). Obviously, Level 4 requires the ability to think abstractly and becomes possible only after a long history of healthy social interaction patterns, some of which can be provided, even belatedly, in pair therapy.

■ Movement Up and Down These Levels

In actual social interactions a movement toward higher and lower levels of interaction is possible and is dependent on the social strategies employed by the partner as well as other contextual factors. Thus, one person's strategies can bring down those of the other person (often aggravating an existing disequilibrium) or they can raise them (defusing the equilibrium). Many adolescents regress quickly to lower levels of interpersonal functioning when teased, frustrated, under stress, or when "baited" by lower level strategies from others. For troubled adolescents, such precipitous decline to lower levels when under stress or when confronted with limits is a common occurrence in pair therapy. The degree of regression may reveal the severity of the problem, and also the precariousness of the higher level equilibrium.

When a higher level attempt at other-transforming does not work, the self, unable to cope with the frustration, might move to increasingly lower levels. Kate, a 10-year-old, sees another child with whom she wants to play. Kate flatters the other child: "Hey let's play kickball now . . . I know you are very good at it" (Level 2). The flattery works and the play begins. A short while later an argument ensues and Kate, now regressing to Level 1, orders the other child, "Give me that ball" (Level 1). Kate's command is frustrated and the other child refuses to yield the ball. Kate's face turns red; she runs over, grabs the ball out of the other girl's hand (Level 0), and runs across the field (Selman & Schultz, 1990).

To facilitate movement to higher levels requires a great deal of patience, tolerance, and the ability to refrain from a power struggle. This is likely accomplished by a therapist, a teacher, a parent, or a more mature friend. Thus, the child who doesn't get his or her way and screams: "Shut up, shut up, shut up . . . I hate you . . ." and then runs toward the door (Level 0), can be guided into higher levels of responding. An understanding mother might respond: "I know how you feel . . . and it is all right for you to hate me . . . I still love you. Let's talk about it." Mom might then receive a somewhat higher level response, such as: "I don't believe you love me," or "What is there to talk about," or some other small indication that internal self-dialogue has been set in motion: "I don't care, I am still very, very angry at you."

■ The Relationship Between Social Cognitive Thought and Interpersonal Interaction

The relationship between the cognitive structure of interpersonal perspective taking (thought) and actual social-emotional behavior in a conflictual interpersonal situation has been studied extensively and is implied in the title of a journal article, "Bridging the Gap Between Interpersonal Thought and Action in Early Adolescence," by Schultz and Selman (1989). The assumption, based on structural developmental theory (e.g., Piaget and

Kohlberg), is that cognitive structure (thought) under normal circumstances is a prerequisite for consistent social behavior. Among normal eighth-graders, the interpersonal negotiation strategies on a given cognitive dilemma (thought) and on a social-emotional behavioral level (action) were significantly correlated. That is, adolescents who can give age-appropriate answers to interpersonal dilemmas tend to use their knowledge to actually negotiate real-life social issues, such as problems, dilemmas, conflicts. A consistent gap between higher level thoughts and lower level actions appears to be a configuration related or contributing to social deviancy and may be associated with developmental pathology. When the interpersonal negotiation strategies in thought are significantly more advanced than those displayed in actual action, the psychodynamic processes are less differentiated and hence, less mature. Thus, action based on a gap between high-level thought and low-level action might be considered neurotic (Schultz & Selman, 1989).

In actuality, a reverse gap between low-level thought and high-level action is relatively rare as theory predicts, and when the gap exists, it tends to be smaller.

Two different patterns of deviancy in social strategies have been identified. In the first instance, the adolescents can reason relatively coherently and correctly about interpersonal relationships. In other words, on a strictly cognitive level the individual can provide the kind of answers that are age-appropriate and normative for a Level 2 or Level 3 adolescent. However, in real-life situations, his or her behavior represents lower-level strategies, such as perceiving his or her social world in a unilateral, one-way fashion, in which friends are told what to do (Level 1) and expected to comply. In other words, the social/emotional manifestation in peer interaction falls substantially below the level of cognitive awareness. An inability to translate this age-appropriate understanding into actual behavior may produce internal conflict because individuals will be aware of the disequilibrium and hence judge themselves negatively. The gap between a cognitive understanding (e.g., knowing what friendship is supposed to be) and actual social interactions (acting in a friendship-building way) often is the most crucial clinical issue when working with troubled youth in pair therapy.

In the second instance of pathology, the individual should be at Level 3 in terms of his or her age, while he or she actually functions both in thought (cognitive level) and in action (social emotional level) at Level 1, with limited awareness of the needs and perspectives of others. Obviously, therapeutic interventions might be more difficult if the adolescent has no awareness of the interpersonal negotiation strategies commonly utilized by the peers.

In diagnosing and interpreting the developmental meaning of peer relationships and the nature of their social interaction, this distinction becomes important. Do children understand, at least on a cognitive level, what is expected of others their age—even if they do not have the social emotional structure to implement such knowledge? Or do they lack both the cognitive as well as the personal social emotional understanding of what might be considered appropriate social strategies for their age?

EDUCATIONAL IMPLICATIONS

Selman, working at the Manville School of Boston Judge Baker Children's Center, has genuinely been concerned with the educational implications of social cognitive theory for education, for schools, for the curriculum, and for the regular classroom teacher. Because his theorizing about interpersonal negotiation strategies [INS] and his pair therapy deals with the social competence of adolescents in a school setting, he writes more explicitly about the educational implications of his theory than virtually any other scholar discussed in this book. His approach is not only theoretical but has increasingly become more practical, clinical, and educational. His concern is not limited to pair therapy as an effective intervention program for emotionally disturbed adolescents but also includes a broader, more general "promotion of social problem-solving skills in school aged children" (Yeates & Selman, 1989: 64). Nevertheless, Selman maintains that less has been written about the teaching of interpersonal negotiation skills in the regular classroom and fewer investigations have been conducted with normal children.

Selman emphasizes that regular classroom teachers may benefit as much as pair therapists from understanding not only the cognitive aspects of social perspective taking, but even more so, from the actual utilization of interpersonal strategies and from an analysis of the level of social competence in their classroom. Such an analysis would reveal what may actually contribute to conflict: that is, the level of competence which children utilize in forming friendships and/or how their social actions contribute to the lack of friendship-forming strategies. Thus, teachers would benefit directly since inadequate social behaviors often have disruptive inter- and intrapersonal effects that do have an impact on learning, classroom behavior, classroom atmosphere, and discipline problems.

Teaching children social problem-solving skills in the regular classroom is not a new idea. The assumption of existing training programs that teach social skills is that they will lead to more adequate, age-appropriate forms of social functioning and contribute to an increase in the complexity and effectiveness of social reasoning (Enright, 1976). Marsh, Serafica, and Barenboim (1980) were able to demonstrate that early adolescents could be trained successfully in perspective-taking skills. Participation in such learning activities did indeed have a positive effect on their ability to solve interpersonal problems. Social problem solving was assessed by asking each subject to assume that one of his or her three close friends must be excluded from a rock concert and to develop an appropriate excuse. There were several other interpersonal problems of this nature, and the adolescents had to decide: What is the problem? What factors must be considered? What are alternative ways of solving the problem? What are the consequences for each solution?

Hudson, Peyton, and Brion-Maisels (1976) demonstrated that children who had developed better perspective-taking skills were also more likely to be friendly, helpful, and adept at using social problem-solving behaviors when confronted with a child in need of assistance than were children with less social perspective-taking skills. Others (Shure & Spivack, 1978; Spivack & Shure, 1974) have reported similar positive effects of perspective-taking training on younger children. However, in these studies the perspective-taking part of the program was embedded in a more general social problem-solving context. The Shure and Spivack (1978) interpersonal problem-solving script is designed not only to help children in solving specific problems "now," it is also intended to teach them to cope with a variety of new social problems, which inevitably will arise in the future. The two most important interpersonal problem-solving skills are *alternative-solution thinking* (the social thinking skill that produces many different solutions to a problem), and *consequential thinking* (the social skill to predict what is most likely to happen with each alternative solution).

In reviewing the literature on teaching social problem-solving skills, Selman distinguishes between a functional approach and a structural approach. The *functional approach* is more directly aimed at teaching and practicing specific social skills that are fairly objectively defined and can, at the end of the program, be evaluated by the attainment of objective criteria, so that one can claim that a specific skill has been mastered. The *structural approach* aims at changing the underlying structure of social cognition and its goal is to advance the child's social ability to a higher level of functioning, a move which then would manifest itself in the emergence of many different and diverse interpersonal negotiation strategies. The best illustration of a structural approach is pair therapy where the goal is not limited to any one specific social skill, but is to facilitate movement toward higher levels (or stages) of social competence, without undue emphasis on any one particular social skill. The structural approach is a direct reflection of Piaget's and Kohlberg's theories, where it is not a specific answer that determines the level of moral judgment; for example, whether Heinz steals the drug or not is not important—but the underlying thinking, reasoning and philosophical justifications for one's actions or answers are the key.

In everyday instructional endeavors, many teachers and principals invest much effort and energy in dealing with inter- and intrapersonal conflicts among children. In different classrooms, management and dealing with individual behavior problems may require more time and more skill than the pursuit of strictly academic learning. Social conflicts, often at the root of lack of achievement and dissatisfaction with self and school, contribute to discipline problems. Yet, even though schools provide a unique setting for teaching interpersonal problem-solving strategies, these kinds of social skill learning activities are rarely identified as a primary educational purpose. Teachers obtain substantially less, if any, training, guidelines, and support for promoting social adjustment, and schools frequently do not have a curriculum for developing social competence and conflict resolution. Clearly, the emphasis remains on the academic content, even though it is known that the development of social skills, interpersonal problem-solving strategies, and social collaboration during the school years are powerful predictors of future social, personal, and emotional adjustment.

On a practical level teachers cannot easily assume the role of the pair therapist because they work with larger groups of children and have other teaching obligations. However, using social dilemmas (see Selman et al., 1986: 459 for specific dilemmas) in small group discussions or cooperative learning activities can encourage children to express their own social problem-solving strategies and to receive feedback. Not only will they learn from their peers but they will be encouraged to think about how the other person (protagonist) might feel. Grouping children so that the socially more advanced pupils are just one level (rather than 2 or 3) above the lower-level children has been found to be more likely to enhance development. On the other hand, children who function at a very low level (e.g., Level 0) are unlikely to benefit from a discussion with typical adolescents who may already utilize social strategies at Level 3 (and in rare cases, Level 4).

A teacher familiar with Selman's system of social perspective taking and the developmental levels and self- and other-strategies as applied to friends and peers possesses a powerful conceptual model for understanding developmental growth patterns in social cognition. This knowledge can be used to facilitate growth in social competence, for example, by asking the child who acts socially immature or inappropriate to reflect on his or her behavior, or by injecting growth-inducing comments and redirecting the behavior of both the protagonist and the other person so as to avoid conflict. A teacher needs to be aware that suggesting to a child at Level 0 (flight or fight) the teacher's own problem-solving strategy (which might be at Level 3 or 4), would accomplish nothing or might even exacerbate the problem. Simply channeling the fighting behavior of a Level 0 child into expressing his or her frustration verbally might accomplish more growth, even though the behavior may not be the desirable ultimate goal.

Recognizing the social-cognitive stages of each child may help the teacher in several ways:

1. The teacher can better identify the behavior of the class by understanding how children view social relationships, rights, and obligation.
2. The teacher can better determine realistic expectations for students' developmental goals, and
3. The teacher can help define the affective, as well as the cognitive capacity of children (Selman, 1976a: 310).

Selman's theory of interpersonal understanding obviously supports an educational philosophy that emphasizes affective education, altruism, empathy, social tolerance, conflict resolution, social problem solving, and an increased social awareness. Implying a movement away from a one-sided and limited concern with only the cognitive side of development, social cognitive theory emphasizes an inclusion of social skills training and the facilitation of interpersonal negotiation strategies in the classroom setting.

12

JANE LOEVINGER: EGO DEVELOPMENT IN ADOLESCENCE

LOEVINGER'S METHODOLOGY AND ITS RELATION TO HER THEORY

In her own professional life, Jane Loevinger (1918–   ) moved from being a psychometric psychologist to a developmental theorist. This has profound implications: her theory developed out of research data and has always depended upon empirical results. Loevinger has received widespread praise for providing a sound and well-developed empirical basis for her theory (Snarey et al., 1983) and she has always viewed the interplay between theory and data as the true nature of science (Loevinger, 1993). The best known of her methodological advances is the *Sentence Completion Test* (*SCT*), sometimes also referred to as the *Washington University Sentence Completion Test of Ego Development* (*WUSCTED*) (Loevinger, 1985; Loevinger & Wessler, 1970; Loevinger, Wessler & Redmore, 1970).

The SCT supplies empirical foundation for her theory as well as the data for determining different ego stages, which are identified by scoring the subject's responses. Loevinger (1976: 430) writes: "Perhaps my most distinctive contribution has been devising a means for the mutual feedback of theory and measurement." Since Loevinger's developmental theory did not grow out of a philosophical rationalization but out of empirical findings, theory and methodology are more closely intertwined than in most developmental theories.

Loevinger's *Sentence Completion Test* (SCT) consists of 36 incomplete sentence-stems, each of which is completed by the subject in a single sentence. The SCT usually is administered in written format, although the test has also been administered orally. The administration of the test itself is relatively easy; however, because it is projective, scoring is very complex and requires specialized training. Unlike almost all other theoretically based developmental tests, Loevinger's original version was designed for women and adolescent girls. Later, in response to research needs, she designed a comparable form for men and adolescent boys. The form for men is as much like the form for women as possible without sacrificing the richness of the content (see Figure 12.1). Actually several different forms of the SCT exist. Male and female forms are approximately equivalent. A discussion of validity data of the SCT, including technical data on gender differences can be found in Loevinger's (1985) article.

Sentence Completion Items

Stem

---

1. When a child will not join in group activities
2. Raising a family
3. When I am criticized
4. A man's job
5. Being with other people
6. The thing I like about myself is
7. My mother and I
8. What gets me into trouble is
9. Education
10. When people are helpless
11. Women are lucky because
12. A good father
13. A girl has a right to
14. When they talked about sex, I
15. A wife should
16. I feel sorry
17. A man feels good when
18. Rules are
19. Crime and delinquency could be halted if
20. Men are lucky because
21. I just can't stand people who
22. At times she (he) worried about
23. I am
24. A woman feels good when
25. My main problem is
26. A husband has a right to
27. The worst thing about being a woman (man)
28. A good mother
29. When I am with a man (woman)
30. Sometimes she (he) wished that
31. My father
32. If I can't get what I want
33. Usually she (he) felt that sex
34. For a woman a career is
35. My conscience bothers me if
36. A woman (man) should always

Notes. Stems for men and women are identical except for those with a word in parentheses.

Parenthetical word indicates change used for men's form.

FIGURE 12.1 Loevinger's sentence completion test. (From J. Loevinger (1985). Revision of the sentence completion test for ego development. *Journal of Personality and Social Psychology, 48,* p. 426. Copyright © 1985 by the American Psychological Association. Adapted with permission.)

Jane Loevinger (1918-   )

The assignment of an individual to specific ego stages depends on the subject's response to the incomplete sentence-stems of the SCT. In other words, the definitions of the ego levels, which emerged from empirical data, constitute *empirical stages*. This contrasts with the clinically derived logical stages of Erikson. In Erikson's theory, the creation of specific assessment methods to identify his eight stages of development followed his clinical and theoretical model. Erikson's stages, which preceded empirical verification, therefore, are *logical stages*. The profound underlying methodological differences of these models receive clear illustration in Loevinger's motto: "The scientist follows the data, even if theories fly out of the window."

LOEVINGER'S STAGE MODEL OF EGO DEVELOPMENT

Loevinger's lifework has been a search for a unifying and holistic theme that characterizes human development or character growth during the entire human life cycle. Thus, ego development has become the central construct that Loevinger views as the underlying "framework of meaning" that is imposed subjectively by the individual on his or her changing life experiences. Included are ideas that other theorists have called "moralization," "integration," "self-system," "cognitive complexity" (Hauser, 1976), and "faith development" (see Chapter 13). Loevinger argues that ego development proceeds by advancing to increasingly more sophisticated levels of meaning-making. The more mature ego stages reveal more internalization, objectivity, abstraction, tolerance of ambiguity, integrative processes, and freedom from dependency on others. According to Loevinger & Wessler (1970: 8), the search for coherent meanings in experience "is the essence of the ego or of ego functioning, rather than just one among many equally important ego functions."

Developmental progression is not a smooth, continuous transition from less to more mature levels, but includes major identifiable structural changes in one's self-definition. Increasing age, maturation, socialization experiences, education, and informal life experiences contribute to increasing capacity to control one's impulses, an increasingly more complex perception of self and others, self-evaluation, self-awareness, reflection about events, increased frustration tolerance, adaptation to moral values, and a concern with broader philosophical issues. Specifically, Loevinger's concept of ego development implies discontinuities, and such disequilibria define the transition from one stage to the next. Loevinger hypothesizes that the ego changes developmentally and that the major progressions in ego development constitute the markers for the identifiable and quantitatively different stages. She conceptualizes that (1) these stages appear in a sequential pattern and comprise an invariant hierarchical order (Loevinger, 1976; Redmore & Loevinger, 1979), and (2) that "a correlation exists between ego level at earlier and at later grades" (Redmore & Loevinger, 1979: 2), meaning that those who are more (or less) advanced in their ego level at age 10 will tend to be more (or less) advanced at age 14, 16, or 18. (See Figure 12.2.)

Research supports both of these hypotheses.

1. Ego levels do tend to increase as a function of age during adolescence; nevertheless, the reported speed of ego advancement varies from individual to individual and sometimes even from study to study. For example, in one study (Redmore & Loevinger, 1979), adolescent subjects showed a half-stage gain in a 2-year period and a full-stage gain in a 4-year period, while for another group in the same study the gain over a 4-year period represented only a half-stage. In general, the rate of gain seems to fluctuate, depending on the characteristics of the group, and tends to slow down as the subjects approach the end of adolescence.

2. The test correlations between the ego level at an earlier grade level with the ego level at a more advanced grade proved significant (Redmore & Loevinger, 1979). Each of the stages is more complex than the previous one, and no stage can be skipped in the developmental progression toward maturity. However, the rate and the distance negotiated by any given person in the developmental sequence are individually determined, and even adults may be found at virtually any level with the possible exception of the very early ones. Furthermore, each stage can, once it has become the final or terminal level, turn out to be an adult personality typology or a distinct characterological portrait. By measuring diverse levels of ego development with the same test, the SCT allows one to assess individual differences and to determine the relationship of ego scores to age. In addition, studies have established correlation with numerous other characteristics and functions (such as intelligence and SES) as well as interactions with developmental constructs defined by other theories, such as cognition (Piaget) or moral judgment (Kohlberg) (Hauser, 1976). Because of the enor-

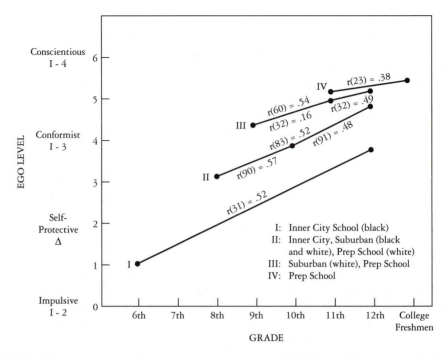

FIGURE 12.2 Average ego level by grade and correlations over 1.5, 2, 3, and 6 years for longitudinal samples. Note: Average SES (0 = high) for Group I = 6, for Group II = 3, and for Groups III and IV = 2. (From C. D. Redmore and J. Loevinger 1979. Ego development in adolescence. *Journal of Youth and Adolescence* 8, p. 18. Permission granted by C. D. Redmore and Plenum Publishing Corporation.)

mous individual variation in the rate and the timing of developmental progression, the relationship between age and ego stage is not a stable one, difficult to define and depends on individual factors. This relationship tends to decline with increasing age because the variance in ego level increases with increasing age during the school years. In addition, ego development advances more rapidly for girls than for boys, primarily during the junior-senior high school years (Cohn, 1991).

Loevinger does not think of the stages themselves as measures of good or poor adjustment. "One cannot use adjustment . . . as clues to ego level as measured by the SCT" (Loevinger, 1993: 10). Physical and mental health are not the same as ego development (Loevinger, 1976). Thus, individuals could score relatively low on the SCT—in relationship to their age cohort—without necessarily appearing abnormal. At each stage, individuals may show signs of mild forms of maladjustment or even more serious mental disturbances. And, although the theory underlying ego development is primarily concerned with the well-adjusted rather than with the pathological person, it reveals that "there may be differences in the kind of pathology or presenting symptoms characteristic for different [ego] levels" (Loevinger, 1976: 427). Although Loevinger did not design the research methodology to assess adjustment problems or abnormality, more recent studies have identified some link between ego development and psychopathology (Hauser et al., 1991). In addition, low levels of ego development have been related to impulsivity (Starrett, 1983), adolescent pregnancy (Hart & Hilton, 1988), authoritarianism (Browning, 1983), and delinquent behavior (Frank & Quinlan, 1976). However, these kinds of findings are not the primary concern of Loevinger's theory which suggests an important distinction between developmental stages and mental health, a distinction that is essential for understanding optimal conditions of development. Responses revealing "good adjustment" are commonly given by conformists and those on the self-aware level. The careless use of "adjustment," "maturity," and "mental health" as being synonymous or even similar to ego development is a stumbling block that will obscure clarity and retard progress. Every stage contains its own "weaknesses, its problems, and its paradoxes, which provide both potential for maladjustment and a potential for growth" (Loevinger, 1966: 200).

THE EGO STAGES

A brief synopsis of the levels of ego development, which consist of six stages and three transitional phases, follows (see Figure 12.3). Emphasis will be on the adolescent period; however, with the exception of extremes on both sides, adolescents can really be found in most stages.

■ The Presocial Symbiotic Stages (I–1)

The very early stages of ego development divide into two component parts.

The presocial phase (0) is an autistic stage in which animate and inanimate objects in the surroundings are not yet differentiated. Infants at this stage have no awareness of the needs and desires of those around them and are concerned only with the gratification of their own needs.

The symbiotic phase (I–1) is different in that a strong symbiotic dependence on the mother (or a mother surrogate) begins to emerge. While the child at this level can distinguish between the mother and the environment, he or she cannot yet differentiate between the self and the mother.

These early stages hardly merit the term *ego stages* since the infant has not yet developed the language skills necessary for assessment of ego development by Loevinger's SCT. An adolescent/adult operating in the presocial stage would not be found functioning in regular society but would be institutionalized or living on the fringe of society (e.g., hobo camps or homeless).

■ Impulsive (I–2)

The next level, the so-called impulsive ego, typical of early childhood, is occasionally observed in junior high, but is rarely found in late adolescence/adulthood, except in traumatic situations or in those who are in some kind of trouble. The impulsive individual might be considered at the lower limit of true ego function. The impulsive orientation is exploitative and grossly self-indulgent in that the young person perceives other people as potential

Some Milestones of Ego Development

Stage	Impulse Control, Character Development	Interpersonal Style	Conscious Preoccupations	Cognitive Style
Presocial		Autistic		
Symbiotic		Symbiotic	Self vs. non-self	
Impulsive	Impulsive, fear of retaliation	Receiving, dependent, exploitative	Bodily feelings, especially sexual and aggressive	Stereotyping, conceptual confusion
Self-Protective	Fear of being caught, externalizing blame, opportunistic	Wary, manipulative, exploitative	Self-protection, trouble, wishes, things, advantage, control	
Conformist	Conformity to external rules, shame, guilt for breaking rules	Belonging, superficial niceness	Appearance, social acceptability, banal feelings, behavior	Conceptual simplicity, stereotypes, cliches
Self-Aware	Differentiation of norms, goals	Aware of self in relation to group, helping	Adjustment, problems, reasons, opportunities (vague)	Multiplicity
Conscientious	Self-evaluated standards, self-criticism, guilt for consequences, long-term goals and ideals	Intensive, responsible, mutual, concern for communication	Differentiated feelings, motives for behavior, self-respect, achievements, traits, expression	Conceptual complexity, idea of patterning
Individualistic	*Add:* Respect for individuality	*Add:* Dependence as an emotional problem	*Add:* Development, social problems, differentiation of inner life from outer	*Add:* Distinction of process and outcome
Autonomous	*Add:* Coping with conflicting inner needs, toleration	*Add:* Respect for autonomy, interdependence	Vividly conveyed feelings, integration of physiological and psychological causation of behavior, role conception, self-fulfillment, self in social context	Increased conceptual complexity, complex patterns, toleration for ambiguity, broad scope, objectivity
			Add: Identity	
Integrated	*Add:* Reconciling inner conflicts, renunciation of unattainable	*Add:* Cherishing of individuality		

NOTE: "*Add*" means in addition to the description applying to the previous level.

FIGURE 12.3 Some milestones of ego development (from Jane Loevinger, *Ego Development*, 1976, pp.23-24, Table 1. Copyright 1976 by Jossey-Bass, Inc., Publishers. Reproduced with permission).

sources of personal benefit. The focus is on the satisfaction of personal needs, physical appetites, and getting one's way. Inner controls are unreliable or ineffective; hence, the young person keeps the uninhibited seeking of self-gratification in check only by immediate reward and/or the fear of punishment; there is no sense of personal guilt. Delinquent adolescents commonly function in the impulsive stage. The impulsive individual may confuse and mix up such concepts as "clean" and "dirty" with the ideas of "good" and "bad," reinterpreting the former with the meanings of the latter. The interpersonal world is dichotomized into those who are "good," meaning "helpful to me," and those who are "mean," meaning "nasty to me." Some aspects of impulsive ego needs may remain stable even in later life, for example, as evidenced in outbursts of temper tantrums. The representative trait adjectives are: demanding, primitive, undiscriminating.

■ Self-Protective, Formerly Referred to as the Opportunistic-Stage (Delta)

In the opportunistic-hedonistic transitional stage, the primary concern is still with the self and with immediate gratification, but self-control is beginning to emerge. There also appears a desire to gain control and dominance over others. While the pleasure-pain principle still seems to govern behavior, the young person now understands that there are rules and manipulates them for personal advantages. What the self-protective person sees as "bad" is not breaking the rules, but being caught. Even when at fault, the individual tends to use a hostile sense of humor to protect the self and to blame others rather than to assume responsibility. The dependence on others, characteristic of the earlier stages, may now yield to a "who-needs-them?" attitude. These patterns of defensive self-protection tend to decline before the end of high school. The representative trait adjectives are: wary, complaining, cynical, manipulative, exploitative, power-oriented.

The Delta/3 phase, which is a transitional phase, has relatively few specific, defining attributes. When the subject's responses are not advanced enough to receive the next highest rating of "conformist," this phase designation is appropriate.

■ Conformist (I–3)

The phenomenon of adolescent conformity, which has been addressed by philosophers and has received much theoretical and research recognition elsewhere, is a characteristic commonly ascribed to early adolescence. Hence, this level of ego development is common in junior high school. Conformists identify their own welfare with the welfare of others because they themselves care greatly about social approval and social acceptance. They are preoccupied with what others think of them; therefore, appearance and superficial niceties are important. The conformist's sense of self depends almost entirely upon the evaluative feedback received from others. Physical appearance, material possessions, and reputation give the conformist and his or her peers criteria with which to evaluate others. The conformist is very much interested in material things. Belonging to the proper group or groups matters greatly, and the individual may go to extremes to become an accepted group member. Some will probably reject those who are not part of the group. The conformist perceives interpersonal relationships in terms of actions and concrete events rather than in terms of feelings and motivations.

Conformists attempt to imitate others in their group and seek their approval. Interpersonal reciprocity based on the Golden Rule becomes possible. However, thinking still includes simplified moralistic cliches and stereotypes, as if "one size fits all." This is evident through certain cognitive simplicities, which manifest themselves in SCT responses; the subject places people into simple demographic categories. Illustrations from the SCT include: All women should . . . "work," or all women should . . . "stay home and care for their family." All men . . . "like football games" and all college students should . . . "join fraternities (or sororities)." The individual is now beginning to internalize social rules and obeys them because they are "the rules." By the end of high school or the beginning of college, the conformist approach has declined and yields to the next higher ego level. The representative trait adjectives are conventional, moralistic, stereotypical, rule-bound.

■ The Self-Awareness Level (I–3/4)

This is a transitional phase, which was also referred to as the *"conscientious-conformist level."* Conscious self-awareness is beginning to replace the other-imposed standards that are characteristic of the conformist stage. Now becoming aware of their own individuality and of individual differences, persons are more sensitive to interpersonal interactions. They may show concern with masculinity and femininity. The young person makes a deliberate distinction between an individual person and a norm. The earlier emphasis on group values and approval begins to give way to concern with individual values; the subject recognizes exceptions to rules. The subject at this stage perceives "rightness" as being influenced by the contextual variables of time and space. The individual becomes introspective and self-critical and may become aware of not living up to social rules or family expectations, ideas which may contribute to feelings of guilt and a sense of loneliness or self-consciousness. Originally, Loevinger identified this stage as the *self-conscious stage*, but she renamed it, since the term *self-conscious* carried the unintended implication of adjustment problems. Several studies (Holt, 1980; Loevinger, 1976) have reported that more people of all ages are in the self-awareness phase than in any of the other stages. In a group of 1,000 young people ages 16 to 26, the average score fell into the self-awareness stage. These data imply that, for many individuals, the self-awareness phase becomes a stable and permanent adult position. The representative trait characteristics are: capacity for self-criticism, awareness of interpersonal differences and interactions, and multiple possibilities.

■ Conscientious (I–4)

A more complex view of the interpersonal world emerges. The conscientious person is no longer opportunistic, as was characteristic of earlier stages. A clearer sense of inner self crystalizes; internalized moral imperatives are becoming more important than group-sanctioned rules. The individual now sees people as having different needs, diverse behavior patterns, and unique traits. At this stage, feelings and motives rather than actions have become more significant in interpersonal relationships. There is a preoccupation with tolerance for different people. However, this may still lead toward a paradoxical intolerance toward those who are prejudiced against others, such as Ku Klux Klan members or Neo-Nazis. The capacity for self-criticism expands, and long-term goals and commitments develop. The individual has internalized rules but perceives that both rules and roles are multifaceted and capable of changing. The sense of responsibility expands from family and friends to include the larger society. Work begins to be evaluated in terms of the opportunities it can provide, rather than as just being onerous, as the preconformist might view it. Patterns of behavior are more firmly established by now and traits are more stable. This level of ego development is common among late adolescents. The representative trait adjectives are: responsible, empathic, psychologically minded, self-respecting, and conceptually complex.

For all of the preceding stages, the transition from a lower to the next higher level is characterized by a corresponding decline in the attributes ascribed to the lower ego level and an increase in the new attributes of the higher ego stage. Following the conscientious stage, the advance in ego level is no longer a simple replacement of already acquired attributes but the cumulative addition of more complex and more abstract ego qualities to those already acquired in the preceding stages. In addition, responses are becoming more complex rather than changing in fundamental orientation. This makes the scoring process more difficult, especially because any person who is at a lower stage has great difficulties in appreciating and/or comprehending the thinking of ego levels above his or her own.

■ Individualistic (I–4/5)

During this transitional phase, respect for individuality and tolerance for different types of people increases further. There is substantial awareness that different people fulfill different roles. This level of ego development is found only among the more mature late adolescents. The representative trait characteristics are: truly tolerant, appreciative of paradox and irony, interested in process, aware of conflicting emotions.

■ Autonomous (I–5)*

The autonomous individual thinks in terms of psychological consequences and shows increasing tolerance toward those who are different. For autonomous individuals, impulse control is no longer an issue. They display inner-directed behavior and have the ability to tolerate ambiguity and cope with inner conflict. They are beginning to recognize conflict as an inevitable aspect of the human condition. The autonomous individual has the courage to admit to and deal with conflict, rather than ignoring it or projecting it onto others. Moral issues arise from dealing with inner conflicts, conflicting needs, conflicting duties, and the conflict between needs and duties. While the mother in the conscientious stage "feels obliged to prevent her children from making mistakes, . . . a typical autonomous mother recognizes their need to learn from their own mistakes" (Loevinger, 1966: 200). The representative trait adjectives are: complex, objective, discriminating, self-realizing, respectful of others.

■ Integrated (I–6)

This ego level is rarely found in a random sample of adult people; in most social groups probably no more than 1 percent are "integrated." Individuals in this advanced stage are

---

*Loevinger's autonomous stage should not be confused with Erikson's second stage of "autonomy vs. shame and doubt," which is much closer to Loevinger's opportunistic stage.

what Maslow has referred to as "truly self-actualized." Their personal identity is strong, and they integrate personal needs with social reality. There is both a willingness and an effort to improve oneself and society, with an appreciation of inevitable limitations and fallibilities. Individuals take responsibility both for their motives and their actions. When Piaget asked children which offense is worse, breaking ten cups by accident or one cup while stealing cookies, most made a decision one way or the other. The integrated person assumes responsibility for both actions. The representative trait characteristics are: wise, broadly empathic, able to reconcile inner conflicts, cherishing individuality, able to reconcile roles to find identity.

This last stage is so rare that Loevinger has proposed stopping the developmental sequence with the autonomous stage and using the integrated stage simply as a suggestion that there is the possibility for more advanced development. A problem arises because fully appreciating and understanding an ego level that is two or more stages beyond one's own is virtually impossible. Even the task of defining and describing the more advanced stages becomes increasingly difficult.

Though Loevinger's development follows a sequential pattern, her developmental stages do not correspond as closely to specific age levels as do many other developmental stage theories. Not everyone who is at the same age level is also at the same ego level; indeed, there may be considerable variation between age level and ego level. Adolescents may be found in a wide range of stages, anywhere from self-protective to individualistic. While adolescents rarely fall in the preconformist stages, neither do they commonly fall in the autonomous or the integrated stages. Most adolescents tend to be classified between the conformist and the conscientious stages, consistent with the notion that, with increasing age, adolescents move away from imitating others (conformist stage) and toward an internalization of values (conscientious stage). Increasingly, they begin to make independent decisions, see themselves as the initiators of actions, and accept responsibility for their behavior. The data represented in Figure 12.4 demonstrate a progressive movement toward higher ego levels with increasing age; however, the data also reveal that ego level and age do not progress at the same rate, but that the rate of progression in ego level development is an in-

Ego/Self Stage of Development (Loevinger)

AGE GROUP	PREDOMINANT STAGE
Early adolescence, ages 12–15	Δ
	1–3
	1–3/4
Middle adolescence, ages 15–18	1–3
	1–3/4
	1–4
Late adolescence, ages 18–21	1–3/4
	1–4
	1–4/5

FIGURE 12.4 Ego/Self stage of development   (From N. Sprinthall and W. Collins. *Adolescent Psychology*, 3rd ed. (1995), McGraw-Hill, Inc. Published with permission of McGraw-Hill, Inc.)

dividual matter. Loevinger does not even attempt to answer the commonly asked question, "What age does each stage correspond to?" because "the average stage for a given age is not the same as the average age for a given stage" (Loevinger, 1976: 13).

■ Polar Aspect of Ego Development versus Milestone Sequences

Ego stages as well as personal attributes and corresponding behavior can change or develop by two distinctly different patterns. Some of the attributes and behaviors related to these stages of ego development tend to emerge as an individual approaches a specific stage, reach their peak, and become the dominant characteristics while the individual remains in that stage, and then begin to fall off as the individual becomes more mature and approaches the subsequent ego level. Loevinger refers to this pattern of ascending and later descending developmental progression as the "milestone sequence," and her ego stages must be viewed as milestones that peak at a given level of ego maturity rather than as polar variables. The peak of the curve represents the milestone for that characteristic, it begins to decline (descend) as the next higher ego stage emerges. Like an inverted U-shaped curve, it has three identifiable points: the low point before it ascends, a maximal or high point when it peaks, and another low point when it declines at the end of the curve. A good illustration of such a milestone manifestation is "conformity" since it falls in the middle of all stages and is a typical ego issue of early adolescence. Conformity might begin to manifest itself, albeit in limited scope, in the ascending self-protective stage. It is a major issue in the "conformity" stage, where it peaks and it is likely to remain prevalent, but at least begins descending in the transitional self-awareness stage. Spontaneity and impulse expression follow similar milestone patterns.

However, other behaviors and attitudes tend to follow a *polar or two extreme point pattern* in that they increase constantly during the developmental period, often most dramatically during the beginning of development; then, further growth continues at a slower pace as development progresses. Ego development over the range of all stages follows a polar growth pattern. Polar variables appear in the two extremes. A specific illustration might be the tendency to stereotype or overgeneralize, an attitude that declines with increasing ego maturity. Thus, slowly but steadily during the entire period of development, the ability to consider and value individuality replaces the inclination to think in terms of stereotypes. Other illustrations include the developmental progression from an egocentric to a sociocentric view of the world, from autistic to realistic thinking, and from intolerance toward tolerance.

■ Reliability and Validity of the SCT

The individual's level of ego maturity is assessed by a 36-item Sentence Completion Test (SCT) (see Figure 12.1). Each response to the incomplete sentence is individually assigned to one of the nine ego levels, six main and three transitional stages, on the assumption that basically different responses to the same stem reflect different ego levels. An illustration might be the responses expressing similar ideas, but indicating different levels of social awareness and tolerance: " . . . having a big mouth"; " . . . saying the wrong thing"; " . . . being too outspoken." From the specific scores, a *Total Protocol Rating (TPR)* is derived.

While responses to specific stems may reflect different ego levels, the TPR is assumed to represent the combined core of the functional level of ego development.

The reliability of the SCT, as measured by the correlation between two TPR scores, with each testing evaluated independently by two trained raters, is r = .85; this is high for a projective test of this nature.

Item validity—that is, how valid is each stem—is not defined by an outside criterion, but by the correlation of the ego level assigned on each specific stem with the overall ego rating on the entire protocol (TPR). The median correlations are r = .44.

LOEVINGER'S EGO STAGES IN COMPARISON TO OTHER DEVELOPMENTAL THEORIES

Comparing the progressive movement through different stages of development as identified by different stage theories, in spite of numerous methodological complications (e.g., different numbers of stages), has been the object of several research studies (Adams & Shea, 1979; Sullivan et al., 1970). One major issue is, of course, that different developmental theories focus on different aspects of personality, e.g., Freud on psychosexual and Erikson on psychosocial development, Piaget on cognition, Selman on social cognition, Kohlberg on moral judgment. Loevinger cites Freud and Piaget, but especially Kohlberg and Harry Stack Sullivan as the intellectual ancestors of her own theoretical conceptualizations. The closest conceptual relationship seems to exist between ego development (Loevinger) and moral judgment (Kohlberg). However, important distinctions characterize each theory's focus: Loevinger sees moral development as one aspect of the more encompassing conception of ego development, whereas Kohlberg might reverse the order and see the ego as the mediator between moral judgment and moral behavior. Different studies using different methodologies report overall correlations of .66 (Sullivan et al., 1970) and .80 (Lambert, 1972) between moral judgment and ego level; this supports the generalization that a relationship between ego developmental stages and moral judgment stages does exist. (The correlations would be lower if the influence of age were removed.)

Loevinger's theory of ego development reveals many conceptual parallels to Kohlberg's theory of moral judgment: her preconformist stages correspond to his preconventional level; her conformist and conscientious ego levels encompass his conventional level. Loevinger's most mature stages, "autonomous" and "integrated," parallel Kohlberg's postconventional level. Kohlberg, whose theory emphasizes form more than content, criticized Loevinger's theory for not having an inner logical structure, and hence for not distinguishing sufficiently between form (structure) and content (the latter is what the SCT assesses). Loevinger sees her position as being partly consonant, but partly oppositional to a strict coherence to the concept of structure since she is committed most of all to the results of her measurements. Loevinger (1993: 14) states, "the fact that our method yields results not anticipated on the basis of stage titles is its strength; it is a method of discovery."

Because Loevinger does not conceive ego development in the limited psychoanalytic sense, which covers only the first two to three years of early childhood, her theory encompasses the entire human life cycle and reflects the way a person assimilates diverse experiences, feelings, and behaviors. Loevinger's use of the term "ego development" is inconsistent with the traditional psychoanalytic definition of ego functions, for her the ego is an organic unit and a major aspect of individual differences at all ages.

Adams and Shea (1979) compared levels of ego development to Marcia's (1966, 1967, 1968) stages of identity formation during late adolescence. The data support the hypothesis that the students who are ego-diffused have a much higher probability of also being in the lower levels of ego development. The reverse also holds true, those students who have achieved an identity are much more likely to be in the more advanced ego stages.

In general, Loevinger (1976) devotes more space than do most other theorists to a systematic discussion of similarities and differences between her construct of ego development and the place and definition of ego, ego components, ego development, and related concepts or beliefs held.

Another fundamental distinction between Loevinger's and many other stage theories, especially those with a life-span orientation, is the idea that normal development does not inevitably progress to the final (most mature) stage, as it does for Erikson, but finds an equilibrium earlier, usually in the conscientious stage. For Loevinger (1976), ego development quite frequently stabilizes far below the highest, "integrated level" of ego development (p. 311), just as in Kohlberg's theory, many adults never advance to the postconventional level of moral judgment, and in Fowler's theory they never reach the more advanced faith development stages (see Chapter 13).

Environmental conditions may play a major role in inhibiting or advancing changes in ego level. Thus, a child who lives in a dog-eat-dog family/community/setting may find it exceedingly difficult to move above the self-protective stage. A positive change of setting can help to produce development; for example, moving from a traditional, conformist family/community/setting into a stimulating liberal arts college will probably enhance progression in a student's ego development.

THE CONCEPT OF EGO DEVELOPMENT IN LOEVINGER'S THEORY

Loevinger appears somewhat evasive, at times outright reticent, in defining the unique meaning of "ego development," even though she writes a great deal about the different uses of the construct of the "ego" as conceptualized in other, especially psychoanalytic, theories. Rather than defining "ego development," she often prefers the use of appropriate metaphors and emphasizes that ego development is a process rather than a thing: "The ego is in a way like a gyroscope, whose upright position is maintained by its rotation" (Loevinger, 1976: 58). She also uses the metaphor of the arch. Architects say "the arch never sleeps," which implies that the arch keeps its form and supports the structure above through thrusts and counterthrusts. In a most general sense, ego development refers to what other psychologists might consider the development of the self, a personal frame of reference by which the individual extracts meaning from experiences. For Loevinger (1969), ego encompasses the organizing, synthesizing, and integrating properties of psychic functioning. At one point, she provides what amounts to an operational definition: " . . . what I mean is what is going on as the person goes from impulsive, to being self-protective, to being conformist, to being conscientious, and so on" (Loevinger, 1979b: 3). Thus, ego development becomes, on the one hand, a change in self-definition in each of the successive stages, but on the other hand, it also becomes a succession of increasingly more complex views of the world. Specific behaviors can rarely be related to any specific level of ego functioning. Ego levels are not so much defined by actual physical behaviors as they are by psychological processes, attitudes, values, characteristics, capacities, and meaning-making. Loevinger's use of the term "ego development" involves, at least in part, ideas described and/or implied in other developmental theories, such as the complexity of moral judgment (Kohlberg), the changing nature of interpersonal relations (Sullivan), the organizational patterns with which one perceives oneself and others as people (Selman), faith development (Fowler), and character development (Peck and Havighurst). However, the term "character development" has the association of becoming moral, or even becoming "good," a connotation Loevinger wants to avoid.

Loevinger rejects the psychoanalytic notion that the ego is a superstructure that supports or supplements and, in turn, is supported by a collection of subordinate or related structures (e.g., id, superego in Freud's theory). This idea was particularly prevalent in psychoanalytic theory and its derivatives. It has even become part of implicit psychological assumptions in that the ego is immediately associated with id and superego. Other subordinate structures in Freud's system include: ego ideal, self, introjected object images, and self-images. In Jung's system, subordinate structures include persona, shadow, the personal unconscious, the collective unconscious, archetypes, anima, animus, magicians, and demons.

For Loevinger, however, the ego is not a collection made up of substructures but, metaphorically speaking, it is a single organ, "a process, a structure, social in origin, functioning as a whole, and guided by purpose and meaning" (Loevinger, 1976: 67). She views ego development "not as an interesting personality trait among many, but as the master trait" (Loevinger, 1966: 205). Loevinger's "ego concept" is the overall frame of reference "that provides more specific traits with their meaning and around which the whole edifice of personality is constructed" (1976: 41). Because of this idea, "ego development" has become the defining concept that gives her theory its name. But it must be distinguished from other psychological dimensions. It is not the same as intellectual or cognitive development (Piaget), and the assessment of intellectual functions is not the same as the assessment of ego functions. Ego development is distinctly different from psychosexual development, physical development, and psychological adjustment. Furthermore, Loevinger insists that developmental ego stages must be distinguished from chronological age. For good reasons, Loevinger refuses to attach age-specific references to any of her developmental sequence of ego stages because individual differences cut across several stages at every age level. Since the stages do constitute a sequential developmental continuum, there is, of course, some general linkage to age. However, Loevinger borrows from Piaget the idea that there exists "an inner logic of ego development, an invariable sequence. Each stage builds on, incorporates and transmutes the previous one" (Loevinger, 1966: 204). Only after the developmental sequence of ego stages has been established does Loevinger begin to entertain some of the age-focused questions: What is the typical age for a given age transition? The optimal age? The earliest and latest possible ages? What conditions other than mere age are essential or favorable for each transition? Cohn (1991) has convincingly demonstrated that during junior and senior high school, gender is such a factor, strongly favoring the ego development in girls.

■ Gender Differences

As indicated earlier, Loevinger designed and standardized original SCT forms using only female subjects. This accounts for such initially included stems as "A woman's body . . ." or "A pregnant woman . . . ." Different forms of the test were later developed for men, for children, and for a combination of both sexes.

Two different types of stems comprise the test, those that begin with the *first-person pronoun* such as "I am . . ." or "My father . . ." and *impersonal incomplete sentences* such as "Education . . ." or "Rules are . . ." or "Usually . . . ." Both first-person and impersonal stems are equally valid for women. For men, in contrast, the impersonal incomplete sentences tend to be more valid (Loevinger, 1985), which means the ego level of these impersonal stems correlates more highly with the Total Protocol Rating (TPR) than those that begin with personal pronouns. This may imply that, for men, the more personal (first-person) life experiences are less well integrated with the ego as a whole than for females.

Actual gender differences in the level of ego development are relatively small for children and adults. However, from the junior high school up to the end of high school and the beginning of the college level, young women tend to be significantly more advanced in their levels of ego development. Gfellner (1986) and Redmore and Loevinger (1979) report a half-stage, and Cohn (1991) a full stage, difference favoring girls during adolescence. However, gender differences tend to disappear among adults. Apparently, men tend to catch up to women toward the end of their college careers (Loevinger et al., 1985; Redmore, 1983; Cohn, 1991).

Loevinger remains aware that the content of some of the items are more appropriate for women. Indeed, they may also have somewhat different meanings for men. Examples include, "The worst thing about being a woman is . . ." and "A good mother . . . ." Even changing these stems for the men's form into "The worst thing about being a man is . . ." and "A good father . . ." does not make them entirely equivalent. For some of the specific stems, developing truly equivalent items for both sexes may be virtually impossible.

■ Ego Development, Intelligence, SES, and Cross-Cultural Research

Several studies (Redmore & Loevinger, 1979) have assessed levels of ego development against scores on traditional intelligence tests. The correlations reported in different studies vary considerably and, therefore, no dependable conclusion can be drawn. However, most of these studies report a positive correlation of rather diverse magnitudes; furthermore, the relationship may vary for different ego levels. Apparently, a minimal level of intellectual ability appears to be a prerequisite for certain levels of ego development. Most of the sixth and eighth graders with IQs below 90 were Impulsive. Twelfth graders and college students who were above the Conscientious level had IQs of over 115. In general, for younger children and children with lower intellectual ability, the correlation between intelligence and ego level tends to be higher (Redmore & Loevinger, 1979). Most researchers seem to assume that the SCT is not simply an assessment of verbal fluency or intelligence, even though the level of ego development and intelligence are somewhat related, especially in the extreme ranges. Nonetheless, the ego characteristics measured by the SCT are really quite different from intelligence (Hauser, 1976; Loevinger, 1979a). Loevinger (1976) perceives ego levels and intellectual levels as conceptually dissimilar constructs.

Similar parallels exist for the relationship between SES and level of ego development. Several, but not all, studies show a significant correlation between these two variables. However, these relationships are relatively minor and much less pronounced than generally expected.

Loevinger's methodology to assess levels of ego development has been applied to a variety of different cultures, including those of Curaçao, Israel, Germany, rural India, Japan, and French-speaking Quebec. Apparently, the test is applicable to such countries, and the results provide support for the broader cross-cultural relevance of Loevinger's theory of ego development. However, as a scientist committed to empirical data, she has never claimed—as many of the less empirically committed theorists have—universal or cross-cultural validity for her research (Snarey et al., 1983).

■ Implications: Improving Levels of Ego Development

A question that touches upon social, political, and educational implications is one Loevinger is frequently asked by her students: "Since the world is in so much trouble nowadays, are you not obligated to devote yourself to raising the general ego level?" (Loevinger, 1976: 429). Theory of ego development does not have an easy solution to such broad and complex social issues. Apparently it is difficult, if not impossible, to permanently raise the intelligence of children. Similarly, to change the level of ego functioning deliberately through training or intervention programs is ostensibly difficult: "Ego development is growth, and there is no way to force it. One can only try to open doors" (Loevinger, 1976: 426). Loevinger does not maintain that her ego development theory provides an easy solution to major social problems, and she is pessimistic that her theory could easily be programmed into the existing school curriculum, even if such instructional procedures had actually been written. "The world could be incinerated or its resources exhausted in less time than it would take to learn how to foster ego development through the public school system and to have such a program accepted over the protest of those who would consider it radical and subversive" (Loevinger, 1976: 429).

Even in introductory college and university courses, where professors or administrators might make it their goal to facilitate the progression of their students to a higher level of ego development, the task is never an easy one. Simply presenting an "Autonomous Point of View" (representing the stage where the professor might be) to a class of freshmen, who probably are in the self-awareness stage, may be counterproductive, create misunderstanding, encounter lack of comprehension, and possibly even provoke rebellion. A more carefully planned educational approach requires, first of all, an assessment of the current level of ego development of the students who are enrolled in the professor's class—including some genuine sensitivity to the degree of individual variation in ego functioning that is likely to exist in such a class. Second, the instructor would have to commence at the level of most students and advance slowly and in small increments to the next higher level of ego development, rather than presenting a position that is two or three levels above that of the majority of students (Loevinger, 1990). Finally, the method would require a change from the traditional didactic to a more dialectic mode of teaching.

Much of the relevant research to improve levels of psychological functioning comes from studies dealing with moral judgment. Apparently, growth may be facilitated when an individual is confronted with arguments and is encouraged to participate in a discussion of conflicts or dilemmas one level above his or her own (Rest, 1973). Being faced with arguments considerably above one's own self level appears futile, since they are not meaningful to the person at the lower level. The underlying thought processes and ego structure of the more advanced levels of ego development are difficult, if not impossible, to comprehend for those who function at lower levels—a situation having implications even for those scoring the test. Instructors or proctors who are several levels advanced beyond those of the learner may be less effective as facilitators of ego growth than those only slightly more advanced. Although no specific curriculum exists to foster ego development, a "natural environment" that can stimulate ego level growth appears to be the liberal arts college (Perry, 1970).

13

JAMES FOWLER'S THEORY OF FAITH DEVELOPMENT WITH EMPHASIS ON ADOLESCENCE

RELIGIOUS DEVELOPMENT DURING ADOLESCENCE

Religious education has been an important issue to theologians, philosophers, and educators for centuries, but almost no one has shown much concern for placing it in the context of developmental changes and developmental theory. An exception is G. Stanley Hall (1916) (Chapter 1), a theorist often referred to as the father of a "psychology of adolescence" who devoted a whole chapter to the "Adolescent Psychology of Conversion." For Hall, it is no accident that the age of personal religious awareness and that of sexual maturity and love coincide; he compares the awakening of love in adolescents to their love for God. His studies about the religious experiences of adolescents have led him to identify this period as one of religious intensification that results in an emotional-religious crisis leading to a new commitment to religion. As a result of his work, the terms "religious awakening" and "religious conversion" have become popular. However, while such rather sudden religious conversions do occur—more in some denominations than in others—they are usually not as dramatic as Hall's early description of conversion implied. Certainly, they are not the norm today. Adolescents are in a period of life during which they may experience an existential or religious crisis and may begin to evaluate their religious upbringing, religious ideas, and the role and function of religion in their personal lives. In other words, it is more or less characteristic for adolescents to move from a "received faith" (received from parents, religious teachers, the church, a cult, or a group of believers) to a personal, existential commitment to a belief system, to challenge, to replace or abandon their "received faith."

On a more general level, Philip Rice (1987) effectively summarizes extensive information about "adolescence and religion" by distinguishing five major dimensions. Much of the extant research literature addresses these issues:

1. The ritualistic dimension addresses the extent to which adolescents actively participate in the services, rituals, and sacraments of their churches/synagogues. Among protestants, about three out of ten high school students actively participate in some form of religious service or education on a weekly basis. Figures of about one-third are commonly reported even for other religious groups.

2. The experiential dimension, in contrast, focuses on the personal-emotional component, that is, the extent to which religion plays a significant role in the ideological belief system and the life of youth. While a majority of adolescents seem outwardly to rebel against the traditional religious institutions, and less than two-thirds demonstrate high loyalty to their church, many do experience personal existential questions about the nature of God and their relationship to an Ultimate Being.

3. The ideological dimension assesses the acceptance or rejection of church dogma. Adolescence is a period of questioning and searching for meaning in one's life and in one's relationship to God—95 percent of American adolescents ages 13 to 18 believe in a Supreme Being, 75 percent in a personal God (these figures may be declining) *(Religion in America,* 1980). Apparently the majority of adolescents have not rejected the traditional dogma about the existence of God.

4. The cognitive dimension examines the adolescent's information and knowledge about his or her own religion and other religions. Findings suggest that adolescents have a rather undeveloped personal faith and reveal limited knowledge about specific religious concepts, such as the Ten Commandments.

5. The consequential dimension investigates to what extent religious beliefs, attitudes, and participation influence the behavior in other areas of the adolescent's life. Religious practices based on personal commitment, such as regular prayer, church attendance, and participation in religious rituals (now less controlled by parents than during childhood) do have a rather strong inhibiting effect in such areas as sexual behavior, use of alcohol and drugs, and participation in antisocial/delinquent behaviors. However, youths maintain that church, as an institution, reveals only limited concern with sexuality and chemical education.

Against this very brief background of traditional information about religious issues during adolescence, a much more recent approach that builds primarily on the developmental theories of Erikson, Piaget, and Kohlberg reflects the attempt to conceptualize the nature of developmental changes in youths' relationship to God or an Ultimate Being. This approach has led to a theory of religious/spiritual or faith development.

Several theories that focus on the faith, spiritual, religious, and metaphysical aspects of development exist, such as Helmut Reich's emphasis on "complementarity reasoning" in religious development (1991, 1992), Fritz Oser's (1991a, 1991b) more empirically grounded theory of religious judgment, and Ana Maria Rizzuto's (1979) psychoanalytically oriented study of the origins of children's images of God. Because of lack of space, these theories will not receive the attention they deserve. Of these recent attempts to develop a theory of religious development, Fowler (1981, 1987, 1991a, 1991b) has taken a significant theoretical initiative in defining stages of faith development. In addition, he has subjected the concept of faith to scientific investigation and theoretical formulation. Fowler's faith development theory constitutes a major advance in the integration of theology and psychology and is therefore presented here. His theory, with its emphasis on faith, is more universally applicable than some of those listed above, since it is designed not only in terms of different traditional religions, but is uniquely applicable even to faith in a secular sense: Marxism, existentialism, materialism, etc.

FOWLER'S FAITH DEVELOPMENT THEORY

James W. Fowler (1940–   ) is an ordained minister and a professor of theology and human development at the Candler School of Theology at Emory University in Atlanta. Trained as a theologian, Fowler attempts to combine in his faith development theory two often separated academic disciplines: theology and developmental psychology. Numerous scholars from both disciplines have influenced Fowler's creation of faith theory; thus, faith development theory integrates quite different strands of thoughts. On the developmental-psychological side, Fowler's faith development theory reflects the influences of J. Mark Baldwin and John Dewey, and is especially inspired by the developmental theories of Erikson,

James W. Fowler (1940-   )

Piaget, Kohlberg, and Selman. Fowler undertakes the rather complex task of integrating into his theory of faith development both the structural cognitive model of Piaget (and his followers) and the more social-emotional-oriented maturational approach of Erikson. In 1972 Fowler spent a semester at Harvard University studying developmental psychology, an experience that led to an association and close friendship with Kohlberg. In fact, Fowler credits Kohlberg as providing the most pronounced influence on the developmental component of faith theory. Nevertheless, Fowler is first and foremost a theologian, not a developmentalist. His intellectual roots on the theological side go back to the works of the evangelical theologian and philosopher Paul Tillich; he is especially influenced by the theologian, ethicist, and political philosopher, H. Richard Niebuhr, and the nineteenth-century liberal German theologian Friedrich Schleiermacher. In addition, his philosophical thought also reflects the ideas of the earlier German philosophers Kant and Hegel. However, Fowler's blending of religious theological concepts and language with the structural approach of developmental psychology tends to blur the traditional boundaries of these two disciplines (Fernhout, 1986; Nipkow, 1991).

Any theory of religious development encounters one major obstacle: How one can determine the range of its applicability from one narrowly defined denomination of a specific religion (e.g., Christianity), to all major world religions, to personal beliefs in an Ultimate Being, to atheism, and to secular humanistic faith. The more encompassing and more inclusive the theory, the more difficult it becomes to do justice to the content of the unique characteristics of any one particular belief system. Furthermore, the more inclusive the theory, the more difficult it becomes to generate evidence that either definitively supports or challenges the theory. Critics have admonished: "For him [Fowler], religious development includes everything, from the cognitive to the social and moral and finally to the symbolic. But in the end it is hard to say for Fowler what religion really is if it is not just everything taken together" (Schweitzer, 1991: 81). Well aware of this criticism, Fowler has selected by design the generic term "faith development" for his theory. Nevertheless, he continues to speak of religion and God and to draw most of his illustrations from Christianity.

■ **Man the Meaning-Maker**

Human beings are continuously involved in a complex cognitive-affective process of meaning-making: "One characteristic all human beings have in common is that [they] can't live without some sense that life is meaningful" (Fowler, 1983: 58). This is a very basic psychological assumption which has been previously expressed by Sigmund Freud, Carl Jung, and Viktor Frankel. As the quotation implies, and as Fowler emphasizes, human beings are meaning-making creatures. Human beings perceive faith as the dynamic way to go about making and maintaining meaning. Fowler shares the concept of meaning-making with Loevinger's (see Chapter 12) theory. For Loevinger, the essence of ego development "is the search for a coherent meaning in experience" (Loevinger & Wessler, 1970: 11). For Fowler, faith becomes the pivotal concept of developmental theory: "Our culture strips away the power of faith by using the word as a static noun, rather than an active verb." Fowler claims, "one doesn't 'have faith' or 'lose faith.' Faith continually grows and changes" (Fowler, 1983: 56).* These growing and changing dimensions of faith as a function of cognitive develop-

---

*In Greek, faith (πίστς) has a verbal form (πιστενείν), usually but inadequately translated "to believe."

ment, maturation, religious and life experiences become the focus of Fowler's theory. Indeed, each major, dramatic, structural advance in faith defines the progression through the seven specific stages (to be discussed in detail later) of faith development.

>Stage 0: Primal Faith (birth to age 2 or 3)
>Stage 1: Intuitive-Projective Faith (early childhood, ages 2–8)
>Stage 2: Mythic-Literal Faith and the Imperial Self (childhood and beyond)
>Stage 3: Synthetic-Conventional Faith (adolescence and beyond)
>Stage 4: Individuative-Reflective Faith (young adulthood and beyond)
>Stage 5: Conjunctive Faith and the Interindividual Self (mid-life and beyond, if at all) [paradoxical-consolidative stage]
>Stage 6: Universalizing Faith

■ Fowler's Concept of Faith

"Faith development," as defined by Fowler, is pluralistic and universal; faith is an attribute that applies even to the faith of a nonreligious person. Not necessarily limited to the traditional ideas of religion and belief, faith in Fowler's theory emphasizes individual differences and diversity as well as the universality of faith as a human experience. Faith in Fowler's rather global and comprehensive (and at times imprecise) use becomes almost synonymous with *meaning-making*. Fowler (1986: 15) repeatedly emphasizes: "Faith has to do with the making, maintenance, and transformation of human meaning." On its more mundane level, "Faith is a coat against . . . nakedness" (Fowler, 1981: xii). On a more sophisticated level, "Faith is a person's . . . way of moving into the force field of life. It is our way of finding coherence in and giving meaning to the multiple forces and relations that make up our lives. Faith is a person's way of seeing him- or herself in relation to others against a background of shared meaning and purpose" (Fowler, 1981: 4). Faith is a kind of wholistic knowing that involves both reason and feeling. "Faith . . . is a mode of knowing and constructing" (Fowler, 1980: 64). Through faith we compose, construct, invest, and commit ourselves to a center of values which then determine our relationship to objects, people, and ultimately, to God. Thus faith always takes place in relationships; it involves trust in or loyalty and attachment to somebody, and/or to values, and/or ultimately to God. Through faith our world is shaped and vested with meaning.

■ The Master Story, the Center of Values, and the Images of Power

The faith orientation of individuals is influenced by their master story, their center of values, and their images of power. These three organizing principles of faith are closely interrelated. Most essential is the master story which people use to interpret the events in their lives. Out of the master story emerges a center of values to which people are loyal and which influences the choices and decisions they make. "Our choices and explanations of choices . . . reflect . . . attachments to meaning-giving images and centers of value and power" (Fowler, 1980: 62). The images of power are the third component which determine in whom we place trust and whom we approach with suspicion and fear.

The Master Story

As individuals make meaning of life and of life's experiences, they develop for themselves a unique master or core story that incorporates their fundamental values and orientation toward life and serves as a guiding compass. The master story contains the crucial ideas that the individual draws upon to give meaning to his or her life. In his theory of transactional analysis, Eric Berne has referred to such fundamental all-encompassing guiding principles as the "script." Such a script is usually formed very early in childhood and, even though modifiable, it seems to take on a life of its own. In Fowler's theory, the "master story" takes on some of these functions and aids in forming and shaping our lives. As the individual matures, he or she becomes increasingly aware of the master story until it emerges more explicitly as ideas, goals, and purposes to which the individual is committed. As an illustration, Fowler reports that among the inmates of federal prisons, about 60 percent had their master story tattooed onto their skin in words and symbols; the story revealed the theme "born to lose."

The master story contains an individual's answer to fundamental questions: "What is life all about?"; "Who is in charge over my life?"; "How do I make my life worthwhile?"; "What goals do I pursue to give meaning to my life?" The answers to these questions determine what choices one makes, how one relates to the world and to other people: "We form and shape our lives in relation to master stories" (Fowler, 1991b: 22). The master story (what literary critics call "character story") also helps the individual comprehend and interpret traumatic events in life. Our master story also determines the group of people with whom we form allegiances and alliances and with whom we join in our effort to make meaning out of life. Such stories belong to communities as well as individuals. The Passover Haggadah does all these things for the faithful Jewish community.

A Center of Values in Life

Fowler assumes that we invest faith in a center of values in our lives. Centers of values are made up of ideas, values, attitudes, and behaviors that are consciously or unconsciously of greatest significance to each of us and may emerge as underlying themes in our master story. While such values may be religious in content, they do not necessarily have to be, as Fowler's use of the more generic term "faith" is supposed to convey. A person maintains the center of values over time and invests them with trust and loyalty. We attach our trust and loyalties and "our affection to those persons, causes, ideals, or institutions that promise to give worth and meaning to our lives" (Fowler, 1991a: 32). This core of values, which becomes embedded in our master story, and which gives meaning to our life, does have a guiding, organizing, and ordering influence on many of the decisions we make. What constitutes a particular center of value or values is unique to the individual; the center of values grows out of a master story. For some, a center of values may be the family; for others, career and success; for still others, an ideological belief. On a more mundane level, still others may understand their center of values as money, material possessions, sexuality, power, and influence over others. From a religious point of view, "God or transcendent reality is meant to be the supreme center of value in our lives" (Fowler, 1991a: 32).

Images of Power

Depending on our interpretation of life events and world affairs, we live in a more or less dangerous world. The crucial question becomes: "Who, in our evaluation or imagination, has the power to protect, to harm, or to destroy us, and how much trust or loyalty do we devote to seeking or avoiding these powers?" Fowler (1991b: 23) provides three telling illustrations of images and realities of power with which people align themselves. For example, consider "The Lord is my Shepherd, I shall not want." The Twenty-Third Psalm expresses a belief in the Judeo-Christian definition of God as being the center of power and values. In contrast "My stock portfolio is my shepherd, I shall not want" shows that the love of money has become the image of power that controls. Or, collectively, Americans went through a period where they believed and paid for "The Star Wars missile defense system is our shepherd, we shall not want." For others, such images of power may be more ominous, creating worries and tactics of avoidance; for example, if one believes in images of power in which criminality, the devil, the drug lords, or the seduction of the mass media play a major role, life becomes more worrisome and dangerous.

■ Faith, Religion, and Belief

Fowler distinguishes among faith, religion, and belief and selects the term "faith development theory" for his approach because he perceives his theory as representing religious pluralism and as being applicable to faith as a universal phenomenon, even without religion. Faith is, of course, the most inclusive and general term among these three concepts. A human universal, it is not limited to any one specific religion. It can include ideologies such as communism, materialism, or secular humanism, or even what Fowler refers to as the "center of values" in our lives. A person can have faith that is not religious faith; many people struggle with the issue of faith even though they have no personal access to a viable form of worship or religious tradition (Fowler, 1981). Elaborating on insights of Niebuhr, Fowler considers "faith as a *human phenomenon*, an apparently generic consequence of the universal human burden of finding or making meaning" (Fowler, 1981: 33).

Religion is more narrowly defined than faith and manifests itself through the revelations of holy persons. Formalized through theology, it is passed on through the accumulation of tradition, is expressed in art, music, architecture, and literature, is practiced by a group of like-minded people in a church/synagogue as well as in the home. Thus, religion is only one of the more common forms and patterns through which faith finds expression. Faith in that instance becomes the foundation for forming a personal relationship with God based on established religious traditions.

Faith includes, but is not limited to, religious faith and finds expression through belief. The term "belief" applies to the endorsement of propositions that no one can verify directly by scientific evidence. Empirical data produce knowledge; belief requires trust, loyalty, commitment, and a more personal "leap of faith." Fowler maintains that faith is deeper than belief: "We hope that our beliefs are congruent with and expressive of our faith, but faith is deeper and involves unconscious motivations as well as those that we can make conscious in our belief and in our actions" (Fowler, 1991b: 22). Belief can also be defined as the intellectual articulation of faith.

One of Fowler's contributions to faith theory is his distinction between the content of faith (the "what" of faith) and the psychological processes that deal with the content (the "how" of faith). Faith content includes the beliefs and values endorsed by a church, a religion or a person's *Weltanschauung* (a person's world view), and might include the gospel, the Talmud (Torah), or the Koran. The psychological processes that make the content personally meaningful are cognitive (Piaget), affective (Erikson), and social (Selman). In other words, thinking, feeling, and social processes modify the personal, existential meaning of the content and are responsible for the progression in faith development which Fowler studies, even if the content remains the same. Fowler studies the psychological processes of faith development regardless of faith content and makes them the building blocks of the increasingly more complex stages of faith.

FOWLER'S SEVEN STAGES OF FAITH

Fowler has organized the developmental progression in faith into seven structural-developmental stages of knowing, or major "styles" of faith, which in many ways parallel Loevinger's stages of ego development (see Chapter 12). They serve to unify various aspects of development into a whole. Fowler's stages of faith development are not primarily maturational stages for which age provides an automatic impetus toward a higher level. Faith structures allow for diversity and place far more emphasis on individual differences than do purely maturational theories like Gesell's, and even Erikson's; not everyone reaches the more advanced faith stages. The distinction between age and development explains why there often exists heterogeneity of faith development in religious classes and even in congregations. The structural developmental models advanced by Piaget and Kohlberg greatly influenced the formulation of these stages of faith as did the broader psychosocial crises that are characteristic of Erikson's more functional approach to human development. Fowler's stages—sometimes referred to as "soft stages"—differ from the developmental models of Kohlberg and Piaget, which are organized around the rigorous logical structures of Piaget (hard stages). Obviously, Fowler's stages and those of Piaget, Kohlberg, and Selman correspond. However, as has been demonstrated empirically, the relevant level of cognitive function à la Piaget is *a necessary but not sufficient prerequisite* for the corresponding levels of moral development and perspective taking. The same relationship appears to hold true for Fowler's stages of faith development, although the empirical data to substantiate this have not yet been collected. Empirical evidence does exist that focuses more specifically on the child's development of the concept of God (Nye & Carlson, 1984). The findings suggest that the child's concept of God parallels Piaget's general model of cognitive development.

Fowler places greater emphasis on feelings, affections, and imagination, but freely combines the insights of Piaget, Kohlberg, Selman, and Erikson with those of theology. According to Fowler, cognitive maturation creates a dissonance in our system of meaning-making, which requires resolution. The cognitive personal faith-work that is necessary to resolve the dissonance propels the individual to more advanced stages in faith development. "We believe that the sequence of equilibrated stage-like positions we have identified is developmentally related. We believe that the order of appearance is sequential and that the sequence will prove to be invariant. Each new stage builds and incorporates into its more elaborate structures the operations of previous stages" (Fowler, 1980: 65).

The classification of any one individual into Fowler's seven stages depends on a semistructured, semiclinical faith interview that takes about 2 1/2 to 3 hours. The resulting protocol can be scored. Inter-rater reliability in scoring such protocols produced 85 percent to 90 percent agreement. Over a 10-year period, 359 semistructured interviews were collected; this data base has led to the formulation of the structural stages of faith development. However, since the critical composition of this sample is not described in sufficient detail, critics have raised the question whether the findings are generalizable to the entire population. The interview itself is organized into four different parts. Illustrations of a few selected questions (Fowler, 1981: 310–312) include:

> *Part 1: Life Review.* Included in the first part are biographical information and a request to identify the major segments or chapters in one's life, e.g., "What gives your life meaning?"; "What makes life worth living for you?"
>
> *Part 2: Life-Shaping Experiences and Relationships.* The questions here are concerned with existential life-issues or histories, e.g., "What experiences have affirmed your sense of meaning in life?"; "What experiences have shaken or disturbed your sense of meaning?"
>
> *Part 3: Present Values and Commitments.* Questions in this part address the subject's ability to reflect on the influences that are drawn upon in making decisions: "When you have an important decision or choice to make regarding your life, how do you go about deciding?" Thus, the crucial issue is not what the actual decision is, but the process, e.g., "Can you describe the beliefs and values or attitudes that are most important in guiding your life?"
>
> *Part 4: Religion.* It is only in Part 4, toward the end of the interview, that religious issues are directly addressed, e.g., "What feelings do you have when you think about God?"; "Do you consider yourself a religious person?"

Fowler's major book, *Stages of Faith* (1981), defines his theory and contains numerous, well-chosen excerpts from interviews providing representative insightful responses from individuals at various stages of faith development. Ages for each of the stages are provided as rough approximations only, because progression in faith development is a highly individual matter. The stages identify only the form of faith, consequently each stage may encompass a great variety of values, individually determined meanings, and life-styles (Fowler, 1980). Many individuals reach a more or less stable equilibrium in their religious development long before they actually reach the higher, more advanced, stages. (See Figure 13.1.)

■ Stage 0: Primal or Undifferentiated Faith (Birth to Age 2 or 3)

This early and basically undifferentiated, prelanguage stage of faith development cannot be assessed by Fowler's interview but is quite compatible with Erikson's definition of "basic trust" in the first two years of life. A trusting attachment to caretakers essentially constitutes "faith" in another person, which later becomes the foundation for all faith. Fowler has designated it as Stage 0. "Primal faith" builds on Erikson's idea of the infant becoming a trusting rather than a mistrusting individual. Such trust depends on experiencing love, regularity in the basic rituals of care, meaningful interpersonal exchanges, and mutuality in relationship to others, especially parents: "Our first *pre-images* of God have their origins here" (Fowler, 1981: 121). This first acquisition of trust constitutes the earliest and most rudimentary—but nonetheless lasting—foundation of faith. Primal faith—faith in others—aids in coping with the anxiety that is associated with separation experiences during this early stage of development.

■ Stage 1: Intuitive-Projective Faith (Early Childhood, Ages 2–8)

The progression in "intuitive and projective" faith development encompasses what Piaget has referred to as "preoperational thought." Children in the intuitive-projective phase master language, which aids them greatly in meaning-making. Stories, symbols, and gesture, all of which are still largely unrestrained by logical thought, help to precipitate meaning-making. Instead, perceptions, creativity, fantasy, dreams, imagination, fear, and hope shape these vehicles of communication and meaning-making. Such powerful early images can produce long-lasting feelings about the nurturing as well as the disturbing powers of life. Though a restricted sense of self-awareness emerges, this self-awareness is still basically egocentric in that the child assumes that his or her experiences and perceptions are the only available perceptions and are of general validity. Self-awareness introduces a concern with sex and death, however, these are often insulated from personal social reflection by cultural and family taboo.

During this early stage of faith development, images, symbols, and impressions contribute to the master story and become welded to profound and long-lasting emotions in faith orientation—feelings that carry over into the later stages of faith development. These powerful images can foster the development of moral emotions and an awareness of both what is taboo and what is sacred. In the process, mental images of God are formed, partly based on everyday experiences with parents and significant others and partly based on the symbolism, the narratives, and the teaching of the church. In the child's imagination, God becomes someone with human attributes (as expressed quite trustingly by Dennis) who resides in the sky to govern the world. A beginning appreciation of cause-effect relationships accompanies the emergence of logical thinking skills toward the end of the early childhood period and contributes to a dissonance in the existing faith structure. Resolving the disharmony may enhance progression to the next higher stage.

■ Stage 2: Mythic-Literal Faith and the Imperial Self (Childhood and Beyond)

As the child's development progresses, concrete operational thinking abilities emerge that include the facility to think logically. Piaget explains that the operational child acquires skills—such as the ability to understand reversibility, conservation, and the ability to classify—and to order things, experiences, and the world into categories of space, time, and number. This newly developed ability in thinking aids the child in more clearly separating the real world from fantasy, imagination, and make-believe. Thus, belief in Santa Claus, the Easter Bunny, and the stork declines during this stage; the child even questions religious miracles. In addition, the child begins to take the perspective of others into consideration. Stories and narratives still remain the major vehicle of building, maintaining, and sharing meaning. Many children at Stage 2 continue to hold onto the anthropomorphic image of

*"I'm going to say my prayers.
Does anybody want anything?"*

"Dennis the Menace" ® used by permission of Hank Ketcham and
© by North American Syndicate.

God as the all-knowing, benevolent, wise, old Saint who rules the world. Stories or myths, both cultural and religious, are utilized in finding meaning and coherence in experiences. "For this stage the meaning is both carried and 'trapped' in the narrative" (Fowler, 1980: 70). For the concrete thinking child, the story does not allow the extraction of deeper conceptual meanings. Some adolescents, and even a few adults, reach a more or less permanent equilibrium in mythical-literal faith and thus, remain there, unless challenged in a rather fundamental way. The mythic-literal child perceives God as rewarding people who do right and obey him, and punishing those who do wrong and disobey him. The underlying theme is reminiscent of Kohlberg's preconventional morality as if God were treating people on an "eye-for-an-eye" basis. Awareness of one's own dispositions, motives, needs, and wishes increases as an early undifferentiated sense of selfhood and autonomy begins to emerge. This movement toward increasing independence contributes to the progression to the next higher stage.

■ Stage 3: Synthetic-Conventional Faith (Adolescence and Beyond)

The faith system of an individual who is in Stage 3 is "conventional," in that the conventional believer perceives his or her own faith system as being similar to everybody's, or even to an entire congregation's. In addition, it is conceptualized as being "synthetic," which means it still absorbs major faith elements from others. Thus, in an existential sense, it is not yet truly a genuine personal faith structure. Furthermore, it is not yet analytic, but emerges as a "sort of unified, global wholeness" (Fowler, 1981: 167) that synthesizes values and information from different sources.

Stage 3 typically has its ascendency during adolescence; however, for some it stabilizes at this age into a more or less permanent equilibrium and the curve depicting Stage 3 in Figure 13.1 declines relatively slowly with increasing age. As the cognitive ability of adolescence expands and formal operational thinking opens the mind to abstract ideas and concepts, mutual, interpersonal perspective taking becomes possible. This kind of recursive thinking might be expressed as: "I see you seeing me: I see the me I think you see" (Fowler, 1991a: 37). We see ourselves as others see us and begin to integrate this new social perspective into our own identity. Even falling in love and seeing oneself through the eyes of one's lover contributes to the formation of a new and more reflective sense of self and faith.

The young person in Stage 3 can integrate diverse roles and self-images into a coherent identity. The identity crisis that Erikson and Marcia postulate as a crucial adolescent experience in general tends to become, in the process of faith development, a religious or spiritual identity crisis. The typical identity question "Who am I?" thus expands to include the additional existential, religious components: "Who is God?"; "Who am I in relationship to God?"; "Does God know me?"; "Does God watch me?"; "Does God love me?"; "Does God care about me as a unique individual?" These searching questions, designed to define a new and explicitly personal relationship to God, raise the same issue which Hall (1916) referred to as "religious awakening" during adolescence. Finding answers to these questions leads to a religious identity and to a more personalized and autonomous way of meaning-making: "A

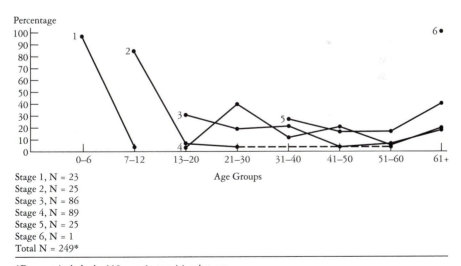

Stage 1, N = 23
Stage 2, N = 25
Stage 3, N = 86
Stage 4, N = 89
Stage 5, N = 25
Stage 6, N = 1
Total N = 249*

*Does not include the 110 cases in transitional stages.

FIGURE 13.1 Line graph of stages of faith by age groups. (From Figure B.1, page 320 from *Stages of Faith: The Psychology of Human Development and the Quest for Meaning* by James W. Fowler. Copyright © 1981 by James W. Fowler. Reprinted by permission of HarperCollins Publishers, Inc.)

personal and largely unreflective synthesis of beliefs and values evolves to support identity and to unite one in emotional solidarity with others" (Fowler, 1983: 58).

The young person gives more systematic consideration and reflection to past personal experiences and examines them for meaning. But meaning and symbol are still inseparable. The synthetic-conventional believer views an attack on a significant symbol (e.g., burning the flag) as a desecration of the sanctity for which the symbol stands. At the same time, the adolescent gives more focused thought to his or her personal future: "Who do I want to become?" One's future work, career or vocation, interpersonal connections, and relationship to God all receive attention. The adolescent at this stage feels a need to be known and loved in relationship to God: "God is believed to know who I am and what I am becoming, and as Divine Other, to sustain and fulfill my selfhood" (Reich, 1992: 160). The progression to the next higher stage evolves from the awareness that one can disagree with the perceptions of others, including the perceptions of those in authority, and one can also "take into oneself . . . the authority one previously invested in others for determining and sanctioning one's goals and values" (Fowler, 1987: 68).

For the adolescent, who typically would be classified as being in Stage 3, the ease or the difficulty of the transition to the next higher stage of faith development may well be influenced by contradictions in preaching and practices, in personal conflict with faith authorities, and by the stage of faith development of his peers, his family, and his church (Fowler, 1981) because faith develops in relationship to others.

■ Stage 4: Individuative-Reflective Faith (Young Adulthood and Beyond)

The transition from Stage 3 to Stage 4 is a critical one, in that the by now late adolescent or young adult begins to take a more personal existential responsibility for his or her own beliefs, commitments, and life-styles (Fowler, 1980). The remaining three stages depend upon formal reasoning ability, defined by Piaget as a kind of cognitive prerequisite for faith development; progression through these stages reveals increasingly more sophisticated levels of abstract thinking. However, not all individuals who have reached Piaget's formal reasoning stage will necessarily progress in their faith development in accordance with Fowler's theoretical model. The further an individual progresses in faith development past Stage 3, the greater the likelihood of an increased personal commitment to faith. Simultaneously, and especially in the transition from Stage 3 to Stage 4, the "received faith" is transformed into a personal, existential faith commitment, or to say it differently, this transition in particular constitutes a major reorganization in that the motivation for faith changes from extrinsic (received from others) to intrinsic (personal, existential).

As the name of this stage implies, the ability to critically reflect on one's beliefs and values and one's self-understanding creates a profound awareness of one's existence in the world. As this reflection reaches outward, it also enhances one's understanding of others and, more generally, of social systems, including religious institutions; thus it contributes to the next step in faith development. Individuals begin to critically evaluate the conventional value systems of their family, their community, and their church. Such evaluation involves a process that can produce a personal tension, but also a kind of emotional distancing, and for some, a loss in the intensity of religious beliefs (and even a denunciation of religion). The individual increasingly assumes personal responsibility for identifying choices, meaning-making, forming commitments to others, developing a vocation, estab-

lishing a personal life-style, and an ideology, and most importantly, for taking full responsibility for his or her religious development. With this increased autonomy, the individual
can take a third-person perspective, involving the awareness that the points of view expressed by other people are relative to them and unique to them, and therefore limited. All
of this leads to a critical examination of one's own background, traditions, beliefs, symbols,
and values, including religious ones. The individual is more firmly aware of what he or she
knows and believes and is able to argue his or her position. There is a conscious effort to
question and examine critically the values and beliefs in one's life to make them explicit, to
make them one's own, and to invest them with personal meaning. Often, this involves a
searching and challenging look at other options, including one's own past meaning-making efforts and one's center of values. Fowler characterizes this process of making beliefs and
commitments explicit as "demythologization." This means a diminishing of some of the
emotional and personal power of symbols, myths, and rituals, which are characteristic of
faith in the earlier stages. Now "meanings can be separated from the symbols that bear
them" (Fowler, 1981: 163).

Theologian and cultural analyst Harvey Cox—as reported by Fowler (1981)—tells the
story of his loss of faith in the symbolic meaning of communion:

> In one period he [Cox] had been dating a Catholic girl a year or so older than he. She
> went off to college while he stayed at home to finish high school. When she came back
> for Christmas vacation Harvey went with her to a beautiful midnight Christmas Eve
> mass. As the mass climaxed and people were receiving the Eucharist, Harvey said his
> college-aged girl friend, who had just completed Anthropology 101, turned to him
> and whispered, 'That's just a primitive totemic ritual, you know.' Harvey said, 'A
> what?' She replied with great self-assurance, 'A primitive totemic ritual. Almost all
> premodern religious and tribal groups have them. They are ceremonies where
> worshipers bind themselves together and to the power of the sacred by a cannibalistic
> act of ingesting the mana of a dead god.' Communion, Cox said, was never the same
> again. A symbol recognized as a symbol is a broken symbol (pp. 180–181).

In the previous synthetic-conventional stage, roles and relationships to others primarily shape the person's identity. A true advance to Stage 4 is based on breaking away from
reliance on significant others and external authority, which is still characteristic of Stage 3.
In the individuative-reflective stage of faith development, the identity becomes much more
autonomous and more individualistic. The individual strips away the support of social roles
and ego-defining relationships to others to define himself or herself. What emerges is a kind
of existential nakedness, a confrontation with the "self" unencumbered by social roles:
"Who am I when I am not defined by being my parents' son or daughter?"; "Who am
I when I am not defined by being so-and-so's spouse?"; "Who am I when I am not defined
by the work I do?"; "Who is the 'I' that has those roles and relations but is not fully
expressed by any one of them?" (Fowler, 1991a: 39). Most people have great difficulties in
answering the "Who am I" question when social roles, interpersonal relationships, group
membership, organization, vocation, and avocation are excluded. Adolescents who can
think abstractly, often for the first time in their life, are confronted with the great existential and spiritual questions, contemplating isolation, the consequences of death, meaning-
lessness, and death.

■ Stage 5: Conjunctive Faith and the Interindividual Self (Mid-Life and Beyond, if at all)

Stage 5, sometimes referred to as the *Paradoxical-consolidation stage*, is more complex and multilayered, and even Fowler (1981) admits his initial difficulties in capturing and describing the basic features of this stage. The individual at this stage—and, as Figure 13.1 reveals, only a relatively small proportion of the population ever reach this stage—can confront polarities in his or her life and make multiple-level interpretations of events that occur in his or her life and in reality. While Stage 4 may show dichotomized thinking of an either-or nature, Stage 5 accepts, appreciates, and combines multiple perspectives of many of the important issues and seeks truth in a multidimensional, dialectic, dynamic way. The possibility for appreciating and resolving opposites, polarities, and paradoxes emerges at this level and contributes to a higher level of meaning-making: "Symbol and story, metaphor and myth (from one's own tradition and others'), are newly appreciated as vehicles for grasping truth" (Fowler, 1983: 58). The power of the symbol is once again combined with its spiritual and conceptual meaning. God no longer appears as a benevolent, uncomplicated, unidimensional father figure who is just and fair to all. The essence of God appears difficult to define and God seems at times full of contradictions and unresolved paradoxes. Philosophically, the thinking of the Danish theologian and early existentialist Soeren Kierkegaard reflects this stage of faith development. Kierkegaard's writings focus on God as the paradox; he even describes the Bible as full of paradoxes and contradictions that need to be accepted and become part of a continuously challenged faith.

This dynamic picture of God as undefinable and as full of paradoxes makes our relationship to God a more active, dynamic, and challenging one, but at times also a more disturbing one requiring the courage to make a commitment even in the face of uncertainty, an idea which Kierkegaard defines as a "leap of faith" and Tillich as "the courage to be." In this stage, "God is both immanent and transcendent, God is both omnipotent and a self-limiting God" (Reich, 1992: 161). Stage 5 is hard to attain, but even more difficult to maintain because the ability to appreciate the paradox of God requires higher cognitive ability, sustained effort, great courage, and the ability to deal with uncertainty. The notion of religious pluralism and multiplicity of values and life-style in a secularized world enters the psychological constructions of the individual and makes him or her vulnerable to a conceptualization of religious relativism: "Stage 5 is characterized by the open-minded *understanding of the plurality of truth claims* as they are expressed in different faith attitudes" (Nipkow, 1991: 85). This dynamic open-mindedness toward other religions may be difficult to reconcile with the trust, loyalty, commitment, and faith in one's own belief system.

■ Stage 6: Universalizing Faith

Individuals who reach the stage of universalizing faith are truly rare, perhaps less than 1 percent of the population and the dot identifying Stage 6, in the upper-right-hand corner in Figure 13.1 does represent just one case and should not be read as 100 percent. Those who attain this level have reached a very high degree of functioning: "Beyond paradox and polarities, persons in this stage are grounded in a oneness with the power of being. Their visions and commitments free them for a passionate yet detached spending of the self in love, devoted to overcoming division, oppression and brutality" (Fowler, 1983: 58). The preservation of the self at any cost, which is so common in our culture, and which is characteristic of all the preceding stages, is no longer the primary meaning in life. The self becomes subordinated to a larger personal commitment to a selfless goal, such as overcoming injustice and oppression. Universalizing faith does include a relationship with God. Fowler's illustrations of individuals who have reached the universalizing faith development stage include the German reformationist Martin Luther, the civil rights leader Martin Luther King toward the end of his life, Dag Hammerskoeld, Dietrich Bonhoeffer, Mahatma Gandhi, and Mother Theresa. Critics have questioned whether "universalizing faith" really can be conceived as part of a developmental end point or goal that follows as a natural progression in the pattern of the preceding stages, or whether it presents a different dimension or a different quality and is not really the apex in a normative hierarchical structure.

Critics have also pointed out that this stage is being both "elegant and attractive," but also "antipluralistic and condescending" and "too highly shaped by the lifeworld of the theorist" (Hoehn, 1983: 79). It seems to constitute a meta-religious position, which (a) is rare, and (b) is limited to selected leaders with a personal commitment to a specific religious mission, or to the mystics who devote their lives to God.

THE TRANSITION FROM ONE STAGE TO THE NEXT

Faith development normally progresses in a hierarchical, sequential pattern identified by these seven stages and the transition from one stage to the next deserves particular attention. The movement from the lower and smaller faith stages of childhood to the increasingly larger circles and the process of the transition from stage to stage can be presented in a graphic illustration (see Figure 13.2) as a pattern of rising spirals. The process of faith development is thus depicted by Fowler (1981: 274) as dynamically interconnected, "each successive spiral stage linked to and adding to the previous ones." Since faith has to deal with recurring major life issues, "the spiral movements in part overlap each other, though each successive stage addresses the issue at a new level of complexity" (p. 274), increased differentiation, and inclusiveness. The spiral also represents a movement outward (toward the right). The outward movement symbolizes a movement toward increasing individuation, which culminates with Stage 4 and a renewed turn inward during the last two stages.

Some of the truly major transitions are generally experienced during adolescence; the transition from Stage 2 to Stage 3 generally occurs during early adolescence, while the more fundamental transition from Stage 3 to Stage 4 happens in late adolescence and often marks the transition from adolescence to adulthood. Since most children eventually move from Stage 2 to Stage 3 and since few adults move from Stage 4 to Stage 5, the major normative faith transitions actually fall in the period between late childhood and early adulthood. For the sample studied these changes in Stages of Faith are depicted in Figure 13.1. For the majority of religious believers, the transformation from a "received faith" into an autonomous, personal, existential belief system takes place during adolescence. Thus, faith development is an adolescent issue *par excellence* and the resolution of faith transformations during the second decade of life sets the pattern for much of adulthood. All of the stages are dynamically connected.

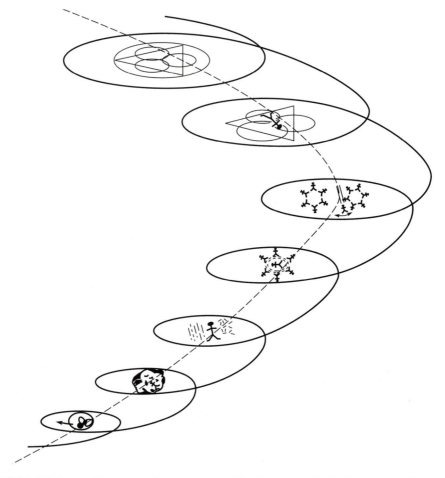

FIGURE 13.2 Stages of faith. (From Figure 5.1, page 175, *Stages of Faith: The Psychology of Human Development and the Quest for Meaning* by James W. Fowler. Copyright © 1981 by James W. Fowler. Reprinted by permission of HarperCollins Publishers, Inc.)

Being in a particular faith stage implies that the patterns of meaning-making are relatively equilibrated; at least they are stable for an extended period of time. The majority of people find a more or less lasting equilibrium in their faith development in this spiral, frequently in Stage 3 or 4. A relatively small group reaches Stage 5, usually relatively late in life, and Stage 6 is rarely attained.

The impact of major challenges, new experiences, exposure to new or different ideas, a drastically changed environment, biological maturity, or cognitive development can throw the existing equilibrium into a disequilibrium. Such a disequilibrium is characteristic of the transition phases. The process of working through such an emotional-cognitive dissonance usually is an emotionally and cognitively intense, dramatic, protracted, dislocating, and sometimes even abortive experience. Often, transition experiences are identified in the faith interview (see page 270) and become the "markers" that divide an individual's life history into clearly identifiable segments. In the past, "markers" were more clearly defined socially (e.g., graduation, confirmation, bar mitzvah) and served to delineate social status, expectations, roles, and behaviors. Elkind (1984) bemoans the declining significance of such transition markers and the blurring of clearly identifiable distinctions that used to organize life into clearly recognizable segments. These markers, especially religious markers, have become more of an individual matter based on individual experiences, rather than a social matter based on age, or an achievement or a communal ritual. With the faith development theory, such transition markers may involve changes in the master story, the images of power, and the center of values. Furthermore, such religious transition may be associated with receiving a "calling," religious conversions, coming forward in a ceremony and giving one's life to the Lord, or some other dramatic shift in faith commitment. In other words, major religious transition experiences often result in rather fundamental reorientations and a new and different form of trust, loyalty and commitment at the next stage of faith development. While age and maturity certainly are necessary prerequisites for such transitions, especially in the sequence of the earlier ones (up to Stage 3), transitions to the more advanced stages (especially past Stage 3) are neither inevitable nor automatic.

The progression along the spiral is thought of as sequential, invariant, and hierarchical* just as the developmental sequence of Piaget's, Kohlberg's, and Loevinger's stages are assumed to be sequential, constant, and building on each other. However, researchers have noted that as people approach old age, some regression to earlier stages of faith development occurs. But even in normal development and among younger people, a movement backward in the progression of faith development may occur and may imply a reworking of faith issues in the preceding stage. For such a developmental reversal, Fowler (1981) prefers the expression "recapitulation in the service of faith development" rather than regression. Empirical evidence that faith development is an invariant sequential progress is still lacking.

CRITIQUE, CONCLUSIONS, IMPLICATIONS

The methodology underlying Fowler's theory of faith development raises an issue central to religious education and pastoral care. Fowler's semistructured interview—or a revised and shortened version thereof—could be used as a diagnostic-educational assessment tool, which would allow religious instructors and institutions to identify the stage of faith development of any one adolescent or group of adolescents, such as in a Sunday school setting. While it might not make all that much difference to individual adolescents to know whether they are in Stage 2, 3, or 4 of faith development, such information might be a considerable aid to their teacher, both in directing specific questions to adolescents and in selecting instructional material. Also, knowing the mix of stages of faith development in a given group of students (or a congregation) might be useful in understanding group dynamics and in guiding group discussions, and could contribute to designing a religious education curriculum for individuals in different faith stages. Fowler devotes less time and ef-

---

*"Hierarchical (each successive stage carrying forward in modified and augmented form the operations of the previous stage) and invariant (each stage building on the previous one so that none can be skipped)" (Fowler, 1987: 26, 36).

fort to the implications of his theory for religious instruction than one might expect; indeed, he almost rejects the idea of using the developmental stages as "educational or therapeutical goals toward which to hurry people" (Fowler, 1981: 114). However, in a more recent work, Fowler specifically addresses the issue of pastoral counseling (Fowler, 1987). Nevertheless, the usefulness of the insight that faith developmental theory can provide— especially to the teacher who deals with children in specific stages of faith—should not be underestimated.

In respect to the earlier stages (0–3), it appears as if ideas previously advanced by Erikson, Piaget, Kohlberg, and Selman interact and merge with those from Fowler's theory of faith development. Therefore, distinguishing the uniqueness of Fowler's contributions from those earlier theories becomes difficult. And Fowler's theory can be both praised and criticized for rather freely combining the structural model of cognitive developmental theories with the more emotionally and socially based model of an invariant, biological maturational theory (Erikson).

Faith development theory, even though designed to focus on faith structure and to be indifferent to religious content, does draw many of its conceptualizations and illustrations from traditional Christianity. The critical reader tends to ask himself or herself: How would this aspect of faith development (or this stage) look to a Jew, a Muslim, a Taoist, a Confucianist, and especially to a Buddhist, an agnostic, or an atheist? Fowler argues that, while the faith content would be different, the underlying faith structure that his interview assesses is uninfluenced by content. Through this distinction of content and process, faith theory permits such a broad spectrum of applicability. Faith structure would fit into the stages of all faith systems in the pattern outlined by faith development theory. The evidence for the cross-cultural (and cross-religious) applicability of faith development theory is limited in scope and anecdotal; in fact, when asked whether his structural stages of faith development apply to Eastern religions, Fowler replied "I don't know" (Fowler, 1981: 296).

Very little information is available about the faith development of religious instructors, ministers, rabbis, congregations, and churches. The question naturally arises as to what impact the stage of faith development of teachers, church leaders, and significant others has on the developmental progression of a congregation or even of an individual. Can a fundamentalist minister, who believes in the Bible as the literal expression of God's will, move his or her congregation to a Level 4 or Level 5 of faith development? Or would he or she interfere with advances in faith development? The answer to these questions has consequences: "Many religious groups . . . reinforce a conventionally held and maintained faith system, sanctifying one's remaining in the dependence on external authority and derivative group identity of Stage 3" (Fowler, 1981: 178). Fowler does point out that many of those adults who have been interviewed may have found a lasting equilibrium (a term implying "terminal stage") in Stage 3, suggesting that the likelihood of major advances is reduced. This contributes to the orderly function of organized religion: "In many ways religious institutions 'work best' if they are people with a majority of committed folks best described by Stage 3 . . . . Much of church and synagogue life in this country can be accurately described as dominantly Synthetic-Conventional" (Fowler, 1981: 164). Applying Fowler's idea of "stages of faith development" to the developmental level, the congruency or the diversity of entire congregations does pose interesting questions.

14

THE CONTRIBUTIONS OF ALBERT BANDURA'S SOCIAL COGNITIVE THEORY TO AN UNDERSTANDING OF ADOLESCENCE

THE HISTORICAL BEGINNING OF SOCIAL LEARNING THEORY

Social learning theory consists of rather diverse thoughts that range from Clark Hull's drive reduction theory, to Skinner's reinforcement theory, to Freud's psychoanalytic theory. Social learning theory's effort in combining such diverse points of view has been described as the merging of the clinically rich psychoanalytic concepts with the scientifically rigorous behavioristic constructs. Concerned with the relationship between psychoanalytic and behavioristic theory, psychologists such as Miller and Dollard (*Social Learning and Imitation*, 1941) and Mowrer and Sears systematically attempted to bridge the gap between these divergent points of view. Their efforts opened new horizons and gave an early impetus to studies using an approach to basic human, social, and developmental problems that later coalesced into social learning theory. As a result, imitation, modeling, observational learning, and especially the idea of bidirectional influences (from parents to child, but also from child to parent) became the cornerstone of social learning theory. The biodirectionality of social influences, especially that of children themselves being active contributors to their own development, has, under the influence of social learning theory, become a core concept in ecological and contextual theories of development.

Sears, Maccoby, and Levin, in *Patterns of Child Rearing* (1957), contributed a considerable amount of information to the understanding of parenting practices and their influence on the social development of children. However, the focus of their work has been on child-hood rather than adolescence. They concentrated their efforts on the study of both the antecedents and the consequences of early child development, and while initially the parents' behavior is seen as the antecedent and the child's behavior as the consequence, both behaviors later increasingly become a matter of interaction. Antecedent-consequence statements are characteristic of social learning theory, since it is the relationship between social and environmental antecedents and their behavioral consequences that is the focus of investigations and theorizing. A well-known early hypothesis in this regard is Miller's (1941) statement that frustration is the inevitable antecedent of aggressive behavior.

The explicit concern with adolescence comes primarily through the work of Bandura (1925-   ) and Walters (1918–1967), who conducted a number of studies that emphasize the application of social cognitive theory, or as they refer to it, a sociobehavioristic approach to adolescent aggression. Bandura, a student of Sears, has remained closer to Sears, while

Albert Bandura (1925-   )

Walters seems to have been closer to Skinner. Their major works relevant to theories of adolescence are *Adolescent Aggression* (Bandura and Walters, 1959) and, concentrating more specifically on children, *Social Learning and Personality Development* (Bandura & Walters, 1963). After Walter's tragic and untimely death, Bandura advanced the theory further in *Social Foundations of Thought and Action* (Bandura, 1986) and *Social Cognitive Theory* (Bandura, 1989b), as well as in innumerable research papers. Bandura and Walters, more than other social learning theorists, were concerned with the period of adolescence; therefore, the major emphasis in this chapter will be on the collaborative efforts of these two scholars. It would be incorrect to identify Bandura and Walters' contribution as a "theory of adolescence" in the narrow sense of the word, since they are convinced that there is continuity in development from infancy to adulthood. Indeed, one of the contributions of social learning theory to an understanding of adolescence is that it seriously questions the widely held assumption that adolescence is a distinct developmental stage that has its own unique characteristics and requires its own set of theoretical explanations. In that respect social learning theory has much in common with the idea of cultural relativism advanced by anthropology (Chapter 6), and more recently, contextualism (Chapter 16). A sociobehavioristic approach to adolescence implies that the principles of learning that help explain child development (Sears, 1951; Sears et al., 1957) are equally applicable to adolescent and adult development, since no fundamental qualitative differences exist between children, adolescents, and adults. What may differ at different age levels are sociocultural attitudes, expectations, and pressures. In the United States, sociocultural expectations are quite commonly different for children and adults, and adolescents frequently are influenced by models that are quite different from those of children.

Social learning theory, with its unique implications for child and adolescent development, has, therefore, emerged as a developmental theory over the last four or five decades. Baldwin (1967) described it as "a theory in the making," partly because its formalizations are not as dogmatically stated as those of behavioristic or psychoanalytic theory and partly because, from its inception, social learning theorists have been firmly committed to verification of hypothetical relationships by way of empirical research. This continuous openness to new evidence and new ideas is also reflected in the identification of what started out as "Social Learning Theory" now being referred to by Bandura (1989b) as "Social Cognitive Theory." Since social learning theorists have objected to the use of theoretical constructs without empirical support, they have been thoroughly committed to a position whereby theory and empirical research findings are viewed as closely interrelated and interdependent. However, since research findings in relatively complex forms of social behavior frequently do not systematically and unequivocally support specific theoretical hypotheses, revisions of theoretical postulates have been and continue to be an essential characteristic of social learning theory. Hence, more than with any other theories, one needs to consider at what point in time a particular proposition had been advanced.

Clearly, social learning theory is eclectic in that it draws on concepts, hypotheses, and methodology from a variety of different psychological sources. While social learning theory develops its own theoretical constructs, of which modeling and observation/imitation are the most important, it draws freely on constructs of behavioristic learning theory, especially reinforcement. But even Skinner's concept of direct reinforcement is expanded to include important social dimensions: vicarious reinforcement and self-reinforcement. Consequently, the concerns of social learning theorists go far beyond those of the narrow connection between a stimulus and a response and include the contributions of the mother-child (and the child-mother) relationships to personality development, the importance of models, the role of cognitive processes, and the imitation of models in the learning process. In addition, the relationship of the individual to the social group and the mutual influences are of unique importance: "Individual and group behavior are so inextricably intertwined, both as to cause and effect, that an adequate behavior theory must combine both in a single internally congruent system" (Sears, 1951: 476).

Bandura attended a small Canadian high school where only two teachers taught the entire curriculum. He and his peers formed small groups to educate themselves. After graduation Bandura worked in the "wilderness of Yukon territory" with a diverse group of individuals. From these early experiences emerged his conviction about the power of self-directedness, a concept which finds expression in many of his theoretical constructs: Self-regulation, self-efficacy, self-reinforcement, and self-evaluation.

In short, the realm of investigation for the social learning theorist is the whole spectrum of socialization processes (e.g., imitation, modeling, instruction, reward, and punishment) by which children learn (and to which children contribute), often through indirect teaching. Over the last three decades, psychologists have explored contextual models for understanding human growth and development. This means that they examined the individual's temperament, parental reactions to the individual, and social and cultural influences on the individual. As a result, they postulated that all components of a person's life can influence all others (Ford & Lerner, 1992). The contextual approach (see Chapter 16) refocused scholarly attention from mechanistic and organistic exploration of human growth and development to include both in interaction. The significance of the socializing agents as "a source of patterns of behavior" has often been neglected in other theories, even though observational and empirical evidence indicate that this social aspect of the learning process is fundamental to socialization and personality development.

RECIPROCAL TRIADIC DETERMINISM

In the earlier conceptualization, social learning theory assumed that "person variables and environmental variables operate independently to produce behavior" (Phares, 1994: 438). More recently, Bandura (1977a, 1977b, 1982, 1986, 1989a, 1989b) proposed a complex model of causation that identifies a reciprocal relationship among three major variables that interact biodirectionally. This interactive view of causative factors in learning and development is referred to as "Triadic reciprocal determinism." The three determinants, which reciprocally influence each other, are:

E = the external and social environment (Skinner's stimulus),

B = behavior (which is influenced by prior learning) (Skinner's response), and,

P = the person. P represents internal characteristics, the biological make-up of the person, cognition, and other internal qualities such as intelligence, motivation, self-control, self-perception and beliefs that influence perception and action. (See Figure 14.1.)

P (the person), the new cognitive dimension that has received increasingly more recog-

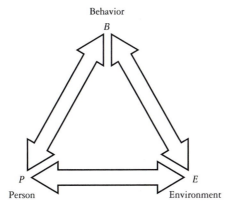

FIGURE 14.1 Model of causation. Schematization of triadic reciprocal determinism. *B* signifies behavior; *P* the cognitive, biological and other internal events that can affect perceptions and actions; and *E* the external environment (from Bandura in Vasta [1989b], Vol. 6, p.2).

nition, represents Bandura's movement away from a strictly behavioristic S–R (stimulus-response) conceptualization of learning and closer to cognitive theory. Illustrations might clarify the biodirectional influences of E, B, and P.

P↔B The physiological and neural structures (P) of an organism affect which behaviors can and cannot be conducted. No matter how hard we try, we cannot flap our arms and fly. However, these structures, in turn, are modified by behavioral efforts (B). Self-control in dieting and rigorous exercise are behavioral efforts that can change biological structure.

E↔P Socially assumed or conferred roles (P) can become both, the result of the social environment (E) as well as the shapers of the social environment (E). Adolescents who have acquired the social reputation of being tough, touchy, and aggressive will elicit quite different reactions from their peers than adolescents perceived as being shy, timid, and weak.

B↔E Environmental influences (E) are activated and modified by appropriate or inappropriate behavior (B). What actually constitutes an environmental event may indeed be modified by an individual's actions. The effect of a presentation in a classroom is greatly dependent on the student's behavior: (a) not attending, (b) attending but daydreaming, (c) paying attention but not participating, (d) actively participating in the discussion, and (e) actually making the presentation to one's peers. Thus, these students are not really in the same environment, but shape the particular environmental events by their different actions. People are influenced by their environment, but as the idea of reciprocal causality implies, these environments are constructed differently by different people. Three weeks of sunshine without a drop of rain is a different environment for the delighted tourist than it is for the worried farmer.

Each individual exists in a very complex web of relationships, which are always changing and being changed by internal, external, and social influences. Thus, neither inner drives and forces nor external determinants of the environment alone can satisfactorily explain the individual's development and behavior (Bandura, 1977b, 1986, 1989b). "This conception of human functioning then neither casts people into the role of powerless objects controlled by environmental forces nor free agents who can become whatever they choose. Both people and their environments are reciprocal determinants of each other" (Bandura, 1977b: vii). As social learning theory has been modified and expanded, self-referents have taken on an increasingly more pronounced role. Bandura describes self-regulatory systems, self-generated-activities, self-control, etc.: "The capacity to exercise control over one's own thought processes, motivation, and action is a distinctively human characteristic" (Bandura, 1989a: 1175). He believes that self-generated activities constitute the core of causal processes. Thus, actions, feelings, motivations, and judgments are at least in part self-determined, and people can bring about changes in themselves and changes in their situations. And it is this sense that cognitive processes (P) are continuously modifying the environment (E) and the behavior (B), or the stimulus and the response. This is truly a major step away from the traditional S–R model since the behavior (B) is no longer seen as solely a function of environmental stimuli (E), but as being codetermined by the person (P) with his or her characteristics.

THE MAJOR TENETS
OF SOCIAL COGNITIVE THEORY

There is no single social learning theory; Bandura has been selected for this chapter because of his work on adolescence. All versions, however, emphasize that individuals learn from others; thus, the social causation as the determinant of learning and behavior change is the primary tenet of social learning theory. Social influences may take different forms: modeling, observing the model, imitation, vicarious and actual reinforcement, and punishment; however, increasingly the importance of internalized self-regulatory functions and cognitive processes are being recognized.

Since social learning theory does not use developmental stages or age-related changes, and is, as the name implies, more of a "learning" than a "developmental" theory, it appears appropriate to elaborate on some of social cognitive theory's major principles that describe the determinants of behavior. These principles are equally applicable to child, adolescent, and adult development. Adolescents behave differently only to the extent that social expectation, social pressure, peer modeling, and other social factors assert different influences on them.

■ Learning by Vicarious Reinforcement

The maintenance of learned response patterns in the behavioristic sense depends on direct external reinforcement. This traditional behavioristic view held that behavior was modified as a consequence of a person's actions. Bandura expands this traditional concept of reinforcement to include vicarious reinforcement. Vicarious reinforcement depends not on what the observer does, but on the positive or negative consequences that the subject observes in others—that is, in the model. Observing social models being rewarded for aggressive behavior increases the likelihood of this behavior occurring in the observer, just as aggressive behavior being punished in the model inhibits (at least temporarily) the same behavior in the subject. Observing and thinking about what happens to other people as they behave in certain ways can be as effective as having the experiences ourselves. As our images of reality are increasingly shaped by scripts the media feeds us, we learn a great deal by the consequences experienced by media characters as a function of their behavior. Young viewers can learn a great deal from these images: social skills, vocabulary, language, dress code, gender roles and gender relationships, racial stereotypes, sexual behavior, and the use of aggression in solving problems. From a social learning theory point of view, mass media provides adolescents with heavy doses of vicarious learning experiences, in which the viewers are only passive observers.

Social learning theory highlights the importance of learning from the observation of others performing or demonstrating a task. If the imitation of an observed behavior is reinforced, that behavior will be strengthened, maintained and learned in the observer.

1. Attentional Processes

The age and cognitive ability of the child influences attention. Young children may have difficulties in paying attention to multiple aspects of the modeled behavior at the same time. They are also more easily distracted by irrelevant events in the situation. The child must pay attention to the person or agent modeling a behavior pattern in order to accurately perceive the modeled behavior. The more focused the attention is, the greater the probability that the observed behavior will be imitated and adopted. The following variables (Ford & Lerner, 1992) influence such attentional processes:

a. The characteristics of the model (e.g., appearance, status, age). One is more likely to imitate a person with desirable attributes, one who is perceived as being an expert, knowledgeable, respected, and friendly. Also, the mode in which the model is presented (i.e., as a cartoon character, or as an actor in a film, or a live presentation) may influence attention.

b. The environment's reaction to the model. Children will learn the behavior but they will be less likely to imitate a specific behavior if the model is punished for it rather than rewarded for it. This is vicarious reinforcement.

c. The past learning history of the child. Is the model someone whom the child knows, is the model someone who has commanded attention in the past, etc.? What experiences has the child had or observed with similar behavior in the past?

d. Circumstantial factors, e.g., specific directions from an instructor who brings to the child's awareness specific characteristics or cues to look for while observing (Bandura, 1981, 1982). Teachers use this technique to gain attention when they say: "Watch carefully how I do this . . . because you will be asked to do it later."

2. Retention Processes

If children do not remember what they hear or see, their future behavior will hardly be influenced by the event. To remember what they have seen, children must employ cognitive processes for encoding, storage, and retrieval of the information (Ford & Lerner, 1992). The observed behavior must be transformed into verbal or symbolic representation and stored in memory. Without sufficient memory ability and memory strategies (repeating, reviewing, imagining, categorizing, forming associations, chunking, etc.), retention of what was observed cannot take place, and hence, there is no learning.

3. The Behavioral Reproductive Processes

After the behavior has been observed and remembered, it must be imitated or translated into personal actions that are similar to what was being observed. To do this, children must have the prerequisite motor, social, language, or cognitive skills to actually transform the observed and remembered behavior into their own personal action. Furthermore, children must be able to evaluate the accuracy of their performance in terms of what they remember of the modeled behavior. On the first reproductive attempt they might make errors and may need more modeling and/or corrective suggestions. Hence, as every teacher knows, complex tasks must be modeled repeatedly and reproduced repeatedly before they become usable skills. Self-regulation plays an essential role in social learning theory, since children do not simply respond to external stimuli but select, organize, symbolize, and transfer them. For example, a teacher drawing a turkey for illustration purposes and then asking the children to draw their own utilizes better teaching strategies than if the teacher were to provide each child with a premade outline of the same turkey.

4. Motivational Processes

After observing a model, an individual must have sufficient incentive to actually perform the same behavior. This is more likely to happen if the outcome appears to be valuable, useful, and personally appealing. Also, if a model experiences positive consequences as a result of the behavior, the observer receives vicarious reinforcement and is more likely to imitate it. Intrinsic motivation (Bandura, 1986) results when the individual experiences satisfaction from completing difficult tasks, achieving high standards, and perceiving oneself as skilled and competent. However, Bandura points out that what appears to be intrinsically motivated behavior may, in fact, not actually be that. Students might willingly work long, hard hours, not because of pure love of learning, but in anticipation of some faraway future reward (e.g., getting into a first-rate college, preparing for a prestigious profession, fame). Bandura (1986: 243) describes intrinsic motivation as a "highly appealing but elusive construct."

Bandura (1977b) has noted the significant influences of observational learning on *gender role development*. He maintains that gender role development results from two processes.

1. Direct reinforcement of gender-appropriate and/or gender-stereotyped actions by parents, teachers, peers, companions, etc. For example, fathers may encourage boys to play with trucks and girls to play with toy versions of household items such as dishes, brooms, irons, etc. Parental support (or the lack of it) for certain toys, play activities, and even bedroom decor (sports paraphernalia or automobile models for boys, dolls and lace and pink colors for girls) exerts a major influence on gender role development.

2. Observational learning of gender-appropriate behavior by same-sex models (parents, relatives, siblings, teachers, companions, etc.) (Bandura, 1977b, 1986). Children can observe gender-appropriate or inappropriate behavior live or through TV models, or they can read about it and notice consequences of such behavior. Until the age of 6 or 7 children may not actually look to same-sex role models as the appropriate source to imitate gender-suitable behavior. For example, some boys at about age 4 or 5 still play with trucks even after they have observed girls playing with them, but they are less likely to play with dolls, even if they have observed other boys playing with them. Preschool boys respond more to the gender label given a toy ("for boys" or "for girls") than to who actually plays with such items. But once the children are 6 or 7, gender roles become solidified and they realize that their sex will not change over time and is not dependent on clothes, hairstyle, or other contextual features (Schiamberg, 1988).

■ Symbolic Activities

Symbolic activities serve as the vehicles of thoughts and help in the creation of images. A simple, quite unrealistic, but easily visualized image is "the cow jumped over the moon." A major tenet of social learning theory is that humans do use symbols to represent events and will reuse these symbols in order to communicate the events to others, such as using language or gestures to share the story of a movie with a friend. Cognitive and personal factors determine what was observed and what was remembered, so that two people seeing the same movie and—independently of each other—telling the story to a common friend, may actually tell two quite different stories.

Symbolic activities involve the cognitive and language processes which a person uses to internalize experiences and events, to share with others, to use in working on problems, and to help in anticipating future events and structure future behavior. Children acquire language through listening, observing, and imitating their parents and caretakers. A wide spectrum of research studies has demonstrated that imitation is essential for the learning of language; indeed, Bandura emphasizes the social factor in language learning.

Parents and, later, teachers continuously present new components of language (e.g., words, phrases, sentence structures, etc.), and at the same time, speak in a manner that the child can understand. Parents may also restructure a child's ungrammatical sentence with a simple but grammatically correct version, or repeat an adolescent's offensive statement in its polite form. Once children can talk, however simply, their peers also serve as models in the process of language development. These social factors have received scanty attention, considering the great importance of modeling and imitation in language development (Bandura, 1986, 1989b). But the social factors, including imitation, do not explain completely the process of language acquisition. Many of the statements youngsters make have no relation to the model presented to them, even in very simplified form. For example, "All gone sticky" (Schiamberg, 1988) bears no resemblance to adult speech but communicates the child's thought. Many verbal statements made by small children reveal thoughts, but are not grammatically correct and are only intelligible to family members. The freshman writer, who begins many sentences with "It," may be able to recall what each "it" represents, but has created an impossible task for other readers, since there are no clear referents in the preceding sentences. And even when children do imitate the language of their parents and others, they sometimes devise their own constructions.

■ Forethought Activity (Cognitive Anticipation of Consequences)

Having a future time perspective and goals or purposes for the future require the ability to anticipate, i.e., forethought activity. Bandura (1986) noted that influences from the environment and conditioning from past experiences do not control human behavior though they contribute to it. Increasingly with age, the ability to imagine what might happen if such-and-such were to occur regulates most human behavior. Human behavior is greatly influenced by goals people strive for or consequences they try to avoid; thus, behavior is shaped by forethought activities. Adolescents can predict and consider the possible results of their behaviors before they actualize them. Adolescents use forethought activity to a large extent in order to choose a course of study, a college, a vocation, a friend, or a lover. For some, direct experiences in classes or clubs (such as Future Teachers of America) might provide a realistic context for making such decisions. For others, forethought might be based more on wishful thinking, such as the student who struggles to get Cs, but proclaims to everyone who will listen that his goal is to become a lawyer. Forethought activities motivate individuals to certain courses of action that seem instrumental in promising a favorable outcome in the future. Images of positive happenings in the future influence individuals to choose a course of action that will contribute to making those imagined events actually take place in the future. Thus, a young person who wants to become a medical doctor will take challenging science courses in high school and in college because these are prerequisites for reaching that goal. Thus, forethought activities actually help adolescents to control and direct their behavior in the present.

■ Self-Regulatory Capabilities

During early childhood, socialization processes are guided by parents through their modeling of behavior, their explanations, and their instructions. As development progresses, these external controls gradually need to be replaced by inner control, so that by the time individuals reach adolescence they have developed the ability to self-regulate. Self-regulatory capabilities include self-demands in goal setting, self-motivation and self-direction in reaching the goals, and self-evaluation in assessing errors, shortcomings, and problems. Self-regulation means that individuals can monitor their own behavior through cues and feedback from the outside world as well as from internal cognitive assessment processes. However, Bandura (1977b) points out that even though individuals can self-regulate their own behavior, the likelihood of certain behavior appearing increases if a reward follows and decreases if a punishment follows. In other words, while self-regulation becomes increasingly more important with increasing age, actual functioning is always regulated by both self-regulation and external forces, as well as social environmental consequences.

■ Self-Reflecting Capability

Ford and Lerner (1992) maintain that social and moral judgments regulate social relationships within families, work and school groups, and society. *Evaluative thoughts* provide internal sources for regulating behavior: "How am I doing?" "How might I do?" "Is it good or bad?" These regulating, evaluative thoughts help a person judge his or her actions and provide evaluation of future actions.

Ford and Lerner (1992) identify four types of self-reflective thoughts:

1. *Performance evaluation.* Individuals compare their actual performance with the desired behavior and evaluate how well or poorly they correspond.

2. *Good-bad evaluations and moral judgments.* Individuals compare various methods available for reaching their goals in terms of the social consequences. For example, people might discuss the advantages and disadvantages of gun control or the moral implications of abortion.

3. *Efficacy evaluations.* This kind of evaluative cognitive process involves consideration of which alternative is likely to yield the best results.

4. *Self-evaluative cognition.* Bandura affirmed that no type of thinking is more important than individuals' ability to assess their capability to handle various situations well. Since the belief people have "about their capabilities to exercise control over events that affect their lives" (Bandura, 1989a: 1175)—that is, self-efficacy—has become so central and so pervasive, it will be discussed separately below.

All of the evaluative processes allow individuals, especially adolescents, to regulate their behavior by considering what might happen "if." Adolescents can imagine various outcomes and consequences, "If I do this . . . then that might happen," without having to experiment directly for themselves. This is particularly important in terms of potentially dangerous or predictably dangerous behaviors such as speeding, unprotected promiscuous sex, drug and/or alcohol use, etc.

■ Self-Efficacy

Self-efficacy can be defined as confidence (or lack of confidence) in one's ability to do something or to learn something new. "Self-efficacy beliefs determine how people feel, think, motivate themselves, and behave" (Bandura, 1994: 71), what kind of choices they make, and their efforts and persistence when confronted with obstacles. Individuals consider their capabilities and the positive and/or negative effect that the environment might have on their performance. Human accomplishments thrive on the belief in one's ability and in the worth of what one is doing. Because this concept is so crucial for the success of the learning efforts, schools may be well advised to pay more attention to self-efficacy. Individuals who have a strong sense of self-efficacy will view difficult assignments as a challenge to be conquered rather than as a threat to be avoided (Bandura, 1994). Research has shown that "higher levels of perceived self-efficacy are accompanied by higher performance attainments" (Bandura, 1992: 4).

The concept of self-efficacy is sometimes used in combination with specific attributes, such as "self-efficacy about helping others," an idea which then becomes an individual's assurance that he or she knows how to be helpful and has the ability to help. If a person actually helps somebody, the willingness to help and the belief in one's ability to help might be modified by the feedback that person receives from the social environment: appreciation, gratitude, recognition, and rewards would enhance self-efficacy, while negative feedback would have the opposite effect.

As children develop, their self-efficacy is shaped by several factors and past experiences: (1) Their successful past performance on related or similar endeavors contributes to self-efficacy. People will not usually set goals unless they believe they have the ability to reach those goals. Having succeeded in the past, most children develop greater confidence so that they will try a similar but more difficult task. (2) Vicarious experiences shape self-efficacy. Seeing others (especially if they are similar to oneself) perform and succeed increases the observer's confidence in trying the task. (3) Verbal persuasion that they can do the task encourages children to try it. Teachers, coaches, and parents often use such persuasion: "I know you can do it. . . . Give it a good try." Such encouragement actually enhances self-efficacy. Unfortunately, lack of encouragement and negative comments are equally effective in reducing a child's sense of self-efficacy. (4) A realistic assessment of one's physical and cognitive strength and weaknesses may contribute to self-efficacy.

The idea of self-efficacy actually may go beyond these specific attributes to include the conviction of a sense of mastery over one's environment, especially one's social environment. The belief that the behavior of other people can be predicted and that one can influence other people to do what one wants them to do are expressions of self-efficacy.

As Figure 14.2 shows, Bandura distinguishes between *efficacy expectation* and *outcome expectation*. Outcome expectation is one's assessment that, for most people under normal circumstances, specific actions will actually lead to certain results. Efficacy expectation, in contrast, is the belief that one personally has the ability to perform a specific task well. In other words, one can be aware that a certain behavior leads to a known outcome. An adolescent successfully diving off a 30-foot diving board for the first time will achieve self-respect and social recognition, yet prior to that act that individual may have serious reservations about his or her ability and courage to engage in such behavior. Many individuals shy away from challenging tasks, not because they do not have the ability to perform the assignment, but because they doubt their ability, dwell on their deficiencies, and give up without trying; in other words, they lack self-efficacy. The distinction between efficacy expectation and outcome expectation is crucial; the extent to which a person will try to attack a difficult or dangerous task or problem may not depend on "outcome expectation" (which many parents and teachers emphasize), but on "efficacy expectation," which takes into consideration not only confidence and courage, but also fear, worries, intimidation, and the feeling of being totally overwhelmed by the task. As social learning theory emphasizes, self-efficacy is different from the ability to perform a task. Thus, in observing adolescents, one can find an overconfident youngster, full of self-efficacy, who literally has persuaded himself or herself that he or she can do anything and will actually try impossible tasks. This is in stark contrast to the bright, but shy, intimidated individual who will avoid difficult tasks because he or she lacks self-efficacy, but which in all probability he or she could do

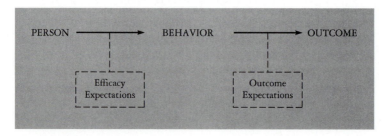

FIGURE 14.2 Diagrammatic representation of the difference between efficacy expectations and outcome expectations. (From A. Bandura, *Social Learning Theory* © 1977, p. 79. Reprinted by permission of Prentice-Hall, Inc., Englewood Cliffs, N.J.)

well. Adolescent girls in the past often seem to have limited "their interests and range of career options by self-beliefs that they lack the necessary capabilities for occupations traditionally dominated by men, even though they do not differ from men in actual ability" (Bandura, 1992: 31). Such self-limitation can be the result of perceived inefficacy rather than actual inability.

■ Self-Reinforcement

Self-reinforcement means that learners actually reward themselves for work that they consider of good quality. Adolescents can be taught to actually reward themselves with positive feedback (pride, satisfaction, feeling of success, etc.) for a job well done or punish themselves with negative feelings (frustration, shame, etc.) for a task poorly completed (Ford & Lerner, 1992). People frequently administer to themselves verbal self-praise, even subvocal compliments, thus utilizing self-reinforcement. Bandura claims that "most human behavior is altered and maintained in the absence of immediate reinforcement" (Bandura, 1971: 248). In a variety of experiments, children gave themselves candy or tokens for attaining self-selected levels of performance in a miniature bowling game. The standards for their self-reinforcement were adopted from the comparison model (Bandura & Kupers, 1964; Bandura & Whalen, 1966); if the standards of the model are stringent, self-reinforcement is infrequent, but if the standards of the model are lenient, self-reinforcement is generous. Actually, self-reinforcement and social reinforcement are equally effective, and both are significantly more effective than noncontingent reward or nonreward.

Once the performance of a desirable response has acquired a positive value, such as an adolescent shooting baskets, the person can administer self-reinforcement by producing the desired basket and feeling good about the improving skill. Common observation illustrates that this kind of self-reinforcement can keep the behavior (i.e., shooting the baskets) going for several hours on a Saturday afternoon. Adolescents are learning to set their own level of performance; reaching that level makes them feel proud or satisfied and, therefore, carries its own reward. In other words, as an individual grows more mature and self-reinforcement patterns stabilize, he or she becomes less and less dependent on parents, teachers, and bosses to get rewards. Children increasingly judge the appropriateness and the quality of their own performance and then reward themselves accordingly. Successful socialization requires that the self-judgment of one's work becomes a more important reinforcer than an outsider administering praise, candy, money, or other reinforcers. Mature adolescents may be able to make themselves feel good about work well done—that is, provide self-reinforcement— even though a critical teacher or an impatient father expresses dissatisfaction. In contrast to Skinner's emphasis on direct external reinforcement, often contingent on fairly specific types of responses, social learning theorists maintain that the more important reinforcers in terms of mature complex social behavior are self-administered.

MODELING, IMITATION, AND IDENTIFICATION

Through a variety of experiments, Bandura and his collaborators have repeatedly demonstrated that children watching the behavior of a model are quick to imitate specific responses as well as the generalized response patterns of a model. Furthermore, personal observations of children and adolescents imitating mannerisms, language idiosyncrasies, and habits of their parents and teachers, at times to the embarrassment of the model, are commonplace. The process of learners' observing the behavior of a model and imitating the behavior observed is such an ancient and common-sense form of learning that it is surprising that it has only become a major theoretical concern in the middle of the twentieth century. The potency of watching and imitating a model in altering response patterns has been demonstrated in some quite divergent areas, such as moral judgment, altruistic behavior, self-imposed delay of reward pattern exhibited by the model, and self-reinforcement patterns that closely follow those of the model.

Modeling functions on different levels:

1. The "modeling effect" is the commonly used educational practice. Especially used in teaching a variety of specific skills, it refers to the already described phenomena that a learner learns by observing a model and imitates the behavior observed.

2. The "inhibitory or disinhibitory effect" is dependent on the consequences of the modeled behavior. If the model experiences a positive outcome, the observer, who may have been reluctant to even try that behavior, experiences a disinhibitory effect. The more inhibited subject will imitate the behavior of an admired peer, especially if the behavior generated peer approval. The factor that most accurately predicts drug use in an adolescent is whether or not friends use drugs. Bandura and Walters' (1959) findings suggest that adolescent boys and girls may be more likely to engage in sexual intercourse when double and multiple dating, thereby imitating the sexual advances of each other. Apparently, an "if he can do it, I can do it" viewpoint prevails. According to Bandura, a great variety of social learning phenomena are acquired because a learner observes a model's behavior, loses his inhibitions and anxieties, and imitates the behavior observed.

3. The "eliciting effect" refers to the additional use of cues provided by the model. Teachers may generate cues by expressing their standards and their high expectation for students' work.

As children grow older they tend to imitate different models from their social environment. The young child usually identifies with parents and attempts to imitate their behavior, including language, gestures, and mannerisms as well as more basic attitudes and values. Identification with a teacher is not uncommon for the child entering school or for the preadolescent. Children imitate speech patterns and mannerisms observed in their teacher. Ideas about social or community issues that the child expresses in dinner conversations and that are new to the family are often those of the teacher. With the onset of adolescence, parents and teachers frequently decline as important models, at least in regard to issues and choices that are of immediate consequence. During adolescence it is the peer group and selected entertainment and sport heroes who become increasingly important as models, especially if communication between the adolescent and his or her parents breaks down. The adolescent's peer group is particularly influential as a model in many of the daily school and leisure time related activities—such as hair style, clothing, language expressions, food, music, and entertainment preferences—as well as in regard to decisions that relate to some of the rapidly changing social values. Some of the problems that arise during adolescence may be the result of an individual modeling the behavior of an admired peer who may have more prestige but may not be more knowledgeable, intelligent, mature, and wise than the individual himself or herself.

Related to modeling and of similar importance in Bandura's social learning theory are the concepts of identification and imitation. In his earlier writing, Bandura frequently uses the concept of identification, but later he rejects it as lacking specific content. Different definitions have been advanced for the concepts "identification" and "imitation." Although there is no complete agreement about the specific meaning of these concepts, identification is viewed as a more general way of taking on the behavior of another person even without the person's presence. Identification includes the incorporation of the model's values, beliefs, roles, and attitudes. Imitation, on the other hand, refers to the specific reproduction or mimicry of behavior sequences, while the person whose behavior is imitated is or was personally present. Experimental psychologists speak of "imitation," whereas personality theorists speak of "identification." Bandura and Walters (1963) discuss the difference in existing definitions but prefer to use the more behavior-oriented term "imitation," which they define as referring to "the occurrence of matching responses."

The role of imitation has been recognized since antiquity as an important method of learning, and it is indeed surprising that behavioristic learning theory has not shown more concern for imitation and modeling. Imitation is particularly relevant for learning complex social behavior, such as language, self-control, altruism, aggression, sexual behavior, and so on. Imitation also plays an essential role in the learning of basic perceptual-motor skills, such as handwriting. Much of the learning in the gymnasium and on the sports field is the result of observing and imitating a model who demonstrates how to play correctly. In many languages, the term "to teach" is synonymous with "to show" or, as in Hebrew, has the same root, revealing that modeling, or showing, is the basic method of teaching when the emphasis is on skills that can be acquired through observational learning (Bandura & Walters, 1963). The adolescent who wants to learn to drive a car does so first of all by observation and imitation. A youth totally naive in the use of cars would endanger his or her life and those of others if he or she were to attempt driving solely on the basis of trial and error or reinforcement. Bandura (1962) reports that natives in a Guatemalan subculture learn to operate a cotton textile machine by observing the correct operation of the machine for a number of days. During this training period the youthful trainees ask no questions and are given neither verbal instruction nor reinforcement. Yet, when they feel confident that they can master the process themselves, they take over the operation of the machine and usually succeed on the very first trial in operating the machine without any difficulties and without further instruction. This kind of learning is based only on the apprentices observing an appropriate social model and imitating the behavior of the model.

■ The Shift from Social Learning to Social Cognitive Theory

With the realization that modeling and imitation are not sufficient to explain social learning fully, Bandura (1977a, 1977b, 1989b) and Mischel (1973) turned increasingly to cognitive constructs and renamed the theory "social cognitive theory." In observing and imitating the behavior of others, an individual draws on various cognitive processes (e.g., memory, language, thinking, evaluating, anticipating consequences, etc.) in order to adapt the observed behavior to the self. Children and adolescents "operate cognitively on their social experiences" (Grusec, 1992: 781), by abstracting, evaluating, and integrating what they observe, and mentally representing these experiences. The revised theory recognizes much more explicitly that these cognitive processes are necessary for learning and contribute to subsequent developmental changes.

SOCIAL LEARNING THEORY CONTRASTED WITH STAGE THEORIES

Stage theories of development, such as those postulated by Freud, Erikson, Kohlberg, Loevinger, and even Piaget, have set forth fairly specific age-related qualitative behavior changes that follow an invariant developmental sequence, possess cross-situational consistency, and claim to be more or less universal and predetermined. Social learning theory, in contrast, assumes that behavior is primarily determined by the social and environmental factors operating within a particular situational context. Consequently, social learning theory focuses on the interrelationship between environmental and social changes as antecedents and the behavioral changes that occur in a given individual as consequences of the situation rather than as a function of age. Descriptions and statements about adolescence are not of such a general, all-encompassing nature as in Erikson's theory, which assumes that an adolescent will experience an identity crisis, or Piaget's prediction that adolescent thought processes will begin to absorb formal logic and become increasingly more abstract. Rather, social learning theory statements are predictions of relationships between external factors and behavior. The strong emphasis in the sociobehavioristic approach on the influence of social conditions and cultural expectations, even on adolescent sexual behavior, becomes obvious in a statement such as: "In North American society, the marked increase in heterosexual behavior in middle and late adolescence is certainly due less to hormonal changes than to cultural expectations" (Bandura & Walters, 1963: 150). Bandura recognizes that changes in adolescent sexual behavior occur in our society. However, he explains the phenomena as being primarily the result of social expectation and vicarious modeling (such as on TV or the movies), rather than being just a matter of hormonal changes. In general, pronounced changes in behavior may occur during adolescence not because of internal maturational forces but because of sudden changes in the social training situation, family structure, school setting, peer expectations, or other environmental factors.

Bandura, in "The Stormy Decade: Fact or Fiction?" questioned the validity of the stage theory assumption that adolescence is a turbulent decade inevitably characterized by "storm and stress, tension, rebellion, dependency conflicts, peer-group conformity, black leather jackets and the like" (Bandura, 1964: 224). While he does not deny that some of these behaviors occur in some individuals, such behaviors are due to cultural conditioning and social expectation rather than being inevitable developmental phenomena characteristic of the period of adolescence per se. Aggressive behavior in adolescence—when it does occur—is viewed as the consequence of specific antecedent conditions in the childrearing pattern and the parent-child relationship rather than as the result of adolescent adjustment problems. Consequently, with the current public concern over aggressive behavior, social learning theory suggests that it may be more productive to look at the antecedents of such behavior (TV models, lack of supervision, dysfunctional families, etc.) rather than to perceive it as more or less normal adolescent development. Whenever such behaviors occur, social learning theory views them as being lawfully related to existing situations or to the preadolescent social situation—that is, antecedent environmental conditions. The prototypical adolescent with turmoils and anxieties, sexual tensions, compulsive conformity, and acute identity crisis so commonly described in the literature, according to Bandura (1964), fits only the actual behavior of perhaps "the deviant ten percent of the adolescent population"; Bandura assumes that such deviant behavior is the result of some antecedent events. Indeed, the "myth" that such behavior is believed to be a normal aspect of adolescent development is due more to cultural expectations and the sensationalized representation of teenagers in movies, literature, and the mass media than to actual facts. Bandura (1964) does find, as does Offer (1969), that responsible, happy, well-adjusted, parent-respecting youth are more common than had been assumed. However, such positive findings are also interpreted not as characteristics of adolescence per se, but as the result of antecedent home conditions which provided a warm, supportive preadolescence where firmness and socialization pressure slowly gave way to increasing autonomy during adolescence.

As a general principle of social and personal development, social learning theory assumes that while individual variations exist, there is continuity in human growth patterns and in the learning process, and no basic changes or clear-cut new stages in the mode of thinking appear at any one age level. Bandura and McDonald (1963) tested Piaget's (1932b) theory that objective moral judgment, which considers the material damage in an act, gives way at about age 7 to subjective moral judgment, which considers the intent of the wrongdoers rather than the amount of damage. Bandura and McDonald did not find a distinct or abrupt change in the moral responses of their subjects, but there was a pronounced increase in subjective moral judgment and a decrease in objective moral judgment as a function of age. Bandura and McDonald consider changes in moral judgment to be primarily the result of changes in reinforcement contingencies in combination with the effects of modeling, rather than a function of maturation or a change from the preoperational to the operational stage in logical thinking. Bandura and McDonald (1963) demonstrated further that age-specific social responses such as moral judgment can be modified through the utilization of appropriate models and the application of social learning principles. Since the age-specific behavior postulated by Piaget's theory of two distinct stages of moral judgment can be modified through modeling and social reinforcement, the theory casts some doubt on the validity of the stage concept. The social learning theory assumption is that external social experiences have greater impact on behavior changes than the internal maturation forces postulated by stage theorists.

In contrast to stage theories, social learning theory is concerned with *interindividual* rather than *intraindividual differences*. Some of the environmental variables that are responsible for interindividual differences in behavior include: intelligence, sex, age, race, socioeconomic status, culture, home atmosphere, past experiences, exposure to models, and different reinforcement schedules. "To the extent that children representing such diverse backgrounds experience differential contingencies and schedules of reinforcement, as well as exposure to social models who differ widely in the behavior they exhibit, considerable interindividual behavior variability would be expected" (Bandura & McDonald, 1963: 274).

COGNITIVE SOCIAL LEARNING THEORY CONTRASTED WITH BEHAVIORISTIC THEORY

Social learning theory also recognizes the very limited applicability of reinforcement theory to a wide variety of especially complex forms of social behavior, such as language learning. Bandura (1962) dismisses the use of operant or instrumental conditioning as "tedious and ineffective" for most complex human learning. Skinner and others have assumed, without sufficient empirical verification, that reinforcement principles based on the findings of studies in highly structured laboratory situations apply equally to complex social situations. Bandura (1962) feels that people would not be socialized and many vocational and recreational skills would never be learned if they depended solely on reinforcement. A new repertoire of complex behaviors can best be learned from observing a model exhibiting that behavior and matching or imitating the behavior modeled. Operant conditioning effectively explains how the learned behavior is maintained and strengthened but not how it is initially acquired. The initial acquisition of a response pattern is more effectively explained by imitation, and this kind of observational learning can take place without direct reinforcement. Similarly, trial-and-error learning can be eliminated, or the number of trials greatly reduced, by providing an opportunity to observe the necessary behavior performed by an appropriate model. This process of observing a model and imitating the behavior observed constitutes the cornerstone of the sociobehavioristic approach. "What you know and how you behave depends on what you see and hear and not just on what you get" (Mischel, 1971: 71).

Social learning theory makes a clear and important distinction between the *acquisition of potential response patterns* and *actual performance*, or responding. The acquisition of potential response patterns is a function of observing the behavior of others and storing the observed information in memory, so that it will be retrievable at a later time. When, where, and whether this potential response pattern will be used depends on social conditions and cognitive processes. In social learning theory, reinforcement certainly has its place, but it is delegated a secondary, supportive role in the learning process. Most complex learning is viewed primarily as social—namely, the imitation of social models, especially in the learning of novel response patterns. The difference between acquisition and performance may be illustrated by the fact that most adolescent boys may know how to use lipstick and cosmetics—the response patterns having been acquired through observation. However, because these responses have never been reinforced, their probability of occurring is very low and may be zero, except as a charade or clowning-around performance, to make an audience of peers laugh. Many response patterns are acquired through observing a model but are not expressed as long as the learned behavior is not functional. However, if the social situation changes so that the acquired response pattern becomes functional, the previously acquired behavior may be performed without further observation, without trial and error, and without reinforcement. When social situations change, for example, children may surprise parents with language patterns or language skills that were acquired earlier but had never been used before. When adolescents or older children visit their relatives without their parents, they suddenly show courtesy, behave politely, and perform voluntarily a number of tasks which they may never have done at home.

That modeling may be more important in inducing behavior changes than reward and/or punishment is illustrated by the way children learn aggressive behavior. One persistent research finding is that parental punitiveness toward aggressive behavior appears to be associated with more rather than less aggressive behavior in the child.

Parental modeling behavior may often counteract the effects of their direct training. When a parent punishes a child physically for having aggressed toward peers, for example, the intended outcome of this training is that the child should refrain from hitting others. The child, however, is also learning from parental demonstration how to aggress physically and this imitative learning may provide the direction for the child's behavior when he is similarly frustrated in subsequent social interactions [Bandura, 1967: 43].

"Do as I say, not as I do" is exactly the reverse of what social learning theory predicts will happen. The imitation of the model, the "as I do" part, apparently is psychologically more potent than the reinforcement or the punishment provided by the "as I say" part. And many adolescents complain about their parents' "hypocrisies," since their "model" behavior belies their verbal recommendations and admonitions. Actually, most manuals on discipline emphasize that the modeling of desirable behavior is a much more potent influence than any verbalization or reward-punishment technique. And the most valid general rule in regard to the training of children and adolescents is: "There is no sure way to guarantee that your child will grow up to be the kind of person you would like him to be. The most likely way is for you to be the kind of person you would like him to be."

THE ANTECEDENTS OF ADOLESCENT AGGRESSION

Aristotle believed that emotional expression releases the emotions. Similarly, hydraulic models hold that as long as the cause of aggression is within the individual, the aggressive energy must find an outlet, since aggression is assumed to be reduced by aggressive behavior. Therapy and various forms of sport provide safe and approved outlets for aggression. Bandura (1973) rejects all hydraulic motivational theories of aggression—such as Freud's aggressive instinct theory and Lorenz's aggressive urge theory—since these theories view aggression as a natural response to frustration.

Plato, in contrast, held that the overt expression of emotion arouses rather than reduces emotions. Bandura agrees with Plato and feels that he provides the more appropriate model. Social learning theory postulates that the causes of aggression are external, social, and environmental. Their origin can be found in the dependency training in childhood, imitation of aggressive models, and lack of internalization of social values.

As an alternative to the frustration-aggression hypothesis, Bandura assumes that rather than frustration leading to aggression, it produces

emotional arousal that can elicit a variety of behaviors, depending on the types of reactions people have learned for coping with stressful conditions. When distressed, some people seek help and support; others display achievement behavior; others show withdrawal and resignation; some aggress; others exhibit heightened somatic activity;

others anesthetize themselves with drugs or alcohol; and most intensify constructive efforts to overcome their problems [Bandura, 1973: 204].

Bandura and Walters' interest in adolescence finds its most explicit manifestation in an extensive study, *Adolescent Aggression* (1959). As its subtitle, "A Study of the Influence of Child Training Practices and Family Interrelationships," suggests, the study is concerned with the antecedent variables in the parent-child relationship that contribute to the development of antisocial aggressive behavior. The specific antecedent home conditions investigated stem from social learning theory hypotheses and involve the socialization process and its effects on such variables as dependency training, sex attitudes and behavior, the handling of discipline in the home, and identification processes. The socialization process is viewed as "the development of habitual response patterns that are acceptable in the society in which the individual lives. The learning of such *habits,* or cue-response associations, requires the presence of some kind of *drive* or motivating process and the occurrence of a reward or *reinforcement*" (Bandura & Walters, 1959: 23).

The conditions that contribute to effective socialization include the development of a dependency motive so that the child desires approval and affection from others. In addition, since dependency alone is not sufficient, socialization pressure needs to be exerted by way of demands and limitations—in short, through discipline—so that the child learns to conform to the patterns of society. This socialization process is facilitated by the amount and quality of personal contact parents give to their child and by withholding secondary rewards such as approval and attention, while at the same time keeping the child in a dependent relationship. The socialization process is delayed or disrupted if dependency behavior is punished or discouraged, if parental discipline methods are inconsistent, and if the parents' values are in conflict with the prevalent values of the community and society. One basic assumption of Bandura and Walters' study is that antisocial aggression develops from a disruption in the adolescent's earlier dependency training in relationship to parents. Dependency needs could be frustrated by lack of affectional nurturance, by parental rejection, or by lack of close dependency ties with one or both parents. An impairment in the development of healthy dependency relationships may directly contribute to feelings of hostility and to aggressive behavior. In addition, children without dependency motives experience less guilt and lack the capacity to control aggressive feelings sufficiently when aroused.

Bandura and Walters obtained their data from two groups of carefully selected boys aged 14–17. Twenty-six pairs of boys were matched on a one-to-one basis in regard to age, intelligence, father's occupation, and area of residence. They differed in that the aggressive boys had a history of antisocial, aggressive patterns of behavior, and many of them were on probation. The nonaggressive boys in the control group were neither markedly aggressive nor withdrawn. Both groups came from intact families, had average or above-average intelligence, did not live in a high-delinquency neighborhood, and were free from neurotic tendencies to withdraw, known organic involvement, or other psychiatric problems. Data were collected through extensive personal interviews of both groups of adolescents as well as their parents. In theoretical orientation and in methodology, the study may actually be considered an extension of Sears, Maccoby, and Levin's *Patterns of Child Rearing* (1957).

Sociological approaches relate incidence of delinquency to population density, poverty, broken homes, deteriorated houses and neighborhood, lack of recreational facilities, and social and personal discontent. These investigators, in contrast, looked at the nature of the parent-child relationship and related it to the absence or presence of aggressive behavior in the adolescent subjects, controlling most of the sociological factors by matching procedures. In contrast to the psychodynamic disease model of deviant behavior, Bandura and Walters assume that both deviant and prosocial behavior are governed by the same learning principles rather than by hidden, subconscious, internal dynamics or aggressive traits. Their assumption is that external stimulus conditions control normal as well as deviant behavior.

Furthermore, since social learning theorists believe in the continuity of human development, antisocial aggressive behavior in adolescent boys is seen not as a problem that emerges with puberty or as related to hormonal changes, but as a failure in the socialization process that often begins very early in childhood and continues during development.

The first group of hypotheses developed from social learning theory compared the dependency behavior, dependency anxiety, feelings of rejection, and aggressive behavior in the aggressive adolescents with those of the nonaggressive controls. In general, there was no significant difference in mothers' warmth and affection with both groups of boys. However, the aggressive boys were, as social learning theory predicts, less dependent on their fathers, felt more rejected by their fathers, and spent less time with their fathers than the control boys.

The fathers of the two groups of boys did not report any difference in the amount of overt aggression directed toward them. Only a few of the mothers of aggressive boys reported physical aggression directed toward them, but they also admitted that they were more tolerant of aggressive behavior. The control mothers had firmer limits in the amount of aggression they would tolerate. In general, the differences in expression of aggression toward parents and parents' tolerance of aggressive behavior between these two groups were not very pronounced. However, it became quite obvious that both the fathers and the mothers of the aggressive adolescents actively encouraged their sons to show aggression outside the home, to use their fists and to stand up for their rights. In addition, the fathers seemed to get some vicarious enjoyment from the aggressive acts of their sons. This difference, especially between the fathers of aggressive sons and the control fathers, was most pronounced. In a follow-up study of aggressive and inhibited preadolescent boys, Bandura (1960) found that the parents of the inhibited boys were nonpermissive and nonpunitive toward aggressive behavior, which means that they neither reinforced nor modeled aggressive behavior. The parents of aggressive boys, in contrast, were nonpermissive and punitive when the aggressive behavior was directed toward themselves, but they encouraged aggression toward other children and permitted sibling aggression.

Aggressive boys had more dependency anxiety—that is, they were less willing to express their dependency, seek help, talk about their problems, and show affection, even though they did have dependency needs. The dependency anxiety generalized from parents to peers and school. The control boys sought and appreciated help from their fathers more; and they also showed more help-seeking and approval-seeking behavior in relationship to their peers. In contrast, the feeling of being rejected in relationship to school and peers was more pronounced among the aggressive boys.

No difference was found in the handling of sexual behavior in both groups of parents, except that the fathers of the aggressive boys were more permissive concerning sexual behavior. However, it was found that the aggressive boys had had significantly more heterosexual experiences and expressed less anxiety about sex. Apparently, the permissive attitude in the fathers contributed to the greater sexual experience of the aggressive boys.

Several significant relationships were found in respect to the handling of rules, limitations, and disciplining of these two groups of boys. The control parents used more reasoning as a disciplinary method and had higher achievement expectations for their sons. The control mothers were more consistent in enforcing rules and were more restrictive—that is, they used more socialization pressure, at least in the home. The methods used significantly more often in disciplining the aggressive boys were physical and verbal punishment by their fathers, isolation, and more deprivation of privileges, although the latter method was common in both groups. The relationship between punitive parents and aggressive behavior in their children has been reported repeatedly in the literature. Apparently, the more children are punished at home for aggressive behavior, the more aggressively they act toward their peers (Eron, 1987; Sears, Maccoby, & Levin, 1957). The mothers of the aggressive boys reported that their sons resisted their demands, and the aggressive boys themselves admitted that they ignored parental requests and refused to do what they were told to do. The parent-child relationship of the aggressive adolescents may best be described as lacking in warmth and affection.

The crucial question from a social learning theory point of view relates to the identification of these two groups of boys with their parents and the internalization of controls. While there was no difference in terms of identification with the mother, control boys identified more strongly with their fathers. The control fathers were more demanding of masculine behavior in their sons. However, the aggressive boys experienced more disruption in affectional relationships between their fathers and their mothers and also more of a disruption in the emotional relationship between themselves and their parents, especially their fathers. In terms of internalization of controls, the nonaggressive group experienced more guilt when they transgressed, whereas the aggressive boys did not. The conscience of the aggressive boys showed the following different patterns from that of the control boys: When confronted with temptation, the behavior of the control boys was governed by guilt, an internal avoidance. The aggressive boys, in a situation involving transgression of rules, were not governed by guilt, but if they were inhibited at all, it was by fear of punishment. Since identification is not encouraged and rewarded in the aggressive boys, the internalization of values seemed to suffer.

In summary, aggressive boys seem to imitate their aggressive parents, who tend to use more physical punishment as a method of discipline and who encourage and reward the aggressive behavior of their sons, at least outside the home. By reinforcing aggressive behavior outside the home, by inhibiting aggressive behavior inside the home directed toward the parents, and by modeling aggressive behavior through physically punishing the boys, these parents "fostered displacement of aggression toward objects and situations eliciting much weaker inhibitory response" (Bandura, Ross, & Ross, 1961). These findings resulting from the study of aggressive behavior of adolescent boys in their natural environment are quite consistent with the results of laboratory studies of aggressive behavior of young children (Bandura, Ross, & Ross, 1961; 1963b; 1963c). Antisocial aggressive behavior in adolescent boys is the consequence of identifiable socialization variables which include parental discipline, parental endorsement of aggressive behavior, and the lack of dependency in the parent-child relationship.

EFFECTS ON THE OBSERVER'S BEHAVIOR OF WATCHING A VIOLENT MODEL

Early studies investigating the effects of watching a model exhibiting violent/aggressive behavior on the uninvolved observer, especially the circumstances under which the behavior was imitated, were inspired by social learning theory. The purpose of these studies was to demonstrate the theory, namely, that antisocial aggression is learned, and that a demonstrable relationship between the modeled and the imitated behavior exists. Aggressive behavior is ideal for such research since it can be defined—an act that injures or irritates another person (Eron, 1987). Observational modeling theory assumes that in order for the observed behavior to affect the viewer, the following conditions must prevail: (a) The viewer must pay attention to the depicted behavior. (b) The viewer must comprehend—at least to some extent—the content. (c) The viewer must internalize the script of the observed event and adopt the behavioral tendencies. The early studies dealt with real-life aggression and aggression in films. Only later did the political and public policy issue of aggressive behavior, depicted on TV, enter into the debate. Investigations have led to the recognition that entertainment TV really has become a major teaching agent, and therefore, plays a widely unrecognized but potent influence on the development of children. Television watching is part of modeling behavior and part of social learning in today's world. Most obviously, the effect of TV on the behavior of the viewer is the basic assumption underlying the sale of spots for commercials. A half-minute spot during prime time may cost as much as $250,000. The media try to have it both ways, cashing in on the effect of advertisement on purchasing decisions, but maintaining that the content of the show is simply entertainment without the powerful influence of the modeled behavior that may be imitated.

Bandura, Ross, and Ross's classic and still quite frequently cited studies gave the impetus to the current "violent-TV-shows contribute to the imitation-of-violent-behavior" controversy as well as the follow-up research and the more broadly conceived concern with the effects of TV watching on the viewer. The depiction of violence on TV has received the greatest amount of attention from the research community. However, the implications of the findings go beyond aggressive behavior and could be applied similarly to sexual behavior, gender and racial stereotyping, but also to the learning of prosocial behavior, vocabulary development and usage, historical and geographic knowledge, etc.

Bandura, Ross, and Ross (1963b) demonstrated that watching unusual aggressive behavior heightened children's aggressive responses significantly when compared to controls who had observed a nonaggressive model. The first experimental group watched a real-life aggressive model; the second group saw the same model portraying aggressive behavior on film; the third group observed an aggressive cartoon character depicting the same behavior. Many of the children's responses in the test situation were rather accurate imitations of the unusual aggressive acts of the model, especially of the real-life and the film model. The overall increase in aggressive behavior was highly significant and about the same for all three experimental situations, but the cartoon aggressive model elicited less precise imitation. Walters and his associates have shown that the increase in aggressive behavior as a result of watching an aggressive model is not limited to children; similar findings were seen with high school students, young women, and male hospital attendants. Related follow-up studies (Eron,1987; Singer & Singer, 1984; Van Evra, 1990) have repeatedly demonstrated that aggression is learned behavior and that exposure to the aggressive behavior of models does indeed increase subsequent aggressive behavior in the observer. Media violence is one method of teaching aggressive behavior.

In addition to its establishment, the maintenance of response patterns or learning in the behavioristic sense does not depend only on direct external reinforcement as in Skinner's theory. Bandura expands the traditional concept of reinforcement to include vicarious reinforcement and also self-reinforcement. Vicarious reinforcement depends on the positive or negative consequences that the subject observes in others—that is, in the model. Observing social models that are rewarded for aggressive behavior increases the likelihood of this behavior occurring in the observer, just as aggressive behavior punished in the model inhibits the same behavior in the subject.

Bandura, Ross, and Ross's (1963c) second experiment is based on the concept of vicarious reinforcement. Two films of Rocky the Villain exhibiting almost identical aggressive behavior were shown to groups of children. In one instance the aggressive behavior of Rocky was rewarded and in another it was punished. Children who watched the movie and saw the aggressive behavior of Rocky being rewarded were quick in imitating both the physical violence and the verbal abuse that they had observed. Actually, they showed about two times as much aggressive behavior as a control group. However, in the situation in which the children observed that the villain was punished after his aggressive act, they showed little immediate imitation of the behavior they had watched. However, even though punishing the villain inhibited the overt learning effects that resulted from observing the "bad" model, it did not suppress the latent tendencies. Children did acquire these response patterns and could describe them with considerable accuracy, even though they did not spontaneously perform them, unless such response patterns became functional under either the impact of provocation or the prospect of rewards.

A real-life survey by Eron (1987) supports the findings of these laboratory studies. Eron interviewed 600 8-year-old children, their parents, their peers, and their children 30 years later, in Columbia County, New York, to investigate the development of aggressive behavior over time. The results were interpreted within a social learning theory framework and are consistent with much of the research on watching violent shows. The study has several unique features that set it apart from most of the TV watching studies. The study followed a longitudinal design, base data were attained when the children were 8, repeated ten years later, about a year after high school graduation, and again 22 years after the initial interview. Aggressive behavior of those who frequently watched violent shows not only persisted but actually increased over time. The study was not conducted in a laboratory, but used parents, peers (peer-nominated index of aggression), and later, police and court records as assessment methods. The initial focus of the study was not on TV watching but on the boys' identification with their father and the level of punishment (high level of punishment + low level of identification = high aggression; low level of punishment + high level of identification = low aggression). However, the astonishing finding revealed a highly significant relationship between the amount of violence these children watched at the age of 8 and their peer-nominated aggression score. The more aggressive these children were judged by their peers in school, the more violent the content of their TV programs. The correlation between watching violent TV at age 8 was higher at age 19 than it had been at age 8. The highly aggressive children at 8 were three times as likely to have police records than those who were not rated as violent at 8. Of all the factors studied, watching violent shows at age 8 was the best predictor of aggressive behavior at 18. The 22-year follow-up data revealed similar patterns.

These social learning theory studies on imitation of aggressive behavior seen on TV clearly demonstrate that long-term exposure to TV violence relates significantly to more aggressive behavior in children. This research has been influential in awakening social concern about the potential danger of children and adolescents repeatedly watching aggressive behavior on TV, since "exposure to filmed aggression heightens aggressive reactions in children" (Bandura, Ross, & Ross, 1963b: 9). A major initiative along these lines came when the Surgeon General's Office called for studies on how TV affects children and adolescents in terms of their aggressive and violent behavior. Consequently, the connection between TV violence and aggressive behavior has become the focus of much research. Some of the contemporary concern with the relationships between observing violent behavior and actually engaging in such behavior has been inspired by the above-cited research studies. As a result, these relationships have become increasingly clearer. However, correlations between two variables, such as TV watching and aggressive behavior suggests, but do not prove, causality; other contextual factors need to be considered.

Some frequently cited statistics may put the issue in perspective. More than 95 percent of American homes have television; by the time adolescents reach the age of 18, they have watched, on an average, 15,000–20,000 hours of TV, representing more than any other single activity, except sleeping. TV has become "a compelling medium for capturing and holding attention" (Grusec, 1992: 781). In 1985, the National Coalition on TV Violence reported in *Five Decades: 1980's* (1989) that typical American youngsters will experience approximately 50,000 attempted or completed murders on TV before their sixteenth birthday. For an adolescent, that may include an average of 6–8 acts of violence and 2 murders per night. The violence of cartoon characters on children's programs is substantially higher, even though the images are more humorous and less realistic, so that the aggressive acts appear sugar-coated. The same coalition identified a 300 percent increase in TV violence since 1957. Similarly the American Academy of Pediatrics has reported a tripling of television violence in the 1980s. Hearold (1986) argues that viewing violence affects not only the child's behavior but, over an extended period of time, underlying values and attitudes as well. Heavy viewing of violent behavior on TV has rather extensively documented effects: (1) It does increase the violent behavior in the observer. (2) In addition, it makes the observer more tolerant toward an aggressive person displaying violent behavior against others. (3) Heavy adolescent viewers perceive their world as a place that cannot be trusted.

Viewing violence as entertainment has a disinhibiting effect on the tendency to imitate that behavior, since it decreases the kind of social and moral inhibitions that viewers normally draw upon to control aggressive impulses. Repeatedly watching TV violence makes viewers insensitive to the suffering violence produces. Calvin in the cartoon (p. 306) dramatically illustrates how TV violence has influenced and desensitized him. There exists considerable evidence (Himmelweit et al., 1980) that prolonged viewing of violence actually has a disinhibiting effect and over a period of time habituates and desensitizes people to violence, so that viewers even become more tolerant to the person who perpetuates violent crimes on others. With repeated exposure to violence, the probability is higher that aggressive thoughts will be activated, and further, that the idea will emerge, at least for a period of time, that aggression is acceptable. Cross-national investigations, in as diverse

countries as Australia, Finland, the Netherlands, Israel, Poland, and the United States, have replicated the observation that children who watched more violent behavior exhibited more aggressive behavior themselves. Williams (1986) notes that the real-life experiences of children may also determine the effect that TV watching has on their behavior. Young frequent viewers may have little real-life experience with violence except for exposure to it on TV. Huesmann (1986, 1988) argues that if children see TV characters use aggressive solutions to solve their problems and, as is frequently the case, get rewarded for it (at least temporarily), they too will attempt to solve their problems that way. The more frequently children experience violence being depicted on television, the more likely it is that they will recall the violent behavior they have seen and will also behave aggressively.

Bandura, Ross and Ross's (1963b) findings—that even watching cartoon violence could lead to aggression—have been replicated. Since 1955 approximately 1,000 studies have established a correlational link between television violence and aggressive behavior. In addition, there appears to be no difference between violence on TV and violent video games on aggression (Silvern & Williamson, 1987). Obviously, the concerns raised by TV and cartoon watching research are not limited to these media, even though they have been researched most extensively, but should include the newer media: cable TV, MTV, VCR, interactive video, and increasingly, even computer internet systems and computer games. Other media, such as the information highway, may enter the arena in the future. Easy access to phone-sex and computer bulletin boards are already an issue.

While the finding that aggressive models increase violent behavior in the observer holds true for all age groups, older viewers can more easily make distinctions between reality and fantasy, while the younger ones cannot. However, this developmental difference is modified by the frequency of TV viewing. Even young adolescents who are frequent viewers believe that TV depicts families the way they are in real life. And the conviction that TV depicts reality increases the potency of its influence. Younger children are emotionally aroused more easily and respond more directly (Hearold, 1986). For young children the connection between the entire story and the violent behavior is often only partially understood.

Gender differences exist in the selection and preference of programs and the frequency of watching violent shows. Turner et al. (1986) have found that sex differences exist in the influence of TV violence watching by contributing to a long-term increase in aggression in boys, but not in girls.

Preexisting aggressive tendencies seem to be a determining factor in how a child responds to TV violence. Josephson (1987) found that boys who already were highly aggressive tended to exhibit more aggressive behavior after they had viewed violent TV shows and been shown a cue (e.g., a walkie-talkie used by police before the violent action) that had been associated with the violence on the screen than did those who viewed violent content on TV but received no subsequent cue.

Violent programs have a tendency to trigger latent inclinations rather than teach aggressive behavior directly, according to Messaris (1986). However, this also tends to work the other way around, in that the children with more aggressive dispositions tend to select more frequently aggressive TV programs than their less aggressive counterparts (Huesmann, 1986; 1988). Children's aggressive predispositions may determine their viewing preferences (Zillman and Bryant, 1985). Adolescents who experience difficulties in their social relationships, especially with their peers, tend to turn to TV and become heavy watchers. Viewing much violence on TV may also provide a model for later behavior when the individual faces personal frustration in real-life situations (Singer & Singer, 1984).

Singer and Singer (1983) found a connection between undesirable social behavior and the viewing of TV violence. Poor adjustment in school and heavy TV viewing and aggressive behavior are linked. They suggested that the following combination of variables increases a child's risk of problem behaviors: (a) home in which parents do not control the TV viewing, (b) heavy TV viewing during the preschool years, (c) heavy TV viewing of aggression and violence, (d) parents whose child rearing emphasizes physical discipline, and (e) parents who do not describe themselves as creative, curious, and imaginative might not suggest viable leisure time alternatives to TV watching, nor do they suggest alternative behaviors to the aggressive actions depicted in many TV shows.

The issue of the influence of TV violence on the aggressive behavior of children is not without some controversy. The National Broadcasting Company (Milavsky et al., 1982) has sponsored research that challenges the notion of a simple causal relationship between violent TV programs and actual violent behavior. However, even in the general social science literature, the relationship between watching violent shows and aggressive behavior is not unequivocally supported. Nevertheless, the most influential theoretical explanation of why repeated watching of TV violence might be a major contributing factor to adolescent aggressive behavior comes from Bandura's social cognitive theory. The crucial theoretical constructs are modeling, imitation, and the disinhibitory effect.

However, the same social learning theory principle (i.e., we learn by observing a model) can also be applied to imitating prosocial behavior, such as in *Mister Rogers' Neigh-*

borhood, and positive cognitive development, such as *Sesame Street*, especially if such shows are viewed with others (older children, adults, parents, teachers) who can later reinforce the ideas presented. Television does have great potential to model social skills, teach knowledge, and portray human diversity and reduce intergroup hostility.

AN EVALUATION OF
SOCIAL COGNITIVE THEORY

Social learning theory has been praised by some for its integrative contribution to a better understanding of learning and human development, but it also has been criticized by others for being descriptive rather than explanatory. Grusec (1992) feels that social learning and social cognitive theories have lost their central position today, as compared to the sixties and seventies, when they had their heydays. Frequently voiced evaluative aspects are:

1. Many of the major tenets and insights gained from social cognitive theory and research have been accepted into psychology in general and become an implicit part of psychological thinking. In other words, much of the information uncovered by social cognitive theory actually appeals to and agrees with common sense.

2. An illustration of such a common-sense insight is the explanation that stimuli are much more than just external realities, since stimuli can also be—especially since the addition of cognitive processes—internal operations or events, such as symbols, language, concepts, and thoughts that allow individuals to control their own behaviors and make decisions (Schiamberg, 1988). The self-regulatory capacity of the person certainly sets social learning theory apart from traditional behaviorism.

3. Family members, teachers, and other adults are recognized as making major contributions to human growth and development through modeling, explaining, reward, and punishment. That humans can and do learn from each other through the entire life span is the most significant feature of social learning theory, since it emphasizes the "social" dimension in human development. The contribution of social interactions in learning and in development were neglected or delegated to a secondary role in other developmental theories prior to the emergence of social learning theory (Schiamberg, 1988; Phares, 1994).

4. Cognitive social learning theory draws on concepts and insights derived from behavioristic, psychoanalytic, and more recently, cognitive theory—theoretical positions that, generally speaking, have been considered in opposition toward one another. Thus, social learning theory attempts to utilize the more successful and researchable constructs of other theories and recombines them into a complementary rather than oppositional system. In other words, through this cross-fertilization and utilization of diverse elements from the whole spectrum of psychology, social cognitive psychology might be considered more eclectic than the traditional theories.

5. Social learning theorists have not yet adequately explained in sufficient detail the cognitive processes (e.g., memory, thinking, evaluating) which, they maintain, are essential for learning. Since these factors seem to depend on situational factors, the

organism's push toward growth by maturational forces does not receive sufficient recognition.

6. Social learning theorists eschew the use of development stages and do not focus on the influence of age-related changes on behavior. Instead, they insist on the idea that development is continuous and that there are no major qualitative changes during development, only quantitative ones. Even though specific developmental issues and developmental changes are a neglected part of the theory, social learning theorists do acknowledge the necessity for more advanced cognitive and psychological processes that are dependent on the age or the development of the child. One never really finds out how experiences, maturation, and age interact and affect development. Bandura (1981, 1982, 1986, 1989b) insists on the importance of cognitive processes, and in his revised theory, he asserts that cognitive function is a major determinant of learning. But there are no stages of development to explain the differences among the attempts to communicate of a 3-month-old, a 3-year-old, and a 13-year-old.

7. In the model of causation, called "Triadic Reciprocal Determinism," biology is recognized as one of the three causal factors. However, biology is combined with "cognitive and other internal events," thus revealing its subordinate role in the theory, even though it is considered a strong force in much of contemporary developmental thinking. Physical changes and physical appearance are not important developmental issues in their own right; however, they are highly significant factors insofar as physical changes and appearance induce changes in social attitudes, social expectations, and social demands made by others in the environment.

8. To these criticisms one might add that social learning theory has not been particularly systematic or comprehensive, and the theoretical focus has been more on the social factors of the learning process than on human development. Phares (1994: 438) maintains that it does not provide "a well integrated set of concepts" that identify specific reasons for choices people make. Social cognitive theory has stimulated empirical investigations yielding findings that had major impacts on public policy and social consideration that go beyond strictly theoretical considerations: (a) aggression—especially the effect of TV on aggressive behavior, (b) sex-typed or gender role development, (c) the processes of imitation and identification, (d) peer social competences, (e) childrearing, (f) education, (g) behavior modification, (h) therapeutic intervention based on modeling and guided participation, (i) self-efficacy, a powerful way to reduce anxiety, fear, defensiveness, and neurotic behavior. Hence, the unsystematic and open-ended qualities of the theory that make summarizing it so difficult have given it vitality and flexibility.

9. When analyzing the influence of a set of social relationships there are always a great many situational and contextual factors that need to be taken into consideration and that make it fairly difficult to advance theoretical predictions. For example, the theory does not predict—although research studies have thrown some light on the issue—why some adolescents are likely to become aggressive after watching violent TV shows, while others do not. Or, why some adolescents so quickly and easily yield to peer pressure, while others do not. To say that such out-

comes depend on contextual or situational factors are commonplace statements, which do not even suggest identifiable variables.

However, within social learning theory, there is diversity rather than unanimity in point of view, both in emphasis and in some rather basic conceptualizations. Even though Sears had an influence on Bandura, and both men were at Stanford University at the same time, their social learning theories have moved in different directions. Some theorists tend to be closer to S–R (stimulus-response) explanations, whereas others are more oriented toward psychoanalytic constructs, and still others increasingly identify with cognitive theory. This cross-fertilization and open-mindedness to the ideas of other systems has given social learning theory its vitality. Common to all appear to be the application of behavioristic constructs to basic social and developmental problems and a belief that environmental, situational, and social, rather than biological and maturational, factors are primarily responsible for learning and development. Social learning theorists emphasize that the rewarding of imitative responses is the psychological explanation of the socialization process.

EDUCATIONAL IMPLICATIONS

Social learning theory's basic assumption is that children and adolescents learn most complex skills more effectively by imitating the behavior of their parents, teachers, and peers rather than by reinforcement, trial and error, and in certain situations, even better than by verbal instruction. Verbal instructions and verbal cues, if they represent the modeling behavior symbolically, can facilitate the learning process, at least for behavior already in the subject's response repertoire. An often neglected aspect of the role of the teacher is the effective model role, demonstrating correct response patterns to be imitated. Only secondarily is the teacher a good reinforcer who uses reinforcement to shape and maintain already learned response repertoires. A teacher serves the model function, and some pupils will imitate this behavior regardless of whether or not the teacher consciously chooses them to do so. Teachers cannot limit their influence on students to academic instruction only, but must be aware that some pupils will be influenced by their personal habits, values, and other nonacademic activities. Studies have shown that the effects of instruction and modeling on the altruistic behavior of preadolescent children is indeed effective. However, in eliciting altruistic responses in students, what the teacher actually did was more important than what the teacher said. Apparently, altruistic behavior can be elicited more effectively by modeling than by verbal instruction. Bandura and McDonald (1963) demonstrated that modeling procedures, especially when both the model and the observer are reinforced, are very powerful in changing preadolescents' moral judgments. Live and symbolic models have been found to have a significant influence on the learning of self-control (Bandura & Mischel, 1965).

In addition to the influence teachers exert through the cognitive, instructional academic curriculum that relates to subject matter and teaching methods, teachers have an indirect but potent influence in shaping values and attitudes of children and adolescents. Teachers can indirectly encourage altruism, moral values, social conscience, and human decency by exhibiting these virtues themselves. Even though adolescents as a group may reject teachers in general as identification models, it is not at all uncommon for an individual student to feel respect, admiration, infatuation, and adoration of an individual teacher. Furthermore, an adolescent may imitate the behavior of a teacher, even though a more general identification with the teacher as a person is lacking. Consequently, it is important to consider the conditions contributing to the imitation-identification process. First, the behavior to be imitated must be within the subject's perceptual and motor capacity. Furthermore, studies have shown that the identification process is facilitated if the model is warm, friendly, and supportive rather than cold and rejecting. However, each of the factors that generally contributes to imitation and learning must be evaluated in relationship to other factors and the overall context. For example, an overindulgent teacher or parent, providing too much warmth and giving the child too much nurturance, may inhibit rather than facilitate the learning or behavior that demands effort, autonomy, and self-denial.

Learning is more likely to occur if imitative or matching responses are directly rewarded, so that modeling and reinforcement jointly contribute to the acquisition of response patterns. Imitation, or matching of responses, can be further enhanced by vicarious reinforcement—that is, if the model who is being observed is also being rewarded.

Social power and the control of rewards are other variables that influence imitation. These factors are of importance in the school situation where teachers who have social power control the rewards. In an experiment, Bandura, Ross, and Ross (1963a) utilized an adult model who controlled the distribution of highly attractive toys. A second adult model received some of these toys, as did the children who served as subjects. Consequently, the children might have viewed the second model as a rival. Bandura observed that the children were much more likely to imitate the behavior of the first model who had the control over the toys than the behavior of the second model who was the recipient of toys. Related to the findings of this study is the common observation that the higher-status model is much more likely to be imitated than the lower-status model. President Kennedy contributed to the popularity of rocking chairs and President Reagan to that of jelly beans.

It appears crucial that adolescents have teachers with whom they can and want to identify. Since much learning occurs inadvertently due to the fact that the teacher serves as a socializing agent, it becomes more important that teachers are selected in the light of their qualities as models for youths and their potential for positive identification. The demand of some that black students be taught by black teachers—since black children tend to identify better with black teachers—seems to receive some implicit support from social learning theory. Bandura (1962) has also pointed out that the sex of the model and the sex of the subject can influence the imitation of behavior. The power of imitating a model is so great that children will imitate sex-stereotypical play behavior of a same-sex model. Boys watching a male model play with a toy stove increase their stove-playing behavior when the model is gone, just as girls increase their truck-playing behavior after having observed a female model play with the truck (Wolf, 1973).

Social learning theory provides an explanation of why school integration works and produces results—although often only modest ones—that are more effective than other compensatory reforms. When children move into academic settings in which peer models value learning, take school seriously, and aspire to academic success, their own attitudes and behavior will change to the extent that they accept and imitate the academic striving of their new peers.

C H A P T E R

15

URIE BRONFENBRENNER'S ECOLOGICAL PERSPECTIVE OF HUMAN DEVELOPMENT

Urie Bronfenbrenner (1917-   ) has advanced a basically new theoretical position: *An Ecological Theory of Human Development*. Through his seminal theoretical works, "Toward an Experimental Ecology of Human Development" (1977), *The Ecology of Human Development* (1979), "Ecological Systems Theory" (1989), "The Ecology of Cognitive Development: Research Models and Fugitive Findings" (1993), he has essentially changed the agenda of developmental psychology. Though his ecological approach encompasses the entire life span and though many of his illustrations come from the early childhood period, Bronfenbrenner's theory does have specific, significant implications for adolescent development. In addition, Bronfenbrenner's theory provides a more interesting perspective than most other theories of development on the nature of the interrelationship between theory and research. According to Bronfenbrenner, the decisions that determine the nature of a research design and the selection of specific methodology indicate fundamental theoretical assumptions. Moreover, Bronfenbrenner's analysis of developmental research models deserves consideration here, since these models are integral to his theory.

BRONFENBRENNER'S ECOLOGICAL MODEL

Ecology investigates the complex system of interlaced and interdependent relationships between the biological organism and the social/physical setting which forms the organism. The idea of interaction between the organism and the external world becomes the cornerstone of ecological theory and contains its explanatory power. Darwin's story of the relationship between the cats and clover provides an interesting illustration.

Apparently, humblebees alone can fertilize red clover, because no other bee can reach the nectar in that variety:

Urie Bronfenbrenner (1917-   )

The inference is that if the humblebees became extinct or very rare in England . . . red clover would become very rare, or wholly disappear. However, the number of humblebees in any district depends in a great measure on the number of field mice, which destroy their combs and nests. It is estimated that more than two-thirds of them are thus destroyed all over England. Near villages and small towns the nests of humblebees are more numerous than elsewhere and this is attributed to the number of cats that destroy the mice. Thus next year's crop of purple clover in certain parts of England depends on the number of humblebees in the district, the number of humblebees depends upon the number of field mice, the number of field mice upon the number and enterprise of the cats (Park, 1936: 2).

To this ecological chain, probably with tongue in cheek, someone has added that the number of cats depends on the number of people who keep cats.

This amusing story may serve to set the stage for Bronfenbrenner's (1977, 1979, 1989) ecological theory of human development. Like biological changes, social interactions always exist as part of the larger ecological system in which they occur. For each individual, a continuously interacting set of complex social relationships exists; these cannot be reduced to simple one-to-one relationships. Past attempts to provide a unifying concept to identify and analyze the simultaneously operating multiplicity of sociocultural and environmental factors and their relationships to the growing person have not been very successful. Bronfenbrenner's model makes this explicit: "Development never takes place in a vacuum, it is always embedded and expressed through behavior in a particular environment" (1979: 27).

To make the simultaneous multiplicity of variables obvious, Bronfenbrenner rejects the traditional laboratory research approach as inadequate. He maintains that a study of the ecological field must supplement the limited laboratory approach so that all variables can be conceptualized—and, hopefully, in the future—investigated. The traditional, well-controlled research methodology in which an experimenter (E) manipulates and measures the changes in the subjects' (S) behavior under various prescribed conditions led to Bronfenbrenner's observation that "much of contemporary developmental psychology is the science of the strange behavior of children in strange situations with strange adults for the briefest possible periods of time" (1977: 513). The fact that (S) might influence (E) often receives no consideration, and the relationship of (S) to parents, siblings, friends, teachers, and neighbors, or other more encompassing ecological systems is usually not part of the research design. Yet, not only may these factors be relevant, they may actually be the more significant variables influencing the outcome of the research. As various people exert influences on an individual, different ecological systems remain in continuous and complex interactions. These interactions may be a more important process than S's measurable responses to specific predetermined stimuli provided in a laboratory. For example, evidence (Sroufe, 1970, and Tulkin, 1972) indicates that lower-class families may experience considerably more anxiety in a laboratory setting than do middle-class families. As a result, the so-called objective, scientific, and controlled setting of the laboratory may produce social class differences in the quality of the father-infant interaction that are not at all representative of the father-infant interaction in the home. Because the laboratory setting is an ecological system with its own properties, results/behaviors will necessarily differ in significant ways from those observed in the home.

To understand human development, Bronfenbrenner argues, we need to go beyond directly observable or measurable behaviors involving one or two people in a laboratory setting. We must expand our perspective beyond any single setting to the "examination of multiperson systems of interaction," taking "into account aspects of the environment beyond the immediate situation containing the subject" (Bronfenbrenner, 1977: 514). Development results from the continuous changes over time in the way that a person matures and perceives and interacts with the immediate environment. The question then becomes, how children and adolescents adjust to an ever-changing interrelated social and cultural environment. To incorporate these interacting and interrelated factors into a coherent developmental theory, Bronfenbrenner (1977) developed his "ecological model."

An ecological approach takes into account both the interrelationship of the growing organisms and the ever-changing social and physical environment. Of the environmental influential factors, the immediate environment (also referred to as "proximal processes," to be discussed later in more detail), has recently received considerable attention in Bronfenbrenner's theory (1993). The ecological model conceptualizes the influences as simultaneous and reciprocal from the outset. Because the model goes far beyond present parameters, it demands new perspectives and generates new hypotheses. This model pushes developmental research from the clearly defined, easily controllable, but somewhat sterile and static research laboratory to the study of development in real-life settings. Bronfenbrenner defines the ecology of human development as "the scientific study of the progressive, mutual accommodation, *throughout the life course*, between an active, growing human being, and the changing properties of the immediate settings in which the developing person lives, as this process is affected by the relations between these settings, and by the larger context, in which the settings are embedded" (1989: 188). Thus, Bronfenbrenner elevates the idea of a continuous interaction between the growing human organism and the changing social and physical environment as the cornerstone concept of his theory: "In ecological research, the principal main effects are likely to be interactions" (1977: 518).

"UPON THE SHOULDERS OF GIANTS"— WHO INFLUENCED BRONFENBRENNER?

Although Bronfenbrenner's ecological model is new in many of its major conceptualizations, this pioneer has readily and generously recognized the influence of other writers on his thinking. He himself humbly uses the metaphor, "we stand on the shoulders of giants, and mistake the broadened vision for our own." The fact that the biological organism is always adapting to and interacting with environmental conditions provided the cornerstone of Darwin's theory of evolution (Chapter 1), which introduced the concept of ecology into biology.

Other historical "giants" who have been influential in the formation of Bronfenbrenner's theory are Lev Vygotsky, with his social historical evolution of the mind theory, George Herbert Mead with symbolic interactionism, and Jean Piaget with his theory of cognitive development. In addition, because they have provided significant theoretical ideas, the works of Sigmund Freud and Edward Tolman deserve mentioning. Thus, Bronfenbrenner's theory owes a debt to diverse disciplines.

However, the single theory that pervades much of Bronfenbrenner's thinking is Kurt Lewin's Field Theory (1931, 1935, 1936, 1946, 1951). Lewin's classical behavior formula (see Chapter 7) provides the initial paradigm upon which Bronfenbrenner built his theory. Lewin highlighted the interplay between person and environment. His behavioral formula captures the nature of the organism-environment interaction on the growing individual, which becomes the connecting link to Bronfenbrenner's theory. According to this formula, Behavior (B) is a joint function (f) of the person (P) and the environment (E). In short: $B = f(PE)$. This field theoretical formulation depends upon the important assumption that the relationship between person and environment is interactive. Not only does the environment influence the person, but the person also affects and modifies the environment.

Bronfenbrenner systematically elaborates the idea of the interaction between the person and the environment and makes it the core concept of his theory. Because Bronfenbrenner is concerned with behavior changes as a function of growth and development, he substitutes (D) development for (B) behavior and maintains that conceptually, "behavior" and "development" differ substantially. Thus, according to the revised formula, "development" is a joint function of person and environment: $D = f(PE)$.

This modification of Lewin's equation is significant since Lewin's "behavior" implies a static concept in which only present field forces matter, not the passage of time. In that sense Lewin took an ahistorical position. "Development" (D) introduces the dimension of time into the equation and incorporates the kinds of changes that characterize development over extended periods. For Bronfenbrenner, development is "the phenomenon of constancy and change in the characteristics of the person over the life course" (1989: 190). However, the introduction of (D) into the formula does not refer to the phenomenon of just individual development per se, but to the interaction of the growing organism with the changing physical/social environment and the resulting developmental outcome at a particular point in time.

An important distinction needs to be made in regard to the use of the concept of time in ecological theory/research. Research in the past has viewed time primarily as manifesting itself in the fact, that with the passage of time the individual develops, changes, and functions more effectively. In that sense, time is synonymous with increase in chronological age. The ecological model would emphasize the influence of time not only on the changes in the surrounding physical environment (home, car, TV, computer, etc.) but in the social environment as well (parents, siblings, peers, etc.).

Adding time requires an additional modification of the formula: $Dt = f(t-p)(PE)(t-p)$. The symbols added to the formula are "t," the time at which a developmental outcome is being observed, and (p), the period during which person and environment are influencing the outcome. With this modified equation, the general theoretical paradigm to study human development in context is defined. Expressed as a sentence, the formula becomes: "The characteristics of the person at a given time in his or her life are a joint function of the characteristics of the person and of the environment over the course of that person's life up to that time" (Bronfenbrenner, 1989: 190).

In this quote, the phrase "the characteristics of the person" appears twice, which implies that the "developmental outcomes of today, shape the developmental outcomes of tomorrow" (Bronfenbrenner 1989: 191). Specific environmental factors may contribute to different developmental patterns, outcomes that depend not only on the environment but also on the characteristics of the person living in that environment. In other words, not only does the ecological context influence the person, but the person also influences the ecological field. These influences are simultaneous and mutual.

FROM LEWIN TO BRONFENBRENNER: RESEARCH MODELS IN THE DEVELOPMENTAL SCIENCES

Lewin (1931) had already distinguished between two basically different kinds of research paradigms, and thus had provided a conceptual frame of reference to classify research approaches. Both Lewin and Bronfenbrenner differentiated the Aristotelian or classtheoretical model from which processes are missing as contrasted with the Galilean or field-theoretical model. Both men attempted to advance science by advocating the latter, which contributed to identifying the processes underlying developmental phenomena.

■ Aristotelian or Class-Theoretical Models

In the *Aristotelian* or *class-theoretical model*, phenomena are "explained" primarily by the specific categories or classes to which they belong. The class-theoretical categories are primarily static concepts. Aristotle's four fundamental elements (earth, air, fire, and water) provide an illustration. Bronfenbrenner maintains that class-theoretical research designs are easier to conceptualize and to execute than ecological process-oriented research. Class-theoretical research designs contribute greatly to the exploration of unfamiliar terrain; they are more popular and, historically speaking, come earlier than ecological research designs. Under this model, the most common developmental research design focuses on two or more specific, clearly defined environmental categories (the independent variables) and measures different developmental outcomes (dependent variables). For example, the effect or the outcome of living in different socioeconomic classes has been studied for well over a hundred years using the class-theoretical model. In terms of the behavior formula, the (E) environmental variables are defined (such as family structure, SES, race, gender, or educational level), but the developmental outcome is explained simply as a product of the environmental factors. The processes underlying the outcomes are not even considered, or if considered, left to speculation.

The Social Address Model (E Is Focus of Research)

Bronfenbrenner identifies the type of research design when the environment (E) is the focus of the research as the *Social Address Model*. Social address research investigates the developmental outcome as a result of living in different environments. Commonly researched social address categories or environmental variables are:

> social class
> family size
> birth order (ordinal position)
> rural or urban setting
> male or female sex
> nationality or ethnic groups
> religious affiliations, etc.

In addition to these traditional social address categories, Bronfenbrenner also identifies the "new demographic social addresses," such as:

> one- or two-parent family
> mother's and father's employment status
> number of times parents remarried
> types of school attended (public, private, parochial), etc.

Much of the research, both past and current, reports information about how children who live in different environments (E) with different "social addresses" differ from one another. However, by themselves, these social address categories have no special explanatory power since they do not consider the underlying mechanisms or processes. Bronfenbrenner is skeptical of the continued value of such research findings because of their major limitations: "One looks only at the *social address*—that is, the environmental label—with no attention to what the environment is like, what people are living there, what they are doing, or how the activities taking place could affect the child" (Bronfenbrenner & Crouter, 1983: 382-383). Thus, although social address model findings do offer a starting point, they are— from an ecological perspective point of view—only suggestive because they do not investigate the underlying mechanisms or processes responsible for social address label differences. Social address research makes the major omission of neglecting to ask or to identify what specific processes in the environments account for the findings.

The Personal Attribute Model (P Is Focus of Research)

Another basically class-theoretical or Aristotelian research design focuses exclusively on the person (P) instead of the environment (E). Bronfenbrenner refers to this model as the *Personal Attribute Model* or, more recently, as the *personal stimulus characteristics*. In this model, development becomes a function of certain attributes that a person had at an earlier age; the question then becomes how these past attributes relate to his or her current characteristics. Except for the rather numerous studies that have investigated the constancy of IQ over time, or of certain other "traits" over time, this type of research design is less common than the social address research type.

The Person-Context Model (Finding Ecological Niche)

Bronfenbrenner expanded these models and combined the social address and the personal attribute models. What emerges from this combination is the *Person-Context Model*, which takes into account both the social address or the social environmental context as well as the characteristics of the person. The person-context model refines the specificity of research findings and helps in identifying what Bronfenbrenner refers to as "ecological niches," but it still remains only class-theoretical. Ecological niches are more narrowly defined regions in the environment that depend upon the intersection of two or more social addresses and two or more personal attributes that may have favorable or unfavorable influences on the development of the individual. A powerful illustration of the ecological niche is the research that predicts the likelihood of a mother giving birth to a low-birth-weight baby (less than 2,500 gr). Data exist that indicate that the probability increases if the mother (a) lives in the inner city, (b) is unmarried, and (c) has less than a high school education (three social address factors). The predictive power increases substantially by including information about personal attributes. Knowing that the woman is (d) still a teenager doubles the probability and knowing that she is (e) African-American doubles the probability once more (two personal attribute factors). Combining these five factors identifies the ecological niche which indicates a high probability that a woman will deliver a low-birth-weight baby.

However interesting and relevant these pieces of information may be, they do not answer the more fundamental question: "What are the processes or the mechanisms that actually influence the low-birth-weight outcome?" More specifically, if one had two women defined by all of the same variables identified above, and one gives birth to a normal-birth-weight baby, the other to a low-birth-weight baby, what are the distinguishing features? To find an answer to this process-question leads into the field-theoretical or ecological model of research.

■ Galilean or Field-Theoretical Models

Lewin referred to the *Galilean* or *the field-theoretical approach,* which Bronfenbrenner advocates and which constitutes the basis for his ecological theory. The field-theoretical model supercedes physical and static variables, delves into psychological functions, and focuses on the mechanism or the process through which changes in development occur. Such an approach provides more valid information for intervention, education, therapy, and public policy.

Bronfenbrenner (1988) reports that some process-oriented data do exist for the illustration of mothers giving birth to low-birth-weight babies. They are:

1. The earlier the mother receives prenatal care, the lower the probability of her delivering a low-birth-weight baby.
2. Mothers who never receive prenatal care have the highest frequency of premature babies. Thus, in predicting the birth weight of babies, the timing and the quality of prenatal care available to the mother suggest some of the crucial process variables as opposed to the more static variables that identify the mother's age, ethnicity, marital status, education, and place of residence. These process variables are easier to modify than the personal address variables, a fact important in terms of intervention. Other relevant process-oriented factors may still be unknown.

The Process-Person-Context Model

Congruent with Lewin's field theoretical approach, Bronfenbrenner proposes a *Process-Person-Context Model* where developmental outcomes are a function of both the environment (E) and the person (P). Bronfenbrenner thus takes into account all of the elements of Lewin's behavior equation [Behavior = f(P, E)], but transformed and modified it into a truly ecological model. Such a research design requires the observation and experience of at least two groups of people, in at least two environmental settings, and during at least two points in time (Clarke-Stewart, 1985: 46). Ecological psychology goes beyond the description, classification, and investigation of environmental variables. It focuses instead on the mutual interdependence between person and environment and on the relevant interaction effects and their consequences. The model differentiates the power of proximal processes by identifying personal characteristics (e.g., mental ability, school achievement) and context variables (parental monitoring, family structure, or SES). Thus, the design itself makes clear what the significant processes are, and as a result, the process now becomes the more important variable. Variations in the developmental processes are conceptualized "as a joint, synergistic function of the characteristics of the person and the environment" (Bronfenbrenner, 1993: 20).

The relationship between low-birth-weight babies and their later psychological development may illustrate the process-person-context model. This phenomenon can be viewed both from the personal attribute model and the process-person-context model. General information based only on the personal attribute (i.e., "low-birth-weight baby") reveals that such a person is at considerable developmental risk in terms of physical growth, number and frequency of illnesses, intellectual development, ability to use intellectual potential, behavior problems, and later, school problems. These deleterious effects tend to be more common among males than females. However, in the ecologically based research model, the interaction between the birth weight and the quality of maternal care (defined as the relationship with the infant), family health practices, and general home and child care management receives consideration: "[T]he more effective the maternal care, the better the development of the young child, particularly for low-birth-weight children. In other words, where the mother is willing and able to make the effort, she can do much to reduce the developmental risk that this handicap entails" (Bronfenbrenner, 1989: 198).

The Chronosystem Research Model ("t" Is Important Research Variable)

The major elements of Bronfenbrenner's behavior formula, and especially the process-person-context model, require that the dimension of time, represented by the symbol "t," receives major attention. Much past and current research assesses the individual at a fixed point in time, or if conducted longitudinally, assumes that personal attributes and environmental setting remain unchanged. In other words, time used to be perceived as synonymous with changes in chronological age. In the ecological model, the constancy or change over time (of both E and P) is essential to assessing the nature of changes during the life course. To conceptualize the importance of time as a crucial variable in the developmental process, Bronfenbrenner introduces a research design that he refers to as *the Chronosystem Model*. Although time has generally been recognized as a factor in human development, and pretest/post-test research designs have been used for years, Bronfenbrenner's unique use of time as contributing to change emphasizes both the simultaneous effect of time on the (E) environment and the (P) person. Furthermore, he emphasizes the interacting nature of these changes, and it is the interacting nature of (E) and (P) that Lewin and more explicitly, Bronfenbrenner, have brought to our attention. Developmental changes often depend upon life events and life experiences: "These experiences may have their origins either in the external environment (e.g., birth of a sibling, entering school, divorce, winning the sweepstakes), or within the organism (e.g., puberty, severe illness)" (Bronfenbrenner, 1989: 201). Research has begun to look at the interacting nature of life events for a person and the changing environment as a result of time.

Chronosystem research might investigate the influence of the arrival of a new baby on the parents' interaction with each other or with the older children. By assessing the mother's interaction (with the older siblings) before, during, and after pregnancy, research suggests that the mother's interaction patterns change rather noticeably as a function of these pregnancy/child-bearing conditions.

The studies by Steinberg and Hill (1980) demonstrate how the advent of puberty not only changes the individual but the family's interaction and communication patterns as well. During puberty, both parents and adolescent sons explain themselves less and interrupt each other more than in the pre- or post-puberal periods. Similarly, divorce is a life-transition event that disrupts the interaction and communication patterns between mother/

father and child. Even after divorce, mother/father seldom regain the influence with their children that they had earlier. During and after divorce, the peer group tends to become more influential, frequently not in a beneficial manner. Such changes in the behavior of children of divorce may be a result of both of these processes in interaction and may depend on the age and the time period of the transition. Such developmental changes become obvious through chronosystem research, when the changes are assessed before, during, and after both environmental and/or person-related life events or experiences.

THE PHENOMENOLOGICAL BASIS OF BRONFENBRENNER'S THEORY

Like Charles Horton Cooley, George Herbert Mead, Harry Stack Sullivan, and Kurt Lewin, Bronfenbrenner takes a phenomenological approach to the study of human behavior and development. Phenomenologists maintain that meaning and significance arise in the interaction of the individual's subjective perception of what is objectively there. The way an object or an event is perceived does not depend solely on experience of the thing-in-itself, but is interpreted in the context in which it is seen. Human beings bring to any situation their own individual perceptions, interpretations, feelings, expectations, and intentions, all of which are significant shapers of their evaluation of the situations. Psychologically speaking, these person-generated "shapers" are the crucial variables.

As an illustration, consider a group of adolescents attending the same history class. Their evaluations of the teacher's presentation of the Civil War may differ substantially, depending on their perceptions, schemata, and expectations. To some, the unit is stimulating and challenging, inspiring them to go to the library to read independently or to request that their parents plan a family trip to a nearby Civil War battlefield. To others, although the lessons are interesting and entertaining, they are unrelated to their own life and needs and hence, inconsequential. Still others see the unit as boring and useless, something to be forgotten. Finally, there are those who view history as something to be endured, because it is a prerequisite for graduation. For all, the "objective reality" is the same, but the personal experience is very different indeed.

Phenomenology emphasizes that one's personal and therefore subjective interpretation of the experience—the individual's definition of the situation—is the crucial determinant of that person's reality and hence, of his or her behavior. Thomas and Thomas (1928: 572) emphasized the phenomenological view in their famous quote, which Bronfenbrenner refers to as approaching an "immutable law": "If men define situations as real, they are real in their consequences." What matters psychologically speaking are not the objective properties as defined by physical reality, but the significance attached to these properties by the individual in that environment. Human perception of reality is selective and evaluative. The factors in the environment that shape the behavior and development of the person are those that the individual in that setting endows with personal meaning. One of Bronfenbrenner's propositions captures the essence of the phenomenological argument: "A setting becomes ecologically valid for research on human behavior and development only when the following two conditions are met: the psychological and social meaning of the subject's experience in the setting is investigated and becomes known to the researcher, and the subjective meaning of the research situation corresponds to the environmental experience to which the investigator wishes to generalize" (1979: 125). Regardless of its status in the research model, the setting remains phenomenologically important for the individual.

BRONFENBRENNER'S FOUR ECOLOGICAL SYSTEMS

Lewin (1946) conceptualized the environment as a topological region with different territories that define the psychological field; however, Lewin's psychological field is vacant of any specific content. The content and the forces, which the researcher inserts only on an individual basis, differ for each case. Bronfenbrenner addresses this omission by defining different ecological environments more precisely. He conceptualizes the so-called environment by identifying four major ecological-environmental levels or systems that constitute a model of nested interdependent, dynamic structures. The conceptual labels applied to these nested structures are: *the microsystem, the mesosystem, the exosystem*, and *the macrosystem*. They range from the proximal process, such as mother-child interaction in the family setting, to the more distal influences comprising broader social context categories, such as law, government, and culture (Bronfenbrenner, 1993). Each is contained in the other from the more immediate to the more remote, like a set of Russian dolls that fit into each other. The nature of these structural systems is interactive; their influence operates in a reciprocal pattern. The relationship and the impact of each of these structures change as a function of development. The infant is aware only of his or her immediate environment, the microsystem. For the adolescent who has mastered formal operations and who can reason beyond direct, personal experiences and think in terms of "principles" and "ideals," the exosystem and the macrosystem becomes increasingly important.

■ The Microsystem

Bronfenbrenner insisted that the microsystem be viewed as the intimate social and immediate physical environmental setting; therefore, at times, he also refers to it as the "proximal level of environment," and the intimate, interpersonal interaction patterns within the microsystem as "proximal processes." According to Bronfenbrenner, "a microsystem is a pattern of activities, roles, and interpersonal relations experienced by the developing person in a given face-to-face setting with particular physical, social, and symbolic features that invite, permit, or inhibit, engagement in sustained, progressively more complex interaction with, and activity in, the immediate environment" (Bronfenbrenner, 1993: 15). Illustrations of specific microsystem settings include: first, the home and family, later, the playground, the school, the peer group, summer camp, and church. For many adolescents in societies other than the United States—U.S. adolescents stay in school longer—the workplace also emerges as an important microsystem. More specifically, the microsystem of the adolescent consists of a familiar and often intimate social network of interpersonal relationships involving direct face-to-face interactions. These interactions in the immediate environment, especially if they occur fairly regularly and over an extended period, are referred to as "proximal processes." They take place with people who have a lasting relationship with the adolescent and who are influential in the adolescent's life. In turn, the adolescent influences those individuals in his or her microsystem.

For more adolescents, the family is the primary microsystem, followed closely by a group of friends and peers in schools, clubs, sport teams, and church (see Figure 15.1). Other microsystems could include the siblings (as part of the family), teachers and coaches (as part of the school), neighbors, as well as members of the church and other social groups (as part of the larger community) with whom the adolescent has enduring, meaningful, personal, social interactions (see Figure 15.1).

Microsystems are continually changing because of the aging process, not to mention changing life experiences that constantly affect people. However, from an ecological perspective, these changes should be conceptualized not only as the maturation and development of the adolescent being studied but also as significant transformations in the other people (parents, peers, teachers, etc.) with whom the adolescent interacts, as well as transformations of the specific settings that make up an adolescent's microsystem. Individuals may move in and out of important environmental and social settings; hence, certain microsystems may become more or less significant as the adolescent joins an athletic team or stops attending church. Moreover, the adolescent is also changing as a function of development and as a function of social and environmental interaction. Thus, the importance of parents may decline during puberty, while the importance of peers may increase. Still later, the importance of the peer group may decline as the importance of a romantic partner becomes all-pervasive.

As development progresses, the complexity of the multiple microsystems increases. The child's progression from a self-contained classroom in elementary school to a subject-

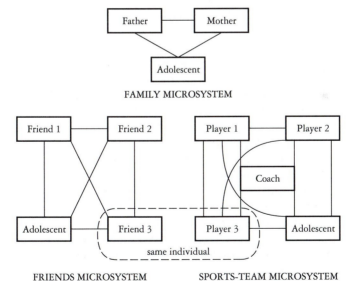

FAMILY MICROSYSTEM

FRIENDS MICROSYSTEM   SPORTS-TEAM MICROSYSTEM

FIGURE 15.1 The microsystem. An adolescent belongs to a number of different microsystems. Depicted are a family microsystem, a friends microsystem, and a sports-team microsystem. One person can play a role in more than one microsystem. For example, friend 3 is also player 3.

matter classroom organization in high school illustrates this phenomenon most convincingly. Figure 15.1 illustrates that an adolescent belongs to a number of different microsystems, although only three are depicted. Clearly, as the child matures, his or her selection of friends becomes based less on play activities and family interests and more on personal attributes. In general, the peer microsystem during adolescence becomes more differentiated (Brown, Lohr, & Trujillo, 1990) and influential, and provides powerful social rewards in terms of status, prestige, friendship, popularity, and acceptance. However, the peer system also can assert a powerful negative influence by encouraging or rewarding detrimental behavior such as cheating, stealing, smoking, using a gun, drinking, drug use, and irresponsible sex. Healthy microsystems are based on reciprocity, as when parents concur with the reasonable requests of their adolescents and the adolescents reciprocate by honoring the reasonable requests of their parents. When reciprocity breaks down, as in the parent-adolescent communication pattern, the quality of the microsystem declines. This results in an information-poor and exploration-inhibiting microsystem.

In contrast, if a microsystem is rich in information, it enhances learning and development by providing opportunities in which questions are asked and answered, exploration and experimentation encouraged, and guidance provided. When these positive proximal processes assert consistent, development-enhancing influences and are permanent, they will foster opportunities for success in later life.

■ The Mesosystem

Several microsystems in interaction constitute the mesosystem. A fundamental ecological assumption is that what happens in a person's microsystem is interrelated to and interacts with what happens in his or her other microsystems. The mesosystem is composed of a network of relationships between the various overlapping and interacting microsystems in a person's life: "A mesosystem comprises the linkages and processes taking place between two or more settings containing the developing person (e.g., the relationship between home and school, school and workplace, etc.). Special attention is focused on the synergistic effects created by the interaction of developmentally instigative or inhibitory features and processes present in each setting" (Bronfenbrenner, 1993: 22). Mesosystem interaction is the simultaneous multiple role participation of the adolescent as son or daughter and friend and student and band player, part-time worker, and camp counselor; it places each individual in each microsystem in the proper contextual perspective. Such a conceptualization accounts for the overlapping microsystem roles in their mesosystem interactions.

The idea of people playing different roles in different contexts—and changing roles as a function of time and as a function of moving from one context to another—is crucial to Bronfenbrenner's theory. This awareness of almost simultaneously playing different roles permeates his mesosystem concept. Clearly, people play different roles when they participate in various microsystems. Social roles are defined as behaviors and expectations associated with various interpersonal relationships and positions in society, such as son or daughter at home, friend in the peer group, student in school, athlete on the sport field, worker in the workplace, and romantic partner in intimate relationships. These social roles imply that another person is playing the complementary role of father or mother, teacher, coach, boss, and lover: "Roles have a magiclike power to alter how a person is treated, how she acts, what she does, and thereby even what she thinks and feels. The principle applies not only to the developing person, but to others in her world" (Bronfenbrenner, 1979: 6). Roles have a transformative effect on the developing adolescent as well as on all those with whom he or she interacts.

Bronfenbrenner (1974) observed that, during the second half of this century, when high school attendance became the norm, "age segregation" became more pronounced, and the peer group plays a more dominant role in the life of adolescents. The idea of "age segregation" implies that the linkages between microsystems that include adults and those that include peers have weakened, and concurrently adolescent problem behavior seems to have become more pronounced. Bronfenbrenner's applied work and his efforts to influence public policy to improve the lives of children have focused on the linkage (mesosystem) between several overlapping microsystems, especially the family, the school, and the parents' workplace. The richness or impoverishment of the mesosystem depends upon the number and the quality of such interrelating links and the values they do or do not share. For a typical 12-year-old, these connecting links may consist of several microsystems, such as family, school, friends, church, and camp. For an 18-year-old, the quality and the relative importance of these microsystems will have changed; new ones (such as a girlfriend or a boyfriend and their respective families) may have become important, while camp is no longer relevant (see Figure 15.2).

A mesosystem analysis examines the quality, the frequency, and the influence of such interactions as family experiences on school adjustment. If family and school share an effective, mutual communication system, and if parents are involved in school activities and decision making of their elementary school children, students receive higher grades and show greater initiative and independence, even later in adolescence when they enter high school. Surprisingly, the influence of the family/school interaction process was actually found to be greater than those of socioeconomic status and race (Epstein 1983a, 1983b).

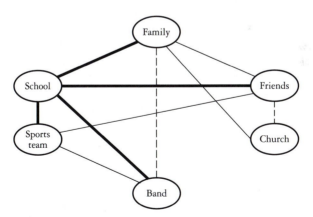

FIGURE 15.2 The mesosystem. The interacting microsystems constitute the mesosystem. Some microsystems may be more heavily interrelated with others (e.g., family-school, school-band, school-team, etc.), while others may only show limited interaction (e.g., friends-church, family-band, etc.). Finally, there may be relatively little interaction, as for example, between church and band or church and sports team.

Bronfenbrenner emphasizes that the effects of proximal processes can be and often are more powerful than those of the environmental context, especially in the more advantaged ecological niche (family with two biological parents and more than a high school education). Proximal process has an impact on an individual's need to conform to peer group pressures. The negative relationship between church attendance and early intimacy with the opposite sex constitutes another mesosystem illustration of the process-person context model. Like the microsystem, the mesosystem focuses on actual interpersonal relationships but emphasizes the linkage, or the mutual interrelationship, between different microsystems. Several microsystems that make up a mesosystem can operate in a congruent pattern to reinforce each other, or they may be quite divergent. For example, the values of parents and peers may harmonize or conflict with each other. School performance suffers if peers discourage school achievement and parents are nonsupportive in regard to their offspring's school work. Obviously, a congruent system of values exerts a more powerful and consistent influence and produces less stress than do conflicting systems of values.

An analysis of the relationships between a microsystem and mesosystem reveals three possibilities for problems and risks:

1. In an impoverished mesosystem, there are few or no meaningful linkages between existing microsystems. The life of the individual appears highly compartmentalized. Illustrations include parents who do not know their children's friends; the adolescent's personal friends who do not attend the same school; and the youth whose church attendance is isolated from friends, neighbors, and maybe even parents.

    Bronfenbrenner has repeatedly expressed concern that, as schools lose their neighborhood character as a result of relocation to the outskirts of town and grow larger and more impersonal, they become increasingly isolated from the home. These trends imply that teachers and parents are less likely to know each other as individuals. Some parents avoid contact with their son's or daughter's school and show no interest in the adolescent's schoolwork. In such cases, meaningful and significant mesosystem links become reduced and stripped of their potential for powerful positive contributions, not only to school learning and achievement, but to overall adjustment. Bronfenbrenner's pessimistic view finds strong expression in the claim that schools have become "one of the most potent breeding grounds of alienation in American society" (1979: 231). Among other factors, as this sense of alienation becomes more pervasive, it may contribute to a progressive decline in adolescents' achievement test scores and an increase in homicide, suicide, drug use, and delinquency. Ecological research that identifies these underlying processes of alienation and the deteriorating linkages of mesosystem interactions may point to the value of ecological research for public policy that Bronfenbrenner has repeatedly proposed.

2. A potential danger exists when different microsystems endorse divergent values. For example, the peer group may glamorize, encourage, and reward drinking, smoking, drug use, or early sexual behavior while parents and church may view these behaviors negatively and disapprove of or punish them.

    Kandel (1986) tested these theoretical propositions of divergent and convergent parent-peer value systems by assessing the power of parent influence versus peer influence on adolescent drug use. Kandel analyzed the drug use of the focal adolescent not only vis-a-vis marijuana use of his peers, but also vis-a-vis the use of alcohol and medically prescribed psychoactive drugs consumed by his parents. She found that the drug use of both friends and parents has an independent effect on the drug use of the focal adolescent. However, the drug use of peers appears to be a stronger influence than the alcohol use of parents. Kandel's findings can be summarized briefly and very convincingly: If both parents (alcohol) and peers (marijuana) use drugs, 70 percent of the focal adolescents smoke marijuana. If the friends smoke marijuana but the parents do not drink, 58 percent of the focal adolescents use marijuana. If the friends do not use any drugs but the parents drink, 22 percent of the focal adolescents smoke marijuana. Finally, if neither the friends nor the parents use drugs or alcohol, only 12 percent of the focal adolescents smoke marijuana. While the drug use of peers provides the more potent influence, the drinking behavior of the parents has a strong modifying effect on the use of marijuana by their adolescent offspring. The same pattern of relative influence of peers versus parents emerges when the crucial behavior of the focal adolescent is not marijuana use, but the drinking of hard liquor. The sequence described above remains the same, but with slightly modified percentages (61 percent, 52 percent, 39 percent, and 31 percent) (Kandel, 1986).

In a more general sense, parents may disapprove of the values, attitudes, and behaviors of the adolescent's friends and restrict opportunities to socialize with them. When basic values between different microsystems diverge, tensions develop in the mesosystem that can pull the individual's loyalties in different directions. Such clashes between values produce intrapersonal as well as interpersonal stress because the adolescent has to make choices between different sets of microsystem values or has "to pretend" to follow both or change his behaviors, attitudes, and values as he or she moves from one microsystem (home) to another (peer group).

3. Problems will arise if the mesosystem, which is composed of interlinking microsystems, endorses or mutually reinforces deviant or delinquent behavior that conflicts with the macrosystem, that is, with the community at large. As an illustration, consider a situation in which both parents and peers encourage cheating to succeed in school, or the selling of drugs to make money, or driving without a license. If the adolescent conforms to such antisocial pressures from peers and/or parents, conflicts result, for example, with teachers, the police, or the neighbors. To the extent that the adolescent yields to such pressures, he or she risks jeopardizing his or her place in the larger community, since the exosystem does not condone such behaviors.

■ The Exosystem

The structure of the larger community, especially its decision-making political and business bodies, provides numerous illustrations of what Bronfenbrenner refers to as *the exosystem*. The exosystem is the larger community setting in which the adolescent lives. Using the metaphor of the series of nesting Russian dolls, the exosystem constitutes a more *distal environmental influence*. Although the adolescent does not directly participate in exosystem decision making, these decisions do have a direct and sometimes an indirect (via the parents or the school) influence on the life of the adolescent. Events and decisions that take place outside the settings of which the person is a part may profoundly influence the individual's development: "The exosystem comprises the linkages and processes taking place between two or more settings, at least one of which does not contain the developing person, but in which events occur that indirectly influence processes within the immediate setting in which the developing person lives" (Bronfenbrenner 1993: 24). The three most significant developmental exosystem influences are: the relationship between one or both of the parents and their workplace, the parents' circle of friends, and neighborhood/community influences on family functions. Illustrations of other social settings and institutions that comprise part of an adolescent's exosystem include the relationship between the school and neighborhood groups, the mass media, the school board, the local government, the transportation system, churches, civic groups, industry, etc. (For a partial illustration, see Figure 15.3.)

The exosystem may impoverish or enrich the quality of the micro- and the mesosystem of an adolescent through exosystem decisions that affect what an adolescent can or cannot do. Thus, the parents' world of work and their work conditions—of which the adolescent is not a part—may have a profound impact on the conditions under which the adolescent lives. For example, the superiors in the parents' workplace determine where the parents work, when parents work, how much money they earn, how much vacation time they get, when they can take their vacations, and whether or not to allow flexible working hours. More significantly, employers may decide to move the father or the mother from the East Coast to a new position on the West Coast or to terminate employment altogether, decisions that may have a profound influence on the micro- and the mesosystem of the adolescent. As studies have repeatedly demonstrated, factors such as whether one or both parents work, the parents' working conditions, their roles in the workplace, their levels of responsibility, and participation in decision-making processes have a direct and profound influence on the parents' socialization efforts toward their offspring. Adolescents who were living in families where the work status of their parents had declined were, all things being equal, less competent in school and exhibited more disruptive behavior than their peers from stable families or those who had experienced a work status recovery (Flanagan & Eccles, 1993).

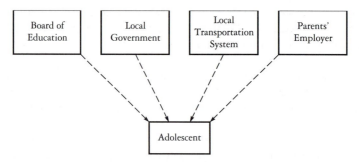

FIGURE 15.3 The exosystem. The board of education, local government, local transportation system, and parents' employer exemplify the exosystem. Some exosystem decisions affect the individual adolescent. However, these influences are primarily impersonal, indirect, and one-way. The exosystem decision maker usually does not know the individual adolescent, and vice versa.

The ecological systems approach goes beyond obvious and direct questions. For example, numerous studies have investigated how maternal employment affects children and adolescents. These studies have failed to identify meaningful, clear-cut, consistent findings. An ecological approach would look not only at the exosystem variables, but also at the relevant meso- and microsystem variables and how they interact. Some relevant questions include:

1. What is the nature of the mother's work, her attitude toward work, and her satisfaction or dissatisfaction with her work?
2. What is the father's attitude toward the mother's employment? Does the fact that the mother works change the way in which the father behaves toward the children?
3. Is the mother's motivation to attain employment based on strictly financial needs or do personal and career development needs play a role?
4. Is the effect of maternal employment the same for boys as for girls?
5. Is the effect of maternal employment dependent on the age of the children?
6. How does family constellation, for example, whether the child is the oldest or youngest, modify the effects of maternal employment?

Ecological research would analyze these variables in terms of behavior and developmental outcome in children.

Another illustration of an exosystem reaching right into the living room and asserting a substantial influence is TV programming, especially MTV, which is geared toward the preadolescent and adolescent population. We know more about the quantifiable aspects of TV watching than the developmental outcomes: before graduating from high school, the average child has watched 22,000 hours, about twice the time he or she will have spent in formal instruction in school. From what we know, TV influences occur on two distinctly different levels:

1. The content of the program and what it suggests. In an average evening, the viewer will witness 6-8 acts of violence and 2 murders. During a typical prime time program, the regular viewer in the course of a year will witness 9,230 instances of actual, suggested, or implied sexual intercourse or innuendos of it, usually outside of marriage. The question is whether and to what extent these entertainment models influence the behaviors of the young viewers. (See Chapter 14, pages 303–307.)
2. Nevertheless, the more serious effect of TV may be not in what it shows, but in what it inhibits. TV watching is known to change the interaction pattern between family members substantially. Since the attention is focused on the screen except during commercials, the family members' speech and actions are frozen. Thus, TV watching inhibits family leisure time activities characteristic of the past: conversations, games, reading, crafts, and even arguments, all of which are likely to enhance development. Consider the implications of the fact that 60 percent of viewers report no other activity while watching. Contemporary TV viewing patterns may well be one of the contributing factors to parents spending 40 percent less time in direct interaction with their children in 1990 than they did in 1965.

Child abuse and neglect studies suggest the significance of exosystem variables as a contributing factor. Inadequate housing, unemployment, and prolonged poverty are all exosystem factors that may be beyond the control of the parents but which, nonetheless, increase the probability of abuse and neglect. Preventive factors may also exist in the exosystem; for example, a functional kinship support network and church attendance tend to reduce the probability of abuse and neglect.

For most adolescents, a major exosystem variable is the educational system that sets school policy. The Board of Education decides what school adolescents will attend and what courses and extracurricular activities will be offered. In order to balance the budget, the Board might close the library, suspend the driver education program, reduce the art or music budget, or eliminate after-school activities, even though these opportunities may be very important to a majority of adolescents. Whether or not the local government opens or closes a youth center, or the neighborhood community association opens or closes the swimming pool will affect adolescents' available recreational resources. Adolescents in several of these examples can write a letter and complain about the actions taken, but in most instances, they are relatively powerless. Later, as they become older and participate in community affairs, they will have a direct voice. At that point, part of the previous exosystem would become their mesosystem. Obviously, adults need to question whether or not exosystem decisions are made with adolescents' best interests in mind. Unfortunately, budgetary or political considerations are often the more influential factors in making such decisions. Bronfenbrenner's theory encourages researchers to question: How do those exosystem decisions that influence the life of adolescents actually affect their development? Bronfenbrenner's maxim, "Where exosystem was, mesosystem shall be" implies that development is enhanced, if the adolescent actually enters into the exosystem wherever appropriate, becomes involved in community and political affairs, and begins to make his or her voice heard in exosystem decisions.

■ The Macrosystem

The macrosystem does not impinge directly on the life of the individual adolescent; however, it contains an overarching societal ground plan for the ecology of human development. It asserts very powerful, albeit indirect, influences: "The macrosystem consists of the overarching pattern of micro- meso- and exosystems characteristic of a given culture, subculture, or other extended social structure, with particular reference to the developmentally instigative belief systems, resources, hazards, lifestyles, opportunity structures, life course options and patterns of social interchange that are embedded in such overarching systems" (Bronfenbrenner, 1993: 25). The macrosystem includes a core of general cultural, political, social, legal, religious, economic, and educational values and most important, public policy. As such, a macrosystem may be thought of as a societal blueprint.

In general developmental research, the macrosystem is usually limited to identifying social address labels (such as social class, urban versus rural, ethnic groups) so commonly used in the traditional research design. Such research commonly involves two groups of children and/or parents from different backgrounds as defined by their social address labels. The findings focus primarily on differences in behaviors, values, attitudes, or child-rearing practices. While such data are useful, they are limited because they fail to assess the process responsible for the observed differences.

A study by Bronfenbrenner (1967), "Response to Pressure from Peers versus Adults among Soviet and American School Children," may serve to illustrate how macrosystems influence the nature of peer group conformity quite differently in different societies. The USSR, at the time of the research, embraced different macrosystem values than the United States. In the Soviet Union, where peer group and adult values seem to converge around a core of politically endorsed and socially accepted values, the adolescent experiences fewer cross-pressures between the expectations of the peers and the expectations of the important adults. In the United States, the divergence of peer group and adult values is more pronounced and the adolescent may feel pressured in different directions (see Figure 15.4).

When one refers to the Judeo-Christian culture, a socialistic country, Catholicism, capitalism, an industrial country, a constitutional democracy, the Protestant work ethic, a monarchy, etc., one is referring to concepts that have macrosystem qualities. Historical, social, technological, cultural, and subcultural forces (e.g., wars, treaties, elections, legislation) shape and modify the macrosystem. Macrosystem values, in turn, find expression in social customs and in what is considered fashionable. Journalists identify subtle macrosystem trends by writing entertaining articles about what is currently "in" and "out." The macrosystem suggests standards for physical attractiveness and defines appropriate and inappropriate behavior for each sex. The dispersion of medical knowledge can influence health practices by identifying which foods are healthy and which may have a detrimental effect on health, by increasing social and legislative restrictions on smoking, or by encouraging

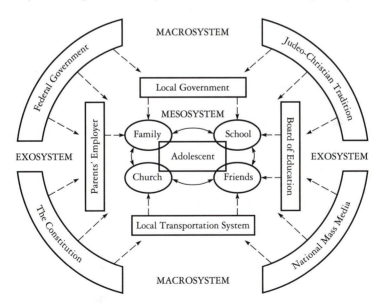

FIGURE 15.4 The macrosystem. The individual is part of several microsystems, and several microsystems form the mesosystem. Interactions at the mesosystem level are personal and direct. The mesosystem is embedded in the exosystem and the more general social cultural macrosystem; effects at this level are impersonal and often indirect.

the advertisement and the use of condoms to avoid AIDS and pregnancy. Macrosystem values can contribute to adolescent eating disorders such as anorexia and bulimia by equating thinness with beauty and sexual attractiveness (Muuss, 1990).

Through legal and economic measures, the macrosystem determines who actually is an adolescent and distinguishes between adolescence and adulthood. Although local customs and state legislatures (exosystems) may modify some of these criteria, short of a violent revolution or an invasion as a result of war, the macrosystem changes slowly. Nevertheless, industrialization, urbanization, democratization, tax reform, civil and equal rights legislation, women's increasing participation in the work force, and the women's liberation movement illustrate fundamental, though slow, changes in the macrosystem.

Seldom, except in anthropological research, are the developmental aspects of the macrosystem the primary purpose of research projects. Furthermore, only rarely do the interaction of the micro-, meso-, and exosystems as well as macrosystem changes and their impact on individual development become the primary object of research. However, the mutuality of these influences is crucial to the ecological model; a functional interdependence exists between the individual and the immediate social and physical environment and the more remote environmental systems. The most powerful illustration of the functional interdependence between individual and family, meso-, exo-, and macrosystems comes from Elder's (1974; Elder & Caspi, 1988) reanalysis of archival data, "Children of the Great Depression." This study has the added advantage of looking at two age cohorts of these "Depression children" and not only following them longitudinally through much of their adulthood, but also through three generations. Half of the families had experienced considerable loss of income (35 percent) as a result of the Depression while half had not experienced deprivation.

The purpose of the research was to study the developmental effects of the economic Depression (macrosystem) on children who lived, at least temporarily, in poverty. In addition, two longitudinal research studies were conducted in different settings, allowing the differential assessment of profound social/economic changes at two different age levels: those who were adolescents during the Depression (born in the early 1920s) and younger children born just before the Depression (born in the late 1920s). The data allow a comparative analysis of the impact of economic deprivation on these two age groups. Because the findings were quite different for both age groups, they highlight the importance of children's age in relationship to ecological variables. The findings support the basic hypothesis that the "Depression entailed more adverse and enduring developmental outcomes in the lives of men who encountered this event as young children than as adolescents" (Elder and Rockwell, 1978: 251).

Adolescents of families deprived by the effects of the Depression compared to nondeprived adolescents based on pre-Depression SES had no choice but to take on family responsibility, to work in the home, and to contribute to the subsistence of the family through outside jobs. However, they were likely to benefit from taking on adult responsibility early because they developed more self-reliance, independence, desire to control their futures, firmer vocational commitments, and ambition, and they became hard-working and responsible adults. They entered full-time employment earlier and married earlier than more privileged peers. The experience of the Depression seems to have motivated them to desire a grown-up status early and to enter the world of adult roles sooner.

However, the effects on the children who experienced the Depression at a preschool age tended to be more negative and showed almost the opposite pattern to that of the older group of adolescents. These children did less well in school, their work history was less successful, and some of them showed emotional and social difficulties later in life. The negative effects were more pronounced for boys than for girls. In contrast to the patterns for the two male groups, the effects on the girls were almost the reverse; the older girls in particular were at greater risk.

The detrimental effects were especially aggravated for a subgroup of families whose fathers (microsystem) were irritable and explosive, characteristics that increased marital discord noticeably after the father lost his job (exosystem). The result of the father's cranky and uncontrolled behavior had negative effects on the younger children that persisted into adulthood. When they became adults, they too tended to be more ill-tempered. Their own marital relationships and later, even their child-rearing practices showed these effects. Thus, the combined effect of the economic Depression and the father's ill-temperament had a negative impact not only on the life course of his children but on that of his grandchildren as well. In contrast, a more stable and happy home helped defuse the negative impact of economic hardships.

■ The Ecological Transition

Bronfenbrenner speaks of an "ecological transition" as a major change in which part or all of a system or a combination of systems undergoes some major transformation. Such ecological shifts occur naturally throughout the human life span. However, major transformations heighten sensitivity and anxiety and may enhance or impair development; hence, transition experiences do provide insight into the relationship between ecological changes and developmental processes. The most common transition experience involves modification of the mesosystem as old microsystems become defunct and as new ones emerge. Such "ecological transitions" involve shifts in role definition. Illustrations include the subject entering school; changing from elementary to junior high school or from private to public school; dropping out of school; graduating; forming new friendship groups or new romantic attachments; converting from one church affiliation to another; or moving to another part of the country. Not only are these ecological changes the consequences of developmental processes, but beyond that, they also become the instigating events of new developmental processes. Such changes can constitute real challenges for the individual since they require adjustment to a new mesosystem: "An ecological transition occurs whenever a person's position in the ecological environment is altered as a result of a change in role, setting, or both" (Bronfenbrenner 1979: 26).

Children of army officers, as well as those whose parents work in industries where they have to move frequently to other parts of the country, may experience a traumatic "ecological transition." The older, more traditional research has tried to identify the negative effects of such transitions on developing children. In contrast, ecological researchers have been more interested in differentiating the transition effects to see whether and what family processes may actually be responsible for the outcome. While some adolescents quickly adapt to and fit into a new mesosystem, others seem to suffer during the process, as well as afterward. The ecological model raises the question: What are the crucial processes that may make such a transition smooth or problematic? In the case of the frequently relocated Army officer, the overall well-being of the family microsystem seems to play a major role in determining whether such an ecological transition is smooth, difficult, or traumatic.

Parental divorce is another example of a major ecological transition. The literature abounds with evidence that divorce has detrimental effects on the children when compared to those from intact families. Generally speaking, this widely dispersed "social label research" finding seems true. However, ecological systems research looks at the effects of divorce not just in terms of the impact of the divorce itself—as if there were a simple, one-dimensional, uniform child development outcome of parental divorce—but in terms of the interrelationship with other microsystems. For example, when the ex-husband/ex-wife relationship after the divorce becomes part of the research design, current field theoretical research findings suggest that the detrimental effects are mitigated, if the ex-husband remains supportive of his ex-wife and maintains a caring and loving relationship with his children.

The ecological transition may also be the result of macrosystem adaptations or transformations. For example, after a landslide election victory, the newly elected President and the more powerful Congress may change the tax, welfare, educational, and health-care system in significant ways and thus, contribute to the reduction in unemployment and spending patterns, ultimately fostering a more optimistic economic outlook. On a more personal level, visiting another country, making friends with people of a different background, falling in love or marrying an individual from a different social class or a different ethnic background, all reflect different degrees of macrosystem transitions. The high school student who studies abroad for a year crosses major macrosystem borders and needs to adapt to such a transition. Emigrating from a third world country to a Western society is the ultimate macrosystem transition. Awareness of such different macrosystem patterns contributes to an appreciation of cultural diversity. Ecological transitions are "examples par excellence of the process of mutual accommodation between the organism and its surroundings" (Bronfenbrenner, 1979: 27), and constitute the essence of the ecology of human development.

HILL'S CONTEXT-BASED MODEL
OF ADOLESCENT DEVELOPMENT

The ecological perspective developed by Bronfenbrenner (1977, 1979, 1989) and applied to adolescence by Garbarino (1985) serves to set the stage by providing the background for an ecological model. The heuristic value of Bronfenbrenner's theory is already reflected in numerous research approaches and the further theory building by Jay Belsky, Richard Lerner, Nan Crouter, Larry Steinberg, and especially, John P. Hill. John P. Hill (1936-1988), a colleague and friend of Bronfenbrenner, built in his own way upon the ecological theory and advanced an applied model of adolescent development that can be used to organize much relevant information about the second decade of life. Hill's model (1980) conceptualized the interactive nature of (a) individual changes, (b) the microsystem contexts, and (c) developmental issues. Hill viewed his model as a framework for organizing our knowledge about this unique period of life. The goal of the model was "to make sense out of adolescence as a whole."

Hill identified three *primary changes* within the individual that mark the transition from childhood to adolescence:

1. The physical transformation of puberty results in dramatic changes in body size and shape, the appearance of secondary sex characteristics, and the growth in primary sex characteristics. These changes all require a readjustment of the body image and bring about an increase in sex drive.

2. Since these physical changes in the appearance of the body modify the way the individual views himself or herself and the way others see and evaluate him or her, changes in social expectations and social role definitions are inevitable. Peers may begin to evaluate the individual as a potential date or a sex partner, and parents and/or adolescents suddenly feel that kissing or cuddling at bedtime is inappropriate. The immense variation in onset, duration, and completion of puberty complicates social definitions.

3. Cognitive changes characterize the transition from childhood to adolescence. They include the emergence of thinking that can deal with more complex and more inclusive processes, processes that give full and systematic consideration to possibility and probability and that include the development of abstract reasoning ability.

All of these primary changes interact with the environment; they take place within the context of the adolescent's microsystem. A cluster of such microsystems constitutes the individual's mesosystem; the most common and the most representative are family, peer group, and school, although not mutually independent, they are interactive. The events at home or with peers influence the adolescent's performance in school, just as the successes or failures at school affect the adolescent's life at home and with peers.

The interaction between the primary changes and the microsystems (family, peer group, and school) has a major impact upon what Hill referred to as the *secondary changes*. Although in no way limited to adolescence, these secondary changes become major tasks for the developing individual in adolescence. Reminiscent of Robert Havighurst's *Developmental Tasks*, they are the crucial issues around which theories of adolescence have been developed. In addition, they are issues that have set much of the research agenda for that period of life. The secondary changes identified by Hill (1980) are:

1. Attachments change, thus transforming family relationships. Most adolescents go through some level of disengagement from their parents and struggle to maintain a precarious balance between attachment and disengagement. This is not always easy. Nevertheless, most normal adolescents preserve strong attachment to and respect for parents.

2. Autonomy is based on the ability to make independent decisions, to assume increasing responsibility, to become self reliant, and to extend self-initiated activities into an ever-increasing number of endeavors. Disengagement and autonomy are not synonymous; actually, those adolescents who are more independent report more positive relationships with their parents.

3. With puberty, sexuality emerges as a major issue requiring that affection for parents be modified. This involves a transformation of social roles, the establishment

of gender roles, the development of new attitudes toward the opposite sex, and the desire for sexual activities with others.

4. Intimacy necessitates the transformation of acquaintanceship into genuine friendship and includes mutual disclosure of personal experiences, feelings, and attitudes. Sexuality and intimacy are different experiences; in addition, they may have different meanings for males and females, because girls in the past appear to have been more socialized for caring and intimacy (Gilligan, 1982).

5. Identity requires a transformation in the definition of the self. It involves gender identity and requires an acceptance of one's past, one's uniqueness and one's current social relationship, solidarity with a group, and an orientation toward the future. It is based on accommodating the primary and secondary changes described here.

6. Achievement means focusing identity and ambition into the formation of educational, vocational, and personal goals and involves choices that now are becoming more realistic and future-oriented.

The more mature forms of intimacy may take their initial impetus from physical maturation, but they require either a new self-definition or new formal-operational interpersonal skills. These take place within an approving or disapproving family, a peer context, and often involve partners who were school acquaintances.

Hill represented this model through a three-dimensional cube ($3 \times 3 \times 6$), which identifies all of these categories, but does not visualize the interactive nature of primary changes with the context variables and with the secondary changes. The model below attempts to capture the interactive nature of these dimensions. Even though it may look confusing, this model does depict the concept of ecological interaction more precisely than Hill's cube (See Figure 15.5).

Hill, Steinberg, and Holmbeck have produced numerous empirical studies which have examined the impact of puberal and cognitive changes in the individual adolescent upon the parenting style and the parents' communication pattern within the family microsystem. Thus, puberty modifies not only family behavior patterns but also the secondary issues of autonomy, identity, and, achievement. Hill, Steinberg, and Holmbeck's findings suggest that, during puberty, parental behavior toward the offspring alters as a function of physiological changes. Steinberg (1993: 139) effectively summarizes the findings of these studies: "Family relationships change during puberty, with conflict between adolescents and their parents increasing—especially between adolescents and their mothers—and closeness between adolescents and their parents diminishing somewhat." Adolescents and their parents work toward forging a new relationship, one in which the balance of power will become more and more equal.

FROM ECOLOGICAL THEORY VIA
RESEARCH TO PUBLIC POLICY

Bronfenbrenner's ecological perspective implies a reaction against the more narrow scope of traditional laboratory research by advocating the inclusion of and the concentra-

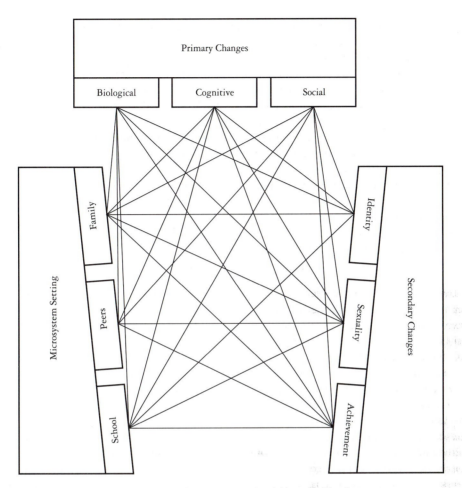

FIGURE 15.5 Hill's ecological model of changes in early adolescence. The three common microsystems (family, peers and school) interact with the primary developmental changes of early adolescence (identified here as biological, cognitive and social) and both contribute to secondary changes in such areas as identity, sexuality, and achievement as well as others not depicted here.

tion on the ecological field (Bronfenbrenner, 1977). Due to its remarkable impact, over the last two decades the ecological perspective has changed the developmental research agenda from the limited concern with the influence of one variable (A) on another variable (B), to a concern with the interaction of these variables, the possibility that (B) may also influence (A), and the more explicit ecological concern with the probability that other factors [beside (A) and (B)] in the field may influence the child. In addition, as both (A) and (B) change over time, the developmental outcome may also change. Bronfenbrenner emphasizes that children can and do change their environment (as does Bandura and other contextual theorists). "Species *Homo Sapiens* appears to be unique in its capacity to adapt, to tolerate, and especially to create the conditions in which it lives and grows" (Bronfenbrenner, 1994:

1647). A happy, friendly, helpful, and cooperative adolescent creates a positive and supportive attitude in others and thus contributes to the making of his or her own social environment. Instead of focusing on the association between two variables, the ecological theory focuses on the interaction effects of numerous variables: biological, psychological, social, cultural, and economic conditions. A different way of viewing these interaction effects is by considering how the micro-, the meso-, the exo-, and the macrosystems interact. Thus, ecological theory brings to full awareness that what happens to an individual in his or her family (microsystem) can only be understood by the relationship of the family to school, the church, the neighborhood (mesosystem), the parents' work setting (exosystem), and society at large (macrosystem). As ecological, process-oriented research data bring to awareness the interacting nature of variables, the complexity of developmental implications for educational practice and child and family policy come to the foreground. For Bronfenbrenner the importance of ecological theory is that it advances developmental knowledge from strictly conceptual constructs to operational models, models that simultaneously stimulate the nature of ecological research design, but beyond that, reveal the implications of such findings for education and public policy (Bronfenbrenner, personal correspondence). It is Bronfenbrenner's goal to live up to Lewin's dictum: "There is nothing as practical as a good theory." Ecological models shun simple solutions to major social issues, such as sex education as the answer for teenage pregnancy, or gun control as the means to prevent crime; these one-dimensional approaches remain only partial solutions as long as the underlying processes are not considered.

When children and adolescents are at risk for developmental, educational, and social problems, an ecological perspective would not just look at one or two of such factors in isolation (such as low birth weight, poverty, or abusive parents). It would take into account the different expectations, pressures, demands, and experiences that are made on the individual, and would view the factors that influence him or her within the context of the home, the family, friends, neighbors, the parents' world or work, the peer group, the school, and the community at large. Each of these contextual variables is defined by a number of factors that might be influential.

16

RICHARD M. LERNER'S DEVELOPMENTAL CONTEXTUALISM

Developmental contextualism constitutes a new, powerful perspective of human development different from those proposed in the past. The only model in this book with which contextualism shares some essential ideas—and by which it was influenced—is Bronfenbrenner's ecological theory (see Chapter 15). During the seventies and the eighties, contextualism emerged as a developmental philosophy, rapidly gaining acceptance and becoming increasingly influential. However, the concept of contextualism is not new; it has roots in symbolic interactionism and systematic philosophy. For example, "Contextualism," the title of a chapter in S. C. Pepper's (1942) *World Hypotheses*, constitutes one of Pepper's hypotheses about the world itself and implies that behavior has meaning only in relationship to its social, cultural, and historical context. Contemporary psychologists (R. M. Lerner, K. F. Riegel, T. C. Schneirla) have formed a theory of human development that derives its name, "developmental contextualism," in part from Pepper's philosophy. It shares with Pepper's writing such essential concepts as plasticity, process, change, and the reciprocal relationship between an active organism and an active event: "Events are all intrinsically complex, composed of interconnected activities with continuously changing patterns" (Pepper, 1942: 233); "The ineradicable contextual categories may thus be said to be change and novelty" (p. 235). This idea can even be traced to the ancient Greek philosopher Heraclitus who maintained, "Nothing endures but change." In Pepper's view, the ceaseless changes in the world are interrelated and produce dynamic, constantly interacting events of which the active organism is a contributing agent. In addition, it is the context itself that gives meaning to an event, to the whole, and to the parts that comprise it.

Developmental contextualism focuses on the interaction between the growing, that is, the continuously changing individual, and the ecological context within which that person lives. The person most directly linked with a "developmental contextual view" as a theory of development is Richard M. Lerner (1946-   ), the director of the Institute for Children, Youth, and Families at Michigan State University. Like several other models discussed in

Richard M. Lerner (1946-   )

this book, Lerner's developmental contextualism is not limited to adolescence. To the contrary, it encompasses the entire span of human life, and actually is a life-span developmental theory that shares many ideas with the life-span developmentalists Baltes, Reese, Nesselroade, and others. Thus, contextualism constitutes a conceptual tool that fosters a comprehensive awareness of diversity and a greater understanding of the individual in the multiple contexts in which he or she lives. In addition to presenting the basic life-span theory, this chapter attempts to highlight some of the model's applications and implications for adolescent development.

General assessment methods, as well as clinical evaluations and some contemporary investigations, increasingly ask contextual questions. The purpose is to advance our knowledge of specific factors and subfactors and emphasize how their interactions contribute to the developmental process. The focus will be on "context" in contrast to earlier theorizing, which emphasized mechanistic-environmental or maturational biological models (with the exception of Bronfenbrenner and Bandura). The family context may serve as one limited illustration here, i.e., the relationships between parents and adolescents (Galambos, 1992). While many or all of the factors have been researched in the past, often in isolation, contextualism views the interdependence of all these factors as its theoretical agenda. More specifically, family diversity refers to a multitude of conditions and circumstances under which different families live and its members interact. Family structure, family size, socioeconomic resources of the family, etc., are categories that have the potential for influencing parent-adolescent relationships as well as more general adolescent development.

They may either enhance positive development, or they may contribute to adolescent problem behavior, such as smoking, drinking, drug use, early sexual behavior, and delinquency. Each of the broad categories could have a number of significant contextual subcategories.

Family structure Family structure comprises a fundamental aspect of family organization. Different family structures constitute different contexts and contribute to differential developmental outcomes, at least in terms of probability. Much research reveals the advantage of living in an intact family with two natural parents, versus a one-parent family with only a mother (or a father), or a divorced, or a reconstituted family. Since family structures are changing, an awareness of the resulting influences becomes increasingly more important.

Family climate and decision making Family climates may constitute quite different contexts in which an individual develops. For example: One kind of parent may be permissive, another authoritative, and still another authoritarian. In addition, the meaning of different family climates and the psychological impact of each of these climates vary for different ethnic groups, as the research by Dornbusch et al. (1987) and by Steinberg and Brown (1989) has demonstrated. Another contextual variable is the extent to which the adolescent participates in family decisions and the extent to which he or she is encouraged to make his or her own independent choices.

Family recreational and leisure time activities Only one illustration will be included here: television. Today, TV has become such an unprecedented leisure time activity (surpassed by no other activity except sleep and maybe school) that it requires consideration both in terms of the rather passive nature of TV watching behavior and of the content depicted. Television simultaneously illustrates how family activities are embedded in historical change— an idea of paramount importance in developmental contextualism—and how changes in family interaction patterns are a function of technological inventions.

Family size Contextual variables might include the number of parents; number, age, and sex of siblings; children at home or away from home; other family and nonfamily members residing in the family; birth order. As families become smaller, the number and patterns of potential interactions have changed. Growing up in the extended family of the past (two parents, six siblings, and a grandparent) in the same house provides a totally different family context than a working mother and her teenage daughter living in the same apartment.

Socioeconomic variables Family income, family assets, whether or not one or both parents are employed or unemployed and what type of work the parent(s) perform(s), are all important contextual variables.

Quality and level of supervision The extent to which parents monitor where their children are, what they do, and with whom they associate, as well as the quality of care for latch-key children are all factors to be considered.

Family harmony and cohesion Families differ in terms of whether or not they do things together; whether or not parents and perhaps older siblings help the younger children with homework; whether or not each family member contributes to the maintenance of the home in some appropriate way.

Geographic and socioeconomic location of the home Other significant contextual variables are whether the residential area is urban, suburban, or rural, and the socioeconomic characteristics of the neighborhood (single home, row house, apartment, etc.).

Clearly all of these variables—as well as others not listed—have been described and researched in the past. The specific contribution of contextualism is its focus on:

(a) the continuous interaction patterns of most of these factors;
(b) the influence of the continuous changes over time, historically speaking (e.g. the emergence of TV after World War II, etc.) and the changes from day to day, such as the emotions or moods of family members;
(c) the conceptualization that the adolescent (or the child) is a major contributing factor in shaping the family context.

The research agenda of contextualism is not so much to add to our already substantial knowledge of any of these variables in isolation, as to elevate the interaction patterns and the bipolar direction of these influences to the analysis of development.

Much of the contemporary research focuses on the significance of the family in parent-adolescent relations and in adolescent problem behavior. According to developmental contextualism, however, to obtain meaningful findings, the specific context requires clear definition and exploration not only in terms of the broad categories, but in terms of increasingly minute, and at times even evasive, subcategories and their interactions. In addition to all of the above-outlined family variables, families must be viewed in relationship to their respective communities. Furthermore, communities are embedded in an overarching social, cultural, legal, and political macrosystem that is shaped by historical changes.

Since contextualism claims to synthesize much of the theoretical knowledge advanced in the past, developmental contextualism becomes meaningful only in relation to the developmental theories that precede it. Lerner characterizes his theoretical model in a subchapter, "Developmental contextualism as a 'compromise' between mechanism and organicism" (Lerner, 1986). Under the concept of "organicism" he combines all those theories of development that rely heavily on biological and/or endogenous explanatory principles of systematic changes from within the human organism (Gesell, Freud, Erikson, Piaget, Werner, etc.). In contrast, the term "mechanism" applies to those theories that define the forces for the developmental processes as coming primarily from external, environmental, and experiential variables (Skinner, Bijou, Baer, behaviorism, social learning theory, etc.). Lerner's developmental contextualism advocates neither "nature," as the organicism theories do, nor "nurture," as the mechanistic theories do, but instead emphasizes the idea that dynamic interactions and reciprocal relationships between the organism and the context always exist and shape development.

However, Lerner, at times, appears too quick in classifying all other theories into groups such as "organicism" and "mechanism." Thus, Erikson is placed in the "organicism" group, even though his approach was a life-span developmental one and he emphasized interactions between the epigenic ground plan and psychosocial influences, making him more of an interactionist than Lerner acknowledges.

■ Three Streams of Thought

Three major streams of thought that shaped Lerner's thinking and his conceptualizations were incorporated into his developmental-contextual approach. They are:

1. *Comparative Psychology* (Theodore C. Schneirla; Ethel Tobach; Gilbert Gottlieb, and Z. Y. Kuo). These comparative psychologists have rejected the maturational notion that biological changes can take place without the modifying influences of the psychosocial setting. Instead, they have stressed the idea that "bidirectional, reciprocal, or dynamic interactional relations among biological, psychological, and social processes" are responsible for development (Lerner, 1985: 356).

2. *The Life-Span View of Human Development* (Paul Baltes, John Nesselroade, and Werner Schaie). This view involves the study of changes over the entire span of the individual's life. Life-span development emphasizes that change, and therefore, development, does not come to an end with adolescence, but that it is a continuing, fundamental aspect of the human condition that ceases only at death: "Humans have a capacity for change across the entire life span" (Brim & Kagan, 1980: 1). Quite similar arguments have been advanced by George Herbert Mead (1934), who focused on socialization and the continuous process of social interaction which contribute to the development of the self.

3. *The Ecological Approach by Urie Bronfenbrenner* (see Chapter 15). Bronfenbrenner highlights the importance of the reciprocal relationship between developing individuals and the various contexts (e.g., the micro-, meso-, exo-, and macrosystem) within which they live. Bronfenbrenner has already defined the processes of human development as a function of context, and similarly he emphasizes the complexity and interdependence of the individual and the major ecological systems within which he or she lives.

CONTEXT DEFINED

For Lerner, context is conceptualized as the central idea of the theory of contextualism and is an interactive system of social variables that are, in large part, responsible for development. Lerner's recurring idea of context is broad and inclusive. The fact that its derivatives provide the name for the entire theory of "developmental contextualism" indicates its paramount significance. However, for Lerner, the term "context" goes beyond often-applied synonyms like "setting," "surrounding," "milieu," or "environment." Even expanding the term "context" to include such social variables as family, parents' co-workers, peers, teachers, and participants in leisure time activities, does not sufficiently capture Lerner's broader meaning. A theoretical understanding of the nature of context in developmental contextualism requires an awareness of the Four Meanings of Context (Dannefer, 1992):

1. Most commonly, context is defined as the physical setting, the surroundings, the environment or milieu, all of which contribute to part of the concept. Specifics include the location of the home with its rooms and furnishings; the school building with its classrooms, offices, bulletin boards, etc.; the church and the community with their recreational facilities, etc.

2. More important perhaps than the physical setting, context also includes numerous social components, such as family, peers, dating partners, teachers, and other significant people, who all are part of the individual's life and who all influence and are influenced by that individual.

3. Though this tends to be overlooked, the developing person is also part of this contextual setting, a fact that receives special emphasis in Lerner's theory. Interaction takes place simultaneously in two directions. Not only are developing individuals influenced by the physical and social contextual variables that surround them, but they assert an influence on those contextual variables, including other people. Thus, through their behavior, physical appearance, verbal expressiveness, etc., they change the context in which they live.

4. Context variables change as a function of the progression of time, that is, people become older and mature, or gadgets break down and are replaced by new ones, or new schools are built or equipped with new and better technology, and economic conditions change from "bullish" to "bearish," etc. The movie *Back to the Future* depicts, in a fictitious and humorous way, adolescent changes in musical taste as well as more general social changes as functions of time. In addition, context variables include the everyday life events that take place within the social and physical setting: parents quarrel; the adolescent falls in love or is rejected by a lover; he or she receives an academic honor, or fails a course, etc. The context inevitably changes and takes on different meanings for the developing person primarily as a function of time and experiences. For example, parental divorce or the remarriage of the custodial parent has a different impact on the preschool child, the elementary school child, and the adolescent. The remarriage of the mother during her offspring's puberty is especially problematic. In addition, the long-range effects of divorce depend on the time interval that has elapsed since the divorce.

Thus, developmental contextualism can only be understood as a dialectic process in which environmental settings and social systems not only influence each other, but also influence and are influenced by the individual. All of these component parts change over time. The interactional nature of these component parts is depicted in Figure 16.1 and will be discussed in more detail later. Lerner emphasizes that human development can only be understood as a function of its reciprocal relationship to the changing context and "that organism and context are always embedded each in the other" (Lerner, 1986: 59).

■ Contextual Relativism, or ". . . It All Depends . . . on the Context"

As a theory, developmental contextualism—or more specifically, contextual relativism—appears almost "content-free" in that the model does not postulate general developmental rules, specific developmental stages, or developmental tasks or milestones: "One cannot assume that general rules of development either exist for, or apply in the same way" to all social settings, children, adolescents, and their families (Lerner & Miller, 1993: 356). Lerner does make references to stage concepts advanced by other theories, such as Piaget's "formal thought processes." However, even if Lerner incorporates developmental stage concepts from other theories, he describes them as being probabilistic in nature. Lerner sees the stages defined by traditional theories as constituting a predetermined epigenesis in that such stages are defined as universal, invariant, and driven by internal organismic forces.

In contrast, contextual relativism deemphasizes the significance of stages (so fundamental in the theories of Freud, Erikson, Piaget, Kohlberg, and others), and views them as occurring with a high degree of probability, but not as predetermined, invariant, or predictable. Specific adolescent issues are conceptualized in terms of the contextual variables that influence an individual. They appear in the framework of specific research findings or a research hypothesis that illustrates the effects of contextual variables, not in terms of universal theoretical generalizations or theoretical predictions that apply to all adolescents. Contextual relativism literally maintains that "it all depends on the context." Developmental contextualism allows for ever-changing relationships among many variables: temperament, innate constitutional factors, physical strength and appearance, interactions between parents and adolescents, past school experiences, or broader events in the community or in the nation, as well as the strictly physical environment. Scarr (1986: 566) summarizes the issue rather critically, but quite appropriately: "Everything determines and is determined by everything else." Because context always changes and because context is the variable that modifies development, "change" is an inevitable part of existence that affects each individual differently. "Change" as defined by Pepper becomes the cornerstone of Lerner's theory.

The theory does bring to full awareness the complex, multilevel, multifaceted, reciprocal nature of all the forces that shape development, including the individual himself or herself: "Growth is more individualistic than was thought, and it is difficult to find general patterns" (Brim & Kagan, 1980: 13). In this sense, developmental contextualism may be more of a vehicle for stimulating research and explaining research findings or behaviors than traditional (or one-dimensional) theoretical conceptualizations of human development. Conceptualism provides a broad view of the nature of development rather than the identification of specific developmental rules, valid principles, regularities, and universal laws. In that sense, it really takes a postmodernistic stance toward development. Lerner's theory does not even attempt to provide universal generalizations that apply to all children, but emphasizes plasticity in human nature, individuality, diversity, and uniqueness, as well as the complex and multileveled interconnections between individual and context.

■ Dynamic Interaction Within Developmental Contextualism

The dynamic interactions between the organism and its characteristics, and the various components of the social and physical setting, constitute an essential element of development and delineate a core concept of Lerner's contextualism. As Lerner emphasizes, this idea is so crucial that it has appeared under quite diverse terminology: "transactionalism"

(Sameroff, 1975); "relational" (Looft, 1973); "fusion," "probabilistic epigenesis" or simple "dialecticalism" (Riegel, 1975); "dynamic interactionism" (Lerner, 1978, 1979, 1985). Even the word "contextualism," as used by Lerner, is based on the defining idea of a continuous, reciprocal, dynamic interaction between the organism and the context. All of the above-cited authors stress "that reciprocal interchanges—most importantly, between an individual and the others in his or her world—are inevitable components of behavior development and functioning" (Lerner, 1979: 272).

■ Why Individual-Social Interactions Are Reciprocal

Dynamic interactionism conceptualizes the organism with its biological-genetic predisposition as being embedded in a sociocultural context. Biological or organismic "variables both influence and, reciprocally, are influenced by contextual ones" (Lerner, 1992a: 379). This relationship and its influences are always mutual and reciprocal and "are always embedded in each other." "No existing form of life is truly solitary and no organism is completely independent of others at all times in its history" (Tobach & Schneirla, 1968: 505). Human life involves reciprocal relations with people, because human behavior has an interactive component. Development, by its very nature is, first and foremost, a social interaction phenomenon (Lerner, 1979). A common illustration of one context influencing another in a reciprocal fashion is the child's poor performance in school which influences the child's mood, attitude, and behavior at home and may change the quality of the interaction between child and parent, because the parents, in turn, are influenced by the child's mood, attitude, and behavior. Subsequent parental restrictions placed on the child may limit his or her opportunity to more freely explore, to play, and to develop social skills. Similarly, in a home setting that is abusive, a child can be so disturbed by his or her difficulties that the child does not function successfully at school. The child's poor report card can also trigger abusive rage in a parent. Such events can create a "circular function" whose influences are felt in both directions. The influences between school and family are biodirectional in nature and exist in an interdependent context. These influences are operative, even if the nature of these influences often are more subtle than in the illustration and are not directly obvious to the child, the parent, and the teacher. As the growing individual influences other persons, such influences proceed in a circular, continuing fashion so that the other person, in turn, influences the first, and so on, *ad infinitum*.

■ How Characteristics Have Consequences

The nature of such an individual-social interaction pattern has actually been researched (Thomas et al., 1963, 1970). The design involved a comparison of the parental responses to the behavioral and temperamental styles of two groups of young infants who differed in their biological-organismic disposition. One group was adaptable, rhythmic, with a prevalent positive mood, while the other was unadaptable, arrhythmic, and with a frequently negative mood. The influence of these temperamental characteristics on the behavioral reactions of the parents was the focus of the investigation. The positive characteristics of the infant's temperament elicited approach-behavior and interpersonal warmth. The negative qualities invited avoidance and coldness from parents. To elaborate on the circular function of the nature of interaction, those children who elicited negative feedback from their parents had a greater probability of developing psychological difficulties later in life. Thus, their own temperamental qualities influenced the parents' behavior, which in turn became a contextual factor contributing to their own development.

■ Why the Reciprocity of Relations Is Crucial to Understand

An awareness of such reciprocal relations and interactions has allowed researchers to better understand human behavior and to study development without the kind of distortions that can result when influences are perceived as unidirectional. To assume that parents unilaterally "socialize" their child without any consideration of the influences that the child may have—through his or her responses or lack of responses—on his or her parents is to ignore the reality of the context. According to dynamic interactionism, the nature of human development cannot be understood without considering the mutuality of the social relationships in which children and adolescents and adults find themselves. In other words, developmental contextualism perceives development as "the confluence of many interrelated and changing systems and subsystems, including the biological, social, cultural, and historical" (Looft, 1973: 51).

HOW CONTEXT AFFECTS PUBERTY

Freudian and other biologically-maturationally-oriented theories have postulated that there exists a direct, "unmediated" biological influence on emerging characteristics of the individual, in that behaviors emerge independent of environmental experiences or context. For example, pubertal changes have often been assumed to directly affect such changes in the adolescent as sexual fantasy, sexual behavior, independence assertion, aggressiveness, etc. In contrast to the notion of an "unmediated influence" of puberty, Lerner advances a more contextual model, which he calls the "mediated effect model." Implied is the idea that the specific changes of puberty involve characteristics of the individual that influence and are "mediated" both by endogenous maturational processes and by interactions with people, and with social, religious, and moral values, in short, the context. Lerner rejects the idea that puberty by itself produces an "unmediated" direct, predictable, and inevitable effect on the psychological functioning and social behavior of adolescents (Lerner 1992a).

Thus, peer group expectations, parent-adolescent relationships, media models, and general sociocultural norms all "mediate" the influence of puberty and modify the psychosocial behavior and development of the person. Accepting the concept of "dynamic interaction" and the "mediated effects model" leads to the conclusion that the effect of pubertal maturation on psychosocial development may differ considerably under varying contextual conditions. Social pressure or stress, which is culturally related to pubertal changes, may be one such contextual condition. Applied to adolescents, the interactional model implies that the characteristics and behaviors of different individuals create quite different reactions in others. In the long run, all of these reactions shape future development in that they create feedback mechanisms, which then may either contribute to or detract from the well-being of that person. Much evidence exists to support such a conclusion.

■ How Contextual Researchers View Reciprocity

The bidirectional and reciprocal nature of adolescent-context interaction receives recognition in much of the contemporary adolescent research literature. Although rarely have researchers specifically focused on the reciprocal nature of these influences, some studies do exist that illuminate the process. However, these studies usually focus on only one of the directions of such influences, not both. Lerner actually distinguishes between the different directions in the influences of such studies, some are social context $\rightarrow$ adolescent studies while others are adolescent $\rightarrow$ social context studies.

A large body of research has investigated the social context $\rightarrow$ adolescent influences. Although this research is too voluminous to cite, an example would be the influence of parental demands or childrearing attitudes on adolescents. Another category of this research includes studies by Simmons and Blyth (1987), who have evaluated the effects of the school organization as a social context, especially the effect of school transition on adolescents (based on the different patterns of elementary, junior high, and high school grades, such as 6-3-3 vs. 5-3-4 or 8-4). But again, the transitional effects need to be viewed in the context of other variables, such as the timing of puberty, gender differences, and self-concept, to mention just a few. A quite different cluster of social attitude $\rightarrow$ adolescent influence studies have assessed cultural beliefs about menarche (female onset of puberty) and their influence on the menarcheal experience of girls (Brooks-Gunn & Ruble, 1982).

The second group of studies looks at "the-adolescent-as-stimulus" effect, and here the interactional effect begins with the characteristics of adolescence and asks what the response of other people is to these characteristics. Some of the adolescent $\rightarrow$ social context studies start by identifying such extensively researched characteristics of the adolescent as early and late maturation, physical attractiveness, body type (ectomorphic, endomorphic, or mesomorphic), and temperament.

HOW DEVELOPMENTAL CONTEXTUALISM USES THE RESEARCH

Developmental contextualism views the findings of such studies as the first link in what will become increasingly the reciprocal, bidirectional, interaction effect. To appreciate the nature of bidirectional interactions, one needs to be aware of the three directions in which such influences can flow:

1. How the attributes, characteristics, maturity status, and physical features of the adolescent influence others. It is the adolescent $\rightarrow$ social context reasearch that examines this topic.
2. How the features and characteristics of the setting influence the adolescent. The social context $\rightarrow$ adolescent research examines this point.
3. The third component is relatively new and constitutes the unique contribution of developmental contextualism: What are the effects of the continuous, reciprocal, bidirectional $\longleftrightarrow$ interactions of individual attributes and contextual features. This component implements Pepper's idea of "contextualism" and constitutes the type of research advocated by Lerner. It is the type of analysis that developmental contextualism brings to bear on contemporary research.

■ Physical Attractiveness

Lerner and Korn (1972) have demonstrated that endomorphic (chubby) 5-, 15-, and 20-year-olds not only receive more negative evaluations than their mesomorphic (muscular-average) peers, but that these evaluations actually influence the quality of interpersonal interactions. This finding held true for males and females and for American, Mexican, and Japanese cultures. Neither the age (5, 15, 20) of the person whose appearance was evaluated nor the age of the evaluator made any difference; moreover, the same stereotypes emerged even when the subjects evaluated just pictures of people of different body types.

In terms of actual social responses, the mesomorphic individuals were more likely to be approached by others, while the chubby children tended to be avoided. In addition, chubby appearance generally received low evaluations in physical attractiveness. Dion and Berscheid (1972) found that children who were assigned low attractiveness ratings exhibit more maladjusted behaviors such as fighting with, and even yelling at, the teacher than their more attractive classmates. The peers of the less attractive students were less likely to choose them as leaders and more likely to exclude them from their activities, while the behavior of the attractive children was evaluated as more congruent with school adjustment. The late-maturing male and female adolescents who were evaluated as less attractive had lower self-concepts. Jackson and Huston (1975) report that physically attractive females received higher ratings on positive behavioral attributes than those who were less attractive.

The evaluation of physical attractiveness may change both historically and cross-culturally. For example, social norms may become more tolerant and more accepting of chubbiness (reflected in the voluptuous female figures in Rubens' paintings). Within a different cultural context, such standards vary to a considerable extent; for example, obesity may be the feminine beauty ideal, as it is in some parts of Central Africa (Benedict, 1934). Even in Western societies the ideal fashion model reveals a thinner body configuration than the romanticized, highly eroticized and physically well-developed ideal of the movie industry.

■ Early and Late Maturation Influences and Is Influenced by the Context

The research literature of early and late maturational changes during adolescence reveals the importance of considering contextual factors. The status of physical maturity during puberty becomes a powerful context variable to demonstrate (1) how the timing of an individual's physical development influences other people, and (2) how the reactions of others to the adolescent's degree of physical maturation shape the future development of that individual. The two groups, those who mature early and those who mature late, receive quite different evaluations from their peers and from adults. Late-maturing boys, in particular, receive less positive evaluations from others. They are described as immature and less effective in interpersonal relationships. Late maturers experience a longer latency period, since their puberty is deferred. They show dependency needs, but their social status and social acceptance are lower. They exhibit a negative attitude toward parents and tend to have a low self-concept; in the process, they also may become more resourceful and more flexible in dealing with problems. In contrast, early maturers, who look more like adults, receive more positive evaluations from others and show more positive signs of adjustment. They are more athletic and are often more socially successful. Longitudinal research indicates that some of the effects of early maturation for males go beyond adolescence and actually influence adult adjustment and social relationships in later life. However, there is also a negative side to early maturation: as adults they tend to be more rigid, moralistic, and conforming. In contrast, later in life, late-maturing boys are better able to cope with ambiguities and to deal with new problems.

The meaning of early and late maturation is also embedded in a sociocultural context. At least some evidence suggests that these effects may be a function of cultural patterns. For adolescents born to Italian parents, the contextual meaning of early and late maturation may differ. In the traditionally authoritarian Italian family, where parents provide warmth and affection, encourage family dependency, and place less emphasis on physical size and strength than do American parents and peers, early maturation may lose its advantage. Mussen and Bouterline-Young (1964: 188) demonstrated that for Italian adolescents the personality variables associated with differential pubertal growth rates "may vary with—and be modified by—the cultural context."

Early and late maturers may also seek different role models, peer-group friends, and dating partners. The early-maturing girl whose body appears more sexually mature and whose physical development is substantially more advanced than that of same-age boys may elicit unique biodirectional relations between herself and her social context. For example, she tends to date earlier, become sexually active earlier, marries earlier, and has a greater probability of divorce. Apparently, the biological characteristics of an early-maturing girl interact with the social evaluations, social expectations, and social behavior, so that the timing of puberty tends to set in motion different life-course patterns. The interaction between physical appearance and social feedback leads to differences in the timing of when adolescents enter the dating game and become sexually active. Thus, research confirms an interrelationship between personal characteristics and social pressures that produces different developmental outcomes.

In the case of the physically unattractive adolescent, frequent negative evaluative feedback will elicit negative responses from the targeted person. These may lead to a self-fulfilling hypothesis: Those evaluated as low in attractiveness or as physically immature (late maturers) may respond by displaying poor social, school, and interpersonal adjustment, by manifesting lowered self-concepts, and by developing negative feelings toward themselves. The end result of this circular reciprocal interaction may contribute to behavioral and adjustment problems during adolescence. Cavior and Howard (1973) have reported that, as a group, juvenile delinquents received a lower physical attractiveness rating than nondelinquents, a finding suggesting that physical unattractiveness, resulting in social rejection, may be one of the contextual factors contributing to delinquency.

These illustrations indicate how physical characteristics, such as body type, physical attractiveness, and early or late maturation are evaluated differently by the social world and may elicit varying responses from different people in the adolescent's social setting. During adolescence, these evaluations are of paramount importance because the young person has become highly sensitive to any kind of social feedback, but he or she does not yet have the firm identity necessary to dismiss negative, inappropriate, or malicious evaluations. These evaluations and responses from significant others comprise the social context and constitute powerful feedback that will influence the future development of the target person. This idea, that early in life "significant others" and later "generalized others" through their actions—and the individual's reaction to these actions—continuously modify the person, also constitutes a significant part of G. H. Mead's (1934) theory of social interactionism as well as Cooley's "looking-glass self," that is, the self as reflected through the eyes of others.

INDIVIDUAL DIFFERENCES AND HUMAN DIVERSITY

Probably no other contemporary development theory recognizes, appreciates, highlights, and emphasizes the idea of individual differences and its corollary of human diversity (such as race, ethnicity, gender, physical handicapping conditions, socioeconomic status as well as national and cultural variations) as much as Lerner's developmental contextualism. As children possess different genetic dispositions, grow up in diverse environmental settings, and contribute uniquely to their own development, these contextual factors do shape children differently, thus turning the focus inevitably toward diversity. Since the theory does not seek the universal patterns identified by the traditional stage theories and since it rejects the notion of predetermined stages, the primary issues conceptualized by the theory are individuality, individual differences, and diversity. Individual variations become the cornerstone for understanding human development. Each individual child is unique and becomes increasingly more unique as development progresses through the course of life: "That is, the unique fusion of biological, psychological, and sociocultural levels makes the person individually distinct; this individuality provides the basis of further, distinct interactions with the context and promotes the continued development of an individual developmental trajectory" (Lerner & Miller, 1993: 353).

The increasing attention to studying the variation of contextual variables and their respective divergent influences leads to an increasing appreciation of the diversity of patterns that research has shown to exist in individual and family development. These concerns become even more pronounced when one begins to consider not only individual developmental trajectories, but also more global, social categories of diversity. "Such diversity—involving racial, ethnic, gender, physical handicaps, national and cultural variation—has not been a primary concern of empirical analysis. Unfortunately, this is detrimental to the human development knowledge base" (Lerner, 1992b: 12). Because cultural diversity has become an influential aspect of life in the modern world, Lerner advances a forceful critical argument against the state of our developmental knowledge. He maintains that theory and research in the past have been too one-sided, focusing on the white, Anglo-Saxon, middle-class male, and that our knowledge about children and adolescents is really slanted toward that narrowly defined subgroup, a group that seems to have been the primary subject of researchers and theorists for more than a century. The diversity of the human condition and of developmental patterns has not been the primary concern of the empirical and theoretical literature, even in situations where existing data are relevant to diversity.

Lerner proposes to end this one-sided neglect and actually make diversity the focus of the research in the study of human development. Recognizing the significance of diversity as a focus for research requires the researcher to assume that few, if any, general developmental laws apply equally to all adolescents. Therefore, unlike past research, Lerner's scholarship agenda is designed less as an attempt to discover laws, rules, or patterns of development than to make the study of diversity the agenda of integrated, interdisciplinary research. Lerner argues that diversity must become the issue if we want to achieve a deeper understanding of the human condition. Furthermore, to fully understand the importance of diversity, we must focus more on the different contexts that create diversity than on attempts to abstract universal laws from existing (at times limited) data. To be successful, such research efforts demand interdisciplinary collaboration across all of the disciplines investigating the development of adolescents and the impact of contextual factors (such as biology, family, school, community, ethnicity, culture, and history) on the process of development.

THE GOODNESS-OF-FIT MODEL
OF PERSON-CONTEXT INTERACTION

The goodness-of-fit model is another essential concept in Lerner's (1983) developmental contextualism; it constitutes one of the substantive models or paradigms. Although Erikson did not use the term, for him too developmental progress is dependent on the "fit" between the epigenic plan and the psychosocial demands. Goodness-of-fit identifies the circumstances that enhance development and adjustment (that is, when the fit is good) or impair growth and well-being (that is, when the fit is bad or when there is a lack of fit).

The concept goodness-of-fit takes into consideration the relationship (or more precisely, the match) between an individual's personality (including temperamental attributes, values, attitudes, beliefs, skills, and propensities) and the corresponding characteristics of the significant other people, such as parents, siblings, friends, peers, teachers, lovers, and later co-workers and bosses who constitute the social context within which behavior takes place. Using this level of analysis it becomes obvious—and research has demonstrated—that, whether a developmental outcome is positive or adaptive does not just depend on the characteristics of the child/adolescent. Neither does the developmental outcome simply depend on the characteristics of social and/or the physical context. The goodness-of-fit model maintains that the outcome of the interaction is most of all dependent on the congruence or the match between individual and context. If an individual's temperament and personality is congruent with or constitutes a good fit with the social context, the result would be an adaptive, constructive, development enhancing outcome. However, if the individual's characteristics are mismatched or incongruent with the context, the outcome would be unfavorable and could impair social relationships and even development.

For example, applying the goodness-of-fit construct to the relationship between adolescent temperament and parental characteristics helps explain the outcome of both family harmony in some families (namely, those in which there is a good match), or in cases where they are incongruent, family discord. Looking at behavior from a goodness-of-fit perspective avoids simplistic generalizations about the cause and the effect, such as the statement that overly strict parents tend to raise aggressive adolescents. Developmental contextualism would view the parental childrearing style and parental expectation in relationship to the adolescent's temperament, pubertal status, and the young person's need and respect for parents. Lerner presents much research data to support the generalization, "that at a given point in development neither children's attributes per se nor the demands of the setting per se are the key predictors of their adaptive functioning" (Lerner, 1983: 289). Instead, what seem to matter most of all is the goodness-of-fit or the match between the children's attributes and their home, peer group, and school context.

Lerner notes that "just as a person brings his or her characteristics of physical, emotional, and behavioral individuality to a particular social setting, there are demands placed on the person by virtue of the social and physical components of the setting " (Lerner, 1986: 72). The question becomes, therefore, how well do the person's characteristics "fit it" or mesh with the setting or with the characteristics of others (parents, siblings, peers, lovers, teachers, etc.). If there is a good fit, meaning that the individual characteristics are congruent with the characteristics or demands, or are compatible with the expectations of significant others, then the positive adjustment that results enhances development. If the organism and context do not fit, that is, if individual characteristics and the social demands are incongruent or incompatible, there will be negative adjustment, friction, lack of development, and in more prolonged or extreme situations, maladjustment. Thus, "if a person's characteristics of individuality match (or 'fit') the demands of a particular setting, adaptive outcome in that setting will accrue. Those people whose characteristics match most of the settings within which they exist should receive supportive or positive feedback from the context and should show evidence of the most adaptive behavioral development. In turn, of course, mismatched people, whose characteristics are incongruent with one or more settings, should show alternative developmental outcomes" (Lerner, 1986: 72).

■ Goodness-of-Fit as a Powerful Explanatory Tool

What follows are common everyday experiences whose meaning can be enhanced by viewing them as a "goodness-of-fit" issue, rather than as something that is anybody's fault, shortcoming, or bad intention.

1. The goodness-of-fit concept can be applied to the love relationship of two adolescents who fall in and out of love. Initially, there is the strong attraction to the other person, and the desire to continuously be close to each other. They seem to be a good fit, a perfect match. As mundane life experiences accrue, and one says the wrong thing or as the idiosyncrasies of one partner begin to annoy the other, the relationship moves from the initial good fit (feelings of true love) to a lack of fit, which eventually results in a break-up of the relationship. Many an adolescent could benefit from viewing the break-up of the relationship as the result of a poor fit, rather than as rejection or as anyone's fault.

2. Some children fit well into a structured educational setting but might feel uncomfortable in a less demanding, relaxed, easy-going, unstructured setting. The reverse could be equally true. Thus, school success and school satisfaction do not only depend on the characteristics of the child, the teaching skills of the teacher, or the nature of the curriculum, but may be a function of the goodness-of-fit between the child's need for structure and the school's philosophy with respect to structure versus freedom.

3. Lewis (1987) examined whether children who preferred gender-inappropriate play behavior, such as a boy dressing a doll and combing her hair, were more likely to be maladjusted later. He observed children who were invited to play with gender-stereotyped toys and classified their play behavior as gender-appropriate or gender-inappropriate. The study revealed no social adjustment difference between those who showed gender-appropriate and gender-inappropriate behavior. However,

when the mother's gender role preference for the child's behavior was taken into consideration, significant adjustment differences did occur. In cases of an androgenous mother, the child's gender-appropriate or inappropriate behavior did not relate to later adjustment. However, if the mother preferred appropriate gender role behavior and the child showed gender-inappropriate behavior, the child was likely to show signs of maladjustment later. Apparently, gender-inappropriate behavior of children does not constitute a good fit with a mother's preference for gender-appropriate behavior.

4. In the New York Longitudinal Study (as cited by Lerner, 1983) two groups of children were compared over an extended period of time. One focus of the study was the impact of low regularity (arrhythmicity) in regard to the sleep-wake cycle on subsequent adjustment in the family and later in school. One group of children consisted primarily of white, middle-class families of professional parents. The second group came from Puerto Rican children of working-class parents. The temperamental attribute of arrhythmicity during early infancy was equally distributed in both groups. The Puerto Rican parents were quite tolerant of their children's irregularity and adapted their life to their children's sleeping patterns. In the first five years of life the children's arrhythmicity was unrelated to any adjustment problems. Apparently the fit between the child's temperament and the parents minimal demands was quite good. In contrast, the middle-class parents insisted on a rhythmic sleep pattern. The arrhythmic children did not fit into their parents expectations, consequently irregular sleep patterns became a predictor of problem behaviors during their first five years. However, middle-class parents took steps to change their children's sleep-wake cycle into a more rhythmic pattern and actually were quite successful, so that their children encountered no adjustment problems by the time they entered school, nor in school later. For the Puerto Rican children the outcome changed as they entered school. Their irregular sleep pattern interfered with getting sufficient sleep, getting to school in time, and remaining alert; subsequently they failed to do well in school. Thus for the Puerto Rican children arrhythmicity in the school situation constituted a poor fit and actually predicted adjustment problems.

THE NATURE AND LIMITS OF PLASTICITY

Lerner's book title, *On the Nature of Human Plasticity* (1984), suggests the significance that developmental contextualism attaches to the idea of the plasticity and modifiability of the organism. In accordance with its roots in life-span developmental psychology, developmental contextualism assumes that an essential attribute of the human organism is plasticity and that individuals are continuously in the process of changing and developing, and contextual events continuously contribute to this process. A developing organism is, by definition, a changing system since developmental processes are not predetermined, fixed, stereotyped, rigid, or immutable. The theoretical conceptualization of plasticity that emerges portrays a quality that affects the human organism not only during childhood and adolescence, but throughout the entire life span. Without plasticity, the organism could not adapt to the changing conditions of the environment, and as Darwin maintained more than a century ago, without variability and adaptability in the evolutionary process, survival would not have been possible. Such a notion of plasticity across ontogeny contrasts sharply with commonly held theoretical assumptions that the human personality, traits, and behavior characteristics complete their development by the end of adolescence (Peter Blos, 1962). Other developmental theorists have also maintained that human personality is no longer available for major alterations after adolescence. Although Lerner agrees that children and adolescents are much more malleable than older people, and although he believes that the ease and the degree of malleability may decline as a function of age, Lerner maintains that plasticity remains an all-pervasive attribute throughout the entire life span.

The concept of plasticity provides an optimistic suggestion that a developing person can change relatively easily through appropriate, deliberate intervention; therefore, the lives of people can be improved through education and therapy. Properly planned intervention can produce beneficial effects, so that long-range improvement becomes the goal. The emphasis on the concept of plasticity implies the idealistic hope for human perfectibility—or, at least, ongoing improvement. Obviously, planned early intervention, therapy, retraining, and education appear to be more effective than later intervention simply because the younger organism is more malleable than the older organism (Scarr, 1986). And, the current efforts to provide early intervention programs for very young children with disabilities is based on that assumption, and increasingly solid research evidence, that: "Infancy is the most malleable, rapid changing and least organized period of human development. Never again will there be the same potential for establishing the basic forms of understanding, style, and feeling in all domains of experience. Early experience is the primary matrix from which all of later development is generated" (Fowler, 1975: 341).

Critics have not so much questioned the fundamental premise that developmental plasticity exists, as life span developmental psychologists have always maintained, but they have posed such questions as: What are the limits of human plasticity? To what degree can human behavior be modified? What characteristics are particularly malleable? Which traits are less plastic? What is the most efficient age or time to produce which type of change? Are some skills better taught at a later time, as the maturationalists have maintained? Are there "critical periods" when certain functions need to be acquired, or at least are the best time for acquiring them? In a review of Lerner's book dealing with human plasticity, Scarr (1986: 565) states: "Anyone who knows anything about evolution acknowledges some genetic constraints on species' developmental patterns. Without contraints there would be no species." Lerner acknowledges the existence of genetic constraints by repeatedly referring to the "organism," or, more precisely, to the organism context interaction. Thus, as developmental contextualism emphasizes, developmental plasticity is a function of the organism and its surroundings (e.g., context). The issue of the limits of human plasticity is not addressed, nor is the question as to what characteristics, skills, or knowledge will most effectively change through education and interventional procedures, nor is much information given as to the optimum time/age range to attempt such change. Obviously, no amount of experience or training can make a goldfish sing! While young circus performers learn to execute amazing stunts, there are distinct limitations placed on acquiring such skills later in life. Similarly, plasticity of the human species is restrained by genetic limitations. However, the potential for human variation is also considerable: Different contextual experiences create considerable diversity among humans. Humans not only can create their own environments, they also can adapt to them (Lewis, 1992).

In the past, as part of the more traditional research agenda, scholars assumed that parents socialized their offspring in a fairly static and unidirectional pattern. In traditional research, parents were seen as responsible for shaping the behavior, personality and social development of their offspring. More recently, psychology is conceptualizing the nature of social influences as reciprocal, a perspective that has been influenced by developmental contextualism. Individuals' relationships and interactions with other people constitute the context in which development takes place. These mutual influences flow in both directions, and the interactive nature of such relationships has been researched. Does the child have an effect on the parent? The answer is obviously "yes." But the more specific question as to the part the child plays in these two-directional social interaction processes (Lerner, 1979) still needs to be resolved.

Questions naturally arise about how much the context influences the individual and how much the individual modifies the context. The answer may well depend, as does almost everything else in developmental contextualism, on the specific contextual setting. It may also depend on the characteristics under consideration. Lerner's somewhat over-optimistic assessment of the power of the individual in shaping his or her own development may be summarized in the following: ". . . the organism as much shapes the context as the context shapes it" (Lerner & Kauffman 1985: 322). The idea that people shape others as well as their environment is a reminder of the rather extensive "Locus of Control" research literature (Rotter) that divides personalities into those who shape their own world (Internalizer) and those who believe they are controlled by powerful others/fate, etc. (External Locus of Control). Apparently, there are personality differences in terms of those who actively shape their context and those who are more passively shaped by their context. Therefore, even "Locus of Control" needs to be viewed as a contextual personality variable.

■ Predetermined Epigenesis versus Probabilistic Epigenesis

Developmental contextualism differs from the traditional organicism theories with their treatment of epigenesis. Epigenesis, a concept borrowed from embryology and applied to human development, means a gradual unfolding, a progression from simpler to more complex levels of organization in development resulting from internal organismic forces. It implies that the emerging developmental progression is predetermined and that, in the normal course of development, every individual moves through the sequence of invariant stages. The epigenetic principle of development (see Chapter 3) has become popular through its use in Erikson's stage theory of development. Erikson is not strictly a maturationalist, since he sees the epigenetic ground plan as interacting with psychosocial events. In the final analysis, Erikson seems to be much more in tune with Lerner's developmental contextualism than Lerner is willing to give him credit for.

In contrast, developmental contextualism does not recognize developmental stages, regardless of whether they are Eriksonian or Piagetian stages, as being rigidly fixed and inevitable, but postulates that contextual factors determine their manifestation; hence, they can be modified. Lerner accepts the notion that many individuals do go through such stages, especially white, middle-class, Anglo-Saxon, male adolescents. Nevertheless, Lerner believes such stages suggest only one possible developmental trajectory which, even though it may have a high probability of occurrence, is neither inevitable nor universal. Furthermore, the nature, speed, and quality of stage development are more plastic and more diverse than has hitherto been assumed.

Lerner differentiates the concept of *predetermined epigenesis* from *probabilistic epigenesis*. The term "predetermined epigenesis" applies to all those stage theories (Erikson, Piaget, Kohlberg) that postulate an invariant and inevitable sequence of stages, a universalistic conceptualization of human development that is alien to developmental contextualism. Lerner claims that such stages do occur in the described sequence, but only in terms of probability. They are never universal, inevitable, or invariant; therefore, he prefers the term "probabilistic epigenesis" as being more appropriate for his theory. A critic might question the idea that an adolescent could possibly become an operational thinker, without having gone through a stage or demonstrated the behavior known as "concrete operations." Not everyone reaches the ability to think operationally; however, for those adolescents who reach this stage the sequence is not probabilistic, but inevitable.

ILLUSTRATION OF LERNER'S DYNAMIC INTERACTIONAL MODEL OF ADOLESCENT DEVELOPMENT

Lerner has designed a diagram, which he has modified repeatedly and which he uses extensively in his publications. The figure represents visually the nature of development as theorized in his contextual, interactional model (see Figure 16.1). It identifies the major dimensions of the integrated and independent nature of forces that can be conceptualized as shaping development of levels of organization.

The three large outer circles within which all development is embedded constitute the larger sociocultural milieu. These all-encompassing circles are organized in descending order (they include what Bronfenbrenner refers to as the "macrosystem"): culture, society, and community. The arrow moving from left to right through the entire figure symbolizes changes over time. Historical events and the impact of technological inventions (such as the availability of the TV, the computer, the pill, the automobile, or the airplane) not only produce slow but, nevertheless, dramatic changes in culture, society, and community, they also influence the more narrowly defined context of the family, parents, and adolescents, and the networks within which they interact. Anthropological data provide a powerful illustration that patterns of individual lives and those of entire societies change dramatically over time as a function of technological changes. Anthropological data collected 50 years ago are no longer accurate today. For any society that has changed from a preindustrial way of life into a more modern and technological pattern, such changes are fundamental and far-reaching. The experiences, attitudes, and behaviors of the Hopi adolescent toward the end of the nineteenth century are fundamentally and in far-reaching ways different from those of a Hopi adolescent today because Hopi society has changed. However, beyond that, the Hopi's macrosystem context has changed (Schlegel & Barry, 1991).

In Figure 16.1, the inside circle on the left represents the adolescent and that on the right, the parents. The inside segments of these circles identify various characteristics that are broadly defined. Each adolescent has distinct biological (e.g. timing of pubertal changes,

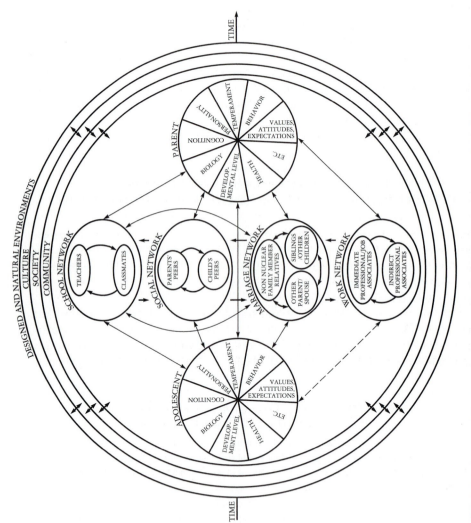

FIGURE 16.1 Lerner's dynamic interactional model of adolescent development. (From R. Lerner, *America's Youth in Crisis*, page xx, copyright © 1995 by Sage Publications, Inc. Reprinted by permission of R. Lerner and Sage Publications, Inc.)

menarche, semenarche, etc.), personality, temperamental, behavioral, cognitive, and health characteristics. Lerner objects to these characteristics being viewed in isolation, but emphasizes that only by considering the interacting nature of these characteristics will we ever achieve an understanding of the whole child. Also, each parent has his or her own distinct corresponding set of characteristics. Adolescent temperament may dovetail, be modified by, or clash with parental temperament. An individual adolescent may receive different kinds of feedback, which in turn, lead to responses from the adolescent that might escalate or de-escalate conflict. Thus, temperament needs to be viewed in accordance with the goodness-of-fit-model. This fit or the lack-of-fit between parents and adolescent could account for quite different interactional patterns and, in the long run, different developmental outcomes.

The smaller, inside circles in the center of the figure represent the most important networks in and with which the parents and adolescents interact. Bronfenbrenner refers to such interactions of networks as the mesosystem. On top is the school network (teachers and classmates), followed by the social network (adolescent's peers, parents' peers), the marriage network (siblings, other children, relatives, and other family members) and at the bottom, the parents' work network (supervisors and work associates of the parents). Although the parents' work obligations usually have only an indirect impact on the adolescent, they can, nevertheless, be very significant (parents' salary, work hours, and vacation time). The multiplicity of arrows both within and between these circles serves as a powerful illustration of the dynamic interactive characteristic of Lerner's contextual model, which moves, and hence, changes over time. That all of the arrows have two arrowheads, one on each side, means that the influences are reciprocal, the interactions are bidirectional. Thus, the dual arrows suggest influences that work in both directions, on virtually all levels of interaction.

The extant research literature provides plenty of evidence for the existence of many of these influences depicted by arrows in the model. However, in the past, research has usually pursued the influence that flows only in one direction, e.g., the influence of the parental disciplinary style on the adolescent or the adolescent's physical maturity status on the parents. Relatively few studies have investigated the simultaneous directionality of such relations. Lerner's model encourages the investigation of the biodirectionality of these influences.

IMPLICATIONS FOR PROGRAMS, INTERVENTION, AND EDUCATION

Developmental contextualism makes suspect any simple rules as well as specific guidelines that traditional theories have so often advanced, advising parents and educators how to effectively raise their children and adolescents. Contextualism does not advance all-encompassing guidelines to childrearing questions, but views issues of training, control, and obedience as being dependent on contextual factors. In other words, one needs to ask specific questions about relevant variables, such as age, sex, ethnicity, past experiences, self-concept, temperament, as well as the goodness-of-fit between child and task or between child and parent and/or educator, etc., before one can provide specific advice on how to proceed in a critical childrearing situation. As Bronfenbrenner also emphasizes, the interaction process has to be understood before suggestions for intervention become meaningful.

Much research in the past has been correlational in nature and, as such, has identified general relationships "between poor or inappropriate child rearing patterns" and the corresponding developmental, interpersonal, and behavioral outcomes in children. While such relationships exist, they are probabilistic in nature and do not apply to every child or every situation. Even at the time of birth, children are different from one another, they change as a result of time and experiences, and they respond differently in different situations and to different people. The theoretical understanding of developmental contextualism brings the complexity of causation to full awareness and emphasizes the suggestive rather than the compelling nature of such correlational findings.

When assessing the result of life events for the adolescent, simple cause-and-effect explanations are inappropriate. Parents need to become aware that childrearing, like other forms of complex human interaction, occurs within a given context. This context may have different meanings, depending upon the child's genetic or temperamental make-up as well as past experiences. Therefore, simple suggestions, provided by well-meaning outsiders— suggestions that may have worked well for them in a different context—may not work for a different child in a different context.

In his position as Director of the Institute for Children, Youth and Family at Michigan State University, Lerner has become increasingly concerned with the application of developmental contextualism and the human ecological perspective to the persistent and pervasive problems of the nation's children and youth (Miller & Lerner, 1994). Public policy and intervention programs, as well as the research agenda of government, universities, and faculty, are not sufficiently attuned to the variations in diversity and context of the critical issues facing the next generation. And, as some recent research has shown, rather than becoming more attuned to diversity, we seem to be losing ground. An analysis (Graham, 1992) of six prestigious APA journals reveals a steady decline over the last 20 years in both the number and the percentage of articles dealing with African Americans. In the 1970-1974 period African Americans were identified as research subjects in 5 percent of the 3,913 articles. In the 1985-1989 period only 2 percent of the articles identified African-American subjects. Hagen and Conley (1994), analyzing ethnicity and race in the journal, *Child Development*, from 1980-1993, similarly conclude that the number of journal articles studying only African-American, Asian, or Hispanic/Latino subjects has really been quite low and relatively constant during the 14-year period. Many of these scholarly investigations focus on the behavior of children in laboratories and not on real-life issues in which contextual variables determine the outcome. As Lerner likes to point out, the research community is becoming less, rather than more, concerned with diversity, and African Americans are increasingly marginalized in psychological research publications, even though they experience a disproportional number of psychosocial risk factors and contribute disproportionally to such issues as school dropout, delinquency, and other teenage problems. The existing diversity in the child and adolescent population is poorly represented in our research literature, even though it has been estimated that at some point in the twenty-first century more than half of all children in the United States will have become, what are currently referred to as "minority groups." A rather fundamental assumption of developmental contextualism is that identifed generalizations about human behavior and development do not permit "*a priori* assumptions that characteristics identified in one or even several samples exist in the same way in another group" (Miller & Lerner, 1994: 24). Lerner rather forcefully and repeatedly suggests that the implications of diversity have to be considered as a major focus in the study of human development. The meaning of diversity is that it is no longer defensible to assume that generally valid patterns of development exist or that developmental rules can be applied in the same fashion to all children and/or all families. Acknowledging diversity requires an awareness of the contributions that different social conditions make to development and an appreciation of the uniqueness that context makes to development (Lerner & Miller, 1993). Lerner, therefore, pleads that scholars need to change their research agenda by focusing less on disciplinary-based research, and by devoting more time and effort to integrated multidisciplinary research. He suggests a shift to a more problem-oriented and diversity-focused research agenda. In addition, he feels that researchers should become more involved in applications, policies, and programs. The personal and social problems of youth are no longer a matter of a few individuals having gone astray. Actually, a frightening 50 percent of today's youth are involved in two or more risk factors, such as "poverty, school failure, underachievement, and drop out, unsafe sex, teenage pregnancy and teenage-parenting, drug and alcohol use and abuse, and delinquency, crime and violence" (Miller & Lerner, 1994: 24). To this list one might add: feelings of hopelessness, despair, depression, suicide, suicide attempts, running away from home, homelessness, and abuse. While these risk factors have existed in the past, they have become much more pervasive and occur at historically unprecedented levels; in addition, they are occurring among increasingly younger age groups (Muuss, 1994), which means that they are more likely to solidify and are more likely to lead to other risk-taking behaviors. The age of beginning risk-taking behavior is an important contextual variable that influences the success of intervention programs. All of this suggests that the risk-taking behavior of the nation's youth is no longer an individual or a family issue but has become an all-encompassing social concern, which has to be recognized in its broader context of social and historical events. Data on adolescents' risk-taking behavior, according to Lerner, suggests that nothing short of a "generational time bomb is confronting American society." Lerner strongly argues that policies and programs need to become much more sensitive to the variations in context and the diversity of the human condition than they have been in the past (Lerner & Miller, 1993).

17

AN ANTHROPOLOGICAL
PERSPECTIVE OF ADOLESCENCE

The current upsurge of interest in the nature of adolescent development and theories of adolescence has brought to the foreground the significant issues of diversity (specifically, ethnic and cross-cultural differences) and of cross-cultural commonalities, yes, even of universals. Questions naturally arise about how and to what extent different cultural contexts shape and modify major life events and behaviors of adolescents.* In the past, cross-cultural and multicultural issues have rarely received the unifying theoretical attention they deserve in developmental psychology, especially in the study of adolescence. "The study of culture and related variables occupies at best a secondary place in American (mainstream) psychology" (Betancourt & Lopez, 1993: 629). This obvious neglect is based on the incorrect assumption "that the study of culture . . . contributes little to the understanding of basic psychological processes or to the practice of psychology in the United States" (Betancourt & Lopez, 1993: 629). Furthermore, the psychological and anthropological knowledge about cross-cultural influences that does exist is only minimally integrated into a broad developmental theory. The empirical and general descriptive cross-cultural development knowledge of adolescence has been accorded a limited place in theories of adolescence in the past. Even though some of the issues addressed in this chapter are controversial, the purpose is to include cultural commonalities and cultural differences in the analysis of adolescence, thus the necessity for adding an often neglected anthropological perspective.

Often unintegrated, knowledge from different disciplines about development in preindustrial societies is widely dispersed; however, the extensive knowledge about specific cul-

---

*The terms "culture" and "social" are used throughout this chapter; while they are different abstractions from the same phenomenon, their distinction is important and requires definition. According to Geertz (1973) and Keesing (1981), "culture" is a system of meanings and symbols that reveals an underlying framework of beliefs, standards, and values. It is within and by this cultural structure that social actions are guided and interpreted and, more generally, that social interactions take place. Social actions include the meaning attached to behavior for those who act in certain ways. The cultural system represents the background of beliefs, values, meanings, and symbols and reveals how they contribute to the functioning of the social system.

tural groups is seldom brought into a coherent and unifying developmental theory of cross-cultural comparison. That some developmental theories too readily claim "universality" for their respective statements and speak of universal stages without the necessary anthropological support is especially problematic. In actuality, theories in the past often presented insufficient cross-cultural evidence to support their broad claims of universality. The dilemma of developmental and cross-cultural psychology has received poignant articulation from Betancourt and Lopez (1993: 634). "The main limitation of mainstream theories is that they ignore culture and therefore lack universality. The limitation of a segregated cross-cultural psychology is that it fails to use experimentation and develop theory."

With the exception of Margaret Mead's somewhat romanticized (and recently challenged) description of adolescence in Samoa half a century ago (Mead, 1950), and the popular anthropological topic of *rites de passage*, that is, various and sometimes exotic puberty or initiation rituals (Muuss, 1980), the differential effect of cross-cultural socialization of adolescents remains widely neglected. Even mainstream textbooks on adolescence frequently present only limited coverage of adolescence in preindustrial societies and in cross-cultural perspective.

CROSS-CULTURAL SOCIALIZATION PATTERNS

Actually, more is known about the cross-cultural socialization patterns of children (Whiting & Edwards, 1988) than of adolescents. The reason is that the meaning of adolescence, the length of adolescence, and even the question of whether all cultural groups recognize adolescence as a distinctly identifiable period have been controversial. To some extent, the cross-cultural aspect of this vacuum is filled by the publication of a welcome and insightful, theoretical analysis by Alice Schlegel (1934-   ) and Herbert Barry, III (1930-   ): *Adolescence: An Anthropological Inquiry* (1991). This study is the result of an interdisciplinary effort that combines the expertise of Schlegel, an anthropologist, and Barry, a psychologist. While Schlegel's original research proposal set out to "develop a cross-culturally valid theory of adolescence as a universal social stage with generic characteristics," the goal of the actual investigation appears somewhat more modest. However, the debate about cultural diversity and the role that the cultural context plays in the emergence of individual and group differences and universalities receives a meaningful and stimulating impetus through Schlegel and Barry's analysis. Contextualists and social cognitive theorists may question the assumption that universal stages exist and are found in all cultures. Any future debate about cultural commonality and diversity and about the significance of cross-cultural influences on adolescence will need to consider the findings and the theoretical implications advanced by these scholars. They provide an elaborate picture of adolescence based on a broad and representative sweep of diverse cultural groups.

■ Methodological Information

For their data bases, Schlegel and Barry have relied on systematically collected anthropological information: The Standard Cross-Cultural Sample (SCCS). Extensive and widely used, this anthropological data base compiled by Murdock and White (1969, 1980) in-

Alice Schlegel (1934-   )

cludes information on 186 different societies. The cross-cultural (or hologeistic) method employed by anthropologists allows the systematic utilization of "the breadth of the ethnographic record" (Schlegel & Barry, 1991: 15). The societies included in the SCCS cover a broad and quite representative worldwide sample. All geographic regions and all cultural types receive attention, incorporating into the study different degrees of sociocultural complexities, subsistence technologies, family structures, and social organizations; therefore, the sample is quite representative of all human societies, with the exception of modern cultures which are included more for comparison and illustration than for systematic analysis. A total of 340 variables dealing with a great variety of adolescent issues were coded. Some are tallied with "yes" or "no," such as: "adolescents are significant socializers of young children." Other codes offer several options, such as, "Full sexual intercourse" can be coded: prohibited, tolerated, expected with limited number of partners, and with large number of partners. A partial listing of the more important codes are included in Appendix II of Schlegel and Barry's (1991) volume. While the use of such coded information obviously has methodological limitations, it is still much less skewed by the interacting influences

Herbert Barry, III (1930-   )

of ethnic, racial, social, and cultural factors that Betancourt and Lopez (1993) address, because these are the very factors that complicate cross-cultural research in the modern world.

In addition, Schlegel and Barry draw freely on the findings and observations of the wealth of other ethnological data and their own extensive anthropological field experiences and previous investigations. Schlegel has a long-standing research commitment to the life of the Hopi adolescent at the turn of the century, and she draws on that experience to present numerous illustrations. In addition, the authors include even some relevant ethnological data on primates. For example, gender differences in the range of activities and the geographic radius of movement are generally greater for boys than for girls. According to Schlegel, in all primate groups the males manifest a greater range of activities and a wider geographic radius of operation. Schlegel and Barry's analysis emphasizes social adolescence, the cross-cultural differences, and commonalities that almost universally characterize the transition from childhood to adulthood. Since these anthropologists have provided virtually the only broadly based cross-cultural approach to adolescent development theory, much of the subsequent material comes from their studies unless otherwise noted.

Many of the preindustrial societies that were part of this investigation have either vanished or have undergone such major transitions that they no longer can be considered preindustrial. Furthermore, the coded information no longer represents current social practices and cultural beliefs. These changes are due to the global impact of technology, communication, education, tourism, and the movement toward industrial production.

THE DEFINITION OF ADOLESCENCE

In modern society, adolescence is generally understood as a prolonged transition period between childhood and adulthood that prepares the young person for occupation, marriage, and mature social roles. The popular, widely used synonym "teenager" seems more closely allied with a specific age range. In ethnographic research, social roles, expectations, level of maturity, and the ability to function independently are the important variables, not age per se, since people in preindustrial societies may not even know their chronological age. Social adolescence frequently, but not necessarily, begins with puberty (menarche, semenarche), typically after the age of 11. Of those cultural groups for whom this information was available, the social recognition of adolescence begins at puberty for boys in 72 percent and for girls in 82 percent of the societies. And even in those societies in which social adolescence commences prior to puberty, such as the Aranda of Australia, the Copper Eskimo of Alaska, and the Yanomamo of Venezuela, adolescent initiation rituals may be tied to early body changes preceding puberty, such as the development of the girl's breasts among the Aranda. Obviously, the biological markers of puberty such as menarche, semenarche, changes in body configuration, and breast development in girls are the most common defining characteristics of the beginning of social adolescence. The end of adolescence is always defined by social criteria such as marriage, having one or several children, and being able to provide for a family. It commonly culminates with marriage, especially for girls, although marriage is not a universal indicator of adulthood.

Various academic disciplines have approached the definition of adolescence differently. Within psychoanalytic theory, the emphasis falls on resolving early childhood conflicts and learning to control aggressive and sexual impulses as well as achieving affective detachment from parents, often referred to as the "individuation process." Cognitive developmental psychologists see the major defining characteristics as cognitive reorganization (Piaget) and the emergence of higher-level thinking skills that characterize cognition after puberty. Sociologists and social psychologists, in contrast, see adolescence as a period of anticipatory socialization for adult roles and statuses. Of these three disciplines, the first two view adolescence from a psychological child development perspective, emphasizing the psychogenic causes of change, whereas the sociological approach investigates adolescence as a special training period leading to adult social roles and functions and focusing on the external environment, especially sociogenic causes of behavior.

Anthropologists understand adolescence not only as a time for learning new adult roles, as sociologists commonly do, but also as a time for learning the "situational needs of society." This perspective often finds expression in the symbolism of rituals and the underlying themes of initiation ceremonies. In addition, anthropologists see this period of life as one during which individuals often make important contributions to society. While the sociologist is asking how society affects the adolescent, the anthropologist is likely to add the complementary question: "How do adolescents affect society?" (Schlegel & Barry, 1991: 6). What contributions do adolescents make to society as workers, as helpers in the subsistence of the family, as entertainers on the stage and in the sports arena, and as bargaining assets in the negotiation of marriages?

Like psychologists' psychogenic definition and sociologists' sociogenic definition, Schlegel and Barry (1991: 8) define "adolescence as a social stage intervening between childhood and adulthood in the passage through life." However, anthropologists do not portray adolescence merely as a transitional or marginal period squeezed between childhood and adulthood. They see this crucial time as a period in its own right, with its own significance and meaning, best characterized as a period of "unlearning and relearning." Sociologists' definitions imply a period of learning social roles. However, Schlegel and Barry view this process as much more than a continuation of the kind of learning that had begun in childhood, including the most essential and important learning of dependency, subordination, and social asexuality. For these anthropologists, adolescence becomes a period of time characterized by much necessary unlearning of some of the attitudinal and behavioral patterns acquired during childhood. Such unlearning appears to be crucial for the individual in order to move toward independence, autonomy, and social sexuality, and to establish patterns essential for adult roles.* Schlegel and Barry (1991: 11) perceive adolescence as a period "during which these processes of reorganization get underway" but do not necessarily come to completion. Long after the termination of social adolescence, these reorganization processes continue well into adulthood. Sociologists argue that such reorganization processes do continue until we die—they involve learning new occupational roles, marital roles, retirement, old age, and whatever preparations a society offers for death.

Schlegel and Barry's idea that adolescence operates as a period of unlearning and relearning is analogous to Ruth Benedict's (1934) concept which much earlier had identified "cultural discontinuities" as an essential component of adolescence. Thus, from this perspective, adolescence becomes not so much a time during which earlier learning moves toward completion, but a time during which a great deal of unlearning, reorganization, and new learning takes place. The underlying dynamics that contribute to such processes of reorganization are the rapid biological changes of puberty and the almost universal incest taboo that prohibits sexual gratification within the family of origin, a taboo that propels adolescents to prepare for intimate relationships with partners outside of their own immediate family. (However, some societies encourage first cousin relationships.) G. H. Mead (1934) would add that it is the newly emerging ability to understand complex social relationships that allows individuals to understand the significance of the incest taboo. To accomplish all of this, the adolescent must unlearn family dependency, family subordination, and asexuality. The relearning that ensues inevitably contributes to the reorganization process of adolescence.

---

* Social psychologists, like G. H. Mead, also view adolescence as significantly different from childhood, because at about age 12 humans are able to see the interconnection between complex roles. At about this age, they begin the process of incorporating "the generalized other" into their self. Consequently, the period of adolescence is conceptualized as more than merely a continuation of previous learning.

■ The Peer Group and the Process of Reorganization

In many societies, peers play an important role in the socialization process of adolescence. The peer group encourages and supports "trying out"—often playfully, experimentally, and without being taken too seriously—some of the new roles and activities of adulthood without the direct interference or censure of the family; this occurs within the proximity of the potential shelter of the family, which provides a safe haven to which the young person can return. In the majority of earlier societies, adolescents actually spent most of their day with the same-sex parent or elsewhere with kin because their labor contributed to the livelihood of the family.

Regardless, most adolescents spend more time with peers of their own age, and even if this is not the case, the peer group acquires greater salience than it had for children. "Universally, . . . an important . . . structure is the peer group, comprising members of the same sex . . . [so that] the peer group becomes central to socialization in adolescence" (Schlegel & Barry, 1991: 9). Schlegel and Barry's study supports Bronfenbrenner's contention that an inverse relationship exists between the attachment of adolescents to their families and their dependency on the peer group. Both adolescent males and females around the world belong to a group of peers; however the degree of involvement differs for the genders. The influence of the peer group generally is more pronounced in the socialization of male adolescents than that of female adolescents. Males spend more of their time in peer group activities devoted to leisure activities than do females. The male peer group tends to be somewhat larger than the female peer group. In general, females participate in multi-age social settings and associate more with their mothers and other older females in most societies and hence, experience more influence from them than do males from their fathers and older males. For males, most leisure time peer group interaction takes place without older adults participating. According to Schlegel and Barry, these differential patterns of associating with adults (girls) or peers (boys) contribute significantly to gender differences.

The peer group may also function to lighten the burden of some work responsibilities. For example, Hopi girls who have been instructed to grind corn may make a party of the job by meeting in someone's house to talk and to joke while doing their cumbersome task.

PARENT-ADOLESCENT CONFLICT IN ANTHROPOLOGICAL PERSPECTIVE

G. Stanley Hall (Chapter 1) proposed that the period of adolescence is inevitably a period of storm and stress. Similarly, psychoanalytic theories have emphasized the universal nature of parent-adolescent conflict, and Erikson (1968) ascribes "a normative identity crisis" to the period of adolescence. Anna Freud (1958) with her often-quoted dictum, "To be normal during the adolescent period is by itself abnormal," takes the most radical position. However, more recently, the assumption that adolescence necessarily initiates a period of crisis and major conflict has been challenged. The pendulum apparently has swung to the other side: some researchers (Bandura, 1964) have labeled as fiction the idea of adolescence as "the stormy decade," a phrase that provided the title of an earlier publication (Mohr & Despres, 1958). In particular, Offer (1969, 1975) has advanced the idea that the period of adolescence is no more stressful, no more conflictual, and no more turbulent than any other period of development and that, if conflicts do arise, they result from external, situational factors. The rather extensive literature on adolescent risk-taking behavior (Muuss, 1993, 1994) does imply that adolescents in modern societies are confronted with unique adjustment problems. One well-known contextual factor contributing to conflict is the single-parent household. While the divorce is harder on children, remarriage is harder on adolescent girls.*

The issue remains controversial, and Montemayor's (1983) review of the research literature does suggest that some conflict may be a normal, healthy, growth-producing component of growing up. Brooks-Gunn and Reiter (1990) postulate that hormonal, endocrinological factors contribute to excitability, arousability, emotionality, and mood fluctuations, all of which may have a disquieting effect on parent-adolescent relationships. A well-tuned, careful analysis of the variations and the factors responsible for the stressful or smooth passage of adolescents can be found in Colton and Gore (1991). Thus, the issue of adolescent storm and stress, crisis, parent-adolescent conflict, and developmental turbulence may depend on the particular definitions of these terms and on the social structure of kin relationships. That is, how much pathology or how much normality is the observer willing to attach to such terms as "storm and stress," "crisis," "conflict," "turmoil," and "turbulence?"

According to Schlegel and Barry, the process of giving up some of the earlier patterns that parents have instilled during childhood and the efforts of acquiring new attitudes, values, and behavior that parents may have discouraged during childhood is not without some tensions to both adolescents and their families. Changing roles and changing expectations during social adolescence often become points of friction with potential for disagreements. Parents have to cope with adjusting their own attitudes, demands, and expectations to their maturing offspring. In addition, inevitably, some ambiguity and ambivalence confuse the process of interpreting the adolescent's developmental status in terms of where the individual stands in respect to dependency, subordination, and sexual maturity. Besides experiencing their parents' ambiguity and ambivalence, adolescents themselves have their own ambiguities and ambivalences, as do their families and the larger community. Because of the ongoing process of adolescents' unlearning and relearning and reorganizing major attributes and social roles, Schlegel and Barry (1991: 12) maintain how "unlikely [it is] that adolescence can be a stress-free time" for the growing individual as well as for the parents. In addition, the body changes accompanying puberty require major psychosocial adjustments; therefore, tensions resulting from internal hormonal changes, changes in body configuration, mood changes, social pressures, and newly emerging sexual needs intensify the process of social reorganization. How well these new adolescent realities fit into the social contexts or clash with family and community expectations and values becomes crucial. As a result, some social awkwardness and intrafamilial stress are not at all uncommon for adolescents, regardless of their national and cultural background.

While parent-adolescent relationships are unlikely to be stress-free, Schlegel and Barry do not find that conflicts commonly escalate into serious problems, emotional trauma, or pathology. On the other hand, discord over mundane issues are sufficiently common to be

---

* In some matrilineal societies, if such conflicts exist, they occur between adolescents (especially males) and their maternal uncle, whose role is that of authority figure and disciplinarian. In such societies, the biological father has a lesser degree of authority.

considered part of a general cultural pattern characteristic of social adolescence. Often, conflicts are temporary, emerging from petty issues, such as household chores, disobedience, and freedom of movement away from parental supervision, especially for girls. If, however, the parental control* of property and economic resources becomes a way of giving and withholding property to influence or control marriage choices and even control the possibility of marriage, then discord is likely. A somewhat extreme illustration cited by Schlegel and Barry (1991: 61) is the father in a pastoral society who may prefer the use of some of his cattle for bridewealth in order to acquire a second wife for himself rather than a first wife for his son.

A conflict between parents and adolescents may also arise if parents insist on the adolescents' contribution to household obligations, farm labor, or other economic contributions to the family's sparse resources at a time when society introduces adolescents to the opportunity of continued formal education. The disagreement becomes one between the needs of the family for significant labor contributions from their offspring, and the adolescent's desire to take advantage of educational opportunities and pursue an education to improve his or her status in society and better his or her life. Schlegel reports that this conflict occurred among Hopi youth at the beginning of the twentieth century when secondary school education became an option. This kind of discord was not at all uncommon among lower class boys in modern societies during the late nineteenth century; it became an issue for girls somewhat later. In general, when the elders tend to hold onto established, traditional, religious, ceremonial, and family values and practices and consequently, resist the propensity of youth toward change, modernization, technology, and education, conflicts are bound to arise.

Based on their analysis of data from 186 societies, Schlegel and Barry do not claim that storm and stress is an inevitable and universal characteristic of adolescence, but neither is it a calm or harmonious period; some conflict is not uncommon. The nature, duration, and intensity of such conflicts are quite variable, depending on the sociocultural context.

■ Cross-Cultural Factors, Gender, and Parent/Adolescent Stress

Schlegel and Barry identify some specific contextual anthropological variables that contribute to, or subtract from, parent/adolescent stress. In other words, they not only endorse the notion that contextual variables contribute to cross-cultural variability in parent-adolescent conflict and stress, they go one step further. Based on their sample of numerous societies' known operative contextual variables that may be responsible for more or less conflict between adolescents and their parents—even more specifically, between father-son, father-daughter, mother-son, and mother-daughter—Schlegel and Barry identify conditions and relationships likely to produce contention. The relationship between social conditions and discord provides insight into the nature of conflict.

Anthropologists have used several constructs to classify preindustrial societies. In their analysis of parent-adolescent relationships, Schlegel and Barry are primarily concerned with the following patterns of social organization:

---

* In matrilineal societies the control of the property may fall under the authority of the mother's brother, not her husband.

1. *Subsistence technology:* foraging, pastoral, horticultural, agricultural, and industrial
2. *Control over property:* private ownership or community property
3. *Structure of household:* matriarchal and patriarchal; nuclear or extended

Various subsistence technologies have different labor requirements that directly influence the extent of the contact between parents and offspring. The diverse requirements of subsistence technologies also determine differential or equal involvement of the sexes in household chores, family work activity, and more general economic productivity. Where the subsistence economy is based on private property, adolescents tend to be highly dependent on their parents for longer periods of time; therefore, opportunity for conflict is greater than in tribal societies with collectively owned property.

The three classification groups identified above are not independent of each other but are usually—although not always—interrelated. In foraging societies where individuals or small groups gather food, go hunting or fishing, private property is rare; in agricultural societies where families own, control, and cultivate the land, private property tends to be the norm.

In *agricultural and pastoral societies*, contacts between fathers and adolescent sons tend to be high. The crucial variable is the ownership of private property, which is rather common in such societies. The father manages and controls the property, but the son's labor contributions are essential in order to maintain the productivity necessary to support the family. In addition, the son needs training in the management of the property since he eventually will inherit it. However, as long as the father owns and controls the property, he plays the dominant role in relationship to his inexperienced son. Consequently, in this cultural pattern, father and son work together and thus have much contact, but the son occupies a subordinate role as an apprentice, a helper, and a laborer. As a result, disagreement between father and son tends to be high since (a) there is much personal contact, (b) the role relationship is dominant-father and subordinate-son, and (c) the issue of ownership may become a factor in the marriage of the son and his status in the community. Ownership of the property allows the father to determine how things are done and gives him status in his family and in the community, a position that he may be reluctant to relinquish. For example, in some farming communities in rural Ireland, fathers postpone turning over the ownership of the land to their sons as long as possible in order to maintain their status as landowners and to avoid becoming part of the powerless old-age group. Under such circumstances, discord between father and son appears inevitable.

In *foraging and horticultural societies*, the contact between fathers and sons, in comparison, is low. In horticultural societies, boys often have the task of tending cattle some distance away from the home and the father so that direct contact during the working day is limited; hence, there is little opportunity for disagreement. The individuals tending the animals, often in the vicinity where the sons of other families tend theirs, are basically on their own and have to learn to make major decisions early in life, for example, where to graze them, how to avoid dangerous locations, how to rescue a lost or injured animal, and how to fend off wild animals. Furthermore, the grazing land may be community property, another factor which contributes to the removal of the son from daily dominance by his father.

Conflict between parents and their daughters follows a somewhat different pattern and depends on somewhat different contextual circumstances. In many tribal societies, fathers tend to be generally more distant than mothers from their adolescent offspring of both sexes. However, beyond that generalization, a father's relationship with his offspring and his attitude toward them tends to be more differentiated than the mother's. The relationship with boys is more likely filled with discord, and the issue of dominance and subordination will probably loom large, especially in agricultural and pastoral societies. The father's relationship with his daughters tends to be more intimate. Perhaps because girls spend much more time with their mothers than do boys, they are also more intimate with their mothers than their brothers. But girls also show more subordination to mothers than do boys. In matrilineal/matrilocal societies, the transfer of household responsibility and the transfer of ownership of property from mother to daughter is more gradual and less conflictual than similar kinds of transfer in patrilineal/patrilocal settings. In an earlier study with preadolescent subjects Barry et al. (1957) found that the majority of societies socialized girls toward compliance—toward responsibility (61 percent) and nurturance (82 percent), boys toward achievement (87 percent) and self-reliance (85 percent).

While some of the relationships between parent-adolescent conflict and social organization are more pronounced than others, much variability exists, depending upon the cultural norms. Nevertheless, the data presented by Schlegel and Barry (1991) indicate that the nature of parent-adolescent relationships in general and parent-adolescent conflicts in particular are a function of such social-cultural variables as subsistence economy, ownership of property, and family structure. In general, Schlegel and Barry found relatively little evidence of severe conflict between adolescents and their parents in most societies and certainly no evidence of an inevitable period of "storm and stress."

ADOLESCENT SEXUALITY

With the advent of puberty and physiological maturity, sexuality increasingly becomes a personal need as well as an issue of societal concern. Preindustrial societies take rather divergent positions in regard to the degree of permissiveness or restrictiveness that governs adolescent sexual behavior during the period between puberty and marriage, for example, during social adolescence. Since in many preindustrial societies girls marry early and marriage provides adulthood status, the stage of adolescence for them may be relatively short. Adolescent sexuality may find overt expression in heterosexual intercourse, masturbation and/or homosexual acts. However, more systematic anthropological information is available about the heterosexual behavior of adolescents than about other sexual outlets and the research has focused more on the social norms applied to sexual behavior of girls than for boys. Even in permissive societies, the social and the parental concern with the girl becoming pregnant before marriage remains an issue and may indirectly contribute to parents' encouraging their daughters to marry early. Early betrothal would free them from the supervisory responsibility and avoid the possible family shame of a premarital pregnancy. However, there is considerable variation in courtship pattern and in social attitudes toward premarital sexuality. Some encourage, or at least tolerate, premarital sex and some do not even associate premarital pregnancy with shame.

A few samples may illustrate the wide range of social norms and/or attitudes toward adolescent sexuality:

- In some traditional Muslim societies, the girl is particularly restricted. She is not allowed to speak to a man outside her family; she is required to wear a veil to cover her face in public; she is aware that the social concern with premarital chastity is strong and that loss of virginity would bring great shame to her and her family. In fact, should that occur, she might become a social outcast or she might even be killed by a male relative. Stoning to death was still practiced in rural areas of some societies.
- A stark contrast can be found among the boys and girls in some societies of Polynesia, who live a more carefree existence with more permissive attitudes. Both sexes attend joint festivities, dance and enjoy clandestine amorous encounters without serious social sanctions.
- The peak of permissiveness, according to Schlegel and Barry (1991), is found among the Ifugao and Bontoc tribes of remote mountain areas in the Philippines and the Murai in central India. These people provide an adolescent social organization that allows boys to live unsupervised in a dormitory type of place, where girls join them in the evening for talk, games, dancing, and massages. Eventually, those who intend to have intercourse retire to a separate hut. The couple practices *coitus interruptus* to avoid pregnancy. Adolescents experience a highly eroticized life. However, even in this permissive setting, not everybody has a partner, which may result in jealousy.
- An interesting compromise used to be made among the East African Kikuyu, who permit their adolescents considerable freedom to experiment sexually, but in spite of this, they also insist that girls maintain their virginity. In earlier times, girls came to the boys' dormitories to join them in festivities, which involved much heavy petting, and at least for the boys, orgasm, but without penetration because the girls would always keep on their leather pubic aprons. Similarly, the Nyakyusa practice interfemoral intercourse to assure the virginity of the girl.
- In rural Haiti, a different kind of social inconsistency has been observed. While the overall social attitude toward premarital sex is quite permissive, this changes if the girl gets pregnant, in which case strong social disapproval and threat of punishment emerge (Herskovits, 1971). In addition, the family of the pregnant girl is shamed.

■ Sexual Permissiveness versus Sexual Restriction

In general, for the large number of preindustrial societies for which reliable data are available, more societies take a permissive position toward premarital sexual intercourse rather than a restrictive approach. Usually, those societies that are restrictive toward the expression of sexuality for one sex also have restrictive attitudes for the other sex (N=29). However, there are some inconsistent societies that have different standards for boys and girls. Most of the societies with inconsistent standards (N=14) are coded as being permissive for males while prohibiting sexual intercourse for females; the reverse pattern, allowing girls to engage in sexual intercourse but prohibiting it for boys, is rare (N=2). Permissive societies are generally permissive for both sexes (N=108), but often not to the same degree because the parental and social concern for a girl losing her virginity or becoming pregnant is an issue, even in permissive societies. Therefore, in the past, anthropological research has focused much more extensively on the socially defined premarital sex norms for girls. Parents may have ambivalent feelings toward their daughter's sexuality, insofar as they may very well admonish or scold the girl for being sexually active, but they may actually do very little to restrict her contact with boys.

Schlegel and Barry add a crucial theoretical-anthropological dimension to the discussion of adolescent sexuality because they perceive the level of sexual permissiveness or social restrictiveness not only as an individual or family concern, but as a function of cultural variables and patterns of social organization. The theoretically significant theme is that cultural attitudes and norms for premarital sexual intercourse are related to other kinds of adolescent behavior and other aspects of a society's culture, including: "simpler subsistence technology, absence of stratification, smaller communities, . . . absence of belief in high gods, . . . high female economic contribution, little or no property exchange at marriage, and ascribed rather than achieved status" (Schlegel & Barry, 1991: 112). In addition, when the period of social adolescence ends early (i.e., within two years after it begins), marriage follows relatively soon after menarche. Sexual permissiveness is more likely to be found in those societies in which adolescence is short than in societies where social adolescence is prolonged. One of the reasons may well be that postmenarchial intercourse during the first year, because of adolescent sterility or subfecundity, is unlikely to result in pregnancy (Ashley Montagu, 1957; Mills & Ogle, 1936). All of the factors related to sexual permissiveness tend to be interrelated with one another and generally are characteristic of less complex societies. Premarital female sexual intercourse is not so much a matter of biology as a correlate of social organization and socially prescribed norms.

Premarital sexual restrictiveness results from another set of cultural values and/or social structures. The relationship between such cultural norms for sexual behavior and these social variables (discussed below) is more pronounced for girls than for boys. In social groups in which girls are highly subordinated to, and hence highly supervised by, their mothers, sexual behavior is likely to be more restricted. Also, when parents or kin assert strong control over the selection of their offsprings' marriage partners, the standards for the sexual behavior of their children tend to be restricted because the sexual attachments that youths might form on their own would likely interfere with the family's marriage plans for them.

When some form of property transfer, such as dowry, indirect dowry, or gift exchange is part of the marriage arrangement—commonly found in more complex societies—families are more concerned about maintaining their daughter's virginity, and by implication, her desirability as a marriage partner; hence, they take a more restrictive posture. Many dowry-giving societies, such as those in the Mediterranean area (ancient Greece, Egypt, Rome) maintain the "honor-shame complex," whereby the family's honor is linked to the girl's chastity and loss of virginity before marriage results in loss of honor and invites social shame: "If no property accompanies marriage, there are likely to be few sexual restrictions" (Schlegel & Barry, 1991: 131).

When social status is an important issue for the family—as it tends to be among those who have attained a relatively elevated social position and have acquired some level of wealth—the likelihood that some restrictions will govern the girl's sexual activity is greater because parents in such situations desire that their daughter marry into an equal or higher social status level. This is especially true if girls marry relatively late. Virginity in such situations remains a major concern, because lower status boys would have much to gain and nothing to lose if they can claim that they are the father of the child of a girl of high social status and/or of wealth. Even in Samoa, which is generally perceived as a very permissive society, the daughter of the chief must maintain her virginity until after marriage: "Virginity is a legal requirement for her" (Mead, 1950: 70). Mead reports that even for the average girl in Samoa virginity adds to her attractiveness and prestige for her and her bridegroom's family.

There is some evidence that the degree of sexual freedom or restriction during adolescence is related to the frequency of adultery and divorce in adulthood. When adolescent boys enjoy sexual freedom, they are more likely to be adulterous later in adulthood. Similarly, if adolescent girls have the freedom to be sexually active, they later as adults are more inclined to be unfaithful. In other words, the sexual behavior patterns established during adolescence tend to show consistency with sexual behavior as adults (Barton, 1969; Schlegel & Barry, 1991).

Sexual restrictiveness is widely related to the presence of a double standard, while permissiveness tends to be associated with the absence of a double standard. To the extent that the sexual activities of adolescent boys and girls and women are restricted, a more general social "control over subordinate persons" (Schlegel & Barry, 1991: 109) may be found. This is most common is societies in which boys, girls, and adult women are subordinated to the control of the men; thus, "sexual freedom is one of the privileges accorded to dominant adult men only."

Sexual permissiveness is not without its own set of drawbacks and social and psychological consequences. The adolescent without a sex partner may feel more threatened than he or she would in a more restrictive setting and may experience feelings of jealousy or personal inadequacy. Most social groups disapprove of adolescent premarital pregnancy. Thus, sociocultural sexual patterns that allow sexual experimentation short of vaginal intercourse have emerged, such as *coitus interruptus*, interfemoral intercourse, and heavy petting, with the girl keeping her leather pubic apron in place. These kinds of social-sexual behavior patterns permit sexual experimentation but greatly reduce the chance of pregnancy.

Homosexual behavior was frequently not reported, so that the available data do not permit conclusive generalizations. However, for those societies that report homosexual activity among adolescents, it is more commonly permitted or tolerated rather than forbidden, even in societies where it is disapproved for adults. The evidence that is available does not suggest that homosexual experiences during adolescence lead to homosexual preferences among adults later. In general, where homosexuality was observed, it was viewed as a substitute for sexual involvement with the opposite sex or was simply shrugged off as childish behavior which the individual would outgrow (Schlegel, 1995).

HOW SOCIETIES RECOGNIZE ADOLESCENCE AS A DISTINCT STAGE

Societies use different means and methods in their recognition of social adolescence as a unique developmental phase that serves as a demarcation from both childhood and adulthood. Clear recognizable social "markers" delineate and define the transition from childhood to adolescence and sometimes even adulthood.

■ Descriptive Expressions

Specific language expressions that would be inappropriate to describe children or adults are used to refer to individuals who are socially recognized as adolescents, expressions that would be equivalent of such English words as "adolescent," "teenager," "juvenile," "youth," or "student." The Navaho Indians refer to the girl between childhood and adulthood as a "ch'ikeet" and the boy as "tsikeet." Corresponding language expressions to identify and differentiate the unique developmental phase of social adolescence exist in the languages of many cultural groups, but not all. Newman (1988) observes that some societies refer to the short period of passage from one status to another status role, commonly celebrated in the form of initiation rituals, as a "period of liminability." This period of transition during which one's status is not clearly defined is characterized by ambiguity, and others are expected to avoid the person during this period.

■ Rites and Ceremonies

In many preindustrial societies, the entry of boys and girls into adolescence is marked by *rites de passage*, puberty rites, or initiation ceremonies. Schlegel and Barry (1980: 698) define such initiation rituals "as some social recognition, in ceremonial form, of the transition from childhood into either adolescence or full adulthood." These public and sometimes private celebrations recognize social adolescence and publicly focus the community's awareness upon the individual's changing social roles and/or sexual status. Of the societies for which information exists, 68 percent conduct transition rituals for boys, 79 percent for girls. Apparently, social recognition of role changes and changes in sexual status are more common for girls. The girls' puberty rites are linked closely to physiological changes (e.g., menarche) and are more likely to be conducted for a single individual. In the case of boys, these initiation ceremonies may be major community celebrations and often involve a group of boys. However, the term "puberty rites" may be a misnomer since the initiates, especially among boys, may constitute rather diverse age groups (and the age may vary in different societies by as much as 8-10 years), and can range from prepubescence through pubescence and beyond. Such developmental diversity is less common for girls for whom the ceremony is more likely related to other developmental events, such as menarche, defloration, betrothal, or marriage. Consequently, physiological puberty and the ceremonial admission into social adolescence may be separated in time, but the latter is more important in conveying a new social status. For girls, such initiations tend to be more individual, private and family-oriented, but with many exceptions. Eliade (1958) identifies some common gender differences in the initiation of both sexes. For boys, it reflects an introduction into the world of his culture. For the girl, the message tends to be more a revelation of the meaning of menstruation, sexuality, and childbirth. For both genders, such ceremonies emphasize the social separation from the family, contact with the spiritual world, bonding among peers and the society of adults, and very importantly, the deflection of sexuality away from the family and toward members of the opposite sex. The theme of ritual death and rebirth is relatively rare but can be found in the Congo and Loange regions of Africa. The 10-to-12-year-old male initiates are required to drink a potion that makes them unconscious. Subsequently, they are carried into the jungle, where they are circumcised and ritually buried. It is assumed that upon awakening they have forgotten their past.

The most common ceremonial themes for both sexes are: responsibility (adult duties), fertility, and sexuality, and less common, valor and wisdom. Usually, these themes are tied to the nature of the contributions that the initiate is supposed to make later in life and to the complexity of social organization. Among foraging societies, productivity and, for girls, fertility are the most common ceremonial messages. Horticultural societies are more likely to emphasize fertility as the ceremonial theme for both sexes. Advanced agricultural societies are less likely to celebrate the transition into puberty as an event deserving public recognition. Thus, one way in which the transition between childhood and social adolescence is clearly recognized and through which the initiates are incorporated into sexually defined social categories, at least in a large proportion of preindustrial societies, is through such rituals (Schlegel & Barry, 1980).

Confirmation, bar and bat mitzvahs are religious initiation rituals that denote changes in religious status, but they do not convey a generally recognized change in social status. However, high school graduation provides a socially recognized diploma, and for many adolescents, prom night is a significant event; especially among lower-class youth, high school graduation commonly constitutes such a "marker" and denotes the end of adolescence. For the individual youth, attaining his or her first driver's license often has the personal meaning of such a "marker." Elkind (1981) bemoans the disappearance of clear social markers in Western societies since they provided public recognition of the individual's developmental level. This encouraged parents and educators to respect the uniqueness of the developmental stage of the young person. In contemporary society, the pressure is on children to be independent and successful and to look and act like adults; pushing children to succeed, society neglects to provide them with the structure and the time to simply grow, learn, and develop.

■ Visual Markers

Visual markers also may distinguish the adolescent from a child, and in some societies, from an adult (Schlegel & Barry, 1991: 37). For example, a change in the hair arrangement for girls is such a visual marker for the Hopi female. The child displays a miniature version of the butterfly hair arrangement. Following a private initiation ritual, the adolescent girl changes her hair into large butterfly wings on each side of her head. This changed hair style signals that she now is approachable for courtship. After marriage, the hair is worn in the style of adult women, consisting of two braidlike ropes. For the Chatino Indians of Oaxaca, Mexico, the visual marker is a shawl. With the social recognition of adolescence, the small *rebozo* (shawl) worn by children is replaced by a large *rebozo*, large enough to carry babies, a common task of adolescent girls. This author, growing up in a rural, Protestant farming village in Northern Europe, remembers that all boys wore short trousers, even in winter, with long socks to keep their legs warm. Only after religious confirmation, which coincided with leaving school and beginning an apprenticeship for most, did boys begin to wear adult-style trousers.

As a generalization, the boys in 86 percent and the girls in 88 percent of the cultural groups studied do indicate their transition from childhood to adolescence through such visual markers. Visual markers for the transition from adolescence into adulthood are less common. That transition usually comes much earlier for girls than for boys in the form of marriage and parenthood. In 63 percent of the cultural groups, girls marry at approximately age 16. As a general pattern, the period of social adolescence is longer but less clearly demarcated for boys and involves the acquisition of work skills and the establishment of reproductive relationships.

■ New Social Roles

Societies recognize social adolescence as a period that differs from childhood by the changes in obligations, responsibility, work tasks, display of sexual attractiveness, marriageability, and new social roles. Often similar changes (less dramatic) identify the changes from adolescence to adulthood through the assignment of new and different social, economic, and religious tasks. Of the 78 societies for which this information is coded, in 64 societies (82 percent) adolescents assume new obligations and tasks in the community. These roles involve economic productivity (specific work tasks in the household, the farm, or the shop); military training (participation in actual warfare is reserved for late adolescence); the permission to participate in religious functions, rituals, and obligations (e.g., Communion); and other ways of contributing to the welfare of the community. Such role changes are less frequently coded for girls (45 societies have information on this) and less community involvement is required of girls (60 percent of those coded).

Marriage, parenthood, and full reproductive adult status define the end of adolescence functionally. In addition, for the male, the ability to provide for a wife and children constitutes a clear social marker for the beginning of adulthood.

HYPOTHESES REGARDING HUMAN UNIVERSALS

Two major hypotheses regarding human universals and gender differences, for which much support is presented, guided the inquiry of Schlegel and Barry.

The period of adolescence, specifically referred to as social adolescence, constitutes a universal or near universal stage in the human life cycle. Adolescence is one of the four major demarcations—infancy, childhood, adolescence, and adulthood—in the human life cycle worldwide. The treatment and the status of the individual in the community and even within the family changes in identifiable ways for each of these four basically different social stages. "Some measurable differences exist across cultures between the treatment of girls and that of boys, corresponding to a universal distinction between the sexes in social roles and cultural perception" (Schlegel & Barry, 1991: 12).

The issue of "human universals" seemed to have been laid to rest with the contributions of the earlier anthropological works of Boas, Benedict, and Mead, and the contributions of some social psychologists and developmental contextualists. But forceful argument espousing human universals has emerged through Schlegel and Barry's research. In addition, it appears as no coincidence that in the same year Schlegel and Barry's book was published, another anthropologist, Donald E. Brown (1991), published *Human Universals*. The major assumption of this book is that there are indeed innumerable human universals; thus, Brown's volume constitutes another major challenge to any theory of simple cultural relativity. Brown addresses many universal patterns without focusing on adolescence in particular.

All societies recognize a period of social adolescence as a distinct stage that confers a unique status for boys; almost all societies also do this for adolescent girls. Social adolescence divides childhood from the full recognition of an individual as an adult by the respective social-cultural criteria for adulthood (e.g., marriageability, self-supporting ability, hunting, going to war). The criteria for "social adolescence" vary for different cultural groups, but the fact that they exist appears to be universal. For example, boys in foraging societies have to prove their ability to provide meat for a wife and children.

Schlegel and Barry "do recognize the disjuncture between biological maturity and social maturity" (Schlegel & Barry, 1991: 11); they also acknowledge that the onset of adolescence usually parallels those biological changes identified as "puberty." However, in some societies, childhood ends and social adolescence begins before puberty.

The Exception to the Rule

One society provides the exception to Schlegel and Barry's claim for universal social adolescence: the Gros Ventre Indians, for whom there exists no social adolescence for girls. Two belief systems that the Gros Ventre Indians hold explain this phenomenon: (1) that the first menstruation occurs only as a result of having experienced sexual intercourse, and (2) that girls must be virgins at the time of marriage. Consequently, the young girl marries before puberty because of the conviction that sexual intercourse is the essential prerequisite for menstruation. As a wife, the young prepubertal girl actually is required to perform those tasks expected of her as a housewife; in the larger community, she takes on the legal and social status of an adult even though she is only 9 or 10 years old. If the prepubertal girl is the co-wife in a polygamous household, she may receive special consideration from her husband's other wives, who treat her almost as a little sister. However, even in this somewhat more protected situation, she does have full adult status in the community. But the Gros Ventre Indians present the exception: All other societies in the sample studied recognize a period, sometimes of relatively short duration, of social adolescence distinguishable from childhood and adulthood. The period of social adolescence generally falls between puberty and the assumption of socially defined adult roles, which, for girls, usually is marriage.

■ The Controversy of Universality versus Adolescence as a Modern "Invention"

Schlegel and Barry seriously challenge the widely held contention (Ariès, 1962) that, historically speaking, adolescence, as a distinct developmental stage, is a modern phenomenon, basically a creation of the Industrial Age. They maintain that almost all nonindustrialized societies recognize a period of adolescence as one of the four generally, socially acknowledged life stages: infancy, childhood, adolescence, and adulthood. Obviously, the proposition that adolescence is a universal phenomenon is a controversial one, rooted in theoretical axioms not unrelated to the nature-nurture issue, and has been debated for almost a century. Among theories of adolescence the claim that it is a universal phenomenon has been both a popular one, but also one that has been seriously challenged and questioned. The best-known early proponents of the universality of adolescence were G. Stanley Hall and Sigmund Freud. Most stage theorists who postulate that the developmental process consists of a sequence of universal stages, such as Erikson, Piaget, Kohlberg, Selman, Loevinger, and Fowler, assume that the period of adolescence constitutes one (or several) stages in that sequence. Stages that define the unique quality of adolescence in all probability exist in all societies. The title and the content of Kiell's (1964) *The Universal Experience of Adolescence* support the idea—based on an analysis of literature, autobiographies, diaries, etc., both cross-culturally and historically—that adolescence is a universal phenomenon. Thus, many scholars from different perspectives have come to the conclusion that adolescence is universal.

Opposing positions of which Leta Hollingworth (1928) was an early proponent have emphasized continuity in development: "The child grows by imperceptible degrees into the adolescent, and the adolescent turns by gradual degree into the adult" (p. 1). More recently, social learning theory postulated that development is continuous and that changes in social status, role, employability, and marriageability are determined by social expectations (or social norms) and not by universal, biological patterns. In addition, there are those who view adolescence—especially the prolonged period of adolescence—as a relatively recent cultural "invention," and claim that the attributes of adolescence have changed greatly over time and from one location to another. In line with that reasoning, Fasick (1994) has proposed a theory that adolescence is really not more than an "invention" of modern times. Accordingly, adolescence, as we know it today, did not exist in preindustrial societies, did not exist in historical earlier periods of time, and thus is not universal. Under the impact of technological inventions, the Industrial Revolution, and the improved economic conditions which it generated, structural and demographic changes have taken place, especially in Western-industrial societies, which greatly prolong the transition period from childhood to adulthood. These recent changes are seen as the causes of the "invention" of adolescence. The general availability and the increasingly compulsory nature of secondary schools have removed adolescents from the workplace and placed them in an educational setting with a cohort of peers, thus removing them from much interaction with adults and shifting the primary social orientation to peers. It is the life-style created by the secondary school that conveys the image of adolescents as we know them today. The more stable, economically better-off and smaller family structure created by the Industrial Revolution make adolescents dependent on their family longer, being high school students virtually mandates living at home with parents. Specialization and diversification of occupational roles in the modern world poorly equip adolescents to become financially independent without education. In addition, state-imposed child labor and school attendance laws literally deprive the adolescent of the kind of meaningful responsibility and meaningful work roles which are taken for granted in primitive societies. In colonial and antebellum United States, these patterns of meaningful responsibility and genuine labor contributions were still the common pattern for those young people who today are referred to as "adolescents." Today, otherwise biological and sexually mature individuals are deprived of adult roles and adult privileges; they are excluded from the workplace, are forced to attend school, are not allowed to smoke, to vote, to drink, and are deprived of other adult privileges, and hence remain in a state of both deprivation and dependency on their parents. According to Fasick, it is this socially enforced immaturity that has contributed to the "invention" of adolescence.

The distinction between these different schools of thought on the nature of adolescence is an interesting one; taken at their extreme, they represent truly important differences. On the other hand, the prolonged period of adolescence in modern urban-industrial society, which according to Fasick results from deprivation, is certainly different from the often short and more natural (less deprived) period which Schlegel and Barry describe. However, Fasick is fully aware that there is a merging of these positions and actually concludes his "invention" argument with a statement that could just as well have come from Schlegel and Barry: "It is probably true that the transitional period between childhood and adulthood is recognized in *all societies* [italics mine] as, in some sense, a distinct time in life" (Fasick, 1994: 20). Thus, the notion of a prolonged period of dependency with legal deprivation for work opportunities and legal school requirements may be more the identification of a specific modern pattern of prolonged adolescence unique to Western-industrial society rather than any solid evidence that this is the sole pattern of true adolescence. Or are we to believe that Schlegel and Barry's universally recognized period of adolescence and Fasick's modern "invention" of adolescence are two rather diverse ways of experiencing and defining adolescence? Schlegel and Barry argue that adolescence is not really a modern invention, but a well-documented social phenomenon throughout human history even though some of the specific social manifestations may differ both historically and cross-culturally.

GENDER DIFFERENCES

Studies of cultural groups suggest that the sexes are commonly treated differently: "Measurable differences exist across cultures between the treatment of girls and that of boys, corresponding to a universal distinction between the sexes in social roles and cultural perception" (Schlegel & Barry, 1991: 12). Furthermore, the commonalities in the patterns in which boys and girls are treated tend to be more pronounced than the differences. Socialization practices are not sufficiently different, "to produce for example, aggressive boys and passive girls" (Schlegel & Barry, 1991: 183). In contrast, gender differences frequently can be explained on the basis of different relationships that male and female adolescents have with adults versus peers.

Gender differences commonly manifest themselves in family and peer group patterns:

1. Many societies tend to separate boys and girls at puberty, but the patterns for boys and girls differ. The adolescent male is much more likely to be excluded from recreational adult male activities. The girl, in contrast, is encouraged to participate in the activities of adult females, interacting with them and spending much time with them. Consequently, girls experience more family continuity and more involvement in home activities than do boys. This finding of gender differences in social interaction patterns is a compelling generalization emerging from Schlegel and Barry's data and analysis.

2. Adolescent girls, who are much more likely to maintain intensive attachments to their families, especially same-sex relatives, are more actively involved with them than are adolescent boys. Boys spend time working with men, but in their social and leisure time activities they experience social and physical separation from the male cohort and tend to interact with each other and form their own social group, the peer group.

3. The social distinction between girlhood and womanhood is less pronounced than the differentiation between boyhood and manhood, a factor that is sometimes highlighted in the male initiation ceremonies. This lack of noticeable differentiation for females facilitates the development of relatively smooth social relationships between girls and women, much more so than those between adolescent boys and adult men. For boys, the relationships are frequently work-oriented and have a hierarchical quality to them, in that the older male gives orders while the adolescent is the subordinate.

4. Girls are directly and personally involved with their mothers and, consequently, with other adult females in the community. In contrast, boys tend to be much more intently and extensively involved with their peer group than with their fathers and other adult models, for whom they work; hence, they are less a part of the adult male group. With puberty, the significance of the peer group increases for both sexes, but much more so for boys than for girls, and the boys' peer group may actually encourage antisocial behavior while the girls' peer group is more likely to reinforce existing socialization patterns.

5. Adolescence is of similar importance for males and females; however, the period of social adolescence, worldwide, tends to be considerably longer for boys than for girls, partly because girls marry at a younger age. In many societies, the difference in length of adolescence for boys and for girls is as much as two to four years.

6. The adolescent's contact with the father carries a different meaning for male and female offspring in most societies. Fathers tend to treat their sons differently than they do their daughters. For sons, fathers require subordination, a behavior that can lead to conflict. Fathers' interactions with their daughters are more likely to involve intimacy. Among preindustrial societies, differential treatment of sons and daughters is much more characteristic of fathers than it is of mothers. Similar findings are frequently reported for lower-class parents in the Western world.

■ Universals or Near-Universals: Romantic Love

Basing their analysis on the same SCCS as Schlegel and Barry, Jankowiak and Fischer (1992) raise the additional issue of whether romantic love is a unique Euro-American phenomenon and a historically recent one. Philippe Ariès (1962) and Stone (1988: 16) had maintained: "If romantic love ever existed outside of Europe, it only arose among the nonwestern nation-states' elite who had the time to cultivate an aesthetic appreciation of subjective experiences." Jankowiak and Fischer (1992: 150) define romantic love as an "intense attraction that involves the idealization of the other, within an erotic context, with the expectation of enduring for some time into the future." Among the 166 cultures that Jankowiak and Fischer considered, the existence of romantic love—most likely, adolescent love—received clear documentation in 147 societies (88.5 percent). For the remaining 19 cultures (11.5 percent), they found no specific evidence for or against the presence of romantic love. However, this by itself is hardly convincing evidence that love did not occur. In fact, for 18 of this subgroup of 19 cultures, evidence reveals that sexual affairs did indeed occur, although the motives for such sexual affairs, whether lust or love, were not revealed by the data. Jankowiak and Fischer (1992: 153) concluded that in almost every culture, "some individuals, often in the face of some severe negative sanctions, do fall in love." This analysis not only puts into question the notion that romantic love is a unique Western cultural and Industrial Age phenomenon, but also suggests that youthful love "constitutes a human universal, or at least a near-universal" (p. 154). In very few societies, however, is romantic love the major basis for marriage.

■ Reproductive Maturity and the Avoidance of Incest

Culturally, the most significant of the biological changes of puberty is the "transformation from a nonreproductive state to a reproductive state" (Schlegel & Barry, 1991: 18). Reproduction and the social control issues related to it provide one key for understanding adolescence. Reproductive maturity creates "the problem of fertile daughters and the lusty sons," which each society must address unless it wants girls to be married at puberty or to become pregnant without the economic support for mother and child that marriage commonly provides. The social mechanisms for controlling reproduction deeply influence the lives of adolescents because they form part of a system of kinship and marriage arrangements that are themselves part of the larger sociocultural organization.

Schlegel and Barry (1991) use one fundamental principle to unify and explain many of their findings, especially those related to gender differences. That is, the social control of sexuality and mate selection frequently highlights the significance of cultural deterrence for "close inbreeding." A fundamental near-universal cultural concern is the avoidance of incest, a goal accomplished by social mechanisms that lower the chances for in-family breeding. The incest taboo almost universally applies to the prohibition of the mating of parents with their children and the mating of siblings. Beyond that, societies use different standards in the definition of incest and permission/prohibition of mating and marriage of more distant blood relationships (e.g., cousins). The idea that incest is a near-universal human taboo, but that the specific definition as to whom it includes varies greatly, is expressed by Benedict (1934/1959: 32–33): "The relatives to whom the prohibition refers differ utterly among different peoples, but all human societies are alike in placing a restriction. No human idea has received more constant and complex elaboration in culture than this of incest."

Many two-sexed species seem to have developed various strategies for reducing "close inbreeding." Two mechanisms help in accomplishing that goal: (1) The dispersal of the young, once they can fend for themselves, in relatively distant locations; and (2) a kind of genetically preprogrammed "sexual repulsion" (e.g., in mice), which occurs between parents and offspring as well as between siblings. The almost universal cultural taboo against incest in humans does not totally prevent its occurrence. (The widespread breach of the incestuous taboo in Western society has only recently been recognized as a major social, legal, and mental health problem, one that appears to be much more prevalent than had been assumed.) Some societies provide much more stringent sanctions against breaking the incest taboo than others. In a few very rare instances, such as the incestuous marriages of Egyptian and Hawaiian royalty and some African noble clans, incest was tolerated because it was intended to maintain the purity of the bloodline.

However, the more global social issue remains: How to ensure that sexually mature males and females avoid incest. The most common strategies to avoid "close inbreeding" have already been identified: Societies separate the sexes during most of the day and encourage daughters to associate with mothers and other females, whereas sons are expected to associate with adult males and with same-sex peers outside the family. Other related strategies include: Males and females often are in the company of other people, girls with adult females, boys with their fathers or their peers. Societies emphasize the significance of the peer group, especially for males. Through the avoidance of unapproved mating patterns among family and relatives, societies attempt to control inappropriate incestual relationships. Strategies revolving around "incest avoidance" thus become the ethological basis for the almost universal dichotomy in the roles, activities, and expectations of the two genders during adolescence, and thus contribute to the formation of gender differences. In addition, marriages are arranged in a way that encourages the formation of social alliances across kin groups, which minimizes the likelihood of conflict between these groups. Some anthropologists have argued that this is an important reason for the incest taboo—as well as the fact that incest inevitably creates jealousy and conflict within the family unit.

VARIATIONS (AND COMMONALITIES) IN ADOLESCENT BEHAVIOR ACROSS CULTURES

Even though much current theorizing emphasize the diversity of adolescent experiences, the meanings attached to these experiences depend on family, social, ethnic, and cultural contexts. Schlegel and Barry (1991: 12) give credence to diversity, but in contrast to Lerner, they emphasize commonalities at least as much if not more: "The empirical evidence is weighted on the side of commonalities across culture," and, apparently, the commonalities and the universals provide the impetus for Schlegel and Barry's theoretical model. Brown (1991) also makes a convincing argument for a great number of human universals.

Many of the specific structures and activities of the adolescent's life differ from culture to culture. Variations in the specifics of adolescent behavior, in particular, depend upon sociocultural structural factors, or more precisely, on the cultural values and the cultural patterns that determine the social organization:

- The social organization and the kinship system
- The family structure and/or the type of marital exchange
- The types of economic mode and technology
- The religious practices and traditional values of the community

Schlegel and Barry (1991) are identifying consistent patterns of cultural practices and beliefs and their influence on specific adolescent adjustment and behavior patterns. Thus, in a roundabout way, findings relating cultural patterns to variations in adolescent values and behaviors from an anthropological perspective highlight the significance of the cultural context in influencing the developmental outcome of adolescence. Obviously, the organizational structure of society is at least as, or even more important than, the maturational biological forces for understanding adolescence.

■ Limitations

In spite of the dust jacket promise that claims "the authors address the implications of their findings for contemporary adolescent life in Western society," one of the limitations of Schlegel and Barry's anthropological inquiry is that their systematic analysis almost exclusively focuses on preindustrial and primitive societies. Indeed, the relationship to and the implication for modern Western society receive much more general treatment. References to the adolescent in the Industrial Age remain incidental and anecdotal and serve as illustrations and contrast, but do not become part of the systematic analysis. Regrettably, the contemporary American adolescent did not constitute part of this cross-cultural inquiry, and Schlegel and Barry only loosely relate the existing knowledge about contemporary American adolescents to their detailed and systematic findings about growing up in preindustrial societies. However, the complexity of such a comparison would be a Herculean task, as Betancourt and Lopez (1993) dramatically demonstrate, since social class, race, ethnicity, and culture are all interrelated and constitute compounding variables, each requiring consideration. Studying the process of adolescence in the less complex preindustrial societies provides a more manageable task and allows the identification of the influence on development of specific social structures.

SUMMARY

Schlegel and Barry provide extensive information about variations in the treatment and the outcome of "social adolescence." Although such differences become especially obvious if economic factors, family structure, and social organization are taken into consideration, they surprisingly, again and again, find, report, and theorize about commonalities. Their basic orientation can best be summarized in their own words: "We have taken a universalistic rather than a relativistic approach to adolescence" (Schlegel & Barry, 1991: 198). In all cultural groups, adolescence is a socially recognized stage that falls between "nonreproductive childhood and reproductive adulthood."

Communication, transportation, education, and tourism have reached the most remote parts of the world and have created social dissonance. For example, several years ago this author visited the Cuna Indians on the remote San Blas islands on the Atlantic coast of Central America, near the Panama Canal. For a long time, untouched by the technological advances of the Western world, these islands conveyed to the visitor the feeling of stepping into a preindustrial society of centuries ago. More recently, major cruise lines have put these islands on their itinerary, anchoring a mile off-shore and tendering their passengers to the island. The delicate needlework of the Cuna women is displayed for sale. As a result of the influx of cash, the natives now have equipped the dugout boats with modern outboard motors. The first TV antennas emerge from the palm-leaf thatched huts, and babies wear diapers with Ninja Turtle designs. Under these circumstances, the rapid movement from the eighteenth into the twentieth century appears inevitable.

Are these patterns of variations and commonalities irrelevant to understanding the growth and behavior of the modern teenager, since these social organizations frequently no longer exist but have become an issue of anthropological academic curiosity?

Schlegel and Barry answer that question with a resounding "We think not." Critics have claimed that Schlegel and Barry have opened perspectives that may require us to rethink our view of adolescence in the modern world. Their presentation "makes a major contribution to our efforts to understand what aspects of adolescence are universal, or nearly so (there are some real surprises here), and what aspects vary widely as a result of differences in social organization, family structure, and type of economy, among other influences" (Conger, 1991).

REFERENCES

Adams, G. R. (1992). Introduction and overview. In G. R. Adams, T. P. Gullato, & R. Montemayor (Eds.), *Adolescent identity formation* (Vol. 4). Newbury Park, CA: Sage.

Adams, G. R., & Fitch, S. A. (1982). Ego stage and identity status development. *Journal of Personality and Social Psychology, 43,* 574–583.

Adams, G. R., & Shea, J. A. (1979). The relationship between identity status, locus of control, and ego development. *Journal of Youth and Adolescence, 8,* 81–89.

Aebli, H. (1963). *Über die geistige Entwicklung des Kindes.* Stuttgart: Klett.

Ainsworth, M. D. S. (1991). John Bowlby—A memoir. *SRCD Newsletter,* Spring, 1–3.

Ala'ilima, F. (1984). Derek Freeman, Margaret Mead and Samoa. *Pacific Studies, 7,* 91–92.

Archer, S. L. (1981). Ego identity development among early and mid-adolescents. Paper presented at the Eastern Psychological Association, New York.

Archer, S. L. (1982). The lower age boundaries of identity development. *Child Development, 53,* 1551–1556.

Archer, S. L. (1985). Career and/or family: The identity process for adolescent girls. *Youth and Society, 16,* 289–314.

Archer, S. L. (1989a). Gender differences in identity development: Issues of process, domain and timing. *Journal of Adolescence, 12,* 117–138.

Archer, S. L. (1989b). The status of identity: Reflections on the need for intervention. *Journal of Adolescence, 12,* 345–359.

Archer, S. L. (1993). Identity status in early and middle adolescents: scoring criteria. In J. E. Marcia, A. S. Waterman, D. R. Matteson, S. L. Archer, & J. L. Orlofsky (Eds.), *Ego identity: A handbook for psychosocial research.* New York: Springer.

Archer, S. L. (1994). An overview. In S. L. Archer (Ed.), *Interventions for adolescent identity development.* Thousand Oaks, CA: Sage.

Archer, S. L., & Waterman, A. S. (1988). Psychological individualism: Gender differences or gender neutrality. *Human Development, 31,* 65–81.

Archer, S. L. & Waterman, A. S. (1990). Varieties of identity diffusions and foreclosures. *Journal of Adolescent Research, 5,* 96–111.

Ariès, P. (1962). *Centuries of childhood.* (R. Baldick, Trans.). New York: Vintage.

Aristotle. (1925). Magna moralia. In W. D. Ross (Ed.), *The Works of Aristotle* (Vol. 9). Oxford: Clarendon.

Aristotle. (1941a). Ethica Nicomachea. In R. McKeon (Ed.), *The basic works of Aristotle.* New York: Random House.

Aristotle. (1941b). Historia animalium. In R. McKeon (Ed.), *The basic works of Aristotle.* (D. W. Thompson, Trans.). New York: Random House.

Aristotle. (1941c). Politica. In R. McKeon (Ed.), *The basic works of Aristotle.* (B. Jowett, Trans.). New York: Random House.

Aristotle. (1941d). Rhetorica. In R. McKeon (Ed.), *The basic works of Aristotle.* (W. R. Roberts, Trans.). New York: Random House.

Arlin, P. K. (1975). Cognitive development in adulthood: A fifth stage? *Developmental Psychology, 11,* 602–606.

Ashley Montagu, M. F. (1957). *The reproductive development of the female with especial reference to the period of adolescent sterility.* New York: Julian.

Ausubel, D. P. (1958). *Theory and problems of child development.* New York: Grune & Stratton.

Bacon, M. K., Child, I. L., & Barry, H. (1963). A cross-cultural study of correlates of crime. *Journal of Abnormal and Social Psychology, 66,* 291–300.

Baldwin, A. L. (1967). *Theories of child development.* New York: Wiley.

Ball, W. B. (1967). Religion and public education: The Post-Schempp years. In T. R. Sizer (Ed.), *Religion and public education.* Boston: Houghton Mifflin.

Bandura, A. (1960). Relationship of family patterns to child behavior disorders. Progress Report, U.S.P.H. Research Grant M-1734. Stanford: Stanford University Press.

Bandura, A. (1962). Social learning theory through imitation. In M. R. Jones (Ed.), *Nebraska symposium on motivation* (Vol. 10). Lincoln: University of Nebraska Press.

Bandura, A. (1964). The stormy decade: Fact or fiction? *Psychology in the Schools, 1,* 224–231.

Bandura, A. (1967). The role of modeling processes in personality development. In W. W. Hartup & N. L. Smothergill (Eds.), *The young child: Review of research.* Washington, DC: National Association for the Education of Young Children.

Bandura, A. (1971). Vicarious and self-reinforcement processes. In R. Glaser (Ed.), *The nature of reinforcement.* New York: Academic Press.

Bandura, A. (1973). Social learning theory of aggression. In J. F. Knutson (Eds.), *The control of aggression.* Chicago: Aldine.

Bandura, A. (1977a). Self-efficacy: Toward a unifying theory of behavioral change. *Psychological Review, 84,* 191–215.

Bandura, A. (1977b). *Social learning theory.* Englewood Cliffs, NJ: Prentice-Hall.

Bandura, A. (1981). Self-referent thought. In J. H. Flavell & L. D. Ross (Eds.), *Social cognitive development: Frontiers and possible futures.* New York: Cambridge University Press.

Bandura, A. (1982). The self and mechanisms of agency. In J. Suls (Ed.), *Psychological perspectives on the self* (Vol. 1). Hillsdale, NJ: Erlbaum.

Bandura, A. (1986). *Social foundations of thought and action.* Englewood Cliffs, NJ: Prentice-Hall.

Bandura, A. (1989a). Human agency in social cognitive theory. *American Psychologist, 44,* 1175–1184.

Bandura, A. (1989b). Social cognitive theory. In R. Vasta (Ed.), Six theories of child development. *Annals of Child Development* (Vol. 6, pp.1–60). Greenwich, CT: JAI Press.

Bandura, A. (1992). Exercise of personal agency through the self-efficacy mechanism. In R. Schwarzer (Ed.), *Self-efficacy: thought control of action.* Washington, DC: Hemisphere.

Bandura, A. (1994). Self-Efficacy. In *Encyclopedia of Human Behavior* (Vol. 4). New York: Academic Press.

Bandura, A., & Kupers, C. J. (1964). Transmission of patterns of self-reinforcement through modeling. *Journal of Abnormal and Social Psychology, 69,* 1–9.

Bandura, A., & McDonald, F. J. (1963). Influence of social reinforcement and the behavior of models in shaping children's moral judgments. *Journal of Abnormal and Social Psychology, 67,* 274–281.

Bandura, A., & Mischel, W. (1965). Modification of self-imposed delay of reward through exposure to live and symbolic models. *Journal of Personality and Social Psychology, 2,* 698–705.

Bandura, A., Ross, D., & Ross, S. A. (1961). Transmission of aggression through imitation of aggressive models. *Journal of Abnormal and Social Psychology, 63,* 575–582.

Bandura, A., Ross, D., & Ross, S. A. (1963a). A comparative test of the status envy, social power, and secondary reinforcement theories of identificatory learning. *Journal of Abnormal and Social Psychology, 67,* 527–534.

Bandura, A., Ross, D., & Ross, S. A. (1963b). Imitation of film-mediated aggressive models. *Journal of Abnormal and Social Psychology, 66,* 3–11.

Bandura, A., Ross, D., & Ross, S. A. (1963c). Vicarious reinforcement and imitative learning. *Journal of Abnormal and Social Psychology, 67,* 601–607.

Bandura, A., & Walters, R. H. (1959). *Adolescent aggression.* New York: Ronald Press.

Bandura, A., & Walters, R. H. (1963). *Social learning and personality development.* New York: Holt, Rinehart & Winston.

Bandura, A., & Whalen, C. K. (1966). The influence of antecedent reinforcement and divergent modeling cues on patterns of self-reward. *Journal of Personality and Social Psychology, 3,* 373–382.

Barry, H., Bacon, M., & Child, I. (1957). A cross-cultural survey of some sex differences in socialization. *Journal of Abnormal and Social Psychology, 55,* 327–332.

Bart, W. M. (1978). Issues in measuring formal operational reasoning. *The Genetic Epistemologist, 7,* 3–4.

Barton, R. F. (1969). Ifugao law. Los Angeles: University of California Press.

Baucom, D. H., Besch, P. K., & Callahan, S. (1985). Relation between testosterone concentration, sex role identity, and personality among females. *Journal of Personality and Social Psychology, 48,* 1218–1226.

Beilin, H. (1989). Piagetian theory. In R. Vasta (Ed.), *Six theories of child development. Annals of Child Development* (Vol. 6, pp. 85–131). Greenwich, CT: JAI Press.

Beilin, H. (1992). Piaget's new theory. In H. Beilin & P. Pufall (Eds.), *Piaget's theory: Prospects and possibilities.* Hillsdale, NJ: Erlbaum.

Benedict, R. (1934). *Patterns of culture.* Boston: Houghton Mifflin.

Benedict, R. (1938/1980). Continuities and discontinuities in cultural conditioning. In R. E. Muuss (Ed.), *Adolescent behavior and society* (3rd ed.). New York: Random House.

Berzonsky, M. D. (1989). Identity style: Conceptualization and measurement. *Journal of Adolescent Research, 4,* 268–282.

Betancourt, H., & López, S. R. (1993). The study of culture, ethnicity, and race in American psychology. *American Psychologist, 48,* 629–637.

Bilsker, D., & Marcia, J. (1991). Adaptive regression and ego identity. *Journal of Adolescence, 14,* 75–84.

Blackman, N. (1980). Inner space revisisted and outer space reconsidered in the preadolescent. Unpublished manuscript.

Block, J. H. (1973). Conceptions of sex role: Some cross-cultural and longitudinal perspectives. *American Psychologist, 28,* 512–526.

Blos, P. (1962). *On adolescence: A psychoanalytic interpretation.* New York: Free Press.

Blos, P. (1965). The initial stage of male adolescence. *In the psychoanalytic study of the child.* (Vol. 20). New York: International Universities Press.

Blum, L. (1990). Universality and particularity. In D. Schrader (Ed.), *The legacy of Lawrence Kohlberg.* San Francisco: Jossey-Bass.

Boas, F. (1928/1950). Foreword. *Coming of age in Samoa.* New York: New American Library.

Bosma, H. A., & Gerrits, R. S. (1985). Family functioning and identity status in adolescence. *Journal of Early Adolescence, 5,* 69–80.

Bourne, E. (1978). The state of research on ego identity. *Journal of Youth and Adolescence, 7,* 223–251.

Boyd, W. (1965). *The history of Western education.* New York: Barnes & Noble.

Brim, O. G. Jr., & Kagan, J. (1980). Constancy and change: In O. G. Brim, Jr., & J. Kagan (Eds.), *Constancy and change in human development.* Cambridge, MA: Harvard University Press.

Bronfenbrenner, U. (1967). Response to pressure from peers versus adults among Soviet and American school children. International Journal of Psychology, 2, 199–207.

Bronfenbrenner, U. (1974). The origins of alienation. *Scientific American, 231,* 53–61.

Bronfenbrenner, U. (1977). Toward an experimental ecology of human development. *American Psychologist, 32,* 513–531.

Bronfenbrenner, U. (1979). *The ecology of human development.* Cambridge, MA: Harvard University Press.

Bronfenbrenner, U. (1986a). Alienation and the four worlds of childhood. *Phi Delta Kappan, 67,* 430–436.

Bronfenbrenner, U. (1986b). Ecology of the family as a context for human development: Research perspectives. *Developmental Psychology, 22,* 723–742.

Bronfenbrenner, U. (1988). Foreword. In A. R. Pence (Ed.), *Ecological research with children and families* (pp. ix-xix). New York: Columbia University Teachers College Press.

Bronfenbrenner, U. (1989). Ecological systems theory. In R. Vasta (Ed.), *Six theories of child development. Annals of Child Development* (Vol. 6, pp. 187–249). Greenwich, CT: JAI Press.

Bronfenbrenner, U. (1993). The ecology of cognitive development: Research models and fugitive findings. In R. H. Wozinak & K. Fischer (Eds.), *Scientific environments.* Hillsdale, NJ: Erlbaum.

Bronfenbrenner, U. (1994). Ecological models of human development. In T. Husen & T. N. Postlethwaite (Eds.), *International encyclopedia of education* (2d ed.). New York: Elsevier.

Bronfenbrenner, U., & Crouter, A. C. (1983). The evolution of environmental models in developmental research. In P. H. Mussen (Ed.), *Handbook of child psychology: Vol. 1. History, theory, and methods* (W. Kessen, Vol. Ed., pp. 357–414). New York: Wiley.

Brooks-Gunn, J., & Petersen, A. C. (Eds.). (1983). *Girls at puberty: Biological and psychosocial perspectives.* New York: Plenum.

Brooks-Gunn, J., & Reiter, E. O. (1990). The role of pubertal processes. In S. S. Feldman & G. R. Elliott (Ed.), *At the threshold: The developing adolescent.* Cambridge, MA: Harvard University Press.

Brooks-Gunn, J., & Ruble, D. N. (1982). The development of menstrual-related beliefs and behaviors during early adolescence. *Child Development, 53,* 1567–1577.

Broughton, J. M. (1983). Women's rationality and men's virtues: A critique of gender dualism in Gilligan's theory of moral development. *Social Research, 50,* 596–642.

Brown, B. B., Lohr, M. J., & Trujillo, C. (1990). Multiple crowds and multiple life-styles: Adolescents' perceptions of peer-group stereotypes. In R. E. Muuss (Ed.), *Adolescent behavior and society* (4th ed.). New York: McGraw-Hill.

Brown, D. E. (1991). *Human universals.* Philadelphia: Temple University Press.

Brown, L. M., & Gilligan, C. (1992). *Meeting at the crossroads: Women's psychology and girls' development.* Cambridge, MA: Harvard University Press.

Browning, D. L. (1983). Aspects of authoritarian attitudes in ego development. *Journal of Personality and Social Psychology, 45,* 137–144.

Bruner, J. S. (1960). *The process of education.* New York: Vintage.

Burk, D. (1973). *Piagetian attainment kit.* Monterey, CA: Publishers Test Service.

Byrne, D. F. (1974). The development of role-taking in adolescence. *Dissertation Abstract, 34,* No. 11, 5647B.

Byrnes, J. P. (1988). Formal operations: A systematic reformulation. *Developmental Review, 8,* 66–87.

Byrnes, J. P. (1992). Meaningful logic: Developmental perspectives. In H. Beilin & P. Pufall (Eds.), *Piaget's theory: Prospects and possibilities.* Hillsdale, NJ: Erlbaum.

Calhoun, J. F. (1977). *Abnormal psychology: Current perspectives* (2d ed.). New York: CRM/Random House.

Campbell, R. L., Bickhard, M. H., & Mark, H. (1986). *Knowing levels and developmental stages.* New York: Krager.

Case, R. (1992). Neo-Piagetian theories of intellectual development. In H. Beilin & P. Pufall (Eds.), *Piaget's theory: Prospects and possibilities.* Hillsdale, NJ: Erlbaum.

Cavior, N., & Howard, L. R. (1973). Facial attractiveness and juvenile delinquency among black and white offenders. *Journal of Abnormal Child Psychology, 1,* 202–213.

Chalmers, J. B., & Townsend, M. A. R. (1990). The effects of training in social perspective taking on socially maladjusted girls. *Child Development, 61,* 178–190.

Chandler, M. J. (1973). Egocentrism and antisocial behavior: The assessment and training of social perspective-taking skills. *Developmental Psychology, 9,* 326–332.

Clarke-Stewart, A. (1985). Urie Bronfenbrenner: An ecological evaluation. G. Stanley Hall Award Presentation. APA Convention, Washington, D.C.

Cohn, L. D. (1991). Sex differences in the course of personality development: A meta-analysis. *Psychological Bulletin, 109,* 252–266.

Colby, A., & Kohlberg, L. (1984). *The measurement of moral judgment.* New York: Cambridge University Press.

Colton, M. E., & Gore, S. (Eds.) (1991). *Adolescent stress: Causes and consequences.* New York: Aldine de Gruyter.

Comenius, J. A. (1923). *The great didactic* (M. W. Keatinge, Ed. and Trans.). London: A. & C. Black. (Originally published 1657.)

Conger, J. J. (1977). *Adolescence and youth* (2d ed.). New York: Harper & Row.

Conger, J. J. (1991). Dustcover Evaluation. Schlegel, A., & Barry, H. III. *Adolescence: An anthropological inquiry.* New York: Free Press.

Constantinople, A. (1969). An Eriksonian measure of personality development in college students. *Developmental Psychology, 1,* 357–372.

Copeland, R. (1988). *Piagetian activities: A diagnostic and developmental approach.* Eau Claire, WI: Thinking Publications.

Corsini, R. J. (1977). *Current personality theories.* Itasca, IL: Peacock.

Côté, J. E. (1992). Was Mead wrong about coming of age in Samoa? *Journal of Youth and Adolescence, 21,* 499–527.

Côté, J. E. (1994). *Adolescent storm and stress: An evaluation of the Mead-Freeman controversy.* Hillsdale, NJ: Erlbaum.

Dannefer, D. (1992). On the conceptualization of context in developmental discourse. In D. L. Featherman, R. M. Lerner, & M. Perlmutter (Eds.), *Life-span development and behavior.* Hillsdale, NJ: Erlbaum.

Darwin, C. R. (1859). *On the origin of species by means of natural selection.* London: J. Murray.

Dion, K. K., & Berscheid, E. (1972). Physical attractiveness and social perception of peers in preschool children. Mimeographed research report.

Dodge, K. A. (1980). Social cognition and children's aggressive behavior. *Child Development, 51,* 162–170.

Donenberg, G. R., & Hoffman, L. W. (1988). Gender differences in moral development. *Sex Roles, 18,* 701–717.

Dornbusch, S. M., Ritter, P. L., Leiderman, P. H., Roberts, D. F., & Fraleigh, M. J. (1987). The relation of parenting style to adolescent school performance. *Child Development, 58,* 1244–1257.

Dreyer, P. H. (1994). Designing curricular identity interventions for secondary schools. In S. L. Archer (Ed.), *Interventions for adolescent development.* Thousand Oaks, CA: Sage.

Dulit, E. (1972). Adolescent thinking à la Piaget: The formal stage. *Journal of Youth and Adolescence, 1,* 281–301.

Dyk, P. A., & Adams, G. R. (1987). The association between identity development and intimacy during adolescence. *Journal of Adolescent Research, 2,* 223–235.

Eckstein, S. G., & Shemesh, M. (1992). The rate of acquisition of formal operational schemata in adolescence. *Journal of Research in Science Teaching, 29,* 441–451.

Elder, G. H. Jr. (1974). *Children of the great depression.* Chicago: University of Chicago Press.

Elder, G. H. Jr., & Caspi, A. (1988). Human development and social change: An emerging perspective on the life course. In N. Bolger, A. Caspi, G. Downey, & M. Moorehouse (Eds.), *Persons in context: Developmental processes.* New York: Cambridge University Press.

Elder, G. H. Jr., & Rockwell, R. C. (1978). Economic depression and postwar opportunities in men's lives. In R. A. Simmons (Ed.), *Research in community and mental health.* Greenwich, CT: JAI Press.

Eliade, M. (1958). *Birth and rebirth; the religious meaning of initiation in human culture.* New York: Harper & Brothers.

Elkind, D. (1961a). Children's discovery of the conservation of mass, weight, and volume. *Journal of Genetic Psychology, 98,* 219–227.

Elkind, D. (1961b). Quantity conceptions in junior and senior high school students. *Child Development, 32,* 551–560.

Elkind, D. (1967). Egocentrism in adolescence. *Child Development, 38,* 1025–1034.

Elkind, D. (1981). *The hurried child.* Reading, MA: Addison-Wesley.

Elkind, D. (1984). *All grown up and no place to go.* Reading, MA: Addison-Wesley.

Enright, R. D. (1976). Social cognition in children. *Counseling Psychologist, 6,* 65–70.

Epstein, J. L. (1983a). *Effects on parents of teacher practices of parent involvement.* Baltimore: Center for Social Organization of Schools, Johns Hopkins University (Report #346).

Epstein, J. L. (1983b). Longitudinal effects of family-school-person interactions on student outcomes. *Research in Sociology of Education and Socialization, 4,* 101–107.

Erikson, E. H. (1950). *Childhood and society.* New York: Norton (2d ed. 1963).

Erikson, E. H. (1959). Identity and the life cycle. *Psychological Issues.* Monograph 1, No. 1, New York: International Universities Press.

Erikson, E. H. (1962). *Young man Luther.* New York: Norton.

Erikson, E. H. (1965). Youth: Fidelity and diversity. In E. H. Erikson (Ed.), *The challenge of youth.* Garden City, NY: Doubleday/Anchor.

Erikson, E. H. (1968). *Identity: Youth and crisis.* New York: Norton.

Erikson, E. H. (1969). *Gandhi's truth.* New York: Norton.

Erikson, E. H. (1970). Autobiographic notes on the identity crises. *Daedalus, 99,* 730–759.

Erikson, E. H. (1975). *Life history and the historical moment.* New York: Norton.

Erikson, E. H. (1982). *The life cycle completed.* New York: Norton.

Eron, L. D. (1987). The development of aggressive behavior from the perspective of a developing behaviorism. *American Psychologist, 42,* 435–442.

Fasick, F. A. (1994). On the "invention" of adolescence. *Journal of Early Adolescence, 14,* 6–23.

Fernhout, J. H. (1986). "Where is faith? Searching for the core of the cube." In C. Dykstra & S. Parks (Eds.), *Faith development and Fowler.* Birmingham, AL: Religious Education Press.

Fisher, S., & Greenberg, R. P. (1977). *The scientific credibility of Freud's theories and therapy.* New York: Basic Books.

Five decades: 1980's. (1989) *People Extra.*

Flanagan, C. A., & Eccles, J. S. (1993). Changes in parents' work status and adolescents' adjustment at school. *Child Development, 64,* 246–257.

Flavell, J. H. (1963a). *The developmental psychology of Jean Piaget.* New York: Van Nostrand.

Flavell, J. H. (1963b). Piaget's contributions to the study of cognitive development. *Merrill-Palmer Quarterly, 9,* 245–252.

Flavell, J. H. (1974). The development of inferences about others. In T. Mischel (Ed.), *Understanding other persons.* Oxford: Blackwell.

Flavell, J. H. (1977). *Cognitive development.* Englewood Cliffs, NJ: Prentice-Hall.

Flavell, J. H. (1992). Perspectives on perspective taking. In H. Beilin & P. Pufall (Eds.), *Piaget's theory: Prospects and possibilities.* Hillsdale, NJ: Erlbaum.

Ford, D. H., & Lerner, R. M. (1992). *Developmental systems theory.* Newbury Park, CA: Sage.

Fowler, J. W. (1980). Faith and the structuring of meaning. In J. W. Fowler et al. (Eds.), *Toward moral and religious maturity.* Morristown, NJ: Silver Burdett.

Fowler, J. W. (1981). *Stages of faith: The psychology of human development and the quest for meaning.* San Francisco: Harper & Row.

Fowler, J. W. (1983). Stages of faith. *Psychology Today,* November, 56–62.

Fowler, J. W. (1986). Faith and the structuring of meaning. In C. Dykstra & S. Parks (Eds.), *Faith development and Fowler.* Birmingham, AL: Religious Education Press.

Fowler, J. W. (1987). *Faith development and pastoral care.* Philadelphia: Fortress.

Fowler, J. W. (1991a). Stages in faith consciousness. In F. K. Oser & W. G. Scarlett (Eds.), *Religious development in childhood and adolescence.* San Francisco: Jossey-Bass.

Fowler, J. W. (1991b). The Vocation of faith development theory. In J. W. Fowler, K. E. Nipkow, & F. Schweitzer (Eds.), *Stages of faith and religious development: Implications for church, education, and society.* New York: Crossroad.

Fowler, W. (1975). A developmental learning approach to infant care in a group setting. In B. Z. Friedlander, G. M. Sterritt, & G. E. Kirk (Eds.), *Exceptional infant-assessment and intervention* (Vol. 3). New York: Brunner/Mazel.

Frank, S., & Quinlan, D. M. (1976). Ego development and female delinquency: A cognitive-developmental approach. *Journal of Abnormal Psychology, 85,* 505–510.

Freeman, D. (1983). *Margaret Mead and Samoa: The making and unmaking of an anthropological myth.* Cambridge, MA: Harvard University Press.

Freud, A. (1931). *Introduction to psychoanalysis for teachers.* London: Allen & Unwin.

Freud, A. (1948). *The ego and the mechanisms of defense* (C. Baines, Trans.). New York: International Universities Press.

Freud, A. (1958). Adolescence. In *The Psychoanalytic Study of the Child* (Vol. 13). New York: International Universities Press.

Freud, S. (1925). Three contributions to the sexual theory. *Nervous and Mental Disease Monograph Series,* No. 7. New York: Nervous and Mental Disease Publishing Co.

Freud, S. (1949). *The infantile genital organization of the libido* (Collected Papers, Vol. 2). London, Hogarth. (Originally published 1923.)

Freud, S. (1950). *Analysis, terminable and interminable* (Collected Papers, Vol. 5). London: Hogarth. (Originally published 1937.)

Freud, S. (1953). *The interpretation of dreams* (Standard ed., Vols. 4 & 5). London: Hogarth. (Originally published 1900.)

Freud, S. (1957). *The unconscious* (Standard ed., Vol. 14). London: Hogarth. (Originally published 1915.)

Freud, S. (1961). *The ego and the id* (Standard ed. Vol. 19). London: Hogarth. (Originally published 1923.)

Freud, S. (1962). *Further remarks on the neuro-psychoses of defense* (Standard ed., Vol. 3). London: Hogarth. (Originally published 1896.)

Freud, S. (1964). *New introductory lectures on psycho-analysis* (Standard ed., Vol. 22). London: Hogarth. (Originally published 1933.)

Furth, H. G. (1970). *An inventory of Piaget's developmental tasks.* Washington, DC: Catholic University Center for Research in Thinking and Language.

Furth, H. G., & Wachs, H. (1975). *Thinking goes to school.* New York: Oxford University Press.

Gaffney, L. R. (1984). A multiple-choice test to measure social skills in delinquent and non-delinquent adolescent girls. *Journal of Consulting and Clinical Psychology, 52,* 911–912.

Gaffney, L. R., & McFall, R. M. (1981). A comparison of social skills in delinquent and non-delinquent adolescent girls using a behavioral role-playing inventory. *Journal of Consulting and Clinical Psychology, 49,* 959–967.

Galambos, N. L. (1992). Parent-adolescent relations. *Current Directions in Psychological Science, 1,* 146–149.

Garbarino, J. (1985). *Adolescent development: An ecological perspective.* Columbus, OH: Charles E. Merrill.

Geertz, C. (1973). Ritual and social change: A Javanese example. In C. Geertz (Ed.), *The interpretation of cultures.* New York: Basic Books.

Gfellner, B. M. (1986). Ego development and moral development in relation to age and grade level during adolescence. *Journal of Youth and Adolescence, 15,* 147–163.

Gilligan, C. (1977). In a different voice: Women's conceptions of self and morality. *Harvard Educational Review, 47,* 481–517.

Gilligan, C. (1979). Women's place in man's life cycle. *Harvard Educational Review, 49,* 431–446.

Gilligan, C. (1982). *In a different voice: Psychological theory and women's development.* Cambridge, MA: Harvard University Press.

Gilligan, C. (1994). Getting civilized. *Fordham Law Review, LXIII,* 17–31.

Gilligan, C., & Belenky, M. F. (1980). A naturalistic study of abortion decisions. In R. Selman & R. Yando (Eds.), *Clinical-developmental psychology.* San Francisco: Jossey-Bass.

Gilligan, C., Kohlberg, L., Lerner, J., & Belenky, M. (1971). Moral reasoning about sexual dilemmas. *Technical Report of the Commission on Obscenity and Pornography* (Vol. 1). Washington, DC: U.S. Government Printing Office.

Gilligan, C., Lyons, N. P., & Hanmer, T. J. (Eds.) (1990). *Making connections: The relational worlds of adolescent girls at Emma Willard School.* Cambridge, MA: Harvard University Press.

Gilligan, C., & Murphy, J. M. (1979). Development from adolescence to adulthood: The philosopher and the dilemma of the fact. In D. Kuhn (Ed.), *Intellectual development beyond childhood.* San Francisco: Jossey-Bass.

Gilligan, C., Taylor, J. M., Tolman, D., Sullivan, A., Pleasants, P., & Dorney, J. (1992). *The relational world of adolescent girls considered to be at risk.* Monograph. Cambridge, MA: Harvard Graduate School of Education.

Graham, S. (1992). Most of the subjects were white and middle class. *American Psychologist, 47,* 629–639.

Gray, W. M. (1990). Formal operational thought. In W. F. Overton (Ed.), *Reasoning, necessity, and logic: Developmental perspectives.* Hillsdale, NJ: Erlbaum.

Grotevant, H. D. (1993). The integrative nature of identity: Bringing the soloists to sing in the choir. In J. Kroger (Ed.), *Discussions on ego identity.* Hillsdale, NJ: Erlbaum.

Grotevant, H. D., & Cooper, C. R. (1985). Patterns of interaction in family relationships and the development of identity exploration in adolescence. *Child Development, 56,* 415–428.

Grusec, J. E. (1992). Social learning theory and developmental psychology. *Developmental Psychology, 28,* 776–786.

Haan, N., Langer, J., & Kohlberg, L. (1976). Family patterns of moral reasoning. *Child Development, 47,* 1204–1206.

Hagen, J. W., & Conley, A. C. (1994, Spring). Ethnicity and race of children studied in *Child Development*, 1980-1993. *SRCD Newsletter, 6–7.*

Hains, A. A., & Miller, D. J. (1980). Moral and cognitive development in delinquent and non-delinquent children and adolescents. *Journal of Genetic Psychology, 137,* 21–35.

Hall, C. S. (1954). *A primer of Freudian psychology.* New York: World.

Hall, G. S. (1916). *Adolescence* (Vols. 1–2). New York: Appleton.

Harris, D. B. (1958). The climate of achievement. *Child Study, 34,* 8–14.

Hart, B., & Hilton, I. (1988). Dimensions of personality organization as predictors of teenage pregnancy risk. *Journal of Personality Assessment, 52,* 116–132.

Hartshorne, H., & May, M. A. (1928–1930). *Studies in the nature of character* (Vols. 1–3). New York: Macmillan.

Hauser, S. T. (1976). Loevinger's model and measure of ego development: A critical review. *Psychological Bulletin, 83,* 928–955.

Hauser, S. T., Borman, E. H., Bowlds, M. K., Powers, S., Jacobson, A., Noam, G., & Knoebber, K. (1991). Understanding coping within adolescence: Ego development trajectories and coping styles. In E. M. Cummings (Ed.), *Life-span developmental psychology: Perspectives on stress and coping.* Hillsdale, NJ: Erlbaum.

Healy, W., Bronner, A. F., & Bowers, A. M. (1930). *The structure and meaning of psychoanalysis.* New York: Knopf.

Hearold, S. (1986). A synthesis of 1043 effects of television on social behavior. In G. Comstock (Ed.), *Public communication and behavior.* Orlando, FL: Academic Press.

Herskovits, M. J. (1971). *Life in a Haitian valley.* Garden City, NY: Doubleday.

Hickey, J. E. (1972). The effects of guided moral discussion upon youthful offenders' level of moral judgement. *Dissertation Abstracts International, 33 (4-A),* 1551.

Higgins, A. (1991). The just community approach to moral education: Evolution of the idea and recent findings. In W. M. Kurtines & J. L. Gewirtz (Eds.), *Handbook of moral behavior and research* (Vol. 3). Hillsdale, NJ: Erlbaum.

Hill, J. P. (1980). *Understanding early adolescence: A framework.* Chapel Hill, NC: Center for Early Adolescence.

Himmelweit, H. T., Swift, B., & Jaegor, M. E. (1980). The audience as critic: A conceptual analysis of television entertainment. In P. H. Tannebaum (Ed.), *The entertainment function of television.* Hillsdale, NJ: Erlbaum.

Hobbes, T. (1651). *Leviathan.* London.

Hoehn, R. A. (1983). Review of Fowler 1981. *Review of Religious Research, 25.*

Hollingworth, L. S. (1928). *The psychology of the adolescent.* New York: Appleton-Century.

Horner, M. S. (1972). Toward an understanding of achievement-related conflicts in women. *Journal of Social Issues, 28,* 157–175.

Hudson, L. M., Peyton, E. F., & Brion-Maisels, S. (1976). Social reasoning and relating. In H. Furth (Chair), Integrations of development in social cognition and social behavior. Symposium presented at the American Psychological Association Convention, Washington, DC.

Huesmann, L. R. (1986). Cross-national communalities in the learning of aggression from media violence. In L. R. Huesmann & L. D. Eron (Eds.), *Television and the aggressive child.* Hillsdale, NJ: Erlbaum.

Huesmann, L. R. (1988). An information processing model for the development of aggression. *Aggressive Behavior, 14,* 13–24.

Inhelder, B. (1966). Cognitive development and its contribution to the diagnosis of some phenomena of mental deficiency. *Merrill-Palmer Quarterly, 12,* 299–319.

Inhelder, B., & DeCaprona, D. (1990). The role and meaning of structures in genetic epistemology. In W. F. Overton (Ed.), *Reasoning, necessity, and logic: Developmental perspectives.* Hillsdale, NJ: Erlbaum.

Inhelder, B., & Piaget, J. (1958). *The growth of logical thinking from Childhood to Adolescence.* New York: Basic Books.

Jackson, D. J., & Huston, T. L. (1975). Physical attractiveness and assertiveness. *Journal of Social Psychology, 96,* 79–84.

Jankowiak, W. R., & Fischer, E. F. (1992). A cross-cultural perspective on romantic love. *Ethnology, 31,* 149–155.

Jennings, W., & Kohlberg, L. (1983). Effects of just community programme on the moral development of youthful offenders. *Journal of Moral Education, 12,* 33–50.

Jones, R. M. (1960). *An application of psychoanalysis to education.* Springfield, IL: Charles C Thomas.

Josephson, W. L. (1987). Television violence and children's aggression. *Journal of Personality and Social Psychology, 53,* 882–890.

Josselson, R. (1987). *Finding herself: Pathways to identity development in women.* San Francisco: Jossey-Bass.

Kagan, J. (1993). The meanings of morality. *Psychological Science, 4,* 353–360.

Kamii, C., Clark, F. B., & Dominick, A. (1994). The six national goals: A road to disappointment. *Phi Delta Kappan, 75,* 672–677.

Kandel, D. B. (1986). Processes of peer influences in adolescence. In R. K. Silbereisen et al. (Eds.), *Development as action in content.* Berlin: Springer Verlag.

Kaplan, L., & Baron, D. (1952). *Mental hygiene and life.* New York: Harper.

Kauffman, K. (1990). The prison as a just community. In D. Schrader (Ed.), *The legacy of Lawrence Kohlberg.* San Francisco: Jossey-Bass.

Keasey, C. B. (1971). Social participation as a factor in the moral development of preadolescents. *Developmental Psychology, 5,* 216–220.

Keating, D. P. (1978). A search for social intelligence. *Journal of Educational Psychology, 70,* 218–223.

Keating, D. P. (1980). Thinking processes in adolescence. In J. Adelson (Ed.), *Handbook of Adolescent Psychology.* New York: Wiley.

Keating, D. P. (1990). Structuralism, deconstruction, reconstruction: The limits of reasoning. In W. F. Overton (Ed.), *Reasoning, necessity, and logic: Developmental perspectives.* Hillsdale, NJ: Erlbaum.

Keating, D. P., & Clark, L. V. (1980). Development of physical and social reasoning in adolescence. *Developmental Psychology, 16,* 23–30.

Keesing, R. M. (1981). *Cultural anthropology—A contemporary perspective* (2d ed.). New York: Holt, Rinehart and Winston.

Keniston, K. (1965). Social change and youth in America. In E. H. Erikson (Ed.), *The challenge of youth.* Garden City, NY: Doubleday/Anchor.

Keniston, K. (1971). The tasks of adolescence. In *Developmental psychology today.* Del Mar, CA: CRM Books, chapter 20.

Kiell, N. (1964). *The universal experience of adolescence.* New York: International Universities Press.

King, M. L. (1964). *Why we can't wait.* New York: Harper & Row.

Kitchener, R. F. (1986). *Piaget's theory of knowledge: Genetic epistemology and scientific reason.* New Haven, CT: Yale University Press.

Kitzinger, C. (1994). Listening to a different voice. *Feminism & Psychology, 4 (3),* 408–419.

Kohlberg, L. (1963). The development of children's orientations toward a moral order. *Vita Humana, 6,* 11–33.

Kohlberg, L. (1964). Development of moral character and moral ideology. In M. L. Hoffman & L. W. Hoffman (Eds.), *Review of child development research* (Vol. 1). New York: Russell Sage.

Kohlberg, L. (1967). Moral and religious education and the public schools: A developmental view. In T. R. Sizer (Ed.), *Religion and public education.* Boston: Houghton Mifflin.

Kohlberg, L. (1969). Stage and sequence: The cognitive-developmental approach to socialization. In D. A. Goslin (Ed.), *Handbook of socialization theory and research.* Chicago: Rand McNally.

Kohlberg, L. (1970). Moral development and the education of adolescents. In R. F. Purnell (Ed.), *Adolescents and the American high school.* New York: Holt, Rinehart & Winston.

Kohlberg, L. (1981). *The philosophy of moral development* (Vol. 1). San Francisco: Harper & Row.

Kohlberg, L. (1984). *The psychology of moral development* (Vol. 2). San Francisco: Harper & Row.

Kohlberg, L. (1985). Resolving moral conflicts with the just community. In C. Harding (Ed.), *Moral dilemmas.* Chicago: Precedent.

Kohlberg, L., & Blatt, M. (1972). The effects of classroom discussion on level of moral development. In L. Kohlberg & E. Turiel (Eds.), *Recent research in moral development.* New York: Holt, Rinehart & Winston.

Kohlberg, L., & Elfenbein, D. (1981). Capital punishment, moral development, and the constitution. In L. Kohlberg (Ed.), *The philosophy of moral development.* San Francisco: Harper & Row.

Kohlberg, L., & Kramer, R. (1969). Continuities and discontinuities in childhood and adult moral development. *Human Development, 12,* 93–120.

Kohlberg, L., Levine, C., & Hewer, A. (1984). The current formulation of the theory. In L. Kohlberg (Ed.), *The psychology of moral development* (Vol. 2). San Francisco: Harper & Row.

Kohlberg, L., & Mayer, R. (1981). Development as the aim of education: The Dewey view. In L. Kohlberg (Ed.), *The philosophy of moral development* (Vol. 1). San Francisco: Harper & Row.

Kohlberg, L., & Nisan, M. (1984). Cultural universality of moral judgment stages: A longitudinal study in Turkey. In L. Kohlberg (Ed.), *The psychology of moral development* (Vol. 2). San Francisco: Harper & Row.

Kohlberg, L., & Power, C. (1981). Moral development, religious thinking, and the question of a seventh stage. In L. Kohlberg (Ed.), *The philosophy of moral development* (Vol. 1). San Francisco: Harper & Row.

Kohlberg, L., Snarey, J., & Reimer, J. (1984). Cultural universality of moral judgement stages: A longitudinal study in Israel. In L. Kohlberg (Ed.), *The psychology of moral development* (Vol. 2). San Francisco: Harper & Row.

Krebs, D., Denton, K., Vermeulen, S., Carpendale, J., & Bush, A. (1991). Structural flexibility of moral judgement. *Journal of Personality and Social Psychology, 61,* 1012–1023.

Kroger, J. (1993). On the nature of structural transition in the identity formation process. In J. Kroger (Ed.), *Discussions on ego identity.* Hillsdale, NJ: Erlbaum.

Kubie, L. S. (1958). *Neurotic distortion of the creative process.* Lawrence: University of Kansas Press.

Kubie, L. S. (1960). Introduction. In R. M. Jones, *An application of psychoanalysis to education.* Springfield, IL: Charles C Thomas.

Kuhn, D. (1979). The significance of Piaget's formal operations stage in education. *Journal of Education, 161,* 34–50.

Kurtines, W. M., & Gewirtz, J. L. (Eds.) (1991). *Handbook of moral behavior and development* (Vols. 1–3). Hillsdale, NJ: Erlbaum.

Lambert, G. B., Rothschild, B. F., Atland, R., & Green, L. B. (1978). *Adolescence: Transition from childhood to maturity* (2d ed.). Monterey, CA: Brooks/Cole.

Lambert, H. (1972). Comparison of cognitive developmental theories of ego and moral development. *Proceedings: 80th Convention of the American Psychological Association, 7,* 115–116.

Lapsley, D. K. (1992). Pluralism, virtues, and the post-Kohlbergian era in moral psychology. In F. C. Powers & D. K. Lapsley (Eds.), *The challenge of pluralism education, politics and values.* Notre Dame, IN: University of Notre Dame Press.

Lapsley, D. K., Enright, R. D., & Serlin, R. C. (1989). Moral and social education. In J. Worell & F. Danner (Eds.), *The adolescent as decision-maker.* San Diego, CA: Academic Press.

Lavatelli, C. (1970). *Early childhood curriculum: A Piaget program.* Boston: American Science and Engineering.

Lawson, A. E. (1985). A review of research in formal reasoning and science teaching. *Journal of Research on Science Teaching, 22,* 569–617.

Lerner, R. M. (1978). Nature, nurture, and dynamic interactionism. *Human Development, 21,* 1–20.

Lerner, R. M. (1979). A dynamic interactional concept of individual and social relationship development. In R. L. Burgess & T. L. Huston (Eds.), *Social exchange in developing relationships.* New York: Academic Press.

Lerner, R. M. (1983). A "goodness of fit" model of person-context interaction. In D. Magnusson & V. L. Allen (Eds.), *Human Development: An Interactional Perspective.* New York: Academic Press.

Lerner R. M. (1984). *On the nature of human plasticity.* New York: Cambridge University Press.

Lerner R. M. (1985). Adolescent maturational changes and psychosocial development: A dynamic interactional perspective. *Journal of Youth and Adolescence, 14,* 355–372.

Lerner, R. M. (1986). *Concepts and theories of human development* (2d ed.). New York: Random House.

Lerner, R. M. (1992a). Dialectics, developmental contextualism, and the further enhancement of theory about puberty and psychosocial development. *Journal of Early Adolescence, 12,* 366–388.

Lerner, R. M. (1992b). Diversity. Winter *SRCD Newsletter, 2,* 12–14.

Lerner, R. M., & Brackney, B. E. (1978). The importance of inner and outer body parts attitudes in the self-concept of late adolescents. *Sex Roles, 4,* 225–238.

Lerner, R. M., & Busch-Rossnagel, N. A. (1981). Individuals as producers of their development: Conceptual and empirical bases. In R. M. Lerner & N. A. Busch-Rossnagel (Eds.), *Individuals as producers of their development.* New York: Academic Press.

Lerner, R. M., & Kauffman, M. B. (1985). The concept of development in contextualism. *Developmental Review, 5,* 309–333.

Lerner, R. M., & Korn, S. J. (1972). The development of body-built stereotypes in males. *Child Development, 43,* 908–920.

Lerner, R. M., & Miller, J. R. (1993). Integrating human development research and intervention for America's children: The Michigan State University Model. *Journal of Applied Developmental Psychology, 14,* 347–364.

Levine, C. (1976). Role taking standpoint and adolescent usage of Kohlberg's conventional stages of moral reasoning. *Journal of Personality and Social Psychology, 34,* 41–46.

Levine, C. (1979). Stage acquisition and stage use: An appraisal of stage displacement explanations of variations in moral reasoning. *Human Development, 22,* 145–164.

Levine, C., Jakubowski, L., & Côté, J. (1992). Linking ego and moral development: The value consistency thesis. *Human Development, 35,* 286–301.

Lewin, K. (1931). Environmental forces in child behavior and development. In C. Murchison (Ed.), *Handbook of child psychology.* Worchester, MA: Clark University Press.

Lewin, K. (1935). *A dynamic theory of personality.* New York: McGraw-Hill.

Lewin, K. (1936). *Principles of topological psychology.* New York: McGraw-Hill.

Lewin, K. (1939). Field theory and experiment in social psychology. Concepts and methods. *American Journal of Sociology, 44,* 868–896.

Lewin, K. (1942). Field theory and learning. In *The Psychology of Learning.* The Yearbook for the National Society for the Study of Education, 41, part II.

Lewin, K. (1946). Behavior and development as a function of the total situation. In L. Carmichael (Ed.), *Manual of child psychology.* New York: Wiley.

Lewin, K. (1948). *Resolving social conflicts.* New York: Harper.

Lewin, K. (1951). *Field theory in social science.* New York: Harper & Row.

Lewis, M. (1987). Early sex role behavior and school age adjustment. In J. M. Reinish, L. A. Rosenblum, & S. A. Sanders (Eds.), *Masculinity/Femininity: Basic perspectives.* New York: Oxford University Press.

Lewis, M. (1992). Commentary. *Human Development, 35,* 44–51.

Linn, M. (1982). Theoretical and practical significance of formal reasoning. *Journal of Research in Science Teaching, 19,* 727–742.

Locke, J. (1753). *An essay concerning human understanding.* London.

Loevinger, J. (1966). The meaning and measurement of ego development. *American Psychologist, 21,* 195–206.

Loevinger, J. (1969). Theories of ego development. In L. Berger (Ed.), *Clinical-cognitive psychology: Models and integrations.* Englewood Cliffs, NJ: Prentice-Hall.

Loevinger, J. (1976). *Ego development.* San Francisco: Jossey-Bass.

Loevinger, J. (1979a). Construct validity of the sentence completion test of ego development. *Applied Psychological Measurement, 3,* 281–311.

Loevinger, J. (1979b). The idea of the ego. *The Counseling Psychologist, 8,* 3–5.

Loevinger, J. (1985). Revision of the sentence completion test for ego development. *Journal of Personality and Social Psychology, 48,* 420–427.

Loevinger, J. (1990). Ego development in adolescence. In R. E. Muuss (Ed.), *Adolescent behavior and society* (4th ed.). New York: McGraw-Hill.

Loevinger, J. (1993). Measurement of personality: True or false. *Psychological Inquiry, 4,* 1–16.

Loevinger, J., Cohn, L. D., Bonneville, L. P., Redmore, C. D., Streich, D. D., & Sargent, M. (1985). Ego development in college. *Journal of Personality and Social Psychology, 48,* 947–962.

Loevinger, J., Wessler, R., & Redmore, C. (1970). *Measuring ego development* (Vols. 1–2). San Francisco: Jossey-Bass.

Looft, W. R. (1973). Socialization and personality throughout the life span. In P. B. Baltes & K. W. Schaie (Eds.). *Life-span developmental psychology.* New York: Academic Press.

Lovell, K. (1961). A follow-up study of Inhelder and Piaget's *The growth of logical thinking. British Journal of Psychology, 52,* 143–153.

Lyons, N. P. (1983). Two perspectives: On self, relationships, and morality. *Harvard Educational Review, 53,* 125–145.

Marcia, J. E. (1966). Development and validation of ego-identity status. *Journal of Personality and Social Psychology, 3,* 551–558.

Marcia, J. E. (1967). Ego identity status: Relationship to change in self-esteem, "general maladjustment," and authoritarianism. *Journal of Personality, 35,* 118–133.

Marcia, J. E. (1968). The case history of a construct: Ego identity status. In E. Vinacke (Ed.), *Readings in general psychology*. New York: Van Nostrand Reinhold.

Marcia, J. E. (1976a). Identity six years after: A follow-up study. *Journal of Youth and Adolescence, 5,* 145–160.

Marcia, J. E. (1976b). Studies in ego identity. Unpublished research monograph, Simon Fraser University.

Marcia, J. E. (1980). Identity in adolescence. In J. Adelson (Ed.), *Handbook of adolescent psychology*. New York: Wiley.

Marcia, J. E., & Friedman, M. (1970). Ego identity status in college women. *Journal of Personality, 38,* 249–263.

Marcia, J. E., Waterman, A. S., Matteson, D. R., Archer, S. L., & Orlofsky, J. L. (1993). *Ego identity: A handbook for psychosocial research*. New York: Springer.

Markus, H. R., & Kitayama, S. (1991). Culture and the self: Implications for cognition, emotion, and motivation. *Psychological Review, 98,* 224–253.

Marsh, D. T., Serafica, F. C., & Barenboim, C. (1980). Effect of perspective-taking training on interpersonal problem solving. *Child Development, 51,* 140–145.

Martorano, S. C. (1977). A developmental analysis of performance on Piaget's formal operations tasks. *Developmental Psychology, 13,* 666–667.

Matteson, D. R. (1972). Exploration and commitment: Sex differences and methodological problems in the use of identity status categories. *Journal of Youth and Adolescence, 6,* 353–374.

Matteson, D. R. (1974). Alienation vs. exploration and commitment: Personality and family correlates of adolescent identity status. Report for the Project of Youth Research. Copenhagen, Denmark: Royal Danish School of Educational Studies.

Matteson, D. R. (1993). Differences within and between genders. In J. E. Marcia, A. S. Waterman, D. R. Matteson, S. L. Archer, & J. L. Orlofsky (Eds.), *Ego identity: A handbook for psychosocial research*. New York: Springer.

Mead, G. H. (1934). *Mind, self and society*. Chicago: University of Chicago Press.

Mead, M. (1928/1950). *Coming of age in Samoa*. New York: New American Library.

Mead, M. (1935/1950). *Sex and temperament in three primitive societies*. New York: New American Library.

Mead, M. (1949). *Male and female*. New York: Morrow.

Mead, M. (1953). *Growing up in New Guinea*. New York: New American Library.

Mead, M. (1961). The young adult. In E. Ginzberg (Ed.), *Values and ideals of American youth*. New York: Columbia University Press.

Mead, M. (1970). *Culture and commitment*. New York: American Museum of Natural History.

Meilman, P. W. (1979). Cross-sectional age changes in ego identity status during adolescence. *Developmental Psychology, 15,* 230–231.

Messaris, P. (1986). Parents, children and television. In G. Gumpert & R. Cathcart (Eds.), *Inter/Media: interpersonal communication in a media world* (3d ed.). New York: Oxford University Press.

Milavsky, J. R., Stipp, H. H., Kessler, R. C., & Rubens, W. S. (1982). *Television and aggression: A panel study.* New York: Academic Press.

Miller, J. G., & Bersoff, D. M. (1992). Culture and moral judgement: How are conflicts between justice and interpersonal responsibilities resolved? *Journal of Personality and Social Psychology, 62,* 541–554.

Miller, J. R., & Lerner, R. M. (1994). Integrating research and outreach: Developmental contextualism and the human ecological perspective. *Home Economics Forum, 7,* 21–28.

Miller, N. E., & Dollard, J. (1941). *Social learning and imitation.* New Haven, CT: Yale University Press.

Mills, C. A., & Ogle, C. (1936). Physiologic sterility of adolescence. *Human Biology, 8,* 607–615.

Mischel, W. (1971). *Introduction to personality.* New York: Holt, Rinehart & Winston.

Mischel, W. (1973). Toward a cognitive social learning reconceptualization of personality. *Psychological Review, 80,* 252–283.

Mohr, G. J., & Despres, M. A. (1958). *The stormy decade: Adolescence.* New York: Random House.

Montangero, J. (1985). *Genetic epistemology: Yesterday and today.* New York: CUNY, Graduate School and University Center.

Montemayor, R. (1983). Parents and adolescents in conflict. *Journal of Early Adolescence, 3,* 83–103.

Moshman, D. (1993). Adolescent reasoning and adolescent rights. *Human Development, 36,* 27–40.

Moshman, D., & Franks, B. A. (1986). Development of the concept of inferential validity. *Child Development, 57,* 153–165.

Moshman, D., & Timmons, M. (1982). The construction of logical necessity. *Human Development, 25,* 309–323.

Mullahy, P. (1970). *Psychoanalysis and interpersonal psychiatry: The contributions of Harry Stack Sullivan.* New York: Science House.

Murdock, G. P., & White, D. R. (1969). Standard cross-cultural sample. *Ethnology, 8,* 329–369.

Murdock, G. P., & White, D. R. (1980). The standard cross-cultural sample and its code. In H. Barry III & A. Schlegel (Eds.), *Cross-cultural samples and codes.* Pittsburgh: University of Pittsburgh Press.

Murphy, J. M., & Gilligan, C. (1980). Moral development in late adolescence and adulthood: A critique and reconstruction of Kohlberg's theory. *Human Development, 23,* 77–104.

Murray, F. B. (1990). The conversion of truth into necessity. In W. F. Overton (Ed.), *Reasoning, necessity, and logic: Developmental perspectives.* Hillsdale, NJ: Erlbaum.

Mussen, P. H., & Bouterline-Young, H. (1964). Relationships between rate of physical maturing and personality among boys of Italian descent. *Vita Humana, 7,* 186–200.

Muuss, R. E. (1962). *First-aid for classroom discipline problems.* New York: Holt, Rinehart & Winston.

Muuss, R. E. (1980). Puberty rites in primitive and modern societies. In R. E. Muuss (Ed.), *Adolescent behavior and society* (3d ed.). New York: Random House.

Muuss, R. E. (1990). Adolescent eating disorders: Anorexia nervosa and bulimia. In R. E. Muuss (Ed.), *Adolescent behavior and society* (4th ed.). New York: McGraw-Hill.

Muuss, R. E. (1993). Zunehmendes Risikoverhalten unter Jugendlichen. *Biologische Medizin, 22,* 3–8.

Muuss, R. E. (1994). Ursachen and Interaktionen jugendlichen Risikoverhaltens. *Biologische Medizin, 23,* 214–217.

Nakkula, M., & Selman, R. (1991). How people "treat" each other: Pair therapy as a context for the development of interpersonal ethics. In W. M. Kurtines & J. L. Gewirtz (Eds.), *Handbook of moral behavior and development: Vol. 3 Application.* Hillsdale, NJ: Erlbaum.

Newman, K. (1988). *Falling from grace.* New York: Free Press.

Nipkow, K. E. (1991). Stage theories of faith development as a challenge to religious education and practical theology. In J. W. Fowler, K. E. Nipkow, & F. Schweitzer (Eds.), *Stages of faith and religious development: Implications for church, education, and society.* New York: Crossroad.

Nisan, M., & Kohlberg, L. (1982). Universality and variation in moral judgment: A longitudinal and cross-sectional study in Turkey. *Child Development, 53,* 865–876.

Nucci, L. (1982). Conceptual development in moral and conventional domains: Implications for values education. *Review of Educational Research, 52,* 93–122.

Nucci, L. (1989). Challenging conventional wisdom about morality: The domain approach to values education. In L. Nucci (Ed.), *Moral development and character education: A Dialogue.* Berkeley, CA: McCuthan.

Nucci, L., & Weber, E. K. (1991). The domain approach to values education: From theory to practice. In W. M. Kurtines & J. L. Gewirtz (Eds.), *Handbook of moral behavior and development* (Vol. 3). Hillsdale, NJ: Erlbaum.

Nye, W. C., & Carlson, J. S. (1984). The development of the concept of God in children. *Journal of Genetic Psychology, 145,* 137–142.

Offer, D. (1969). *The psychological world of the teenager.* New York: Basic Books.

Offer, D., & Offer, J. B. (1975). *From teenage to young manhood: A psychological study.* New York: Basic books.

Ojemann, R. H., & Pritchett, K. (1963). Piaget and the role of guided experiences in development. *Perceptual and Motor Skills, 17,* 927–940.

Orlofsky, J. L. (1975). Intimacy status: Relationship to interpersonal perception. *Journal of Youth and Adolescence, 5,* 73–88.

Orlofsky, J. L., Marcia, J. E., & Lesser, I. M. (1973). Ego identity status and the intimate versus isolation crisis of young adulthood. *Journal of Personality and Social Psychology, 27,* 211–219.

Oser, F. K. (1991a). The development of religious judgment. In F. K. Oser & W. G. Scarlett (Eds.), *Religious Development in Childhood and Adolescence.* San Francisco: Jossey-Bass.

Oser, F. K. (1991b). Toward a logic of religious development. In J. W. Fowler, K. E. Nipkow, & F. Schweitzer (Eds.), *Stages of faith and religious development: Implications for church, education, and society.* New York: Crossroad.

Overton, W. F. (1990). Competence and procedures: Constraints on the development of logical reasoning. In W. F. Overton (Ed.), *Reasoning, necessity, and logic: Developmental perspectives.* Hillsdale, NJ: Erlbaum.

Parikh, B. (1980). Development of moral judgement and its relation to family environmental factors in Indian and American families. *Child Development, 51,* 1030–1039.

Park, R. E. (1936). Human ecology. *American Journal of Sociology, 42,* 1–15.

Patterson, H. O., & Milakofsky, L. (1980). A paper-and-pencil inventory for the assessment of Piaget's tasks. *Applied Psychological Measurement, 4,* 341–353.

Patterson, S. J. (1992). The inner space and beyond: Women and identity. In G. R. Adams (Ed.), *Adolescent identity formation* (Vol. 4). Newbury Park, CA: Sage.

Pepper, S. C. (1942). *Word hypotheses.* Berkeley: University of California Press.

Perlmutter, R., & Shapiro, E. R. (1987). Morals and values in adolescence. In V. B. Van Hasselt & M. Hersen (Eds.), *Handbook of adolescent psychology.* New York: Pergamon.

Perry, H. S. (1982). *Psychiatrists of America, the life of Harry Stack Sullivan.* Cambridge, MA: Belknap.

Perry, W. G. (1970). *Forms of intellectual and ethical development in the college years.* New York: Holt, Rinehart & Winston.

Petrone, F. R. (1976). *The developmental kindergarten.* Springfield, IL: Charles C Thomas.

Phares, E. J. (1994). Social learning theories. In R. J. Corsini (Ed.), *Encyclopedia of Psychology* (2d ed., Vol. 3). New York: Wiley.

Phinney, J. S. (1990). Ethnic identity in adolescents and adults: A review of research. *Psychological Bulletin, 108,* 499–514.

Phinney, J. S., & Alipuria, L. L. (1990). Ethnic identity in college students from four ethnic groups. *Journal of Adolescence, 13,* 171–183.

Phinney, J. S., & Chavira, V. (1992). Ethnic identity and self-esteem: An exploratory longitudinal study. *Journal of Adolescence, 15,* 271–281.

Piaget, J. (1929). *The child's conception of the world.* New York: Harcourt, Brace.

Piaget, J. (1930). *The child's conception of physical causality.* London: Routledge & Kegan Paul.

Piaget, J. (1932a). *The language and thought of the child* (2d ed.). New York: Harcourt, Brace.

Piaget, J. (1932b). *The moral judgement of the child.* London: Routledge & Kegan Paul.

Piaget, J. (1947a). The moral development of the adolescent in two types of society, primitive and "modern." Lecture: United Nations Educational, Scientific and Cultural Organization, Paris.

Piaget, J. (1947b). *The psychology of intelligence.* New York: Harcourt, Brace.

Piaget, J. (1952). *The child's conception of number.* New York: Humanities.

Piaget, J. (1953). *The origins of intelligence in children.* London: Routledge & Kegan Paul.

Piaget, J. (1955). *The construction of reality in the child.* London: Routledge & Kegan Paul.

Piaget, J. (1957). Programme et méthodes de l'épistémologie génétique. In E. W. Beth et al. (Eds.), *Etudes de l' épistémologie génétique.* Paris: Presses Universitaires de France.

Piaget, J. (1962a). *Play, dreams and imitation in childhood.* New York: Norton.

Piaget, J. (1962b). Three lectures. *Bulletin of the Menninger Clinic, 26,* 120–145.

Piaget, J. (1963). The attainment of invariants and reversible operations in the development of thinking. *Social Research, 30,* 283–299.

Piaget, J. (1971). *Biology and knowledge.* Chicago: University of Chicago Press.

Piaget, J. (1972). *Essai de logique opératoire.* Deuxième édition du traité de logique. Paris: Dunod.

Piaget, J. (1973). *To understand is to invent.* New York: Viking.

Piaget, J. (1977). Logique génétigique et sociologie. In *Etudes sociologiques.* Geneva: Librairie Droz.

Piaget, J. (1980). Intellectual evolution from adolescence to adulthood. In R. E. Muuss (Ed.), *Adolescent Behavior and Society* (3d ed.). New York: Random House.

Piaget, J. (1985). *The equilibration of cognitive structures.* Chicago: University of Chicago Press.

Piaget, J. (1987a). *Possibility and necessity: Vol. 1. The role of possibility in cognitive development.* Minneapolis: University of Minnesota Press.

Piaget, J. (1987b). *Possibility and necessity: Vol. 2. The role of necessity in cognitive development.* Minneapolis: University of Minnesota Press.

Piaget, J., & Garcia, R. (1991). *Toward a logic of meanings.* Hillsdale, NJ: Erlbaum.

Piaget, J., & Inhelder, B. (1967). *The child's conception of space.* London: Routledge & Kegan Paul.

Piaget, J., & Inhelder, B. (1969). *The psychology of the child.* New York: Basic Books.

Pinard, A., & Laurendeau, M. (1964). A scale of mental development based on the theory of Piaget. *Journal of Research in Science Teaching, 2,* 253–260.

Plato. (1921). *The Republic* (B. Jowett, Trans.). Oxford: Clarendon.

Plato. (1953). Laws. In *The dialogues of Plato* (B. Jowett, Trans., 4th ed., Vol. 4). Oxford: Clarendon.

Pollak, S., & Gilligan, C. (1982). Images of violence in thematic apperception test stories. *Journal of Personality and Social Psychology, 42,* 159–167.

Power, F. C., Higgins, A., & Kohlberg, L. (1989). *Lawrence Kohlberg's approach to moral education.* New York: Columbia University Press.

Prose, F. (1990). Carol Gilligan studies girls growing up: Confident at 11, confused at 16. *The New York Times, January 7,* 13–15, 25–29, 45–48.

Rank, O. (1964). *Will therapy and truth and reality.* New York: Knopf.

Redmore, C. D. (1983). Ego development in the college years. *Journal of Youth and Adolescence, 12,* 301–306.

Redmore, C. D., & Loevinger, J. (1979). Ego development in adolescence. *Journal of Youth and Adolescence, 8*, 1–20.

Reich, K. H. (1991). The role of complementarity reasoning in religious development. In F. K. Oser & W. G. Scarlett (Eds.), *Religious Development in Childhood and Adolescence*. San Francisco: Jossey-Bass.

Reich, K. H. (1992). Religious development across the life span. In D. L. Featherman, R. M. Lerner, & M. Perlmutter (Eds.), *Life-span development and behavior* (Vol. 11). Hillsdale, NJ: Erlbaum.

Reid, B. V. (1984). An anthropological reinterpretation of Kohlberg's stages of moral development. *Human Development, 27*, 57–64.

Religion in America, 1979–1980 (1980). Princeton, NJ: Princeton Religious Research Center.

Rest, J. (1973). The hierarchical nature of moral judgment. *Journal of Personality, 41*, 86–109.

Rest, J. (1983). Morality. In J. H. Flavell & E. Markman (Eds.), *Manual of child psychology: Vol. 3. Cognitive development* (4th ed.). New York: Wiley.

Rice, F. P. (1987). *The adolescent* (5th ed.). Boston: Allyn and Bacon.

Richards, F. A., & Commons, M. L. (1984). Systematic, metasystematic, and cross-paradigmatic reasoning. In M. L. Commons, F. A. Richards, & C. Armon (Eds.), *Beyond formal operations*. New York: Praeger.

Riegel, K. F. (1975). Toward a dialectical theory of development. *Human Development, 18*, 50–64.

Rizzuto, A. M. (1979). *The birth of the living God*. Chicago: University of Chicago Press.

Rothbart, M. K., Hanley, D., & Albert, M. (1986). Gender differences in moral reasoning. *Sex Roles, 15*, 645–653.

Rotheram-Borus, M. J. (1989). Ethnic differences in adolescents' identity status and associated behavior problems. *Journal of Adolescence, 12*, 361–374.

Rousseau, J. J. (1911). *Emile* (W. H. Payne, Trans.). New York: Appleton. (Originally published in 1762.)

Rubin, K. H., & Schneider, F. W. (1973). The relationship between moral judgment, egocentrism, and altruistic behavior. *Child Development, 44*, 661–665.

Sameroff, A. (1975). Transactional models in early social relations. *Human Development, 18*, 65–79.

Scarr, S. (1986). How plastic are we? *Contemporary Psychology, 31*, 565–567.

Scarr, S. (1994). Fighting gender politics. *Contemporary Psychology, 39*, 699–700.

Schenkel, S., & Marcia, J. E. (1972). Attitudes toward premarital intercourse in determining ego identity status in college women. *Journal of Personality, 40*, 472–482.

Schiamberg, L. B. (1988). *Child and adolescent development*. New York: Macmillan.

Schlegel, A. (1995). A cross-cultural approach to adolescence. *Ethos, 23*, 15–32.

Schlegel, A., & Barry, H. III. (1980). The evolutionary significance of adolescent initiation ceremonies. *American Ethnologist, 7*, 696–714.

Schlegel, A., & Barry, H. III. (1991). *Adolescence: An anthropological inquiry*. New York: Free Press.

Scholnick, E. K. (1990). The three faces of it. In W. F. Overton (Ed.), *Reasoning, necessity, and logic: Developmental perspectives.* Hillsdale, NJ: Erlbaum.

Schultz, L. H., & Selman, R. L. (1989). Bridging the gap between interpersonal thought and action in early adolescence. *Development and Psychopathology, 1,* 133–152.

Schweitzer, F. (1991). Developmental views of the religion of the child: Historical antecedents. In J. W. Fowler, K. E. Nipkow, & F. Schweitzer (Eds.), *Stages of faith and religious development: Implications for church, education, and society.* New York: Crossroad.

Sears, R. R. (1951). A theoretical framework for personality and social behavior. *American psychologist, 6,* 476–483.

Sears, R. R., Maccoby, E. E., & Levin, H. (1957). *Patterns of child rearing.* Evanston, IL: Row, Peterson.

Selman, R. L. (1971a). The relation of role-taking to the development of moral judgment in children. *Child Development, 42,* 79–91.

Selman, R. L. (1971b). Taking another's perspective: Role-taking development in early childhood. *Child Development, 42,* 1721–1734.

Selman, R. L. (1976a). Social-cognitive understanding. In T. Lickona (Ed.), *Moral development and behavior: Theory, research, and social issues.* New York: Holt, Rinehart & Winston.

Selman, R. L. (1976b). Toward a structural-developmental analysis of interpersonal relationship. In A. D. Pick (Ed.), *Minnesota symposia on child psychology* (Vol. 10). University of Minnesota Press.

Selman, R. L. (1977). A structural-developmental model of social cognition. *Counseling Psychologist, 6,* 3–6.

Selman, R. L. (1980). *The growth of interpersonal understanding: Developmental and clinical analyses.* New York: Academic Press.

Selman, R. L., Beardslee, W., Schultz, L. H., Krupa, M., & Podorefsky, D. (1986). Assessing adolescent interpersonal negotiation strategies. *Developmental Psychology, 22,* 450–459.

Selman, R. L., & Byrne, D. F. (1974). *A structural-developmental analysis of levels of role-taking in middle childhood. Child Development, 45,* 803–806.

Selman, R. L., & Schultz, L. H. (1990). *Making a friend in youth: Developmental theory and pair therapy.* Chicago: University of Chicago Press.

Selman, R. L., & Selman, A. P. (1979). Children's ideas about friendship. *Psychology Today,* October, 71–80, 114.

Selman, R. L., Jaquette, D., & Lavin, D. R. (1977). Interpersonal awareness in children. *American Journal of Orthopsychiatry, 47,* 264–274.

Shantz, C. U. (1975). The development of social cognition. In E. M. Hetherington (Ed.), *Review of child development research* (Vol. 5). Chicago: University of Chicago Press.

Shantz, C. U. (1983). Social cognition. In P. H. Mussen (Ed.), *Handbook of child psychology: Vol. 3, Cognitive development* (4th ed.). New York: Wiley.

Shure, M. B., & Spivack, G. (1978). *Problem-solving techniques in childrearing.* San Francisco: Jossey-Bass.

Shure, M. B., & Spivack, G. (1980). Interpersonal problem solving as a mediator of behavioral adjustment in preschool and kindergarten children. *Journal of Applied Developmental Psychology, 1,* 29–44.

Shweder, R. A., & Haidt, J. (1993). The future of moral psychology: Truth, intuition, and the pluralist way. *Psychological Science, 4,* 360–365.

Shweder, R. A., & Much, N. (1991). Determinations of meaning: Discourse and moral socialization. In R. A. Shweder (Ed.), *Thinking through cultures: Expeditions in cultural psychology.* Cambridge, MA: Harvard University Press.

Silvern, S. B., & Williamson, P. A. (1987). The effects of video game play on young children's aggression, fantasy, and prosocial behavior. *Journal of Applied Developmental Psychology, 8,* 453–462.

Simmons, R. G., & Blyth, D. A. (1987). *Moving into adolescence.* New York: Aldine de Gruyter.

Singer, D. G., & Singer, J. L. (1983). Learning how to be intelligent consumers of television. In M. I. A. Howe (Ed.), *Learning from television.* New York: Academic Press.

Singer, J. L., & Singer, D. G. (1984). Intervention strategies for children's television. In I. P. Murray & G. Salomon (Eds.), *The future of children's television.* Boystown, NE: Father Flanagan Boystown.

Snarey, J., Kohlberg, L., & Noam, G. (1983). Ego development in perspective: Structural stage, functional phase, and cultural age-period models. *Developmental Review, 3,* 303–338.

Snarey, J. R., Reimer, J., & Kohlberg, L. (1985). Development of social-moral reasoning among kibbutz adolescents. *Developmental Psychology, 21,* 3–17.

Spiegel, L. A. (1951). A review of contributions to a psychoanalytic theory of adolescence: Individual aspects. In R. S. Eissler, A. Freud, H. Hartman, & E. Kris (Eds.), *The psychoanalytic study of the child* (Vol. 6). New York: International University Press.

Spivack, G., & Shure, M. B. (1974). *Social adjustment of young children.* San Francisco: Jossey-Bass.

Sprinthall, N. A., & Collins, W. A. (1995). *Adolescent psychology* (3d ed.). New York: McGraw-Hill.

Sroufe, L. A. (1970). A methodological and philosophical critique of intervention-oriented research. *Developmental Psychology, 2,* 140–145.

Starrett, R. H. (1983). The conceptual commonality between impulsiveness as a personality trait and as an ego development stage. *Personality and Individual Differences, 4,* 265–274.

Steinberg, L. (1993). *Adolescence* (3d ed.). New York: McGraw-Hill.

Steinberg, L., & Brown, B. B. (1989, March). Beyond the classroom: Parental and peer influences on high school achievement. Paper presented to the Families as Educators special interest group at the meeting of the American Educational Research Association, San Francisco.

Steinberg, L., & Hill, J. (1980). Family interaction patterns during early adolescence. In R. E. Muuss (Ed.), *Adolescent behavior and society* (3d ed.). New York: McGraw-Hill.

Stephen, J., Fraser, E., & Marcia, J. E. (1992). Moratorium-achievement (Mama) cycles in lifespan identity development. *Journal of Adolescence, 15,* 283–300.

Sternberg, R. J., & Powell, J. S. (1983). The development of intelligence. In P. H. Mussen (Ed.), *Handbook of child psychology: Vol. 3. Cognitive development* (4th ed.). New York: Wiley.

Stone, L. (1988). Passionate attachements in the West in historical perspective. In W. Gaylin & E. Person (Eds.), *Passionate attachements.* New York: Free Press.

Sullivan, E. V., & Hunt, D. E. (1967). Interpersonal and objective decentering as a function of age and social class. *Journal of Genetic Psychology, 110,* 199–210.

Sullivan, E. V., McCullough, G., & Stager, M. (1970). A developmental study of the relationship between conceptual, ego, and moral development. *Child Development, 41,* 399–411.

Sullivan, H. S. (1947). *Conceptions of modern psychiatry.* New York: Norton.

Sullivan, H. S. (1950). The illusion of personal individuality. *Psychiatry, 13,* 317–332.

Sullivan, H. S. (1953). *The interpersonal theory of psychiatry.* New York: Norton.

Sullivan, H. S. (1964). *The fusion of psychiatry and social science.* New York: Norton.

Sullivan, H. S. (1972). *Personal psychopathology.* New York: Norton.

Sund, R. B. (1976). *Piaget for educators: A multimedia program.* Columbus, OH: Charles E. Merrill.

Sutherland, P. (1992). *Cognitive development today: Piaget and his critics.* London: Chapman.

Thomas, A., Chess, S., & Birch, H. G. (1970). The origin of personality. *Scientific American, 223,* No. 2, 102–109.

Thomas, A., Chess, S., Birch, H. G., Hertzig, M., & Korn, S. J. (1963). *Behavioral individuality in early childhood.* New York: New York University Press.

Thomas, W. I., & Thomas, D. S. (1928). *The child in America.* New York: Knopf.

Tietjen, A., & Walker, L. (1985). Moral reasoning and leadership among men in Papua New Guinea society. *Developmental Psychology, 21,* 982–992.

Tobach, E., & Schneirla, T. C. (1968). The biopsychology of social behavior of animals. In R. E. Cooke & S. Levin (Eds.), *Biologic basis of pediatric practice.* New York: McGraw-Hill.

Toder, N. L., & Marcia, J. E. (1973). Ego identity status and response to conformity pressure in college women. *Journal of Personality and Social Psychology, 26,* 287–294.

Triandis, H. C. (1994). *Culture and social behavior.* New York: McGraw-Hill.

Tulkin, S. R. (1972). An analysis of the concept of cultural deprivation. *Developmental Psychology, 6,* 326–339.

Turiel, E. (1969). Developmental processes in the child's moral thinking. In P. H. Mussen, J. Langer, & M. Covington (Eds.), *Trends and issues in developmental psychology.* New York: Holt, Rinehart & Winston.

Turiel, E. (1983). *The development of social knowledge: Morality and convention.* Cambridge: Cambridge University Press.

Turiel, E., Killen, M., & Helwig, C. (1987). Morality: Its structure, functions, and vagaries. In J. Kagan & S. Lamb (Eds.), *The emergence of morality in young children.* Chicago: University of Chicago Press.

Turner, C. W., Hesse, B. W., & Peterson-Lewis, S. (1986). Naturalistic studies of the long-term effects of television violence. *Journal of Social Issues, 42, no. 3,* 51–73.

Unger, R., & Crawford, M. (1992). *Women and gender: A feminist psychology.* New York: McGraw-Hill.

Uzgiris, I. C., & Hunt, J. McV. (1976). *Assessment in infancy: Ordinal scale of psychological development.* Urbana: University of Illinois Press.

Van Evra, J. (1990). *Television and child development.* Hillsdale, NJ: Erlbaum.

Vygotsky, L. S. (1986). *Thought and language.* Cambridge, MA: MIT Press.

Walker, L. J. (1982). The sequentiality of Kohlberg's stages of moral development. *Child Development, 53,* 1330–1336.

Walker, L. J. (1984). Sex differences in the development of moral reasoning: A critical review. *Child Development, 55,* 677–691.

Walker, L. J. (1989). A longitudinal study of moral reasoning. *Child Development, 60,* 157–166.

Walker, L. J. (1991). Sex differences in moral reasoning. In W. M. Kurtines & J. L. Gewirtz (Eds.), *Handbook of moral behavior and development* (Vol. 2). Hillsdale, NJ: Erlbaum.

Waterman, A. S. (1982). Identity development from adolescence to adulthood: An extension of theory and a review of research. *Developmental Psychology, 18,* 341–358.

Waterman, A. S. (1985). Identity in the context of adolescent psychology. In A. S. Waterman (Ed.), *Identity in adolescence.* San Francisco: Jossey-Bass.

Waterman, A. S. (1993). Finding something to do or someone to be: A Eudaimonist perspective on identity formation. In J. Kroger (Ed.), *Discussions on ego identity.* Hillsdale, NJ: Erlbaum.

Waterman, A. S., Geary, P. S., & Waterman, C. K. (1974). A longitudinal study of changes in ego identity status. *Developmental Psychology, 10,* 387–392.

Waterman, A. S., & Waterman, C. K. (1970). The relationship between ego identity status and satisfaction with college. *Journal of Educational Research, 64,* 165–168.

Waterman, C. K., & Nevid, J. S. (1977). Sex differences in the resolution of the identity crisis. *Journal of Youth and Adolescence, 6,* 337–342.

Weikart, D., Roger, L., & Adcock, C. (1971). *The cognitively oriented curriculum.* Washington, DC: National Association for the Education of Young Children.

White, R. W. (1960). Competence and the psychosexual stages of development. *Nebraska Symposium on Motivation* (Vol. 8). Lincoln: University of Nebraska Press.

Whiting, B. B., & Edwards, C. P. (1988). *Children of different worlds.* Cambridge, MA: Harvard University Press.

Williams, T. M. (1986). Summary, conclusions and implications. In T. M. Williams (Ed.), *The impact of television: A national experiment in three communities.* Orlando, FL: Academic Press.

Wolf, T. M. (1973). Effects of life modeled sex-inappropriate play behavior in a naturalistic setting. *Developmental Psychology, 9,* 120–123.

Yeates, K. O., & Selman, R. L. (1989). Social competencies in the schools: Toward an integrative developmental model for intervention. *Developmental Review, 9,* 64–100.

Youniss, J. (1975). Another perspective on social cognition. In A. D. Pick (Ed.), *Minnesota symposia on child psychology* (Vol. 9). Minneapolis: University of Minnesota Press.

Youniss, J. (1980). *Parents and peers in social development: A Sullivan-Piaget perspective.* Chicago: University of Chicago Press.

Youniss, J., & Damon, W. (1992). Social construction in Piaget's theory. In H. Beilin & P. Pufall (Eds.), *Piaget's theory: Prospects and possibilities.* Hillsdale, NJ: Erlbaum.

Zillman, D., & Bryant, I. (1985). Selective-exposure phenomena. In D. Zillman & I. Bryant (Eds.), *Selective exposure to communication.* Hillsdale, NJ: Erlbaum.

NAME INDEX

SUBJECT INDEX